D0076279

DEMOCRATIC TRANSITIONS

DEMOCRATIC TRANSITIONS

....

Conversations with World Leaders

Edited by SERGIO BITAR AND ABRAHAM F. LOWENTHAL

International Institute for Democracy and Electoral Assistance
Stockholm

....

JOHNS HOPKINS UNIVERSITY PRESS • BALTIMORE

© 2015 International Institute for Democracy and Electoral Assistance
(International IDEA)
All rights reserved. Published 2015
Printed in the United States of America on acid-free paper
9 8 7 6 5 4 3 2 1

Johns Hopkins University Press
2715 North Charles Street
Baltimore, Maryland 21218-4363
www.press.jhu.edu

Library of Congress Cataloging-in-Publication Data

Democratic transitions : conversations with world leaders / edited by Sergio Bitar
and Abraham F. Lowenthal.
     pages cm
 Includes bibliographical references and index.
 ISBN 978-1-4214-1760-8 (pbk. : acid-free paper) — ISBN 978-1-4214-1761-5 (electronic)
 — ISBN 1-4214-1760-x (pbk. : acid-free paper) — ISBN 1-4214-1761-8 (electronic)
 1. Political leadership—Case studies. 2. Democratization—Case studies. I. Bitar,
Sergio. II. Lowenthal, Abraham F.
 JC330.3.T73 2015
 321.8—dc23   2014046776

A catalog record for this book is available from the British Library.

*Special discounts are available for bulk purchases of this book. For more information, please
contact Special Sales at 410-516-6936 or specialsales@press.jhu.edu.*

Johns Hopkins University Press uses environmentally friendly book materials,
including recycled text paper that is composed of at least 30 percent post-consumer
waste, whenever possible.

About International IDEA

The International Institute for Democracy and Electoral Assistance (International IDEA) is an intergovernmental organization that supports democratic institutions around the world.

International IDEA produces practical knowledge products and tools on electoral processes and constitution building that support political participation and representation as it relates to gender, diversity, conflict, and security.

International IDEA brings this knowledge to people who are working at both a national and regional level for democratic reform—and facilitates dialogue in support of democratic change.

In its work, International IDEA aims for:

- increased capacity, legitimacy, and credibility of democracy;
- more inclusive democratic participation and accountable representation; and
- more effective and legitimate democracy cooperation

Based in Stockholm, Sweden, International IDEA has offices in North Africa, sub-Saharan Africa, Asia, the Caribbean, Latin America, and the Pacific.

CONTENTS

FOREWORD

On December 17, 2010, Mohamed Bouazizi, a young jobless Tunisian man, set himself on fire and made all Tunisians—not to mention the entire world—aware of the miserable human rights situation in Tunisia. Meanwhile, the political regime promoted the image of a happy country where people had few worries about their lives, future, and freedom, and of economic growth and prosperity providing chances for all. But it was all a lie. The uprising of December 17, 2010, to January 14, 2011, exploded in an atmosphere of invisible repression. Tunisia used to be a country that had a "legal" political opposition decimated by its eternal divisions, limited projects and ambitions, and an "illegal" opposition that was either imprisoned or forced to leave the country for indefinite periods of time.

The regime collapsed swiftly. But 330 people died in the events that immediately followed December 17, 2010, while the state structures managed to resist the waves of the revolution in which people were claiming reasonable and unreasonable changes.

The Tunisian revolution was not just a local event. It was the starting point of a large wave that changed realities in the whole region. Indeed, since late 2010, when Tunisians decided to take to the streets and make a determined bid to regain their dignity and build democracy, a wave of transitions to democracy has been sweeping the Arab region. The citizens of Egypt, Libya, and Yemen, in addition to Tunisia, were able to topple long-standing dictators, thus opening a window of hope for a young population devastated by frustration and lack of opportunity. It was clear from the beginning, however, that some dictatorships were not ready to listen to their people and that they would continue to oppose fierce resistance, thus causing continued human suffering.

Soon after the initial euphoria felt by young generations thirsty for freedom, reformers throughout the region discovered that building democracy is much more complex, challenging, and multifaceted than expected. When dictators fall, people come to realize that the dictators were not as strong as they were thought to be and that only fear made the people believe that the dictators were controlling everything. People also discover that the dictator was not the only one to blame for their problems.

Dethroning dictators is only a first step in a much longer path toward making real change. What paves the way to democratic transition is change in concepts, mentalities, values, and behaviors. Especially in the Arab region, this is proving to be critical, and unless seriously considered, democratic governance that meets the aspirations of the people, allows space for all, and is able to consolidate and sustain itself may be only an illusion.

In this context, frank and free speech is also vital. Those who find themselves involved in the leadership of a country during a difficult transition must defend their freedom of expression and use it to tell the truth. They should be ready to criticize themselves and their partners in order to correct the course of things that a difficult social and security situation may impose. Leaders must anticipate the future of the nation and prioritize its interests. Regardless of the difficulties they face, they must avoid excessively inflating people's expectations, both because it is their ethical duty and also because it is a wise way to maintain their credibility with citizens expecting quick results from the revolution.

But goodwill, dedication, and sacrifices made by many—leaders and citizenry alike—seem not to be enough. Systematic work to identify, introduce, and apply reforms that become the solid roots of a democratic society is a critical requirement. This entails the development and use of multiple skills and techniques that can benefit greatly from the accumulated experiences of others who have faced the same variety of challenges while being mindful of important contextual differences.

As a leader of the first link of the chain of transitions in the West Asia/ North Africa (WANA) region, I believe *Democratic Transitions: Conversations with World Leaders* is an exciting book that gathers insights and reflections of preeminent political leaders who have played a major role in their countries' transitions toward effective democratic governance. It contains probing interviews with 13 world transition leaders over the past four decades who address the dilemmas they faced, the choices they made, the implications of their critical decisions, and what they regard as their pivotal successes.

This innovative publication is a unique and timely contribution to current debates about how to promote, inspire, and manage a peaceful transition from authoritarianism to democracy. Its content will be of great value to leaders currently steering transition processes, democratic movements, and the democracy-building community.

I appreciate the message of this book: that while popular mobilizations can spark transitions, skillful, steady, and sensitive leadership over the long term is required to reconcile fragmented political and social contexts; build the capacities of government institutions; and guide a country through a critical transition period.

The book has a particular importance for the WANA region because the lessons that can be learned from the leaders interviewed for this study are of exceptional value for all those who strive to cement the founding conditions for democratic governance, inclusiveness, and dignity. This includes those of us in an Arab world that has suffered for centuries from real deficiencies in relevant democratic experience. But it is also true that the potential benefits of these lessons are far reaching and intended to help democracy builders worldwide.

Human rights are becoming the ideology of our times. I believe this is what all of humanity really needs: a world in which all individuals simply enjoy all basic rights as human beings. I think the WANA region is opening a new era in human history, in which it is called on to demonstrate that the path to democracy can be opened by all people, whatever their culture or history. There is no culture that refuses or resists the avidity of people to change toward democracy. In all countries and cultures, people generally aspire to choose their rulers, without imposition or repression.

MOHAMED MONCEF MARZOUKI
Former President of the Republic of Tunisia

PREFACE

....

In 2015, International IDEA celebrates its 20th anniversary, marking two decades of supporting stronger democratic institutions and processes worldwide. During those 20 years, we have contributed valuable technical information to those who are seeking to build sustainable democracy around the world. We have prepared and widely distributed comparative knowledge about the organization and conduct of elections in particular, and also on constitution building, democracy assessments, and political parties. What neither we nor others have thus far contributed is first-hand testimony from top political leaders about how transitions toward democracy have been achieved in different continents. This exciting publication fills that critical gap.

Political leaders play a pivotal role in determining the outcome of transitional periods. While democracy is about inclusive processes, democratic transitions are also about those critical decisions that ultimately rest with the person at the top. These critical decisions often rest with one person because transition processes are disruptive. They are disruptive because they do not fit within the established frameworks and procedures for collective decision making, because they relate to a problem that is being experienced for the first time, and because the weight and size of the situation and challenge may prevent other decision makers from taking responsibility. Most important, they are disruptive because they change the course of history.

These disruptive dilemmas and challenges confront the political leader with the quintessence of leadership and responsibility—to respond, to decide, to lead on the basis of a good personal assessment of the situation, of the pros and cons of the possible options, of the public interest that is at stake, and on the basis of the set of values that underpin a leader's engagement.

These decisive times and moments of true leadership require a forward-looking approach, the courage to confront resistance and to take personal risks, and the patience to wait for positive results, all on the basis of being responsive and accountable to the country's citizens and their representatives.

International IDEA is therefore proud to present a book that captures lessons from 13 political leaders who faced such challenges. *Democratic Transitions: Conversations with World Leaders* examines the critical role of political leadership in promoting and achieving democratic transition, and provides contemporary leaders with comparative experiences on a broad range of issues of central importance during transitions to democratic governance.

There are many excellent contributors to this publication, particularly the political leaders who have shared their unique experiences. But my greatest thanks must go to my predecessor, Vidar Helgesen, for his vision and conviction that the experiences of leaders who helped to achieve democratic change need to be shared. My thanks also go to Senator Bitar and Professor Lowenthal, who prepared for and conducted the interviews and provided the intellectual acumen and political insights needed to drive this project; we greatly appreciate their commitment, energy, and skill.

It is our hope at International IDEA that this rich volume will serve as a source of inspiration, reflection, and guidance for a new generation of leaders in the decades to come as they carry out transitions from authoritarian and exclusionary rule toward democratic governance.

YVES LETERME
Secretary General
International IDEA

DEMOCRATIC TRANSITIONS

Introduction

SERGIO BITAR AND ABRAHAM F. LOWENTHAL

This book reveals how 13 former presidents and prime ministers from 9 countries—2 each from Africa, Asia, and Europe as well as 3 from Latin America —helped achieve successful transitions from authoritarian rule toward democratic governance. We know of no comparable source of practical insights and considered judgments on the challenges such transitions present and how they have been confronted.

Between January 2012 and June 2013, we interviewed Fernando Henrique Cardoso of Brazil, Patricio Aylwin and Ricardo Lagos of Chile, John Kufuor and Jerry John Rawlings of Ghana, B. J. Habibie of Indonesia, Ernesto Zedillo of Mexico, Fidel V. Ramos of the Philippines, Aleksander Kwaśniewski and Tadeusz Mazowiecki of Poland, F. W. de Klerk and Thabo Mbeki of South Africa, and Felipe González of Spain. The interviews provide extensive presentations, and in one case the first presentation, of the leaders' perspectives on their roles in these historic transformations.

The interviews cover a range of transitions from diverse authoritarian regimes that led to sustained—and thus far unreversed—democratic governance.* Every transition is unique, so each leader played a distinct role. De Klerk, Habibie, and Zedillo were key figures in autocratic regimes of varying types who helped move their countries toward legitimate democracy. Aylwin, Cardoso, González, Kufuor, Lagos, Mazowiecki, and Mbeki were prominent in opposition movements that helped end authoritarian rule, and they then helped construct democracies in their place. Kwaśniewski, Ramos, and Rawlings were bridge figures, straddling the divide between autocracy and democracy. All made significant contributions to their countries' democratic transitions.

The interviews shed fascinating light on what these chief executives did and why. The leaders discuss the sources and characteristics of effective actions, both to end authoritarianism and to craft democratic governance. They recall how they understood and confronted the principal problems they faced,

---

* Because we did not launch this project until 2012, we could not interview such historic figures from these nine cases as Nelson Mandela, Corazon Aquino, Wojciech Jaruzelski, and Ulysses Guimarães, nor could we include outstanding leaders from other salient democratic transitions of this period such as Vaclav Havel or Raúl Alfonsín.

what specific goals they aimed to achieve, what strategies and tactics they developed, and how and why these changed.* They illuminate the crucial—and sometimes anguishing—decisions they had to make. And they reflect upon lessons that can be drawn from their experiences for current and future transitions, and on differences between today's opportunities for democratization and those in their own generation.

The interviews make it clear that many issues of continuing significance must be faced in such transitions: how to organize and unite divided political and social forces to confront an authoritarian government; how to reinforce movement within an authoritarian regime toward political opening; how to forge workable compromises, both among different opposition groups and, when possible, between them and elements of the old regime; and why (and how) to strengthen political parties and build democratic institutions. The leaders reflect on the influence of civil society organizations and international actors as well as the constraints on their respective roles.

They also take up such thorny questions as how to assure civilian control of the armed forces and police and intelligence agencies; how to balance the need for transitional and restorative justice with the imperative of coexisting with former adversaries; how to bolster confidence and attract investment from the business sector while responding to popular demands and expectations for equity and redistribution; and how to develop consensus around constitutional principles and electoral procedures. In their own voices and terms, these exceptional figures offer something that is missing in most studies of democratic transitions: experienced political wisdom.

Transitions toward democracy are not achieved solely, or perhaps even mainly, by those at the top of the political order. Mass movements, civil society organizations, and the instruments they employ—strikes, protests, street demonstrations, and other bottom-up pressures—have also been crucial in virtually all transitions. In different ways and degrees, this is true of each of these nine transitions, from the demands for *diretas já* in Brazil to "people power" in the Philippines to the massive demonstrations against Soeharto in Indonesia to the general strikes by the Solidarity workers' movement in Poland and the student protests of 1968 in Mexico. Political parties, trade unions, women's movements, students, professional associations, religious organiza-

---

* What political leaders (or others) say in retrospect to explain their decisions and assess the consequences of their actions is not necessarily completely accurate, of course. Even if they sincerely strive to be perfectly honest, they may not exactly remember the situations they faced years ago or how they perceived conditions at the time and acted upon them, and they may have misjudged the forces at play. On the whole, we believe these interviews have the ring of authenticity and that they provide valuable perspectives, often not available from any other source. They may play down mistakes and underline achievements, but they illuminate decision making and agency in ways that are sometimes obscured by other methods of analysis. There is no better way than probing interviews to tap into this unique source.

tions, and international pressures helped bring about changes in these countries. Socioeconomic structures, demographic and geopolitical realities, and deep national histories and cultures also shaped demands for democracy and the obstacles that had to be overcome to achieve it.

Yet these interviews demonstrate compellingly that political leadership also counts. Individuals were key at all stages of these movements from authoritarian rule toward democracy. One cannot imagine the South African transition without Nelson Mandela, F. W. de Klerk, Oliver Tambo, and Thabo Mbeki. Nor can one understand the Indonesian transition from the long Soeharto regime without the decisive role of B. J. Habibie; comprehend the Chilean transition without the special contributions of Patricio Aylwin and Ricardo Lagos; appreciate the Spanish transition without taking into account the crucial parts played by King Juan Carlos, Adolfo Suárez, and Felipe González; or assess the Polish achievement of democracy without examining the distinct roles played by Lech Wałęsa, Wojciech Jaruzelski, Tadeusz Mazowiecki, and Aleksander Kwaśniewski. Structures are important, but so are human agents. Political scientists tend to downplay the importance of leadership. This book highlights it.*

The heart of this book is the interviews themselves. We prepared for these discussions, which ranged from two to five and a half hours in length, by reading intensively and consulting country experts. We concentrated on common themes and issues as well as the important special circumstances of each case. We did not use a rigid questionnaire but rather engaged the individual political leaders in dynamic conversations, guided by our aim to understand their country's transitions and to elicit their reflections on how these were achieved and what lessons can be learned.

With each executive's approval, we edited the transcripts to avoid needless repetition, thematically organized their comments, and condensed our own

* There is surprisingly little academic literature on political leadership, perhaps because it is so difficult to capture with the instruments and measures of modern political science. An exemplary exception is Juan J. Linz, "Innovative Leadership in the Transition to Democracy and a New Democracy: The Case of Spain," in *Innovative Leadership in International Politics*, ed. Gabriel Sheffer (Albany, N.Y.: State University of New York Press, 1993). See also the recent volume by Archie Brown, *The Myth of the Strong Leader: Political Leadership in the Modern Age* (London: Bodley Head, 2014). Brown notes that those political figures he characterizes as "redefining" or "transformational" leaders are the exception rather than the rule, but that they can make a profound difference. While stressing the dangers of placing faith in a "strongman," he advances arguments in favor of collegial and inclusive leadership. In personal correspondence, Brown notes that this type of leadership is especially needed during transitions, an observation that is well illustrated in these interviews. Marshall Ganz provides another perspective in "Leading Change: Leadership, Organization and Social Movements," in *Handbook of Leadership and Practice*, ed. Nitin Nohria and Rakesh Khurena (Boston: Harvard Business Press, 2010). Ganz defines leadership as "accepting responsibility to create conditions that enable others to achieve shared purposes in the face of uncertainty." Most of the leaders interviewed in this volume personify that concept.

questions and comments. In two cases (Ramos and Habibie), we included relevant passages from the interviewees' published writings to more fully present points that were briefly stated in the interview. We also introduced subheads and bold typeface to facilitate the reader's review, added brief clarifications, and provided guides to suggested further reading for each case, and on the comparative and theoretical literature we think most useful. We furnished time lines to help situate specific references to leaders and people, parties, and events and prepared brief biographical sketches on all the leaders. The interviews are preceded by context-setting essays, written by leading academic experts on each country, discussing its transition and the role of each leader.

Unfortunately, there are no surviving women leaders of these transitions, and few of our interviewees provided much insight about women's participation in them. International IDEA, at our suggestion, asked Georgina Waylen of the University of Manchester to prepare a separate chapter on this topic, drawing on interviews she has conducted over several years and some new interviews with women activists who played significant roles in these countries, although not at the chief executive level.

Our own concluding essay distills main principles about how authoritarian rule can be ended and democratic governance constructed. Transitions from authoritarian rule toward democracy face recurrent challenges. Lessons learned from these cases are highly relevant for future leaders and activists. This book should be valuable for current and future political leaders and citizens around the world who are still striving to establish democratic governance; for activists in civil society organizations; for the media and the international community; and for all who want to understand foster, conduct, and support democratic transitions.

Conducting these interviews together and reflecting jointly on what we learned has been a wonderful experience, primarily because of the continuing importance of the questions we explored and the extraordinary experiences and human qualities of those we interviewed. Our own long-term friendship deepened as we drew on our shared values and different life experiences to carry out this work.

With great appreciation to International IDEA for initiating and supporting this project as well as deep gratitude to the leaders who allowed us to draw out their recollections, we invite readers to join us in learning from them.

Chapter 1

BRAZIL

....

Brazil's Transition: From Constrained Liberalization to Vibrant Democracy

FRANCES HAGOPIAN

The Brazilian military ruled Brazil from 1964 to 1985; for half of that time, the opposition patiently played by the regime's rules in a protracted transition to democracy. Brazil's experience with democratization is instructive for the lessons it offers about the strategic decisions taken by both autocrats and democrats that can result in a peaceful transition—and how, in time, constraints on effective democratic governance imposed by institutional and substantive compromises can be overcome.

Democracy and Dictatorship

Brazil established a competitive political system at the end of the 19th century, but during decades of oligarchical rule the overwhelming majority of Brazilians were denied the effective rights of citizenship. Even as the political system opened to broader political participation and competition after World War II, the urban lower classes were well controlled, rural workers were not allowed to organize unions, and the illiterate could not vote. Although the country prospered in the late 1950s with infrastructural investment, import substituting industrialization, and the construction of a new national capital in Brasília, the political system began to strain. Institutional weakness—exemplified by a highly fragmented political party system and an ineffective Congress—did little to assuage the fears of an elite threatened by the mobilization of peasant leagues, the electoral advance of a populist labor party, and the president's leftist rhetoric.

At the height of the Cold War in April 1964, the Brazilian military, guided by doctrinal fears of Communist-inspired insurrection and civil war, reacted to the perfect storm of soaring inflation and dwindling foreign reserves, demands for land reform, the apparent ineptitude of civilian leaders, and intensifying labor and student unrest by staging a coup and imposing a military authori-

5

tarian regime. Military rulers then stabilized the economy, strengthened the state and expanded its role in the economy, abolished existing political parties, and turned harshly repressive, suspending habeas corpus—the right to be released from unlawful detention and not to suffer prolonged incarceration without a formal charge—and imposing press censorship and a state of siege. Like other Latin American militaries during this period, the Brazilian regime subjected enemies—real and imagined—to arbitrary detention, torture, exile, and even death. Nonetheless, even at the height of the repression, it was less brutal than its neighbors. Military courts routinely handed down "not guilty" verdicts, only about 500 politicians lost their political rights—including to hold office (as compared with 15,000 in Uruguay)—and the government was responsible for "only" 333 deaths, a per capita death toll 50 and 100 times lower than Chile and Argentina, respectively.

It was hugely important, as Fernando Henrique Cardoso stresses, that the Brazilian military regime clung to a veil of legality, staged regular legislative and municipal elections, and permitted representative institutions (including Congress and a pro-government official opposition party) to function. Although the regime cancelled elections for state governors and mayors of state capitals, manipulated electoral laws, and divested elected positions of meaningful constitutional powers, competitive elections ultimately paved the way for Brazil's particular path to democratization.

The Political Transition

The Brazilian transition to democracy was gradual, launched from above, and tolerant of restricted partisan and civic mobilization. A fissure between "hard-line" military officers (who believed Brazil needed indefinite military rule to realize its potential) and "soft-liners" (who saw military rule as custodial and temporary and feared the future loss of civilian support for the military as an institution if the hard-liners' repressive power was not restrained) created the opening for political liberalization. In early 1974, the new soft-line president General Ernesto Geisel signaled that he would "relax" military rule, ease up on press censorship, and allow a freer expression of ideas and elections. Seven years of double-digit growth, political and social stability, and an opposition so dispirited that it had considered disbanding in 1972 gave Geisel confidence that the regime could win competitive elections.

The opposition faced a familiar dilemma: boycott elections that could not possibly result in the unconditional transfer of power or use the space afforded by the regime to organize, advertise positions, and mobilize support for a democratic opening. It chose the latter. Facing accusations that they were legitimizing the dictatorship, Cardoso and others effectively argued that participating within the system—and indeed using the system to their advantage—was the surest path to democratic change. They were proved right. The opposition immediately won 16 of the 22 contested Senate seats in 1974, increased its share of seats in the lower chamber from 28% to 44%, and took control of 5 additional state legislatures. This result was a stinging defeat for the government; Cardoso points out that it was not a result of a popular thirst for democracy but rather the opposition's effective campaign protesting bread-and-butter economic issues—notably the erosion of the purchasing power of workers' salaries amid an economic boom. Over the longer term, contesting elections strengthened the opposition's capacity to mobilize voters and pressure the government to stay the course of its political opening. Adhering to the logic articulated by Cardoso—the transition would not take place via a frontal assault on the regime's fortress but by laying siege to it until those on the inside were ready to deal—the opposition persisted even as the regime adroitly rewrote the rules, time and again, to manipulate the political process to its advantage in municipal (1976), congressional (1978), and, eventually, gubernatorial elections (1982). The opposition also understood that structural change and time were on its side. Economic growth and industrialization had moved millions of Brazilians into cities, created a strong middle class that was able to consume a range of durable goods from refrigerators to cars, and expanded the size of the working class to nearly 30% of the population.

A vibrant civil society also emerged in the space created by the political opening. Influential segments of elite opinion were the first to express reservations about authoritarian rule. The hierarchy of the Roman Catholic Church notably condemned repression, kept records of state-sponsored murder and violence in the countryside, sheltered striking workers, embraced democracy, and promoted grassroots groups that fostered the norms of participation. The death in October 1975 of prominent Jewish journalist Vladimir Herzog in the custody of the Intelligence Unit of the Second Army in São Paulo provoked the normally docile Association of Brazilian Lawyers to issue a statement charging the government with torture, and Cardinal Evaristo Arns bravely held a joint Catholic-Jewish ceremony for Herzog in the São Paulo cathedral that turned into the first mass protest against the military regime. A group of prominent entrepreneurs also courageously waged an anti-statism campaign in 1974, and a few years later drew a direct link between a strong interventionist state and arbitrary rule, and called for democracy as the only solution when the state controlled society rather than the other way around.

As political space opened, grassroots religious groups, neighborhood associations, and a powerful women's movement pressed for specific interests as well as greater political freedom. In the late 1970s, Luiz Inácio (Lula) da Silva led a new union movement that was suspicious of state intervention and drew strength from its connections to the shop floor instead of state patrons; the movement impressively mobilized thousands in the industrial heartland of São Paulo to strike for higher wages and collective bargaining rights. Civil society mobilization in elite circles, the streets, factories, and polls strengthened the bargaining hand of the political opposition. Against a military that had suffered no defeats in war or plebiscite and had negotiated its exit from a position of strength, the irrepressible tide of democratic fervor empowered the democratic opposition.

The transition accelerated with the gubernatorial elections of 1982. Seeking to reverse the plebiscitary quality that elections had assumed since 1974 by dividing the opposition, the regime allowed new parties to form beginning in 1979. The opposition predictably split into five parties, ranging from Lula's Workers' Party (Partido dos Trabalhadores, or PT) on the left to a short-lived moderate party on the right (which dissolved itself in 1981 after the government imposed yet another set of rules forbidding electoral alliances), but the opposition's decision to contest elections in the face of the blatant manipulation of electoral rules once again bore fruit. With annual inflation raging at over 200% and the economy mired in a deep recession caused by the mounting cost of servicing a staggering foreign debt, opposition parties elected 10 governors in the most industrialized and developed states of Brazil, which accounted for three-fifths of the national electorate and three-quarters of the gross domestic product, including São Paulo, Minas Gerais, and Rio de Janeiro. Thereafter, a slim opposition majority in the lower chamber compelled the government to negotiate controversial bills, and even regime party governors became more accountable to their constituencies than to the military government.

Even after these electoral setbacks, the military, convinced that the regime candidate would prevail in an Electoral College that was stacked with thousands of pro-regime mayors and state assemblymen, stayed on course to hand power to a civilian president in 1985. In 1984, with the goal of passing a constitutional amendment to force direct presidential elections, the opposition mobilized the campaign for Direct Elections Now that drew millions of protesters chanting "Direct Elections Now" in massive street demonstrations sequenced in major state capitals across Brazil, beginning in São Paulo in January. The military did not interfere. Although the opposition narrowly failed to win the two-thirds congressional majority needed to change the constitution, it opted to contest the indirect election. The military regime's party nominated a highly controversial presidential candidate that set in motion an avalanche of defections among the political class, which helped opposition candidate Tancredo Neves (the moderate governor of the important state of Minas Gerais and a commanding, consensus-building politician) win the election.

Building a Democracy: The Role of Fernando Henrique Cardoso

The Brazilian transition to democracy continued after the military handed over power to a civilian president in 1985, and Brazilians faced the hard challenges of constructing a democratic regime. The first challenge was to establish civilian control over the military without triggering a military backlash. The military wished to avoid prosecution for human rights abuses (after the Argentine government put top military officers on trial, all Latin American militaries harbored such fears), retain control over military affairs (promotions, budgets, and weapons procurement), and continue to play a constitutional role in "guaranteeing internal order." Although no military officers were prosecuted, in time, civilian governments opened the archives of military repression and compensated the families of 265 victims who had been killed or disappeared under the military regime. Civilian governments also curbed the military's national security ambitions in the Amazon, clamped down on political comments by active duty officers, suspended purchases of jet fighter planes, and halted the country's nuclear enrichment program. Most notably, at the end of his first term as president, in a brilliant sequence of steps laid out in his interview, Cardoso definitively reduced the power of uniformed military officers in the cabinet when he abolished three separate service ministries and named a civilian to head a new Ministry of Defense.

Democratic leaders also had to balance demands for economic redistribution and justice with the need to establish property rights and assuage the fears of economic elites. The issues of agrarian reform and property rights were particularly explosive, as agrarian elites and cattle ranchers often met land seizures carried out by the Movement of Those without Land (Movimento dos Trabalhadores Rurais Sem Terra) with ruthless violence. Ultimately, the questions of redistribution and rights were settled in the Congress, which (doubling as a Constituent Assembly) drafted, debated, and ultimately promulgated a new democratic constitution in 1988. The right effectively turned the tide against agrarian reform in Congress, but other rights that were written into the constitution—including labor rights, indigenous rights, and the universal right of all citizens to health care—became permanent commitments of Brazilian democracy. A president was finally elected by popular vote in 1989.

Throughout the years of transition, Fernando Henrique Cardoso was the opposition's intellectual leader and one of the most outspoken and influential critics of the military regime. Striking a middle ground between radical and moderate camps, Cardoso helped to prevent the opposition from splintering. He backed labor strikes and Lula's release from prison but restrained the opposition from pushing for too much too fast. He admired the Spanish model. A visible figure in the campaign for Direct Elections Now from the outset (he delivered the opposition's keynote Senate speech in favor of the constitutional amendment), Cardoso—who believed there was a real possibility of defeating the government's candidate despite the obstacles—persuaded the opposition not to withdraw from the elections and convinced Ulysses Guimarães, a key opposition leader, to help coordinate Tancredo Neves's campaign. Cardoso also played an important role in drafting the democratic constitution of 1988 as the rapporteur of the Internal Rules Committee and the Commission of Systematization. In 1993, as finance minister, he worked with a team of academic economists to develop the Real Plan to curb inflation and then used his persuasive talents to get the plan adopted, implemented, and accepted at a time, he reveals, when the Congress was weak. In 1994, a public grateful for his role in vanquishing inflation elected Cardoso president. His administration's economic reforms laid the foundation for economic and democratic stability.

The Brazilian transition to genuine democratic governance was ultimately in some ways harder than other transitions, such as Argentina's, where military defeat undermined the credibility of the armed forces. But Brazil's complex social structure, highly urban society, and political culture shaped by the country's politicoelectoral history made pressure for gradual democratization through the electoral process entirely viable. The democratic opposition accepted the regime's rules and pace, and made countless compromises along the way. Whether these compromises unnecessarily prolonged the transition, as some argued at the time, we cannot know for sure. But with hindsight it is now clear that they did not permanently constrain democracy. Civilian control was unambiguously established over the military, social welfare provisions were dramatically expanded, more equitable economic growth has occurred, and today democracy in Brazil is vibrant, innovative, and deeply entrenched.

Biosketch of Fernando Henrique Cardoso, President of Brazil 1995–2003

PHOTO: YASUYOSHI CHIBA / SCANPIX

Fernando Henrique Cardoso made his initial professional reputation as a sociologist; his dissertation and first book were on race in Brazil. He soon displayed his political and administrative talents in the governance of the University of São Paulo. Deprived by the military regime of his tenured position there, Cardoso went into exile in Chile, where he coauthored a landmark volume on dependency and development. He turned down attractive international academic posts to return to Brazil in 1968. With help from the Ford Foundation, he cofounded CEBRAP (Centro Brasileiro de Análise e Planejamento, or Brazilian Center for Analysis and Planning), an independent social science research center, where he led the development of research on urban São Paulo, focusing on income distribution and other themes with policy implications that challenged the military regime. Cardoso entered elective politics in the partially free 1978 congressional elections, then played an increasingly important role in Congress as a member of the opposition, and cofounded the Social Democratic Party of Brazil.

As an opposition leader in Brazil's gradual transition, Cardoso built bridges among opponents of the military regime and then in the country's successive democratic governments. He served as rapporteur of the congressional committees that fashioned Brazil's 1988 constitution. As finance minister, beginning in 1993, he drew upon academic expertise to curb inflation with the Real Plan and won public support by articulating the new economic approach to the broad citizenry. The success of the Real Plan strongly aided his election as president in 1994. Cardoso then used his personal and relationship-building skills to forge a governing coalition. He also drew on his family's extensive military background to understand the mores of the Brazilian officers and win their support for important reforms, including the establishment of a civilian Ministry of Defense. He served two presidential terms, oversaw market-opening economic reforms and active international diplomacy, and then led a seamless transition to the longtime left and labor leader Luiz Inácio (Lula) da Silva, elected in 2002, who continued and extended many of Cardoso's economic and social policies.

Interview with President Fernando Henrique Cardoso

What were the critical factors that contributed to the transition from military rule to democratic governance in Brazil?

First, one must bear in mind that the Brazilian transition was carried out during the Cold War, with a world divided in two. The military coup of March 31, 1964, cannot be explained otherwise. The thawing of the Cold War, in turn, helped the transition. In other words, international circumstances matter —even though they are not the essential factor.

It is the internal factors that are essential. Brazil's experience shows the importance of combining social pressure with occupying institutional spaces, even when these are narrow at first. The military in Brazil kept the Congress running, except for a brief period. They did not prohibit political party life; they suppressed the previous parties but created two new parties during the same time as they established mechanisms typical of arbitrary rule. Under the national security directive, the military could not (and did not want to) let go of the appearance of liberal institutions. The existence of these institutions was fundamental to the dynamics of the transition. Social pressure could find expression in the elections. Partial gains, in turn, reinforced the social pressure against the regime.

In this process a new society gradually emerged and found new forms of unarmed struggle. Armed struggle was a disaster and served as a justification for the worst period of political repression by the military regime, which took place from 1968 to 1973.

Social Mobilization

How did you become involved in the political process?

I threw myself into this struggle at great risk. My path was from society to politics. In 1973, I began to have a strong public voice. The Brazilian Society for the Advancement of Science, which was a sort of conglomerate of independent opposition people—professors, scientists, and other independent intellectuals who criticized the regime—was a forum for discussion and criticism that was important for undermining the regime.

The CEBRAP was also a major instrument for intellectual mobilization. We created this center with support from the Ford Foundation, which brought considerable internal debate because the Ford Foundation is a US organization. People had doubts as to whether it was legitimate for a US foundation to provide support, but I had already worked at ECLA (United Nations Economic Commission for Latin America), and I didn't share this apprehension. CEBRAP became an important center, and many people who later played a key role in Brazil's intellectual life went through there, including Pedro Malan, José Serra, and Luciano Coutinho [who later became finance minister, governor of São Paulo and presidential candidate, and president of the National Development Bank, respectively]. We didn't belong to any party, but we did accept people who were getting out of prison on the condition that they end their association with the armed struggle. There we worked with the Church, especially with the Cardinal of São Paulo, Dom Paulo Evaristo Arns. I gave many talks at convents, and in 1975 I wrote a book with other researchers from CEBRAP called *São Paulo: Growth and Poverty*, which denounced Brazil's social situation at the time.

Even though economic growth was 7% annually, the social situation was worsening due to internal migration and huge population growth. The state did not have the wherewithal to provide more health care, education, or transport. In addition, there was a get-tough policy to hold wages down.

How did the sense of freedom awaken and connect with social movements? How did the political forces begin to organize?

There was political space for social criticism—opposing torture, for example—and the Catholic Church did a lot. The Cardinal Bishop of São Paulo, Dom Paulo Evaristo Arns, was a very active man, and opposed torture. In 1975, we held a very large demonstration when they killed the director of TV Cultura, Vladimir Herzog. Dom Paulo was very bold when he made the decision to organize a protest mass with Rabbi Henry Sobel and Presbyterian Pastor James Wright. The governor of São Paulo (appointed by President Ernesto Geisel, 1974-79),

Paulo Egídio Martins, was a friend of ours who had a conservative liberal position. Dom Paulo sent a messenger to speak with the secretary of interior, and he answered, "you know, you can cause a massacre," and Dom Paulo called me and we spoke. In the end, he decided to go forward with the mass, which was the first popular mobilization against the regime. He gave a hard-hitting homily; Cardinal Helder Cámara was in attendance, and I participated with the priests at the altar.

Building a Coalition

In 1974, there was already a major change in the opposition. The opposition leader was a legislator by the name of Ulysses Guimarães, an extraordinary man from the former Partido Social Democrático (Social Democratic Party), the main government party before the military coup. Ulysses had conservative origins, and little by little he emerged as a leader of the redemocratization effort. He wanted to breathe new life into the Movimento Democrático Brasiliero (MDB, or Brazilian Democratic Movement), the only legal party opposing the dictatorship. In 1974, there were elections, and he came to see me at CEBRAP with his friend, another legislator. Ulysses had read my articles, where I mentioned that it was time for the left to grow closer to the MDB. At that time, that proposal was a sin in the eyes of many. Colleagues argued that we had to be pure—that the genuine opposition should not make contact with an opposition that enjoyed the consent of the regime. In the article, I had argued that it would not be possible to break the military domination without an alliance among various sectors. Ulysses Guimarães came to my office without knowing what CEBRAP was; we were a research center, not a political organization. For us to act politically, one had to ask who was ready and willing. Some of my colleagues agreed to prepare a campaign program for the MDB in 1974. Among those working together were Francisco Weffort and Francisco de Oliveira, both of whom would join the Workers' Party (PT, or Partido dos Trabalhadores) years later; Bolivar Lamounier; Professor Maria Hermínia Tavares de Almeida; and Paulo Singer, who is with the PT to this day. That program was a framework for future programs. It wasn't enough to criticize the violence and torture and to talk about democracy; one also had to speak of women, blacks, indigenous peoples, civil society, and the trade unions, and to respond to the intense social pressure to seek redress for grievances. It was a social democratic program.

Creating a Consensus for Change

At that time, some of our group thought that social democracy was a betrayal. Nonetheless, in practice I no longer thought so. Ulysses Guimarães invited Chico Oliveira and me to Brasilia to present the program to the leaders of the

MDB—the old political leaders who had fought with the military government, including Tancredo Neves and André Franco Montoro, among others. We did not think they were going to accept it, but to our surprise, all adhered to the program. For them it was mainly important to include more people in the opposition, and they weren't very concerned about the program, except for Ulysses Guimarães.

Then came the 1974 elections. The opposition won 16 of the 22 seats up for grabs in the Senate and elected 161 members of the lower chamber—less than the government party but much more than in the 1970 elections. These results were a total surprise for the regime. It turned out well for the opposition because the economic situation of the masses was poor, not because they opposed the regime. Then the opening began. Golbery do Couto e Silva was Geisel's lead political minister even though he was a military man. In 1964, he had established the National Information Service, which played a key role in the repression. Yet Golbery returned to the government concerned about limiting the power of the extreme right and the repressive apparatus.

Geisel had an ambiguous attitude. On one occasion, the police came to CEBRAP and arrested several researchers. They were not involved in any subversive movement, yet they were tortured at the police facilities in São Paulo. When they were released, I took them to the home of a friend of mine, Severo Gomes, who at the time was one of Geisel's ministers; he was later a senator for the opposition party. Severo asked me to write a letter to Geisel about what had happened, and he took it to him. Geisel told Severo that I was also a Communist. "What do you mean, 'a Communist'?" answered Severo. Geisel was a tough person, but he was influenced by Golbery do Couto e Silva. With a certain easing-up of the regime, the press began to take more risks. There was a daily newspaper called the *Gazeta Mercantil* that was influenced by people who had been Communists; some were major intellectuals. In 1977, I believe, they created a forum of the 10 most important business leaders of Brazil. They began to criticize the excessive gigantism of the "entrepreneur state." It was unusual, for the press had invented a leadership that was, in fact, dispersed. It was not a question of leadership of the business associations, but rather of major individual business leaders, who were themselves economically strong.

The voice of the press had repercussions in the government. The two leading daily newspapers of São Paulo played a role in this. Ever since the 1968 Institutional Act 5 (AI-5),[1] O Estado de São Paulo had protested press censorship by publishing several verses by the poet Luís de Camões in place of articles the government had censored. The mobilization against censorship (and in favor of repealing AI-5) picked up momentum. It was Golbery, mainly, who perceived the need to move forward with liberalizing the regime. The idea was to proceed with liberalization with the slogan "slow, gradual and sure." But we opposed that; we wanted to proceed more quickly, even if it wasn't so sure. The transformation wasn't linear; there were moments when Geisel was under considerable pressure, and others when he enjoyed more freedom of action to liberalize.

In 1977, other interesting events ensued. Ulysses had been the anti-candidate for president, going up against Geisel in the Electoral College, which was controlled by the dictatorship. At the same time, a movement of unionized workers emerged, which was not linked to the Communist Party or to any other part of the preexisting left. Then Lula appeared; he was the secretary general of the São Bernardo union, and then its president. He did not have a political formation and opposed the idea of political parties, but he had considerable skills as a speaker. As he did not come out of the left, his way of seeing things was not the usual perspective. With support from the German unions, which were very strong in the automobile sector, the new union began to stage strikes around economic demands without a broader political program. Yet the economic grievances came to present themselves as claims for rights. A group of lawyers associated with the unions—among them Almir Pazzianotto, who was later Sarney's labor minister—played an important role in this regard. With this new approach, these unions grew.

In 1977, I entered the MDB. The next year I went to Lula's union, for the first time, as a precandidate for the Senate. Lula sent me a message saying he wanted to support me. I was impressed because he had a powerful apparatus. The unions began to become politicized. Some of Lula's strikes, especially in 1978–79, mobilized people, the Church, the intellectuals, and part of the MDB.

Defeating the Authoritarian System from Within

In 1978, there were new elections for Congress. The opposition did not obtain a majority in either the Chamber of Deputies or the Senate [in 1977, the government had introduced the so-called bionic senator, elected indirectly, to ensure that it would not lose its majority in the Senate]. Nonetheless, the opposition got a very good number of votes, especially in the most socially and economically dynamic states and localities. The idea then came about to run a dissident member of the military in the elections to succeed Geisel. We knew the likelihood of winning in the Electoral College was very slim. Despite the growth of the opposition in Congress, especially in the lower house, the regime had the Electoral College under its control—including, among others, representatives to the provincial legislative assemblies. Our objective was not to win, but to show strength vis-à-vis the regime in its own court.

I was in Rio with Severo Gomes, who had already stepped down from the government and moved to the opposition, and he suggested that we go to the home of General Euller Bentes Monteiro, who appeared to oppose the government candidate, General João Batista de Figueiredo. At that first meeting, General Euller Bentes told us that he would agree to be the opposition candidate, and Severo told us to consult with Ulysses Guimarães. Ulysses's reaction was cold because he was promoting a civilian candidacy—that of the former governor of Minas Gerais, Magalhães Pinto, who distanced himself from the regime and had begun to embrace a new position. Ulysses wanted Magalhães to be the candidate because he was a civilian, and, although he was close to the regime, he represented internal opposition to it. On one occasion, when I was a senator, Magalhães called me. He asked me if I knew that our children were dating, and added that he didn't want it to be known. Afterward, my son married his daughter. They've divorced, but my grandchildren are also his grandchildren.

Ulysses had the idea of opening a breach in the regime using Magalhães, and now this Army general was coming forward who also wanted to be the candidate. I preferred the general because he would crack the regime closer to its foundation. Some time elapsed without Ulysses making a decision. He called me and asked, "What do you really think of this general?" I replied, "I think you are holding back your support." He did not like my response at all and told me, "but you know that São Paulo is civilian oriented." "I know," I answered, "but this is a military regime and it's the first time an active duty four-star military officer has switched sides, and we are not going to win without breaking them from within as well."

My conception was always that the transition would not occur without a direct confrontation. I always used the following image: they are a fortress; we have to surround the fortress, and if we impose a strong cordon, those on the inside will get hungry and seek us out. Then the transition will occur as the result of a sort of confluence of forces that break away from the government to join the opposition. It will not be the opposition alone. My view, however, was considered by many to be a position that could be taken advantage of by the regime.

I believe that my perspective eventually won out. Euller was the candidate, but he lost—it was an election to be lost—for there was no way he could have won, but the breach remained.

What was the military's strategy, and how did they act to counter a growing opposition?

At first, Golbery wanted a slow transition. The votes won by the opposition in 1974 and 1978 were surprising. The government reacted by delaying the return to elected state governments, which had been anticipated for 1978. It brought the two-party political arrangement to an end in 1979. This measure was aimed at dividing the opposition front. It was in this context that the PT arose. At first, the new union movement was looked upon favorably by the government; never before had a trade union leader appeared on the front pages of the magazines as Lula did. Because Lula was new, he was not associated with the Cold War or with the old left; he represented something new. The most moderate sectors of the MDB also tried to create another party called the PP—Partido Popular—with the encouragement of the government, under the leadership of Tancredo Neves. Olavo Setúbal, who had been appointed mayor of São Paulo by Geisel and was a major banker, joined the party. Yet the PP was short lived; its cadre returned, for the most part, to the MDB, which came to be called the PMDB (Partido do Movimento Democrático Brasileiro, or Brazilian Democratic Movement Party).

How was the struggle for democracy activated in this new stage of the transition?

At that time, other movements emerged: a very strong movement for amnesty, even at the end of the Geisel administration, plus the strikes organized by Lula. Interestingly, Lula did not support the amnesty because he said that a real amnesty for workers would be ending Vargas's labor legislation, which tied the state to the unions. The new union leaders had a more independent outlook, with a more Catholic and non-statist influence. The new unionism sought to break the ties with the government. They fought for a more autonomous union. We were involved in the struggle for political amnesty. The major figure in that struggle was Senator Teotônio Vilela, a relative of mine on my mother's side. He also supported the regime but changed his views at the end. People began to change positions. Teotônio became a hero of the opposition; the name of my party's foundation is Teotônio Vilela, even though he was with ARENA (Aliança Renovadora Nacional, or the National Renewal Alliance Party), the government party under the two-party system.

The Amnesty Law was adopted at that time. The return of those who'd been in exile had an impact on the formation of the new parties, especially the PT and the PDT (Partido Democrático Trabalhista, or Democratic Labor Party), the party created by Leonel Brizola. [The military succeeded in taking the former PTB, or Partido Trabalhista do Brasil, from him; it was left in the hands of Ivete Vargas, the great-niece of President Getúlio Vargas.] Golbery and the government maneuvered for her, and not Brizola, to carry the symbolic banner of the PTB.

The Experience of Exile

In many transitions there are tensions between the exiles and the leaders of the opposition on the inside. What lessons does Brazil's experience offer in this regard?

There is always tension between the people who are in the country struggling against the regime and those who are outside, the exiles. I was outside and inside at different stages. Those inside, who are experiencing the situation on a day-to-day basis, are more able to realize what's happening at different stages in the process, yet at the same time they are scornful of those who are outside.

I clearly recall a talk in Paris with Brizola. He insisted that as soon as he returned to Brazil, the MDB would become the PTB, which was his and Getúlio Vargas's old party. He did not believe in the continuity of the MDB and thought the PTB was going to return as strong as it had been earlier. Time went by, and after the amnesty he returned to Brazil. We went to the home of a journalist by the name of Claudio Abramo, at a gathering of young people, and others who were not so young, with Brizola. All of a sudden, one man got up and corrected a number of things Brizola said about the trade union movement. Brizola became irritated and challenged him: "What do you know about that? Who are you?" It turns out he was the lawyer for Lula's union, Almir Pazzianotto. Brizola was recalling the trade union world of his time, without realizing that we were in another time; he thought that on returning he was going to retake everything. He had retaken something, but it was never the same, and the MDB was much stronger than Brizola's party.

I recall that Ulysses Guimarães, the great leader of the redemocratization movement, looked down on Brizola and Arraes, old-school politicians who were in exile. Ulysses was going to Europe but did not intend to speak with them. There was a certain tension between the opposition leadership here and there, and since I had contact with both, to some extent I served as a bridge. Ulysses once called and told me that Arraes, who (according to Ulysses) was the head of the Communist Party, was going to return. There's always that failure to find common ground, and it was not easy to get the two groups to work together.

Defeating the Authoritarian System from Within

How did you come to be senator and Franco Montoro become governor?

I ran for the Senate in the 1978 elections. There was considerable doubt as to whether the electoral authorities would allow my candidacy. AI-5 got me thrown out of the university in 1969. I was forced into retirement; I was 37 years old and a professor at the University of São Paulo. The law did not permit me to be accepted as a candidate. That allowed me to assure my wife that, for me, being a candidate was just a protest and not the beginning of a political career.

At that time there was a system of incorporating internal party elections into the general election, known as the system of *lemas*. As in Uruguay, each political party could nominate up to three candidates for Senate, and those candidates' votes were added up to decide which party won; of the three, the one with the most votes would win the seat. The objective of my candidacy was to increase the vote for the MDB by drawing in younger people, intellectuals, artists, etc. So they held a meeting at the home of a friend of mine, José Gregori, who was later minister of justice in my administration; at that time he was a member of the Church's Justice and Peace Commission. Those present reached the conclusion that I was the only one who had a certain presence in society, although that wasn't so obvious then, because I wasn't a legislator and I didn't have a political life. The courts of São Paulo rejected my candidacy and the Court of Appeals also rejected it. Then, just two weeks before the election, the Federal Supreme Court accepted it. A judge agreed with the argument that university tenure is for life, and that no one can be condemned to lose their political rights for life.

I received 1,300,000 votes, more than the ARENA candidate and less than Montoro. So from 1978 on they invented the notion that I was the alternate senator. There was no such position. When they introduced us, Montoro's ticket had one alternate and I had another; mine was chosen by Lula. My alternate was Maurício Soares, who was associated with the metallurgical workers' union. Montoro's was the mayor of Campinas.

In 1982, Montoro became governor and I replaced him, taking his place as senator. I was in Berkeley, as a visiting professor, and Professor Robert Bellah called me to offer me a permanent position in the university. I turned down the offer because I had decided to return to Brazil to become a senator.

The Campaign for Direct Election of the President

Another moment in the struggle for redemocratization began, a struggle in the streets: the campaign for Direct Elections Now (Diretas Já). This happened because, in the 1982 elections (when, for the first time since 1965, there were also elections for state governors), the opposition won São Paulo with Montoro, Minas with Tancredo, and Rio with Brizola.

The movement for Direct Elections Now emerged in this context: the regime was operating from the trenches of Brasilia, with governors allied with it in the states that had less social mobilization and economic dynamism, while the opposition had won new bases of power: the governors' offices of Brazil's three leading states. André Franco Montoro, governor of São Paulo, was decisive in the Diretas Já campaign.

With Montoro elected governor of São Paulo, I assumed office as senator in 1982. I also became the chairman of the PMDB in São Paulo because the sitting chairman, Mário Covas, was appointed mayor of the city of São Paulo by Montoro (direct elections for the state governments preceded direct elections for mayors of the state capitals). I was the chairman of the MDB at the time of the campaign for direct elections, and I tell you that to reiterate how important Montoro was. In late 1983, Montoro called and told me the time had come to hold a major rally in favor of direct elections to the presidency of the republic. I told him that I didn't think the conditions were right. I consulted the party; the Executive Committee unanimously decided that it was insane, that we were going to expose ourselves. So I suggested to Montoro that we speak with the other parties; I sought out the PT, but the PT wanted to go it alone, for they opposed alliances at that time.

The PT held a rally in October or November 1983 in favor of direct elections; I went. They didn't jeer when I asked for a minute of silence for the death of Teotônio Vilela. It was a very small rally, a very sectarian thing of the PT. Montoro wanted to do something much broader, with Brizola, Lula, Ulysses, and all leaders of the parties opposing the government. And so he called a rally of the different opposition groups for January 25, 1984, in the plaza in front of the great Cathedral of São Paulo.

January 25 is the date of the founding of the city of São Paulo and of the University of São Paulo, so I went as a professor to the celebration of the university. We were there when José Gregori (then a legislator), who was in the plaza at the cathedral, called me by phone and said, "come here, because there's quite a crowd." The loudspeakers were not enough for all the people; the crowd continued to grow despite the rain. So we went, and we were surprised by the number of people. It was the first large rally, to be followed by others. Everyone came together there: Lula, Montoro, Tancredo. The people harassed the TV Globo vehicles; Globo had taken a long time to give the campaign coverage proportional to its significance and size. Then came the huge campaign of support for a constitutional amendment reestablishing direct elections for president of the republic, called the Dante de Oliveira amendment, the name of the PMDB legislator from Mato Grosso who introduced it.

In April 1984, the amendment went to a vote before the Congress. It won by a wide majority in the Chamber of Deputies but failed to gain the number of votes needed to change the constitution. So the question arose as to what to do next. A few weeks went by.

Having failed to secure approval of direct presidential elections, how did you react?

I went to the Senate and gave a speech with the message "change now," which meant that we were going to fight in Congress for the election of a new president. **We would accept that once again the election could be indirect. It was not an easy decision. We intended to use the instruments of the regime to change it, but if we were not successful, we could end up helping the regime gain legitimacy.** At a dinner that brought four or five of us together, including Ulysses, I told him that of those of us who had come together, I had paid the highest price under the military regime because I went into exile, lost my position at the university, was imprisoned, and had been targeted by threats. The others present had not suffered all this. I said that I was not willing to see the situation in Brazil continue any longer, that I believed there was an opportunity to win through indirect elections and bring about a change. Ulysses, whom I admire profoundly, told me that we should make the decision but that he was not going to follow that path—he continued to believe that we should insist on mobilizing to support direct elections.

Defeating the Authoritarian System from Within

Our candidate for the direct elections was Ulysses, but not for the indirect elections, because he had fought a lot with the military, was harsher in his criticism, and had fewer votes in Congress. Montoro or Tancredo could win congressional approval. We wanted direct elections, but once we lost that battle, we decided to wage the fight in Congress. Thus began a new stage: how could an opposition candidate win in the Electoral College? Who was going to be the candidate? There were two possible choices: Montoro and Tancredo.

Montoro was the governor of São Paulo and had more popular votes than Tancredo, but Tancredo had a better chance in terms of votes in Congress. His outlook was more acceptable, including for the military, and he was a more agreeable person than Ulysses. Once when I was president of the party in São Paulo, Ulysses came to see me at the headquarters, which was a mansion. We approached the window, near a large tree. He asked me what I thought about the fact that Montoro's secretary of interior had given an interview to *Veja* magazine in which he said he could support Tancredo. "Do you believe that Montoro also supports Tancredo?" he asked me. "Well," I told him, "I think so; to win, it's Tancredo." He didn't like my answer, but he was a great man. He asked me, "What do you think I should do?" I told him that he should support Tancredo and run the campaign. He answered that he wanted to hear that directly from Montoro.

We had a terrible dinner at the palace—with Montoro, his secretary of interior Roberto Gusmão, Ulysses, and me—at which Ulysses demanded that each person around the table state what he really thought. Ulysses realized it was Tancredo's moment. He was a formidable guy, and he agreed to embrace Tancredo's campaign completely. Winning in Congress required wider support from other factions of those who were backing the government. So a group was formed called the Frente Liberal, which separated from the government party. It had already changed its name when multiparty politics was established. Having been known as ARENA, it came to be called the Partido Democrático Social (PDS), and then the Partido del Frente Liberal (PFL) emerged from the PDS.

We wanted the vice presidential candidate to be Aureliano Chaves or Marco Maciel, but the PFL came up with Jose Sarney. Sarney had recently stepped down as chairman of the PDS. He wasn't our first choice. Nonetheless, that was the decision. If we wanted the support of the Frente Liberal, it was with Sarney, so the ticket was Tancredo-Sarney. It was very difficult to win approval of this ticket in our party, the PMDB. More than 100 of the 500 voting delegates at the convention that approved the Tancredo-Sarney ticket voted against it. In January 1985, Tancredo was elected president in the Electoral College.

Ulysses carried considerable weight in the selection of president-elect Tancredo's cabinet ministers. I had a very good relationship with both of them. Sometime between January and March, when the new president was to take office, Tancredo took me to his office one day at the Fundação Getúlio Vargas in Brasilia and told me, in his style, "I'd like to invite you to be a minister, but I have four ministers from São Paulo, and if I were to appoint you, I'd have a fifth." I answered that I did not aspire to the cabinet post. It would be difficult for me to give up my seat in the Senate, and I wanted to be the leader of the PMDB in the Senate if the cabinet appointment of the other candidate for leader in the Senate, Pedro Simon, was confirmed. Simon was then appointed by Tancredo, and the person who was seeking the presidency of the Senate for my party, Humberto Lucena, lost his election but wanted to continue in his leadership position within the party. That's why Tancredo asked that I give it up.

Two or three days before turning over the helm of the party, I was called by Ulysses, who said that Tancredo had just appointed me leader of the pro-government forces in Congress. I was surprised, because the position did not exist. I then went to speak with Tancredo. He was at his ranch with Miguel Arraes. He finished speaking with Arraes and then he came to me. I asked him what the appointment was about and he told me, "don't worry, I already called the Senate and I told them to tear down some walls so your office will be the largest in the Senate. That way everyone will know you're in charge. Moreover, it's more important to be a leader than a minister." And we went to have lunch: Tancredo, his wife, Arraes, and I. Arraes was a leader of the left, but a very close friend of mine and Tancredo's good friend as well.

Setbacks

The sudden illness and death of president-elect Tancredo Neves must have been a shock for the process of democratic transition. What happened when it became necessary to replace him as the first civilian president after the military regime?

On the eve of the inauguration, I was at the Embassy of Portugal with Mário Soares, Ulysses Guimarães, and other political leaders when we were advised by phone that Tancredo had been taken to hospital. Several of us went to the hospital to find out what was going on. There was a waiting room. The physician went through to perform surgery, and there was great uncertainty. Then a discussion ensued about who would replace Tancredo on an interim basis. Sarney, who was very skillful, said that it would not be he, and suggested Ulysses, arguing that he had not yet been sworn in as vice president, and that the next in the line of succession was the speaker of the Chamber of Deputies, who was Ulysses. Ulysses, however, argued that Sarney should occupy the presidency until Tancredo recovered. The discussion unfolded at the hospital. There they decided to go to the home of the chief of staff of the presidency, Leitão de Abreu. He was an ultraconservative jurist from southern Brazil, but a very decent man. It was he, when he was serving as a justice of the Supreme Court, who had handed down the ruling that allowed for my Senate candidacy in 1978.

Ulysses, José Fragelli (president of the Senate), General Leônidas (appointed minister of the Army), and I all arrived at one o'clock in the morning. Leitão de Abreu was asleep. He woke up and got dressed, even putting on a tie, very formal, and the discussion began. He too believed that Ulysses should become interim president. I recalled the case of president-elect Rodrigues Alves, who died before taking office and was replaced by his vice president in 1918, but I did not know the exact circumstances. The decision, basically made by Ulysses and Leitão de Abreu with the consent of the president of the Senate, was clear: José Sarney would replace Tancredo Neves.

We left Leitão de Abreu's house and went to the Congress. We met in the office of the president of the Senate. Other legislators and politicians joined. My party was furious because they wanted Ulysses, not Sarney. I remember that the speech by Afonso Arinos was decisive. Arinos was a renowned constitutional scholar in addition to being the biographer of Rodrigues Alves. He said that it should be Sarney. I don't know why Ulysses wanted Sarney. People say that it was because he calculated that if he himself were to assume the presidency, he would not be able to be a candidate for the next presidential term. The truth is that no one knew that Tancredo was going to die: for us it was a matter of one week. We were not discussing who was going to be the future president of Brazil; we discussed who could occupy the position in the interim, causing the least possible harm. So Ulysses wasn't in fact worried about the next election, but he was fearful of provoking a very strong reaction from the military. Ulysses was quite confrontational with the military; he was a grandiose guy, so the issues being debated were never small.

This illustrates the uncertain circumstances of the transition. We were approaching the succession to the military government, and we were still very cautious. **Transitions are very complicated; one must do a lot of calculating because you never know what's going to happen the next day. You have to maintain an overall view and always keep your eye on the main objective.** The main objective was to win power, but how? Under what conditions? When? What are the preconditions for being able to govern? With whom is an alliance acceptable, and with whom it is not? And how to go about that? There's never any certainty. In our case, Tancredo died and Sarney became the first nonmilitary president, he who had been one of the political leaders of the authoritarian military regime! The situation was extremely delicate and continued to be so throughout Sarney's term in office; Sarney inherited a cabinet put together by Tancredo in collaboration with Ulysses. Ulysses was the big leader, and Sarney did not have effective strength in Congress, at least at the beginning of his term.

What were the most important decisions Sarney made, and how was it possible to maintain the cohesion of the democratic forces?

Once Sarney had become president, Ulysses hosted a dinner at his home with all the ministers, except the minister of the treasury, Francisco Dornelles, since he was not from the PMDB. I went to Dornelles's house to explain to him that the dinner was not a meeting against him. Ulysses brought together all the ministers, so it was almost a challenge to Sarney. At one point Sarney did not know what to do, and while Tancredo was alive it was very difficult. Sarney was—and yet wasn't—in charge, and the time came when we were telling him to start governing, because Tancredo was not coming back. But he was fraught with indecision, and we were afraid. Sarney was very skillful. I resigned my fictitious position as leader of the Congress, but Sarney asked me not to because it was going to seem as if he were losing people, above all because he needed people for the dialogue with the left. So I stayed on for a year as Sarney's leader in Congress. It was very difficult due to the political tensions between Sarney and Ulysses. Each time there was a crisis, Sarney sought the support of the military. He was very close to the military; he knew the generals well.

New Constitution and System of Government

Under pressure, but by his own decision, Sarney called a national Constituent Assembly. This had been one of the issues of the opposition: to truly change the previous regime, and the constitution that had been decreed by the military. It was a very important moment for the country. The assembly lasted almost two years, from early 1987 to late 1988. Most of the old opposition wanted a very social democratic constitution, in which full rights and liberties would be guaranteed and social rights would be expanded. Sarney organized a group that was more conservative.

Of the political issues, the big topic of debate was whether the presidential system should be replaced by a parliamentary one. Part of the PMDB was parliamentarianist—those of us who would later form the PSDB. Ulysses was presidentialist, like Sarney, and like the military, whom I sought out to explain how the proposed parliamentarian system would work. (I recall a major debate with the minister of the Army.) The discussion of the system of government was combined with a debate on the duration of Sarney's term. The term inherited from the previous constitution was six years. Sarney did not want the assembly to change the duration of his term, but most of the opposition defended a term of four years. Sarney was able to organize a sufficient base of support to ensure a five-year term. His minister of communications, Antonio Carlos Magalhães, played a key role in this effort. Like Sarney, ACM, as we called Magalhães, had been a major political figure in the military regime.

Role of the Military in Constitutional Reform

I believe the military were reasonable; they appointed advisers for the constitutional process. If one reads the constitution, there is only one point that talks about the military. There the big discussion was trying to figure out whether the armed forces would be limited to defending the country's borders and territory, or whether they were also to play a role in maintaining internal order. The text approved by the assembly establishes that the armed forces are for the defense of the homeland and of the constitutionally established authorities and are responsible, upon the request of these authorities, for maintaining internal order. A state of siege, for example, can only be decreed at the request of the president, after consulting the Council of the Republic, and with the authorization of Congress.

Political and Social Rights

We made progress in relation to both political and social rights. The result was a good constitution, despite being national-statist from an economic point of view, and therefore not concerned about maintaining a balanced budget. Many crazy things happened at the assembly; many benefits were created without having the fiscal basis to pay for them. For this reason the constitution had to be amended during my administration. Without amendments there would have been no stabilization or modernization of the economy. In any event, the 1988 constitution represents political and social gains. I don't know if it would have been possible to make it as social democratic if Tancredo had been president. He was more conservative. So was Sarney, but he didn't have the political strength to confront most of the old opposition in his effort to "address the social debt" of the military regime.

First Direct Elections for President

The first direct elections for the presidency of the republic were held in 1989, under economic conditions that were quite unfavorable for the government. At the end of the Sarney administration we went to the brink of hyperinflation. The government was very much weakened politically. Against it were Lula and the PT, and Brizola and the PDT; Sarney's support in the PMDB was residual. Franco Montoro, Mário Covas, José Serra (who had been elected a federal deputy in 1986), and I had left the PMDB the year before to found the PSDB.

Even within the PMDB, we had fought for parliamentarianism and for a four-year term for Sarney. We saw that the PMDB, growing closer to the state, was increasingly becoming a traditional political force. With the PSDB we were out to build an alternative social democratic party. Serra and I in particular were concerned about the country's isolation in relation to the transformations in the international economy. For this reason he and I wrote a document that was an important piece in the campaign of Mário Covas, our candidate in the 1989 elections. It was called "The Capitalist Shock" and advocated the position that Brazil should be integrated into the world.

Yet it was Collor de Melo who won the elections. He won in the second round, defeating Lula. The PSDB decided to support the PT in the second round. It was up to me to conduct the negotiations with the PT. They had 13 major points. My interlocutors were José Dirceu and Plínio Sampaio, whom I knew well. They were advocating direct agrarian reform without government intervention, and proposed that newspapers should be directed by a committee of editors. These were such radical proposals that I decided to speak with the old Communist leader João Amazonas, president of the Partido Comunista do Brasil and a member of the coalition backing Lula, to tell him that this was an election, not a revolution. We didn't come to an agreement, so my party's decision was to vote for Lula even though we were not committed to this program. There was excitement because, if Lula won, we would become part of the government. But Collor won. We were all very lucky, as it turns out; Lula has said so on more than one occasion: he was lucky to lose because he couldn't have governed with the ideas he had at that time.

So a common theme during a transition is that there is a lot of luck and surprise?

Yes. **When the inevitable approaches, the unexpected comes up. I always say that. Politics, like life, is like that.** Collor was a very interesting guy. He had tried to become Covas's vice presidential candidate. Now he is more cautious, but back then he made very big mistakes. Recently, Collor, who's now a senator, gave advice to our current president, Dilma Rousseff: "don't do what I did; I was contemptuous of Congress."

Collor wanted to govern without the parties. He had clashes with his younger brother, who in mid-1992 made serious allegations of corruption in the government. In Congress, a commission was established to look into them. The PT assumed a leading role in the commission. With the press against him, and without the support of Congress, Collor was impeached. The PSDB voted in favor of the impeachment. I didn't expect this to be the outcome. I said at some point during that time that recourse to impeachment is like the atom bomb: it's best not to use it. But Collor's situation became unsustainable.

Collor was very young. He opened the economy abruptly and made some major changes without any negotiation. We all criticized that, but I believe if it weren't for those changes, the Brazilian economy never would have opened up. When I was minister of finance, after Collor, the industrialists of São Paulo and the economists strongly advocated more state, more protection, more subsidies. That's the predominant culture, but it's not modernization. Collor made changes and completely dismantled the public administration. He had innovative ideas, but his actions made no sense in that they did not take stock of reality. **Change does not happen through sudden ruptures; one must accumulate forces to win.** Collor wanted to change the country all of a sudden, but failed. He lost his base of support in Congress and was impeached.

So Itamar Franco, Collor's vice president, became president (1992–95). He was an unusual character; he had been Tancredo's opponent in Minas Gerais state politics. He did not want to vote for Tancredo in the Electoral College. He was from the PMDB but did not follow it; he voted on his own, and when we all thought he was going to support Covas, he went for Collor. Yet he was a man of good faith and organized a coalition government. The PFL and PT remained in the opposition. A prominent woman from the PT agreed to serve as a minister, and for that reason she was expelled from the party.

Itamar Franco, a man with a nationalist outlook, admired me at that time and called me to his office when it was clear that the Chamber of Deputies was going to conduct a proceeding against Collor. As a result, the president was suspended and the vice president took his place. Itamar was fearful of São Paulo since he was from Minas, and during our conversation in his office he asked me what people from São Paulo thought of him. I told him I thought he was stubborn, insistent in his ideas, and that he wanted to be involved in everything all the time. He asked me if I thought he was thick skulled. I told him no, but that I thought he was stubborn. There we began to talk, and when we wrapped it up, he authorized me to give an interview to a newspaper from São Paulo to convey the idea that he would be a sensible president.

Responding to Economic Crisis

With the first president dead and the second impeached, it must have been very difficult to stabilize the economy and consolidate the transition. How did the new president manage to deal with economic troubles?

First he appointed me foreign minister, and seven months later minister of finance—the fourth in seven months. The situation was complicated; inflation was accelerating and the government was not finding its way. A new expectation was created when I assumed the ministry of finance. I knew—and said—that fighting inflation was the priority, but that I was not willing to adopt a new stabilization package with price controls, frozen salaries, etc. We had to build an alternative.

I formed a small team of economists close to me. There was considerable skepticism among them about whether we could do anything more than just manage the situation. They were not willing to repeat the "mistakes of the past," and they feared that Itamar would not be able to resist the temptation to adopt a new shock plan against inflation. In addition, the Congress was experiencing its own crisis, for in mid-1993 a scandal broke out in the powerful budget committee that involved many parties and legislators. How could it be possible, for example, to approve fiscal adjustment measures without the firm support of the president and with party leaders who were on the defensive due to a scandal that no one knew how (or when) it would end?

I tried to convince the economists that the crisis gave us an opportunity to approve an agenda of measures that, in normal situations, the Congress would not accept. As for Itamar, he was an unpredictable politician, but we had been colleagues in the Senate, we got along well, I knew what he was like and how he thought, and he trusted me. I also had the support of my party, especially of Mário Covas and Tasso Jereissati, and this too was decisive for convincing the economists to come work with me on a stabilization program. In that context, it wasn't a chimera.

I assumed the post in May, but only in December 1993 did we announce to the country a program that provided for an emergency fiscal adjustment and an innovative monetary mechanism for transitioning to a new currency. The innovation was that, for the first time, an effort would be made to stabilize the economy without surprises and with total transparency as to how to do so. Success depended on congressional approval of the fiscal adjustment and the voluntary accession of the economic actors to the monetary mechanism that would lead to the issuance of the new currency.

There were plenty of problems from May to December. Inflation continued to be high, and trending upward. The pressure within the government and from society for immediate responses from the Ministry of Finance was mounting all the time. Itamar grew angry over a minor issue with the president of the Central Bank, and fired him. I took that occasion to expand my team, and I convinced the president to appoint Pedro Malan as president of the Central Bank. Itamar also had a problem with the president of the BNDES (Banco Nacional de Desenvolvimento Econômico e Social, or National Bank for Economic and Social Development), and I convinced him to appoint Persio Arida to replace him.

Persio was identified as one of the "fathers" of the Cruzado Plan, which had brought considerable popularity to the Sarney administration for a year, but which had failed at the end of the day. Itamar may have seen in Persio a signal that I might be ready to reissue a plan like the Cruzado Plan. That is why he did not oppose Persio's appointment as president of the BNDES. I didn't know that Persio was very critical of the Cruzado Plan, but he and Andre Lara Resende would play a key role, along with Edmar Bacha, in the theoretical formulation of the mechanism that made possible the transition to the currency known as the *real*. It was up to me to talk to the country, to explain what we intended to do, to convince Itamar that there were risks but that we were on the right path, and to negotiate the approval of the fiscal adjustment measures with the parties.

We approved the fiscal adjustment measures in February, and then we moved on to the transition to the new currency. We did not set a date for its issue. It was open ended and depended on the degree of trust the economic actors had in the Unidade Real de Valor (URV), a proto-currency without inflation. The prices of goods and services were denominated in URV but paid in cruzeiros, the currency tied to inflation, whose value we were adjusting daily. We killed inflation with its own poison. But we didn't know how long full acceptance of the URV was going to take, and by law I had to leave the ministry by April in order to run for office. I feared that an early exit could compromise trust in the success of the stabilization program.

During this process, an alliance began to form between the PSDB and the PFL that would be at the heart of my candidacy for president. Itamar wanted me to be a candidate. At first I very much resisted becoming a candidate. He was right. If the program suffered political orphanhood, this would have been fatal for the stabilization effort. Lula, who was the favorite in all the polls, directly opposed the program. He, his party, and the unions linked to the CUT (Central Única dos Trabalhadores, or Unified Workers' Central) nicknamed the Real Plan an "electoral swindle." This was a serious mistake that cost them the presidency of the republic in October 1994.

Civilian Control of the Armed Forces

How did you handle your relationship with the military before and during your government to subordinate them to the civilian authorities?

I had good relations with Itamar's military ministers. Let me mention an episode to illustrate this point. During Carnival in February 1994, Itamar went to Rio to attend the procession of the samba schools. A wretched legislator arranged for a woman provocatively dressed as a policewoman to enter the presidential box, where the president was viewing the show. It was a setup. The photographers, who were below the presidential box, took photos of the woman next to the president. Itamar fell in love with her. The next day he was preparing to phone her in front of television cameras.

I was in Brasilia and General Cahim, minister of administration, sought me out, saying that he was there on behalf of his colleagues in the armed forces. They were scandalized by the president's behavior, and he told me that he and his colleagues supported replacing Itamar in Congress. They thought there was a legal way to have him replaced by Senator Jarbas Passarinho, a respectable man, a former Army colonel and a conservative. They wanted to know if I would agree to continue in the ministry under the new circumstances. I put a halt to the situation and I never told Itamar of the plan by his military ministers to depose him. At that time, the military no longer had the say they had had in the times of Sarney, at the beginning of the return to democracy. I suggested to Itamar that he find out more about what was happening in the military milieu, that things were ugly due to the photograph and the phone call, that it would be worth investigating whether there were military officers involved in the trap that was laid for him in Rio, etc. He didn't do anything, but he did not step down. He was a good guy; at the end of the day, people knew he was naïve, and that he hadn't acted with any negative animus.

When I was elected president of the republic, I decided to create the Ministry of Defense. I called each of the military officers that I was going to appoint minister of the Navy, Air Force, Army, and Joint Chiefs of Staff, and I told them that I would appoint them on the condition that they cooperate with the formation of the new Ministry of Defense. It took three years to create it. I had only one problem. It was, I believe, in 1998, in the final stage of implementation of the Ministry of Defense, when I was trying to choose commanders for the branches of the armed forces to serve under the minister of defense, who would be a civilian. The minister of the Navy asked to speak with me at my official residence; he came in uniform. He wanted to be the commander of the Navy. I told him that I was not appointing him, but that I wanted to appoint the number-two man in the Navy, Admiral Lacerda. General Alberto Cardoso, a minister in the military cabinet, invited Lacerda on my behalf but he said that he would not accept the position. So I called Cardoso again and I told him, "we're going to appoint the third admiral, Sergio Chagastelles. If he also says no, then imprison all three of them, because it's insubordination, not rejection." The third candidate accepted the post.

In 1999, once the Ministry of Defense was established, I had the commander of the Air Force, Brigadier Lieutenant Walter Brauer, step down for making certain statements to TV Globo that gave the impression that he was calling into question the authority of the civilian minister of defense. I called the head of the high command of the Air Force and told him that I had dismissed Brauer for what he said to the reporters. Nothing happened; there was no reaction on the part of the active duty military officers. A few retired officers hosted a luncheon for him as a gesture of solidarity.

Justice and Reconciliation

Early in my administration, in 1995, I dined at the home of the minister of the Navy with all the other military ministers and General Alberto Cardoso. There were five generals and myself; we were going to toast democracy. I told them that I had been a prisoner for one day in Operation Bandeirantes, a clandestine initiative of the dictatorship in which those imprisoned were tortured. I told them that I had seen some people tortured, and that for me human rights represented more than merely a rhetorical concern. I also told them that I was going to establish a commission to make reparations and offer apologies in the name of the Brazilian government for the violence perpetrated by the state.

I established a commission to review the punishments imposed without any legal trial during the dictatorship. Many people who demanded them received reparations until the time came for the promotion, postmortem, of a military officer by the name of Carlos Lamarca. He became a guerrilla fighter who had killed a military officer and was himself killed later. His family received a pension, but the commission tried to promote him to colonel, which was an exaggeration. So the representative of the armed forces on the commission, a retired general, asked to come to my home to speak with me. He told me he was a member of the reparations commission but that his opinions always lost out. He said that the commission was prejudiced but that he continued to serve on it, and that he had established a committee to support me in his city during my campaign. He told me that he had great respect for me but that he could not continue if they were going to promote Lamarca. I told him that when I established the commission I gave it full powers, and that I was going to abide by its decisions. Personally, I thought the promotion of Lamarca to colonel was an exaggeration, but if the commission approved it, I would carry it out. However, his resignation would cause me major political damage. The general was so proper with me that he did not step down from the commission even though they approved Lamarca's promotion.

The only active duty officer who protested the commission's decision was a general who was in command of the Army in the northeast. We quietly relieved him of his command; he was transferred to the reserves without any major incident. In other words, the military officers made the transition to obeying, and continued in that vein with Lula and now with the new president, who has established a Truth Commission to clarify responsibilities for events that occurred under military rule. **The transition to democracy was slow, gradual, and unsteady, but now there is no longer the looming threat of a military coup.** The military had the custom of celebrating April 1 (the date they called the revolution and we called the coup d'état); this ended during my administration. The military stopped talking about its role in "recovering democracy"; during my administration there were no more such references or celebrations.

Civilian Control of the Armed Forces

The Brazilian transition took several years, and the relationship between the armed forces and the civilian government took decades to work out. In contemporary Egypt, it would be very difficult to accept that the military question is going to take 25 years to resolve. Might it have been possible to move forward more quickly on this front in Brazil? Would doing so actually have endangered the process?

The thing to emphasize is that here the armed forces were never defeated by the opposition. There was an internal change, within the regime, and an external one, in society. In Argentina and Uruguay, the military split. In Chile, the armed forces were not defeated either. Pinochet stayed on for eight years. Here the process was gradual; there was never a rupture. The first sign of a rupture was the Constituent Assembly in 1987–88, because up until then the transition essentially unfolded in keeping with the rules of the authoritarian regime, albeit modified by mounting pressure from the opposition.

One point remained unresolved: the reciprocal amnesty. The Amnesty Law was adopted in Congress in 1979, but it was still the military regime, without the right to vote, without full freedoms. Today there is a controversy over amnesty for all—those responsible for torture and the torturers. About two years ago, the Supreme Court decided that the amnesty covers all of them. With the establishment of the Truth Commission, the issue heated up again. To get the military to calm down, it was determined that the commission will clarify the facts and not impose sanctions on those responsible.

Was there fear at any time of military interference that could provoke a turnaround? What role did social organizations play to inhibit military intervention?

Once he was elected president, one of the first steps taken by Tancredo Neves was to appoint the minister of the Army, a general who very likely would have protected and defended us from a possible military reaction. I already referred to him General Leônidas Pires Gonçalves. He was not a hard-liner but a typical professional military man, and he somehow assured Sarney, after Tancredo died, that there would be no turning back. The head of the information service, which was a key position, was also an even-handed man. From that point on, when the Constituent Assembly began to deliberate, we did not think there would be any backsliding; the assembly acted as if there were (and indeed there was) full freedom.

The military never embraced an authoritarian ideology, in that they always said they were going to govern for a brief time, to ensure a future democracy. It was hard for them, too. Staying in power created problems for the armed forces as an institution. Geisel sought to reestablish control over the sectors most associated with torture, which had gained strength in the most brutal period of repression. He succeeded in reestablishing the military hierarchy. Yet internal resistance to the opening did not come to an end. In 1980–81, the far right carried out several attacks with the direct participation of members of the military.

Sarney played an important role in ensuring there would be no backsliding, for he was a conservative liberal and had served the military regime. All of a sudden, he began to meet openly with representatives of the left. He would receive them at the palace, for example. That type of gesture was important for sending a signal that the years of guns and bullets were a thing of the past. Then came the fall of the Berlin Wall in 1989, and the Cold War was over, so much so that when Lula was running for president against Collor, the workers' movements and others were very much out there, and there was no longer fear of a military coup.

Many transitions face problems with the police and security apparatuses inherited from military regimes. What was Brazil's experience in this regard?

Under the military regime, the state police were placed under the direct control of the Army. So the military police were maintained in each state—some of them very powerful, as in São Paulo and Minas—in the hands of the Army. This influence continued even after the direct election of governors in 1982. It was only with the new 1988 constitution that governors' command over the military police of their respective states was legally established.

Did people criticize the police and call for the prosecution of those involved in repression? What was the solution?

Yes, of course. It's the whole controversy around the Amnesty Law. No changes were made to the law. But now, every time someone who belonged to the repressive groups is appointed to a position, there is enormous pressure against them. The press and the groups that defend human rights are very attentive, so neither appointments nor promotions of these officers can take place without close scrutiny. These officials have not been imprisoned, but their careers have been more or less contained.

How did the military view you—as a politician who was the son and grandson of military men? Did this help you understand the dynamic?

Yes, my family background helped me understand the codes. I gave great consideration to the military. They wanted to improve their salaries and obtain materiel—artillery, airplanes, and so on. Yet I didn't have money for it, not even to improve their salaries or buy very much. They wanted attention. I attended the celebrations of the important days for the military; I often went to naval maneuvers with the Navy. I went to the jungle and spent the night there to observe the Army's training, and each time an officer was promoted to general, I went with my wife. That is a high distinction, because they also came with their wives. I would make a short speech, giving them instructions; in this way we began to design a Brazilian defense strategy, which did not really exist.

Did they consider you part of the military family?

In a way, yes. It wasn't explicit, but they did know that there were about 10 or 12 generals in my family, two or three of them ministers of the armed forces. There was a tradition, but my family was also very progressive, from my grandfather to my father. From the war with Paraguay, the military opposed slavery and participated in the campaign against it. They felt themselves to be a sort of "father of the homeland," responsible for the country. The military always kept its distance from business; the state yes, the market no. My father was an attorney in addition to being a military man.

Ruth, my wife, who was from São Paulo—and who was very anti-military— was invited to the military academy to give a class. She was delighted because she realized that much had already changed, that the armed forces had modernized. They had also changed a lot in a technical sense, especially the Navy: they sent many people to study abroad in the United States. The wives and children of military officers pursued university studies. Their relationships with their wives and children gradually changed the mentality of the military officers. Today I doubt there is a segment of the military with authoritarian political thinking, or that claims to stand above the rest as the only pure defenders of the homeland.

Constitutional Reform

Did you create a Constituent Assembly? What were the most important political issues you dealt with? What changes were made in the electoral system? What could have been done differently?

There was a major discussion as to whether there was going to be a specific Constituent Assembly or whether there would be a normal assembly with the powers to rewrite the constitution. In the end, it was a normal assembly with the power to draft the constitutional provisions. The difference is somewhat subtle, because in both cases the representatives are elected, but then the regular assembly grants constituent powers to those who at the same time are thinking about their reelection.

This formula was decided upon during the Sarney administration and met with the approval of Congress. In other words, the following was declared: in the upcoming (1986) elections, the deputies and senators elected will have a constitutional mandate to approve a new original constitution by simple majority (50% plus 1).

The big political issues in this Congress with constituent capacities had to do with the federal question. The concern was that the military had centralized everything, including the tax system, and that they had suffocated the state and local levels. Even before the Constituent Assembly, under Figueiredo, there was already major pressure from the localities, and certain taxes were assigned to the local governments so they could have more revenue. The process of decentralizing revenue was accentuated with the new constitution. The tax base of the local and state governments grew, and the share of federal taxes earmarked for the subnational governments also grew. Half of the revenues from the two main federal taxes came to be distributed to state and local governments, based on the criteria of population and income. The question of how to distribute taxes was a major topic of debate in the assembly.

At a certain point, then-President Sarney made a speech in which he said that Brazil would become ungovernable because the new constitution had decentralized revenues but had not transferred responsibilities proportionally. All social security continued in the hands of the federal government, now expanded by the social rights created by the Constituent Assembly. This forced us, during my administration, to increase federal taxes that were not shared with the states and localities. The tax burden grew.

Electoral System

The constitution also defined the electoral system. The disproportionate representation of the states in the federal Chamber of Deputies, a legacy of the democratic regime of 1946–64 and accentuated by the military, was maintained. São Paulo has only 70 members of the Chamber of Deputies; it should have more than 100 if the system were to respect the principle of "one person, one vote." The system overrepresents the most backward states, where society and the electorate have little autonomy in relation to the local de facto powers.

I believe that it would have been good if we had insisted, as a minimum, on reducing the distortions in proportional representation. Looking back, I think the best thing would have been to introduce a system of votes by districts. In the Constituent Assembly, the district-based system was not highly regarded by the "progressive" forces. They imagined that it would reinforce the rule by local political bosses. We didn't realize that with the migration from rural areas to the cities this reasoning was no longer so well founded. If the vote were by district and proportional to the population, the persons living in the country's urban metropolises (where more than one-third of the population lives and where people are more "progressive") would have greater political representation. Today the constitution prohibits district-based voting. The vote must be proportional.

System of Government

The system of government was also discussed. Parliamentarianism was approved in the committee that discussed the issue but was rejected in the plenary of the assembly. We were able to establish that a plebiscite on the system of government would be held within five years. In 1993, the PSDB advocated parliamentarianism with a mixed district-based system, like Germany's. Yet presidentialism won when the electorate was asked to vote on the issue in a plebiscite.

Going back to the Constituent Assembly, we created an instrument inspired by the Italian parliamentary system—provisional measures to replace the decrees of the dictatorship. We were concerned about giving the executive an instrument with which to act and not being held hostage to impasses in Congress. This would have made sense in a parliamentary system and was created under the assumption that parliamentarianism would ultimately be adopted. But this isn't what happened, and provisional measures ended up in the presidential system. This gave excessive agenda-setting power to the president and is one of the factors behind the weakening of Congress. If Congress took the power it has seriously, it would take much more initiative. Actually, every time there is a desire to discuss ministers' accountability some discussion does take place, but most of the legislators prefer to exchange favors rather than exercise their oversight role with respect to the executive.

Today it would be very difficult to govern with parliamentarianism. In a federal system with such strong localities, a dispersed population—with so much inequality and with so many competing interests—the president is practically a power broker. When it comes down to it, the president of Brazil is like a monarch who has to avoid fragmentation. The people vote for a president, which gives him or her considerable symbolic and actual strength. I would say that the president of Brazil has much more power than the president of the United States to set the agenda.

Mechanisms for Constitutional Reform

How did giving Congress powers to draft the constitution work? What lessons did you take away from that experience?

The speaker of the Chamber, Ulysses Guimarães, was elected president of the Constituent Assembly, and he named me to draw up the rules that were going to define how the assembly would operate. It was very difficult to adopt a set of rules, given that the legislators thought that such rules would diminish their power. The prevailing attitude among the deputies reminded me of when I was a professor in France in 1968, when there was so much talk of "prohibiting prohibitions," to the point that it was thought one must start from zero prohibitions, with full freedoms. A preliminary draft was rejected that was drawn up by a group of notables under the command of Afonso Arinos, a respectable jurist who, after chairing the government commission to prepare a preliminary draft constitution, was elected senator for Rio de Janeiro.

We followed the model of Portugal. Eight thematic committees were created: rights and guarantees, organization of the branches of government and the political order, the economic order, the social order and social rights, etc. And there were 24 subcommittees. This defined the model of the constitution from a formal standpoint. Each party appointed its members to these committees and subcommittees (proportionate to the number of seats they held in the legislature). In addition, a committee on systematization was established to consolidate the proposals of the various committees. Senator Bernardo Cabral was elected the general rapporteur of the constitution to consolidate a more organized proposal. That committee was at the heart of the new constitution. They say that the constitution, with nearly 250 articles, is lengthy. And indeed it is. One mustn't forget, however, that it would have had another 2,000 articles if it had been based on all the texts approved in the committees and subcommittees. The committee on systematization had to make a Herculean effort to put the hundreds of proposals into a more reasonable form.

We elected a liberal and parliamentarianist jurist, Senator Afonso Arinos de Mello Franco, to chair the committee on systematization. Senator Jarbas Passarinho and I, plus a deputy from Rio de Janeiro, were appointed ad hoc executive vice chairpersons. The first proposal by the general rapporteur was pro-parliamentarian. We voted on it in the committee on systematization, and parliamentarianism won.

Balance of Powers

That victory provoked great national confusion because Sarney did not want parliamentarianism. At one point a shorter presidential term of five years was proposed on the condition that the president appoint a parliamentarian prime minister. The leader of my party at the time, Mário Covas, did not accept the proposal, which might have made parliamentarianism possible. In response, Sarney organized and established a group called Centrão, or Broad Center. This group was the most conservative in the Constituent Assembly, and that was the end of parliamentarianism. The presidentialist system ultimately came to a vote and was approved. Yet as I said earlier, the institution of the provisional measure, when joined with presidentialism, gave the president immense decision-making powers.

This measure enables the president, in the event of a very important or urgent matter, to make the decision he wishes until the Congress states its views. The Congress has 30 days to establish a committee to evaluate whether the provisional measure corresponds to the criteria of urgency and relevance. No committee was ever established to evaluate the hundreds of provisional measures sent by the executive, however. At the end of my administration, Congress sought to limit the reissuing of provisional measures (the main provisional measure for the Real Plan, for example, was reissued for several years until it won legislative approval). It was determined that the provisional measure would be in force for a maximum of 60 days, and that as of the 45th day the congressional agenda would be blocked until the pending provisional measures were voted on. Instead of increasing the initiative of Congress, however, this change increased the executive's agenda-setting power. So, in practice, it is the president of the republic who legislates. It has reached such a point that now the Supreme Court has forced Congress to form committees that must vote to allow the provisional measures to stand.

The effective counterweights to the executive are the judicial branch and the Public Ministry (Ministério Público) [the body of public prosecutors working at both the state and federal levels], both of which were strengthened in the 1988 constitution. The Supreme Court has really become a constitutional court; it is not simply passive in relation to constitutional review. It has the power to force Congress to make decisions when it deems that the lack of a decision, in practice, impedes the implementation of a constitutional provision. Moreover, the constitution grants complete autonomy to the Public Ministry. Its members are in charge of defending the diffuse rights of society. They can investigate and accuse a governor, president, or minister and bring them before the judicial branch to answer accusations. And they do so independently of the executive, which is good, and it works. At first, they were very politicized. They were practically a branch of the PT, which was then in the opposition. But the Public Ministry has evolved in recent years. It is an important component of the system of checks and balances, which is necessary because the power of the executive is very great in Brazil.

We have a complicated system that gives the president considerable power while also creating other mechanisms that subject politics to considerable judicial checks. Congress approves a law, but this may be futile, since someone can appeal to the court, saying that the new statute is at odds with the constitution. The whole decision-making system is very cumbersome.

Economic Context

What was the role of the economic situation in the Brazilian transition? To what extent did it help social mobilization? To what extent did it weaken the military government? Did it pose a risk to the transition?

Initially, the private sector organizations issued appeals to support the coup. In 1964, the first military president, General Castelo Branco, made major economic reforms to promote a new stage of growth: inflation was reduced, the tax system was streamlined, and new mechanisms were put in place to finance the government and its enterprises. The results bore fruit in the second military administration, from 1968 to 1973, when the so-called economic miracle occurred. Growth was spectacular, but its benefits were concentrated disproportionately in the hands of the owner classes and the middle classes.

The beginning of the easing of tensions by the regime coincided with the end of the economic miracle. The first oil crisis [1973] hit Brazil very hard because we imported almost all the oil we consumed. Even so, the economy continued to grow because the government decided to go into debt abroad, taking advantage of the availability of so-called petro-dollars, and implemented an ambitious investment program. This program provoked the business sector's first major negative reaction to the regime. A more liberal sector thought the government—at that time under the command of General/President Ernesto Geisel—had become too statist. Some of these people grew closer to the opposition. They didn't like the mix of super economic statism and political authoritarianism. In this period of growth, rapid external indebtedness inflation accelerated. That began to undercut the purchasing power of wages, which breathed new life into the trade union movement and was reflected in the congressional results of 1974 and 1978, in favor of the opposition party.

The economic situation moved into a new stage with the second oil shock and the abrupt hike in the interest rate in 1979. Inflation climbed to more than 100% annually, and growth fell off sharply. In 1981, Brazil entered a recession for the first time since the mid-1960s, which spurred the campaigns of the parties opposing the state governors. The struggles for democracy and to regain economic growth and wages became linked. In 1982, Brazil asked the International Monetary Fund (IMF) for help because it could no longer make the interest payments on its external debt. IMF aid had a high political cost for the government. I recall that we stopped the approval of a decree on salary reductions that was imposed by the IMF and sent to Congress by the executive. Another opposition senator and I pressured and convinced the president of the Senate, Nilo Coelho of the government party, to approve the Chamber of Deputies' decision to vote against the decree. This was a decisive blow. One week later the president of the Senate suffered a massive heart attack; the political situation was so dramatic it cost him his life.

After 1982, the regime clearly lost its main source of legitimacy: economic growth. The business class no longer feared the armed left; it had been repressed and defeated from 1968 to 1976. Without the fear of disorder on the one hand, and without prospects for growth on the other, the business class was willing to gamble on the end of the military regime. Yet, except for the more liberal and bolder among them, business leaders in general were latecomers.

At their outset, many new democratic governments have faced serious economic difficulties. Inflation climbs once again, making people think that democracy is of no use to improve the economy. Did that happen?

Yes and no. Indeed, democracy did not bring about an improvement in the economic situation. On the contrary, inflation continued to rise, interrupted only temporarily by successive stabilization plans, each of which failed to control inflation. However, politics continued to spawn new agendas and new hopes, with the Constituent Assembly, the return of direct elections for president of the republic, and the impeachment of the first elected president.

Inflation was terrible, but it did not completely disrupt the economy or society. Brazil had the unique experience of controlled hyperinflation, so to speak. There was an "indexing" of assets [assets and wages were adjusted] by means of a correction of deposits and debts based on an official indicator of inflation. The hyperindexing of the economy made possible some degree of "normalcy," albeit unstable, given that it made growth difficult and was regressive in terms of distribution. Understanding this "strange normalcy" of the social and economic situation—and the possibility of overcoming it—was essential for creating the Real Plan.

Social Mobilization

How did social movements—the Catholic base communities, lawyers, workers, business executives, women—relate to the political parties that made the transition? And what happened after the transition to direct election of the president? Did the social organizations weaken?

During the transition, all civil society was very active, and the parties sought to have contact with all those groups. Then the parties sought to *control* them. It's what the PT did, and it controlled the movements so much that it killed them. Many of the civil society groups became subordinated to the party's political project; they became part of the party apparatus and were bureaucratized. When the PT won the presidency, they benefited with more public resources but at the price of their autonomy. Some of these organizations have become almost state organizations. The Movimento dos Trabalhadores sem Terra (Movement of Landless Workers), which radicalized, is a partial exception.

The trade unions lost the ability to mobilize, especially in the private sector—in part for structural reasons, and in part because they were co-opted by the state. Lula was in the position to reinforce the autonomy of the unions vis-à-vis the state. When he rose to prominence as a union leader, his main banner was ending the compulsory union tax and the requirement that unions must be recognized by the state in order to officially exist. As president, he maintained the compulsory union tax, earmarked part of those revenues to the trade union federations, and made the Ministry of Labor a tool for securing political support through recognizing new trade union organizations.

Did women's movements play a role during the transition?

Yes, women played an important role, mainly in the campaigns for amnesty and direct elections. Many of the artists and intellectuals who became involved were women. But women continued to have a small presence in the political parties and the private sector trade unions. The industrial workers' unions are very *machista*.

The parties are now seeking to better reflect women's role in society. A growing number of heads of household are women, and women's participation in the labor force has increased considerably. There is a law that requires political parties to have a minimum percentage of women on their slates for candidates to Congress.

Yet policies and laws change slowly, much more slowly than changes in society. President Rousseff may accelerate the process of change by her own example and because she has appointed many women to important positions in the state.

Contemporary Transitions

How do you see democratizing trends today in the Arab world and elsewhere? What impact will the new communications technologies have? How do you view the dominant forces affecting transitions now? And what lessons are useful, looking to the future?

The new technologies allow people to express themselves. The problem with all this is that it is easy to mobilize to destroy, but much more difficult to rebuild. The new technologies are not sufficient by themselves to take the next step forward. Institutions are needed, along with the capacity to understand, process, and exercise leadership that is sustained over time. How the new technologies can be used to build something new isn't clear. When a country is closed and authoritarian, and also has economic problems, it is easy to mobilize. For us, television was fundamental. When TV Globo began to publicize the mobilization for direct elections, everything changed. Now you no longer need television; the Internet now facilitates mobilizing. But what is to be done next?

This is a complicated moment because we are witnessing an enormous crisis in the democratic capitalist system, with varying degrees of depth and recovery. There's a fascination with the Chinese model, which is authoritarian. China, Chávez, etc., all represent a kind of statism. Chávez did not have a one-party system, but he would very much have liked to have had one. So there is no single model to follow. There are those who think that Western capitalist democracy has met its demise. That's not what I think, not only because I value political liberalism, but also because I believe that the economic recovery is going to happen as the result of opening up to new sources of investment, technology, and innovation. I believe that the United States has more potential to create and innovate than Europe or China does at this time. Until the economic turnaround takes place, however, authoritarian governments are gaining a degree of prestige.

In Brazil there has been a certain amount of backsliding toward more centralization, with less trust in civil society and more trust in the state. Regulation is always necessary, but at times it can become political intervention, which is detrimental. Argentina is a case in point.

I don't think it's enough to preach democracy. Perhaps the big issues are justice and equality. The time comes when there is such a great distance between the politicians in charge and the people that there is general unrest. The situation is worse when there are cultural and ethnic differences. Here in Brazil, we were able to reduce poverty considerably, and inequality to some extent. In some countries nothing has changed, and it continues to be difficult to promote democracy without a concrete sense of more respect for others, for their citizenship rights and greater equality.

The situation in Africa is troubling in that sense. Although the continent is improving a great deal economically, much remains to be done in other respects. What is happening in South Africa frightens me because there is black racism, enormous corruption, and tribalism. Mandela was exceptional because he was capable of leading his people there, and able to create a system that respected the rights of the white ethnic minority even though that minority lost power.

There is no enlightened path to progress and democracy. Getting rid of the authoritarian regime is easier than establishing a true democratic culture and practices.

Fundamental Principles

If, for example, someone from Russia wishes to promote democracy and came to speak with you and said, "There are many of us in Russia who really believe firmly in democratic liberal ideas with the hope of having a better future; what advice would you give us to improve our chances of achieving what you have achieved in Brazil?" what would you tell them?

Have considerable patience and realize that change comes little by little, because it takes time for democracy to take hold and for the market to become more sophisticated. The problem is that the economy is growing with monopolies and oligopolies in Russia, and that could get worse over time. It is difficult to anticipate what the pace of history will be; looking at it today, one gets the impression that the doors are closed, but we must recall that the Soviet Union came apart quickly. So it is always advisable to say that one should maintain the hope that a better situation is possible. Who would have imagined what has happened lately in the Arab world?

On Russia, I don't think one can entertain the illusion that the whole world is going to become liberal democratic. Bush's mistake was to go forward when he should have stopped, when he should have contained more than trying to advance. This is not the time to *advance* the cause of liberal democracy, but to *defend* it.

Given the great variety in the different transitions and the various personalities involved, what lessons do you think can be learned from previous transitions that may be relevant today and in the future?

In Brazil the change did not occur suddenly. There was no D-Day; it was a process. It was an agreed-upon transition, without formal agreements but with negotiation. We had political struggle and negotiation, a presence in society and institutional spaces, and confrontation with the regime and rapprochement with sectors that were dissatisfied with the regime. We started as a single opposition front. The front fragmented along the way, with the end of two-party politics. **We were able to converge around the main objectives despite the plurality of visions and interests of the different opposition parties that rose up. In this way, a culture of mutual negotiation and dialogue was reinforced as an aspect of Brazilian democracy. But this can deteriorate into co-optation and the accommodation of interests, weakening democratic politics, discouraging the citizenry, and compromising the state's ability to engage in republican action. The style of the transition conditions democratic governance, for better or worse.**

International Influence

What impact did international factors have in the Brazilian transition?

Initially, Spain was the main point of reference. Later on it became Chile, right at the moment of strengthening democratic governance. We were observing what was happening with the Concertación in that country. In Brazil we did not have a single broad coalition like the Concertación, yet the PT and the PSDB realized, as of my administration, that they were both part of a single process of democratization and modernization, even though they might fight a lot. Who emerged as new phenomena after the dictatorship? Lula and I. Our parties have fought over something that is very simple: which of the two is going to be in charge. The fight is political; it revolves around who is going to control the executive branch.

Do the parties fight over which path to take—how best to respond to globalization and to modernize Brazil?

Yes, to some extent. There are differences because, for example, the PT has a state-centered and party-centered outlook. We in the PSDB are more pluralist and less hierarchical. But there is a strong social democratic tendency in both parties. And as for macroeconomic issues, there are no radical differences. They accused us of being neoliberals, but we never were; we accused them of being Stalinists, even though they never were.

It's a shame that Lula let himself be absorbed by traditional Brazilian political culture. He was too accepting of the political dynamics. I, who come from a more traditional context, made an effort to change the political culture. When I left the government the oligarchic groups were weakened; Sarney and Antonio Carlos Magalhães were weakened and had fought me. Lula put them back into politics, and when his second term ended he traveled to São Paulo on the same plane as Sarney, who was the symbol of the oligarchy. There was backsliding during his presidency in that sense. But Brazil's democracy is here to stay; it will not revert to authoritarian rule.

Time Line

Mar. 1964: Amidst mass demonstrations and high inflation, President João Goulart announces redistributive "basic reforms" that anger conservative political factions, including much of the military. In response, the military stages a coup against Goulart on March 31.

Oct. 1965: The military holds gubernatorial elections but does worse than expected. Military hard-liners successfully push to ban existing parties and establish the Brazilian Democratic Movement (MDB) as the sole legal opposition party.

Mar. 1967: Hard-liner General Artur da Costa e Silva is elected president by the military-dominated legislature, with the support of the quasi-official National Renewal Alliance Party (ARENA). He is later replaced by another hard-liner, General Emílio Garrastazu Médici. Repression reaches its height under these leaders.

Dec. 1968: Military government issues Institutional Act 5 (AI-5), giving the president the power to force the national and state-level legislatures into recess, to assume legislative power, to censor the press, and to suspend habeas corpus for "politically motivated" crimes.

Mar. 1974: The legislature elects General Ernesto Geisel, a moderate, as president. He announces *distensão* (limited political liberalization).

Nov. 1974: Campaigning on economic issues, MDB wins 16 of 22 contested Senate seats, 44% of the lower house, and 5 more state legislatures. This validates its controversial decision to participate in the elections.

Oct. 1975: Journalist Vladimir Herzog dies in military custody after torture. Religious leaders hold an ecumenical funeral that transforms into the first demonstration against the military regime. Geisel orders curbs on repression and fires the general responsible for Herzog's death.

Apr. 1977: Government enacts the "April package," which ends direct elections for one-third of the Senate, limits the opposition's access to media before elections, and overrepresents states with a strong pro-government sentiment in Congress.

May 1978: The Novo Sindicalismo labor movement, led in part by Luiz Inácio (Lula) da Silva, holds major strikes to challenge the regime and the labor system.

Nov. 1978: Congressional elections are held. Opposition wins popular vote in Senate but fails to win control of either chamber because of the April package.

Mar. 1979: General João Figueiredo, a moderate, is appointed president by the military-dominated Electoral College. Dissident General Euller Bentes Monteiro runs against Figueiredo, exposing rifts in the military. In office, Figueiredo promotes a policy of *abertura* (opening).

Aug. 1979: Figueiredo announces amnesty, including for crimes committed by the military. Opposition leaders begin returning from exile.

Nov. 1979: The government ends the two-party electoral system, allowing all parties to compete. The MDB is renamed the Brazilian Democratic Movement Party (PMDB), and ARENA becomes the Democratic Social Party (PDS). New parties emerge, including the leftist Workers' Party (PT) led by Lula and others from Novo Sindicalismo.

Dec. 1980: A large group of landless peasants occupies and demands the redistribution of farmland. This begins the Landless Peasant Movement, which formally incorporates and grows rapidly over the next two decades.

Aug. 1982: The Mexican banking crisis spreads to Brazil, severely damaging the economy and provoking public anger and inflation that successive governments struggle to control.

Nov. 1982: In the general elections, the opposition wins a majority of the popular vote in the Chamber of Deputies and most important state governments, forcing the regime to negotiate over legislation. The opposition does not win control of the Senate or the Electoral College.

Jan. 1984: The Diretas Já (Direct Elections Now) campaign for direct presidential elections holds protests that continue through the year and are often supported by opposition governors. A constitutional amendment for direct elections fails to win the required supermajority in Congress.

Jan. 1985: A faction of the PDS defects during an indirect presidential election and forms the Liberal Front Party (PFL), which allies with the PMDB to elect Diretas Já leader and respected Minas Gerais politician Tancredo Neves as president and PFL's José Sarney as vice president.

Mar. 1985: Neves becomes severely ill on the day before the swearing-in ceremony. Sarney is sworn in as acting president, and becomes president when Neves dies shortly thereafter.

May 1985: Congress passes laws making presidential elections direct, extending the right to vote to illiterate citizens and easing registration of political parties.

Nov. 1986: Elections are held for both houses of Congress, which will sit together to form a Constitutional Assembly. The PMDB wins a majority of the seats.

Oct. 1988: The Constitutional Assembly, with Senator Fernando Henrique Cardoso of São Paulo as rapporteur, enacts a new constitution after over a year of deliberation. It expands political and social rights, decentralizes power, restricts the military's role in internal security, establishes strong courts, and continues the presidential system.

Dec. 1989: Fernando Collor de Mello, a small-state governor backed by business and the media, defeats PT's Lula in a direct presidential election. Collor de Mello introduces policies to curb inflation but has little success.

Dec. 1992: Collor de Mello resigns from office rather than face likely conviction via impeachment for alleged corruption in his administration. Vice President Itamar Franco replaces him.

Apr. 1993: In a referendum, voters endorse continuing the presidential system rather than introducing a parliamentary system.

Dec. 1993: Franco and Finance Minister Fernando Henrique Cardoso introduce the Real Plan, a new macroeconomic policy that succeeds in curbing inflation.

Oct. 1994: Cardoso is elected president with Franco's endorsement, winning 54% of the vote and defeating PT's Lula, who receives 27%.

Dec. 1995: Cardoso signs a law acknowledging the government's role in deaths under the military regime and establishes the Special Commission on Political Deaths and Disappearances to provide compensation to victims' families.

Jun. 1997: Congress enacts a constitutional amendment allowing the reelection of the president. Cardoso heavily lobbies Congress for the amendment.

Oct. 1998: Cardoso is reelected with 53% of the vote. Lula, his major opponent, receives 32%.

Jul. 1999: Cardoso establishes a unified civilian Ministry of Defense, abolishing ministries controlled by military personnel.

Apr. 2001: The federal government adopts Bolsa Escola, a widely praised social welfare program that gives poor families cash for sending their children to school.

Oct. 2002: In presidential elections, Lula defeats the candidate endorsed by

Cardoso and wins 61% of the runoff votes. During the campaign, Lula moderates some previous stances, such as a plan to impose conditions on the payment of foreign debt.

NOTE

1. It gave the president the power to force Congress into recess, assume legislative power, censor the press, and suspend habeas corpus for "politically motivated" crimes.

GUIDE TO FURTHER READING

Cardoso, Fernando Henrique. "Entrepreneurs and the Transition Process: The Brazilian Case." In *Transitions from Authoritarian Rule: Comparative Perspectives*, edited by Guillermo O'Donnell, Philippe Schmitter, and Laurence Whitehead. Baltimore, Md.: Johns Hopkins University Press, 1986.

———. *A Arte da Politica: A História que Vivi* [The art of politics: The history that I lived]. Rio de Janeiro: Civilização Brasileira, 2006.

———. "Reconciling the Brazilian Military with Democracy: The Power of Alfred Stepan's Ideas." In *Problems Confronting Contemporary Democracy: Essays in Honor of Alfred Stepan*, edited by Douglas Chalmers and Scott Mainwaring. Notre Dame, Ind.: University of Notre Dame Press, 2012.

Cardoso, Fernando Henrique, and Brian Winter. *The Accidental President of Brazil: A Memoir*. New York: Public Affairs, 2006.

D'Incao, Maria Ângela, and Hermínio Martins, eds. *Democracia, Crise, e Reforma: Estudos Sobre a Era Fernando Henrique Cardoso* [Democracy, crisis, and reform: Studies on the age of Fernando Henrique Cardoso]. São Paolo: Paz e Terra, 2009. See especially chapters by Hurrell and Whitehead.

Fishlow, Albert. *Starting Over: Brazil since 1985*. Washington, D.C.: Brookings Institution Press, 2011.

Gaspari, Elio. *A Ditadura Derrotada* [A dictatorship defeated]. São Paolo: Companhia das Letras, 2004. Fourth volume in an authoritative history of military regime, covering *distensão* and *abertura*.

Hagopian, Frances. *Traditional Politics and Regime Change in Brazil*. Cambridge: Cambridge University Press, 1996.

Hunter, Wendy. *Eroding Military Influence in Brazil*. Chapel Hill: University of North Carolina Press, 1997.

———. *The Transformation of the Workers' Party in Brazil, 1989–2009*. New York: Cambridge University Press, 2010.

Hurrell, Andrew. "The International Dimension of Democratization in Latin America: The Case of Brazil." In *The International Dimensions of Democratization: Europe and the Americas*, edited by Laurence Whitehead. Oxford: Oxford University Press, 1996.

Kingstone, Peter R., and Timothy J. Power, eds. *Democratic Brazil: Actors, Institutions, and Processes*. Pittsburgh, Pa.: University of Pittsburgh Press, 2000.

Lamounier, Bolivar, and Rachel Meneguello. *Partidos Políticos e Consolidação Democrática: O Caso Brasileiro* [Political parties and democratic transition: The Brazilian case]. São Paolo: Editora Brasiliense, 1986.

Moisés, José Alvaro. *Os Brasileiros ea Democracia: Bases Sócio-Políticas da Legitimidade Democrática* [Brazilians and democracy: Socio-political bases of democratic legitimacy]. São Paolo: Attica Press, 1995.

Payne, Leigh A. "Working Class Strategies in the Transition to Democracy in Brazil." *Comparative Politics*, 23, no. 2 (1991): 221–38.

Skidmore, Thomas. *The Politics of Military Rule in Brazil, 1965–1985*. New York: Oxford University Press, 1988.

Sola, Lourdes. "The State, Structural Reform, and Democratization in Brazil." In *Democracy, Markets, and Structural Reform in Latin America: Argentina, Bolivia, Brazil, Chile, and Mexico*, edited by William C. Smith, Carlos H. Acuña, and Eduardo A. Gamarra. Boulder, Colo.: Lynne Rienner, 1994.

Stepan, Alfred. *Rethinking Military Politics: Brazil and the Southern Cone*. Princeton, N.J.: Princeton University Press, 1988.

——, ed. *Democratizing Brazil: Problems of Transition and Consolidation*. New York: Oxford University Press, 1989.

Weyland, Kurt. *Democracy without Equity: Failures of Reform in Brazil*. Pittsburgh, Pa.: University of Pittsburgh Press, 1996.

Chapter 2

CHILE

....

Chile's Successful Transition: From Intense Polarization to Stable Democracy

GENARO ARRIAGADA

In 1970, Chile had a population of about nine million and the third-highest per capita income in Latin America. It was a politically advanced society, and its well-developed political party system, divided into nearly equal thirds, reflected major European influences. The left had two Marxist-Leninist parties; the larger was the pro-Soviet Communist Party, which was the third-largest Communist party in the Western world after those in Italy and France. The predominant force in the center was the Christian Democrats, which was further to the left than its counterparts in Europe and similar in importance to the Christian Democrats in Italy and Germany. The right had a democratic tradition, and its parties were better organized than those of the political right in other Latin American countries. The armed forces had long been under firm civilian control.

This was the context of Salvador Allende's electoral victory in the Popular Unity movement in 1970. Allende won the presidency with 36% of the vote, but his party had a minority in both houses of Congress. Observers still disagree over the real nature of Allende's project. Detractors saw it as an attempt to establish one more "actually existing Socialist" country. For many of his partisans, it was an unprecedented project that sought to construct an alternative and pluralist model of transition to socialism. For others, the Chilean experiment could not escape the "laws of scientific socialism," including the inevitability of a period of "dictatorship of the proletariat." Whatever the Allende government's intent, Chile began sliding toward intolerance; there was a sharpening of social and political conflicts (and violence), both verbal and in the streets.

The Rupture of 1973

The military intervention led by General Augusto Pinochet, which ended in Allende's overthrow and death on September 11, 1973, was extraordinarily violent. Even though there was no armed resistance, approximately 3,000 people were killed in the initial days, the vast majority of whom were summarily executed. The prisons filled up with political prisoners, and several concentration camps were established. No fewer than 100,000 people were forced into exile. Tens of thousands were fired from their jobs in the public administration, universities, schools, and public and private enterprises. Torture became an essential tool of the regime.

The government dissolved the legislature, trade unions, and political parties. It burned the voter rolls and intervened in the universities, appointing active duty military officers as university presidents. It shut down the newspapers that it thought would not give the government their unconditional backing and established censorship of the press and of books. It required all new daily newspapers and magazines to be authorized by the Ministry of Interior. It enforced a curfew for more than a decade.

A coup with this level of brutality should have provoked solid rejection in a country with a democratic record like Chile's. But that is not what happened. The society had become extremely polarized, and political and social hatred permeated the entire social fabric. Disorder in the streets was an everyday occurrence as all sides staged major demonstrations. Industries, universities, and lands were occupied by groups that wanted them to be taken over by the state, or else to be saved from it.

A significant part of the population saw the military coup as a solution—a return to order—and gave it their unrestricted and cross-eyed support (i.e., one eye saw the order and a certain economic prosperity, while the other failed to notice the unfolding human rights atrocities). The business class supported the coup, grateful first for the return of the state-controlled or occupied businesses and then for the application of an orthodox neoliberal economic policy. But it would be incorrect to say that social support for the regime ended there; in different degrees, it extended to all social classes.

A Tough Road for the Opposition

The coup's brutality had the effect of breaking the alliance between the military and the Christian Democrats that had opposed Allende. The magnitude of the human rights violations, and the dictatorship's hatred of political parties, led the Christian Democrats to oppose the regime by late 1973. Pinochet's response was to declare them illegal and seize their properties and offices. Yet this move did not end the antagonism between the Christian Democrats and the alliance of Socialists and Communists; rather, both continued to engage in a poisoned polemic over who was responsible for the breakdown of democracy.

And so a divided opposition characterized the first years of the military regime: the Christian Democratic Party was the strongest at home, while the Socialists and Communists were the predominant force among Chileans abroad.

Yet an interesting confrontation was emerging between the military junta and the opposition. The military intelligence apparatus, acting with no moral or legal oversight, was strong, but a growing number of human rights organizations began to report their crimes. The government had taken absolute control of the universities, but opposition think tanks proliferated that brought together a large part of the intellectual community. The government had created a "yellow trade union movement" after dissolving the trade unions, but it could not do away with the influence of the workers' leaders associated with the left and Christian Democrats, who enjoyed legitimacy in Chile and abroad. The parties, though beaten up by the repression, maintained part of their structures. The Catholic Church, with the acquiescence of bishops and parish priests, provided an umbrella that gave cover to human rights lawyers and a variety of civil society organizations.

Several factors helped the opposition become better organized after 1980. The debate over what group was responsible for the breakdown of democracy was replaced by the parties' recognition of their own faults; intellectuals from different camps contributed to this trend. Most important, within the organizations that struggled against the military regime, those who had been political enemies in the 1960s and 70s began to come together. The political differences of an earlier time, though they persisted, lost urgency in the face of the concrete work of saving lives, denouncing the abuses, organizing demonstrations against the regime, and financing community kitchens to feed the families of the unemployed.

In 1980, the regime called a plebiscite—without lifting the stage of siege and without voter rolls, forums, debate or publicity—to approve a new constitution. The opposition denounced the whole process as fraudulent, but the government's initiative actually provided an opportunity for Socialists and Christian Democrats to work together. A realignment occurred during this time, in Chile and abroad, which changed the nature of the opposition. A majority faction of the Socialist Party broke with the internationalist "Socialist" camp led by the Soviet Union and developed closer ties with the European Social Democratic parties. At the same time, the Chilean Communist Party turned in the other direction, proposing to build an advanced form of socialism through political means as well as paramilitary and military actions, including terrorist acts. A new correlation of forces emerged within the opposition. On one side was the Communist Party; on the other was the expanding common ground between the Christian Democrats and the Socialists, who argued that the regime should be defeated through peaceful social mobilization and by better organization of parties and civil society in order to force a negotiated transition to democracy.

Under these new conditions, the moderate sector of the opposition redoubled its activism, founding the Alianza Democrática and the Asamblea de la Civilidad. The Alianza was a pact among several political parties organized around the Socialists and Christian Democrats. The Asamblea was a social agreement among professional associations, trade unions, student associations, and groupings of small-business interests. A few years later, in 1985, the Church convened a National Accord that included some representatives of the right who previously collaborated with the dictatorship. All these initiatives were organized in support of a moderate program that could win the broadest support of society, excluding only the Communists, who continued to claim "the validity of all forms of struggle," including violence.

In the first half of the 1980s the opposition made notable gains, but they were not able to hide two major failings. The first was their inability to incorporate significant sectors of the right. The liberal right, which had been a constant force during Chile's history as a republic, had been fizzling out since the 1973 coup and had been replaced by a mix of civilian militarists and Catholic integrationists (integristas), who distrusted democracy, and some neoconservatives, whose liberalism was limited to the economy. The second difficulty came from the clash between the strategies of the Alianza Democrática and the Communists, which split the opposition. The discourse of moderation and the invitation to a peaceful solution to the crisis were constantly contradicted by acts of violence, which ranged from excesses in street demonstrations to blowing up high-tension electrical towers and assassination attempts.

This harmful contradiction was played out in protestas, which were demonstrations staged once a month beginning in 1982. Peaceful demonstrations were held during the day, and at dusk pots and pans clanged from houses in the widest array of neighborhoods, filling the city with a deafening noise. But at night, extremist groups clashed with the police, resulting in major destruction and the deaths of young people, usually from the poorest sectors. The ultraleft, meanwhile, appeared to be involved in killing police, placing bombs in the metro, and carrying out acts of vandalism. The government's response was brutal: there were assassinations, including that of trade union leader Tucapel Jiménez; three Communist professors had their throats cut; and on one protest day, two students were sprayed with gasoline and then burned by a military patrol. This climate of violence was welcomed by the most radical sectors of the regime, which sought to justify an "iron-fisted approach" (la mano dura) as the only form of achieving governability and order, and at the same time to characterize the opposition (without drawing distinctions) as an anarchistic force.

Notwithstanding this environment, the moderate opposition continued to pursue its efforts to unify and adopt more sweeping agreements. The Communist Party strategy, by contrast, had its Waterloo. In the second half of 1986, an enormous arsenal was discovered on a remote beach in northern Chile that had been smuggled from Cuba by the Frente Patriótico Manuel Rodríguez (FPMR), the armed wing of the Communist Party. One month later the FPMR attempted to assassinate Pinochet. The operation failed, but half a dozen of the dictator's bodyguards died. Thus 1986 ended with the regime strengthened, Pinochet in absolute control of the Army, and the Communist strategy bankrupt. But the Socialist-Christian Democratic alliance, though rowing against the current of polarization and violence, was strong enough to continue its strategy of social mobilization with the support of civil society and the revitalized political parties.

The Beginning of the Transition

By 1987, the dictatorship's 14th year in power, the picture became increasingly more complex. The government and opposition had reached a tentative balance of power. Pinochet's strength continued to be great; it was mostly state and military power. He was the head of a state that functioned, and also the commander in chief of the armed forces, over which he had absolute power: united, obedient, not meddling in politics, and loyal to their commander in chief. He also had the support of the upper class and businesses.

But things were not going so badly for the opposition. One of the opposition's distinctive features was the strength of its institutions, which meant that its leadership was collective rather than focused on charismatic personalities. Its power was political, social, and international. Parties, though illegal, were well organized enough to call demonstrations that would mobilize hundreds of thousands of people. The opposition also relied on organizations that were independent of the state, such as churches, trade unions, student organizations, professional organizations, women's organizations, and neighborhood associations. It enjoyed the solidarity of international opinion and the near-unanimous sympathy of the governments of Europe, North America, and South America. It also benefitted from the presence of strong personalities who played a fundamental role in bringing together the opposition and designing its strategies. These included Patricio Aylwin and Ricardo Lagos, both of whom emerged as key figures in the opposition to Pinochet and helped build cooperation among center and left parties; both became presidents of Chile after democracy was restored.

In the 1980s, Chile settled into a catastrophic equilibrium. Pinochet was strong enough to stay in power, but not strong enough to crush his adversaries. The opposition, in turn, was strong enough—despite intense pressures, including a state of siege—to continue controlling civil and political society, but it was not strong enough to change the government.

In the second half of the 1980s, the opposition's skillful political leadership managed to define the agenda and refused to be diverted from its objectives. The opposition decided to contest the plebiscite that the Pinochet constitution had set for late 1988 in order to produce a decisive confrontation. A "yes" vote would perpetuate the dictatorship for another eight years; a "no" vote would require holding elections. Although it accepted the 1988 timetable, the opposition struggled insistently to replace the plebiscite with open elections. But when the government gave firm notice that there would only be a plebiscite, the opposition accepted the government's terms, fearing that a competitive election would pose challenges for which they were not yet fully prepared (such as agreeing on a single candidate and a platform), and therefore the best chance of unity would be to say "no" to a continuation of Pinochet's rule. The opposition warned, however, that if minimal conditions for a fair plebiscite were not in place, it would withdraw from the contest and denounce the plebiscite—in Chile and internationally—as fraudulent.

Next came the organization of the "NO" campaign, which required pulling together many political and social forces. The campaign embraced the concept of a peaceful transition to democracy, one that moved away from the idea of a revolution or polarized confrontation and that, rather than seeking "total victory," pledged to build "a homeland for all" (*una patria para todos*) in which everyone (except for those responsible for crimes) would have a "place under the sun"—that is, the same rights and respect for their dignity.

On October 5, 1988, the opposition triumphed. The NO campaign won 56% of the vote, which started the countdown for the dictatorship. In December 1989, in open elections for head of state and both chambers of Congress, Patricio Aylwin was elected president of the republic. Ten years later, Ricardo Lagos was elected president.

A Difficult (Yet Successful) Transition

The Chilean transition presents a curious contradiction. Its beginning was so difficult that it seemed condemned to have meager results; by now, however, it is widely considered one of the most successful transitions.

Politically, the starting point was highly adverse. In 1988, although Pinochet had been defeated electorally, he had still won 44% of the votes. The old regime had left power with an Army staunchly united behind the dictator, and with the militant support of two political parties that also won 44% of the votes in the first legislative elections. The right also had the near-total support of the business class, one of the most conservative in Latin America. Despite the strong support of its partisans, the military regime stepped back, having scored an economic success; Chile was projected to be the model of neoliberal economic reform.

The institutional framework was even worse. According to the constitution, Pinochet would continue to be commander in chief of the Army for eight years, twice as long as Aylwin's presidential term. A "binomial" electoral system ensured a tie between the government and the opposition in representation that could only be broken in districts in which one of the coalitions won twice as many votes as the other (i.e., at least 67% of the vote). The tie in Congress was broken in the Senate so as to favor the forces of the old regime by

Pinochet's appointment of eight senators for life from among his partisans. In addition, the constitution demanded special quorums for the passage of any important law, which made it impossible to amend legislation without the agreement of the opposition. During its final year, the military regime appointed 14 of the 17 members of the Supreme Court and granted itself amnesty with respect to human rights crimes.

If politics had been reduced to what the institutional framework allowed, the Chilean transition would have died before it was ever born. In the struggle to "untie" the inherited framework, the quality, unity, and strength of the Concertación—which was the political instrument of the transition—would be fundamental. The Concertación was successful because it constituted the most significant political alliance that Chile had seen in more than a century. It was Chile's longest-lived government coalition, electing four presidents in a row: Patricio Aylwin, Eduardo Frei, Ricardo Lagos, and Michelle Bachelet. The Concertación participated, united, in all the presidential, legislative, and municipal elections for 20 years. Its leaders, from the presidents of the republic to the grassroots, shared a single political program and ways of approaching it, which enabled successive administrations to give continuity to the essential actions of a transition to (and then a consolidation of) democracy.

As for the human rights abuses of the past, the first great objective was to recognize them, to have official recognition that they really occurred. The creation by President Aylwin of the Truth and Reconciliation Commission was fundamental. It documented the enormous scale of the dictatorship's crimes so that the whole country would know what had happened. Years later, President Lagos created the Commission on Political Imprisonment and Torture, which documented 30,000 cases of human rights abuses. The impact of these reports was enormous, and they gave a moral imprimatur to the democratic administrations.

A similar effort was made to remove the "authoritarian enclaves" that had been created for the explicit purpose of contradicting majority rule by making the Concertación, which had much greater electoral support than the forces of the old regime, into an institutional minority. Under Aylwin and during the first years of his successor Eduardo Frei, three draft constitutional amendments were introduced. All were rejected. Although the right succeeded in blocking these amendments, it was clear that the legitimacy of the "enclaves" was weakening. They were forced to accept rectifications: the repeal of the constitutional provision that outlawed the Communist Party; a reduction of the quorums for passing legislation; and a gradual curtailing of the powers of the Security Council, which, according to Pinochet's constitution, allowed two service chiefs to overrule the president's authority. The most significant reforms were finally achieved under the Lagos administration in 2005, ending the provision for designated senators and the ban on presidents removing the commanders in chief of the armed forces and the police during their four-year terms.

Pinochet's continuation as commander in chief of the Army after 1990 made it difficult for the Concertación to achieve transitional justice. Under the Aylwin administration, Pinochet put troops in the streets in combat gear to intimidate the civilian authorities. The decision of the Frei administration (while Pinochet was still commander in chief) to imprison General Manuel Contreras, chief of the dictatorship's secret political police during its most repressive years, was also challenged.

From Aylwin on, the Concertación governments insisted on subordinating the armed forces to civilian control and the rule of law. They were careful to respect the career service of officers not involved in the past in politics or human rights abuses, and they provided adequate funding to the armed forces. At the same time, however, military intervention in politics was forbidden. These two decisions were complementary: respect for the military profession required its subordination to civilian political authority.

The economic policies of Chile's transition were also successful. Growth, investment, exports, macroeconomic equilibrium, and social policies were all well managed. Chile was able to learn from the transitions in other countries, some of which had been carried away by populist policies that unleashed hyperinflation. From the first days of Aylwin through the last of Bachelet, the Concertación's fiscal discipline did not preclude strong action to address the social demands—many of them accumulated under the dictatorship—of the poorest sectors. Aylwin emphasized the idea of "growth with equity"; "growth with equality" would later be the central slogan of Lagos's presidential campaign. A major achievement was reducing the percentage of persons living under the poverty line from 44% to 13.7% during the 20 years of Concertación government. The Aylwin administration adopted and implemented a new economic strategy: clearly define the rules of the game, reassure business to discourage a revival of their alliance with the armed forces, and hammer out agreements between business and workers to promote tax and labor reforms. A number of free trade agreements were negotiated to facilitate a surge in exports. Production, investment, and employment grew at a sustained pace and contributed to the success of the transition.

The leaders of the Concertación were careful to preserve the ethical appeal that accompanied their rise to power. They implemented policies with a sense of proportion and justice, tolerance and the search for compromise. The Concertación's decisions were based on an ethics of responsibility rather than an ethics of conviction; they accorded priority to results. The leaders saw politics an instrument for attaining liberty, security, and prosperity for all of society, and not as a means for the salvation of souls, mending of hearts, or as a remedy for tedium and malaise.

At the end of the administrations of the Concertación—that is, 20 years after the transition began—Chile appeared to be the most developed and stable country in Latin America. Its per capita income increased threefold to become the highest in the region, and the growth rate of the four administrations of the Concertación was twice the average attained by the military regime in its 17 years. These high growth rates during the period had brought about a dramatic change in Chilean society. Chile had the best Human Development Index of Latin America. The percentage of its population living under the poverty line was the lowest. According to Transparency International, it was among the least corrupt countries in the world. Its Freedom House ranking, which considers both the actual observance and quality of political rights and civil liberties, is in the highest category, along with Uruguay and Costa Rica. And if one examines more complex measurements (e.g., the World Bank or the Bertelsmann Stiftung) that attempt to gauge observance of the law, governability, political freedoms, and the quality of the state, once again Chile was considered the best in Latin America.

These economic and social gains ran in tandem with the satisfaction of two essential elements of any transition. The first was the relationship with the military. Notwithstanding the difficult start, 10 years after the dictatorship ended, Chile had recovered full civilian control over its armed forces on the principles of professionalism, obedience, nondeliberation, and submission to legitimate civilian authority. Among other things, this is attributed to the Army's rehabilitation, with the highest honors, of General Carlos Prats, the commander in chief before Pinochet, who was assassinated in 1974 in Buenos Aires by the regime's political police, and to the promotion to the leadership of the armed forces a generation of officers who, while not adversaries of Pinochet, were at least not tied to him or his government. The second essential element of the transition was the treatment of past human rights abuses; the Chilean transition made an enormous effort to attain truth, justice, and reparations and to recover the memory of those crimes. By mid-2000, charges had been brought against more than 100 members of the military, including all the generals who had held the position of chief of the dictatorship's security apparatus during the Pinochet regime. No transition has achieved full justice for the victims of authoritarian rule, but Chile's persistent efforts to do so stand out among the transitions in Southern and Central Europe, Asia, Africa, and other countries of Latin America as having accomplished the most in this regard.

Biosketch of Patricio Aylwin, President of Chile 1990–94

PHOTO: CLAUDIO SANTANA / SCANPIX

Patricio Aylwin is a constitutional lawyer and professor of jurisprudence with a long background as a centrist Christian Democratic political leader. He served as president of his party and as a member (and president) of the Chilean Senate before the military took power. He was known for his opposition to Socialist President Salvador Allende in the unsuccessful political negotiations that immediately preceded the September 1973 coup by General Augusto Pinochet and the Chilean armed forces that overthrew Allende's Popular Unity government. Despite that controversial stance, Aylwin eventually came to play a pivotal role in bridging differences among major elements of the deeply divided opposition to Pinochet. He helped lead the Coalition for the No, which defeated Pinochet in the 1988 plebiscite, thus opening the way for the transition to democratic civilian rule in 1990.

Moderate and patrician in manner, Aylwin won support for strategic compromises that brought together the center, center left, and center right. He projected a firm commitment to the rule of law and to Chile's long democratic political traditions. As the leader and first president of the Concertación por la Democracia that won the 1989 presidential election and every subsequent national election until 2010, Aylwin moved to exert civilian control over the armed forces in the face of embedded constitutional provisions, imposed by Pinochet in 1980, which made this very difficult. He worked to stabilize the economy and win business confidence, introducing greater attention to social justice. Aylwin operated as a team captain, almost always deferring to trusted advisers. But he took personal responsibility, against advice from his political team, for insisting that a pluralist and representative commission be established to determine the truth with regard to political executions and "disappearances" under the authoritarian regime and, "insofar as possible," to seek justice. That decision, and the resulting Truth and Reconciliation Commission (the Rettig Commission), won legitimacy and stability for the democratic transition, and left open the possibility of future progress toward transitional justice.

Interview with President Patricio Aylwin

The Chilean transition from the Pinochet dictatorship to an extended period of democratic governance and economic advance is often considered a model. Of all the decisions you made to guide this process, which were the two or three that you consider the most important?

First I would say that, beyond the question of those decisions, the history of my country was very important for the transition. Chile is perhaps the Latin American country that had the greatest democratic stability after independence. And when we lost democracy, recovering it became the fundamental task of our process. Those of us who struggled for the return to democracy—in both the left and the center (to which I belonged), the world of the Socialists, and the world of the Christian Democrats, plus the world of the Radicals (what we could call the center left)—what brought us together, beyond a spirit of change and the search for a more just society, was our thirst for democracy.

Civilian Control of the Armed Forces

When I speak of Chile's democratic tradition, I think we also benefited from the fact that—unlike many Latin American countries, where the armed forces have intervened in politics permanently, always conditioning democratic governments—Chile had great stability and the armed forces remained subordinate to the civilian authorities, with few exceptions. Even in times of great social change, attempts to install authoritarian governments did not find a solid base of support in Chilean society.

Defeating the Authoritarian System from Within

Yet responding to your question straight on, I think that one important decision was to attempt to defeat the military using its own rules of the game. In general, what happened in the Latin American countries was that the opposition forces would attempt to overthrow authoritarian governments with another coup d'état. A dictatorship would be overthrown by another dictatorship. **We finally defeated Pinochet within his own institutional framework, without altering too much or compromising what we could call peaceful coexistence among Chileans. It was difficult; it was actually quite complex.**

To do so, we had to learn to act with our feet on the ground. If we had not done so, we would have taken a very heavy fall. The adversary wasn't only Pinochet, who was not at all a fool; he was skillful and had the support of one part of the population, and above all the most unconditional support from the united armed forces: Army, Navy, and Air Force. They believed—and I think they continue to believe—that they fulfilled their duty to Chile by overthrowing Allende. That was their belief at the time of the military coup and throughout the process of recovering democracy in Chile.

Building Trust among the Opposition

You were initially quite critical of President Allende, but in the 1980s you were able to win the trust of people who had supported him. How were you able to work with those who had been your adversaries?

We were adversaries at a moment of great political division and confrontation. It is not common in history for parties that have been adversaries until so recently to be able to reach such an agreement. During the administration of Eduardo Frei Montalva (from 1964 to 1970), the Socialists were a tough adversary of ours, and during the Allende administration (from 1970 to 1973), we waged a strong opposition because we saw in his Unidad Popular government a de facto attempt to establish socialism. Indeed, when the military coup came, many of us felt that it was the inevitable consequence of the situation the government had gotten itself into: a country on the verge of civil war. So we were accused of having supported the military coup.

Yet the dictatorship was so harsh that we ended up finding common ground defending fundamental values, beginning with the defense of human rights.

There were also political initiatives that brought together figures inside and outside of Chile, analyzing how we could rebuild democracy. One of the first such initiatives was called the Group of 24. The group was made up mostly of lawyers or people associated with legal issues; we formed a study group to analyze Chile's problems and to seek a return to democracy, which challenged the government in the process. People with different points of view joined the Group of 24, from a spectrum that ranged from the old Liberal Party to the Socialists and even Communists.

The mind behind the Group of 24 was Edgardo Boeninger. At first we were a group of friends and we would meet in our homes. Almost all of us were academics who, for the most part, were no longer in the universities because the universities had been taken over by (and subjected to) military authority. The group included academics such as Luis Izquierdo of the School of Biology; historian Sergio Villalobos, who won the national history prize; Manuel Sanhueza, who was minister of justice under Allende; Sergio Teitelboim, who was a Communist and the brother of a high-level leader in that party. There were lots of lawyers.

We studied a new constitution, what the new democracy should look like. The group was rather academic. We met in an office in downtown Santiago in full view of, and tolerated by, the government—everyone know about it; we met weekly. That process built up trust among those of us who had been adversaries.

I also think it's important that we assumed our share of responsibility from our different positions; even the Socialists began to recognize the errors of the Allende administration and to revalue democracy, and the Christian Democrats did so as well.

Finally, friendships also helped this come together. For example, I had had many good friendships with Socialists since I was a kid—for example, with Clodomiro Almeyda, a minister of foreign affairs in the Allende government. When he returned from exile, my old friendship with him helped integrate the toughest faction of Socialists into the emerging coalition of democratic parties.

Did the experience of working together in the Group of 24 contribute to building relations of mutual respect and trust among people from very different positions? How did you find common ground?

Exactly, that's right. It was a long process. I have spoken of the "reencounter of the democrats." I wrote a book with that title about how this process of finding common ground unfolded. **There were many ways for us to meet. Discussion circles known as *círculos de diálogo* emerged, and seminars were held in Chile and abroad that brought together the exiles and those of us who were in the country. Analyzing the situation together enabled us to reduce prejudices and build trust.**

The question of human rights was very important, for it brought people together—beyond ideological differences—in defense of human dignity. Those of us working as human rights attorneys were Christian Democrats, Radicals, Liberals, and Communists, and we would meet defending cases in the courts. I argued on their behalf several times, when Jaime Castillo [the former minister of justice and recognized Christian Democrat leader] was exiled, and also for Socialist friends who had been expelled from the country. There was one occasion, I don't recall the case, in which the hearing room was small and the Supreme Court authorized placing loudspeakers outside, and so one heard the arguments in the corridors of the courts. And almost all the trials were lost.

Building a Coalition

Subsequently, the political alliances began to take shape. First came the Alianza Democrática and then the Acuerdo Nacional and the Asamblea de la Civilidad, which were the antecedents of the Concertación de Partidos por la Democracia (Coalition of Parties for Democracy, or La Concertación). There was a great social movement in support of the democratic demands: workers and unionists, university students and women—who played a uniting role defending human and citizen rights. **The women's organizations were very active, and also very bold. They were the first to go out on the streets and act united even though they were from parties that had been adversaries.**

Social Mobilization

The economic crisis and neoliberal reforms of the early 1980s generated considerable poverty and left many worse off and contributed to growing unrest. From 1983 to 1986, the mobilization of civil society, supported by the political parties that existed despite being formally banned, eroded support for the military regime. The mobilizations wore down the dictatorship—until the attempt to assassinate Pinochet in 1986.

There was a major discussion about whether it was possible to put an end to the dictatorship by plebiscite. The Communist Party argued that the end of the dictatorship would have to come about through a broad social mobilization without excluding armed struggle. What was your view?

Social mobilization was actually promoted by the democratic parties. The Communist Party and its armed front supported a strategy of all forms of struggle, including the use of violence. The democratic parties believed in peaceful mobilization, even if we were repressed. When the Communists smuggled arms into the country, which were discovered, and made the failed attempt to assassinate Pinochet, this was the breaking point. Repression hardened, and we realized clearly that we had to commit ourselves to a nonviolent path in order to build broad support.

It was a tense debate, and we all had doubts. I am very much a pacifist and a man of law. Although at that moment I could not bet that things would go well for us, I thought a nonviolent approach was in line not only with the history of Chile but also with the mind-set of Chileans, with the peculiarities of our national character.

There were also two factions within the parties that later formed the Concertación: those who insisted that the Pinochet government was going to fall as a direct result of the social mobilization, and those who believed it would be more effective to get involved in Pinochet's constitution, contest the plebiscite provided for in that document, and defeat him from within via the plebiscite.

I belonged to the latter faction. The social mobilization strategy had indeed begun to erode the regime, but we were concerned that continuing to attempt social revolution and grassroots mobilization was going to have a very tragic end, because the armed forces had the capacity of repression. Those of us who backed one or the other of these theses rejected the strategy of the Communist Party, but its interests were better served by intensifying the social mobilization.

Defeating the Authoritarian System from Within

When there was a plebiscite to approve the 1980 constitution, we denounced the illegitimacy of the procedures—without freedoms and without an electoral list, which had been destroyed by the dictatorship—and therefore of that constitution. **Nonetheless, in 1984, some of us began to propose leaving behind the discussion of the legitimacy of the constitution and accepting it as a de facto reality. The idea was to register the parties under Pinochet's law on political parties, which we didn't like, participate in the plebiscite, which we didn't like either, and defeat the regime using its own rules.**

That was the strategy that ultimately triumphed. Indeed, I was elected president of the Christian Democratic Party, defending the position that the party should be registered as a political party under the dictatorship's law. In our own party, there were people who opposed doing so. Then we struggled for free elections, we registered our parties, and we got seven million Chileans to register to vote. Finally there came the campaign for the "NO" vote and the plebiscite, in which we defeated Pinochet.

Civilian Control of the Armed Forces

You said that the historical tradition of the armed forces helped because the Chilean military was historically obedient to civilian authorities. The Chilean experience is unique because in no other transition has the dictator remained after leaving presidential office as commander in chief of the Army for eight years. How did this relationship with the military unfold? And how did you negotiate with the military? What are the lessons, and what were the problems?

In my first meeting with Pinochet, as president-elect, I told him that I thought it was better for Chile for him to step down as commander in chief. [Smiling and imitating Pinochet] "You are wrong Mr. President, no one is going to defend you better than I will." He was very much looked up to in the armed forces, and it is likely that his staying on prevented uprisings by colonels, as occurred in other transitions.

My relationship with Pinochet was complex, but in the end he submitted to an institutional framework that was not to his liking; he respected it because he had created it. Yet he wanted to skip over many things. For example, in the first meeting I had with him in the presidential palace, La Moneda, once I had been sworn in and taken office as president, he told me that he was going to report directly to me and not to the minister of defense.

So I showed him the constitution and I told him, "Look, General, the constitution that you created says that you are under the minister of defense, so I'm sorry but you have to deal with him." He tried to avoid going through an intermediary, but he had to accept this, and from that point on, he reported through the minister of defense.

Setbacks

There were certain unexpected incidents during your administration aimed at derailing the transition that had a great impact, including the assassination of Senator Jaime Guzmán, a leader on the right, and the kidnapping of the son of Agustín Edwards, the publisher of El Mercurio, the leading newspaper. How did you respond to these incidents?

I would say that I faced them as part of the tense situation we were experiencing. We were thrust into a situation whose outcome we didn't know; there were great risks, there were terrorist acts. We even knew there were civil servants or persons who infiltrated and continued working, as they say, *a la mala* (in the wrong way). I have a very vague recollection of that, but it was discovered that there were connections between La Moneda and a building of the secret police who wiretapped our phone lines.

We experienced many tensions. I recall that once in Punta Arenas I met with the chief of the armed forces from there, one of the most militarized zones, and I told him I wanted to meet with the officers as a show of my will to be president of all Chileans, civilians and members of the military. They put all sorts of obstacles in my way, and said it was very difficult to call them together for the next day. So I said to them: "What is this? And if there's a war, you can't pull the officers together in a matter of hours?" So I met with the officers and I spoke with them about the transition. It was a very representative meeting, with officers from all the armed forces; it was in Magallanes.

How did you react to the two incidents, in 1991 and 1993, when Army troops exerted visible pressure that was apparently intended to intimidate the government into stopping investigations of alleged financial irregularities by Pinochet's son? Did Pinochet control the armed forces?

The one in command was Pinochet, but the armed forces didn't follow him in everything. For example, when the so-called liaison exercise or *enlace* was

conducted in 1991, that day was the graduation and bestowing of special recognition on the best Army officers, and so there was a ceremony and a luncheon at La Moneda in which Pinochet participated as commander in chief of
the Army. When Pinochet left La Moneda, he was given the daily newspaper
La Segunda, which was reporting on an investigation regarding some checks
written by his son, the so-called *pinocheques*, for arms purchases during the
military government. That afternoon, the Army withdrew to its barracks and
then went out into the street dressed for combat.

That afternoon I had the Carabineros officers' graduation ceremony [the
Carabineros is the national police force], and while I was there I was told of the
unfolding situation. Well, I said to myself, we'll see what's happening here. Yet
the ceremony for the Carabineros went normally, and the other branches of
the armed forces did not join. Pinochet had intended to get the government to
stop the investigation into his son's activities. This showed that his influence
was limited to the Army, as the Navy, Air Force, and police did not follow suit.

The second time Pinochet tried something similar was when I was on a visit
abroad. The causes were similar, but the issue of investigations into human
rights cases, which had them worried, was added. He did not get support from
the other branches this time either.

Fortunately, attempts at intimidation by the Army did not succeed, because
the truth is that the commitment to democracy had already taken root in the
national consciousness, so it wasn't easy to turn back: the idea had been established that Chile had recovered its democracy.

Justice and Reconciliation

Yet the greatest tensions with Pinochet were regarding the issue of human
rights. When we convened the Truth and Reconciliation Commission to investigate the disappearances of persons during the dictatorship, Pinochet told
me, "Why are you doing this, Mr. President? That's like when peace has come
to prevail once again in a family, and someone comes to claim the inheritance,
and a family fight ensues." I answered, "we're going to do it," and later, when
the report was released, there was considerable tension. They convened the
National Security Council but did not achieve any more than that.

How did you make the decision to create the Truth and Reconciliation Commission?
What reaction did you expect from the military?

The Truth and Reconciliation Commission was formed to investigate the dictatorship's crimes. I convened it at the beginning of my term. It was fundamentally my initiative. I thought it was necessary, but first I had to convince
my advisers. Neither Edgardo Boeninger nor Enrique Correa, my principal
political advisors, thought it was a good decision, but I was convinced that it

was the way to open doors. If one wanted the military to open up to a solution, I had to be both candid and prudent, so the phrase I used about seeking "justice to the extent possible"—for which I have been much criticized—reflected a degree of prudence, because if justice was going to be total, if it meant trying Pinochet and all his people, there was going to be a civil war. "To the extent possible" was a viable course because there were trials, but not a beheading, not aggressive actions against those who continued to have the power of arms.

Pinochet had said that he was going to be alert, that none of his men should be touched, but the commission's report had an enormous impact because there were still many then who did not believe the accounts of widespread and systematic human rights violations. The commission's report was like an official confirmation. And then came other steps, and we made concrete gains in truth and justice that went further than in many other transitions.

How was that commission formed? Did you choose the members yourself?

I called the persons, one by one, who in my judgment enjoyed prestige and represented different viewpoints, in an attempt to ensure that the commission would have legitimacy. It was chaired by Raúl Rettig, a well-known jurist, a great leader of the Chilean Radical Party. He and I had also been personally close; he had been one of the members of the Group of 24. He stood out because he was highly respected on the right but equally respected on the left.

I recall that I was very interested in persuading a venerable leader of the Chilean conservatives, Francisco Bulnes, to be part of this commission because he was widely respected among those on the traditional right. I even went to his home to ask him, but he said no. It was hard for me to find people on the right who would accept. Finally, the historian Gonzalo Vial accepted; he had been Pinochet's minister of education. We also involved figures from the world of human rights, such as José Zalaquett. All were widely respected.

Constitutional Reform

A crucial moment before you became president, in 1989, was the negotiation of the constitutional amendments with the dictatorship. Many felt that the changes obtained were not significant enough. What is your evaluation, in retrospect? Should you have insisted on greater changes then?

Well, **that phrase that many don't like, but that I consider very realistic— "to the extent possible"—reflected our efforts to move forward gradually. Those reforms were a first step, not all we wanted, but they clearly marked progress.** Considering that Pinochet at the time was the dictator and would continue as commander in chief of the Army and the armed forces, he held very great power.

Many years have passed and I may have forgotten many things, but I would say that I don't hold on to questions like: "Did I do well? Did I do poorly?" No, **I think that we did what we had to do, and fortunately it turned out well, but it also could have failed. We had to give up on certain ideas and take up others.** For example, in the government program of the Concertación, we supported repealing the amnesty law, but when we came into government we weren't able to do so because we needed a super majority, which we didn't have, in order to change that statute. We should recall that Pinochet had the designated senators (who he had appointed under the 1980 constitution), and we didn't have the votes in Congress to shut down those authoritarian enclaves. That's why we created the Truth and Reconciliation Commission. It was an important step for advancing the country's reconciliation, and fundamental for attaining justice.

A central issue for a successful transition is building a strong coalition. You had firm support from the political parties. To what extent was this due to developing a policy program that was agreed upon among those parties?

I believe that our agreed program was the navigational chart, and we tried to operate within this program. I recall that it was a subject I enjoyed discussing with the leaders of the parties: "How do you view what we're doing in relation to what we promised the country?" There were great expectations, but we were careful not to make great promises that could lead to disillusion. We had an ambitious economic and social program for the time, but it was reasonable. Those in charge of implementing it were those who had participated in its design. However, there were always aspirations that we could not satisfy because we had a political system with senators designated by Pinochet who forced us to make concessions, especially on political issues.

Economic Management for Development

The political right has said that the Concertación continued applying the same economic model as Pinochet. But when one observes what has been done in Chile—international treaties, fighting poverty, infrastructure, investment, and seeking "development with equity," as your administration put it—perhaps yours was a different approach. What was your economic approach? And how important was economic policy for maintaining your government?

Pinochet implemented a neoliberal policy to the hilt. We maintained the economic opening; we even took it further, and we have had a responsible fiscal policy. But it is very distinct from the dictatorship's economic model. We promoted a policy, as you say, of growth with equity. In my government we made important reforms in the labor and tax regimes, among others. We created policies to reduce poverty, we improved wages and salaries, and we increased state investment in health and education. We slashed inflation, which ceased to be a problem for Chile. In sum, the results of the economic and social policies of the Concertación that we initiated in my administration are plain to see. Modesty aside, I believe that we did a good job—the job that had to be done—and that we didn't make many serious mistakes. We may have done some things poorly, but I think that in general we had a good administration, and the evidence is that the government had continuity. If one does a bad job in government, most likely the opposition will then come along and win the next time around. We had 20 years—four administrations—of the Concertación.

In the Chilean case, the people exercised a great deal of self-control in making their social demands, for wage increases and improved working conditions, for example. How did you respond to (and channel) those demands?

I think that the success of my administration, and of transition administrations in general, is due not only to the policies followed by the authorities but also to the great support of the national community. I never felt that we were cornered, or that the opposition was greater than we were. At the same time, **we took care to treat the opposition well. In other words, it was important to reach an understanding with the opposition, to take them into account, so they did not feel marginalized, to explain to them what we were doing so they would understand. That helped me win support for the policies we undertook. Indeed, when we began the first international tours, we invited business executives, trade union leaders, opposition and government legislators, so they would form a team. That also generated encounters, for at night they would get together to eat and become better friends, so it was a way to construct civic friendship.**

Social Mobilization

What role did women play in the transition and in your administration?

The women's struggle for democracy was very important. They were very courageous. There were organizations such as Mujeres por la Vida and Mujeres de Detenidos Desaparecidos that mobilized tirelessly looking for their loved ones, reporting human rights violations and demanding liberty and justice. In addition, women organized in local communities seeking forms of solidarity to respond to the economic crisis. The **ollas comunes** (community kitchens for feeding the unemployed) proliferated. At the same time, the women were raising issues of concern to them, such as family violence and inequalities in the workplace and in the civil legislation. During my administration, while we didn't have a high level of representation of women in politics, the National Women's Service (Servicio Nacional de la Mujer) was established; its director has the rank of minister. From there, changes were promoted in civil and criminal legislation, and the problem of family violence was addressed. The foundation was established so that in subsequent administrations one could significantly modernize family legislation and make progress in eliminating gender differences.

International Support

Chile is a very interesting and important case for analyzing the international role in a transition. Could you talk about this?

Chile had considerable international support. It was very important for us. Indeed, we began the administration with the presence of presidents from Latin America, Europe, and also important figures from the United States. We proposed to integrate Chile into the international community beyond the economic opening, because politically we had been very isolated during the dictatorship. There was considerable solidarity with us. It was great support for a government that started out in a difficult situation.

To what extent did you consider previous transitions in order to figure out how to achieve Chile's transition? For example, Brazil was a slow transition, begun from above by the military. In Argentina, the military were discredited and therefore easier to remove, but inflation shot up; the economy weakened; and President Raúl Alfonsín, the first democratic president, had to resign. Were the experiences of other Latin American countries important for your analysis?

Since Chile was the last country to return to democracy in this region, we could learn from the experiences of others. The case of Argentina with Alfonsín, which ended poorly, showed the difficulties we might have to face. Democracy came with many expectations, and it was necessary to have considerable control to ensure that things did not get out of hand. In addition, we were especially concerned with strengthening ties with the governments of Latin America, especially with Argentina. With President Carlos Menem, we made progress in resolving practically all of our border problems. We signed the first free trade agreement with Mexico.

One of the decisions that we made, especially looking at the case of Argentina, was to undertake social reforms, but we did so seeking agreements with the unions to channel the social demands and also by helping workers and business owners reach agreements. We owe a lot, in that respect, to the union leaders, such as Manuel Bustos, who understood the complexity of the process of the transition to democracy.

Fundamental Principles

How did you keep your focus and your equilibrium facing so many complex and difficult challenges, and with so many people and groups having such different views?

That's a good question. **I am a person who commits myself to the things I believe in, for which I'll go out on a limb, but I have a sort of spring mechanism that tells me: "Watch out, be careful, don't allow yourself to be guided only by your impetus, your enthusiasm." That has meant that throughout my political life I have always worked well in teams, and I have forged good human relationships.** One example is my relationship with Edgardo Boeninger. He was an academic who was the rector of the Universidad de Chile. He had not been involved in politics, but after the coup he joined the Christian Democrats. We worked very well together.

I think it's also helped me that I have the ability to sleep well and take a distance from things. I have also tried to preserve time to read and to lead a normal life. I liked driving my own car. I recall that once while president I was driving, with the bodyguards in the car behind me, and all of a sudden the Carabineros stopped us. The Carabineros opened the road for Pinochet. He was accompanied by a security detail much larger than mine!

Contemporary Transitions

What general advice would you have for a political leader from the Arab world, or elsewhere, who wants to help his or her country make the transition from an authoritarian to a democratic government?

I wouldn't dare improvise a response on the spot. It's hard to get a clear idea of what one should do in one's own country, much less give advice to others in distant countries. Yet perhaps, **after periods of much division, one general recommendation would be to place the emphasis on looking more to what unites than to what divides. In this way we were able to reach agreement.** Many of us had been on opposite sides, such as Minister Bitar (who had participated in the Allende administration and was detained and exiled) and politicians who opposed Allende. Yet we reached agreement on defending essential things: the struggle for liberty and individual dignity. We also reached consensus with many of those who had been partisans of Pinochet. Seeking unity was difficult after years during which what divided us was much clearer than what might unite us. In that sense the administrations of the Concertación, beginning with my own, attained a greater degree of convergence between government and opposition, and among the various political sectors, than had occurred in previous decades.

One other aspect to highlight is not to start from zero. It is better to make changes based on what is already there. That was the idea when we proposed defeating Pinochet within his own constitution, rather than starting by saying, "we're going to change the constitution." We were changing the rules of the game from within. We were very realistic about defining our policy; **we had our great dreams—the dream of rebuilding democracy, of achieving the unity of Chileans—but our actions were realistic.** In that sense I think we did what we had to do. And it is interesting, because although we said, "justice to the extent possible," few transitions have had as much justice as we have had over the years in Chile: **what is possible changes over time; not everything can be done at once.**

Biosketch of Ricardo Lagos, President of Chile 2000–2006

Ricardo Lagos was a leader of the student federation at the law school of the University of Chile in the 1960s. Also trained in economics, Lagos developed his career in academia and international organizations, entering politics first

PHOTO: TOBY JORRIN / SCANPIX

in the Radical Party and then in the Socialist Party. Allende nominated him to serve as ambassador to the Soviet Union, a post he never took up because of the 1973 coup. In the postcoup years, living first in the United States and then returning to Chile to work for the United Nations, Lagos became a respected opposition figure known for his acute analysis. He became known as a Socialist representative in the multiparty National Accord and was briefly arrested after the assassination attempt on Pinochet in 1986. He gained stature because of his willingness to challenge Pinochet directly, especially in a memorable television appearance, as a spokesman for the country's long-repressed dissatisfaction.

Lagos took the lead in establishing the Party for Democracy, which helped build cooperation between the moderate left and the Christian Democrats, and played an important role in the Coalition for the No that defeated Pinochet in the 1988 plebiscite and in the subsequent Concertación por la Democracia. He declined to be a candidate for president in 1989, believing that the Concertación was too fragile to risk a divided constituency and that the country was not yet ready for a left candidate; he ran for the Senate that year and lost. Lagos served as minister of education and then of public works in the first two Concertación governments, and he was elected president in 2000, serving until 2006. His administration transformed Chile's infrastructure, achieved important constitutional reforms that reduced the antidemocratic features of the 1980 constitution, and established a commission on political imprisonment and torture that furthered transitional justice.

....

Interview with President Ricardo Lagos

Building Trust among the Opposition

There are four issues in the Chilean transition that have great relevance for contemporary transitions: first, the convergence of social and political forces that made it possible to bring an end to the dictatorship and build the longest-lasting coalition among Western democracies; second, the negotiation to persuade the military to return to their barracks and answer for human rights violations; third, the partial and gradual process of constitutional reform; and fourth, the pursuit of economic development with equality, which led to high growth and poverty reduction. In that context, how did the highly polarized, mutually hostile forces that were opposed to the Pinochet regime manage to come together, cooperate, and together defeat and remove General Pinochet?

First one must explain how, in a country as polarized as Chile was in 1973, the political and social forces eventually came together in a broad understanding. The rupture of Chilean democracy led Chileans to understand that the issues that had divided us in the past were becoming less relevant as the dictatorship continued.

I can illustrate this by reference to my own personal experience. In 1975, when I was lecturing at Chapel Hill, North Carolina, in the United States, we were visited by former Christian Democratic President Eduardo Frei Montalva. That day I told the professor, Federico Gil, "tomorrow I'll be out sick; I won't be able to make it to class." I didn't feel like talking with Frei Montalva. That was a year and a half after the coup, in 1975.

When I returned to Chile in April 1978, things were changing, and my own attitude toward the Christian Democrats and former president Frei Montalva was also evolving. My first activity was to get together with Enzo Faletto, a brilliant sociologist and a member of the Socialist Party, to go to the May 1st Labor Day protest. Supposedly Faletto knew where the protest was to take place, yet when we went out, we encountered a group of men that was—I have no doubt—Pinochet's police. We didn't see anyone protesting in the streets. That night we saw on television that the protests had been held elsewhere. Not even Faletto, who was very well informed, knew where the protest was, because if many people found out, Pinochet would have anticipated and repressed it. In such a helpless situation, we realized it would be best to get together with the Christian Democrats to discuss what we can do going forward.

Let's put it plainly. In order for a dialogue, such as that which was attempted in 1973 between the Christian Democrats and Allende, to be successful, one had to be clear about the consequences of failure—not only the advantages of success. The Christian Democrats entered a dialogue with Allende thinking that six months later, if there were a coup d'état, they would return to power. We embarked on the dialogue thinking that, if there was a failure, there would be a dictatorship for a long time, with all its consequences. So everything that was done was not enough to reach an agreement. This is my perception of how things unfolded in 1973, which helped those pushing for a military coup.

The Christian Democrats began to review their approach only after they realized that the dictatorship was going to last a long time—that the regime had "goals, not fixed time frames," as Pinochet said—and that they would not have any space.

When I went back to Chile in 1978, Tomás Reyes—a former senator who was a major figure in the Christian Democratic party and who was in charge of coordinating with the left—invited me to dinner soon after I arrived, and we began to meet regularly.

In 1981, I wrote an article entitled "El Precio de la Ortodoxia" (The Price of

Orthodoxy) that analyzed what the 1929 crisis had cost Chile. In examining that crisis, in effect I made a head-on criticism of how the Pinochet government was dealing with the crisis of 1981-82. To my surprise, I received a call from former President Frei to congratulate me on the article; we agreed to get together to talk sometime after his upcoming surgery. It had been six years since I had refused to see him. Unfortunately, we never met, for he died. I have always regretted not having gone to see him in Chapel Hill.

The Experience of Exile

This shows how many years it took to create personal confidence and political convergence. What other factors are important to explain how you built cooperation after a period of polarization?

Another factor that favored the formation of our coalition is that many Socialists who went into exile behind the Iron Curtain realized that the system there was not the democracy we had imagined. In East Germany, only those at the top had the right to enter and leave the country. The rest, including exiled Chileans, had to request authorization, which was granted or withheld by the political boss. We weren't accustomed to that in Chile.

For those who were in Chile at that time, as Chilean economist Aníbal Pinto once told me, there was room for only two political positions: the moderates, who called for respect for habeas corpus and the extremists, who demanded free elections. When you are in a dictatorship, you're happy if there's habeas corpus. That's why I always say, "democracy is like the air we breathe, and you feel happy because there's democracy." Well, when I was born, we breathed clean air in Chile. Democracy is the same: when you have it, you take it for granted. So the Pinochet period caused a revaluing of democracy by many Socialists, either because they were in exile or because they were living in Chile under repression.

These circumstances also sparked a discussion about "actually existing socialism" in its different expressions. In 1978-79, an internal discussion began on the process of Socialist renewal. In 1980, an unprecedented series of meetings was held. For eight or ten months we would meet from three in the afternoon until nine at night, the first time at a retreat home of the Schoenstatt religious group, to engage in discussions on the renewal of Socialism. There were 10 or 12 of us who, with the parties of the day, were from the Socialist Party/Almeyda, the renewed Socialist Party, the Christian left, the different lines of the MAPU (Popular Unitary Action Movement), etc. Detailed minutes were taken by Germán Correa [then a member of Almeyda's Socialist party, who later became president of the Socialist Party and Minister of Transportation during Aylwin's administration and minister of interior during Frei

Ruiz-Tagle's administration], which were distributed at the next session, and then we approved them. A document was put together there on the Socialist convergence, as we began to call it, in mid-1980.

At those clandestine meetings it was sometimes fun to discuss, for example, what we would do with the banks if we gained power, whether we would nationalize them or accept private banks, and we would engage in polemics among ourselves on such issues.

Differences within the Opposition

Could you explain the differences that persisted among Socialist sectors that had to be overcome in order to build a broader alliance?

When I returned to Chile in May 1978, I was working for the United Nations. As politics was prohibited and clandestine, I wasn't in violation of any United Nations rule by working in domestic politics, for no one could know that I was engaged in politics after my work day ended. And so I became involved in the phase of the Socialist split. There were the Altamirano Socialists and the Almeyda Socialists, depending on who their leader was; both lived abroad. The Altamirano Socialists were reformed quickly, and the Almeyda Socialists continued in unity with the Communist Party (PC). When the split occurred, I was part of a group of Socialists at VECTOR, a small think tank we had set up to have a place for thinking about the left, because there was also a think tank run by Alejandro Foxley [an economist who later served as minister of finance from 1990–94 under Aylwin] called CIEPLAN, which was associated with the Christian Democratic Party. We had a small office, and Enzo Faletto, Eduardo Trabuco, Eduardo Ortiz, Rodrigo Alvayay, and Heraldo Muñoz [distinguished Socialist intellectuals] would come by. One day Germán Correa came to inform us that there was to be a Socialist Congress and to consult us on our views. We informed him of the situation, and we assumed that information went where it was supposed to go. Three months later, Correa came back to tell us the Congress had resulted in a split in the party. So I asked him to explain what the split entailed, and I asked how we were going to fight Pinochet if we were divided. He asked me whether I accepted Almeyda's instructions, to which I answered that as long as they were divided I would not accept them. My group in VECTOR shared that point of view.

When I traveled to Mexico some months later, for my work with the United Nations, the first thing one had to do was to call on Hortensia Bussi, Allende's widow, who invited me to have lunch at her home with a large group of Chileans. She introduced me and asked that I give a report on the latest events. She then asked what I thought about the Socialist split. I explained to her what the representatives of the Almeyda Socialists had told me, and noted that in VECTOR we refused to accept the split and would not side with either faction. So she answered that I was like the Swiss: "neutral." I hadn't thought about it in those terms; I just said that we could not split. From then on we [who did not recognize the leaders of the split factions] were dubbed "the Swiss."

For a long time, those of us who were "Swiss" ended up being one faction among the many islands that the Socialists, divided into several factions, had become. Later the Political Committee for Unity (Comite Politico de Unidad, or CPU) was formed, which agreed to rebuild a single Socialist party with six factions: Núñez's (the *renovados*), Almeyda's, those who followed Raúl Ampuero, those who followed the coordinating body of the regional sections, one more, and us (the Swiss). I participated in the CPU; it was agreed that we would create a Central Committee, to which each faction would designate 10 members. I informed the Swiss group that we had a problem: we were only seven individuals. In the end, six of us were on the Central Committee; Enzo Faletto, who was our intellectual leader, said that if there was a Central Committee, that meant that "that body held power, and in respect for my anarchist ancestor, I won't accept a position in power." So there were 6 of us on behalf of the Swiss in a Central Committee with 36 members, 6 per faction.

In 1982–83, two processes began to unfold: the Socialist convergence [the incorporation of the two wings of the MAPU and the Izquierda Cristiana (Christian Left)]and the initiatives of the Christian Democrats, led by Gabriel Valdés after Frei Montalva's death. Valdés initiated contact with sectors of the right—such as Hugo Zepeda and Armando Jaramillo, Luis Bossay first and then Enrique Silva of the Radical Party—and then he invited the Socialists.

Building a Coalition

Many other political groups sought to end the dictatorship. How did you gather all sectors and unite them around a common platform?

On August 15, 1983, the Democratic Alliance (Alianza Democrática) was formed at the Círculo Español with a speech by Gabriel Valdés. [The Democratic Alliance—initially formed by the Christian Democrats, Radicals, some Socialists, the MAPU, Christian Left, and personalities from the right—aimed to represent all parties and independents that opposed Pinochet and rejected armed struggle.] Our political committee for Socialist unity designated representatives to the Democratic Alliance from the Almeyda faction (Julio Stuardo and Aquin Soto) and the Núñez faction (Hernán Vodanovic). These designations sparked a dispute in the Almeyda faction. Those who were outside Chile rejected the Democratic Alliance, since they saw it as a group that was willing to negotiate with Pinochet, while they believed that the correct path was to maintain the struggle and understanding with the PC. The PC was not invited to join the Democratic Alliance because it supported the use of violence. Finally, the Almeyda faction decided not to participate, but Julio Stuardo and

Aquin Soto, from that group, decided to stay and were part of the CPU, while others remained outside that committee.

The Democratic Alliance made its first decisions in those days; it defined a revolving chair that would change every month. Initially it was Gabriel Valdés in October; in November it was the Radicals' turn to chair with Enrique Silva; and in December it was to be the Socialists' turn. Aquin Soto and Julio Stuardo, who came from the Almeyda faction, asked if I was willing to be the Socialists' representative to chair the Alianza. I told them no, that my participation was clandestine, since I was working with the United Nations. Later I received a visit from two Socialists representing the *renovados* sector, Julio Stuardo with Hernan Vodanovic, to reiterate that I should chair the Alianza. So I made a very difficult decision. I told my family I was going to resign from my job at the United Nations, and in December I became the president of the Alianza.

On September 4, 1983 (a symbolic date because it was the date that Salvador Allende and all previous Chilean presidents had been elected), the country was informed of the unification of the Socialists in a central committee with 36 members. The enormous attention garnered by the "renewed" Socialist party was a great surprise for me. I gave many interviews to newspapers and magazines, and I began to see that innovative politics could result from collective action, for ideas were expressed through me that had been debated in prior meetings. It became evident that the Socialist Party was changing. There was also the influence of the Mediterranean Socialist parties. Felipe González had been governing since 1982, and Mitterrand had won in France.

International Support

The long period that preceded the end of the dictatorship provided time to rethink while in exile what had happened in Chile and to learn from other experiences. How did European Social Democrats see the new coalition and its strategy, which was also supported by the Christian Democrats?

I recall that when Mitterrand was inaugurated president of France in May 1981, he entered the Pantheon with Allende's widow to his right. I would underline the effect of Allende and the coup d'état against him in the world of the European left. If you spoke with Olaf Palme [Sweden], Gerhard Schroeder [Germany], or Tony Blair [United Kingdom], they would tell you they entered politics motivated by Allende's experience. All Europeans one met would tell you that they would take to the streets to protest for Chile. I also recall when I was in Chantilly and Bordeaux in two meetings with the Socialist convergence abroad, where the exiled Chileans would listen to us with great respect because we were living in Chile. There one encountered those who lived in Sweden, Milan, Paris. One noted the influence of their surroundings, the Renaissance men and women who came directly from Italy, and those who came from Sweden with a Scandinavian mind-set—it was incredible. No one has written about how the experience of exile impacted the political culture. **The process by which Chile's democratic forces reached an understanding took place against a backdrop of changing ideas arising from different sources.**

I recall my visit to the inauguration of Argentine President Alfonsín in December 1983. I was there as chair of the Democratic Alliance because, as I explained, the Socialists chaired it that month. With me were Valdés, Silva Cimma, and Armando Jaramillo. We held meetings with Felipe González, president of the Spanish government; Pierre Mauroy, the prime minister of France; Bettino Craxi, president of the council of ministers of Italy. We set forth our brilliant program to them: a provisional government, Pinochet is out, Constituent Assembly, a new constitution, and elections would be convened. We explained this to Felipe González, and he told us: "This is not a program. With this plan you'll continue for a long time in academia. How can you say provisional government? Is Pinochet going to leave? And how can you appoint a provisional government? Let us assume you are successful and Pinochet submits his resignation, and you are left without any discourse. Before you can do any of this, you have to get yourselves out of the bottom of the well." That meeting really had a major impact; it was very enlightening and very useful.

We then met with Pierre Mauroy, who told us, "I receive you as comrades, companions in struggle, but I can't do much more for you because relations are government to government: the interests of France, the interests of Chile, etc. You have my full support as a comrade, but as prime minister I can do very little." When he ceased being prime minister, Mauroy called and told me, "Now you can count on me; when I go to Chile I'm going to work with you." And he did so before and during the plebiscite that defeated Pinochet. We were learning about politics.

And we got to the meeting with Craxi. We made our speech and he said that "this is very easy. First we need a communications outlet; then, as we are in Argentina, tomorrow we'll ask Alfonsín to give us a place in the Andes on the Argentine side. I'll finance a large antenna and from there we'll broadcast into Chile." The next day Craxi went to speak with Alfonsín, who tried to explain to him that it was very difficult for him to put up an antenna, because he was going to end up fighting with Pinochet. That shows you the three very different mentalities of these three political leaders.

Alfonsín was very important for us. We asked him to intercede with the Cubans to ensure that their friends in Chile [the Communist Party] did not do anything crazy, for if they were to set off bombs they would wipe us out. And he did so. He played a useful role behind the scenes to explain to the Cuban leadership our strategy for defeating Pinochet.

In conclusion, there was a debate between those of us who spoke of social mobilization and protest and the partisans of "all forms of struggle," including violence; in this context we entered 1986, which we thought would be the decisive year.

Defeating the Authoritarian System from Within

The Democratic Alliance was an important step forward, but Pinochet and his dictatorship were still quite strong. How did you plan to put an end to the dictatorship? And what was the role of civil society organizations?

We thought that we should try to get Pinochet out in 1986. Otherwise we would have to confront him in the plebiscite scheduled for 1988, as called for in Pinochet's 1980 constitution. The plebiscite would be held to decide whether Pinochet would continue to govern. In the draft of the 1980 constitution, Pinochet had planned to be in power 16 more years, but his minister of interior, Sergio Fernández, told him, "Don't you think 16 years is too much? Why don't we hold a plebiscite halfway through that period? And then you could continue for eight more years. You will be the candidate of the plebiscite." And who would name him the candidate? The junta of four commanders in chief. "Approved," said Pinochet, and therefore it was agreed that in eight years the junta would designate Pinochet as the candidate.

Aylwin helped to create a constitutional study group, or Group of 24, in 1978, with Manuel Sanhueza as president. That group drew up an alternative constitution during the time that Pinochet was talking about drawing up a new constitution, which he imposed in a referendum in October 1980. In 1984, I had a public debate with Aylwin. We attended a seminar organized by the Instituto Chileno de Estudios Humanísticos, an institution of the Christian Democrats supported by the Konrad Adenauer Foundation. Aylwin said that we had to accept Pinochet's constitution in order to change it later. He said that the constitution is illegitimate and that he would continue saying so until the end of his days because of its origins, and he accepted that there were others who argued that the constitution is legitimate. He said that Pinochet cannot oblige him to say that the constitution is legitimate, and that Pinochet had the right to say that it is. The difference between Pinochet and himself was that Pinochet had the military force. **Aylwin did not want to discuss whether or not the constitution was legitimate, because he claimed we would never reach an understanding among ourselves in this discussion. He said that he understood that when a carabinero issued a speeding ticket, he was obeying an institutional order that begins with Pinochet's constitution and ends with the right to issue a ticket for speeding. Pinochet's constitution was a fact that exists, that is enforced; so if this is the de facto situation, then we can attempt to change that constitution without thereby according it legitimacy.**

I had a major disagreement with him over that. Yet he insisted and said that he accepted Pinochet's constitution, even though he opposed it as illegitimate, and he abided by it because it is the order that emanates from the use of force; it is a fact that exists.

Social Mobilization

There were several attempts to put an end to the dictatorship through social mobilization and political actions. As regards social mobilizations, the first protests in Chile occurred in May 1983 and were organized by the copper workers' federation and an emerging union leader, Rodolfo Seguel. We would meet in the Carlos V building in downtown Santiago, where the Christian Democrats had their offices in a law firm. We told the copper workers that they could go on strike, but we believed that no one else was going to go on strike in Chile. We, the leadership of the Democratic Alliance, together with the leaders of the copper miners, became convinced that it was better to organize a milder protest. The call for the protest said that on the designated day one should not send one's children to school, nor should workers have lunch at work; you should work, but sluggishly. We imported that idea from Argentina, working without putting much into it, but going to work and working. In Argentina they called it "working by the rules." You could go to cash a check at the bank, for example, a check drawn on a large institution that you know has funds, and they would tell you, "I'm going to check if there are funds," then tell you they had doubts about the signature. They would cash the check for you after 15 minutes, and they would do that with everyone; it was insane.

So someone suggested that at night we could bang pots and pans. Before the people in the upper-class neighborhood with rightist political leanings had done so because there was a shortage of goods under the Unidad Popular government. On that day, May 11, 1983, at eight o'clock in the evening, from the apartment buildings in middle-class sectors, such as the *comuna* of La Reina, there was a deafening noise of pots and pans. It was a great surprise, and I had the sensation that something had happened in Chile. Pinochet brought tanks into the streets and imprisoned the leaders who had called the protest. In a subsequent protest, Gabriel Valdés had printed some posters to get people to come out; the posters were found and they arrested him with the others.

In 1985, our respected Cardinal Raúl Silva Henríquez retired, and the Vatican designated Cardinal Fresno as his successor, who observed that there was a very polarized climate between the government and the opposition, so he proposed a great National Accord. The accord involved bringing in representatives to the right and left of the Democratic Alliance. Luis Maira was invited to join; he came from the Christian Left (Izquierda Cristiana) and was part of the Movimiento Democrático Popular (MDP), while representatives of the right such as Fernando Leniz, who had served in Pinochet's cabinet, were also invited to join. The MDP was the political grouping of the PC, PS (Partido Socialista) Almeyda, and other groups, partisans of "all forms of struggle."

The National Accord was an attempt to find a broad political solution beyond the Democratic Alliance. This was important; it was the first time that there was an analysis of what had to change in Pinochet's constitution, and that meant implicitly accepting that constitution.

The Catholic Church played a crucial role—the churches in general, but especially the Catholic Church. We would meet in their places of worship; the church was protection. And **women were very important, because under the slogan of "gender equality" they were also demanding equality in the struggle against the dictatorship.** Then came the idea that "liberty has a human face," which was very true, and that was a significant element. Without doubt, the social movements played an important role.

In 1986, the Asamblea de la Civilidad (Assembly of Civility) was established by trade union leaders and professional associations, such as the teachers' association and the medical association, which was very important. Once the doctors joined it was serious, and the truck drivers also joined. That assembly was organized by Dr. Juan Luis González, president of the Colegio Médico (Medical Association) and a member of the Christian Democratic Party; everyone was involved in it.

Setbacks

The Democratic Alliance also conceived a plan to end the dictatorship in 1986, which was called the decisive year. What happened then?

That year was indeed decisive, but not in the way we thought it would be. It turned out to be much more decisive because the discovery of smuggled arms in Carrizal showed that "all forms of struggle" [i.e., the use of violence] were still being pursued to overthrow Pinochet, and that had a harsh effect. This was an operation that was well financed: a fishing company with two boats and a mining company to exploit an abandoned mine. And the weapons came from the high seas. The two companies operated legally, with managers; they sold the fish, and from time to time they were found with arms. It was said that this information had come from Peru. What is known is that Carrizal was discovered, and that arms were coming into the country in an operation of considerable scale.

When it was discovered, in all likelihood the Frente Patriótico Manuel Rodríguez resolved to accelerate its Plan B, which was an attempt to assassinate Pinochet. They tried on September 7, 1986, but that also failed, for they didn't kill Pinochet, though several bodyguards were killed. The operation was very well organized, yet its failure, plus the Carrizal affair, meant that 1986 ended up being a decisive year, but not in favor of the opposition. I was imprisoned, as were others, among them Germán Correa, a member of the Socialist sector who maintained an alliance with the PC. I asked him whether he knew of the assassination attempt; he said he had no idea. So I told him that his partners were not fair to him because they didn't tell him about it. I realized he was very angry. Many Chileans died in the days after September 7 at the hands of Pinochet's secret police.

In the Democratic Alliance we had created a Private Political Committee (Comité Político Privado) in which the Christian Democrats and the Radical Party participated with Valdés and Silva Cimma, together with the Socialist Party. We would meet with the MDP at a place we would provide to discuss specific operations; for example, how to organize the next protest without violent actions that could serve as an excuse for repression, how to avoid having people hide their faces, and how to ensure there would be no burning of tires, blocking of roads, or other such disruptions.

How did the parties organize for the 1988 plebiscite, which would decide whether Pinochet would remain in power for another term?

We needed to register with the electoral authorities in order to appear on the electoral rolls for the 1988 plebiscite on Pinochet's next term. It was very important when the Constitutional Court decided that, in order to hold a plebiscite, a new voter registry should be established to replace the one that was destroyed after the military coup; that created the need to register voters. Then came the creation of the Committee on Free Elections and the Committee of the Left on Free Elections, for we in the Democratic left were not participating in the Committee on Free Elections. We had to establish our presence and reinforce the alliance of political groups in support of the plebiscite.

Article 8* was repealed, but only after the plebiscite, so we weren't able to run as the Socialist Party. We registered the Party for Democracy. In the end, the Party for Democracy became, in effect, the renewed Socialist Party; it included a group that was leaving the Radical Party and another group of liberals from the republican right, plus some independents, for Almeyda had still not registered.

At that moment the MDP, formed by the Almeyda faction of the Socialist Party plus other leftist groups, adopted the slogan *inscripción-traición* (registration is treason). The Democratic Alliance was no more, or was on the way out, to be replaced by the Concertación. The MDP at that stage began to change; it was called the Izquierda Unida (United Left) in an effort to keep the PS Almeyda with the PC and the Movimiento de Izquierda Revolucionaria

---

* Article 8 of Pinochet's 1980 constitution established that individuals could be held criminally liable for what they think: "political parties and organizations that promote against the family, favor violence, or that promote totalitarian concepts are unconstitutional"; it thus gave the government a basis for repression, bypassing the judiciary.

(Revolutionary Left Movement). I remember having gone with Arturo Valenzuela, an American political scientist, to the *comuna* of Renca on August 15, 1987, to a street market to tell them that they needed to register people to vote. Behind us came a small group shouting *inscripción-traición*—they were people from the PC. So I turned to the ones I knew and told them that we were doing what we could. I asked them not to provoke us, that they should situate themselves on the pavement across the street if they wanted. And they proposed that we meet in the afternoon with their colleagues to discuss the matter of registration. We met in the church, and the Communist colleague gave a speech explaining why registration was treason. When I spoke, I asked them whether they knew what Pinochet's path to staying in power looked like. Before he stayed in power by force, but now he had to win the plebiscite. If we have poll watchers, we could defeat Pinochet, so long as our people register to vote.

What were our calculations? Eight million Chileans can vote; Pinochet shouldn't get more than 40%, and all of his supporters will register. In effect, the first to register was Augusto Pinochet. Therefore they had 3.2 million votes—40% of 8 million. To win, we had to get at least seven million people to register in Chile. I recall that once Ricardo Núñez proclaimed, "today the seven millionth person has registered, we're going to defeat Pinochet." That was the numerical logic, but if there were a boycott and our people did not register, we were lost.

And so it came to pass: the Party for Democracy (Partido por la Democracia, or PPD) registered as a party, and the government moved Clodomiro Almeyda from Chile Chico to Santiago, accusing him under Article 8 of the Pinochet constitution. I visited him in the Capuchinos prison, where he told me, "we have good news; the MDP is going to register for the elections." I told him that now we have to form a political party, we have to create the PPD, for if we don't have a party, who is going to assure the fair conduct of the election and the fair counting of votes? Only the Christian Democrats? The parties would designate poll watchers (*apoderados de mesa*), and I don't want the Christian Democrats to be the only ones monitoring the polls. I want to be counting the votes too. I wasn't able to convince Almeyda to be part of the PPD. Only the PPD, for the left, plus the Humanist party had poll watchers to count the votes. After Pinochet lost the plebiscite, requiring the government to hold elections in 1989, Almeyda and that sector of the left formed the Partido Amplio de Izquierda Socialista (Far Left Socialist Party) to run candidates in the elections.

I remember it well, because when Aylwin was running for president we discovered that only the presidential candidate himself could designate candidates and poll watchers, so we were begging Aylwin to delegate that authority and responsibility to our people. In the end, we were able to have them because we could designate the poll watchers for the candidates for senator and representative.

I am recounting these events to show that achieving this coalition, the Concertación, was the result of a successive accumulation of forces over an extended time, not of a single decision.

Building Trust among the Opposition

The opposition movement had to overcome mistrust and fractured internal politics in order to work together. What were the pivotal moments and decisions that put the opposition on the path to eventually defeat Pinochet?

The first was the decision of the Socialist Party to cooperate with the Christian Democrats, who many of us thought had knocked on the doors of the barracks to provoke the military coup in 1973. I'm not myself saying that's what happened, but many members of the Popular Unity coalition believed that the Christian Democrats had been in favor of and helped to trigger the military coup. This was an obstacle to our cooperation. **We had to overcome deep mistrust to achieve our democratic goals, and we did.**

Defeating the Authoritarian System from Within

The second issue was whether to participate in the plebiscite and, consequently, accept Pinochet's constitution, at least in that respect, and run all the associated risks of an eventual fraud. This decision was made in late 1986 and early 1987, after other attempts to put an end to the military regime had failed and people saw that the plebiscite was right around the corner.

In February 1987, when Clodomiro Almeyda [a leading member of the Socialist Party] returned to Chile, I went to see him in Chile Chico, a remote town in Patagonia, along with Pedro Durán, my brother-in-law, to tell him that it was necessary to register the Socialist Party for the elections. We reached Balmaceda at midnight. The bus in which we were traveling came to a police post, where they made us get out; in those posts the police could interrogate and search you. We didn't know whether they were going to send us back to Santiago, for there was no freedom of movement.

The decision to register in Pinochet's voter rolls and electoral registry was a major one, for who could imagine that Pinochet would ever walk away because he'd lost a plebiscite? I realized that to make things easier I should involve Almeyda, because if he came into Chile by the underground, what would he do? He would go to the courts to avoid being expelled. By doing so, he had in effect accepted the institutional framework of the dictatorship, and he thought that within that institutional framework they wouldn't kill him. Indeed, they took him prisoner and sent him 1,400 km from Santiago, while they pondered what to do with him. He was the declared president of the Socialist Party, but the Socialists were prohibited in Pinochet's constitution, so the government had to decide what to do with him. The easiest thing was to send him to internal exile. You could go and talk with him, because he was allowed to move within the limits of that small town, but he could not leave the place. Registering for the elections and having the support of the Almeyda faction was important. I didn't get such a commitment during that visit. "I need more time to make that decision in the party," he told me.

And the third decision, as a result of the previous one, was to found the PPD. In 1987, Patricio Aylwin won the primary held in the Christian Democratic Party, and he made two fundamental commitments. First, he committed to have a small coalition, without the Socialists, which was a demand of Adolfo Zaldívar [a leader in the Christian Democrat Party], who said he would support Aylwin only on the condition that the Socialists not be included. And second, Aylwin committed that the Christian Democratic Party would register. When I saw those two conditions, I spoke with Aylwin and told him, "if you form a small coalition, you will be Adolfo Suárez and I will be Felipe González." I put it to him that way because once, as we were leaving a meeting, Gabriel Valdés told me, "I'm not going to be Adolfo Suárez so that you can be Felipe González; let's go into the government together because there are many difficult measures to adopt." [By this time, González was president of the government of Spain, and Suárez, the first Spanish prime minister after Franco's death, had already resigned in 1981. The Spanish Parliament elected Leopoldo Calvo Sotelo to serve as prime minister until the elections of 1982, when González's party, PSOE, won by a large margin.]

So while I didn't express my objection to the small coalition to Aylwin, I did question him about registering his own party. But I told him I wasn't accepting that, because one cannot register the Socialist Party since Pinochet's constitution banned it. When Aylwin said he was going to register his party, I went to speak with Enrique Silva of the Radical Party to ask him what he was going to do. He told me, "If the Christian Democrats register, then I'm going to register too." Therefore I called on the solidarity of the democratic-minded people of Chile with the Socialist Party. At that moment I proposed that we form an umbrella party, the PPD, to represent everyone. So I resolved to register the PPD. In an interview in the daily newspaper *El Mercurio* in January 1987, I said that a large party had to be formed, the PPD, that would bring all of us together. I put the idea forward because we were about to register the party. Aylwin told me that in order to win the presidential election he should say that the Christian Democratic Party was registering. And he added that I should rest assured that he would not do so until Article 8 was repealed, so we too can register, and if that article is not repealed, we can form a single party.

Civilian Control over the Armed Forces

Chile was the only case of a transition in which the former dictator stayed for an-
other eight years as commander in chief of the Army, a major obstacle to addressing
human rights violations and getting the military to return to the barracks. What
lessons do you take from your experience in dealing with the armed forces?

Policy with regard to the military has to be based on clear principles:

1. The military and the armed forces are permanent institutions of the
republic, and therefore they will have the full support of the elected civilian authorities, as institutions of the republic.
2. That means that how and when military force is used—as they have the
monopoly on the use of force—is worked out in the civilian world.
3. In exchange, the civilian world must give the military a monopoly over
the use of force and guarantee that its technical and financial needs are
met in order to enable it to do its job of defending the country from external threats.
4. All other benefits or advantages the military may have obtained while
they ruled as a dictatorship should be brought to an end. Institutions of
the republic belong to the whole country, and any special benefits the
dictator gave the military should be ended.
5. Even more important, since the military forces have the arms, they
cannot be involved in politics. If you are an individual who wants to get
involved in politics, you remove the uniform, dress as a civilian; then you
can go before the TV cameras and debate, without arms, to see who's right.

These are the basic principles that you must adhere to from the outset. Now
I know it's easy to say this, but it was tough to sell this message to the central committees of our parties. It wasn't easy when many people wanted to
have some military officers punished for their involvement in human rights
violations.

When Pinochet assumed the position of commander in chief of the Army
in 1990, it was known that it would be for a fixed term. Before, Pinochet gave
orders because he appointed the other commanders in chief of the Navy and
the Air Force. When I became president, Pinochet had already returned from
London, where he had been arrested, and was being prosecuted in Chile for
human rights violations. One day, a few weeks after my inauguration as president, the four commanders in chief went to have lunch together at a restau-
rant in Santiago as a show of unity and solidarity with Pinochet in full public
view. I was furious, but as president I did not yet have the power to remove
them. So the first thing I asked was who was picking up the tab, and they told
me the commander of the Carabineros; I called the commander of the Cara-

bineros, and he confirmed it was so. I told him, and then I repeated it to each of them separately, "Have you ever seen all the commanders in chief enter the White House? Or the three commanders go to see the prime minister in Norway or the Netherlands, or any other democratic country, on their own initiative? With this lunch meeting you have harmed Chile's standing in the world. I will never again accept such a display, and the next time I am going to issue a call from the balcony of La Moneda to relieve all of you of your duties, and we'll see who's in command in Chile." And "I will take the opportunity to tell you one more thing, that the day you decide to call the National Security Council to a meeting on your own, you'll have to seek a place to meet, because as president of the republic I will not attend, and therefore you will not meet in La Moneda; I'm not going to attend." And with such exchanges we gradually came to understand one another. Later, I decided to ask for the resignation of one commander in chief because of his human rights record. He didn't challenge me, although I didn't have the constitutional authority to remove him; he didn't tell me, "you can't ask for my resignation." The situation changed, but that happened over time. In the end, the rightwing opposition in 2005 voted to repeal the constitutional provision that established that the president could not remove the commanders in chief during their four-year terms. But everyone knew that this provision was, in practice, already a thing of the past.

Justice and Reconciliation

How can one explain that Chile made the most progress on transitional justice despite the former dictator being the commander in chief of the Army for eight years?

It's important to define how justice can be carried out in a transition, taking into consideration that human rights were violated. How do you explain to the military that seeking truth and justice is not revenge, and at the same time tell the citizenry, "We will not deny it so we will not have to live it again"? You have to tell the military that we don't want revenge, but to ensure that we never experience it again, let's not deny it happened. The process [of seeking justice and reconciliation], which led us to a plebiscite that finally reformed Pinochet's constitution, at times moved forward slowly, but it continued to progress at a sustained pace.

Frei had a successful initiative, the Mesa de Diálogo, or Table for Dialogue (1999–2001). The table had four sides: you had the generals, represented by the highest-level authority of the Army; across from them the human rights lawyers; then the Church and other moral institutions of the country; and finally a group of people who represented the political spectrum in Chile. You could find people from the center, the right, and the left who were not appointed to that table by the parties but by the president of the republic, and it was around that table that the dialogue began. It started off with a symbolic gesture. The

Army general approached attorney Pamela Pereira, whose father was disappeared, and offered to shake her hand. Pereira did not extend her own hand, instead telling him, "general, I will shake your hand when the dialogue has ended," in other words, when this dialogue session concludes something concrete, not before then. At the end, they shook hands.

I continued the Mesa de Diálogo, and it ended during my administration. The fact that military officers took a seat at that table means that they assumed some responsibility. It took time to get this. The women would go there with photos of their disappeared loved ones.

Moisés Naim, a well-known Latin American political analyst, once asked me, "What was the most difficult decision in your administration?" The most difficult was the decision to produce a report on political imprisonment and torture, because that meant going back and opening a Pandora's box of human rights violations, 13 years after we had won and 11 years after Aylwin had established the National Truth and Reconciliation Commission that investigated politically related deaths and disappearances and released its Rettig Report in 1991, which later served as an example for Mandela. But those who had been in prison continued to argue that no one acknowledged what they had gone through, and that when they asked for their record and it appeared that they had been prisoners, they had to explain that they were prisoners because of their political ideas. In the end I decided to form the Valech Commission.* These were tough decisions. I addressed the country on the conclusions of the report on political imprisonment and torture, which recognized more than 29,000 Chilean men and women who had been tortured and indicated the places of confinement and types of torture. Reading it was a journey to Inferno. Nonetheless, unlike Aylwin's Rettig Report, this report was not called into question by the military. They now accepted it and sought forgiveness for what had happened during the military regime.

Social demands usually rise when freedom returns, but they can complicate the initial political steps of a transition. How responsible were Chilean social movements? Did they help limit expectations to ensure that political change could go forward?

I'm going to share with you an anecdote that conveys a lot about the transition. I was in the Ministry of Education, and one day the secretary told me that I had received a handwritten letter from a place near Valdivia, in southern Chile. The writer first recalled that I had gone through her town during the campaigns; then she described her problem. She said, "We are a group of

---

* The National Commission on Political Imprisonment and Torture, called the Valech Commission, was chaired by Catholic Bishop Sergio Valech, who presided over the human rights organization La Vicaría de la Solidaridad (Vicariate of Solidarity) that operated during Pinochet's regime.

comuneros that knows where our relatives who were shot by the dictatorship are buried, and now we want to go before the judge to tell him to have the corpses exhumed, because we want to give them a Christian burial. Yet some of us think that it shouldn't be done yet, that it is too soon; the military might get mad and overthrow us once again in another coup d'état. Others of us were thinking we are now living in democracy and we can do it. We have waited almost 17 years, and as we have not reached agreement, because we don't know all that well what is going on in the country, we decided to seek your advice. We will do what you tell us to do." That letter had a big impact on me; I found it very moving.

I took the letter to Aylwin. He asked what to do, and I answered that we had to tell them to go before the judge. Aylwin agreed. I sent my chief of staff to tell them so. And they went to the judge, who ordered the exhumation. They dug and they found some bones and a few buttons. The military had already taken the remains. This example illustrates that they were not asking for a wage increase, which you might expect, but for basic human and political rights, which is very powerful. I tell you this anecdote as an example of the sense of both fear and responsibility of the Chilean citizenry.

Fear of the Past

You know when I realized I might lose my Senate race? As I mentioned, I said no to the presidential candidacy in 1989, even though I enjoyed considerable support. It is true that at the time the surveys were not as accurate as they are today, but I was aware that if I became a candidate there could be another coup. I realized I might lose when, in Huechuraba, a poor *comuna* near Santiago, I was winding up a speech to more than 20,000 people and I noted an older woman who was looking at me as if God were speaking. As I was leaving, the woman began to approach the stage, which was elevated. I realized she was not going to reach me, so I jumped down. The people opened the way, and I went to embrace her. She was moved and said, "You convinced me; I'm going to vote for you. I was an Allende supporter, but I was going to vote for Zaldivar, for I thought if you were elected the military might come back, and I suffered a great deal." It had such an impact on me that I asked someone to go speak with the woman the next day, and she told her what had happened to her before with the military forces. That's when I realized I could lose the election. That was the fear: although she supported me, she thought that she should vote for someone else to ensure the military would not return, as long as we were both against Pinochet. That speaks of the maturity of the people, and such maturity can make a transition easier.

Thus far we've been discussing the relationship with the military. What was the role of the civilian political right wing that supported Pinochet?

In Chile the military sought forgiveness, but the political right never sought forgiveness. Many on the political right continue to insist that the coup was called for, and therefore justify the violation of human rights. This continues to be a factor of distrust, and an obstacle to reconciliation and broader agreements.

Electoral System

During the Chilean transition there was an important opportunity after the 1988 plebiscite to amend the 1980 constitution, but the changes were relatively minor, leaving in place many authoritarian enclaves. What happened then, and what is your evaluation today?

A transition requires each group to understand that it cannot demand everything it wants. That is a transition: talking with those who think differently, even if they have been defeated, and working a lot on shared aims, winning the plebiscite, negotiating with the government, repealing Article 8, and so on.

Pinochet's constitution had established a binomial electoral system: two representatives were elected from each district. The political right discovered that this system was fundamental for its political existence, for it leads to political stalemate: you get 60% and I get 40% and we're tied—you elect one and I elect the other. The binomial electoral system also has a major impact on coalitions, because small changes within the coalition can cause the election of all Christian Democrats and none from the PPD, or alternatively of many from the PPD and few Christian Democrats. This effect, in addition to the high quorums required in the legislative votes (which are still in place), in practice give the opposition coalition the ability to veto. After 20 years, there's no longer any need for that. The political cycle of a right wing with the right to veto—in which we govern having won a majority at the polls for 20 years but do not have the majority to change what we want to change because we couldn't muster a quorum or we were stalemated—that's over. How are we going to get out of this impasse? I don't know, because the binomial system continues, and, even if we win the next presidential election, it's not clear to me what is going to be done to change that.

It seemed to me that this had to be repealed, but it wasn't possible to get that. The final negotiation was Aylwin with Jarpa, of Renovación Nacional on the right, along with the Concertación de partidos por el NO, which by then had become the Concertación por la Democracia. We had already won the plebiscite but were not able to change the binominal system.

Constitutional Reform

Pinochet's constitution had a gap. It established a high quorum to amend it: important matters required a four-sevenths majority, and amending some titles of the constitution required a two-thirds majority. Paradoxically, the title that referred to amending the constitution was not among those requiring a supermajority, so you could reform that title of the constitution with a simple majority, and by doing so change the quorums required to change the constitution. It was our only weapon. The discussion was whether we were going to use it or not, which the dictatorship already knew. The alternative was to head into a clash. The military could say that we were making a mockery of them, and they could hit us with a coup d'état once again. Accordingly, going forward in the first session of the Congress was very risky. Ultimately, the military allowed a series of changes, such as the repeal of Article 8 and others. In exchange, a special quorum was imposed to amend the constitution. In other words, they closed the one avenue available to us to make changes we thought were important in the 1980 constitution. But this was a very technical discussion from the standpoint of the public, and I saw that we were headed into a dead end.

I recall that we reached the moment of the final decision on whether to approve the few constitutional changes [that could be negotiated with the military]. Aylwin knew that I opposed it. That was the only time I saw him get angry, for we faced off in a debate. At that moment I had to call for a "no" vote on the new plebiscite to change the constitution that was being negotiated with Pinochet. It was impossible for us to take the initiative, because constitutional changes, in that period, could only be proposed by the junta and approved in a plebiscite. So I had to issue an appeal to vote no.

Aylwin was clearly in favor of a "yes" vote. He insisted that together we were going to change the binomial electoral system later. Then Aylwin concluded his remarks and I asked him, "what guarantees do we have?" He answered that the next day we would go to the home of Ricardo Rivadeneira, the attorney for Renovación Nacional who was drafting the reform. The next day we went to Rivadeneira's but Jarpa, the political boss of the right, didn't show up, so nothing could be done.

A second difference between us came once Aylwin became president-elect. I was a prospective cabinet minister. I had lost my run for the Senate, and in a conversation involving just the two of us, I asked him, "what is your first measure going to be?" And he told me that he hadn't really thought about it, and he asked if I had any ideas. I told him I did, that he should call on Pinochet to resign. To which he answered that Pinochet was not going to resign, and I told him that at that very moment he should send a constitutional reform proposal to the legislature asking for a change in the constitution, announcing that he has decided to remove Pinochet and has asked for his resignation, and that he is not presenting it because the constitution says that he is not obligated to do so. And then we began to discuss the issue, until I told him that he had not mentioned the most important argument for overcoming this difference of opinion. He asked me what it was, and I told him: "You could say to me, 'look Ricardo, you with your way of being, you just became a cabinet minister, I became president.'" Well, it was ridiculous that as cabinet minister I should tell him what he had to do as president. We both laughed and that's as far that "argument" went.

Building a Coalition

How did the Concertación reach agreement when it came to deciding on candidates? It also debated and prepared programs for each new government. What importance do you assign to this practice?

More difficult than making the transition from dictatorship to democracy is what comes after the dictator leaves—for example, reaching agreement on who is going to be the presidential candidate.

Many thought of my name for presidential candidate. It was clear to me that this was out of the question. It was like placing a red cape in front of a bull. That's why two days after the plebiscite I announced that I would not be a candidate for president. **The transition requires that some renounce their possible aspirations.** I recall that after the plebiscite the General Council of the PPD wanted to proclaim me the candidate. Armando Jaramillo and others were very enthusiastic. I thanked them, but I explained that my candidacy would be harmful for the transition. I proposed that we support Enrique Silva as the PPD candidate, and eventually we all supported Patricio Aylwin as the Concertación candidate. And the rest is history.

Setting Policy Priorities

We did not realize at first that there was another, much more difficult, transition—from a poor country to a developed country. We had to ask, "what kind of society do we want?" Not everything can be done right away, so in governing one must set priorities.

Let me give an example. After we won the plebiscite, we were certain that Aylwin was going to win the presidential election. One day I received a call from the Bishops' Conference to ask whether the Aylwin administration was going to press for a divorce law. I told him no, because there were more important things to be done. I explained that in a second administration we would work to get a divorce law passed. Well, we didn't accomplish that either. When I was president, the cardinal asked me, "And divorce?" "This time yes," I told him. So he asked whether he could ask a favor of me. "Why not let the minister of justice be the point man, so that we can argue about it with him and not with you?" They had realized that political conditions were ripe and that change could not be blocked. And a divorce law was adopted in 2005.

We agreed on our priorities and they were expressed in a program prepared during each presidential campaign. These agreed-upon programs helped us maintain unity. A transition has primary political priorities: to change the political system and ensure elections, freedom, and respect for human rights. Then a second process of economic and social change begins to unfold. When you propose growth with equality for all and you look for that growth to reach everyone, that requires new public policies and integrating into the world of free trade. All of that requires having a large majority. So, getting a large majority to defeat Pinochet was the easy part; the large majority to elect Aylwin was the easy part; the hard part was this other transition—the one that does not have a major impact on public opinion comparable to the moment when a dictator removes the presidential sash and places it on a new president who has been elected by the people.

No political party made a formal agreement [after the election of Aylwin as president]; we all operated on the understanding that we had to continue to stick together. We were going to win the election, to govern for eight years, because that was the presidential term under Pinochet's constitution. And we happily agreed to shorten the period from eight to four years. We thought, "we're going to be together no more than four years, and then each can go his own way, and we will go back to fighting it out."

The four years went by quickly, and we went back to the procedure of agreeing on a common candidate. We did so with midterm primaries that we invented along with Eduardo Frei Ruiz-Tagle [the son of former president Frei Montalvo] to ensure that he would win, and we continued to govern. **I believe that was a very important moment, when you realize that the unity to bring down the dictatorship must transition to another stage, a common program of political, economic, and social change.** If you look back, in the decade prior to the plebiscite, we had 10 years to think. So what Alejandro Foxley did afterward as minister of finance, and the economic and social policies he applied to grow the economy and drastically reduce poverty, resulted from common thinking.

The Chilean transition was quite special. Pinochet lasted eight years as commander in chief after the return to democracy, and naturally it was difficult to govern with the dictator remaining in that important position. Some began to anticipate new issues of governance and how to confront them. For example, Edgardo Boeninger, who played a very important role in the transition, told me, "Now we have to see to it that the social movements do not continue to be so active, for otherwise how are we going to govern if they are asking us for more every day? How can we control expectations?"

Economic Management for Development

Chile is an economic success story. How did economic policy help the political transition?

In the modern world, managing the economy must be a serious and responsible undertaking. It is not a question of left or right; one must find an appropriate way to manage the economy. In addition, **in times of transition, in developing countries with poverty, economic management is essential because growth is needed to meet the demands of the disadvantaged sectors. Solid public policies are needed that target spending where it should be, so that people see a change.** If people don't see a change for the better in their lives, they will be disenchanted with the reestablished democratic regime. Many will think that if democracy is not capable of delivering, what use is it? So growth became a key element of our policy. **Every leader of a government in a transition is the main communicator in a country, and that person should explain what he or she is doing and why he or she is doing it,** and whether the country has or has not had sufficient growth. Democracy is a plant that must be watered every day, and the greater the income, the greater the number of demands that can be met.

International Support

In addition to the solidarity offered by Socialists in other countries, did Chile receive additional international support?

International support, on which we were all dependent in one way or another, was also crucial. I recall that something changed in the second Reagan administration, when George Shultz played a key role. The new ambassador, Harry Barnes, went to Chile and said, "I want to meet with the Democratic Alliance." Armando Jaramillo was the president and asked Ambassador Barnes when we could pay him a visit. But he answered no, that he would visit us. We had a very small office, and the ambassador came there. This visit had a major impact on Pinochet; it was an important policy change. I also recall that we and others with Sergio Bitar were invited to a seminar at the State Department in 1985, and we met with Elliott Abrams. It was clear then that the US administration supported a return to democracy and was distancing itself from Pinochet.

Looking toward the Future

Repression and control create fear and may paralyze social struggle and political action. So it was necessary to combat fear. This was the reason why the NO campaign in 1988 focused on happiness and the future: la alegria ya viene (happiness is on its way). What are your lessons on how to face fear when fighting a dictatorship?

The NO campaign, which has been upheld worldwide as an example, was also influenced by friends from the United States. When the public relations experts said we were going to terrify people with all the reports on human rights violations and the like, it became clear that they were proposing that **to win people over you had to look to the future in a positive way, not dwell on the past.** The NO campaign was very important, no doubt, and that was an important lesson.

Contemporary Transitions

With your experience, how do you view today's transitions?

The most important thing is that today's transitions are different from yesterday's, because now you have Twitter and Facebook. When I assumed the presidency of the Democratic Alliance for the second time, in November 1984, there was a protest and Pinochet declared a state of siege. We were marginalized and we could not talk to one another. It was prohibited for us to be interviewed; we ceased to be who we were. Enrique Silva, the head of the Partido Radical, was identified simply as the former comptroller general. Gabriel Valdés, head of the Christian Democratic Party, was referred to as the former foreign minister, and I only as economist Ricardo Lagos. We could not be mentioned with our political party identity. One day, upset, I gave a press conference knowing that nothing would appear. After I made my presentation, a person came up to me and asked me two questions for the *New York Times*. "What do I care about the *New York Times* if my problem is the Santiago *Times!*" I answered, and then I apologized. My outburst was due to the frustration I felt because of the cordon of silence imposed on us by Pinochet.

Recently, the Piñera administration prohibited a march called by student leader Camila Vallejo that had been held weekly on Thursdays. Then one night she said on Twitter we should all beat pots and pans, and that night people beat their pots and pans. Comparing it with the previous transitions, the social networks today are spectacular, but at the end of the day one must go to the plaza. Yet Twitter and Facebook are tools that empower social movements; I haven't the slightest doubt about it. And once you are in government, they use Twitter to ask you to carry out your promises, saying, "I voted for you and look how the government treats us."

Fundamental Principles

Could you very briefly summarize some main points about how to make transitions from authoritarian rule to democracy that capture basic principles that should be understood and remembered?

First, when beginning to make a transition, understand that the starting point is that people fear going back to dictatorship and repression. Second, build the broadest coalition possible, because you need to accumulate all the power you can in order to make a break with the past. Third, **never forget that only in academia can one do and say whatever one wants. In politics you do what you can, and you have to do so with passion, forcefully, so that people see that you truly believe in what you are calling for.** When your appeals are no more than demagogy and expediency, people will sense that, and you will lose support.

....

Time Line

Sep. 1970: Leftist Salvador Allende wins a plurality—but not a majority—in the presidential election. In this circumstance, Congress chooses the president from the top two contenders. US President Richard Nixon orders the Central Intelligence Agency (CIA) to undermine Allende.

Oct. 1970: René Schneider, a military chief known for respecting the constitution, is killed during a botched kidnapping plot (supported by the CIA) to block Allende's election. Congress elects Allende president.

Nov. 1970: Allende begins nationalizing copper mines owned by US firms, accelerating agrarian reform and expanding social benefits, which polarizes society.

Nov. 1971: Fidel Castro visits Chile for 40 days, exacerbating the polarization.

Oct. 1972: After prolonged domestic unrest and a major strike, which was covertly supported by the CIA, Allende nominates a new cabinet incorporating military commanders.

Aug. 1973: Congress and the Supreme Court accuse Allende of ruling illegally through decrees, ignoring judicial decisions, and tolerating armed leftwing groups.

Sep. 1973: Junta led by Army head Augusto Pinochet Ugarte stages a coup and assumes power. Allende dies. Junta bans parties and trade unions, closes Congress, tortures and "disappears" many leftists, and imprisons most of the cabinet. Many opposition leaders flee.

Sep. 1974: General Carlos Prats González, Army head and interior minister under Allende, is killed in Buenos Aires, one of several assassinations by Chile's intelligence service.

Apr. 1975: In response to low growth and high inflation, the government introduces free market reforms led by "Chicago Boys" economists. Gross domestic product drops 15% during the year, and unemployment rises.

Jan. 1976: At the behest of Cardinal Raúl Silva Henríquez, the Catholic Church establishes the Vicariate of Solidarity to provide legal aid, document rights abuses, and publish a magazine that is critical of the government.

Sep. 1976: Orlando Letelier, ambassador and Cabinet minister under Allende, is assassinated in Washington, DC, along with his assistant. The US government condemns the Chilean government for the killing.

Sep. 1980: Chile holds a referendum on a new constitution, which would extend the junta until 1990 and hold a referendum in 1988 on extending the regime until 1998. Amidst censorship, fraud, and a ban on parties, the referendum is approved; the opposition rejects it as illegitimate.

Jun. 1982: The Chilean economy shrinks by 17% in 1982–83, and unemployment rises to 23%. Dissatisfaction with Pinochet rises, pushing him to moderate his economic policies.

May 1983: The opposition stages its first major demonstrations, in collaboration with the miners' union, beginning several years of protests.

Aug. 1983: A broad range of opposition parties establishes the Democratic Alliance, which is committed to peaceful, democratic change.

Mar. 1985: The murder of three Communists by the military police prompts an investigation by the Supreme Court. Several officers are eventually convicted; the police chief, a junta member, resigns.

Aug. 1985: Eleven parties sign the National Accord for Transition to Full Democracy, a Church-backed strategy of gradual political reform through engaging the regime.

Jan. 1986: The Civic Assembly, a coalition of pro-democracy civil society groups, begins.

Aug. 1986: Security forces find a massive arms stockpile in Carrizal Bajo; the government claims it is a leftist plot to overthrow the regime, which gives it an excuse to increase repression and discredit the far left.

Sep. 1986: Leftist guerillas attempt to assassinate Pinochet, killing five. The attack further divides the opposition on the use of violence and prompts a government crackdown.

Apr. 1987: Pope John Paul II visits Chile, criticizing the dictatorship and calling for democracy.

Sep. 1987: The government nominates Pinochet as its presidential candidate for the 1988 referendum, legalizes political advertising, and begins voter registration.

Jan. 1988: The opposition decides to contest the referendum, despite concerns about fairness, and forms the Coalition for the No (Concertación de partidos por el NO). Its professionalism surprises the government and receives broad international support; the US ambassador and others press for a fair plebiscite.

Oct. 1988: Voters reject continuing Pinochet's tenure 56% to 44%. The government negotiates modest constitutional changes with the opposition but insists that Pinochet remain commander of the Army for eight years and then become a senator for life.

Jul. 1989: Constitutional changes are approved in a free vote following intense negotiations. Reforms change the procedure for amending the constitution, restrict emergency powers, let treaties supersede Chilean law, and expand political pluralism, but preserve military autonomy.

Dec. 1989: Chile holds free general elections. Concertación por la Democrácia, the successor to Coalition for the No, wins a majority in Congress. Patricio Aylwin, Christian Democrat and leader of the Concertación, defeats Pinochet's treasury secretary to win the presidency.

Mar. 1990: The government initiates a plan to combine Pinochet-era macroeconomic policy with new antipoverty measures, tax reform, and increased public investment.

Apr. 1990: Aylwin convenes the National Truth and Reconciliation Commission to report on human rights abuses under Pinochet. Its 1991 report identifies 2,279 political killings.

Apr. 1991: Pinochet ally Senator Jaime Guzmán is assassinated by the radical left. Other kidnappings and violence against the right fuel polarization and convince the government to strengthen its intelligence capabilities.

Oct. 1992: Following constitutional changes, the first municipal elections since 1973 are held.

Dec. 1993: Concertación's Eduardo Frei Ruiz-Tagle, a Christian Democrat and son of the former president, is elected president. Concertación keeps control of Congress.

May 1995: Manuel Contreras, former intelligence head, is charged with plotting Letelier's assassination. He is eventually convicted of serious rights violations.

Mar. 1998: Pinochet steps down as Army head. As former president, he becomes senator for life, with immunity from prosecution.

Oct. 1998: Pinochet is arrested in London, on an international warrant, for human rights violations. Frei's government requests extradition to Chile, and a Chilean magistrate indicts him.

Jan. 2000: Ricardo Lagos, a center-left Concertación leader who served as minister of education under Aylwin, is elected president.

Mar. 2000: Pinochet is extradited to Chile. Congress grants him immunity from prosecution but removes him from the Senate. Numerous court cases challenge this immunity.

May 2004: Lagos convenes a commission to identify and compensate people who were imprisoned and tortured under Pinochet. It releases a report six months later.

Sep. 2005: Congress amends the constitution, eliminating nonelected senators and allowing the president to remove military and police commanders.

Jan. 2006: Socialist Michelle Bachelet, Concertación candidate and daughter of a general who opposed Pinochet, is elected Chile's first female president.

Dec. 2006: Pinochet dies at age 91, still the subject of ongoing prosecution.

Jan. 2010: Businessman and center-right politician Sebastián Piñera is elected president, the first time Concertación loses the presidency.

GUIDE TO FURTHER READING

Arriagada, Genaro. *Pinochet: The Politics of Power.* Boston, Mass.: Unwin Hyman, 1988. By the executive director of the Coalition for the No.

Aylwin, Patricio. *El Reencuentro de los Demócratas: Del Golpe al Triunfo del No* [The reunion of the Democrats: From coup d'état to the triumph of the No]. Santiago: Ediciones Grupo Zeta, 1998.

Aylwin, Patricio, Serrano Peréz, Ascanio Cavallo, and Karin Niklander. *El Poder de la Paradoja: 14 Lecciones Políticas de la Vida de Patricio Aylwin* [The power of paradox: 14 political lessons from the life of Patricio Aylwin]. Santiago: Grupo Editorial Norma, 2006.

Barahona de Brito, Alexandra. *Human Rights and Democratization in Latin America: Uruguay and Chile.* Oxford: Oxford University Press, 1997.

Bitar, Sergio. *Transición, Socialismo y Democracia: La Experiencia Chilena* [Transition, socialism, and democracy: The Chilean experience]. Buenos Aires: Siglo Veintiuno Editores, 1979.

Drake, Paul W., and Iván Jaksic, eds. *The Struggle for Democracy in Chile.* Lincoln: University of Nebraska Press, 1991.

Fleet, Michael, and Brian H. Smith. *The Catholic Church and Democracy in Chile and Peru.* Notre Dame, Ind.: University of Notre Dame Press, 1998.

Foxley, Alejandro. "Lessons from Chile's Development in the 1990s." In *Development Challenges in the 1990s: Leading Policymakers Speak from Experience*, edited by Timothy Besley and Roberto Zagha. Washington, D.C.: World Bank, 2005. By Christian Democratic think-tank leader and finance minister under Aylwin.

Garretón, Manuel Antonio. *Reconstruir la Política: Transición Consolidación Democrática en Chile* [Rebuilding politics: Consolidating democratic transition in Chile]. Santiago: Editorial Andante, 1987.

Huneeus, Carlos. *The Pinochet Regime.* Boulder, Colo.: Lynne Rienner, 2007.

Lagos, Ricardo, with Blake Hounshell and Elizabeth Dickinson. *The Southern Tiger: Chile's Fight for a Democratic and Prosperous Future.* New York: Palgrave Macmillan, 2012. By a former president and Concertación leader.

Muñoz, Heraldo. "Chile: The Limits of Success." In *Exporting Democracy: The United States and Latin America*, edited by Abraham F. Lowenthal. Baltimore: Johns Hopkins University Press, 1991.

Ominami, Carlos. *Secretos de la Concertación: Recuerdos Para el Futuro* [Secrets of the Concertación: Memories for the future]. Santiago: Editorial Planeta, 2011.

Oxhorn, Philip. *Organizing Civil Society: The Popular Sectors and the Struggle for Democracy in Chile*. University Park: Pennsylvania State University Press, 1995.

Puryear, Jeffrey M. *Thinking Politics: Intellectuals and Democracy in Chile, 1973-1988*. Baltimore: Johns Hopkins University Press, 1994.

Silva, Patricio. "Searching for Civilian Supremacy: The Concertación Governments and the Military in Chile." *Bulletin of Latin American Research* 21, no. 3 (2002): 375-95.

Tironi, Eugenio, and Guillermo Sunkel. "The Modernization of Communications: The Media in the Transition to Democracy in Chile." In *Democracy and the Media: A Comparative Perspective*, edited by Richard Gunther and Anthony Mughan. Cambridge: Cambridge University Press, 2000.

Valenzuela, J. Samuel, and Timothy R. Scully. "Electoral Choices and the Party System in Chile: Continuities and Changes at the Recovery of Democracy." *Comparative Politics* 29, no. 4 (1997): 511-27.

Chapter 3

GHANA

....

Ghana's Winding Path toward Democracy

KWAME A. NINSIN

Ghana attained independence from British colonial rule in 1957, the first country in sub-Saharan Africa to do so. President Kwame Nkrumah and his Convention People's Party managed the transition from colonial rule to independence and Ghana's conversion to a republic. Nkrumah's government oversaw substantial social, political, and economic advancement but became increasingly authoritarian. In February 1966, the military overthrew his regime. From the first military government (1966-69) onward, Ghana was governed by civilian governments for brief periods and by military governments in 1972-79, briefly in 1979 (about three months), and in 1981-92.

Flight Lieutenant Jerry J. Rawlings led the last two military governments. The Armed Forces Revolutionary Council, led by Rawlings, overthrew the military government of 1972-79, which had become corrupt and notorious for economic mismanagement and the abuse of political and civil liberties. After barely two and a half years of constitutional rule, Rawlings's Provisional National Defense Council (PNDC) overthrew the elected government of the People's National Party, headed by Dr. Hilla Limann, on December 31, 1981.

During the periods of military rule, Ghanaian civil society groups of diverse political persuasion emerged to press for a return to constitutional rule in defiance of the general atmosphere of repression. Professional bodies—including university teachers, a network of Christian churches, and workers and student organizations—usually led these groups. Successive elites of banned political parties also played an active role in calling for a return to constitutional rule and the rule of law. In the late 1980s and early 90s, the community of Western donors also pressured Ghana to return to multiparty politics, and international financial institutions (IFIs) such as the World Bank and International Monetary Fund (IMF) increasingly conditioned their loans and aid on improved governance.

Post-1982 Calls for Constitutional Democracy

When Rawlings seized power from the elected Limann government, he positioned his "revolutionary" PNDC administration in opposition to what he characterized as the corrupt and exploitative political and economic elite. Rejecting multiparty liberal democracy as a Western imposition that had failed Ghana, he sought to create what he perceived to be an authentically Ghanaian form of democracy rooted in the traditional governance model, which is based on consensus and community participation. The people were to be empowered through local nonpartisan self-government structures that addressed shared community challenges, and these structures would form the basis for the national political order.

Like the previous military regimes, the Rawlings administration defied the initial pressure to return to constitutional rule spearheaded by the Ghana Bar Association (GBA), Association of Recognized Professional Bodies, National Union of Ghana Students (NUGS), and mainstream Christian churches. The administration consolidated its rule by bringing the civil service and other state organs under its control and establishing new state organizations such as the Citizens Vetting Committee, National Investigations Committee, and public tribunals. The regime used the investigative committees and the media to prosecute Ghanaian opposition elites for alleged economic crimes against the state: humiliating and intimidating the opposition as well as undermining their legitimacy. The regime also organized workers' defense committees and people's defense committees at workplaces and neighborhoods (in 1984, these were consolidated into the Committees for the Defense of the Revolution). Under the leadership of radical political organizations that supported the PNDC government, the defense committees intervened in the production and distribution of goods and services and settled local disputes concerning land titles, rents, and the price of consumer goods. By the close of 1983, human rights violations were rampant and the political class and their organizations had been suppressed and marginalized in the economy and politics of the country.

In response to the continuing deterioration of the economy, and in a sharp departure from his initial populist economic policy, Rawlings embarked on IFI-prescribed structural adjustment programs, called Economic Recovery Programs, in 1983. This allowed Ghana to tap into international financial loans and aid streams. The next wave of demands for political reform occurred in the second half of the 1980s, following years of austere economic policies prescribed by the IFIs. The social effects of those policies mobilized a broad front of forces against the regime. The Ghana Trades Union Congress (GTUC), NUGS, GBA, the Christian churches, and others demanded the restoration of constitutional rule, respect for human rights, repeal of repressive legislation, and restoration of the rule of law. But the Rawlings government remained impervious to domestic pressures and instead proceeded with the entrenchment of "no-party" politics by establishing district assemblies (local governing bodies) based on nonpartisan local elections conducted in 1988–89. The administration heralded the district assemblies as the building blocks of a national legislative body.

The formation of the Movement for Freedom and Justice (MFJ) in August 1990 changed the dynamics of the calls for constitutional rule. The MFJ was "a broad and open nation-wide movement to campaign for the restoration of democratic rule in our country."[1] Formed by "a group of public spirited Ghanaian men and women representing the whole spectrum of political, ideological, and religious persuasions and from different social, class, occupational, and ethnic background,"[2] its leaders had come from the country's two major political traditions—the Nkrumah and the Danquah-Busia—and from new political groups. The MFJ was joined by a network of other pro-democracy forces, some of which had previously been vociferous in their demand for constitutional rule, including the GTUC, NUGS, GBA, Kwame Nkrumah Revolutionary Guards, New Democratic Movement, African Youth Command, the Christian Council of Churches, and the Catholic Bishops Conference. The activities of this wider coalition of civic groups ignited a social movement for democratic rule. The 1980s therefore closed with intensified political pressure on the PNDC to initiate constitutional reforms. The international donor community—especially the governments of the United States, United Kingdom, and European Union—also exerted pressure for political and constitutional reform as conditions for aid.

Rawlings and the Transition

Despite Rawlings's reservations regarding multiparty democracy, from 1991 the PNDC government showed signs that it was responding to internal and external pressures for political reform. In his New Year's address to the nation on January 1, 1991, Rawlings outlined a number of reforms that indicated movement in that direction. He announced that the National Commission for Democracy (NCD), which had been mandated to undertake nationwide consultations on the form of democracy and governance, would present its report by the end of March. Following the submission of the NCD report, a committee of constitutional experts would be appointed to propose a constitutional outline on the basis of the report and the 1957, 1960, 1969, and 1979 constitutions. Finally, an inclusive Consultative Assembly would be convened to deliberate and vote on a new constitution for the country, which would also draw on the NCD report and the previous constitutions—significant because three of these constitutions were based on the principles of liberal democracy.

But it was also clear from the New Year's message that Rawlings had not entirely abandoned his original agenda of replacing the country's liberal political institutions with populist democratic ones, based on a no-party concept of direct democracy. He stated that his government would now remain focused "on the road towards establishing for Ghana a new constitutional order" that would be consistent with "the democratic processes set in motion on 4 June 1979 and 31 December 1981." This was in reference to the PNDC's original aim of establishing a democratic system in which the lower classes of Ghanaian society would take part in decision-making processes through their own political institutions—previously the defense committees and later the district assemblies. Yet the Rawlings government remained firmly in control of the political and constitutional reform process and did not widely consult the civil society groups that had been pressing for reform. Further, following the work of the Committee of Experts and the Consultative Assembly in drafting the constitution but before its submission to referendum, the PNDC inserted entrenched indemnity clauses regarding actions connected to changes in government (i.e., coups d'état) or any acts or omissions by the PNDC or its appointees during its administration, thereby protecting themselves from any form of legal action by any subsequent governments.

By the close of 1991, the PNDC had proved quite adroit at maintaining its control in the face of mounting opposition from pro-democracy forces. However, the donor community had also intensified its coordinated messages advocating for reform. On the domestic front, the network of civic associations expanded and formed a larger coalition—the Coordinating Committee of Democratic Forces, which comprised about 11 groups—to push for further political and constitutional reforms. The new liberal constitution was approved by a majority vote in a referendum held on April 28, 1992. Following it was a new Political Parties Law that lifted the ban on political party activities (May 1992), the repeal of the restrictive 1985 Newspaper Licensing Law in May 1992, and the establishment of the Interim National Electoral Commission (INEC), which was mandated to register all political parties.

In response to this massive democratic opening, pro-democracy civic associations scrambled to transform themselves into political parties. From April to August 1992, 11 political parties were registered for the multiparty elections, scheduled for November 1992 (presidential) and December 1992 (parliamentary).

By then, Rawlings had established a reputation as a "reluctant democrat." Accordingly, leaders of the political parties were cautious. They formed the Alliance of Democratic Forces (ADF) to fight for thorough constitutional and political reforms. The ADF* took the government to court over provisions of

---

* The leaders included Professor A. Adu-Boahen, B. J. Da Rocha, Dr. Hilla Limann (president of the Third Republic and overthrown in the Rawlings coup d'état of December 31, 1981), Kojo Botsio, Dr. Kwame Safo-Adu, Alhaji Mohmmed Farl, and Bawa Dy-Yaka, who belonged to the Busia-Danquah and Kwame Nkrumah political traditions.

the Political Parties Law, which had placed restrictions on the use of party names, emblems, and slogans if they belonged to political parties banned by previous military governments. The Alliance also used the courts to secure human rights reforms. Meanwhile, private newspapers mushroomed, and the private press emerged as the unofficial mouthpiece of the pro-democracy movement, which also helped to accelerate the reform process.

Over the course of 1992, it appeared that the trajectory of political reforms was irreversible. In anticipation of an eventual transition to a liberal democratic order, Rawlings formed the National Democratic Congress (NDC) party, which he led as its presidential candidate to contest the November presidential elections. He also insisted, against advice by the International Foundation for Electoral Systems and over the protests of the opposition parties, on using an outdated voter registry. Despite such political maneuvers, presidential and parliamentary elections took place in November and December 1992, respectively.

The INEC declared Rawlings the winner of the presidential elections, with 58.3% of the votes cast. The New Patriotic Party's (NPP) presidential candidate, Professor A. Adu-Boahen, came second with 30.4%. The opposition parties vehemently protested the results, alleging widespread fraud. The subsequent boycott of the parliamentary election by the NPP and other opposition parties guaranteed the NDC and its allies a resounding victory. Rawlings and his NDC party won the presidency and formed the first government of the Fourth Republic, and secured control of the new Parliament with 189 of 200 seats.

Institutionalizing Democratic Politics

The boycott of the parliamentary elections by the opposition underscored the disagreements and suspicions regarding the transition process. The National House of Chiefs and leaders of the main religious bodies—both Christian and Muslim—intervened in the stalemate. Their aim was to end the political strife and restore orderly politics. When that failed, the NPP, which was the largest opposition party, took the initiative to end the self-exclusion of the opposition political parties from the nascent democratic politics. It gave notice of its intention to "do business" with the NDC government, and in conjunction with other opposition parties formed a shadow opposition cabinet outside Parliament and engaged the government on a number of policy issues through the courts. The futility of the strategy of boycotting the parliamentary election soon became obvious, as the Rawlings government and the NDC-dominated Parliament governed the nation without the opposition parties. It was clear at that point that the only way to take active part in the country's governance was by getting elected.

In March 1994, the opposition parties readily accepted an invitation to join the Inter-Party Advisory Committee (IPAC), initiated by the Electoral Commission to serve as a platform for interparty dialogue, consultation, and consensus building. Under the chairmanship of the Electoral Commission, the IPAC became a platform for the major political parties to build consensus on reforms that were necessary to boost confidence in the electoral process and enhance its integrity. The result of the dialogue and consensus building was manifested in the 1996 general elections. The NDC won the presidential election as well as the majority of parliamentary seats. This time the political elite reflected the growing democratic culture. John Kufuor, the NPP presidential candidate, conceded defeat without hesitation and congratulated President Rawlings for winning the election. In his acceptance speech, President Rawlings was also gracious toward Kufuor for ensuring a peaceful, free, and fair election and "orderly democratic procedure."

During his presidency, Rawlings "underutiliz[ed] his coercive capacity and invest[ed] in democratic institutions."[3] Further developments, propelled by both domestic and international pressures, contributed to the growth of democratic culture. In 2000, Rawlings demonstrated his commitment to democratic norms and procedures by respecting the constitution's two-term limit for the presidency. John Attah-Mills replaced Rawlings as the NDC presidential candidate in the 2000 general elections. Kufuor ran again as the NPP's candidate and won the presidential election after a second round of voting with 56.9% of the vote (43.1% went to Attah-Mills). The NPP also won control of the legislature with 100 parliamentary seats, compared to 92 for the NDC. Attah-Mills and his NDC conceded defeat, becoming the first incumbent political party in Ghana's postcolonial history to lose power through democratic means.

Kufuor and the Consolidation of Democracy

Despite this peaceful transition, Ghanaian society was polarized into Rawlings/NDC and Kufuor/NPP camps (a division that persists today), and political competition was intensely adversarial. The authoritarian and poor human rights record of the Rawlings/NDC party deepened the political divide. There was also the problem of media freedom. Even though Rawlings's PNDC government had repealed the Newspaper Licensing Law in May 1992, the media continued to be prosecuted under remnants of authoritarian laws dating back to the PNDC years, negatively affecting the freedom of the press.

President Kufuor took steps to heal political wounds and unite the nation. First, he appointed some members of the coalition of political parties opposed to the NDC to various ministerial positions. This policy of inclusive government was not extended to the ranks of the defeated NDC party, however, and therefore did not become a compelling precedent for future governments. Rather, their exclusion legitimized the use of the winner-takes-all rule to monopolize the power and the privileges associated with political office.

Second, President Kufuor's government established a National Reconciliation Commission (NRC) with the mandate to "seek and promote national reconciliation among the people of this country by recommending appropriate redress for persons who have suffered any injury, hurt, damage, grievance or who have in any other manner been adversely affected by abuses and violations of their human rights arising from activities or failures to act by public institutions and persons holding public office during periods of unconstitutional government." The initial hostility shown by the Rawlings group mellowed over the course of the committee's proceedings, especially when it became clear that it was not going to be inquisitorial and that it would balance the search for "peace, democracy, social equity, and the rule of law with criminal justice in the overall interest of a nation in dire need of cohesion and stability."[4] Rawlings testified briefly before the NRC in response to a subpoena. Whether the NRC achieved actual reconciliation is difficult to determine, but the political will that President Kufuor exercised served the cause of the rule of law and enhanced trust in the judiciary.

Kufuor's NPP government also advanced media freedom by repealing the Criminal Libel Law to ensure that the media enjoyed freedom in line with the constitution. Many Ghanaians were emboldened to establish both electronic and print media houses that performed the critical democratic functions of monitoring the governing class, exposing their excesses and holding them accountable. But the sudden gust of freedom also encouraged the media to irresponsibly use the freedom of expression.

The judiciary has continued to enjoy the traditional independence guaranteed by the constitution and has protected citizens' rights through socially responsible judgments. There were, however, a few instances in which President Kufuor intervened in judicial processes. For example, he appointed additional Supreme Court judges when he became president, and later appointed another Supreme Court judge to sit on the case of *Attorney General (No. 2) v. Tsatsu Tsikata* (former chairman of the Ghana National Petroleum Corporation). While not illegal, this move was perceived as an attempt to tilt the court in favor of his government. Even so, the general conduct of the judiciary has resulted in the growing willingness of the Ghanaian political class to submit to the courts for settling disputes such as those involving individual rights, controversy over election results, and the creation of new districts and constituencies.

Like the judiciary, the security agencies have functioned as reliable instruments for protecting and defending the democratic order. They have partnered with the Electoral Commission to guarantee the integrity of elections and have protected citizens' rights and generally ensured peace, order, and the rule of law. In particular, the military has submitted to civilian control in accordance with the constitution and as the result of a process of reprofessionalization started by the Rawlings PNDC government. To consolidate this civil-military balance, both civilian and military authorities are schooled in "democratic management of the security sector" to equip them with the appropriate capacity to effectively play their respective roles.[5] Tests of the military's submission to civil authority occurred in 2008 following the disputed election results, and in 2012 during the events following the sudden demise of President Attah-Mills in office. On these occasions the military submitted to the constitution and civil authority to ensure peaceful transitions of power.

The 2012 election also affirmed the growth of Ghana's democratic culture. Notwithstanding the widespread anxiety about the country's peace and stability, the election was conducted peacefully. The chairman of the Electoral Commission declared former vice president and NDC candidate John Mahama as president-elect with 50.7% of the valid votes cast. Nana Addo Dankwa Akufo-Addo of the NPP received 47.7% of the valid votes. Despite the NPP's rejection of the election results, Mahama was sworn in as the fifth president of Ghana on January 7, 2013, as provided by the constitution. The acceptance of the election results by foreign and local election observers, as well as foreign governments, helped to calm the political waters. A chorus of intercessions and supplications for peace and national cohesion by civil society organizations, including religious bodies and traditional rulers, reinforced the need for civic culture to prevail. The NPP's decision to challenge the presidential results in the Supreme Court signals the growth of democratic culture in Ghana.*

This was not the first time a losing political party challenged the presidential election result. In 2004, leading members of the NDC challenged the result of the presidential election in the Supreme Court and lost. Then, in 2008, NPP presidential candidate Nana Addo Dankwa Akufo-Addo refused to concede defeat until the intervention of a group of religious and civil society leaders persuaded him to reconsider his stand. In all of these instances, the governance institutions that are central to the efficient management of elections and related disputes have survived the test.

Conclusion

The sustainability of Ghana's transition to democracy is anchored in its independent democratic institutions and the respect its political parties and leaders have accorded them. Crucially, since 1992 the Electoral Commission

---

* Article 64(1) of the constitution allows such a challenge within 21 days after the declaration of the election result. On September 29, 2013, the Supreme Court, after about eight months of tortuous adjudication, decided by "majority decision" that John Mahama was the duly elected president of Ghana. The NPP presidential candidate, Nana Addo Dankwa Akufo-Addo, and his co-petitioners accepted this verdict—according to them in accordance with their commitment to democratic principles and the rule of law.

has managed successive elections with skill and diligence. The integrity of the electoral process has contributed to public confidence in governance institutions more generally. The military has fulfilled its role as defined by the constitution, remaining subject to civilian authority and outside the political process. The political class has shown commitment to the rules and norms of democracy, and has resolved conflicts through dialogue and legally defined conflict resolution procedures.

Challenges remain along Ghana's democratic path, however. Although political parties have accepted the mechanisms for arriving at agreements on electoral matters, there is still a great deal of mistrust between parties, and they have not developed a consensus on a shared national development agenda. As a result of this enmity, politicians do not enjoy the same level of public confidence as democratic institutions more generally. The judiciary is widely perceived as a neutral arbiter, but the justice system is also perceived as an expensive process that is beyond the reach of ordinary Ghanaians. In spite of these challenges, Ghanaians have come to accept that building a successful democratic order is a shared responsibility and the only way to guarantee social peace and development.

Biosketch of John Agyekum Kufuor, President of Ghana 2001–9

PHOTO: DESIRE CLARKE

John Agyekum Kufuor, a lawyer of royal lineage from Ghana's majority Ashanti ethnic group, combined national and international experience in business and finance as well as important technocratic roles with years as an opposition leader. He was a minister in the Second Republic government of Kofi Busia (1969–72), an opposition member of Parliament in the Third Republic under Hilla Limann (1979–81), and secretary for local government under the PNDC military government of Jerry Rawlings. Kufuor was a founding member of the NPP, which organized to contest democratic elections in the mid-1990s. He led the NPP as a presidential candidate in the 1996 elections, which he won. Kufuor's accession to the presidency marked the first successful transfer of power from one democratically elected government to another since Ghana's independence in 1957. He was reelected president in 2004, completed the two terms permitted under the constitution, and then turned over power to the newly elected president, John Atta Mills of the NDC, thus deepening Ghana's liberal democracy. Kufuor strengthened Ghana's democratic institutions by significantly reducing restrictions on the freedom of the press and establishing a commission to investigate human rights violations committed under the pre-1992 regimes. As the head of a political party with a long tradition of liberal democratic and free market ideology, Kufuor followed consistent free market economic policies that further integrated Ghana into the world economy.

....

Interview with President John Agyekum Kufuor

Cycles of Military Intervention in Governance

The international image of Ghana is that it has been a successful case of transition to a system in which there have been free and fair elections, alternations of power, functioning electoral institutions, a free press, separation of powers, and effective democratic governance. Is the international reputation of Ghanaian democracy accurate? If so, how was it possible to accomplish it?

The international reputation of Ghanaian democracy is quite accurate, but this reputation is nowhere near perfection. Democracy does not happen naturally. A lot depends on the people, their temperament, and even their culture. I would say the temperament of Ghanaians, among the tribes from the coast to the northernmost parts, from east to west, tends to be that of accommodation. Visitors to Ghana have observed that Ghanaians are very friendly, peaceful, law abiding, and religious. So with this temperament and our history, they have lived together very well from old times; they intermarry and that sort of thing.

With this background, and given good constitutions that prescribed democracy, one would think that it should have been easy for democratic governance to be established. But it was not at all easy in the case of Ghana. Ghana was the first country in sub-Saharan Africa to gain independence, in 1957. But after that, it suffered quite a long period of military intrusions and coups d'état. In Ghana's case I would say that during the 50 years of independence the people have been exposed to various types of governance. The initial constitution was democratic, but then along the way Kwame Nkrumah's government strayed into a one-party system in which people who did not agree with the regime were arrested and put into political detention without trial. So by 1966, when the military coup happened, many people had been detained without trial, without justice. The people did not like that, so the soldiers stepped in, but they brought in a military dictatorship, which again the people didn't like. The military stayed in power for about three years and then handed over to Professor Busia's government in 1969, in which I cut my political teeth. So they gave way for civilians to come in, to rule by a democratic constitution.

The ensuing civilian regime lasted only two years and three months, and the soldiers came back saying that the regime had denied them of their few privileges. They behaved as if once they had tasted power they believed it should be theirs. The military ruled for the next eight years. They destroyed the economy of Ghana and were so corrupt that the people said they wanted a civilian regime again and constitutional democracy.

By the end of that tenure there was a coup among the military, so they removed their own government, and then a young man, an officer [Jerry J. Rawlings], staged a second coup. They killed off the generals, including three former heads of state, before surrendering power to the civilians. That was in 1979. That is also how the Third Republic came in. The civilian regime [headed by President Hilla Limann] that was ushered in by the outgoing military also lasted only two years and three months. Then there was another coup, on New Year's Eve [December 31, 1981], when the whole country was caught up in the celebratory mood of Christmas. The democratic constitution was abrogated so the soldiers could reimpose themselves, this time claiming to be coming in to clean the stables of corruption and so forth. The soldiers came and then stayed in power for the next 10 years or so. It was a total military dictatorship. The country knew no peace. For three years the country was kept under curfew. Social life was upset, and the economy was not working. The private sector was not allowed to grow, so poverty consumed the country and the people.

Transformation of the Authoritarian System from Within

Then toward the end of the 1980s there were changes around the world. The Berlin Wall had fallen, so the East-West syndrome that had also gripped Africa was lifted, and then there was a mood of liberalization all over. Meanwhile, the economy of Ghana was totally in shambles. People did not like it, and under international pressure the Fourth Republican Constitution—which is very democratic, under which we are living now—came into being. When the people got the chance in 1992, they grabbed the opportunity, and since then people have shown patience. The government ushered in the current constitution, with the separation of powers; respect for fundamental human rights; inclusion regardless of tribe, religion, or gender; and recognizing civil society organizations. The constitution establishes the rule of law and judicial review, freedom of the media, a multiparty system, and so forth. That is the constitutional regime we are working on developing.

Since 1992, when this new system came into being, Ghana has succeeded in changing governments. We have had five elections [as of September 2012]. In 2000, the opposition won the election and there was a peaceful surrender of power; that is when I assumed office. Then in 2008 we had another election.

My party lost very marginally. **With an electorate of 9 million voters, my side lost by only 40,000 votes. This would have caused upheaval in many other places, but here we accepted the result of the election.**

The system is not perfect, even the Electoral Commission. If you look at the papers today [September 2012], you will see that many sectors are taking the Electoral Commission to task for wanting to create new constituencies, with only two months until the elections and after the Electoral Register has closed. But one defect of the constitution is that the Electoral Commission was set up without ensuring its accountability to the people. So this is the challenge we are facing now, which the people are now criticizing because of the freedom of the media. The judges are criticizing, the opposition parties are criticizing, and the Trades Union Congress has criticized it, but the government seems to support the Electoral Commission.

So I would say yes, we are improving in pursuing democracy. But a lot of credit should go to the people, because their temper and their histories make for give and take, and "live and let live," and these are essential to democracy. However, I have learned from my experience that freedom is different from democracy. I don't know anyone who wouldn't love freedom. I believe freedom comes naturally to people; everybody wants to have space to express themselves. However, you may have freedom, but if you don't have a democratic culture—which must be cultivated and nurtured—chaos might prevail or some clever clique of people could wend their way to take power and then deny the people democracy.

You told us that the Ghanaian people are by history and nature accommodating, open, and not given to clashes but rather to work things out. But the people as such find it very difficult to work as a unit to produce change. There have to be processes, institutions, and leaders.

The masses cannot construct institutions; that's why leadership is important.

International Influence

You referred to a junior officer, Jerry Rawlings, who overthrew his own military and then went through the various stages you describe. How did he become a leader of a process that led to the democratic outcome that you have described?

The 1989 fall of the Berlin Wall unleashed freedom all over the world, because until then the bipolar system, the East-West ideological divide, was pervasive. By 1989, the forces of liberalism gained ascendancy, and then the Bretton Woods institutions and the other international organizations started putting pressure everywhere, including here. And that was how I believe the military regime under this young officer, which had been in place for about 10 years, was forced to respond to the pressures from the donors. The free media that were expressing themselves everywhere prevailed on the dictators of the continent. So here, too, people began speaking up, and the elements within the regime found that they were also affected, and then they started talking of introducing a new constitution. It did not happen out of the kindness of the heart of anybody within the military regime. It happened because of international pressures. The economy was not functioning well, and Ghana's donors and creditors started introducing conditions.

It occurred in many African countries. Toward the 1990s, even apartheid started to give in to international pressures, and in other places the strongmen also started leaving the scene. Again, Ghana, always setting the pace on the African continent, perhaps was the first to have left behind its military dictatorship for the transition that took place in 1992. But the interesting thing is that the young officer, instead of leaving office with the military dictatorship, somehow converted from the military uniform into a civilian and formed a party [National Democratic Congress] and contested the presidency as its candidate. Before this change, the constitution was introduced and people had been appointed to the institutions of the constitution like the Electoral Commission because it was set up by the outgoing regime and allowed to fail.

Social Mobilization

The events that culminated with the constitution of 1992 show how a process of implicit or explicit negotiations can lead to a nonviolent transformation toward democracy. How did social movements contribute to pressure on the Rawlings government to accept a major change if he was not willing?

In 1988, Adu Boahen, a history professor, gave a memorial lecture for the person who is credited with introducing party politics to Ghana in 1947, J. B. Danquah. Danquah had invited Kwame Nkrumah [first president of Ghana, 1960–66] from abroad to Ghana in 1947. When he came here, Nkrumah ended up abandoning his work for the United Gold Coast Convention to set up the country's first political party. Nkrumah conducted this original group, and then the ensuing politics that led toward independence found Nkrumah leading the majority party, the rest of the people who invited him here becoming the opposition. When Ghana decided to become a republic in 1960, J. B. Danquah, called the doyen of Ghanaian politics, contested Nkrumah for the presidency. In 1964, Nkrumah detained him. Unfortunately, Danquah died in detention in 1965. Exactly a year later, Nkrumah was overthrown in a military coup. The Memorial Lecture has been instituted here in Ghana since Danquah's death. In 1988, this lecture, delivered by Professor Adu Boahen, was titled "The Ghanaian Sphinx—Culture of Silence." In this lecture he said that Ghana suffered from a culture of silence. And truly it was as if the whole country were under a pall spread by the regime. People were afraid to talk. The economy was not working, but people could not express themselves openly. The private sector had been destroyed. Banking confidentiality had been removed. The government could confiscate assets. So the country really wasn't a happy country then. So in 1988, when Adu Boahen gave this lecture, it opened a can of worms. Everybody started talking, and he instantly became a hero. Even though he was not a mainstream politician, that lecture alone catapulted him into my party, and he stood for the presidency in the 1992 elections and challenged Rawlings. The electoral commissioners tried to prevent his candidacy.

Constitutional Reform

Rawlings's chief advisor, Justice Daniel F. Annan, was instrumental in setting up institutions created by the constitution—the Electoral Commission, the Commission on Human Rights and Administrative Justice, the Commission for Civic Education—which have remained entrenched institutions within the constitution. Because the people were so eager to get out of the clutches of the military, the constitutional referendum was approved. In fact, the constitution also included the Transitional Provisions, which gave immunity to the coup makers [Section 34]. It was supposed to be transitional, but it is still part of the constitution. Why? Because the people were willing to pay any price to get away from the clutches of the military. But we still see that as only marginal to the essence of the constitution, which talks of the rule of law, separation of powers, etc.

The First Democratic Elections

So Rawlings converted himself into a civilian to contest the presidency for his party. It seemed like the outcome was predetermined. In spite of that, my party contested the election. When the results were such that my party could not accept them, we wrote *The Stolen Verdict* [a report on the 1992 presidential election released by the New Patriotic Party, founded in 1992, that compiled evidence of electoral rigging]. We felt that the results did not match the mood of the country, and so my party decided to boycott the parliamentary elections, as the presidential and parliamentary elections did not take place on the same day. So, for the whole term, my party was out of Parliament.

What's your evaluation of the opposition's boycott of the 1992 parliamentary elections?

There were elements that were not happy with the boycott even though within my party, across the board, we all felt cheated very badly by the 1992 presidential election.

In 1996, when I contested the presidency against Rawlings, he of course enjoyed the benefits of incumbency. I didn't have any sponsors at all. I had to sell off some of my properties to fund my campaign. Even with fewer resources, the results announced by the electoral commissioners were 39% for an opposition without vehicles, without money, without support from the media. I still got to 39%. And then the results could not be declared for about five days, and people were asking why there was a delay. The electoral commissioner asked for protection. So the question was, "From whom?" When eventually they declared the results, there were elements that were trying to prevail on me to boycott again. I said no, we needed to be in Parliament because the constitution that had been signed by the president provides for only two terms. By that time Rawlings had already served one term of four years. The question was whether he would violate the constitution he had created.

In the 1996 parliamentary election, my party won 61 seats and the government party won 133 seats. In the 2000 presidential elections, John Atta Mills, who served as vice president under Rawlings, became the National Democratic Congress [established in July 1992 as the successor to the PNDC] candidate. I competed as the NPP candidate. I won the second round of voting and then, with the whole world looking, Rawlings conceded his party's defeat.

What I am trying to say is that democracy has come, but we need to remove some rough edges of the institutions. The core of the constitution is democratic. Some people argue that the Transitional Provisions have overstayed their time, but there are others who argue that the beneficiaries of the Transitional Provisions are still here, so we do not want to provoke any social upheavals by removing them. We do not want to sweep the challenges under the carpet. Here we have a media to open the debate. The beneficiaries of the transition are growing old, and they are adjusting to the liberal spirit of the country, even Rawlings. So democracy is growing, and I don't think people want to go back.

Justice and Reconciliation

Your government established a Truth and Reconciliation Commission. How do you evaluate Ghana's experience with reconciliation and justice questions?

Evolving a nation is a long process. There are few nations in the world where you will not find, back in their history, periods when there were high-handed dictators. The main issue is to draw the line somewhere and get the people to look ahead, and then you build from the history. You never forget, but don't leave traces that would rebound to generate retribution. And so when I was elected, for example, I had the bodies of the generals who had been shot by Rawlings exhumed and given back to their families to bury. They were shot and buried in unidentified places, so as part of the reconciliation, their families appealed and asked that they be buried with dignity. So that was done. I believe that went down well.

We set up a Truth and Reconciliation Commission, which was made up of religious leaders and many people who were not in my party; we tried to give everybody a chance to go and say what had gone wrong during those times, and we did not limit the commission's work to the Rawlings period. People from as far back as Kwame Nkrumah's time who had suffered what they considered to be wrongs were allowed to give evidence, and on the basis of the commission's reports, confiscated assets and things like that were given back to those families. This was done through executive powers, but on the recommendation of the commission, which had powers similar to the High Court. The commission made recommendations to give back assets and provide compensation. There were reparations. So what the government could do, we did.

How do you feel about the work of the Truth and Reconciliation Commission now? Would you have gone a little bit further if you had to do it again?

I sleep very well. Today I believe that problem was solved. I don't think there are any extant problems for any government to go back to. The commission sat publicly for long periods and invited people to come and pour out their feelings. Even Rawlings was invited, and some of the people suspected to have committed wrongs were invited. They could go and talk. Some did not use the occasion to tell their stories, but others did, and then at the end the government acted exclusively on the commission's report.

Contemporary Transitions

You have mentioned the role of the international context and international pressure from governments, international organizations and so on, which contributed to the transition in Ghana. What can be learned from Ghana's experience that could help establish guidelines for international actors who wish to support democratic processes?

I think the history of international engagement has tended to raise doubts about even the best intentions. For example, in the Middle East, the United States and the old colonial powers like Britain and France will mostly be suspect in Syria and other countries. That's their history. But to get democratization going, democracy needs to be cultivated or nurtured. In Ghana's case, when the pressures built, we had alternatives to the military regime that had converted itself into a civilian party. Parties should be developed, given that the alternation of power is critical to anchoring democratic government. In Ghana the constitution mentions political parties as essential institutions for democracy. In North Africa the parties have not been properly nurtured. So when Mubarak went, where were the parties, aside from the Muslim Brotherhood? The leaders of Egypt had not really constituted themselves into parties and had not given a vision to the people or given them an aspiration to work toward: a vision as an alternative to Mubarak and even as an alternative to the Muslim Brotherhood.

It is necessary for international actors to understand and emphasize that political parties are important: to organize people, to educate them on rights they should pursue, and to position them to provide alternatives to dictatorial systems when the time comes to pull them out. If there are no parties and the dictators go, yes there will be freedom, but freedom for what? Is it for chaos or for the smart group to quickly take over in the first election and then find a way to undermine democracy? In Ghana we were lucky because our party had always been in the race. This party was founded in 1947, and its tradition has always been strong in Ghana, even though the military regime lasted 19 years.

Civilian Control over the Armed Forces

What measures did you and the previous government take to ensure that the military would not disrupt democratic processes?

How to define the proper role of the military? We didn't make enemies of the military. In fact, when we had the opportunity, we decided to instill pride in their job so they would be proud to be soldiers. They are sworn to be there to defend the nation if we are attacked from outside or when the president, who is the commander in chief, tasks them to do something, but not to come and use their power to take over. So what did we do? I made my brother, Dr. Kwame Addo-Kufuor, minister of defense.

Previously, professional soldiers were just used by politicians. Rawlings, for instance, seized power, and the way he managed the military, at the end of the day, the regular officer was not quite part of the government, but the institution was unduly politicized. So the regular soldier felt that his profession was being polluted.

So what we did to get them to stay in the barracks is we treated them well. For example, Ghana has participated in UN (United Nations) peace missions all over the world for a long time. The allowance for going on peace missions was low: $32 a day. At the time my government came in, soldiers were given only half of that, about $15 or $16 a day. My government raised the allowance to $27 because the soldiers were risking their lives going on these missions. They appreciated that. We ensured their upkeep. We built perhaps the biggest hall in Accra. It's in the barracks, called Burma Hall. We rebuilt it into a fine, very modern hall. We created ICT (information and communication technology) centers in the barracks to train them. We worked to instill pride in them as soldiers, which made them aware that being there did not make them politicians. We made the soldiers understand that they belonged to their own world and that they had sworn an oath to serve the president as commander in chief, a civilian, and that they should be loyal to that oath.

This seems to be working still. The government is not unduly courting soldiers to come and do things they shouldn't do under the civilian system.

Fundamental Principles

What are the lessons from your experience that you try to convey?

I visited Nigeria recently, and people wanted to know how we accepted the outcome of the very indeterminate results of 2008, with 9 million voters and 3 rounds of voting, and in the end the Electoral Commission declared somebody the winner by a margin of only 40,000 votes. But I had foreseen the outcome. After the second round there was one constituency that hadn't voted because of some technical mishap, so that was going to be the decider of the election. In fact, I had gone there to support my candidates, only to learn there that my candidate had gone to court seeking an injunction to prevent the electoral commissioner from conducting the election in that constituency. And we had only 10 days or so between Election Day and the assumption of office by the president-elect. Of course the handing-over date is fixed by the constitution, January 7. So if I had sided with my candidate, then it would have meant that I would have had to declare a state of emergency; that was the only way to constitutionally postpone the dates before handing over the presidency. I looked at the merits of the matter, and I could not in good conscience agree with my candidate. So I told my candidate, "You have gone to court but you did not consult me, because I would have advised against it, because I felt we had a real chance. If the court throws out your application and the election goes ahead, we will certainly lose." So I could not do any campaigning. Rather, I told them without mincing words that I was going to make a statement to the nation that I was prepared to hand over power to the person the Electoral Commission declares the winner. The court did not uphold my candidate's writ, and the commission went ahead with the election in the remaining constituency and declared the NDC the winner with a majority of just over 40,000 votes.

I did it in good conscience. **The constitution says to hand over power to the president-elect, and I obeyed the constitution. So let us all obey the constitution. A good constitution is necessary for the nation, one that prescribes respect for human rights, respect for the ballot, respect for an independent Electoral Commission, respect for an independent judiciary. If you do all these things, you make peace because people truly feel that they are participating in their government. If you deny them that feeling, even-**

tually you have an Arab Spring; that is, sooner or later the people will rise up to promote their rights. So everywhere I go, I say, "let a good constitution be in place." The government must swear by the constitution, respect it, and allow people to talk, allow freedom of the media. The government should be seen to be accountable. If you do that, anybody wanting to usurp power will not have the grounds to do so.

Biosketch of Jerry John Rawlings, President of Ghana 1993–2001

PHOTO: DESIRE CLARKE

Jerry John Rawlings was an Air Force pilot and flight lieutenant in the Ghanaian armed forces. Together with other junior officers, he overthrew Ghana's elected government in 1979, leading to the execution of several high-ranking military officers, including three former heads of state. Rawlings facilitated new national elections in 1979, three months after coming to power. Highly critical of the then-elected government of Hilla Limann and its alleged protection of elite privileges, Rawlings overthrew the new regime on December 31,

1981. He ruled as military dictator until 1992, when he agreed to constitutional reform in response to pressure from both Ghanaian civil society organizations and the international community, and threw his support behind competitive multiparty elections.

Rawlings supervised the adoption of a new constitution, establishing the Fourth Republic, which was approved by referendum in early 1992. He formed the National Democratic Congress party and led it as the presidential candidate in the first multiparty elections in November 1992 and 1996, winning on both occasions. The Fourth Republic constitution established nonpartisan institutions to oversee elections, civic education, the media, and the protection of human rights. During his first term as elected president (1993–95), Rawlings implemented the establishment of these institutions and allowed them considerable power. In 2000, facing term limits and international scrutiny and pressure, Rawlings stepped down after his party's candidate lost to John Agyekum Kufuor, the opposition leader, thus firmly placing Ghana on the path to liberal democracy. Ghana has since managed additional competitive elections and transfers of power, most recently in the December 2012 elections, despite a closely contested outcome.

Although not a constitutional democrat by prior personal conviction or experience, Rawlings upended the oligarchic quasi-democracy that Ghana had before he took power. He connected with mass popular aspirations through political mobilization and socially inclusive policies that brought previously marginal regions of northern Ghana into the development process. Rawlings built political support, first from urban workers and then from rural peasants, and helped channel Ghanaian politics toward more inclusionary and institutionalized democratic governance.

Interview with President Jerry John Rawlings

You entered political life as a young Air Force officer, helped overthrow two governments, and ruled as an unelected military leader for about a decade. Yet you chose to establish multiparty competitive elections in the late 1990s, accepted presidential term limits, recognized the victory of your main political opponent in the elections of 2000, and transferred power to him peacefully, thus contributing greatly to institutionalizing constitutional democracy in Ghana. How do you explain your evolution and your choices related to establishing and strengthening democratic governance?

Let me provide some background about what led to my military government, the challenges, the events, and my efforts that culminated in the institutionalization of constitutional democracy in Ghana.

Cycles of Military Intervention

The 1979 revolt by junior officers that I led was an expression of outrage; something the people alone had not been able to do. In 1979, Ghana was becoming like an overheated kitchen. No soldier would follow any officer to initiate a coup, because the rank and file hated the senior officers at that point in time after seven years of military rule. I remember I used to tell my colleagues, "Let's move. Let's move," two years before 1979. When we finally did, the level of corruption in the military leadership that overthrew Prime Minister Kofi Busia [1969–72] in 1972 had enraged the populace to the extent that not even the execution of the two corrupt heads of state among these generals would satisfy the blood lust of the country.

The political situation by the time of the 1979 revolt was such that all you needed to do was to light a match and throw it into the room. **In modern societies, when the pressure is building up, there is enough integrity and capacity within the institutions to deal with it. So the pressure hardly ever builds up to the point of sparking an explosion. The fear of the buildup and explosion should not be in the air, but when it exists, it means something is wrong somewhere in the political process and institutions.** In our case, when finally it exploded, we did not examine what led to the buildup of the pressure and the explosion; we were asking, "Who lit the match?"

Three months later, after the elections, we handed power over to the Limann [President Hilla Limann, 1979–81] regime, which announced my retirement. And at that point in time I knew where the Limann government were going. They were after my blood because I refused to leave the country. All I had to do was to disobey their announcement of my retirement. I heard it on the radio; I could have disobeyed it and walked straight back to camp and continued working. But that would have created a horrible situation for the government. It could have been the beginning of the end, because the revolt [that Rawlings led against the previous military regime] was more popular than the [Limann] government. But I stayed at home when the government announced my retirement in order to give credibility and authority back to the spoken word, because the use of the word had been so much abused and had lost its credibility for so long. I was still so bent on helping the government that I stayed at home, because for those three months people were so full of anger [against the political, economic, and military elites who were viewed as corrupt and exploitative] that they were not prepared to listen to a second opinion.

When we came back a second time on December 31, 1981 [overthrowing President Limann], some of that outrage of the people had dissipated.

Decentralization

What was left of this energy was channeled constructively, which was the beauty of the process between 1981 until 1992 led by the Provisional National Defense Council government. We needed to channel all the reawakened political power of the ordinary citizens into a formal structure for decentralized local governance. We pursued decentralization rather than devolution because we didn't want to simply give power to local elites; we wanted to give decision-making power to the people. That's why we created more than 40 district assemblies [which were the highest political and administrative body in each district] out of 10 existing subnational administrative units, which afforded people an avenue for democratic expression. The district assembly concept was not partisan; we did not have political parties at that time. We went ahead with nonpartisan district assembly elections [which took place in stages in different regions from December 1988 to February 1989]. So, invariably, people were being elected on the basis of their values, who and what they represented, and the personal respect they commanded in their community.

I reserved 30% of the seats in the assemblies for people to be appointed. We used that opportunity to look for good people, and, in consultation with the chiefs and opinion leaders, we brought in those good people from the grassroots into the assemblies by appointment. District assembly members were also given the opportunity to elect their own chairpersons. I believe around 90% of those who were elected as chairpersons came from the appointed members.

Challenging Entrenched Interests

In 1979 and subsequently in the 1980s, during the first 10 years of my leadership, we had a council of which I was the chairperson. We tackled injustices in the political, economic, and cultural systems. We attempted to streamline the economy and remove rent-seeking activities, because there were people who were exploiting state institutions, rules, and regulations of trade to amass wealth at the expense of the people. The council also established tribunals that took the place of Western conventional courthouses, and the tribunals were presided over by opinion leaders (a councilor from the chiefs, a woman of reputation, etc.), and the chairpersons were lawyers. Cases that used to take 5, 10, 15 years were being solved in a matter of weeks.

The Meaning and Popular Appeal of Democracy

When we were in office, at the end of the 1980s, we were sort of pushed by the US State Department to create a multiparty system. In fact, we had already experienced multipartyism in this country, also a single party under Kwame

Nkrumah [first president of Ghana, 1960-66], capitalism, socialism, coups; none of these regimes were accountable to the people. But, somehow, out of the 1979 revolt by junior Army officers that I headed against the military, which overthrew President Busia, a sense of accountability was emerging, with a creative expression of freedom both mentally and physically. And we needed to protect this as it brought the best out of our people. The Western powers used to call our system of government under the PNDC "nondemocratic," and they call it "democratic" when we went to constitutional rule with a multiparty system in 1992. But democracy was actually being practiced during those 10 years [1981-91]. We just did not have a formal constitution.

We, the National Democratic Congress [established in July 1992 as the successor to the PNDC], won the 1992 presidential multiparty election without much problem because our popularity then was still very high in spite of 10 years of so-called revolution.

After the introduction of constitutional rule in 1992, people said of me, "He had the power and he could have kept it." I couldn't have, even if I had wanted to. Because once you empower people and they get the taste of freedom and justice, it can be difficult to take it away from them. For us who live in the so-called developing world, in Africa, the course of democracy was picking up; people power was gradually gaining momentum, so leaders in Africa could no longer get away with "foolishness" or hardheadedness by refusing to listen to the people. I believed very much in what I was doing. I chose the easier option, the more sensible option, and at least for me there was no other way, there was no other alternative than to have free elections and to step down after my second presidential term. I believe in democracy and I believe in freedom and justice. And quite frankly, that is what the average human being desires and wants to see in their lives. The culture of democracy had already become a part of my leadership style and a way of life of the people before constitutional rule, so it was very easy and natural to be institutionalized in the country.

How did you understand the changes taking place in Ghana in the late 1970s?

It's not as complex as outsiders, or even internal observers, may say. But if you lived it, you would learn that finding the solution should not be that difficult. At that time Ghana was craving a change. We could have had a change through reforms, but the leadership was not waking up to this. So a revolt became the way out [against the military head of state, Frederick Akuffo, 1978-79]; it was not a coup, it was a revolutionary movement that was to put an end to coups and remove the building blocks of exploitation and misuse of power. There was the question of whether to allow the revolt to gain momentum, to have its full course, or to rein it in. We compartmentalized to see in which areas to allow the revolt to have its full life, and in which areas to subject it to reforms. But the important thing was how to allow the human spirit to own the atmosphere.

Some people claim that multiparty democracy is true democracy. No—there are multiple forms of democracy, including participatory democracy. Multiparty democracy has failed Ghana in the past—in our history, we have tasted multiparty democracy. We've lived it, and we've lived under a single-party system. The Socialist economic philosophy, the capitalist economic philosophy, the coups of the generals—none of them was accountable to our people. Eventually that led to the revolt of 1979.

How could a country that has won independence in Africa—a country like Ghana that was under the inspiring leadership of Dr. Kwame Nkrumah, who won independence for us and took us through 10 years under his leadership from independence—be overthrown and then, 13 years or so later, the country was ready for an explosion, where 3 former heads of state and 5 generals had to be executed? And still the country was asking for more blood. Every society grows and builds on ethics, on morality, a sense of justice, freedom, etc. So when you take it away, you create stress. For example, when a daughter or son slaps the mother, this is a serious offense. But the worse offense is when the father returns from the farm and does nothing about that slap. That's when the moral break occurs, when the social fabric begins to collapse; the corrective mechanism may be in place, but the leaders refuse to do something about it.

As soon as we won, we started attempting to fly a kite of freedom. No kite of freedom will fly if the rope of justice is not strong enough to hold it. So here and now in Ghana we are enjoying some form of freedom, but without justice. And the people know it. So the time has come for the test. And we are frightened; we are worried. Freedom and justice are taken for granted in Western countries, because you dare not mess around with it. Governments have been unseated on the basis of the economy. But here in Africa, governments have been unseated because of how much freedom and justice they allow or don't allow.

Transition as the Culmination of a Process

You made the decision to hold a referendum for a new constitution in 1992, which mandated the creation of the Commission on Human Rights and Administrative Justice, ensured the independence of the Electoral Commission, and instituted other reforms to bring about democratic transition. Was there an important change in Ghana that made this transition possible or imperative?

There was nothing extraordinary about 1992, the creation of the constitution, and holding elections. It was a process; the National Commission for Democracy led consultations on the future of Ghanaian democracy, which led to the establishment of district assemblies. Then, as a follow-up to the electoral process for district assemblies that we had instituted and operationalized, the NCD organized another set of public consultations. By that point the IMF and the World Bank were supporting us financially to build new roads, provide water, etc. So, to be quite honest, they were not going to wait for us to come out with an appropriate formula of how to sustain that new culture of [populist, grassroots] democracy in our people. The US State Department also exerted pressure to go multiparty.

After 10 years of an exercise in people's power, my wife and I were not sitting at the castle [Osu Castle, formerly the official residence of the president]. She was spending days and weeks moving around the country. By that action we were demystifying the godly posture of head of state in high office. Demystifying the presidency helped to empower people. Mentalities have changed. And it is not as if we were introducing something new to the people. This was the suppressed good side of people, and our style of leadership brought the best out of our people. I did not perform a miracle. The people performed the miracle. Irrespective of what race or where they came from. Give them the right leadership and they will perform the miracle, not I.

Social and Political Opposition

How did the mobilization of workers, students, parties, and the Movement for Freedom and Justice influence the political transition in Ghana?

The civil society and opposition were weak; they were not strong enough to be recognized by the people. We had divergent views and positions within the PNDC about different issues, including the direction of the government. The internal criticism within the PNDC was strong enough to deal with the governance challenges. We did not need to recognize any sort of institutionalized opposition in the name of a certain party because internal criticism and internal democracy was so high. The government included some democratically minded members of the military, but also civilians with progressive ideals and people from different ethnic groups. Military power was used to establish law and order and to stabilize the situation, but the power was to go to the people.

Transformation into an Elected Leader

You and the NDC had the support of people all over the country when you made the decision to call for elections. You won the presidential election in 1992, and then you were reelected in 1996. Why did you decide to run for presidential elections after the return of multiparty politics?

Unlike most people who sit on the throne and sleep on it, we were tired. Ten years of trying to manage a revolutionary government, instituting reforms to give power to the people, and bringing the economy back from crisis—it was an exhausting business. I was tired. It wasn't until we heard these characters —the opposition—beginning to sing false tunes and to malign us that we realized that we had to form the NDC to stay on. That is the raw truth. So staying active in politics was nothing we enjoyed. It was a duty. I decided we would continue, because we could not have what the people had toiled for be thrown overboard.

So I hoped that I would protect what we had created and what the people had created. That's how I saw myself. We built more roads. We provided electricity and water. For example, we wanted to vaccinate the people very fast to prevent cerebrospinal meningitis. One year, before moving up north to be there to help with the mobilization, the doctors came to vaccinate before I set off. And at that time, my wife and I had been spending so much time talking about family planning and AIDS that when the meningitis issue came up, and we sent the refrigerated drugs, and the nurses were all ready to start their jabs, the masses were all there but nobody was forming a line. Nobody would come and form the queue. They were afraid, so I was asking, "What is going on? We've got to hurry up and move on." They were afraid that we were coming to give them injections that would make them sterile, I think, because I had been talking about AIDS and family planning for so long. So I had to be the first in the line, rolled up my sleeve for a second jab. Then everybody went into the line and it went so fast, so smooth.

I never thought I would see the practice of family planning in my lifetime. I was so privileged to see it. One of the most formidable organizations in this country was the 31 December Women's Movement [an organization to advance the social and economic position of women] that was led by my wife; family planning is one of their areas of focus. Once I had a speaking engagement, and whenever I'm talking, I invite whoever also wants to make a point or ask questions to come on the stage. This particular time there was a lady who offered to say something. She came, and she was encouraging everybody because she has two children and she doesn't see the need to have more, because the six killer diseases have been controlled due to vaccinations.

I don't know when to stop my selflessness and become selfish, to limit myself. I think I have given enough of myself and my life to my environment, to my people, and I should now concentrate on myself. I want to teach others to start being what they are and to catch up, to grow up, so I can go. I am saying, in effect, it's not fair for those in power and for the political class to take advantage of people's naïveté, people's ignorance, and manipulate them the way it has been done, time after time after time, government after government after government. People are to be managed, but not manipulated. Create the environment for them to bring the best out of themselves.

There is a way in which we've used the English language to suppress the cause of democracy, freedom, and justice in this country, because we adopted that beautiful English language without adopting the integrity with which it is spoken in native English-speaking countries. Does that mean that we have no integrity? We have as much integrity, and you will find it even in our local languages and behavioral patterns. But by taking on this colonial language, we leave out the integrity in our political culture. The educated classes that speak fluent English put themselves on a pedestal above others and use language to manipulate the people. Just because someone speaks English fluently does not mean that they are automatically more qualified, will make good decisions, or will not be self-interested; this is false and reduces the integrity of politicians.

International Context

How did the broader global context affect your political choices?

There was a point in time in our recent past that America made a terrible mistake, under George H. W. Bush, when it decided to deal with Saddam Hussein by invading Iraq [August 1990 to February 1991]. Around that time, with the collapse of the bipolar world, America was standing out as the unipolar authority and power. Later, the United States ended Saddam's regime; they didn't have the patience to wait it out. The very act of moving in when they did created extensive damage, and it allowed their right to use their might to override the might of right to override against all the antiwar sentiments from the rest of the world. The minute that happened it was like something had broken the link between the exercise of power and the exercise of authority.

Authority has a morality to it. And the minute that nonlegitimate power was used in Iraq, some of us in power in Africa took a cue, but what happened in my case was to exercise authority that's rightful power: power with morality and legitimacy. As the head of state, I could have used the military force—"the right of might"—at my disposal, but instead I chose to allow the power of the people—"the might of right." I listened to the voice of the people and by so doing exercised authority with morality.

Along with the exercise of political power without morality, as by America in Iraq, something else was happening to Africa: the savagery of capitalism. In advanced economies, there is a check on capitalism, and there is a way in which capitalism is competitive. In America you make your money on the basis of merit, on ability. Here you make your money from influence.

When I was at school, there was a writer, Ayi Kwei Armah, who authored a book called *The Beautyful Ones Are Not Yet Born*. It was a book I really loved. Many years later, as I was getting more and more politically conscious, I realized that, no, the title of his book was wrong. No, the beautiful ones, in my opinion, *are* born. They are here. The main challenge is that the political situation does not give room to these people with the right qualities to take the stage. The [political] situation suppresses them. People with that sense of justice, people with that kind of quality, are also invariably very frightened of standing up on a political platform because those who have monopolized it are dirty and will say false things against their name, and they don't want that, so they keep away. So it is only the criminals, economic criminals, who take advantage of politics and business, thereby leading to disregard for merit in a society, and this amounts to undermining the roots for development.

After the PNDC regime, Western powers and the media kept whitewashing the government's image because Ghana had become a so-called star of democracy, and especially when John Kufuor and the New Patriotic Party came in, it is like the West needed a country that could be projected to the rest of Africa and the world as a success story. So, in spite of all the corrupt things going on, the Western media kept whitewashing Kufuor's government and image. Things are not quite what people outside are made to believe.

Traditional Governance

When you speak about Ghana today, it does not sound like the current political culture corresponds with the values and habits that you attribute to Ghana's people. What do you believe accounts for the differences?

Some may not agree with this, but I believe that unlawful or harmful behavior in society is less constrained today. I think in the old days there was respect in society. You could easily be hauled up by your own people to the traditional ruler for wrongdoing, and you might pay a fine of a sort. But when we became independent, I think one of the unfortunate mistakes Nkrumah made in trying to assert the nation's statehood, the authority and the structure of the state, is that he went about it in a manner that took away the power of the traditional rulers and their ability to punish wrongdoing. We don't have uniformed policemen employed by the state in villages all over the country, and there is diminished recognition of traditional authority. Through little mistakes we destroyed that social sense of responsibility and discipline. In the meantime, we go round in a cycle and come back to appreciate traditional authority, which does not need police and soldiers to make itself respected.

When we were reforming the governance system, there was a conflict between two schools of thought about traditional governance systems. One was that we can learn lessons from these grassroots systems about how to exercise authority in a nonpolitical, nonpartisan way and use this knowledge to advance the course of development. Others, with a more leftist orientation, said that the chiefs are anachronistic feudal institutions that are no longer relevant in a properly defined people's power environment. Because of this clash, when we were structuring decentralization we did not effectively factor in the mobilization force and the moral authority that chiefs have at the grassroots level. Therefore their role in the grassroots governance structure was not defined and properly used. **We were not able to purge what we thought of as the negatives of the traditional system and get to the true value of integration into the governance system, even if they would not replace the executive authority in an area.**

But to illustrate the importance that traditional beliefs still hold, I will share an anecdote. In my last year in office, the opposition was harassing us. It was an election year, and they were accusing one of our regional ministers of doing something that I did not think he would have done. So I invited this regional minister to Accra and asked him if he had done these things he was accused of, and he said no. So I asked him to swear on his traditional gods. Not many will swear on their traditional gods and misbehave. There is integrity within our own traditional languages and behavior. He said he was willing to do it. So he swore and dared those chiefs and people to also swear and repeat the allegation. Nobody accused him anymore.

International Support

Regarding the role of the international community in Ghana, you mentioned, for example, that the US State Department pressured Ghana to return to multiparty elections. Can international organizations and other democratic countries effectively promote institutions of democratic governance?

I would like to give the international community the benefit of the doubt in saying that they genuinely want to see a culture of democracy, globally. But maybe the way they are approaching some of these things is undermining the very objective they are trying to achieve.

For example, the Palestinian problem with Israel and apartheid in South Africa were the two eyesores on screens around the world. Apartheid was removed. So the world's attention is on the issue between Palestine and Israel, because it is horrible what we are seeing. When you take away every chance for a person to fight back, don't be surprised if they risk their life in trying to fight you.

Leadership Qualities

In these last 30 years of your national political experience, what has surprised you? What would you have done differently?

People tend to ask, "What would you have done differently?" I reply that there is nothing I would have done differently. Everything we did was what we could have done under the circumstances. But when I had to come back [in 1981], the rank and file of the military were expecting it because of the persecution that had started against them with President Limann's regime. Limann's government was spreading misinformation among the military and fomenting ethnically based tensions. That could have led to an implosion within the armed forces. I was the one they were looking up to, to step in and stop the decline they were sending the country back to.

I couldn't take that nonsense in our society. When I joined the military academy, I must have been about 19 or so. I come from a modest background, but I grew up with servants. In our homes in those days, servant or no servant, you would also do work in the home. So, in effect, we ended up like we belonged to the same family with the servants. I also used to do holiday jobs. So I've worked with laborers, with so-called ordinary folks, and with people from different tribes. In my tribe we don't have gold and we don't have cocoa. So a lot of people from my area end up in the military or the police. But the military is a place where tribalism, ethnic-based conflict, does not reign. The military is really a great place to be.

An important lesson that I have applied in my life is that in anything you do, be confident, but don't be overconfident, for that can be dangerous. When you are less confident, then go and relearn. Go teach yourself until you feel confident enough. I made a few mistakes where I nearly crashed badly, and it shook me up. Some said I should resign, and leave the Air Force. In my case I had to start again until I could build up my confidence. I did not allow my ego to intoxicate me. You've got to face the reality about yourself and know your limitations. Do you know how many generals insisted that I should promote myself? Do they think I'm stupid? There's nothing greater and better than being true to yourself.

When presiding over the seat of state, you must maintain a high level of integrity and make sure all those below you also maintain a high level of integrity—because it is integrity that brings about so much creativity, so much development, and so much creative energy. But now all that is being replaced with money. Respect is being replaced by money.

The Role of Women

Can you describe the role of Ghanaian women in the building of democracy?

The women of this country are our backbone. Women were the ones who marshaled themselves and literally held the old colonial fortresses under siege and made sure Nkrumah was released. We men have not shown enough appreciation and respect for the power and the value of our women. Thirty-four women were murdered in my last term, and I believe it was politically motivated to create insecurity.

Women did not require money to hit the campaign trail, to hit the road. Five o'clock in the morning, they are ready because the revolution came for the dispossessed, for the underprivileged, for the oppressed, and, to be quite honest, Muslims, northerners, and women and children were the very bottom rungs of society. So we were winning for ourselves our freedom, and the women came along with us.

I don't know whether it was the 1992 or 1996 election, but I ended up in a certain village and, as I finished talking, I asked the chief and his people if anybody had anything to say, or a comment or question. Nobody said anything. Then a young lady lifted her hand. I immediately beckoned her to come to the microphone. She pointed at a cement tower that was behind them and asked if the government could repair this tower for them. At that moment I said to myself, "Why do you think it took this woman to come forward? Why do you think she raised this issue? Why didn't any man talk about it? Why didn't any of the councilors or the chief talk about it?" Because they don't have to wake up at four, five o'clock in the morning to walk two miles to go and fetch water because the water tower is not working. It is the women who have to do that.

What haven't women suffered in this country, this continent? The day the circumstances of women begin to change for the better on this continent, I will know Africa is ready to move. I taught a 13-year-old girl how to fly, my own daughter, and I did it for political reasons. I did it for a deliberate reason, because I wanted to tell people, "Stop underestimating the potential, the mental, intellectual faculties of the youth and the girl child." When Dr. Kwame Nkrumah wanted to create an Air Force, we men thought, "Oh no, no, no, it is only for the white man. Only the white man can do that." So he had to go behind us. Because at that time we looked down on women, he went behind us and picked two women and they were trained how to fly before the men woke up. The men then thought, "if the women can do it, so can we."

Has there been a high proportion of women in the Ghanaian Parliament?

Unfortunately, the leadership of the political parties is so poor that we don't give enough places, even where we have very solid grounds, to women. We're selfishly nudging them out of the way, and yet when it comes to the electoral campaign, if the women don't hit the road to campaign for and support the candidates, they won't be successful. When the men hit the campaign trail, it is like a truck, a lorry, or a car or bicycle. When the women get involved, it is like a train. Everybody is jumping on board.

....

Time Line

Mar. 1957: Ghana gains independence from Britain. Kwame Nkrumah, leader of the colonial legislature and independence movement, becomes prime minister, backed by the populist-leftist Convention People's Party. Over the following years, Nkrumah consolidates power, restricts free speech, and bans opposition.

Feb. 1966: Nkrumah is overthrown by the military; he is exiled and eventually dies abroad but maintains a popular following.

Aug. 1969: The government holds new elections. Nkrumah opponent Kofi Abrefa Busia of the Progress Party wins but is overthrown three years later. Over the next decade, the state-controlled and export-dependent economy deteriorates.

Jun. 1979: Flight Lieutenant Jerry Rawlings leads a coup against the military government but allows scheduled elections while warning against irresponsible civilian politicians. He remains an Air Force officer, keeping his rank until 1992.

Sep. 1979: The Nkrumahist People's National Party, under Hilla Limann, wins democratic elections but subsequently struggles to confront inflation and budget deficits.

Dec. 1981: Rawlings leads a coup, establishes the governing Provisional National Defense Council (PNDC), and bans parties and independent media. The PNDC announces a "people's revolution" of local cadres, paramilitaries, and extrajudicial public tribunals.

Apr. 1983: Facing economic difficulties, the PNDC abruptly embraces market-oriented World Bank–designed economic policies; over the next decade, they are credited for economic growth and enhance Rawlings's popularity. International financial institutions become a major source of government funding.

Jan. 1985: Rawlings creates the National Commission on Democracy (NCD) to study a return to constitutional government. The NCD is mostly quiet for the next five years.

Jul. 1987: Rawlings proposes partially elected, partially appointed nonpartisan local assemblies while criticizing liberal democracy as elitist and conflict based. Assemblies are created and "no-party" elections are held over the next two years despite opposition criticism.

Jul. 1990: Rawlings, under pressure from the United States and international financial institutions to democratize, proposes converting local assemblies into an Electoral College.

Aug. 1990: "Nkrumahist" (leftist-populist) and "Busiahist" (liberal) opposition forms Movement for Freedom and Justice (MFJ), led by Albert Adu Boahen, to criticize "nonparty democracy." MFJ mounts urban protests but does not gain a mass following.

Mar. 1991: The NCD organizes public meetings on its "no-party" democracy plan. The opposition circumvents government control of meetings to criticize the proposal as undemocratic.

May 1991: After confidential surveys show Rawlings was likely to win a free presidential election (in part owing to the strong economy), he abandons his "no-party" proposal, proposes direct multiparty elections, and appoints a constitution-drafting committee.

Apr. 1992: Over 90% of voters endorse the new constitution, although campaigning is restricted during the referendum. The constitution establishes an elected presidency and Parliament.

May 1992: The PNDC lifts the ban on parties. New parties, including the Busiahist National People's Party (NPP), Nkrumahist parties, and Rawlings's National Democratic Congress (NDC), begin their campaigns. The NPP supports liberal economic policies, while the Nkrumahists oppose them.

Nov. 1992: Rawlings is elected president; NPP is main opposition, and the Nkrumahists do poorly. The NDC benefits from government resources, but elections are mostly clean. The opposition protests the results and threatens to boycott legislative elections.

Dec. 1992: The NDC wins 189 out of 200 seats in legislative elections, with the NPP boycotting. International observers describe the elections as fair, but the NPP publishes an account of alleged fraud that international experts consider partially hyperbolic.

Jun. 1993: Rawlings appoints an independent commissioner of human rights and administrative justice following opposition protests against an earlier nominee.

Jul. 1993: The Supreme Court rules that state media must provide equal time to the opposition, and that protests can be held without permits.

Nov. 1993: The NPP ends its boycott and begins "doing business with government" by resolving disputes within the legal system and participating in future elections.

Feb. 1994: The NPP threatens an election boycott over voter registration procedures. The US embassy resolves the issue by paying for improved voter identification cards.

Mar. 1994: The Electoral Commission creates a consultative Inter-Party Advisory Commission (IPAC) of party and civil society officials. IPAC builds trust between parties and enhances the credibility of the Rawlings-appointed Electoral Commission.

Apr. 1995: The opposition mounts protests against the proposed value-added tax. Members of PNDC-era cadres clash with protestors; four die and the government withdraws the plan.

Dec. 1996: Rawlings and the NDC win legislative and presidential elections. The NPP solidifies its role as a major opposition party. International and domestic observers declare contests to be fair; the opposition concedes.

Jun. 1998: Rawlings, indicating that he will respect constitutional term limits, endorses lawyer and former Internal Revenue Service Commissioner John Atta-Mills as the NDC's next presidential candidate.

Dec. 2000: The NPP's John Kufuor defeats Atta-Mills in the presidential election. Elections are mostly fair, despite some misuse of government resources and NDC hints of military intervention. In office, Kufuor strengthens democratic institutions, reinforces market-oriented economic policies, attracts foreign investment, and oversees continued economic growth.

Jul. 2001: The NPP-led Parliament repeals the Criminal Libel Law, encouraging independent media.

Dec. 2001: Parliament creates the National Reconciliation Commission to investigate rights abuses during military rule. It can recommend compensation but cannot prosecute.

Dec. 2004: Kufuor and NPP are reelected in largely clean democratic elections.

Jun. 2007: Major oil fields are discovered in Ghana's territorial waters, improving the country's economic prospects but prompting fears that oil revenues will fuel corruption.

Dec. 2008: New elections are held; Kufuor is ineligible because of term limits. Atta-Mills and the NDC win. NPP initially refuses to concede, but backs down under civil society pressure.

Jul. 2012: Atta-Mills dies in office; Vice President John Dramani Mahama completes his term.

Dec. 2012: Mahama wins a full term. The NPP initially does not concede, but election observers and civil society convince the NPP to launch a legal challenge rather than street protests.

NOTES

1. Movement For Freedom and Justice, "Announcement of the Formation of a Broad-Based National Movement: The Movement for Freedom and Justice," press conference, August 1, 1990.

2. Ibid.

3. Steven Levitsky and Lucan A. Way, *Competitive Authoritarianism: Hybrid Regimes after the Cold War* (New York: Cambridge University Press, 2010).

4. Kwame Boafo-Arthur, "The Quest for National Reconciliation in Ghana: Challenges and Prospects," in *Voting for Democracy in Ghana: The 2004 Elections in Perspectives*, Thematic Studies 1, ed. Kwame Boafo-Arthur (Accra: Freedom Publications, 2006), 136.

5. Eboe Hutchful, *Democratic Governance of Security: Facing Up to Ghana's Fragility* (Accra: IDEG, 2007), 23.

GUIDE TO FURTHER READING

Agyeman-Duah, Ivor. *Between Faith and History: A Biography of J. A. Kufuor.* Trenton, N.J.: Africa World Press, 2003.

Boafo-Arthur, Kwame. "Ghana: Structural Adjustment, Democratization, and the Politics of Continuity." *African Studies Review* 42, no. 2 (1999): 41–72.

———, ed. *Ghana: One Decade of the Liberal State.* Dakar: Council for the Development of Social Science Research in Africa, 2007.

Bratton, Michael, Peter Lewis, and E. Gyimah-Boadi. "Constituencies for Reform in Ghana." *Journal of Modern African Studies* 39, no. 2 (2001): 231–59.

Chazan, Naomi. *An Anatomy of Ghanaian Politics: Managing Political Recession, 1969–1972.* Boulder, Colo.: Westview Press, 1983.

Crawford, Gordon. "The European Union and Democracy Promotion in Africa: The Case of Ghana." *European Journal of Development Research* 17, no. 4 (2005): 571–600.

Crook, Richard C. "'No-Party' Politics and Local Democracy in Africa: Rawlings' Ghana in the 1990s and the 'Ugandan Model.'" *Democratization* 6, no. 4 (1999): 114–38.

Frempong, Alex K. D. *Electoral Politics in Ghana's Fourth Republic: In the Context of Post Cold War Africa.* Accra: A. K. D. Frempong, 2012.

Gyimah-Boadi, E. "Another Step Forward for Ghana." *Journal of Democracy* 20, no. 2 (2009): 138–52.

———, ed. *Ghana under PNDC Rule.* Dakar: Council for the Development of Social Science Research in Africa, 1993.

Handley, Antoinette. "Ghana: Democratic Transition, Presidential Power, and the World Bank." In *Transitions to Democracy: A Comparative Perspective*, edited by Kathryn Stoner and Michael McFaul, 221–43. Baltimore: Johns Hopkins University Press, 2013.

Hearn, Julie. "The US Democratic Experiment in Ghana." In *Africa in Crisis: New Challenges and Possibilities*, edited by Tunde Zack-Williams, Diane Frost, and Alex Thomson. London: Pluto Press, 2002.

Herbst, Jeffrey. *The Politics of Reform in Ghana, 1982–1991.* Berkeley: University of California Press, 1993.

Hutchful, Eboe. "Pulling Back from the Brink: Ghana's Experience." In *Governing Insecurity: Democratic Control of Military and Security Establishments in Transitional Democracies*, edited by Gavin Cawthra and Robin Luckham. London: Zed Books, 2003.

Morrison, Minion K. C. "Political Parties in Ghana through Four Republics: A Path to Democratic Consolidation." *Comparative Politics* 36, no. 4 (2004): 421–42.

Ninsin, Kwame, ed. *Ghana: Transition to Democracy.* Dakar: Council for the Development of Social Science Research in Africa, 1998.

Quarshigah, Edward Kofi. "Constitutional Reform and Democratic Governance in Ghana: An IDEG 10th Anniversary Lecture." Accra: Institute for Democratic Governance, 2010.

Sandbrook, Richard, and Jay Oelbaum. "Reforming Dysfunctional Institutions through Democratization? Reflections on Ghana." *Journal of Modern Africa Studies* 35, no. 4 (2007): 603–46.

Chapter 4

INDONESIA

....

Indonesia's Democratic Venture: Problems, Prospects, and Remaining Challenges

BAHTIAR EFFENDY AND MUTIARA PERTIWI

Indonesia is an archipelago state of more than 13,000 islands that are divided by geography as well as ethnicity, religion, and social class. The country includes 366 different ethnic groups. Islam is the dominant religion, professed by 87% of Indonesians, and there are also communities of Catholics, Protestants, Hindus, Buddhists, and Confucianists. These ethnic and religious divisions have made it hard to attain national consensus and legitimate authority in Indonesia.[1]

The First Democratic Encounter

When Soekarno and Mohammad Hatta proclaimed Indonesia's independence in 1945, elite sentiment generally favored democracy as its system of government. The country's 1945 constitution tilted toward the executive, but it also honored some important basic tenets of democracy. Its preamble emphasized humanitarianism, consultation, and social justice. Under the constitution, sovereignty rested in the hands of the people, to be represented by both the People's Representative Council (DPR) and the People's Consultative Assembly (MPR).* In addition, the constitution stipulated the principles of majority rule, separation of powers, and freedom of religion. These principles were also recognized in the state ideology, Pancasila, based on five principles, including democratic representation; it did not link the state to a specific religion.† The

---

* As the highest body, the MPR is composed of DPR members, representatives of the regions, professional groups, and the military. The primary tasks of this body are (1) to elect the president and vice president, (2) to evaluate the president, (3) to amend the constitution, and (4) to formulate the Broad Guidelines of State Policy.

† Pancasila, introduced by Soekarno on June 1, 1945, comprises five basic principles: (1) belief in one God, (2) just and civilized humanity, (3) unity of Indonesia, (4) democracy guided by the inner wisdom in unanimity arising out of deliberation among representatives, and (5) social justice for all the people of Indonesia.

preference for democracy was strengthened by a plan to hold general elections in January 1946, for which the government issued Declaration X in 1945 to encourage the public to form political parties.[2]

Unfortunately, the plan was never carried out. Even normal governmental activities had to be put on hold as Indonesia was forced from 1945 to 1949 to defend its independence against a threatened return of Dutch colonialism. That struggle ended in December 1949 when the Netherlands, after a series of negotiations, agreed to recognize Indonesia's sovereignty. The new state, working under a parliamentary system of government, was then able to formulate basic laws in line with democratic principles. The country's democratic bias was especially evident in the liberal character of Parliament. Its members enjoyed almost unhindered freedom in their endeavors to function as representatives of the people.

This phase of the democratic journey culminated with the general elections of 1955.* At least 34 political parties and individual candidates contested the parliamentary (DPR) and Constituent Assembly seats.† Of that number, only 28 parties and individual candidates gained one or more seats in Parliament. The Indonesian Nationalist Party, Masyumi, Nahdlatul Ulama, and the Indonesian Communist Party (PKI) emerged as the 4 largest parties, with 22%, 21%, 18%, and 16% of the vote, respectively, with the others ranging from 0.1% to 2.9% of the vote.[3]

Although the elections were free and fair, neither the government nor the Constituent Assembly performed well. From December 1949 (well before the 1955 elections) to March 1957, there were at least eight cabinet or government changes as governments had to deal with issues of national unity rather than focus on the country's serious social, economic, and political problems. The Constituent Assembly also failed to write the constitution or decide whether Pancasila, Islam, or socioeconomy should be adopted as the state ideology.

To solve the gridlock, President Soekarno in 1959 issued decrees returning to Pancasila and the 1945 constitution and dissolving the Constituent Assembly. Because the 1945 constitution had established strong executive powers, Soekarno was able to rule with a strong hand. Supported by General Nasution, who often showed his own (and the military's) dislike of civilian politicians, Soekarno and the military emerged as the dominant players in Indonesian politics from 1959 to 1966. To balance the military's role in politics, Soekarno invited the PKI to join him in governing.

---

* The general elections were held on September 29 and December 15, 1955. The first was to elect members of Parliament (DPR), and the second was to elect members of the Constituent Assembly. See Herbert Feith, *The Indonesian Elections of 1955* (Ithaca, N.Y.: Modern Indonesian Project, Southeast Asia Program, Cornell University, 1951).

† The function of the Constituent Assembly was to formulate the state ideology and write the constitution.

Breakdown of Democracy

Soekarno's 1959 decrees marked the breakdown of Indonesia's first experiment with democracy. At the height of his power, between 1957 and 1966, Soekarno curbed freedom and public liberty, and imprisoned his political opponents without due process of law.

Soekarno's rule, known as Guided Democracy, ended with a coup following the assassination of six senior Army generals, which took place on September 30, 1965. The coup, known as the 30 September Movement, was led by Lieutenant-Colonel Untung Samsuri, a battalion commander of the elite Cakrabirawa Regiment that guarded Soekarno.[4] Together with anticommunist social and political forces, including the Muslims, the Army as the avant garde launched a violent purge that resulted in a high number of casualties on the part of PKI members and its alleged sympathizers.*

Under the leadership of Major General Soeharto, the former commander of the Army Strategic Reserve Command who put down the coup and took control of the September event, the formation of the New Order government was meant to address the failures of the Old Order regime, as the period from 1950 to 1965 was called. The new regime rejected both the Liberal Democracy (1950-57) and Guided Democracy (1957-66) periods as ineffective in meeting public demands for stability and economic growth.

The New Order government aimed to create stability rather than deepen democracy. From 1966 to 1998, Soeharto's New Order government discouraged political competition and installed a "repressive developmentalist regime."[5] Through shrewd political engineering, the government curbed political liberties, limited the number of political parties, and drafted an electoral law that limited competition and controlled election results. The DPR became a rubber stamp. Many in Indonesian society and the international community came to believe that Soeharto's government was just as authoritarian as the Soekarno regime it had replaced in 1966.[6]

To obscure its authoritarian nature, the New Order government regularly conducted parliamentary elections in 1971, 1977, 1982, 1987, 1992, and 1997. The government party, Golkar, always won those elections. Most voters were too intimidated by repression to cast ballots for other parties, allowing Golkar to claim 60%–70% of the vote.

Contrary to its illiberal political approach (and in contrast to the statist ideology of the Soekarno period), the New Order government embraced a liberal

---

* The number of deaths varies from one account to the other, ranging between 80,000 and 3 million. The moderate number is perceived to be around 500,000. See Robert Cribb, ed., *The Indonesian Killings 1965-1966: Studies from Java and Bali* (Clayton, Vict.: Monash University, Centre for Southeast Asian Studies, 1990); Douglas Kammen and Katherine McGregor, *The Contours of Mass Violence in Indonesia, 1965-1968* (Singapore: National University of Singapore Press, 2012).

economic policy. Its turn toward a market economy enabled the government to invite foreign investment and gain the support of international financial institutions. For many years, Indonesia became a "favorite child" of the World Bank.[7]

Transition to Democracy

The MPR reelected Soeharto to his seventh five-year term in March 1998. His supporters claimed that the country still needed his leadership, but Soeharto was sitting on a hot seat. The Asian monetary crisis had hit Indonesia hard, and the devaluation of the rupiah in August 1997 was the main reason for the collapse of the country's economy, which contracted by 18%.[8] Next came riots and bloodshed that resulted in enormous destruction in the capital, Jakarta, and such other cities as Medan, Solo, Jogjakarta, Surabaya, Padang, and Banyuwangi.* The financial crisis in turn set off other crises that revealed Indonesia's social and political as well as economic problems. Soeharto's final term lasted only three months, from March to May 1998.

Soeharto had worked hard to address the crisis. On May 14, 1998, just a week before he abdicated, Soeharto attended the G15 summit in Cairo to seek political and economic support from the United States and other international powers to help him solve the crises. He crafted a plan to reshuffle the cabinet and bring in several reform-minded leaders and nongovernmental organization activists. But these efforts to control the situation did not attract broad support. Even loyal ministers with whom he had shared his power for so many years refused to join his projected new cabinet. Under these circumstances, Soeharto had no choice but to leave the office he had occupied for more than three decades.

After Soeharto resigned on May 21, his vice president, B. J. Habibie, was sworn in as the third president of Indonesia. But Habibie's accession was received with ambivalence. His supporters, the majority of whom were modernist Muslims associated with the Indonesian Muslim Intellectual Association, maintained that Habibie's appointment was constitutional. His opponents saw him as a close confidante of Soeharto, however, and therefore as part of the problem. For this reason, they called for Habibie's resignation.

Lacking broad support, Habibie realized that he needed to make strategic decisions to secure the survival of his presidency.[9] One key choice was to establish civilian control over the military, which had served as the praetorian guard of the state for decades. This was particularly crucial, as Soeharto apparently had a backup scenario should Habibie prove unable to restore national order. General Wiranto, as defense minister and commander of the

---

* See relevant essays in Geoff Forrester and R. J. May, eds., *The Fall of Soeharto* (Singapore: Select Books, 1999).

armed forces, held Soeharto's undisclosed instruction to rescue the nation "by all means necessary" if there were a political emergency. Wiranto himself informed Habibie of the existence of this instruction, and Habibie let the general hold onto it as an option if the situation turned worse, thus showing trust in Wiranto's integrity and winning his loyalty.[10]

Habibie's confidence in General Wiranto grew stronger when the defense minister reported a suspicious movement of troops heading to Jakarta that were led by General Prabowo Subijanto, head of the Army Strategic Reserve Command and Soeharto's son-in-law.[11] In response to this news, President Habibie instructed Wiranto to remove Prabowo from his position, effectively preventing a military coup.* By separating Prabowo from his troops, Habibie secured his presidency against its most likely military challenge. Further changes in the military hierarchy ensured adequate support.

Some of Habibie's opponents accused him of being incapable of managing the government and of being corrupt for preserving the interests of Soeharto's cronies.[12] Others declared Habibie's presidency illegal, arguing that the transition of power required a special session of the MPR.[13] These criticisms increased after Habibie announced his new cabinet. One of his most vocal critics was the National Front (Barisan Nasional or Barnas), composed of some of Soeharto's former cabinet ministers; retired military officers such as Ali Sadikin and Kemal Idris; and civilian figures including Megawati Soekarnoputri (Soekarno's daughter, who would years later become president), Rizal Ramli, and Marsilam Simanjuntak. Another influential group was Nahdlatul Ulama, Indonesia's largest Islamic socio-religious organization, led by Abdurrahman Wahid (also known as Gus Dur), which took a position in moderate opposition to the government.[14]

Habibie's opponents were not united, however. When the MPR special session was held in November 1998, student protests demanded that Habibie resign. But neither Megawati nor Abdurrahman Wahid backed this action.[15] Habibie developed different ways of dealing with each group, which divided them and made the opposition more manageable.

Habibie's Presidency

With fragmented support for his presidency and weak legitimacy, Habibie struggled to retain his post. Meanwhile, investors were still hesitant to return and the rupiah remained weak, trading at 14,000 and 17,000 to the US dollar. About 79 million people (39% of the population) lived below the poverty line in July 1998, and this number was projected to grow to 96 million by the end

---

* On May 22, a rumor circulated that the military would take over Parliament. See Geoffrey Forrester, "A Jakarta Diary, May 1998," in *The Fall of Soeharto*, ed. Geoffrey Forrester and R. J. Mays (London: C. Hurst, 1998), 55, 58–64.

of the year.* In June, the International Monetary Fund projected that the Indonesian economy would contract another 10% during the year. On the street, mass protests still happened occasionally, and the country was by no means politically stable. Separatist movements in East Timor, Aceh, and Papua were still waiting for resolution, complicated by communal conflicts in Maluku and Poso. The early period of transition was characterized by what Richard Robison called "a chaotic market and disorganized democracy."[16]

Contrary to what Soekarno and Soeharto had done in 1959 and 1966, Habibie chose to start by guaranteeing liberties instead of imposing order. He announced his Reformed Development Cabinet on May 22, charging it with democratically reforming the country's economy, politics, and legal system. During the 18 months of Habibie's administration, Indonesia adopted least 68 new laws, 3 government regulations that replaced laws, 109 government regulations, 248 presidential decrees, and 31 presidential instructions.[17]

Political Reform

President Habibie did not have broad support during his presidency but nevertheless proceeded resolutely to relax the political atmosphere. He released 15 political prisoners on May 25, including Sri Bintang Pamungkas and Mukhtar Pakpahan, two of Soeharto's most vocal critics. By the end of his term, Habibie had freed about 150 political prisoners, including known Communists.[18] He declared freedom of the press, revising all regulations that were considered impediments to the promotion of freedom of speech and expression.

Another important political breakthrough in Habibie's early days in office was to transform Golkar into a normal political party. It would no longer be able to mobilize support from either the bureaucracy or the military, as it had in the Soeharto era, and would have to compete with other political parties to maintain its influence in Parliament. The internal reform of Golkar severed the institutional linkage between the party and the military. (The Golkar Congress formally announced and accepted this change in July 1998.)

In June, Habibie ended restrictions that hindered the establishment of political parties in order to assure that the next election would return Indonesia to a liberal multiparty system; within 6 months there were 181 registered political parties. To ensure that elections were held freely and fairly, Habibie formed an Independent Election Commission and an oversight committee (Bawaslu).

---

* The total population in 1998 was about 204 million. See Badan Pusat Statistik, *Tabel Laju Pertumbuhan Penduduk* [Table of population growth] (Jakarta: Badan Pusat Statistik, 2012), http://bps.go.id/tab_sub/view.php?tabel=1&daftar=1&id_subyek=12&notab=2; and Badan Pusat Statistik, *Penduduk Indonesia* [Table of Indonesia's population] (Jakar-ta: Badan Pusat Statistik, 2012), http://bps.go.id/tab_sub/view.php?kat=1&tabel=1&daftar=1&id_subyek=12&notab=1.

As part of this political reform agenda, in the face of popular demands and in negotiation with parliamentary leaders, Habibie moved the date of the general election up from 2003 to 1999. Without Habibie's personal commitment to reform, there would have been no guarantee that the first post-Soeharto elections could be held so soon, less than 18 months after Habibie took power.

Habibie's efforts to curb the military's primary role in politics were fundamental to his political reform agenda. He gradually removed military personnel from the political arena, sending them back to the barracks to be professional soldiers. On September 1, he announced—and General Wiranto reiterated—that "the social and political role of the armed forces will systematically and automatically decline, along with the growth of our civil society."[19] By April 1, 1999, the national police was separated from the armed forces in order to clearly divide the sectors of public order and defense. Further steps necessary to assure civilian control of the military occurred gradually during subsequent years.

In order to provide a strong basis for democracy, President Habibie supported a proposal introduced during the November special session of the MPR to start the process of amending the 1945 constitution. The process began after the 1999 general election; one of the important decisions was limiting the president to two five-year terms.

Political relaxation also provided a greater opportunity to raise women's awareness and promote their activism in politics. Habibie met with a group of female activists and intellectuals to discuss female victims of the May riots.* He agreed to ask for an apology to female victims on behalf of the government and pledged to establish an independent body, the National Commission on Violence against Women, focusing on advocacy and the protection of women.[†]

Decentralization (Regional Autonomy)

The Indonesian state under the New Order had been highly centralized, and the president treated the heads of regional governments as administrative subordinates, both bureaucratically and politically. Although a number of provinces—including Jakarta, Jogjakarta, and Aceh—formally enjoyed special status, regions did not exercise real autonomy in managing their affairs.

---

* There were several reports on rape against Chinese women in Jakarta and several other cities during the May riots. For further accounts, see "Peta Amuk di Kota Hantu," *Tempo*, May 19–25, 2003. See also *The May 1998 Tragedy in the Course of the Nation's Journey: In Denial* (Jakarta: Komnas Perempuan, 2003).

† This agency is now known as Komisi Nasional Perempuan (National Commission for Women's Rights). In 1999, Habibie also ratified the Optional Protocol of the UN Convention on the Elimination of All Forms of Discrimination against Women (CEDAW). See *Independent Report of Non-government Organizations Concerning the Implementation of the Convention on the Elimination of All Forms of Discrimination against Women (CEDAW) in Indonesia* (Jakarta: CEDAW Working Group Initiative, 2007).

Habibie undertook a commitment to decentralization. Under the Regional Autonomy Law (No. 22/1999), regions were authorized to administer their own affairs, with the exception of foreign affairs, defense, and security; monetary and legal affairs; and religion, which remained in the hands of the central government.[20] For each of the provinces in which separatist movements were active—including Aceh, Papua, and East Timor—the government adopted different policies. For Aceh, the plan was to grant special autonomy status, although this did not resolve Aceh's issues with Jakarta, and in fact made the secessionist organization, the Free Aceh Movement (GAM), more popular under the leadership of Hassan Tiro.*

As in Aceh, special status for East Timor did not appear to satisfy a large portion of the Timorese. Habibie opted for a referendum giving the Timorese the right to decide their own future, which resulted in the separation of East Timor from Indonesia. The problem of Papua has still not been entirely resolved. The province was divided into Papua and West Papua, both of which have been granted a great deal of formal autonomy, but some Papuans still support separation.

Promoting the Independence of the Central Bank

The Asian crisis focused attention on the need to improve the management of Indonesia's monetary policy. Based on his experience of living in Germany for 20 years, President Habibie believed that an independent Central Bank was crucial to designing a reliable monetary policy, without intervention from political interests. Both Soekarno and Soeharto, who used the bank to finance the government's programs, violated this principle.[21] Habibie consulted with his economic advisors and invited former executives from the Deutsche Bundesbank such as Dr. Josef Ackermann, Dr. Helmut Schlesinger, and Dr. Wolfgang Kartte to help write new legislation allowing the Central Bank to operate independently.[22]

Promoting Democracy

As mandated by the MPR special session in November 1998, parliamentary elections were held in April 1999. Habibie's role in this was crucial, as he en-

---

* The separatist idea in Aceh was finally resolved through a different arrangement during the Susilo Bambang Yudhoyono-Jusuf Kalla government. Mediated by Marti Ahtisaari, former president of Finland, a peaceful agreement between the government and GAM was reached under the initiative and direction of Vice President Jusuf Kalla in August 2005. With this agreement, Aceh remains part of the unitary state of Indonesia, yet the province was granted autonomy to administer its affairs on the basis of Islamic law. See Fachry Ali, Suharso Monoarfa, and Bahtiar Effendy, *Kalla & Perdamaian Aceh* (Jakarta: *Lspeu* Indonesia, 2008).

acted a series of regulations to ensure that the election would be competitive, free, and fair. These included eliminating the rights of members of the military to vote and removing the obligation of civil servants to vote for Golkar. He also empowered the election oversight committee with the authority to monitor and mediate disputes as well as take legal action against any violation of the electoral rules. This was a major breakthrough, as a similar institution in Soeharto's era was simply part of the Golkar's winning team.

The 1999 election was relatively competitive, democratic, and peaceful; 48 political parties competed. The PDI-P (Indonesian Democratic Party of Struggle) under Megawati's leadership won the most seats in Parliament, with 153. Golkar came in second with 120, followed by 4 Islamic or Muslim-based parties, including the United Development Party with 58 seats, the Nation Awakening Party with 51 seats, the National Mandate Party with 34 seats, and the Crescent Star Party with 13 seats.[23]

Under the 1945 constitution, this election was for members of Parliament (DPR). The president and vice president are elected by the MPR, which is the highest body with the right to evaluate—and impeach—the president, amend the constitution, and formulate the broad guidelines of state policy. The MPR was composed of DPR members, a group of professionals appointed by the president, and regional representatives appointed by the regional government. During the New Order period, "these appointments were all made in processes controlled by Suharto and therefore produced an Assembly prepared to do the president's bidding."[24] This was not the case when Habibie was in power; not all of Habibie's efforts yielded positive rewards for his presidency.

His accountability speech was rejected in the MPR session held in October 1999 by a margin of fewer than 50 votes—the equivalent to losing a parliamentary vote of confidence. There is no definitive explanation of why his speech was rejected. Assembly politics and competing ambitions were perhaps the most important factors; there was also popular discontent with what was perceived to be Habibie's lack of commitment to bringing Soeharto to trial and with his responsibility for the East Timor referendum results. In addition, some felt that Habibie was unresponsive to cases of human rights violations that involved the military.[25]

In any event, it was clear to Habibie that he did not have enough political support in the newly elected Parliament. For this reason he decided not to contest the presidential race in October 1999. A loose coalition of Islamic parties, plus Golkar, elected Abdurrahman Wahid as Indonesia's fourth president. Megawati, leader of the winning party (PDI-P), became the vice president.

Habibie's Democratic Legacy

Habibie lost the immediate political battle during his short period as president, as his contributions were not fully appreciated at the time. But given the problems he inherited and the resources at his disposal, Habibie accomplished a great deal, helping to create the key institutions and practices needed for democracy to work in Indonesia. He established public liberty, freedom of the press, and free speech, and facilitated the emergence of political parties and the holding of the first truly democratic elections in 44 years. More importantly, Habibie was able to keep Indonesia's nation-state relatively intact in the face of a threatened breakup, reduce the political influence of the armed forces, and turn Golkar—the party that had served as the institutional link between the Army and the state—into a normal party in a competitive multiparty system.

His successors benefited immensely from the solid ground Habibie had prepared. There was still a lot to be done when Habibie left office. Efforts to amend the 1945 constitution had just begun, direct presidential and vice presidential elections had not been established, and women were still politically left behind. Yet Habibie helped make Indonesia's transition to democracy relatively peaceful, creating lasting reforms that have proven effective and legitimate. These provided a valuable legacy for Presidents Abdurrahman Wahid, Megawati, and Susilo Bambang Yudhoyono to build on as they continued to develop Indonesian democracy into an effective system of governance.

Indonesia's democracy has now been consolidated. Much has been achieved and improved by Habibie's successors. Party politics remain the core of the country's democracy. But unlike the early years of transition, fewer political parties now participate in the elections and are represented in Parliament. The 1945 constitution has been amended four times, incorporating more rigorously the principles of transparency, accountability, and checks and balances between the executive, legislative, and judicial branches of government. Many have registered complaints about its lack of coherence, however, and are proposing another round of amendments. Since 2004, public officeholders—including the president, governor, district chief, and mayor—have been contested directly. The police and military forces are no longer represented in Parliament, and their members are still not allowed to vote.

Indonesia's democracy seems to be an expensive enterprise. To contest for almost all public offices requires a large amount of funding, which is one alleged or perceived reason why corruption is still rampant despite the fact that the Corruption Eradication Commission has worked vigorously. Significant numbers of public officeholders—including ministers, governors, district chiefs, mayors, members of Parliament, as well as public servants—have been tried and found guilty of embezzling state funds.

Much still needs to be done to make Indonesia's democracy deliver fully on its promises—order, stability, and security on the one hand, and public decency and prosperity on the other. Great progress has been made, nonetheless, especially in the years of B. J. Habibie's presidency and since.

Biosketch of B. J. Habibie, President of Indonesia 1998–99

PHOTO: ADEK BERRY / SCANPIX

As a young man, **B. J. Habibie** had a close personal relationship with Soeharto, who served as the country's authoritarian president for 32 years. Habibie went to Germany in the early 1950s and spent 20 years there as an aeronautical engineer and business executive. Soeharto brought him back in 1974 to run the state-owned aerospace company and advise the government on advancing technology. From 1978 to 1998, Habibie served as minister of state for research and technology. Soeharto gradually gave Habibie broader and more sensitive responsibilities and had him elected vice president in 1998. Habibie was a member of the governing Golkar Party and chairman of the Muslim Intellectual Association. He understood the workings of power in Soeharto's Indonesia, but he had no appreciable power base of his own beyond some in the bureaucracy associated with the Muslim Intellectual Association and was generally unpopular with the military and the opposition.

When the Asian financial crisis of 1997–98 battered Indonesia's previously thriving economy, opposition to Soeharto mounted rapidly, with massive street demonstrations that forced his resignation in May 1998. Habibie reached the presidency through constitutional succession, endorsed by Parliament, which averted a dangerous power struggle among senior military leaders. He immediately exerted personal control over the armed forces, freed most political prisoners, recognized trade unions, and removed censorship and press restrictions. Habibie authorized the formation of new political parties, brought forward the date for new national elections by three years, and removed Soeharto family supporters and several military officers from Parliament. He undertook a program of political and administrative decentralization, appointed a civilian minister of defense for the first time in 50 years, and agreed to a referendum that led to Timor-Leste's independence. Habibie acted mainly on his own convictions, bolstered by religious faith and advice from a team of academics and civil servants. He believed that Indonesia required fundamental reform and recognized that contending power centers would accept these reforms in exchange for the chance to compete in early elections. Habibie ended his presidency in 1999 after his accountability report was rejected by a close vote in the People's Consultative Assembly. The changes he introduced have generally remained in place during Indonesia's subsequent extended construction of democratic governance.

Interview with President B. J. Habibie

Ending of the Authoritarian Regime

After 32 years in power, President Soeharto's government came to an end in 1998. What were the critical factors that ended his regime? How did you understand your own challenges as vice president at that time?

The Soeharto government deteriorated because the president was increasingly acting in the interest of individuals and families who were close to him, and he lost touch with the interests of the majority of the people.

After the deregulation of the banking system in late 1988, banks established by companies were making bad short-term, nonperforming loans, which created economic uncertainty. In July 1997, as the devaluation of the Thai baht started, demand increased for US dollars in Indonesia to pay the interest and principal installments on Indonesia's loans in the international capital markets, and the value of the Indonesian rupiah relative to the US dollar started to fall. As uncertainty increased, the free fall of the rupiah accelerated. Inflation and interest rates rose, and basic necessities became scarce. High school and university students and youth organizations started to join the mass demonstrations in the streets and in front of the People's Consultative Assembly. The financial situation deepened the uncertainty and generated increased economic difficulties that pushed social, political, and military forces in Indonesia to force Soeharto's resignation.

I was never interested in becoming president of Indonesia. I was not even interested in becoming a minister. I was only interested in bringing technology to Indonesia to make airplanes. I made a deal with Soeharto. In 1974,

I agreed that I would come home from Germany to build an Indonesian airplane, through a company that was owned by the government and run like a private enterprise. I did, and I delivered on schedule.

When President Soeharto asked me to join his ticket as the candidate for vice president in the early months of 1998, I told him I was not available because my wife was very sick. But he asked me to run for Golkar to win the election, so I agreed. I was elected vice president by the members of the People's Consultative Assembly, which had five factions: the Indonesian Democratic Party of Megawati; the Islamists (the United Development Party); Golkar, my party; the people representing the provinces, the Regional Representative group (Utusan Daerah); and the military.

Soeharto imposed a regulation that allowed each faction to propose one candidate for vice president, so there was the potential for five candidates. First they elected the president and afterward they elected the vice president. The candidates for vice president are submitted one at a time to the elected president; the vice president must be accepted by the newly elected president. To avoid a long discussion, before proposing a candidate for vice president, the different groups would speak with the president and ask who he thinks he could work with. I was so sure that the president would take seriously my request not to be a member of the cabinet that I didn't consider the possibility of being the vice president. I had already told the president that I did not want to be a member of the cabinet. He said to leave it to God. So while the other potential candidates were lobbying, I was not. I was only interested in my engineering work. But things happened differently. People may plan, but God decides.

Two weeks before the election, the chief of the armed forces, a four-star general, Feisal Tanjung, went to the president. Under the constitution, he had the responsibility to ensure the safety of the president and the new vice president. To prepare and perform this duty, he wanted to know who would be vice president and presented the list of names to Soeharto.

After a discussion with Soeharto, Tanjung came to the conclusion that I would be vice president. This surprised him, since I had already stated that I was not interested in becoming a member of the cabinet. But Soeharto insisted, and pointed to my record of achievement.

Tanjung called my security staff. At that time, I was already the coordinator and the elected chairman of the coalition of three factions—the armed forces, Golkar, and the representatives of the provinces. I was doing that already in 1993.

Setting Policy Priorities

Opposition to Soeharto developed to the point where he didn't have a chance of staying in power. You then succeeded to the presidency without the support of the Soeharto regime, without the support of the opposition, with distrust from the armed forces, and without an independent power base. You had a reputation as a forward looking thinker—somebody who understood technology and industry and who had a close relationship with the Indonesian Association of Muslim Intellectuals—but not as a political leader with broad support. But you were able to initiate many reforms. How was that possible? What can we learn from your experience that may be relevant elsewhere?

That's correct. I never had a political network like Soeharto. Soeharto controlled and built a political network for 32 years. I never commanded the military as Soeharto did. All chiefs of staff in the armed forces and the police were his former aides-de-camp because he was in power for so long, from 1966 to 1998. So he controlled that network and I was aware that I had no similar source of support. The only thing I had is my intelligence and the ambition not to become president or vice president. My ambition was already fulfilled after I had done my engineering work.

But I was suddenly thrust into this leadership role. The first time I realized vividly how powerful the presidency is was when I started to receive a lot of intelligence reports: from the Army, Navy, Air Force, police, the national intelligence agency, the Ministry of Foreign Affairs, the Ministry of Interior, and from the Golkar Party. I read these very detailed reports, which did not match each other. How could I find out which one was correct?

I looked at the strength of the people demonstrating, "people's power." I decided to give them the freedom to express themselves, to demonstrate, and to allow a free press. When I made these decisions, the coordinating minister for politics and security and former chief of the armed forces, General Feisal Tanjung, protested. He said that I would be killed. I said I did not care, because that was the only way that I could balance all of those confusing inputs, with the help of the people themselves. That is why within 24 hours of becoming president I decided to allow a free press.

Suddenly a lot of conflicting information and advice poured in. If I had followed some of this advice, there would have been a violent revolution. The people who would have been most adversely affected by such a revolution were the innocent people who just want a normal life, and I could not allow that to happen.

Because of these concerns, **I decided to lift the laws restricting the freedom of the press. By allowing freedom of expression, I could receive accurate information on the attitude of the people toward my administration.** I did this because I wanted to give power back to the owners of state power: the people of Indonesia. Not to a family or to a man, not to me or my children, but to the people.

I also decided to release all political prisoners, and to reserve prison for criminals, not for those who were simply opposed to the president in power. General Wiranto and the attorney general said that doing this would be dangerous and that there would be demonstrations and perhaps plans to kill me. But I believed that I would only die if God wanted it.

On Thursday May 21, 1998, at 10:00, Soeharto resigned. I had to take over. I began forming my cabinet on Thursday evening. I didn't sleep at all. On Friday morning, I announced my new cabinet. Before doing so, I called the armed forces and told them that I was the president, and they had to follow my orders.

Responding to Economic Crisis

What was your strategy for gaining legitimacy and public support, and for controlling the armed forces and other elements that might have sought a return to authoritarian rule?

I gave the highest priority to solving economic and political problems through quick decisions and by improving transparency through good governance. My priorities were to give the people freedom and the values of human rights, human responsibilities, and the principles of a social market economy by introducing and accelerating evolution and reform instead of revolution.

The main problem we faced was unpredictability in almost all areas of the economy and the financial sectors, including high inflation, the free fall of the value of the Indonesian currency, increasing unemployment, the outflow of foreign direct investment, and the limited availability of basic necessities.

We analyzed suggestions and proposals coming from national and international institutions like the International Labour Organization (ILO), World Bank, other banking organizations, antitrust and monopoly law, and institutions for democratic development, especially those from American and German institutions. We tried to be consistently pragmatic. We believed that appropriate laws must be based on the constitution and approved by the Parliament and the People's Consultative Assembly. One advantage I had was that before the election in May 1999 I had the support of more than 80% of the seats of the still-functioning Parliament.

Setting Policy Priorities

I took several important actions to address immediate challenges. I declared freedom of the press, freedom of expression, and the freedom to demonstrate. The first thing the people did was to come out and demonstrate against me, and that was fine. Because of my close association with Soeharto, some opposed my presidency and questioned my legitimacy. There was a lot of questioning in the country about what would happen now that Soeharto was gone, and there were calls for my resignation. But I wanted to avoid engaging in a public argument.[26] To strengthen my position, I knew my actions had to adhere to the constitution and laws of Indonesia, and that I had to act quickly.[27]

With regard to security, I instructed the commander in chief of the armed forces to be responsible for the safety and security of the former president and his family. I ceased to receive any commander or chief of staff without a request by the chief of armed forces. I read all incoming intelligence reports (from the Ministry of Defense, Ministry of Foreign Affairs, Ministry of Interior Affairs, and the State Intelligence Coordinating Agency) and compared them carefully with information from the free press.

I also made the main basic human necessities available at an affordable market price through subsidies and controls.

I also took many mid- and long-term actions to promote good governance. I fought against corruption and in favor of the rule of law. The law has to apply to everyone equally, including the president. I passed anticorruption, antimonopoly, and antitrust legislation and established an anticorruption institution, the Commission to Eradicate the Crime of Corruption. [The current, more powerful Anti-Corruption Commission was established in 2002.]

I also increased the independence of the Bank of Indonesia so that it was no longer controlled by the president. Other economic issues I addressed included debt restructuring, small- and medium-sized enterprises, agriculture, natural resources, business competition and consumer protection, and the restructuring of state-owned enterprises.[28] I took the initiative to begin the ratification of all ILO principles. I could do that because I controlled the Parliament. [Golkar was the largest party in Parliament at the time.]

Reform of the Electoral System

Then there is the issue of free elections. I did not interfere in the election. I opened the door for foreign NGOs (nongovernmental organizations), and I requested former President Carter to help and observe the elections. The Europeans, the Americans, and the Japanese came. My predecessor had always put his people on the Election Commission. My instruction to the minister of home affairs was that the commission should contain no government officials or political party members, but rather personalities from society who are credible. They protested that I would lose the election, but I told them that I didn't care. The minister of intelligence said that this was a sign that I would lose my party. Again, I said I don't care; I want the winner to be the people, represented by whomever they choose. I created the system. Let the system do it.

Regional Autonomy

I wanted the provinces to obtain the autonomy to govern themselves. Previously, local authorities at both the provincial and district levels were controlled from the center. Those who stood to lose capital, money, and power as a result of decentralization were against it. Some provinces had great natural wealth and contributed to the national GDP (gross domestic product) but still had high percentages of people living in poverty. Other provinces with fewer natural resources had fewer people in poverty due to a focus on developing human resources and economic infrastructure development. By giving greater autonomy, the provinces would be able to improve the equitable distribution of investments in education, opportunities, and wealth. In 1999, laws were passed that devolved a wide range of powers to the local level along with a financing structure. Direct elections were introduced for members of the local Parliament. After the implementation of the decentralization laws, many civil servants were transferred from central to local authority employment.

I advocated for Aceh to be given a special form of autonomy, one that recognized and accepted its values as rooted in their culture, religion, and tradition. Legislation granting autonomy to Aceh was passed in 2001 and was intended to intensify and accelerate the process of the equitable distribution of opportunities, income, and access to justice.

Reform of the Civil Service

I stressed that the bureaucracy must be free from corruption, collusion, and nepotism (the commonly used phrase in Indonesia, KKN, short for *korupsi, kolusi, nepotisme*, refers to this). **The bureaucracy and civil service must be objective, professional, transparent, and proactive in increasing the productivity of the people through improving professionalism, its cultural resilience, and implementing the values of human rights and human responsibilities within the five basic principles of Pancasila** [the philosophical principles of the Indonesian state]. I also banned civil servants from being members of political parties so that they would be impartial in their duties. [Golkar strongly opposed this decree, as civil servants under President Soeharto were obliged to vote for Golkar.]

Reforming the Security Forces

I was aware that the military forces were politicized and not united, and that there were some ambitious groups competing for national leadership among them. I made the commander in chief of the armed and police forces responsible for security in the country and for the security of the former president.

Only the commander in chief, if necessary, would be received by me as president at any time, on any day.

In the New Order system, the military and police had their own faction in Parliament as well as in the People's Consultative Assembly. The military leaders could pursue their vision through their own faction, other political parties, and the free press.

Did you believe that there was a risk of a military coup?

Of course! When I went to the Istana Merdeka [the official residence of the president] on the Friday morning after Soeharto's resignation, I had my new cabinet ready, which I wanted to announce to the public. General Wiranto was waiting for me, and he urgently wanted to speak to me in private. He told me that the commander of the Army Strategic Reserve Command, Lt. General Prabowo, and his troops were entering Jakarta. Members of the Air Force, from the provinces, were flying in the direction of Jakarta. Wiranto told me that my family and I were in danger, that Prabowo's troops had surrounded my residence in Kuningan. So he gathered my family at Istana Merdeka. My wife and sons were also there, where I was supposed to receive Prabowo, so it was very tense. General Wiranto asked for orders, so I knew that Lt. General Prabowo was acting without the approval of General Wiranto. I instructed him to replace Commander Prabowo before sunset, and said that the new commander must send all the troops back. He resisted, but I insisted. He asked me who should take up the position, but I put the decision in his hands.

Lt. General Prabowo is Soeharto's son-in-law, and all the troops surrounding me were also Soeharto's people. But I had an ally, a young man who was also a lieutenant general. He is a Christian, Sintong Panjaitan. Sintong had problems with Soeharto due to the conflict in East Timor. His family came to see me many years ago and asked for help, so I made him my assistant. I was the founder of the Indonesian Association of Muslim Intellectuals, but my family is not known as hard-liners but rather as dedicated Muslims, and I took the initiative to have somebody close to me who is not Muslim. At that time I didn't know it, but Sintong stayed with me all the time. He slept here. He never left me alone. He watched over the whole family.

Some tried to postpone my decision—as the son-in-law of Soeharto, Prabowo was well connected and influential—but I said no. Prabowo came to see me. Sintong disarmed him before he entered my office. General Prabowo pleaded to retain his position, but I remained firm in my decision.

I spoke with the attorney general on Friday, less than 24 hours after I had assumed the presidency, and told him to release all political prisoners immediately. I had to face many issues at once; it was all very confusing. I met with the demonstrators, not to become popular so as to be electable. No, I was not interested in becoming the president. I was only interested in avoiding a revolution that could kill a lot of innocent people. I was interested in only one thing: to give the power back to the people.

While this was happening, I was concerned for the safety of my family. I was surrounded by Prabowo's troops, and I was very aware of what might happen.

So that was the situation. You ask me whether I knew there was a coup attempt; of course I knew. But I had one advantage. I fired the former president's son-in-law—who had a network— within 24 hours. **I acted decisively when I knew that I needed to. So that step helped a lot. I prepared to make the defense minister a civilian, not a general or retired general, and I never put the police and armed forces together under one commander in chief or minister.**

Responding to Political Crisis

Events moved very rapidly. Soeharto stepped down on Thursday. On Friday I announced the new cabinet and my decision to set all political prisoners free. I faced down Prabowo on Friday. On Saturday I swore in the new cabinet members.

Saturday night at eight o'clock I received seven people here: Amien Rais, Emil Salim, Buyung Nasution, and other men who were also civil society leaders of the opposition. They wanted me to call for parliamentary elections in three months, not later than August. I told them no, but that I planned to call for an election after one year, not to wait for the scheduled date in four years, in 2003. They insisted that waiting a year would be a mistake. However, I was at an advantage because they used to be afraid of the president and I inherited that. I had been president for just three days. If I were thinking about myself and my party, then I would have accepted their proposal. **The voters had already known me for 30 years, but the new parties would not have had time to establish themselves. The people would have been the losers. Had I acted on the advice to call elections within three months, this would have had a politically and economically destabilizing effect, and adversely impacted the transition.**

After the cabinet was sworn in, I instructed the interior minister to announce that all people are free to form political parties; I introduced the multiparty system. He said that it was against the constitution, but I told him that we will change the constitution, and the People's Consultative Assembly issued a decree to allow parties. I limited the president to two terms. These are signals to the people that I was not just talking; I was implementing good governance and transparency.

I held a cabinet meeting every day. I would listen, then make a fast decision. We approved an average of 1.3 new laws and regulations every day.

Role of the Legislature

Was the Parliament supportive of your initiatives?

Yes, I used my power in Parliament to get many things done, but I did not misuse it. I would give the President's Accountability Address in the next meeting of the assembly.

But the assembly rejected your accountability speech. Why did they do so?

Before I read my accountability address, some members of the assembly indicated that they would not accept it. I told the people, however, that I would make my accountability address according to the rules, and if the assembly accepted it, then I was available to be reelected. If not, then I was not available. I made many changes to solve a lot of problems; I believed I had done my best. Beforehand I met with a number of influential people in the assembly, the armed forces, and various professions who said that even if my accountability speech were rejected, I could still be nominated to run for the presidency. But because my opponents knew that I would not be available if my accountability address was not accepted, they said they would not accept it. The new parties said that without even reading it; 48% accepted my accountability speech, and 52% rejected it. My wife asked me, "Are you really serious about giving up the presidency?" I answered, "Yes. The best is just good enough. It seems I am not the best." It does not matter whether they are objective.

Reform of the Security Forces

Civil-military relations are an important part of the transition process in many countries. You have said elsewhere that the armed forces and police should concentrate on self-defense and security issues during times of war as well as during times of peace, and should not be active in politics and social affairs. It is easy to say that, and to put it down on paper, but if the armed forces do not want to behave that way, putting it on paper does not make much difference. What did you learn about how to manage civil-military relations that might be relevant to other countries in the future?

After Indonesia declared independence in 1945, the people had to fight against the colonial master to be recognized as an independent state and society. At that time there were no professional military forces; they were all members of Indonesian civil society and were called the "1945 generation." Some of them later joined the armed forces and police. Soeharto used the dual function of the military to maintain power.

I have always stressed that the military should be considered technocrats;

they specialize in developing and applying technologies for preventing war and, if war cannot be avoided, to win the war against any kind of enemy that is disturbing the social and economic development of Indonesia. People of the 1945 generation are fading, so the dual function of the military that was part of their tradition is also fading. Some in the military are interested in maintaining their dual function, but treating the military as technocrats, showing the history of the military and why it exists, can help prevent this.

I think that those who lead a transition from an authoritarian regime to a democracy have to show—not by talking or writing, but by action—the importance of civilian control of the military, which I did with Prabowo. And I was assisted by somebody who was not a member of Islamic intellectual society and was not a Muslim.

We made reforms that barred members of the military from also serving in the civil service and reduced the number of seats they held in the Parliament, thereby decreasing their political influence.

In critical moments, people hesitate. The leader must demonstrate that he is willing to take action. For example, General Wiranto asked me what he should do with Soeharto's decree that authorized him to take whatever action he felt necessary in the national interest, which was almost an authorization to depose the president. I had been president for only a few hours. I told him to keep it. Why? I didn't know what would happen to me. If something happened to me, he would have to act.

Do the armed forces have any political role and influence in Indonesia today? And do they manage part of the budget independently?

They don't have a faction in Parliament, and they do not manage part of the budget independently. When I became president they did, but the constitution was amended. Now the constitution is very difficult to change, because no single faction has 80% of the vote.

Money in Politics

Since your presidency, Indonesia has been very different from how it was during the last years under Soeharto. But despite the functioning of democratic governance and the free press as a countervailing force, despite all the different checks and balances, Indonesia has the reputation of struggling with vast corruption. Why hasn't its political system succeeded in establishing processes of accountability that would make it much more difficult for such corruption to continue?

Corruption is a problem in any system, whether it is authoritarian or democratic, in which people are longing to be the leader and to control, because they need money to gain (and maintain) political power.

Soeharto and Soekarno, both authoritarian, needed money. Where does a political leader get the money? Whether he gets money from outside the country or from a local oligarch and his network, he becomes a puppet.

You lived many years in Germany. The German political leaders need money too. But do you think it is so corrupt there?

In a certain way, yes, and also in the United States, it's no exception. This is the system. You have a meeting, and somebody has to finance it.

I was lucky. I was never financed like that, and everything I earned, I earned very transparently. I paid my taxes. That is why I can sit here. Then I became president. I was not interested in the presidency because I knew I could never collect enough money to become president. What for?

There are so many people who want to be president, or a minister or a governor. They collect money, and people finance them. But their financers need a return of investment; they want their money back. That is the mechanism of all kinds of democracy.

Now what has happened in the world is we have one revolution after another. It is not only due to corruption, because people can access social networks on the Internet, such as Facebook, Twitter, etc. In the Middle East, they have been using social networks during the revolutions. But they were not the first. The first we had here in Indonesia in 1998 using mobile telephones. That's why I made the decision to allow freedom of expression.

So that is the problem, the problem of mankind. How to fight against that? Increase justice, increase transparency, increase productivity. Care more about people or organizations that really create value in society. If I make an airplane, I can add value. But if I provide nonperforming loans, I suck value from society. I could be super rich; then I could be super poor and lose a lot in a moment. It's just gambling. And that is happening now in Europe as well as in the United States, and we have to take care in Indonesia that it will never happen again.

I started the strategic aerospace industry with 20 people in 1974. In 1998, I had to hand it over to another person because it is a government-owned business and the vice president is not allowed to have other functions. I handed over 48,000 people with a turnover of $10 billion. I had signed agreements for assembly lines outside Indonesia.

But we had a problem because of bad loans—not because of me, but due to a lot of manipulation. We had nonperforming loans, and from whom? From private entrepreneurs with artificial projects, from those who bend the rules and who live from that, from brokers.

We had an agreement with the International Monetary Fund. What could I do? I was the president, but I could not break the agreement because it was signed by the former president. I didn't know about it when it was signed; I was not informed. But if I changed the agreement, I would have international and national problems. It could have caused a revolution. Many were expecting me to do so, but I did not break the agreement. I said if this is the price we have to pay, we will pay. I could not trigger a revolution; the majority of people are poor and innocent and they would be the ones who would suffer, and I could not let that happen.

Economic Management for Development

You initiated a new economic policy, and at the same time you launched a social safety network. How important were these measures for the movement toward democracy?

The question is capital formation. Where do you start? One option is a top-down approach. Create laws and regulations in such a way that certain people who are really good control the capital and create jobs. The only mechanism to ensure that there is an equal distribution of income and opportunity in capitalism is education. The other option is a bottom–up method. It was tried by the Soviet Union; this approach is bankrupt. But the top-down approach is almost bankrupt now, and we know that there is a lot of manipulation. An example is how interbank rates are manipulated, starting with LIBOR.

People who deal with so-called private equity and so on in my eyes are just brokers. They move very fast, and they get a commission. And they are free from paying tax, but they do not create wealth. They misuse the wealth created by others to become more wealthy. And if these companies have a problem, then the government comes to their assistance with the taxpayers' money. The majority has to inject capital to rescue those who are super rich. They are the only winners.

I'm not against capitalism. I have an approach, and that is starting in the middle. The middle class must be taken care of, and it must pull up the people under the poverty line and push good people to the top—what I call a "push-pull society." I think there is a chance that we can do it. I use the German way to describe it, the social market economy.

Political Parties

It is a historical accident that you were in the role of president, and you were prepared to act. But you need strong political parties for a democracy to work, and political parties here are very fragmented. What is your thinking about the role of parties in politics?

Soeharto designed the system in this way on purpose. He would only allow two parties in Indonesia [although Golkar contested elections in addition to the two sanctioned political parties], and he had the power. He took over from Dr. Engineer Soekarno and controlled everything. He was the president as well as the chairman of the parliamentary coalition, and he said, "I will have only two powers [political parties]. One will care about life today and one will care about life after death." He called one Partai Demokrasi Indonesia, the Democratic Party of Indonesia. And those who care for the life after death he called Partai Persatuan Pembangunan, the United Development Party for the building of the nation, in the wider sense. And then he made a third group. He did not call them a political party; it was a group of professionals. He called it Golkar (Golongan Karya). Golongan is "group"; Karya is "those who perform." He said that all those who believe in Islam, let them pray what they want and do; it's OK. But the others are a mixture of Islam, Christian, extreme left, extreme right, social, whatever. They quarrel sometimes, so they never win. Smart. The only winners are those who belong to the doers, who perform. So after the election he had to bring in the doers, the professionals, and the two minorities. He also created a so-called military faction. The chairman of the military faction in Parliament and the People's Consultative Assembly reported to the chief of armed forces according to a certain formula. The faction coming from the provinces only has representation in the People's Consultative Assembly, not in Parliament. So, based on these rules of representation, he could control the majority for more than 31 years.

And this party system contributed to stability under Soeharto, but it had to be financed. How to finance it? I was informed by Soeharto that he had a transparent fundraising system to finance the party in which the overhead cost of the system was 10%. If you are transparent, you can get people to cooperate with you, and you can keep 10% of that financing for yourself; the rest is for the party. Soeharto could do that until his children became adults. But after they married and developed their own business interests and surrounding teams, Soeharto could not control the process. His attitude toward limiting corruption was positive; I am convinced about that. But he was fighting against nature.

That is one of the main reasons why my first decision as president was to establish a term limit of two terms. I learned this from the United States. Some here wanted to do a feasibility study, but there was no need. The United States is an example that works. And I could do this because I had the majority—80% of Parliament. I could instruct them, and they had to do it.

Do you think that political party fragmentation makes democratic transition and consolidation more difficult? Do you think the political party law is effective?

The political party law is a good one. Of course, it can always be improved. I made it clear that anyone is allowed to establish a political party as long as the party accepts the constitution and adheres to existing laws. **There is a dem-**

ocratic way to improve the constitution, through existing laws and policies, but the street is not the Parliament. Demonstrations are a democratic means of expression in a civil society, but political leaders have to follow the rules of the game and should make appropriate suggestions for change through the free press or Parliament.

Today only political parties can propose presidential candidates. One change I would make is to have a mechanism so that civil society organizations can also propose candidates; we have to set up a system that makes this possible. This would improve voter participation. For example, in the first round of the recent elections for the governor of Jakarta, 40% of eligible voters did not participate. We must convince the people that they have to vote. I think they are not voting because they believe that they are not represented by the parties, and I think that low voter turnout is bad for them and for Indonesia.

Social Mobilization

Students played an important role in ending the Soeharto government, and then they seemed to disappear. What happens to these students and their mobilization? What do the leaders of those student organizations do?

Historically, from the very beginning, students have been the pioneers of change in Indonesia. And they still play that role.

So when you came to power, what happened to them? Did they suspend their mobilization?

The students came to me and we exchanged views, but they did not suspend their mobilization. Some were very aggressive against me. I listened. Some were supportive. I just listened.

I have never thought of myself as a politician, but I survive in politics. It doesn't mean I don't understand politics; I understand very well. But it is not my vehicle to become what I want to be. My vehicle is engineering, making airplanes and ships.

Advancing Gender Equality

Transitions are periods that can contribute to redefining the role and treatment of women. How did you address the rights of women?

We have human rights organizations, as in every country. The human rights organizations in Indonesia are advocating for the human rights of everybody, women and men. But women are at a disadvantage in many areas. Nobody cares for the women who are raped, and during the time of the transition, many women were raped. So I established the National Commission on Violence against Women (KOMNAS Perempuan).

I also worked with the chairman in Parliament and told him that this group must be taken care of because at least 50% of the population of Indonesia is female, so you should not ignore them.

International Support

Did foreign countries help you develop and implement your program?

The countries that really helped me, not only by talking but by action, were the United States—for example through former President Jimmy Carter leading the NGOs to observe the elections—and Germany, in assisting the restructuring of the Bank of Indonesia by sending the former president of the Deutsche Bundesbank, Dr. Schlesinger.

What do you think is the proper role for external actors during processes of transition toward democracy?

International agencies, governments, and transnational organizations should be proactive in helping people to improve their social care, health care, education, and economic infrastructure, but they should not become involved in domestic politics. International actors all pursue their own interests. Indonesia's social, political, and socioeconomic problems should only be solved by Indonesian people. International actors should act only on request and based on win-win cooperation.

Religion and Democracy

Your tenure of less than 2 years—517 days—changed the direction of the history of Indonesia. Indonesia is the largest Muslim country that has made a transition to democracy. There is a lot of discussion concerning Islam and democracy, and also that Indonesia is different because of Pancasila and because of the tradition of all religions living together and the unity of the nation. What are the lessons to draw from Indonesia concerning the role of religion, and what can be done to enhance the democratic process in countries where Islam is strong?

Democracy is the answer. I opened the door in Indonesia. I have told this to my colleagues in Turkey—Necmettin Erbakan and Abdullah Gül. Gül and I formed the International Islamic Forum for Science, Technology and Human Resources Development together. At that time, Gül was having problems with the military. I told him that he should deepen democracy. It is the people in the democracy who will decide.

Today people around the world are more informed about what is happening and more able to conduct their own analysis based on truth and free access to information. Before, decisions were based on approximations and assumptions. That is why the challenges that we have in the Middle East, the so-called Arab Spring, are not an Islamic problem. They are problems of justice and equitable distribution. Some people use the Islamic hard-liners as a means to get more attention, and money and control.

In Indonesia we have opened the door to allow the hard-liners to compete. But none of the hard-liners, Islamic or non-Islamic, has enough support to enter Parliament.

People—not religion—are the source of the problems; therefore the people must solve the problems. Culture influences how people solve their problems, and culture is much older than any religion. We are captured today by religious approaches and tend to use them to assert universal values and sometimes ignore the cultural background. Islamic values are not always identical with Arab culture and values.

In Indonesia, Muslim and other religious leaders must accept that Indonesia is not an Islamic state but a very religious society based on the Indonesian guiding principles of Pancasila, a philosophy that emphasizes five principles.

1. Monotheism and religiosity
2. Just and civilized humanity
3. Unity of Indonesia
4. Social justice for the whole of the people of Indonesia
5. Social welfare

Perhaps others in the Muslim world can learn from our experience in the Indonesian Association of Muslim Intellectuals. **We discussed common convictions and beliefs and never started by discussing our differences. Through such approaches we increased understanding among us and developed a greater tolerance for further discussion. Indonesia is a religiously diverse country. Generally, Indonesians of different faiths live together peacefully and contribute to (and participate in) Indonesian identity.**

Contemporary Transitions

Reflecting on the Indonesian experience, what do you think are the key lessons and principles for leaders in countries undergoing complex democratic transitions today?

First, they must amend the constitution, if necessary, so that they can implement their reform agenda legally and according to the constitution. Next, **leaders must accept demonstrations as a tool of democracy.** Killings and destruction of public assets should be treated criminally, of course, and **Parlia-**

ment should not become a "street parliament," but demonstrations themselves are important expressions.

- The president should be directly elected and should behave firmly and decisively. He should act inclusively (and not exclusively) and immediately form
a cabinet to help resolve the most pressing problems the society is facing.
Cabinet members should be drawn from all political parties elected to Parliament, represented proportionally, and members of the police and armed
forces.

- Political prisoners should be released, and freedom of speech and freedom
of the press granted.

- Increasing the stability and predictability of politics and the economy is
crucial. This may require some unpopular decisions.

- New elections may have to be called after the political situation is stabilized. Anyone should be allowed to freely form political parties and participate in elections as long as they follow the election criteria and behave
constitutionally.

- The president must treat the armed forces and police as technocrats in order
to limit their role in politics.

- **Above all, the president must be aware that his main duty is to focus on
solving the society's most immediate problems—not to maintain power
and control! The president is responsible to all people, not just his party.**
Transparency and good governance are the keys.

Do you think the Indonesian experience is relevant to Myanmar?

Of course. Myanmar and Indonesia share some similarities in their culture.
The culture of Indonesia, the Javanese, is based on the Ramayana, Mahabhara-
ta, and so on. Islam and Christianity came later. The way many cultures and
religions come together in Indonesia is something that Myanmar can learn
from. They may also observe how we came out from a military-dominated system peacefully.

In Myanmar they need somebody who understands power, has a good background, is educated in Western civilization, etc. Many forces try to influence
politics; powerful families, the armed forces, political parties, and rich individuals all try to influence power. I observed this kind of dynamic for 25 years.
I learned. And, suddenly, God put me in the center; I was surrounded, but I was
not blind. I knew what the people came for.

Time Line

Aug. 1945: Indonesia declares independence from the Netherlands, beginning a four-year war. An interim assembly selects nationalist leader Soekarno and Mohammed Hatta as president and vice president, and enacts a constitution based on Pancasila, a nationalist ideology.

Dec. 1949: The Netherlands recognizes Indonesia's sovereignty; the country becomes a unitary democratic state with a parliamentary government.

Sep. 1955: Indonesia holds its first parliamentary elections, followed by Constituent Assembly elections in December.

Mar. 1957: In response to regional rebellions, Soekarno declares martial law, beginning authoritarian "guided democracy."

Jul. 1959: Soekarno dissolves the Constituent Assembly and reinstates the 1945 constitution, which includes sweeping executive powers, but retains Pancasila as the state ideology.

Oct. 1965: An attempted coup by the 30 September Movement is put down by Army General Soeharto, who is then commander of the Army Strategic Reserve Command. Together with anti–Communist Party of Indonesia forces, including the Muslims, the Army launches a violent purge that kills hundreds of thousands of Communists and alleged sympathizers.

Mar. 1966: With public order decaying, Soekarno gives Soeharto expansive authority to stabilize the country. Soeharto purges Soekarno allies and slowly seizes power over the next two years, eventually placing Soekarno under house arrest and beginning the New Order regime. The government, backed by the military and technocrats, applies export-oriented policies and achieves economic growth over the next decades.

Jul. 1971: Elections are held for the People's Representative Council. The pro-Soeharto Golkar Party wins overwhelmingly amidst repression and fraud.

Jan. 1973: Soeharto forces opposition parties to merge into the nationalist Indonesian Democratic Party (PDI) and the Islamic-linked United Development Party (PPP). Only these parties and Golkar may contest elections.

Mar. 1978: Soeharto appoints B. J. Habibie, director of the state aircraft industry and former engineering executive in Germany, as minister of science and technology.

Dec. 1984: Nahdlatul Ulama (NU), the country's largest Islamic group, withdraws from the PPP. NU chief Abdurrahman Wahid says the NU should focus on religious and social work and avoid practical politics.

Nov. 1990: Soeharto permits the foundation of the Indonesian Muslim Intellectuals Association (ICMI), with Habibie as chairman, to increase support among pious Muslims. Many "modernist" Muslim reformers, linked to Muhammadiyah and future leader Amien Rais, join; most "traditionalist" reformers linked to Wahid and the NU reject it.

Dec. 1993: Megawati Soekarnoputri, Soekarno's daughter, is elected head of the PDI on a platform of secular reform, with support from some in the military.

Jun. 1996: A pro-government PDI faction holds a leadership convention, ousts Megawati, and storms the PDI headquarters, sparking major protests led by Megawati.

Jul. 1997: The Asian financial crisis begins. The value of the Indonesian currency (rupiah) drops rapidly, causing consumer prices, foreign debt, and the cost of credit to rise.

Oct. 1997: Soeharto agrees to reform the banking system in exchange for an International Monetary Fund (IMF) loan. Resulting bank closures damage public confidence in the country's currency and economy.

Jan. 1998: The exchange rate plummets further. Soeharto obtains new IMF loans; he agrees in return to break up monopolies and curb cronyism, but stalls on reforms. The opposition calls for Soeharto to resign or negotiate.

Mar. 1998: The People's Consultative Assembly (MPR) reelects Soeharto and confirms the choice of Habibie as vice president. Soeharto installs a new cabinet that includes family and personal friends. During an MPR session, large student protests begin, calling for Soeharto's resignation.

Apr. 1998: The student protests grow; protesters clash with police. Muhammadiyah leader Amien Rais joins. The military, led by General Wiranto, calls for dialogue.

May 1998: Protests grow, spread outside campuses, and become more violent, driven by the killing of demonstrators and protests of IMF-mandated fuel price increases. The NU and ICMI call for Soeharto to resign. The military allows protesters to storm Parliament and says it will not open fire. Cabinet members threaten to resign, the legislature threatens impeachment, and Soeharto fails to assemble new a coalition government.

Soeharto resigns and turns over power to Habibie, with the support of Wiranto. Habibie forms a coalition including Golkar, PPP, PDI, and reformist and military leaders. He demotes General Prabowo Subianto, Soeharto's son-in-law, to prevent a possible coup.

Jun. 1998: The Habibie government frees most political prisoners, lifts censorship, legalizes trade unions and political parties, and advances scheduled elections. Unrest and sectarian violence continue.

Dec. 1998: The legislature passes a proportional representation election law, preserving nonelected seats. Habibie declares a referendum on East Timorese independence, prompting Army-backed paramilitary attacks on independence supporters.

May 1999: The government enacts a law strengthening regional government powers.

Jun. 1999: Parliamentary elections are held, which are considered free by international observers. Megawati's Indonesian Democratic Party of Struggle (PDI-P) wins 33%, Golkar 22%, and Wahid's National Awakening Party (PKB, or Partai Kebangkitan Bangsa) 12%.

Aug. 1999: East Timor votes strongly for independence. Paramilitary violence kills over 1,000 and displaces nearly one-third of East Timorese. The United Nations deploys peacekeepers, but the military stalls their arrival while violence continues.

Oct. 1999: The MPR rejects Habibie's "accountability speech" in a close vote, in effect a vote of no confidence, with some Golkar legislators opposing Habibie. The MPR elects Wahid as president, backed by Golkar and moderate Islamists, and begins a four-year process of amending the 1945 constitution.

Jan. 2000: The National Human Rights Commission accuses Wiranto of crimes in East Timor. Wahid removes Wiranto and other active duty officers from the cabinet.

Aug. 2000: The MPR amends the constitution to curb the military's role in internal security and MPR, and to strengthen human rights and regional autonomy.

Oct. 2000: A court convicts Soeharto's son Tommy on corruption charges, reversing an earlier acquittal. Tommy flees with police complicity.

Feb. 2001: The MPR censures Wahid over an alleged bribe from the state logistics agency, the first step toward removal from office. The courts free Soeharto from house arrest, citing his poor health, but imprison Soeharto ally Bob Hasan for corruption.

Jul. 2001: The MPR impeaches Wahid, replacing him with Vice President Megawati. Wahid attempts to declare martial law and dissolve Parliament, but the military rebuffs him.

Nov. 2001: The MPR creates a Constitutional Court, an independent Judicial Commission, and a Regional Representative Council. Tommy Soeharto is apprehended and eventually convicted.

Jul. 2002: The MPR creates a directly elected presidency and removes all appointed seats from Parliament, completing major reforms to the 1945 constitution.

Dec. 2002: The Corruption Eradication Commission is established, which proves effective in prosecuting corruption.

Sep. 2004: Former General Susilo Bambang Yudhoyono (SBY) defeats Megawati in a direct presidential election. SBY's government enacts judicial and anticorruption reforms and partial reforms of the armed forces over his two terms.

Aug. 2005: The government signs a peace and autonomy deal with separatists in the province of Aceh.

Sep. 2009: SBY is reelected by a large margin. His party triples its share of seats in Parliament.

May 2012: Modest electoral reforms ahead of the 2014 elections raise the electoral threshold and eligibility requirements from 2.5% to 3.5% and mandate women's representation in party leadership.

NOTES

1. R. William Liddle, "Indonesia's Democratic Past and Future," in *Leadership and Culture in Indonesian Politics* (Sydney: Allen & Unwin, 1996), 181; Herbert Feith, *The Decline of Constitutional Democracy in Indonesia* (Ithaca, N.Y.: Cornell University Press, 1962), 27.

2. Feith, *Decline of Constitutional Democracy.*

3. Herbert Feith, *Indonesian Elections of 1955*, 58–59.

4. Hamish McDonald, *Suharto's Indonesia* (Blackburn, Vict.: Dominion Press, 1980).

5. The phrase was taken from Herbert Feith, "Repressive-Developmentalist Regimes in Asia: Old Strengths, New Vulnerabilities," *Prisma* 19 (1980): 39–55.

6. John Bresnan, *Managing Indonesia: The Modern Political Economy* (New York: Columbia University Press, 1993).

7. Andrew Macintyre, "Power, Prosperity and Patrimonialism: Business and Government in Indonesia," in *Business and Government in Industrializing Asia*, ed. Andrew Macintyre (St. Leonard, N.S.W.: Allen & Unwin, 1994), 244.

8. Richard Mann, *Economic Crisis in Indonesia: The Full Story* (Singapore: Times Books, 1998).

9. Bacharuddin Jusuf Habibie, *Detik-detik yang Menentukan Jalan Panjang Indonesia Menuju Demokrasi* [Decisive moments Indonesia's long road to democracy] (Jakarta: Habibie Center Mandiri, 2006), 55–58, 78–80.

10. "Wiranto: Tidak Ada Perintah Menarik Pasukan," *Tempo*, May 25, 2003; Habibie, *Detik-detik yang Menentukan*, 61.

11. "Current Data on the Indonesian Military Elite," *Indonesia* 67 (April 1999): 136–39; Geoffrey Forrester, "Introduction," in *Fall of Soeharto*, 19–22.

12. Habibie, *Detik-detik yang Menentukan*, 149–56.

13. Marcus Mietzner, "Between Pesantren and Palace: Nahdlatul Ulama and Its Role in the Transition," in *Fall of Soeharto*, 197.

14. Habibie, *Detik-detik yang Menentukan*, 151.

15. "Mampukah Habibie Menjinakkan," *Tempo*, November 24, 1998.

16. Richard Robison, "Indonesia after Soeharto: More of the Same, Descent into Chaos or a Shift to Reform?," in *Fall of Soeharto*, 229.

17. Bilveer Singh, *Habibie and the Democratization of Indonesia* (Sydney: Book House, 2001), 131.

18. Geoffrey Forrester, "A Jakarta Diary, May 1998," 61.

19. Singh, *Habibie and the Democratization of Indonesia*, 94–97.

20. Benjamin Smith, "The Origins of Regional Autonomy in Indonesia," in *Journal of East Asian Studies* 8, no. 2 (May / August 2008): 221–23.

21. Fachry Ali, Bahtiar Effendy, Umar Juoro, and Musfihin Dahlan, *The Politics of Central Bank* (Jakarta: *Lspeu* Indonesia, 2003), 14–54, 76–77.22. Ibid., 72–73.

22. Ibid., 72–73.

23. Kamarudin, *Partai Politik Islam di Pentas Reformasi* [Islamic political parties in the Reform Era] (Jakarta: Visi, 2003), 143.

24. R. William Liddle, "Indonesia's Unexpected Failure of Leadership," in *The Politics of Post-Suharto Indonesia*, ed. Adam Schwarz and Jonathan Paris (New York: Council on Foreign Relations Press, 1999), 20.

25. "Pertanggungjawaban Habibie," *Tempo*, October 11–17, 1999.26. Habibie, *Detik-detik yang Menentukan*, 127.

26. Habibie, *Detik-detik yang Menentukan*, 127.

27. Ibid.

28. Ibid., 345–53.

GUIDE TO FURTHER READING

Aspinall, Edward. *Opposing Suharto: Compromise, Resistance, and Regime Change in Indonesia*. Stanford, Calif.: Stanford University Press, 2005.

Aspinall, Edward, and Marcus Mietzner. "Economic Crisis, Foreign Pressure, and Regime Change." In *Transitions to Democracy: A Comparative Perspective*, edited by Kathryn Stoner and Michael McFaul. Baltimore: Johns Hopkins University Press, 2013.

Bilveer, Singh. *Habibie and the Democratisation of Indonesia*. Sydney: Book House, 2001.

Chandra, Siddharth, and Douglas Kammen. "Generating Reforms and Reforming Generations: Military Politics in Indonesia's Democratic Transition and Consolidation." *World Politics* 55, no. 1 (2002): 96–136.

Effendy, Bahtiar. *Islam and the State in Indonesia*. Athens: Ohio University Press, 2004.

Habibie, Bacharuddin Jusuf. *Decisive Moments: Indonesia's Long Road to Democracy*. Jakarta: Ilthabi Rekatma, 2006.

Hadiz, Vedi R. "Decentralization and Democracy in Indonesia: A Critique of Neo-Institutionalist Perspectives." *Development and Change* 35, no. 4 (2004): 697–718.

Hefner, Robert W. *Civil Islam: Muslims and Democratization in Indonesia*. Princeton, N.J.: Princeton University Press, 2000.

Hill, David T., and Krishna Sen. *Media, Culture, and Politics in Indonesia*. Oxford: Oxford University Press, 2000.

Horowitz, Donald. *Constitutional Change and Democracy in Indonesia*. New York: Cambridge University Press, 2013.

Künkler, Mirjam, and Alfred Stepan, eds. *Indonesia, Islam, and Democracy: Comparative Perspectives*. New York: Columbia University Press, 2013.

Mietzner, Marcus. "The Ambivalence of Weak Legitimacy: Habibie's Interregnum Revisited." *Review of Indonesian and Malaysian Affairs* 42, no. 2 (2008): 1–33.

———. *Military Politics, Islam, and the State in Indonesia: From Turbulent Transition to Democratic Consolidation*. Singapore: Institute of Southeast Asian Studies, 2009.

Mietzner, Marcus, and Edward Aspinall, eds. *Problems of Democratisation in Indonesia: Elections, Institutions and Society*. Singapore: Institute of Southeast Asian Studies, 2010.

O'Rourke, Kevin. *Reformasi: The Struggle for Power in Post-Suharto Indonesia*. Crow's Nest, Australia: Allen & Unwin, 2002.

Robison, Richard, and Vedi R. Hadiz. *Reorganizing Power in Indonesia: The Politics of Oligarchy in an Age of Markets*. London: Routledge Curzon, 2004.

Sulistiyanto, Priyambudi. "Politics of Justice and Reconciliation in Post-Suharto Indonesia." *Journal of Contemporary Asia* 37, no. 1 (2007): 73–94.

Uhlin, Anders. *Indonesia and the "Third Wave of Democratization": The Indonesian Pro-Democracy Movement in a Changing World*. New York: St. Martin's Press, 1997.

Van Klinken, Gerry. *Communal Violence and Democratization in Indonesia: Small Town Wars*. Abingdon: Routledge, 2007.

Chapter 5

MEXICO

....

Mexico's Gradual Democratization: From Above and from Below

SOLEDAD LOAEZA

From 1940 until 1982, amidst rapid economic growth and dramatic social change, Mexico maintained political stability under a single dominant party, the Partido Revolucionario Institucional (Institutional Revolutionary Party, or PRI), which controlled all branches of government at the national, state, and municipal levels. In the late 1970s, the country's president, all state governors, all senators, and at least 80% of deputies in the House of Representatives were from the PRI. Mexico differed from other authoritarian states in that it held regular elections and had a formal separation of executive, legislative, and judicial powers as well as constitutionally stipulated civil rights. In practice, however, its executive power was largely unchecked, the electoral results were preordained, and rights were often unenforced.

After the students' mobilizations and violent repression in 1968, there was a growing belief within Mexican society that political reforms were needed. President Luis Echeverría (1970–76) attempted a return to the populist tradition, but the path toward a democratic transition began with the 1977 electoral reform introduced by President José López Portillo (1976–82) in the context of the oil boom. From then on, pressures from different sectors and parties fueled a process of change that took several decades and culminated during the administration of Ernesto Zedillo (1994–2000).

Mexico's authoritarian hegemonic party rule was shaken in 1982 by a severe financial and economic crisis produced by excessive external debt and public spending. The crisis upset the general population's relatively passive acceptance of authoritarianism and set in motion a series of events that gradually moved Mexico, by fits and starts, toward democratic governance. Increased political mobilization and electoral participation, combined with top–down political reforms in response to recurrent crises, challenged and reduced the government's traditional control over electoral processes. The dismantling of authoritarianism took place over the next two decades under conditions of slow economic growth and interacted with market-oriented economic reforms. In those years, the Mexican economy and political system went through profound—but incremental and peaceful—transformations.

Ernesto Zedillo was the last president who came to power under the PRI-dominant party regime. Following the policies of his predecessor, Carlos Salinas de Gortari (1988–94), Zedillo deepened Mexico's economic liberalization and its integration into the global economy. Zedillo also helped to further open the political system by reducing state intervention, curbing presidential authority, accepting and adjusting to the opposition's political gains, and protecting the institutional integrity and fairness of the 2000 presidential elections.

The Authoritarian Regime

For most of the 20th century, Mexico experienced political continuity and stability (without resorting to military rule) while maintaining democratic appearances. This civilian-dominated authoritarian system contrasted sharply with that of many Latin American countries, where the military often played a central role.

The continuity of the political system was made possible by strong institutions: a coherent state, a powerful presidency, and the virtually unchallenged dominance of a party closely linked to the state. This arrangement was introduced in 1929 when the Partido Nacional Revolucionario (PNR) was created to represent the revolutionary elite. The Partido de la Revolución Mexicana (PRM), which was dominated by leftist trade unions and peasant groups, replaced PNR in 1938. In 1946, this party was in turn succeeded by the PRI, which was founded as a multiclass nationalist organization that represented and pursued the goals and means of the 1910 Mexican Revolution.

The 1917 constitution established a federal state governed by a presidential regime that experienced a separation of powers, but a highly centralized government structure that strengthened the executive's tendency to override the legislative and the judicial branches compromised the principle of checks and balances. This centralization of power also contradicted the principles of federalism.

A weak rule of law and arbitrary public officers, particularly with respect to law enforcement, characterized Mexican authoritarianism. Mexicans never knew whether the law would be enforced or not. Nevertheless, presidents were constrained by some norms that shaped their decisions and set limits on their power. For example, a constitutional ban on presidential reelection was—and still is—a golden rule of the Mexican political system, which every president has respected. This norm has prevented an overambitious politician from staying indefinitely in power and becoming a long-term dictator, and has curtailed the ambition of would-be candidates.

The president's formal powers were enhanced by the informal power afforded to him by the PRI. The party extended presidential authority beyond constitutional limits; for instance, the president chose candidates for elected office at the local, state, and national levels. This prerogative gave him control over the renewal of the political elite and, more importantly, over Congress. The party was at the heart of the clientelistic networks that were the foundation of authoritarian rule. It was also the vehicle of the president's symbolic presence at all levels of society. Thanks to the combination of formal and informal powers, the Mexican president ruled virtually unchallenged during his six-year term.

The PRI was in some ways a weak organization despite its powers. It had limited autonomy; its dominance depended on the president's support and on public resources to maintain its various mechanisms of control—from coercion to corruption. Decisions regarding the party's leadership were all taken personally by the president. The party's influence on policy making was limited, as it was subordinate to the president's political needs and priorities. Its main functions were to mobilize support for the government's decisions and to demobilize the opposition.

The PRI corporatist structure traditionally organized and controlled the participation and representation of workers, peasants, and urban middle-class groups. The party's hegemony was based in part on high rates of electoral abstention that facilitated the control of representation—and, where necessary, of fraud and the manipulation of results—in order to give the PRI consistent majorities of more than 75%, which gave legitimacy to arbitrary presidential rule. Economic development, however, helped create a more urbanized, educated, and diverse society that could not be controlled so easily. By the end of the 1960s, the PRI regime was thus becoming less effective, and as the student mobilization of 1968 showed, Mexicans could turn to nonelectoral forms of participation. This was a strong motivation for successive presidents to engage in political reform.

Nascent Party Competition

Mexico's democratization process followed an essentially electoral pattern, rather than one defined by street protests and mobilizations led by trade unions and other civil society organizations. This suggests that elections in authoritarian times might not have determined political power, but they did socialize the Mexican public in the values and rules of democracy. The government encouraged the existence of opposition parties that represented minor currents of opinion. There were never more than four opposition parties, and for decades they were weak because they could not compete with the almost unlimited resources of the official party. Their regular participation in elections helped sustain the democratic façade that distinguished the Mexican system from outright dictatorships. Opposition parties functioned as limited interest groups rather than genuine political parties.

Over time, however, the electoral competitiveness of the opposition parties slowly increased. The Partido de Acción Nacional (PAN) was for many years the only truly independent political organization. It was founded in 1939 by a group of Mexico City middle-class professionals, many of them involved in Catholic organizations, as a reaction to the radical policies of President Lázaro Cárdenas, such as land distribution and compulsory education with a Socialist orientation. PAN represented the conservative opposition to the revolution. Given its scant resources and the PRI's implacable hostility, for many years PAN barely survived. When PAN did not present a presidential candidate in the 1976 election because of internal conflict, the virtually uncontested election sharply exposed the hollowness of a choiceless vote.

Incoming President Lopez Portillo was concerned about maintaining political legitimacy and providing ways to channel dissent. He introduced an electoral reform in 1977 that relaxed general conditions for party registration and reinforced political representation by allocating proportional representation (PR) seats to minority parties on the basis of their electoral performance at the national level. Seven parties were represented in the 1979 Congress, including the Communist Party. This reform was adopted at a time when military dictatorships were rising in South America, and Mexico itself was facing incipient guerrilla organizations, which made democratic legitimacy more important for the regime.

Electoral reform converged with powerful long-term social trends: urbanization, secularization, and the diversification of Mexican society. The political expression of these changes was the emergence of pluralism and the articulation of demands to recognize citizens' rights to independent organization and participation.

Partido de Acción Nacional was the first party to benefit from the weakening of the PRI. Throughout the 1980s, PAN continued to gain from the official party's missteps in a recurrent pattern in which crises led to reforms and opened space for the opposition. The first crisis was the abrupt expropriation of commercial banks by the Lopez Portillo administration in September 1982, which provoked massive middle-class opposition; in northern states such as Baja California, Sinaloa, Sonora, Durango, and Chihuahua, PAN candidates won local elections between 1982 and 1985, indicating the erosion of the PRI's influence among the affluent groups of Mexican society.

But the main challenge to the PRI's electoral hegemony arose from the party itself. In 1987, as the presidential succession approached, Cuauhtémoc Cárdenas—a distinguished member of the party and son of the revered President Lázaro Cárdenas as well as former governor of the state of Michoacán, senator, and undersecretary of agriculture—demanded transparency in the selection of the PRI's presidential candidate. This designation had previously been the prerogative of the incumbent president. This time, Cárdenas and others in the PRI wanted to open the presidential nomination to competition and public debate in order to alter the direction of the government. They disapproved of President Miguel de la Madrid's neoliberal economic policies, such as joining the General Agreement on Trade and Tariffs (the precursor to the World Trade Organization) and his decision to accept PAN's victories in various municipal elections. The critics called for a return to a nationalist economic policy and traditions of the Mexican Revolution, which they claimed the PRI under President Miguel de la Madrid (1982–88) had abandoned.

Cárdenas's appeal was at its strongest in Mexico City, which had been hit by two major earthquakes on September 19, 1985. This tragic event, in which at least 10,000 people lost their lives, unleashed anti-PRI sentiment because the de la Madrid government seemed paralyzed by the catastrophe. The capital's population turned to independent nongovernmental organizations, and Cárdenas's message reached voters in Mexico City who had until then been mostly loyal to the official party.

Cárdenas was expelled from the PRI and in 1987 founded the Frente Democrático Nacional (FDN), a coalition that was a forerunner of the Partido de la Revolución Democrática (PRD), which in 1989 united various currents of the left into a single organization.

Mexican Democratization after 1987: The Rise of the Partido de la Revolución Democrática

The 1988 presidential election was marked by the emergence of a new major competitor, *cardenismo*, which was organized in the FDN, and by an unexpectedly high independent electoral turnout that could not be handled by the PRI's control mechanisms.

Cárdenas ran a campaign based on traditional nationalist themes; he emphasized the social costs of economic adjustment policies, focusing on poverty and inequality. His followers spoke of *charisma*, and his family name was a party platform in itself; he appealed to the underprivileged and challenged the PRI's monopoly on support from the low- and middle-income sectors. FDN was a dangerous threat to the official party's hegemony because the dispute between these two political forces was over the legacy of the 1910 revolution.

In the last two months of the campaign, Cárdenas, despite scant resources, showed a power to mobilize the public that surpassed that of the other candidates. There was virtually no television coverage of his campaign and the media rarely mentioned his name, but his support increased.

The final official results in 1988, questioned by many observers, gave Cárdenas 30% compared to 50% for Salinas and 16% for Manuel Clouthier, the PAN candidate. Electoral turnout was 49%, which was low compared to the fabricated reports from previous elections, but an unusually high rate of independent participation was generally recognized. The election was plagued by irregularities and allegations of fraud. Many Mexicans and other observers believe that Cárdenas actually won a plurality of the votes. Even according to the official results, his coalition gained 108 of 500 seats in the Chamber of Deputies. Cárdenas then played a decisive role in converting his coalition into a party and positioning PRD as the dominant leftwing party. The emergence of PRD, combined with the consolidation of PAN, altered Mexico's political landscape. For the first time since its foundation (as a successor to earlier parties) in 1946, the PRI was seriously challenged and failed to win its customary large majorities in Congress.

Partido de la Revolución Democrática incorporated members of the former Communist Party and numerous disaffected *priistas*. It took the new party some time to adjust to the rules of parliamentary politics and party competition. But the existence of stronger and more diverse opposition parties transformed Mexico's executive-legislative relations over time, and began to make the mechanisms of checks and balances far more effective.

After the 1988 election, the liberalizing economic and political reforms begun by President Salinas, and later advanced by President Zedillo, transformed the country. The economic reforms ran counter to the PRI's tradition of state intervention, while the political reforms gradually ceded political power to the opposition. The first important defeat acknowledged by the PRI was PAN's success in the 1989 gubernatorial election in Baja California. The 1990 electoral code, known as COFIPE, was the price PAN demanded for accepting Salinas's election in 1988. The most important feature of this legislation was the creation of the Federal Electoral Institute (Instituto Federal Electoral, or IFE), an autonomous permanent body with its own budget and professional administrative staff, which took charge of organizing and administering the electoral process. In 1992, the IFE introduced a voter photo identification (ID) card that soon became the most important and reliable official ID document for all Mexicans.

President Salinas's radical economic reform program contrasted with the timidity of his political reforms. The IFE was a step forward, but the formula to assign PR seats was a regression that favored the majority party because it introduced a so-called governability clause that gave the largest party in the Chamber of Deputies additional seats until it controlled 60% of the representation. President Salinas's constitutional reforms had the support of PAN, but he never concealed his animosity toward PRD. During his administration, Baja California, Chihuahua, and Guanajuato elected *panista* governors, whereas PRD's apparent victories were never recognized.

The 1994 Election

Several extraordinary events in 1994 further contributed to the weakening of the PRI. In January, the poorly organized peasant movement, Ejército Zapatista de Liberación Nacional (EZLN, also known as the Zapatistas), declared war on the Mexican government in the state of Chiapas in southern Mexico, at first in the name of socialism but soon emphasizing the defense of indigenous communities and Indian rights. In March, PRI presidential candidate Luis Donaldo Colosio was assassinated while campaigning in Tijuana, creating an atmosphere of uncertainty.

Salinas had only two choices in appointing a new candidate from his entourage of modernizers to replace Colosio: Pedro Aspe (the finance minister) and Ernesto Zedillo, who had also made a career mainly in the state financial sector, most recently as secretary of planning and budget and secretary of education. Choosing Aspe was not possible, as presidential candidates had to resign their cabinet posts six months before the election. Zedillo met this requirement because he had left the government to become Colosio's campaign manager.

Ernesto Zedillo was an atypical presidential candidate. He was known as a technocrat who was devoted to public service but impatient with the labyrinthine turns of politics. But he seemed likely to continue Salinas's economic reforms, unlike other presidential aspirants such as the president of the PRI, Fernando Ortiz Arana, and Francisco Rojas, the chief executive officer of Pemex. Salinas may also have expected Zedillo to be a weak president who would need his advice and support.

Ernesto Zedillo's Role

An unprecedented 35 million Mexicans (78% of registered voters) went to the polls in 1994. The high turnout was probably a response to both the potential spread of political violence and to important changes in the electoral procedures. To counter the possible appeal of the Zapatista movement, in January all the political parties had agreed to amend the law to enhance the election's credibility by increasing the participation of the legislature in the electoral process at the expense of the executive. Thus the IFE's councilors were replaced by six "citizen councilors," who were elected by a two-thirds vote in the Chamber of Deputies from a list prepared by the political parties. The new photo ID also contributed to voters' confidence in the process.

Ernesto Zedillo took office in an atmosphere of general relief. The election results had been clear and uncontested, accepted by the opposition and public opinion. Three presidential candidates had received 92% of the national vote: Zedillo took 49%, PAN's Diego Fernández de Cevallos received 26%, and Cuauhtémoc Cárdenas 16%. In August the PRI's secretary general, Francisco Ruiz Massieu, was shot and killed, but an investigation found that his killing was related to a personal dispute. This further damaged the party's image, but political violence had largely ceased, and normality seemed to be returning.

Less than three weeks after the inauguration, however, an abrupt financial and economic crisis precipitated the collapse of the Mexican peso, which lost 40% of its value in a month. Inflation and interest rates increased sharply in early 1995, and the economy contracted severely. Millions of Mexicans saw their savings and investments vanish, and many were unable to repay their loans. This reminded many Mexicans of the 1982 crisis, and they held the PRI responsible again. The party was seen as not only corrupt and antidemocratic, but also incompetent. Recovery was relatively fast, thanks in part to a fiscal rescue package from the United States, approved by President Bill Clinton, but the damage had been done, as the 1997 midterm federal elections would show.

In this complex political context, President Zedillo also had to deal with the polarizing effects of the ambitious economic reforms undertaken by Carlos Salinas, which had shaken the foundations of Mexico's traditional economic nationalism. Salinas had signed the North American Free Trade Agreement with the United States, privatized many industries, and reformed two sacred legacies of the Mexican revolution: ending the *ejido*, a collective form of land ownership, and reforming the anticlerical articles contained in the constitution. These historical discontinuities alienated many *priistas*; antagonism between the party and the government elite was part of Salinas's legacy to Zedillo. Personal antagonism also emerged between them, especially after the former president's brother was jailed on charges of corruption and participation in the conspiracy to kill Ruiz Massieu.

The goal of Ernesto Zedillo's political program was democratic normality, by which he meant setting limits on presidential power, loosening the ties between the presidency and the PRI, and assuring the effectiveness of checks and balances. In December 1994, right after taking office, he sent Congress a constitutional amendment to reduce the number of seats in the Supreme Court, modify the election process for justices, and redefine their terms in office in order to assure judicial independence. President Zedillo's political project also aimed to level the electoral playing field with regard to campaign finance and media access.

Zedillo also declared that a healthy distance would separate the PRI from the government. In practice, this meant that the party would no longer enjoy privileged access to the president or state resources in order to maintain its dominance. Zedillo sought to build a democratic presidency that was strictly based on the constitution.

The relationship between the government and the PRI from 1994 to 2000 was marred by strains and mutual distrust. The new president seemed even more ideologically committed to economic reform than Salinas. He had a strong conviction that direct state intervention in the economy was a source of corruption and low productivity, and preferred regulation to direct government intervention. Zedillo showed a lack of confidence in the PRI from the beginning, appointing an active PAN leader as attorney general, who was in charge of investigating the Colosio assassination. The relationship between the president and the PRI elite was also tense because Zedillo made special efforts to establish a dialogue with PRD, rather than rebuffing the party as Salinas had. Nevertheless, President Zedillo expected discipline and support from PRI members. Their votes in Congress allowed him to implement the painful stabilization program in response to the crisis of 1994–95, and the party gave Zedillo the legislative support he needed to continue the economic reform process.

Zedillo outflanked the PRI and negotiated his political program with the opposition parties. He supported a new electoral reform in 1996 to strengthen the autonomy of the electoral authorities. The IFE's general council would have eight members, and the minister of the interior would be replaced as its head by a "member of civil society" who would be elected in the Chamber of Deputies at the proposal of the political parties. This reform also modified the relationship between the public and private funding of electoral campaigns and made the electoral tribunal part of the judiciary rather than the executive branch.

In the 1997 federal elections, which were widely acclaimed as fair, PAN and PRD together won a majority of 247 representatives in the Chamber of Deputies, compared to 239 from the PRI. Cuauhtémoc Cárdenas became the first elected mayor of Mexico City, and PRD won a majority in the local assembly. This was a strategic defeat for the PRI because the country's capital concentrates Mexico's economic, financial, political, and cultural resources.

Between 1994 and 2000, PRD won gubernatorial elections in Sur, Tlaxcala, and Zacatecas, while PAN won Jalisco, Aguascalientes, Querétaro, and Nuevo León, and retained Baja California and Guanajuato. Mexico's diverse political map was enriched by the proliferation of party coalitions that included small parties such as the Partido del Trabajo and the Partido Verde Ecologista de México.

The president's reformist impulse reached the PRI, which chose its presidential candidate for the 2000 election in an unprecedented internal primary, in which Zedillo's involvement was limited. Francisco Labastida, former secretary of energy and governor of Sinaloa, was elected the official party candidate in December 1999, but by then he was already far behind Vicente Fox, the former governor of Guanajuato, who had been campaigning for PAN for a year and had already won great popularity. Fox was able to represent change and appeal to a broad electorate.

On the night of the July 2000 presidential election, the IFE president announced on national television, on the basis of tabulated results and careful projections, that Fox had won the election. President Zedillo immediately congratulated the president-elect even before Labastida had conceded defeat.

Today Mexico has multiparty democratic governance in which presidents, members of Congress, state governors, and mayors are chosen in free and fair elections that are independently, professionally, and honestly administered. Alternating between parties occurs at all levels of government. In 2012, the

PRI was voted back to the presidency after two PAN administrations: Fox (2000–2006) and Felipe Calderon (2006–12).

To govern, the president must negotiate with somewhat independent power centers in Congress, the states, and municipalities. Important private concentrations of power—including large (often oligopolistic) business firms, peak associations, labor unions, media empires, and criminal cartels—all make the governance process complex, but Mexico now has increasingly effective checks and balances.

Much remains to be done to further strengthen and deepen Mexican democracy. The three main parties have formally agreed to undertake major political reform. Discussions are currently underway regarding proposals to permit independent candidates and citizen ballot initiatives; regulate political parties, campaign finance, and government propaganda; introduce a second round in presidential elections; and facilitate coalition governments. Whatever the outcome of these negotiations, they illustrate the increasingly vibrant state of democracy in Mexico today.

Biosketch of Ernesto Zedillo, President of Mexico 1994–2000

PHOTO: LINUS SUNDAHL-DJERF

Ernesto Zedillo was educated at the primary and secondary levels in Mexicali on the Mexico-Texas border, completed undergraduate studies at the National Polytechnic Institute in Mexico City, and then won a scholarship to Yale University, where he completed a PhD in economics and first connected with members of the Mexican elite who were fellow graduate students. Returning to Mexico, Zedillo worked in the state financial sector, developing a reputation for outstanding technical competence rather than political activity. In the presidential administration of Carlos Salinas de Gotari (1988–94), he served as secretary for budget and planning and then as secretary of education. He resigned early in 1994 to become presidential campaign director for Luis Donaldo Colosio, a fellow northerner. When Colosio was assassinated while campaigning, Zedillo was the only cabinet-level member of the ruling party, the PRI, eligible to run for president because Mexican law requires cabinet members to resign months before campaigning for election.

In an election with the highest turnout in Mexican history, Zedillo was elected president in August 1994. Zedillo set out to help Mexico become a "normal democracy" by proposing reforms to strengthen the judiciary and Congress, separate the government from the PRI, and strengthen independent electoral institutions. Despite a severe economic crisis that exploded within weeks of his inauguration, Zedillo undertook reforms in campaign finance rules and media access and accepted opposition control of Mexico City and the national Congress. He called for a "healthy distance" between the government and the PRI and promoted the party's first internal primary process for candidate selection. His administration's decision to prosecute Raúl Salinas, the former president's brother, broke with the precedent of impunity for former presidents and their close relatives. The Zedillo administration also reinforced the liberalization of Mexico's economy that had been initiated by Miguel de la Madrid and accelerated by Salinas and introduced an innovative performance-based poverty-alleviation program, PROGRESA, which provided conditional cash transfers.

On the night of the 2000 election, Zedillo congratulated opposition candidate Vicente Fox as president-elect even before the PRI candidate had conceded. Zedillo has subsequently based his career outside Mexico, serving as director of Yale University's Center for the Study of Globalization and on a number of corporate and nonprofit boards and policy commissions.

....

Interview with President Ernesto Zedillo

Reforming the System from Within

What lessons might Mexico's gradual democratization have for leaders who are attempting to make democratic gains in other countries?

One must first distinguish between the Mexican process and others that involved a move from a totally authoritarian regime to one that is more open or democratic. That was not the case in Mexico. Mexico had a formal democracy with periodic elections going back many years and certain rules for political competition. By the time I was elected president of Mexico, people from the opposition had already held positions at other levels of government, and certainly in Congress, and a series of prior steps had been taken toward a gradual electoral reform to make possible the participation of parties other than the party in power [the PRI]. So there was a meaningful process of learning, I would say.

Some thought this process had been slow; others thought it moved very fast. From my point of view, it had been slow. For some time the citizenry had been ready to live in full democracy. The great challenge for me, and for all the political actors, was to step up the pace of building the bases for competitive, modern, full democracy.

One of the first things I told my colleagues in the party [PRI] after the 1994 election was that this election had been clean and legal, that we had abided by the rules in force, and the votes were counted properly. But the election was not fair because the conditions for political competition were still not fair in Mexico.

And I could make these comments because I didn't have any problem of legitimacy, as the party had performed satisfactorily not only in the presidential election, but in the elections for Congress as well. So the party was able to be receptive to my message. No one was standing up to tell me that I was mistaken, and I was very encouraged that there was no negative reaction from the people in the party at that time, so I thought we could continue to move forward.

The day I took office as president, I announced my intent to work with all the political parties for something that I called "democratic normalcy." We needed the country to achieve a normal democracy, which included having genuine checks and balances in our government, and that can only be achieved democratically.

Going back many years, there was certainly a concern on my part, and on the part of many people, that if we did not undertake to carry out an orderly process for a greater opening and more political competition, that these demands could come, at some point, in a disorderly and chaotic fashion, which at least in the short term could be bad for the country and certainly bad for (and perhaps a mortal blow to) the party.

This concern had long been present in my mind, and it was felt even more strongly by others. After what happened in the late 1980s in Eastern Europe, those of us who shared this way of thinking had one more argument: we realized we should take leadership of such a process, rather than follow in its wake. **Putting up resistance to greater democracy would be a mistake because, sooner or later, based simply on the level of economic development Mexico was attaining, it would have been impossible to maintain autocracy with an alert and demanding citizenry that was already aspiring to democracy.**

Forty or fifty years ago, democracy was not yet a widespread demand of the population, but by twenty or twenty-five years ago there was clearly greater awareness among the citizenry. People were saying, "we want political freedom, we want participation, representation and democracy."

Everyone articulated it differently, but when it comes down to it, that's what they were all saying. Why don't we have democracy, if we believe in it and the citizenry is ready for it and we have organized political parties? I think the big difference between Mexico and other countries that have experienced such changes is that the government understood that it had to be part of that. We couldn't be the obstacle; on the contrary, we had to contribute with our political and intellectual capacities in order for the process of democratization to take place in an orderly manner, in keeping with what the country needed.

There were undoubtedly many people who understood that the PRI needed to respond somehow to the clamors for greater democracy but wanted the PRI to maintain control. You describe wanting not just to manage pressure while maintaining PRI dominance, but also to genuinely open up the political system. These are two very different concepts. Please discuss the process by which both you and Mexican political leadership (in the PRI and outside it) moved from one concept to the other.

I have no doubt that in the party there were different views or interpretations of what advancing in the construction of real, effective, normal democracy meant at that time in Mexico. Surely there were some who were concerned and even wondered, "advance for what purpose?" particularly after clearly winning an election. They said, "Why are we doing this now, we don't have any problem of legitimacy," as had happened at some other times in the past. And perhaps there were other views that we have to modulate the pressure, we have to change so that nothing changes. But there were many others who said, "Why not, if we have what it takes to wage this democratic battle, if we have what it takes to compete?" And there was confidence not only that the country was ready, but that the PRI was also ready to compete under the new rules of the game. I was the one who had won the presidency, so I believe that I not only had the responsibility, but the right, to represent that more modern current in the party. It wasn't traumatic for the country or the party because there were actually people in the party who agreed with that, although some have not wanted to recognize this.

At times there is talk of the PRI as if it were the major opposition to the democracy that was constructed in the 1980s and 1990s in Mexico. The PRI was an integral part of that process, and played a very active role, and it deserves recognition—just as the other parties have been recognized for their contributions as well as the citizen movements, which played a very important role.

Social Mobilization

What was the role, in this process of opening, of the civic and social forces that were pushing in that direction?

If you force me to identify the moment when a group of citizens—and some of them were very young—expressed with great civic force, but not necessarily with great clarity, that there was discontent with the way the Mexican political system was working, I would refer to 1968 [when a student-led protest movement began that was met with violent repression from government security forces].

No political party, whether or not it was officially recognized, clearly sided with the students in 1968. Some of the activists with the banned Communist Party certainly did support the movement, but none of the parties sided with the student movement. So some who were involved in that would claim, I believe, that it was the first citizen movement that questioned how the political system was working.

Unfortunately, like many other things that occurred during the Cold War, a movement of this nature, seen through the lens of those years and from a perspective I would describe as myopic on the part of many, was held in disrepute. And unfortunately the government acted as if the student movement of 1968 was one of the various movements in those years that were seen as a threat, behind which were lurking dark forces emanating from the other side of the Iron Curtain. Some wanted to see it as a threat, and this was often used to inhibit the participation of new political actors in Mexico.

Perhaps the movement did include some people who had their heart on the other side of the Iron Curtain. But basically the movement was for freedom, rejecting authoritarianism and repression. It was a youth movement, and when young people do things, one should not expect a high degree of articulation and ideological or conceptual sophistication. It would have been ideal if their first demand from the government was to say, "We want more democracy," but I think that underlying the movement such a demand was there, and also "Why can't we participate? Why can't we voice our opinions? Why when we march are we called Communists and accused of conspiring against the country's stability?"

In reality this was a movement for political freedom, so I think democratic construction in Mexico arose from a citizen's movement, the 1968 student movement.

For many years it was widely thought that the student movement had failed because it was repressed, because it didn't lead to anything concrete in terms of what the students were demanding, and because there was a high human, social (and probably political) cost in the short run. Forty-five years after this movement began in July 1968, I can say that the movement triumphed, and I hope that will be valued one day. I was a student at the Politécnico [National Polytechnic Institute, a public university in Mexico City] at the time; I was very young, 16 years old.

How did that political event mark your life?

Profoundly. I was already very modestly involved in student politics in high school, when I was 15 to 16 years old. I saw that we could not hold elections in the school with fair rules because there were slates financed by people whose identity we did not know. This was in 1967.

Once we were competing and we thought we had won, we discovered that the votes were not counted properly and therefore we lost, but we were very sure that we had won; we thought we were much more attractive than our competition. And obviously when the student movement came and the government reacted as it did, I think for me it confirmed that something was very wrong, and that what the government was saying about them wasn't consistent with what I saw in my colleagues. They were simply people who were getting an education, who wanted to express themselves, as we wanted to express ourselves in other aspects of life, in our taste for music or literature or in our personal relationships, emotionally and physically, but the environment was totally repressive. But what ended up hurting most was the political aspect, because political repression is normally accompanied by two things—manipulation and violence—and that is what happened in 1968.

A considerable time passed between the 1968 student protest movement and the first visible political change with President José López Portillo [1976–82]. What gains were made from 1968 to 1978?

That's right. I believe that the very considerable lapse helped create this sense of failure, that nothing had been gained. I believe that the student movement helped sow the idea, within the system, that something had to be done. And it is not by chance that among persons within the government who expressed a different (I would say even a dissident) opinion of how the student movement was handled by the government in 1968 was Jesús Reyes-Heroles, the director of Pemex [Petróleos Mexicanos, the state-owned petroleum company]. A few years later, Reyes-Heroles became minister of interior and was President López Portillo's key man for promoting the Federal Law on Political Organizations and Electoral Procedures. As you can see, my hypothesis regarding the relationship between 1968 and Mexico's political progress is supported by more than one item of evidence.

Political Parties

Were there pressures from other social sectors?

I think so, but also in the parties, within and outside the PRI. I can't deny the merit of the Partido de Acción Nacional, which is almost as old as the PRI, and PAN always played according to the rules—let's say the precarious rules of that formal but clearly imperfect democracy—and one of its lines of action was always to call for more democracy. They always did so in a civilized way; they always encouraged participation. We cannot play down the role of the parties other than the PRI; I couldn't say that the Communist Party believed in democracy, because that wasn't a matter of principle for it; on the left it's a different story. Its formal position in favor of democracy took longer to articulate, but I would say that it was equally (and at times even more) decisive than the other political actors because they made major efforts. I would say that in 1968 most of the students' hearts were beating for the left.

The students did not say, "we want this movement to be like the Soviet Union"; they said, "we want to have freedom, not a repressive government. We want a government that will listen to us."

Where do you situate the Partido de la Revolución Democrática in this context?

The PRD itself did not exist until its founding in 1989. After the first democratic reform by President López Portillo, some left parties were established with some historical leaders—for example, the party led by Mr. Heberto Castillo. There were several groups and then parties; you had the heirs of the more orthodox left that followed the Partido Popular Socialista, which had been founded earlier. In the late 1980s, a group of dissidents from my party created a front [the Frente Democrático Nacional] to participate in the elections; that front was joined by other groups and some of the parties of the left. Eventually, over time, that became PRD. But actually those who so far have been PRD's most important figures have come from the PRI, and perhaps from the most conservative wing of the PRI, at least with regard to economic policy. PRD includes people who were always active in the left. There are people who were in the 1968 movement, people who contributed to creating political parties at the time of the first major political reform during the López Portillo administration, and who moreover continue working in their party, and I think they should be given full recognition.

International Context

Among the many important things that happened in the world in 1968, one was the Soviet intervention in Czechoslovakia. For a number of people on the left, this was shocking. Did this incident affect the Mexican left?

I suppose so, but I was never close to the leaders. I was very young, but what I do recall very well is that during the Prague Spring we had meetings at my school. I recall at least one marked by great enthusiasm and great happiness, where two sentiments were expressed—one in which some were saying, "You see, the Russians are not as bad as they say, the Russians are allowing this," and others who said, "Now the Czechs are doing something."

Then came the repression. I don't know what those who were using the Czech Spring to say "you see, the Russians aren't as bad as the Americans make them out to be, or as many people here in Mexico make them out to be" were feeling. I'd like to think—but I have no evidence—that what happened in Prague at that time led some colleagues to reflect a bit more on what the Soviet regime represented.

Electoral System

What other major political changes occurred after the term of López Portillo that culminated during your presidency?

There was also an important reform under President Miguel de la Madrid [1982–88], when the number of seats in Congress filled by proportional representation was increased, giving greater representation to minorities [1986]. We moved to a conventional system of proportional representation, and then a couple more steps forward were taken under President Carlos Salinas [1988–94], especially in terms of how elections were to be organized. A specialized electoral body was established to ensure professional management of elections, and other important features were introduced in the law. But from my point of view there were still great opportunities to build a better system.

Role of Social Forces

In many countries the intellectual establishment—university professors, commentators, essayists, and the Catholic Church—have tended to be ahead of the curve, and they understood the need to open up the system. However, is it correct to observe that the intellectuals in Mexico were generally defending the old system?

I would say that in general terms that is so, but it is also valid to say that we have (or we had) intellectuals who were also far ahead of the curve. The most obvious case is Octavio Paz, who from the 1950s realized what was happening in the Soviet Union, articulated his view, let it mature, and expressed it. During the 1960s, he clearly noted the need for and urgency of having real democracy in the country; he became more active in the 1970s and 1980s.

Some highly reputed intellectuals were more timid when it came to clearly articulating the demand for greater democracy; they were more interested in social justice. They rejected authoritarianism, but it took them time to say it was a question of constructing real democracy.

I'm not going to speak for them, but I suppose that there was still the hope that one could construct a just society, independent of whether there was democracy. The model of Cuba was attractive to many at that time. I think that was part of the problem. Today when we talk about Cuba, at least those of us who try to understand it, it is as a project that didn't work in terms of bringing social justice, progress, and well-being to the Cuban people. But 40 years ago there was still the idea that something positive was happening, and not only the case of Cuba. There were other cases; there were those who said that the most important thing was social justice and not democracy, and I think that ended up inhibiting some. But they came over, and did so in a positive way, and many of them have contributed to constructing the intellectual foundation of what Mexico is today.

Setting Priorities for Reform

During your presidency there were a coherent set of initiatives, including judicial reform, electoral reform, changes to the electoral courts, constitutional reform for the election of the governor of Mexico City, strengthening of the legislature, and the reduction of the president's discretionary financial power. Some argue that these were part of a longer-term trend and would have happened anyway. Yet experiences worldwide reveal that if there is no leadership pushing for action, critical reforms often don't happen. Did you gradually adapt to each problem? Or was there some prior planning and coordination of these reforms?

One did not have to be a genius to imagine what steps would have to be taken, even after winning the elections with over 50% of the votes and with a vote total that stood as a record for many years. For even though there is an ever-increasing number of votes in Mexico, it took 18 years before a candidate won more votes than we had won in 1994. So I didn't have any legitimacy problem, and no one said this election was not legal or anything of the sort.

Yet it was clear that there were at least three problems, some real and others problems of perception. The first problem was equity in the conditions of political competition. If you analyze the reforms prior to the 1996 reform, it is clear that the party in government had big advantages vis-à-vis the other parties in terms of financing, access to the media, and transparency of the resources used in political campaigns. This was an issue pending in Mexican democracy.

There must have been opposition within the PRI to changing that.

Well, surely there was opposition, but it was never strong enough to keep us from reaching an agreement, or for someone to stand up in those months to say that we would not go forward with it. Congress had a PRI majority, and the PRI supported the reform, so I know that people say the PRI probably had people who did not have a positive attitude regarding this. But the majority was in favor, and was there and supported the reform, which was passed in 1996. It wasn't everything at once. Steps had been taken, and more steps had to be taken. We could debate whether these steps could have been taken before; I would have liked it if they had come 20 years earlier, but if it hadn't been done before, it had to be done now.

Electoral System

The other factor was: how could we know that we had an accurate vote count? By then we had a sound electoral system; that was one of the reforms that was undertaken before my administration. Yet there was an original sin in that system, which was that the electoral body continued to come under the authority of the executive. **In a country with a history of suspicions in relation to elections, with a party that had been in power for so many years, having the electoral body as an official agency of the federal executive branch—well, we were obviously never going to overcome suspicion and distrust. One didn't have to be a genius to see that what we needed to create was a body of the Mexican state, not a body of citizens outside the state, which has guaranteed independence from the executive and legislative branches.** It should include people who, on the one hand, are supported by the parties and who, on the other hand, enjoy a solid reputation for probity. That would make it less likely that their actions would be called into question. And this would also help ensure it would be well financed by the state so that it can perform its functions.

The other issue is: who determines the legality of the process? Moreover, if there are disputes, who decides them? Under the previous system, the Congress judged the elections. But obviously that is a conflict of interest, for there you have the parties represented in the Congress, where you have the maximum expression of representation and competition of the political parties over their agendas. So asking the Congress to decide elections was, from my point of view, totally absurd.

Judicial Reform

You mentioned the judicial reform. The second day of my term, I went out and gave a message to the nation to say that if we wanted to have balance among the branches of government and if we wanted justice in Mexico, we would have to undertake an in-depth reform of the judicial branch to make it truly independent. That wasn't all we needed, I said, but it was a very important part of it.

That reform was achieved in the very first month of my administration and was adopted with the consensus backing of all the parties. Just weeks after the initiative was proposed, we had strengthened the federal judiciary to serve the citizens and also—one would have to evaluate the progress—so that the judicial branch would govern and vet itself. We also needed to take the determination of the legality of the elections and put it in the hands of the judicial branch through a specialized court. So it seemed to me that it was important to advance in that direction. These were not isolated acts; all this came to the fore very soon, not only at the initiative of the president of the republic but at the initiative of the parties as well.

Building a Coalition for Reform

The great aspirations and general outlines of the reform were posed from the outset. We experienced a very arduous 18 months with many interruptions, because in the midst of this political reform effort we were battling a serious economic crisis, and we continued to hold elections under the old system. So it was very understandable yet very unfortunate that any excuse would be invoked by the political parties to get up and walk away from the negotiating table.

So it took us 18 months to negotiate this change, which seemed so obvious because the country's situation was difficult and the process of negotiating the political reform was often held hostage to many other interests that were minor or inconsequential next to the major political reforms. So I had to fight hard to keep making progress on the political reforms.

I recall that, once, one of the most important parties got up from the table because there was a dispute over an election in a municipality in the state of Puebla. They were accusing the governor of having intervened in the election and said that if we were negotiating the great political reform, that problem had to be resolved first to prevent such situations or to resolve them in a clear and open manner. If you get up from the table over controversies like that—well, we'd never be able to resolve these problems. And they would return to the table. Finally, a year and a half later, a major political agreement was signed that was then translated into the constitutional and statutory reforms that gave us the legal and institutional framework for the 1997 and 2000 elections.

It is important to have a mechanism for monitoring the elections to ensure that they do not face credibility problems. Yet there's also something else: to have a democracy, you need democrats, and that is something that I believe we are still forming in Mexico. Despite these very solid institutions that we've had, to organize, observe, and judge elections, there have still been huge disputes in Mexico. So when people say "What happened? Did the institutions fail?" I say "no, to the contrary." If it were not for these institutions, the consequences of the misconduct of some political actors, claiming victories that they have not obtained at the polls, would have had catastrophic consequences for the country. The institutions may work, but if certain political actors do not wish to behave like democrats, others will come along who do.

Separation of Powers

After the elections of 2000 established the alternation of power, some Mexican observers seemed ambivalent. They wanted democracy, but they also had a kind of impatience regarding the political process and felt that it ought to be possible for a democratically elected regime to be efficient in resolving problems once the government decides what it needs to do, without taking into account how much negotiation is required to govern in a system with separation of powers. What is your view on this impatience?

There are many people—not just in Mexico—who say that if we had a system in which the president could do things more quickly, many problems would be resolved. I think they're wrong. I have also heard it from my Asian friends, who tell me our problem is that we want to forge democracy in the American or European style and that we are not going to emerge from underdevelopment that way. So my response to them is that for almost 200 years we tried to do what you have done and we always failed; whenever we've had a concentration of power and a lack of checks and balances, the failure has been resounding, the economic, political, and above all human failure.

In Latin America we are experts at that kind of failure. The concentration of power has not brought any good in Latin America, and we can count the lives and even the percent of GDP that this has cost us. So that path must be discarded; we have no path other than democracy, the path of checks and balances among the different branches of government, and learning so that it works.

Octavio Paz said that democracy is a servant of development and social justice. **Democracy does not automatically yield good results; it gives you a form of government that the citizens, parties, and leaders have to use to attain development.** But I am ever more certain that every time we have not instituted checks and balances and accountability in Latin America, because power was too concentrated, we have failed. We have old, recent, and present-day examples.

Democracy is right for Latin Americans. We are going to prove in the future—we are still years off—that we can operate much better in democracy than in authoritarianism. It is not in our spirit to operate well under authoritarianism; it goes against our genes, against many things that we are. Unfortunately, we were not given the opportunity to do so after our independence. If we had had that, we would be a more fully developed region today.

Civil Conflict

What was the impact of the Zapatista movement [a movement in the state of Chiapas in southern Mexico that declared war on the Mexican government in January 1994, invoking Socialist rhetoric but soon emphasizing indigenous rights] on Mexico's political reform and democratization processes? What was its impact on society at large and on the political parties?

The issue of Chiapas was important; it was also taken up with the parties, but what we did was not because of the situation in Chiapas. We came to agree on what I think was a good diagnosis of the situation there. First, the Chiapas movement was not fundamentally an issue of armed rebellion; it was an issue of social discontent. Although it is true that these persons came forward with a revolutionary discourse, including with violence initially, it was evident that it was not a military matter. It was about social discontent, and I think the government understood that the best thing it could do was work to resolve the social problems in Chiapas.

But it wasn't clear with whom one was going to speak, for these persons had supposedly operated in the underground. Once the origins and nature of the movement became clear, a serious dialogue ensued. Unfortunately, the political incorporation of this group into the country's formal political life was never accomplished. But what is clear to me is that the social situation in Chiapas, six years later, was significantly different because we had done a great deal of work. It was one of the places where I spent more time, as president, addressing the state's social problems in normal conditions and in exceptional conditions. Among other things, we had at least two very serious natural disasters in Chiapas, and they had to be tackled head on, just as I tried to address other natural disasters, many of which occurred during my term.

But I would tell you that my aspiration to achieve political reform would have been the same with or without Chiapas; or, I should say, Chiapas was an issue on its own, which merited its own treatment and strategy, and the political reform also stood on its own, and that's why it was accomplished.

Responding to Economic Crisis

In Mexico, political reform was being carried out in the midst of an economic crisis. If you had to discuss Mexico's experience in terms of the relationship between political change and economic policy, what lessons can you draw?

The Mexican case may be special, for before taking office we had already said that we would work with the political parties to carry out political reform. When this was said we had no idea—I had no idea—that we would be confronting an economic crisis such as the one we ended up facing.

At the beginning of the Salinas administration I was minister of budget and planning, and as of 1992 I was minister of education.

But during the campaign, once you were a presidential candidate, did you and your advisers not suspect that a crisis of that magnitude might ensue?

No—well, if we had thought of it, it wouldn't have happened. That's why crises happen, because no one expects them, at least not with the magnitude of the Mexican crisis. To cite a contemporary example, no one predicted that a crisis would erupt in 2008 of such proportions that we continue to feel the negative impact today. It's true, some said that the banking system was very vulnerable; others said that global macroeconomic disequilibria may lead to a financial crisis. But it is not true that anyone was able to predict the magnitude and gravity of the crisis we have been experiencing since 2008, really since 2007, when the subprime mortgage market burst.

The same thing happened with the Mexican crisis. No one anticipated it, because if we had been able to see it coming, those who were in government and those of us who were out of government at that time—well, it would have been possible to do something to prevent it.

The Mexican crisis was the first big financial crisis in this new era of financial globalization and emerging markets. It was very different from the 1982 debt crisis. We were the first guinea pig of financial globalization. I am not criticizing or supporting financial globalization; it's just that when the history of contemporary financial globalization is written, it should say that its first crisis occurred when a sudden turnaround of capital flow occurred and flattened a country, Mexico, in late 1994–95. There is no other case before like it, for the Asian crisis, the Russian crisis, and then the Brazilian crisis came after ours.

We had a commitment and an objective in terms of political reform. The administration began, a great economic and financial crisis set in, and a very important decision had to be made: should this economic crisis hold us back on the political reform so we can focus our attention on the economic issues?

Some said that we could not take on more than the economic issues at that moment. I didn't agree. I said we had to try to do both things, for two reasons. First, because it is what we had committed ourselves to do, and it was what the country needed; it was part of the strategy for the country to develop. And the second, I must admit, was a tactical reason, for I thought that the economic track alone was going to be very complicated when it came to trying to get the other political forces behind it.

Although at first it was very complicated, I thought that I would have a greater likelihood of success in managing the economic track by opening up space for political negotiation. My interpretation is that this was exactly how it turned out. It seems to me, once again, that one needn't be a genius to see why it was important. If the parties that are in the opposition know that because of the inequity of the electoral rules they are doomed to continue in the opposition, why are they going to feel they have a stake in helping to solve, let's say, the immediate problems? Their bias was going to be negative. So it was important to tell them, "look, we need to secure economic recovery. This is a very serious crisis, but it is a crisis that has a solution. We can recover. And through democratic means we are going to decide who is going to take care of this house in three years in the Congress and six in the presidency."

There were even people in the opposition who said we should not discuss political reform at the time because there was going to be a great deal of blackmail, but the reform was attained because it was in everybody's interest. There was a tactical interest on the part of the government, but to validate a strategy for economic recovery there was also a strategic interest, or there should have been, on the part of the other political parties.

Independent Institutions

At the outset of your administration you appointed a person from the opposition PAN as attorney general of the republic. Some characterized that move as aimed at weakening your party. Can you explain how you conceived of the composition of your administration?

The appointment of the attorney general was a very deliberate decision that I made, and one that people tend not to take fully into account. My first attorney general was not a person whom I knew personally, nor had I ever had a word with him, until I called to ask him to consider it. He was the leader of the PAN legislators in the Chamber of Deputies. When I appointed him, I told him, "you are a totally independent attorney general. I am only to interact with you in two major respects: I must appoint you, and if you are not sufficiently competent, in my view, I can fire you. You are free to perform your functions." When he left office, I appointed another man whom I had met, but I was never close to him, who had been named by my predecessor to chair the Commission on Human Rights, but he was not someone with whom I had any bond. He had an excellent reputation as a jurist and great probity, and when the first attorney general left, I offered it to him. So during my whole presidency I had an independent attorney general, which is also important, as is the question with respect to the judicial branch. Some critics said that I had tied my hands—that in addition to seeking the independence of the judiciary, I also appointed an independent attorney general.

It seems to me, in view of the dramatic situation the country was going through at that time, that it was tactically and strategically important to do two things. I say this because, with the passage of time, some very superficial people have made criticisms. The justice system was independent and the attorney general was independent, and that is something of which I'm very proud because I think that tactically it was necessary. But I also believe that the president's power has to be limited, that the president should no longer have imperial power, that his power should be limited to what is provided for in the constitution. I took it a step beyond the constitution in the case of the attorney general, when I acted on my view that the attorney general should enjoy the freedom necessary to be able to perform his functions.

Some argued at the time that a person from PAN investigating the 1994 assassination of Luis Donaldo Colosio [the PRI presidential candidate] would have greater autonomy. Was that your reasoning?

Well, I wanted an independent attorney general. I didn't want there to be any bias; I didn't name a disorganized activist. I named a jurist who had a reputation for being serious; many people recommended him. Once again there's the issue of credibility: how can we rebuild the credibility of the institutions? Law enforcement and the justice system were totally discredited, so I wanted to see how I could take a step forward to begin to reconstruct credibility in law enforcement and show that the justice system was working.

There are several interpretations of your decision to announce the outcome of the election in 2000, which had not yet been announced, as I understand it, by the IFE to the Mexican people.

No, the result *was* announced first by the IFE. The first to announce it was the chairperson of the IFE. For me this is very clear, because that was an institutional decision. The chair of the IFE, with whom I had spoken three times in my life, did not make his way to the IFE because he was my friend, but because he was a person with an unquestionably good reputation. And one of the few times that we spoke was that night. He told me, "Mr. President, the vote count [referring to the IFE's quick-count program] shows that PAN candidate [Vicente] Fox has won, and the IFE considers that it has a solid basis for announcing the election results."

So I told him, "The IFE has to do what it must do by law, so you have my full respect to make your announcement." I told him that a few minutes after the IFE announcement, I would make a statement in support of the announcement by the IFE because I trust the institution that he represented, and the exit polls that I was being shown were saying the same thing.

And so that's what I did. José Woldenberg [president of the IFE, 1996–2003] spoke, and a few minutes later I appeared in order to say what I had to say. So I didn't jump the gun with respect to the IFE, for that would have been a mistake. It would have negated the whole sense of the reform, which required respecting the IFE's independence to say what it has to say. I did congratulate the president-elect; that's why people remember it more. But the chair of the IFE made the announcement before I did.

But what you did was misunderstood, was it not?

Yes, because some have made a whole myth out of that message. And they forget that, once again, you needn't be a genius. What had to be done was obvious; it was what made sense. If we have an electoral body that can announce the outcome of the presidential election with great certainty, with great assuredness, why shouldn't the president make an appearance to congratulate our next president?

Wasn't there fear that the PRI would have some difficulty accepting the outcome? Did the PRI want to delay the announcement?

Well, I believe that all the parties wanted to ensure they didn't lose, and it's natural for them to say, under the pressure of the moment, perhaps the results will change as the count proceeds. Yet those who look at things with a cold mind know about statistical methodologies, and they know there's no way this will change; it would have to be a totally incredible pattern for the direction of the vote to change.

So it is not true that there was opposition in the PRI to me making an announcement, and the facts are there; the PRI candidate behaved very well that night. I understand that some might have wanted to wait until there was more data, more results, so as to give a bit more time, but it was very clear by that time.

There are many myths about that night, and in some I am given more merit or more criticism than I deserve; appearing as I did was no magical act.

We had worked with all the political parties for six years, so that whether the PRI, PRD, or PAN turned out to be the winner, things would turn out well; that was democratic normalcy. Democratic normalcy was having elections without fighting in the streets the next day over the results. And what happened? We achieved democratic normalcy. I used the term "democratic normalcy" on December 1, 1994, and in the elections almost six years later what did we have? Democratic normalcy. Not just for me, but for everyone.

Social Policy

PROGRESA (Programme for Education, Health, and Nutrition) was an innovative social program, the first of its kind in Latin America, to mitigate the social impacts of the macroeconomic adjustments and to reduce poverty. Can you explain its purpose and the results?

PROGRESA has had a very interesting history. When I was campaigning, I said that we needed to begin to think about the whole question of poverty and education more seriously, more scientifically. The tough nut to crack was that there were population groups in the country that had a school, that had teachers, at times textbooks, special support for the teachers, and there were enough of all these things for children to complete their primary and secondary education. Nonetheless, it wasn't happening.

I asked, "Who has thought about examining the connection between education and poverty?" I was given the name of Santiago Levy, and I also called a very smart friend of mine, a PhD in demographics, José Gómez de León, and I asked them separately to begin to work with some ideas. Pilot tests were done. We spent the equivalent of $10 million in research and experimentation to get to the point of configuring the program's basic characteristics.

The advantage of having had José Gómez de León on the team is that he designed a program application that is a pioneer in the social sciences. It has a control population and an experimental population so as to verify, over time, whether the intervention was having the desired impact.

The candidates of the parties other than the PRI criticized PROGRESA and said that they were going to take it away if they came into the government, that it was a program with a political intention. Just before the end of my term we invited renowned social scientists to evaluate PROGRESA. They concluded that the program was yielding results: it improved children's health, reduced the dropout rate, and a bias we had introduced on behalf of girls was working. On the basis of this analysis, the program was continued by the next administration.

Leadership

Prior to your election in 1994, you were not necessarily thought of as a political leader but rather as a very gifted técnico (technocrat). If one thinks of political leadership as being able to understand the underlying forces and tendencies and how they play out, with a vision of how conditions might be improved and with the will and ability to facilitate positive change, you clearly are somebody who played a very important political leadership role. What prepared you for political leadership?

First, I'm not sure that I was an important political leader. I was just president of Mexico, and before that I had other important responsibilities in my country's government. But let me first say something about this distinction, which is a bit artificial, between politicians and technocrats. When people talk about politicians, I don't really know what attributes they are referring to. If people tell me that by politicians we mean people who have a clear taste for power and the exercise of authority, then you can cross me off the list because I never had any attachment or need to have power or authority. If by politician you mean someone who is attracted by the superficial aspects of having political power, the apparatus, the machinery, people around you who say yes to everything, then I'm not a politician.

If you are talking about someone who is always interacting with many people in public—well, I'm shy by nature, so that's very hard for me, but I do it, and indeed in part I make a living from that now, from talking with people.

Now, if you tell me that a politician is someone who has a vocation for public service, I do fit that part. If a politician is someone who thinks more of the general interest, I am a politician; if it's someone who enjoys political competition, yes, I enjoy it.

It seems to me that the distinction between politician and technocrat is a very artificial distinction that, moreover, does not withstand historical scrutiny. Some of the great politicians may have had very deplorable records of accomplishment, and others don't appear to have the attributes of politicians but turn out to be great political leaders. I think it was Carlos Solchaga, minister of finance in the time of Felipe González [president of the government of Spain, 1982–96], who once provided a definition of technocrat—a politician who knows something, who went to school.

Perhaps I was one of those technocrats then. Now I have been neither technocrat nor politician for the last 12 years. I was a technocrat and it doesn't offend me, just as it doesn't offend me when there are people who say all politicians are bad, and who tell me, "The thing is, you're a politician." And I tell them yes, because politics is one of the great inventions of humankind. There are two things that have enabled us to cease being savages: politics first and, second, diplomacy derived from politics. If there were no politics or diplomacy, we would probably still be living in caves, killing one another.

The technocrat is someone who understands the nature of a problem and what needs to be done, but doesn't necessarily have the skills or the social role to bring together diverse forces to support a common vision. That is precisely what a political leader does. Those are different qualities. It is hard to be good at either, but it is particularly hard to be a good political leader. What can you tell a young person who wishes to contribute to democratic changes with respect to the qualities, capacities, or attitudes that are necessary and that one must cultivate to be a political leader?

Almost every semester I give classes, and there are one or two, at times three, young people who come up to me to tell me that when they finish school they want to dedicate themselves to politics, and they ask me what I think. I tell them that first they are on a good path, because they are getting a good education. But one must recall that this is necessary but not sufficient.

Second, along with education you need the conviction that you want to serve people, without expecting anything in return, because that is politics. If you are an honest politician you may or may not have your salary, but you have to have a conviction in total service and serving the truth. Because, for example, the banker serves but charges for his service, and charges a very good price. One who is in public service should be eager to serve for the sake of serving, to do something for the collective good. If your ambition has to do more with notoriety, being recognized, just get into another area of activity. The vocation for public service is fundamental.

And third, as we live in a democracy in this country and many others, one must understand that politics is like the wheel of fortune: at times you're up and at times you're down; at times you're in government and at other times in the opposition. So you have to analyze whether you have the stomach for being down and up, and not everyone does. There are people who prefer certainty, stability, predictability, and immediate reward; and in politics, in public life, you can't always find that.

Yet the component of preparation is very important; nowadays there are geniuses who can do well in politics, and in government they have the instinct or common sense to do well, and experience helps us perform well. But it is a great risk to have people in positions of responsibility who do not have a well-structured intellectual foundation. It's a great risk, for that person and for citizens, and so we have sad and pathetic cases.

International Context

In Latin America, numerous transitions were concluding at that time. Were those other experiences examined in Mexico?

No, in that regard I think that, once again, Mexico is a special case. It's true that, seen in light of the circumstances of the late 1980s and early 1990s, someone might have said that Mexican democracy was more advanced than Brazilian or Argentine democracy. The truth is that we never made the comparison with Brazil or Argentina because we never ceased to have a formal democracy, regular elections, changes in power. In addition, there is something very important that is in the conscience of Mexico: each time some Latin American country had to suffer these military dictatorships, it was Mexico where people could find a place to live and express themselves. Not just from other parts of Latin America, also in the case of Spain. So we never felt as though we were in the same club as our brothers from Argentina, Brazil, Chile; indeed, it would have been offensive for them, because we enjoyed many liberties that our brothers from the Southern Cone simply did not enjoy, and it is true that there were restrictions, there was manipulation, forms of control, and at times repression in Mexico, but it wasn't at all comparable to the dramatic experiences of South America.

So if in 1990 someone wanted to compare Mexican democracy to Brazilian democracy, they'd say about Brazil, "You're in diapers," because in Mexico we have had orderly, regular, periodic changes in government, elections, etc., and we have had great freedom of the press; in other words, things that sadly did not exist until recently in South America. At that time we still didn't know what was going to happen in Chile—now we know that it has been extraordinary. After 20 years, democratic normalcy was attained, but the truth is, we said, "What if Mr. Pinochet decides the day after tomorrow that no [he would not step down from the presidency]," and moreover he had the mechanisms in place if he had tried to do so. So they were not points of reference.

Contemporary Transitions

In contemporary transitions that are unfolding, one sees that communication technologies, the expansion of the middle classes, and higher levels of education will all have an impact on the new processes of democratization. What are your thoughts about future democratization?

In many parts of the world we are still in transition, and with great doubts as to whether these processes are going to crystallize, at least in a reasonable time. In the last 10 years, in part thanks to an improvement in the terms of trade of many African countries and also due to the growing role of the Chinese economy in the world economy, African countries are seeing improved economic performance, and in some cases this is accompanied by better political systems. Yet there is great doubt as to whether it will be possible to sustain this trend in countries that have an incredibly weak institutional framework. **If there is a lesson from Latin America for these countries it is that perhaps the sequence should begin with constructing the institutional framework as the top priority, because without a solid institutional framework, the risk of policies that are not the right ones, or that may be reversed, is very high.** To some extent that is also the problem in Latin America. We cannot deny that there have been setbacks, that in some countries there has been a concentration of power, effectively doing away with checks and balances, with perhaps subtle, not so brutal, limitations on freedom of expression. So it's too soon to declare victory.

I think that we are still on a risky road, and we shouldn't lower our guard. I am confident, nonetheless, that what has been achieved in terms of citizen awakening—that people know not only how to exercise their rights but how to enjoy them, and that people have made progress in learning to play this game with rules—makes it more difficult for us to have episodes of reverting to more authoritarian or less democratic forms of government, but the temptation is always there.

Crisis of Democracy

In advanced democracies, there are also very serious problems. The ideal of democracy, I would say, is stronger than ever in the history of humankind. But if you ask me whether the model for attaining that ideal of democracy is strong enough, I would say no; that's not the case, even in the developed countries. **When I look around, even at democracy in the United States, I see enormous vulnerabilities; I see flanks on which the democratic ideal may be yielding to the influence of certain private or sectoral interests on the configuration of political power, and in the breakdown of decision-making mechanisms.** This is very worrisome, and I think that the way democracy is working in the United States today does not correspond to the democratic ideal.

The idea is to have government *of* the people and *for* the people. Today, who are those people? Those who can influence the results of the elections by contributing money to the political process? In the case of the United States, this is legal; in the case of other countries, it is illegal, but in both cases it is happening. It doesn't matter to me so much in a long-term perspective that it is legal in the United States; it simply seems to me that it is bad for the health of US democracy, just as it seems to me that it is atrocious when it occurs, as it does, illegally in many other countries of the world, including in Latin America.

International Support

Would you like to add anything on your relationship with President Bill Clinton when he supported financing to assist Mexico through the crisis of 1994–95?

I enjoyed the benefit of having a man as intelligent and visionary as President Clinton as my counterpart in the United States. The first time I mentioned to him that we were having serious problems, I was already convinced that this crisis wasn't like others. I told him that this is not just a matter of fiscal or monetary adjustment; this has elements of panic, but it may be something much bigger, it may be systemic. He did not have enough information and he had not yet reached that conclusion. He said he would speak with his advisers on the matter, Treasury Secretary Robert Rubin and his deputy, Larry Summers. Two or three days later he called and told me, "They say you may be right, and I think you are right. This is different. You must do your work. But you also need the support of the international community, beginning with your main partner." In two days, literally, Clinton realized that, and was ready to help. So it was really great luck to have him as my counterpart.

Can international actors constructively contribute to building democratic governance?

Clearly, the geopolitical shake-ups in the world and international events do influence whether or not democratic gains can take place. One cannot deny that communications technology influences how rapidly people can find out what is happening in the world; this has to be taken into account and influences the course of events. As to whether organizations or institutions that promote democracy around the world may have some influence, I would say they can, but frankly it's marginal. If the conditions, aspirations, movements, and leadership for democracy are not present in a country, then practically nothing that comes from outside will make any difference. Now, **if internal conditions are tending to coalesce, the international community can no doubt play a positive role. Yet from my point of view this role will always be subsidiary and secondary, a complement.** In addition one must be very careful, because on occasion the attempt to intervene may end up betraying the purpose of democracy building.

We should never underestimate the nationalism of any country. It's not that I believe strongly in nationalism, yet it is a reality. Nationalism that has been created in some cases for political or cultural reasons, in others artificially, is a real factor. Yet in addition there is a history of imperialism, of interventionism, of double standards, of governments that on the one hand say they are going to intervene in order to support democracy but at the same time support authoritarian regimes, so one must be very careful with this issue. For me, the main point is that what is not born from within is not going to prosper.

So I believe in internationalism and cooperation. I believe that the countries that are trying to work for a better future should be supported, but they should not be supported against their will; the people within have to find their own path to democracy.

....

Time Line

Feb. 1917: The Mexican constitution, enacted during the Mexican Revolution, provides for democracy and extensive social rights.

Mar. 1929: Outgoing President Plutarco Elías Calles founds the Partido Nacional Revolucionario (National Revolutionary Party, or PNR), a broad coalition of revolutionaries that dominates elections at all levels. In 1946, PNR is succeeded by the (similar) Partido Revolucionario Institucional (Institutional Revolutionary Party, or PRI).

Sep. 1939: Conservatives opposed to the PRI's leftist, anticlerical policies found the Partido de Acción Nacional (National Action Party, or PAN). Although PAN initially wins few elections, it becomes the largest opposition party over the coming decades.

Oct. 1968: Following two months of student protests for free speech and government accountability, the Army fires on and kills demonstrators in Mexico City.

Jul. 1976: When internal feuds in PAN prevent it from running a candidate, the PRI's José López Portillo is elected president unopposed.

Dec. 1977: The PRI enacts electoral reforms, easing registration for opposition parties and introducing a proportional representation system that is more favorable to small parties.

Sep. 1982: Lopez Portillo nationalizes banks; the middle class reacts strongly against the decision.

Sep. 1985: A major earthquake strikes Mexico City. The PRI government response is widely criticized as slow; many new civic groups emerge to provide relief and social services.

Jul. 1986: The evidence suggests that PAN rightfully wins the Chihuahua gubernatorial election, but that the results are manipulated by the PRI. PAN begins advocating forcefully for fair elections.

Mar. 1987: Cuauhtémoc Cárdenas, a left-leaning PRI politician and son of former President Lázaro Cárdenas, calls for intraparty democracy to confront the PRI's economically neoliberal wing.

Oct. 1987: Cárdenas is passed over for presidential nomination in favor of Carlos Salinas de Gortari, a Harvard-trained economist and former budget and planning minister. Cárdenas launches a presidential campaign outside the PRI criticizing the PRI's authoritarianism and neoliberal economic policies.

Jul. 1988: Early election results suggest that the PRI may lose and that Cárdenas could win the presidency, but the PRI maintains control after a nationwide power failure requires a change to hand-counted ballots. Despite apparent fraud, the PRI presidential vote falls in the official count from 74% to 51%; it wins only 260 of 500 seats in the House of Deputies.

Dec. 1988: Salinas is inaugurated. In office, he promotes liberal economic reforms and social welfare programs. Some reforms require opposition support to amend the constitution. Salinas initiates limited political reforms in negotiations with PAN: an independent Electoral Commission, more equitable media coverage, and legal recognition for the Church.

May 1989: Cárdenas and his allies found the leftist Partido de la Revolución Democrática (Party of the Democratic Revolution, or PRD). They encounter persistent harassment from government in the following years.

Jul. 1989: PAN wins the gubernatorial election in the state of Baja California Norte, the first time an opposition party wins a state government from the PRI.

Jun. 1990: Formal negotiations begin over the North American Free Trade Agreement (NAFTA) Salinas has promoted. Some US leaders argue that the treaty should require improvement in Mexican political and labor rights.

Aug. 1991: Salinas forces several winning PRI gubernatorial candidates who are accused of fraud to resign. He appoints successors via negotiations with PAN. This pattern continues throughout the decade, giving PAN control of some states, but the PRI refuses to negotiate with PRD.

Jan. 1994: NAFTA comes into effect. Leftist, ethnically indigenous Zapatista National Liberation Army (Ejército Zapatista de Liberación Nacional, or

EZLN) guerrillas known as Zapatistas emerge. Salinas promises campaign finance and electoral reforms in exchange for the opposition denouncing EZLN.

Mar. 1994: PRI presidential candidate Luis Donaldo Colosio is assassinated while campaigning. Few other PRI leaders are eligible to run; Salinas selects former secretary of budget and planning and of education, Ernesto Zedillo (Colosio's campaign manager), as the new candidate.

Aug. 1994: Zedillo is elected with 49% of the vote in a record turnout. PAN wins 26%, and Cárdenas's PRD wins 17%. The elections are generally regarded as mostly clean, although the PRI benefits from many state resources.

Sep. 1994: PRI secretary general José Francisco Ruiz Massieu is assassinated. An investigation later reveals that his murder was plotted by Carlos Salinas's brother Raúl; Raúl's conviction breaks the precedent of immunity for important PRI figures.

Dec. 1994: Upon taking office, Zedillo promises electoral reforms, introduces a constitutional amendment to strengthen judicial independence, and appoints PAN's Fernando Antonio Lozano Gracia as attorney general. Within three weeks, the value of the peso plummets, currency reserves drop, and the government is forced to enact harsh budget cuts.

Feb. 1995: The Clinton administration assembles $50 billion in loans to stabilize Mexico's economy.

Mar. 1995: Congress creates a multiparty commission, including PAN and the previously marginalized PRD, to negotiate with EZLN.

Nov. 1996: Negotiations stall on electoral reforms promised in 1994. The PRI unilaterally passes many proposals for reform: more equitable media and campaign finance laws, a more independent electoral commission, and a directly elected Mexico City mayor.

Jul. 1997: In mostly fair midterm elections, PRD and PAN win a combined congressional majority, giving them control over policy and spending. Zedillo expands cooperation with both parties. Cuauhtémoc Cárdenas is elected mayor of Mexico City.

Aug. 1997: The Zedillo administration launches the Programme for Education, Health, and Nutrition (PROGRESA), a major antipoverty program. It is independently administered, selects recipients transparently, and is regularly evaluated, making it hard to manipulate for political purposes.

Jul. 1998: The PRI wins back the Chihuahua state governorship from PAN after selecting its candidate through its first-ever primary election, helping PRI reformists convince the party to hold a presidential primary the next year.

Jul. 2000: PAN presidential candidate and Guanajuato Governor Vicente Fox defeats Cárdenas and the PRI's Francisco Labastida to become the first president in over 70 years from outside the PRI and its precursors. PRD's Andrés Manuel Lopez Obrador is elected Mexico City mayor.

Aug. 2000: The Supreme Court issues landmark limits on the power of the executive branch.

Jul. 2006: PAN's Felipe Calderón narrowly defeats Lopez Obrador in the presidential election; the PRI finishes third. Lopez Obrador refuses to accept the results, which he attributes to fraud.

Jul. 2012: The PRI's Enrique Peña Nieto is elected president, defeating Lopez Obrador. PAN places third.

GUIDE TO FURTHER READING

Aguayo Quezada, Sergio. "Electoral Observation and Democracy in Mexico." In *Electoral Observation and Democratic Transition in Latin America*, edited by Kevin J. Middlebrook. Boulder, Colo.: Lynne Rienner, 1998. By a leading civil society activist.

Aristegui, Carmen, and Ricardo Trabulsi, eds. *Transición: Conversaciones y Retratos de lo Que se Hizo y se Dejó de Hacer por la Democracia en México* [Transition: Conversations and portraits of what was done and what was not done for Mexican democracy]. Mexico City: Random House Mondadori, 2010.

Becerra, Ricardo, Pedro Salazar, and José Woldenberg, eds. *La Mecánica del Cambio Político en México: Elecciones, Partidos y Reformas* [The mechanics of political change in Mexico: Elections, parties and reforms]. Mexico City: Editorial Aguilar, 2000.

Bruhn, Kathleen, Daniel C. Levy, and Emilio Zebadúa. *Mexico: The Struggle for Democratic Development*. Berkeley: University of California Press, 2006.

Centeno, Miguel Angel. *Democracy within Reason: Technocratic Revolution in Mexico*. University Park: Pennsylvania State University Press, 1994.

Eisenstadt, Todd A. *Courting Democracy in Mexico: Party Strategies and Electoral Institutions*. New York: Cambridge University Press, 2004.

Fox, Jonathan. "The Difficult Transition from Clientelism to Citizenship: Lessons from Mexico." *World Politics* 46, no. 2 (1994): 151–84.

Greene, Kenneth F. *Why Dominant Parties Lose: Mexico's Democratization in Comparative Perspective*. New York: Cambridge University Press, 2007.

Loaeza, Soledad. *El Partido Acción Nacional: La Larga Marcha, 1939-1994: Oposición Leal y Partido de Protesta* [The National Action Party: The long march, 1939-1994. Loyal opposition and party of protest]. Mexico City: Fondo de Cultura Económica, 1999.

Lujambio, Alonso. *El Poder Compartido: Un Ensayo Sobre la Democratización Mexicana* [Power shared: An essay on Mexican democratization]. Mexico City: Océano, 2000.

Magaloni, Beatriz. *Voting for Autocracy: Hegemonic Party Survival and Its Demise in Mexico*. Stanford, Calif.: Stanford University Press, 2008.

Mazza, Jacqueline. *Don't Disturb the Neighbors: The United States and Democracy in Mexico, 1980-1995*. New York: Routledge, 2002.

Middlebrook, Kevin J., ed. *Dilemmas of Political Change in Mexico*. Washington, D.C.: Brookings Institution Press, 2004. See especially Ai Camp on the military and Lawson on the media.

Preston, Julia, and Samuel Dillon. *Opening Mexico: The Making of a Democracy*. New York: Farrar, Straus and Giroux, 2004.

Ríos-Figueroa, Julio. "Fragmentation of Power and the Emergence of an Effective Judiciary in Mexico, 1994-2002." *Latin American Politics and Society* 49, no. 1 (2007): 31–57.

Selee, Andrew, and Jacqueline Peschard, eds. *Mexico's Democratic Challenges: Politics, Government, and Society.* Washington, D.C.: Woodrow Wilson International Center for Scholars; Stanford, Calif.: Stanford University Press, 2010.

Shirk, David A. *Mexico's New Politics: The PAN and Democratic Change.* Boulder, Colo.: Lynne Rienner, 2005.

Trejo, Guillermo. *Popular Movements in Autocracies: Religion, Repression, and Indigenous Collective Action in Mexico.* New York: Cambridge University Press, 2012.

Chapter 6

THE PHILIPPINES

....

The Philippines: "People Power," a Troubled Transition, and "Good Governance"

MARK R. THOMPSON

"People power" overthrew the dictatorship of Ferdinand E. Marcos in the Philippines nearly 30 years ago, which put this Southeast Asian country in the international spotlight. The protest by millions of Filipinos drawn from all social classes—who dramatically held off a government military assault—was broadcast live to a worldwide television audience from February 22 to 25, 1986. Known in the Philippines as EDSA (after Epifanio de los Santos Avenue, the major avenue on which the largest crowds gathered), this uprising influenced a number of other popular revolts against dictatorships in Asia and beyond. South Korean activists in 1987-88, Burmese protesters in 1988, and Chinese students in 1989 all drew inspiration from the Philippine example. Even Václav Havel, the revolutionary idol of the Czechoslovakian uprising in 1989 and later president of the Czech Republic, said during a 1995 visit to the Philippines that people power had been an inspiration to him and his fellow Eastern European dissidents. People power has come to symbolize a peaceful, spontaneous popular revolt that topples an unbending dictatorship. It also presented a challenge to the literature on democratization that, initially focused on South American and southern European examples, had stressed the importance of pacted transitions between regime soft-liners and opposition moderates. People power showed that it was possible to overthrow an unpopular authoritarian ruler without a violent revolution.

Although he became a dictator, Marcos had assumed power as an elected president (he was first voted into office in 1965 and then, more controversially, reelected in 1969). His imposition of martial rule in September 1972, shortly before his second term expired, put an end to the longest electoral tradition in Asia. Some local elections had been held during the late 19th century during the Spanish colonial period, and there was a president and legislature during the short-lived period of independence under the First Philippine Republic (1899–1901). National legislative elections were held in 1907, shortly after the US conquest of the Philippines, which began an unusual experiment in "colonial democracy." Aside from the period of Japanese occupation (1942–45), regular elections were held until independence in 1946. In 1935, the United States established the Philippine Commonwealth, which involved the election of a president and a bicameral Congress. In the post–World War II independence period, presidential elections were held every four years and congressional elections every two years. Two major political parties, the Nacionalistas and the Liberals, competed for political power in fair (if sometimes violent and often expensive) elections; the presidency regularly changed hands between them. Yet the two parties were weak, highly clientelist, and lacked definitive platforms. Politicians often switched sides just before elections. After Marcos's declaration of martial law, one journalist described the Philippines as a "shattered showcase of democracy."

The Impact of Martial Law

The advent of authoritarian rule also occurred at a time when the Philippines seemed poised for economic "takeoff." Marcos—like his South Korea authoritarian counterpart Park Chung-hee, who also declared martial law in 1972—promised rapid economic development. He claimed that to improve the economy, "peace and order," which had frayed in the late 1960s, had to be restored. After the decline of the Hukbalahap (the so-called Huks) Communist-led insurgency in the 1950s, a new Maoist-oriented Communist Party of the Philippines (CPP) was formed along with its armed wing, the New People's Army (NPA), and began waging guerrilla war in outlying rural areas. In the capital, Manila, radical students (some of whom were linked to the CPP) engaged in violent antigovernment protests, the most famous of which were known as the First Quarter Storm in 1970. In the southwest of the country, where the country's Muslim minority is concentrated, a Muslim secessionist movement, led by the Moro National Liberation Front (MNLF), had begun. After martial law was declared, a brutal, full-scale (though little known) war broke out in Mindanao, which resulted in as many as 100,000 deaths. The Philippine military engaged in wide-scale bombing and carried out a bloody anti-insurgency campaign before a temporary ceasefire was arranged under the controversial Tripoli agreement in 1976. The CPP-NPA was largely pushed out of the cities and put on the defensive in the countryside.

Marcos also neutralized political rivals from the landed Philippine oligarchy, led by the Lopez brothers (Fernando Lopez was Marcos's estranged vice president, and Eugenio Lopez was one of the richest tycoons in the Philippines). This opposition elite also included Benigno S. Aquino Jr., who was the son of a famous politician (who served as vice president during the Japanese occupation) and married to Corazon "Cory" Cojuangco Aquino, an heiress to one of the country's largest sugar plantations. Benigno Aquino, as a young opposition senator, had emerged as Marcos's most outspoken pre-martial law political rival. Aquino and a number of other leading opposition politicians were imprisoned under martial rule, and Marcos confiscated businesses from several oligarch opponents, including the Lopezes. Other politicians and big businesspeople quickly decided it was better to collaborate with Marcos than to oppose his authoritarian rule.

The Philippines made rapid economic gains during the early years of Marcos's authoritarianism. Exports were up as Marcos encouraged foreign investment. Technocrats stabilized the economy, launched a massive infrastructure drive, and drew up plans for 11 major industrial projects that were designed to push the country toward industrialization and make it the next Asian "tiger" economy. Much-needed (and overdue) land reform also began. To pay for these ambitious undertakings, Marcos borrowed freely from international markets awash in petrodollars after the oil price increases in 1973. The Philippines' foreign debt rose from $3.8 billion in 1975 to $12.7 billion in 1980.

It soon became evident, however, that Marcos was not an "authoritarian developmentalist" leader of the same caliber as South Korea's Park. A lawyer-politician rather than a soldier-nationalist, Marcos did not distance himself from his loyalists; he ultimately favored them over his technocrats. Instead of using rigorous performance criteria to ensure the country's export performance despite close business-state ties—as Park had insisted on when giving state subsidies to giant conglomerates (*chaebols*) in South Korea—Marcos apportioned large sectors of the economy to his family and friends (or "cronies"). Most Marcos cronies turned out to be inept capitalists who racked up debts in mismanaged enterprises. Land reform stalled, while monopolies in sugar and coconuts impoverished many cultivators. The flight of financier Dewey Dee in 1981 with 700 million pesos in bad debts revealed the shaky state of the crony-dominated economy. The Marcos regime was beginning to unravel.

The Aquino Assassination and Growing Opposition

The assassination of opposition leader Benigno Aquino in August 1983 at the Manila airport, as he was attempting to return from exile, turned economic decline into a full-scale financial meltdown. Revelations that the Central Bank had falsified the country's financial records (much as Greece would be caught doing 25 years later) led to capital flight and caused the Philippine peso to plummet, inflation to skyrocket, and the government to ask for a debt moratorium; the country now owed over $25 billion. The government was forced to accept an International Monetary Fund austerity program in exchange for a bailout. The result was severe economic contraction: gross domestic product (GDP) declined by 15% in just 2 years.

Beginning with a massive funeral procession for Aquino, which included an estimated two million mourners, antigovernment demonstrations proliferated. The first demonstration in the metro Manila business district of

Makati in mid-September 1983, which involved 100,000 (well-dressed) office workers, signaled the business community's discontent with the Marcos regime. Big business, once supportive of Marcos, had begun to turn against him with the rise of cronyism and became openly hostile after the massive financial crisis following the Aquino assassination. Business leaders worked closely with Catholic bishops, led by Manila Archbishop Jaime Cardinal Sin, who had become outspoken in his criticism of human rights violations after the Church abandoned its policy of "critical collaboration" with the regime. They were joined by pre-martial law politicians opposed to Marcos and newly founded "cause-oriented" groups led by middle-class activists. Women's groups were also prominent in the protests, although they were often divided along ideological lines between moderate and leftwing activists. There were also "mass organizations" under CPP leadership, which (having survived heavy repression during the early martial law period) had a rapidly growing base of rural fighters and urban activists. Alternative print and radio media emerged after the Aquino assassination, circumventing government censorship. Even the US government, which had once strongly backed Marcos, given his anticommunist stance and the two major US military bases in the country, began to distance itself from the regime.

"Snap Elections" and the Fall of Marcos

With Marcos unwilling to resign or arrange a transition to democracy (e.g., as rulers of more institutionalized military regimes in South America, such as Brazil, had done), the opposition began to search for a new strategy. One group—composed of politicians backed by the Catholic Church and big business—decided to participate in legislative elections in mid-1984 despite Marcos's past record of electoral manipulation. Although many candidates were cheated, a surprising number of opposition candidates won, which gave them a psychological boost although their power as a minority in the National Assembly was limited. Another group had boycotted the polls and was working to unify "cause-oriented groups." But because of the Communists' insistence on a Leninist-style leadership of the "parliament of the streets," these efforts failed by mid-1985, resulting in a break between the Communist and noncommunist opposition forces. When Marcos—under pressure from the United States and the country's continued economic woes—called a "snap" presidential election for February 1986, all major national opposition groups (except the Communists) decided to participate.

The snap election caught the opposition flat-footed, as it was divided between parties, party coalitions (the biggest coalition was led by Aquino's future vice presidential candidate Salvador "Doy" Laurel), and activist groups. Under pressure from the Catholic Church and big business for the opposition to unite, Corazon "Cory" Cojuangco Aquino (Benigno Aquino's widow) was chosen as the presidential candidate despite her political inexperience and because of the "moral capital" she enjoyed as a "simple housewife" promising to carry on her husband's "struggle for justice and democracy." Like many dynastic female leaders in Asia (such as Aung San Suu Kyi in Burma or Megawati Soekarnoputri in Indonesia) who inherited the charisma of their "martyred" fathers or husbands, Cory was seen as a less self-interested politician who was not caught up in the Machiavellian struggles typical of her male counterparts. Millions attended her campaign rallies around the country, braving government goons and lining up for hours to vote on Election Day due to deliberate delays in the balloting. The National Citizens' Movement for Free Elections, an election watchdog group backed by big business that mobilized hundreds of volunteers, the Catholic Church and civil society groups monitored the polling and produced an independent electoral count showing Aquino had won the election. Marcos's blatant manipulation of the final result embittered robbed voters, who could now be easily mobilized against the regime.

The people power revolution that ousted Marcos was sparked by a failed coup attempt by military rebels who were angered by Marcos's personalization of the military (he had promoted his cousin and former chauffeur, Fabian Ver, to be chief of staff of the armed forces). Facing annihilation by government soldiers and tanks, hundreds of thousands of Manileños, backed by the Catholic Church and cause-oriented groups, rallied around the military rebels. Two defectors from the Marcos government—Defense Minister Juan Ponce Enrile and chief of the Philippine Constabulary and vice chief of staff of the armed forces, General Fidel V. Ramos, who later became the second post-Marcos president—led the dissidents. After a four-day standoff, Marcos fled the Philippines in a helicopter provided by the United States as a final step in a concerted American effort to get the Philippine president to step down from power (Marcos later claimed he was kidnapped by the Americans). The uprising marginalized the Communist opposition, which had boycotted the polls and was absent from people power. Cory Aquino, sworn in as president on the last day of the uprising, assumed emergency powers after Marcos fled, abolishing his constitution, replacing local government officials, and ruling by decree. She arranged for a constitutional commission to write a new basic law that restored a "strong" presidential system with extensive executive powers but also clear guarantees for civil liberties. The draft constitution was approved by referendum, and Aquino set local and national legislative elections (with a bicameral legislature as in the pre–martial law days) for May 1987.

Cory Aquino and a Troubled Transition to Democracy

But the collapse of the coalition between opposition politicians and military rebels who turned against Cory Aquino destabilized the government. After trying to overthrow Marcos, the Enrile–Reform the Armed Forces Movement

(RAM) faction felt cheated of power by Aquino and the civilian politicians who dominated her cabinet, and was angered by overtures made to the Communists and Muslim rebel groups. The Aquino government's early promise to investigate human rights violations was also threatening, as several RAM leaders had been notorious torturers. There were a total of nine coup attempts against the Aquino administration. A military rebellion led by RAM nearly toppled the government in December 1989. The Aquino administration survived as it moved to the right on security, human rights, and social issues (watering down land reform followed by a police shooting of peaceful peasant demonstrators marching toward the presidential palace in January 1987). It also relied heavily on Chief of Staff of the Armed Forces (and later Secretary of Defense) Fidel Ramos to reunite the military in support of civilian rule. Cory's government attempted to recover Marcos's stolen wealth and promised to follow the principles of good governance. The economy gradually stabilized, thanks to macroeconomic reforms undertaken by technocrats to dismantle crony monopolies, lower inflation, and deal with the country's debt burden. The legislative elections of 1987, though marred by violence and dominated by dynastic politicians, were largely free and fair, luring politicians of different political stripes—including Marcos loyalists—back into the electoral arena. In the 1987 congressional election, 62% of representatives elected had relatives in elective office; by the 2001 polls, the number of dynastic politicians in the lower house had risen to 66%. Term limits enacted in the 1987 constitution did not dent clan power, as the wives and children of leading politicians were often elected as their successors. Elections are expensive and often violent, particularly at the local level. But "warlord" politicians remain a relatively isolated (if well-publicized) phenomenon, and votes are seldom simply bought. Philippine elections are competitive and voters are independent minded; well-known political families are often defeated at the local or national level when they became unpopular. But even post-Marcos presidents have often been dynasts: Gloria Macapagal-Arroyo was a president's daughter, and the current president, Benigno "Noynoy" S. Aquino III, is the son of President Cory Aquino.

Democratic Consolidation under Ramos

Ramos's presidency led to the consolidation of Philippine democracy. This was a remarkable achievement, given his narrow victory in the 1992 presidential polls, in which he won less than a quarter of the total votes. Although chosen by Aquino as her successor, Ramos was unable to secure the presidential nomination of what was then the largest political party, Laban ng Demokrat-ing Pilipino (Fight of Democratic Filipinos), led by House Speaker Ramon Mitra. Instead, he founded his own party (further weakening the country's fragmented party system). He appealed to voters on the basis of his military professionalism, loyalty to the Aquino administration, and a promise to carry out further reforms. His closest rival turned out to be a hard-driving anticorruption candidate, Miriam Defensor-Santiago, indicating that the public's concern had shifted away from the fear of authoritarianism to worries about growing corruption in the country's new democratic institutions. Ramos instituted a series of economic reforms focused on deregulation and the privatization of underperforming government assets, which many economists credit with putting the Philippines back on the path of economic growth—through a burgeoning service sector rather than through industrialization. Ramos also restored political stability, securing a peace agreement with the MNLF and negotiating with Communist insurgents and military rebels. Ramos's image as a reformist was so strong that a corruption scandal (the so-called PEA-Amari deal) did not significantly dent his popularity. The Asian financial crisis of 1997–98, although it did not hit the Philippines as hard as other East Asian countries, reversed a number of financial gains made during the Ramos administration, however.

Renewed Instability during the Estrada and Arroyo Presidencies

Although the Philippines' next president, the movie star turned politician Joseph E. Estrada, easily won the 1998 elections, his presidency proved to be much more turbulent than Ramos's. Estrada had successfully wooed the Philippine *masa* (the poor masses) with a persona forged during his years as an action star by transferring his celluloid image as a fighter for the poor onto the political stage. His populist narrative as a friend of the friendless poor was the basis of his 1998 campaign slogan "Erap for the poor." Estrada drew strength from what had been Aquino's and Ramos's greatest weakness: their inability to substantially improve the living standards of the vast majority of Filipinos who remained poor. Although the economy had improved at the macro level, poverty remained widespread, with unemployment (and underemployment) stubbornly high. But Estrada's pro-poor populist narrative, his ties to the old Marcos administration, his broken English, and his openly "immoral" lifestyle antagonized elites and much of the middle class. The Catholic Church and business sector, along with much of the press, became leading critics of his administration. A major gambling scandal prompted many civil society groups to abandon Estrada and led to his impeachment in the lower house. When the Senate failed to convict him, however, a second people power movement formed, this time made up almost exclusively of middle-class protesters and directed against a freely and fairly elected president. The military's euphemistically termed "withdrawal of support" led to a "people power coup" that was sanctioned by the Supreme Court in a controversial ruling. When a few months later Estrada's successor as president, former Vice President Gloria Macapagal-Arroyo, ordered his arrest for corruption, hundreds of thousands of his poor supporters turned out for yet another people power uprising. This "revenge of the masses" had to be suppressed by military force, saving the Arroyo administration but revealing how fragile its legitimacy was.

Arroyo, a trained economist, built on Ramos's macroeconomic reforms to inaugurate a period of high economic growth that has continued for over a decade as of this writing. But her administration's robust economic performance did not buy her political popularity with the poor. This was brought to a head when Estrada's friend and fellow actor Fernando Poe Jr. announced his candidacy for the 2004 presidential election. He faced Arroyo, who (breaking an earlier promise not to run for president) declared her candidacy in defense of the reforms she had undertaken. Although scorned by the elite media and the middle class, Poe, like Estrada, was very popular among ordinary Filipinos. Most wealthy Filipinos greeted Arroyo's victory by over a million votes with relief. A year later, however, the "Hello Garci" scandal, in which Arroyo was caught on tape discussing the electoral manipulation of the 2004 national election with then–Election Commissioner Virgilio Garcillano, revealed the extent of cheating in the balloting. Arroyo's credibility was further undermined by several high-profile scandals, many of which were linked to her husband. Reformists in her cabinet resigned, and civil society activists took to the streets to demand she step down from the presidency. Several military coup plots were hatched. Her popularity ratings plummeted to the lowest level of any post-Marcos president. Arroyo survived only by using political patronage to block impeachment efforts, pampering the top military brass, and winning over key Catholic bishops (whose resolve was weakened by internal divisions, sex scandals, and the material privileges given to leading several top Churchmen dubbed "Malacañang bishops" after the presidential palace). Arroyo's last year in office was marred by the killing of 57 people, including 34 journalists, who had accompanied an opposition candidate's wife as she attempted to register her husband's candidacy for governor. The Maguindanao massacre, orchestrated by the notorious Ampatuan political clan, occurred far from Manila in southern Mindanao. But it was soon linked to the Arroyo administration through her earlier backing of this warlord family as part of an anti-insurgency drive against Muslim secessionists and because of the Ampatuan's crucial role in the ballot box stuffing that ensured Arroyo's "reelection" in the 2004 presidential polls.

The Son Also Rises: Noynoy Aquino's Presidency

The outpouring of national grief that followed Cory Aquino's death from colon cancer in 2009 led to the surprising emergence of her son, Benigno "Noynoy" Aquino III, previously a low-profile first-term senator, as the leading opposition candidate for president. Although Arroyo was constitutionally barred from seeking reelection, Noynoy Aquino effectively used her administration as a foil for his campaign, promising that if corruption were eliminated, poverty would be as well. After winning an easy victory in the 2010 presidential polls, Noynoy promised good governance, helped rebrand the Philippines abroad (with major financial rating agencies providing investment upgrades), and maintained his high opinion poll ratings at home. Neither Aquino himself nor his immediate family has been linked to any major scandals (Aquino has remained a bachelor in office, with no spouse to become a lightning rod for corruption allegations such as Imelda Marcos or Mike Arroyo). But malfeasance in government remains endemic, smuggling has worsened, and local syndicates continue to thrive. At the same time, major structural problems—such as jobless growth, high poverty rates (despite a conditional cash transfer scheme), and the relative decline of manufacturing—remain largely unaddressed. A major pork barrel scandal in 2013 raised the question of whether Aquino has run into a narrative trap: promising reform while using patronage to pass his reformist measures. Even Aquino's great successes, such as the removal of Supreme Court Chief Justice Renato Corona on corruption charges, were apparently only made possible through a generous allocation of presidential patronage to legislators. Nonetheless, Aquino retains the support of key strategic groups in Philippine society (the Catholic Church, big business, many civil society activists, and much of the media and the military). His popularity ratings have remained relatively high and have not declined abruptly, as Arroyo's did after a series of scandals.

From a Troubled Transition to Good Governance?

Philippine people power—in which mass demonstrations in support of a military rebellion brought down the Marcos dictatorship after the stolen 1986 election—led to a troubled transition to democracy. Dissidents in the armed forces who had turned against her administration nearly toppled Cory Aquino's government. While Fidel Ramos was able to bring the military under civilian control during his administration, another period of instability occurred after his presidency. Joseph Estrada was overthrown by an elite-led repetition of people power, although this time is was against an elected president who was popular among the poor. Estrada's successor, Gloria Macapagal-Arroyo, suffered from a legitimacy crisis after taking power in an extraconstitutional manner and then manipulating the 2004 presidential election to "defeat" Estrada's friend and fellow actor-politician, Fernando Poe Jr. But the unpopular Arroyo survived renewed coup attempts and served out her term. This set the stage for the 2010 landslide election of Noynoy Aquino in what was probably the freest and fairest post-Marcos Philippine presidential election.

Noynoy Aquino won the presidency on a promise to return the country to the straight path of good governance and to fulfill the promises of people power embodied by his mother, Cory Aquino. There is little doubt that the Philippines' nearly three decades of democratic transition have seen improved governance in terms of stable macroeconomic policies and serious efforts (although often with limited effect) to reduce corruption. The role of technocrats has been enhanced, economic growth has been rapid, inflation is low, and the country's debt burden has been reduced. A new group of tycoons has emerged with investments concentrated in the rapidly growing service sector, overshadowing the old oligarchy, whose wealth was based on landholdings and basic industry.

But post-Marcos economic governance has failed to reduce poverty and unemployment. This is why even a successful reformist president can be succeeded by a populist, as happened when Estrada took office after Fidel Ramos, whose time in office is generally thought to mark the golden age of political reform in the post-Marcos period. Estrada's strong support among poor voters who swept him into the presidency in 1998 was a product of Ramos's failure, despite his reforms, to do much for the impoverished majority of Filipinos. Estrada's overthrow illustrated the extent of elite distrust of his populism. It seems that the Philippine middle and upper classes are prepared to tolerate populist challenges for power. This may lead to electoral cycling, in which measures to increase economic efficiency through macroeconomic stability and good governance compete with efforts to decrease inequality through job creation and social welfare as the main policy goals of the Philippines' democratic political system.

Biosketch of Fidel V. Ramos, President of the Philippines 1992–98

PHOTO: JAY DIRECTO / SCANPIX

Fidel Ramos is a professional soldier who exercised senior responsibilities in the armed forces and police during the long dictatorship of Ferdinand Marcos, his distant cousin, who ruled the country under martial law from 1972 to 1986. Educated at the US Military Academy at West Point, with a master's degree in civil engineering from the University of Illinois, Ramos served in the Philippine Army and saw active duty in Korea and Vietnam. His role in the Philippine transition derived from his personal stature within the Philippine armed forces; his timely support for Corazon ("Cory") Aquino and the people's power movement that rose in protest in 1986 against the increasingly repressive and corrupt Marcos regime; his close relations with the United States, especially in the Pentagon, where he was known as "Steady Eddie"; and his positive reputation in the Filipino business community.

First as chief of staff of the armed forces and then as Aquino's minister of defense, General Ramos worked behind the scenes to quash several attempted military coups against her. He was elected president in 1992 as Aquino's designated successor with only 24% of the vote in a 7-candidate race, but he quickly built broader popular support with development and infrastructure programs, such as constructing new power stations to end the frequent brownouts that plagued Manila. Ramos extended amnesty to military coup leaders, repealed the antisubversive law of 1981 and thus legalized the Communist Party, and reached out to engage both Communist and Muslim insurgents. He also accommodated himself to traditional Filipino patronage politics while respecting the national cultural legitimacy of democratic institutions.

The Philippines has managed 20 years of contested and generally fair elections, with an alternation of governing authorities, although there has been little change in its underlying oligarchic structure, weak parties and political institutions, and extensive corruption. Some Filipinos criticize Ramos's tolerance for corruption and military insubordination, and for the return to political life of the Marcos family and other traditional oligarchs. But most Filipinos give Ramos credit for reducing the country's political violence, strengthening the democratic processes that were restored under Cory Aquino, and fostering the country's robust economic growth.

....

Interview with President Fidel V. Ramos

Efforts to build democratic governance in countries with authoritarian pasts are occurring around the world. What can people in these countries learn from the experience in the Philippines?

Are people in the Middle East and North Africa willing to listen? They have their own mind-sets and their own cultures. If you look at Syria right now, and before that Libya and Egypt, they could not learn our "lessons" in just 24 hours. They are still fighting their problems.

In the Philippines, we did our regime change in four days, peacefully. Nobody got killed. We tried to record that for our own benefit here. The successors must always build from the lessons learned and the successes (and even the failures) of their predecessors. That is the point of what I am trying to do in the Fidel Ramos Development Foundation. Our main product is a book program. I took it upon myself, after retiring from the presidency, to write about my experiences as much as I could, or to get the help of friends to record them for the sake of the younger ones.

Leadership

It is hard to put these things in a capsule, but good governance and enlightened leadership must be homegrown, because they cannot be outsourced. I could not import Mahathir [prime minister 1981–2003] of Malaysia to run the government of the Philippines, nor could he import me. Nor could I import Patricio Aylwin [president 1990–94] from Chile.

The general principles are good governance and enlightened leadership or visionary leadership, which must lead the way forward with a vision of at least 25 years into the future. We cannot do all that needs to be done during the six-year term of a Philippine president or the eight-year term of a reelected US president. These terms are too short to accomplish all that needs to be done. You have to visualize, be active and imaginative, and have a plan for what happens to water, what happens to energy, what happens to the infrastructure, what happens to education, etc. This is what it means to be a transformational leader—someone who can inspire people with their visions to undertake "bold, transformational change."[1] They can turn crises into "turning points in the nation's life."[2]

This was my mind-set because I had been in government since 1946. I entered government service as a cadet in the US Military Academy as the Philippine representative at 18 years of age. It was a war-torn era. The southern part of Manila was totally devastated by the liberation of the city, which was defended by the Japanese and of course attacked by the Allies (especially the United States) and guerrillas from the Philippines. That's what started my public career. I retired from the armed forces when I ran for the president of the Philippines, after serving as secretary of national defense [1988–92].

On an individual level, I use very simple buzzwords to encapsulate my own approach in three ways—giving, sharing, and daring for others. Address the needs of your family while also caring, sharing, and daring for others and for the country. Daring means to give more than you take: daring to sacrifice for the common good. How many people can dare to do that? "For many, family interests" still take precedence over the well-being of the people and the nation.[3] Leaders must dare to take the tough decisions that the bureaucracy will not take, and show the way forward.[4] Leaders must dare to unite in order to make a difference. Thus a leader must unite the opposition with him so that there is only one national team. If you are talking about the national interest and our vision for a better future in the Philippines, even the opposition is part of the team; for certain things, we must be one team. You can have intramurals in sports, and so it is in politics. When it comes to protecting our interests, let's operate as one team. I refer to unity of purpose, one nation, a big country team, and solidarity in the values of honesty, hard work, love of country, love of God, love of people, and love of the environment.

A strong work ethic is important for leaders. To work 24 hours, 7 days a week is not enough; I refer to 25-8. I have been retired for the last 13 years, and I still work Saturday afternoons. How do you work more than 24 hours a day, 7 days a week? You have to juggle many things all at the same time. Mindanao, South China Sea, the economy, overseas workers, massacre, robbery, UN (United Nations), ASEAN (Association of Southeast Asian Nations). The problem is some leaders are not doing enough; they are not devoting enough time to their duties, but they could really be attending to all of them. They fall off the high wire and the whole country collapses. That has happened here twice already.

You began your career as a cadet at a young age; you spent your professional career, before becoming president, in the armed forces and the police; and had many positions of high responsibility as chief of staff and secretary of defense in a professional armed forces that was well trained and that had promotion by merit. How did you keep your independence in order to open and lead a new path?

Yes, that's the way my career evolved, fortunately for me. I can frankly confess that when I was maybe at the rank of full colonel, the new president here happened to be a second cousin of mine, Mr. Marcos. But before that I had gone up the ranks in the best professional manner I could think of, by commanding troops and serving abroad in hazardous duties in Korea and Vietnam. When I attained the rank of general, it was already during the time of Mr. Marcos, but it was not because he favored me. He was the commander in chief, but I rebelled against him because some of us did not like what he was pursuing, which was imposing martial law and abusing the rights of the people.

Role of the Military

You say, "I rebelled," which raises the question: how can the military be made subject to civilian rule? In the Philippines there were many military plots during the presidencies of Corazon Aquino and Gloria Arroyo. How did you manage the military? How did you produce changes in civil-military relations?

The important thing for me while I was in the military was to maintain my professionalism and not allow politics to enter my decision making, even though there were pressures. As I went up in the ranks, the pressures from politicians increased, including those from the office of the president. But, having been trained in a very professional way, I maintained my cool. I was in charge of one entire major service, the national police. At that time there were four major services in the armed forces—the Army, Navy, Air Force, and national police. But during my time as president, because of the constitution enacted by Cory Aquino, we had to separate the national police into another service under civilian control, under the minister of interior and local government. It became the Philippine National Police, which was distinct from the armed forces.

So I was in charge of the national police while I was second in command of the overall armed forces. And we were subject to the political decisions of our acknowledged leader in the rebellion [1986], who was the secretary of national defense, Juan Ponce Enrile. He is now president of the Senate.

I think what was lacking in the Middle East and North Africa is that the rebellious civilian movement, the young people, the nongovernmental organizations (NGOs), academia, and labor failed to bring a component of the armed forces to their side. It was not preplanned in those countries, but many of the rebellious armed forces, one by one, unit by unit, joined them later on. That happened in Libya; that is still going on in Syria. But in our case, from the very beginning, the rebellious military was already with the civilians. Really, the rebellious military was joined by the civilians; let us put it that way. It was the military that started the first moves to withdraw support from President Marcos's government in the middle of our election campaign when Cory Aquino was the main opposition candidate. We were not really in favor of her over Mr. Marcos. We just withdrew our support from Mr. Marcos.

We were lucky in the sense that we could have been overcome very easily by Mr. Marcos. We were very inferior in comparison to his armed forces. He had the tanks, the helicopters, the fighter planes, the artillery, the marines. We were just a bunch of officers who wanted to go against the regime. But Minister Enrile and I decided that we would split the duties and the management of the operations. I asked Minister Enrile to take care of the political and civilian aspects of our withdrawal from Mr. Marcos. He would be the one to talk to the media, the political leaders, and the political parties. I would take care of the military operations. And that is how it happened. Now of course we overlapped in many areas. Minister Enrile also dealt with some military personnel because he had his own provincial following that included some soldiers. And, of course, as a long-standing general, I also had a sizeable following myself. But generally that is how we divided the work.

So how did we get the loyalty of the great majority of the 110,000 national policemen and another 120,000 from the Army, Navy, and Air Force? We are not a very big armed forces. I had learned to become the good friends of the commanders since they were still junior officers. We got to know each other by calling each other by our first names, playing tennis and golf, going scuba diving, doing road racing, and competing in sports. And of course we did many projects together, because we needed all the services together in many projects. So we had that esprit de corps among us that was maintained and continued up to my time as president; we are still playing golf and having reunions, and we are still talking about many issues that have not been resolved.

In our case, on the fourth day of the rebellion (we started on February 22, 1986, in the late evening) by noon it was finished. Then Cory Aquino took her oath as the new president of the Philippines, which was administered by one of the Supreme Court justices. She appointed Mr. Juan Ponce Enrile as the secretary of national defense and me, Lieutenant General Fidel V. Ramos, as the new chief of staff with one more star on my shoulders, on February 25. The armed forces have always been under civilian authority. **During Aquino's presidency, I led efforts to instill values of a "new armed forces of the**

Philippines," which meant that the armed forces would be nonpolitical and nonpartisan, and would perform their proper role before to maintain law and order. We tried to reconcile and unify the officer ranks, not focusing on the past but on the future, with loyalty to the constitution. Standardizing promotions and assignments was an important reform introduced at this time. We didn't distinguish between those who were pro-Marcos and pro-Aquino; assignments were based on merit and competency.[5]

That sounds so simple, but we understand that there were many attempted coups. Why was this?

There were nine recorded coup attempts from 1986 to 1990 against Cory Aquino. There were various military groups, not just one monolithic group. Some were the very young ones who were at the rank of captain, who had spent many years in the field under extreme hazards, and who probably were not properly recognized and were inadequately paid. Then there were the young colonels like Gregorio Honasan, now a senator, who wanted very much to run the show but could not because there were some generals like me still on top. As the chief of staff initially and then the secretary of national defense, I had to make sure that we put them all down. They were all defeated, but it was also my task to maintain "the unity of the armed forces."[6] We had pledged to recognize Aquino as the elected president of the Philippines.

In March 1986, Cory Aquino issued Proclamation No. 3, the provisional Freedom Constitution, which established the order for the transition. In between February 1986 and February 1987, we were under a revolutionary government. There was no definitive constitution in operation, and she ruled by decree. Congress was abolished during that time. But in any case, there were no big movements or upheavals during that one-year period, except for one failed attempt by Marcos loyalists when they occupied the Manila Hotel.

The military was divided after the revolution, according to the interests of the age levels within the military. The young captains, the very active and ambitious colonels, and then the old generals like me wanted to maintain the status quo and give the civilian government a chance to operate according to the 1987 constitution. When it was my turn to aspire for the presidency, my own people in the armed forces and in the Ministry of Defense said that I didn't have to run for election, that I could just grab the presidency and they would support me. But I said no. I might seize the presidency and keep it for maybe three years, but I would not be able to hold it any longer than that because the people of the Philippines would not allow it. That's how we are here.

I have observed in the Middle East and North Africa that dynasties and rich families and dictators may rule for a time, but they will not endure because the people will not allow it. They may rule for 10, 20, 30, even 40 years, as in the case of Gaddafi, but in the end the people will not allow it.

Why did these plots continue, after your government, against President Gloria Arroyo? Why couldn't they be stopped?

After my time, military rebellion was replicated during the time of President Estrada. He lasted only for two and a half years because of the intervention of the armed forces and the national police. He was removed in January 2001 because he was perceived to be abusive and corrupt. He confined his activities and influence to a select group of cronies. We didn't like that, and so in this case the civilians protested. The Church, academia, workers, NGOs, and the military supported the protests. The civilians were the first to rebel, then the military, and the police supported them.

Then Gloria Arroyo became president. During the first three years of her presidency, she was seen as a heroine, and we had such high hopes, but she reneged on one promise after another. Again the armed forces became very, very unhappy, but there was no military revolution against Arroyo. She lasted for nine years. It is very unfortunate, because in the beginning she was very efficient and hard working. She is still very hard working, but her interests turned around when she started enjoying so much power, which I think is the experience of dictators and despots everywhere. They are all do-gooders in the beginning, and then if they taste power for a while, they enjoy it so much that they want to hang onto it and never let go, by hook or by crook.

When I was president, I wanted to amend the parts of the constitution that addressed economic provisions and the form of government. I was in favor of a parliamentary form of government in which the military and police do not have to be persuaded to side one way or another with a political leader in case of a coup situation. In a parliamentary system, a simple no-confidence vote by the members of Parliament is enough to boot out the incumbent government. That is the system we want, because the military and the police are professionals and should not be drawn into political in fighting. That is my experience, looking at the time between 1987 and 1990. At that time I was already in charge, and of course I didn't want anything to happen to the integrity of the armed forces and the police.

The Davide Commission [chaired by Hilario Davide Jr., who was at that time chairman of the Commission on Elections] convened in 1989 by President Cory Aquino looked into the coup attempts during her administration. Then the Feliciano Commission [chaired by retired Associate Supreme Court Justice Florentino Feliciano] was created in 2003. It investigated the protest movements that occurred during the time of Gloria Arroyo and found that the military's complaints were legitimate. There was favoritism at the higher levels in terms of promotion and assignments, and low pay for the rank and file, especially the corporals and the privates. And there was political interference in many of the military procedures, including procurement. So there was graft and corruption, initially coming from the political superiors, and then some of the military commanders got infected by it and became corrupt also.

One disruption happened in October 1990 and was related to the secession of Mindanao, in which the co-plotters who claimed the Christian, Muslim, and indigenous people of Mindanao—Lumads we call them—wanted to secede to form a Federal Republic of Mindanao, which would be separate from the Republic of the Philippines. But the hostilities lasted for only five days. There was some bloodshed, but it was all settled relatively peacefully and prevented from becoming a wider war by the interventions of us cabinet members during that time.

As I said, there were nine attempts during Aquino's administration, and in January 2001 there was a civilian-military action that removed Estrada. Then, during Arroyo's time, there were three coup attempts. First the Oakwood incident here in Makati [part of metro Manila] in 2003; then, in 2006, a very similar one by disgruntled members of the military led by higher-ranking officers who tried to take over the Makati business district, and therefore force the government to capitulate to them, but that did not work either; and then the Manila Peninsula incident in November 2007.There were no military protest movements during my time in 1992-98, and I was already retired from the service during the Estrada and Arroyo period.

Constitutional Reform

Would you say that the constitution, democratic institutions, and commitment to them are all firmly established?

Today the trouble is that there are some very powerful blocs that have prevented any amendment to the 1987 constitution. These are the followers of the late Jaime Cardinal Sin, the followers and descendants of President Cory Aquino, and some of the authors of the 1987 constitution. This constitution was not based on an elective process, unlike the previous 1935 and 1972 constitutions, in which the people elected the delegates of the Constitutional Assemblies. In 1986, President Aquino chose the 50 brightest Filipinos as delegates. It was elitist in a certain way, but various sectors were represented, including business, landowners, labor, women, the Muslim community and far-left groups, and the delegates who represented the different geographical areas of the country. The referendum to ratify the constitution was approved by 76%. The new constitution introduced a six-year single term limit for the presidency.[7]

The descendants of all of those people have stopped any attempt to amend that constitution even very slightly, as if it were engraved in stone and cannot ever be changed. We cited the US constitution. How many times has it been amended? There have been 27 amendments in the last 200 years. That is an average of maybe one big amendment every ten years. In our case, I recommended amending the economic provisions, which established a 60/40 rule in regard to the development of natural resources and the ownership of public utilities [foreign ownership of companies is limited to 40% of the company], which has had a very negative impact on foreign direct investment and hence economic growth.[8] My other amendment was related to the parliamentary system, but I did not push that one because it would take time for people to accept that they would not directly elect their president. We pointed out that while the United States votes for a president, it is not the counting of their votes one by one that decides who will win; the Electoral College does. Now we have to correct people's mind-set and get them to accept a governance system that provides fair representation, even if not direct voting.

The other amendment that I really fought for was the one against dynasties. The constitution already has a provision: political dynasties are prohibited as may be provided by law. But where is the enabling law? The ones who benefit from political dynasties are the very same people who are in Congress and since 1987 have not passed a law despite some attempts. So I suggested, very simply, that we amend the constitution so that the language of the prohibition is in the constitution itself and is not dependent on an operable law. And where is this happening? It is in the other provisions of the same constitution. It says that the president of the Philippines cannot appoint any officials in the executive branch who are relatives within the fourth degree of affinity or consanguinity.* So we should use that language to prohibit election to public office so that political dynasties are not created. That's all—very simple.

Political Parties

The other aspect of it, because they are related, is changing political parties. Because if you are allowed to change political parties easily, then you provide the seeds for political dynasties to take place. I could have created a dynasty. My father was a politician, but he died before I became a politician. I only ran once and that's it. I don't want to fail as a politician. My sister was a senator before I ran for president. She is an educator, a diplomat, but she was good in her own right and then she retired [she did not run again afterward]. She has a son, but he ran at the provincial level, so that's not a dynasty in the real sense. There are only 24 members of the Philippine Senate, and in the 2013 election only one-half were up for election because the other half is elected through

---

*Article XII Section 13 of the 1987 constitution of the Philippines states that the spouse and relatives by consanguinity or affinity within the fourth civil degree of the president shall not during his tenure be appointed as members of the Constitutional Commissions or the Office of the Ombudsman, or as secretaries, undersecretaries, chairmen, or heads of bureaus or offices, including government-owned or -controlled corporations and their subsidiaries.

2016. So voters here have very little to choose from because the potential candidates come mostly from political dynasties. So where is the democracy then? This "dynasty-ism" must be corrected by the language of the constitution itself; no enabling law will ever be passed by Congress since it would be self-defeating for them.

There is a move now by the House speaker and the Senate president, Feliciano Belmonte and Juan Ponce Enrile, respectively, to reform the constitution little by little, starting with the 60/40 provisions, and then maybe they can throw in some definitions in between. The really big amendment is the form of government. Currently, the 1987 constitution specifies a presidential system and a multiparty system. The two features don't go together. We have about 272 political party-list groups right now in our presidential system, so the people are confused.

There are many political parties in the Philippines, and you formed your own party, Lakas, when you ran for president. Do you think having so many parties is a problem for democracy in the Philippines?

We started Lakas (National Union of Christian Democrats-United Muslim Democrats Party) with seven members in December 1991, and by the February 1992 deadline to register candidates, we had about 1,000. That's how big we became in a short time.

I am asked how I won. I explain that it's like what we call the oil spot theory. One drop of oil will spread so much in a lake that several hundred would be significant. I got 10,000 NGOs to help me. Not political parties, but movements, associations, organizations. I had operatives all over the place because I was a friend to many of these people during my early days in the military, because we were into community development.

The number of political parties is a big problem now, and the president here must attend to that problem. In 2012, the Congress said we must have some amendments, and the president said it's not the time, and they are still quarreling in the media about that. The political parties are not stable; they are based around individuals, so there is no "continuity in public policy."[9] One measure that could support the formation of stable parties is to create a system of public financing.[10] Constitutional reform to a parliamentary system would also strengthen parties and diminish the role of "personalist political leaders."[11]

Building a Coalition

If during your time as president the large number of political parties was not a problem, why is it a problem now?

I did not have a problem because under the legal mechanisms called the LEDAC (Legislative Executive Development Advisory Council) we the leaders discussed our challenges every Wednesday while Congress was in session, at breakfast, so we had productive cooperation among the executive, legislature, and private sector.[12] That meant 35 Wednesdays out of the whole year we were meeting as one family. The president, presiding officer, and maybe five members of the cabinet, depending on the agenda, met together with the majority and minority leaders in the Senate and House, and also NGOs, sectoral leaders, women, youth, elderly, veterans, academia, labor, fishermen, and overseas workers, and we talked as one family. In this way, we managed to develop executive-legislative consultation and consensus.

I would also hold cabinet meetings in the field. For example, if the main subject was energy in Mindanao, I would send five teams out ahead, led by an undersecretary—public works, energy, local government, maybe defense, and then maybe science and technology. You are one team. You go this way. You take the land route. You take the ferry all the way to Davao. I take another team of undersecretaries—maybe education, transportation—we take the island-hopping airplane. Now, in between, as you move, the team must check projects and meet the people in the provincial capitals or city halls and have a dialogue. I might give them three days to make it to the place where we are having the cabinet meeting. I end up having a morning session with them. I learn from them, together with some key cabinet members, also perhaps the executive secretary and maybe the vice president. We learn what happened during their field trips. I would get five different reports, and then we would have a cabinet meeting after lunch. The local governor and the city mayor would join us. They would participate in the discussion when their agenda item came up. And then, before I left the premises at maybe five in the afternoon, I would make a decision, and they were there to learn about it in terms of what it meant for their province, for their region, for their island. And then we left in the late afternoon, which was sometimes very risky because many places do not have nice airports and we would take off at night. So this is how we used to run government—with "hands on."

Did these regular meetings between the executive, legislature, and sectoral leaders occur only during your government? How was this managed during Aquino's government?

Yes, it was only during my time. During President Cory Aquino's time, a law was passed that created the Legislative Executive Development Advisory Council, but she vetoed it allegedly because her brother was in the House as deputy speaker, and she conducted business with the House of Representatives, which has 250 members, only through her brother. In the Senate she had her brother-in-law, Butz Aquino, and she conducted business with him. She did not like to share power. When I heard about this in 1991, I was completely ignorant about these inner workings. I suggested reviving that vetoed bill, and that was the very first law that was passed during my time. It was the very first law that I signed, in December 1992.

I wanted consultation and consensus, and that's what happened for my six years. And we passed 229 reforms or structural laws in 6 years. That's about one every nine days in agriculture, industry, the armed forces, national police, education, empowerment, economic zones, investment, banking, everything. Now we have the reproductive health law that hasn't been passed [signed into law in December 2012], but the issue is integrally linked to the environment and sustainable development.[13] A Freedom of Information bill has been discussed for 12 years, and there still has been no presidential action. During my time, we had a fiscal surplus for four years because we opened up the economy. This goes back to what I said in the beginning: good governance and enlightened leadership cannot be outsourced; it has to be homegrown.

Social Empowerment

You mentioned that during your presidency you had consultative meetings with legislators and representatives of civil society. What was the role of civil society during your time as president?

Well, my vision was always people empowerment. I did not emphasize "people power." I worked on increasing the capacity of each individual, boy, girl, old, young, baby, naturalized citizen, or foreign resident to be able to do better, live longer, and be more energetic. That's what empowering the people means. It is the people who are the most important asset on this planet. It's not land. It's not sea. It's not military power. It's people.

The NGOs consist of many groups, including the Church. During my time, because it was in the constitution, I could appoint six sectoral representatives to the Lower House who had to be confirmed by the Commission of Appointments. That was later phased out because it was only temporary. But we had representatives from the women, youth, overseas workers, veterans, academia, and from the business sector. They were selected by their own community, which then formally informed me. I nominated them on the basis of their being selected from their constituency, and I met with them for six years, during two terms in the Lower House. In the second term I had slightly different representatives, but the younger ones were the same.

Were women's organizations part of the consultations? Was the Catholic Church an important political actor?

Yes, during my time and also during Aquino's time. She organized several councils. I had regular meetings with the women and young people. We had a National Council on the role of Filipino Women and a National Youth Commission; the leader of each group had cabinet rank. We met the female leaders once every two months, really a full-blown meeting, with everybody doing their homework with a secretariat and minutes.

We have a bigger share or percentage of women in legislative positions than any other country in our part of Southeast Asia. Women here are very active in terms of speaking out. All kinds of very effective think tanks and NGOs are run by women. I am writing about one now, called the Philippine Rural Reconstruction Movement, which is still around and works with mass education and countryside development, especially giving poor people good drinking water, three meals a day, and medical care, and it is mostly women who run it.

From the very beginning, even during the Spanish colonial times, we already had women fighting the Spaniards. We had several female generals who were heads of village organizations, and of course female writers and think tankers who were very vocal in the Spanish newspapers. And then when the Americans came, the more the women were liberated. Women's suffrage, or the right of women to vote and occupy political office, was ratified in our country back in 1936. Similarly, we had the National Ecumenical Church Commission with Catholics, Protestants, Muslims, atheists, the Church of Christ (Iglesia ni Kristo), and the independent churches represented. The leadership or chairmanship was rotated every year for six years. We maintained a dialogue with them. This doesn't exist anymore.

Fundamental Principles

You have described many principles and practices you followed as president, but it appears that the usual political practices of the Philippines seem to have little relation to the principles that you believe in, and that you say were practiced when you were president.

Well, of course, I am very sorry about that. It is one of my failures, you see. Because we tried to practice what we think is correct, and we are putting it down in writing and talking about it.

But why is there such a gap between principle and practice in politics?

People learn what they want to learn, but what they cannot swallow or practice regularly, because the prescriptions are not palatable to them, they discard. And yet I've been saying here that nation building is not a matter of adding up successes and failures of a series of presidents or prime ministers. It's a continuous upward process, and nobody must fail. Each incumbent must do better than his predecessor, so his successor is bound to do better than himself.

So I go back to nation building. On a daily time frame you are not only screwing up, although it seems that way. You have all kinds of failures. Things happen. I think in the United States they are saying this also, and if you look at the last 225 years, they have been really going up but in between they are going up and down as well. Now, I think that is the same for every country that has grown up. We can say the same here, because 20 years ago we didn't have high rises, we didn't have the electric train, big boulevards, and big malls. We didn't have the civilian-operated Clark and Subic special economic zones; they were still US military bases.

International Influence

How would you assess the role of the US government, which has such a long record here, and other international actors in the Philippines' democratic transition?

As a whole, I would venture that the experience with the United States was a very good colonial experience for us. But there is still that hidden feeling, and it's not just from the old people, that the United States also stole our independence. When we had already declared our independence, and were about to capture Manila, the Americans came in and dealt with the Spaniards. You see, it was a deal so that Manila would not be destroyed; otherwise, there could have been fighting between the Spaniards and the rebels. In the Treaty of Paris, in 1898, the Philippines was disposed of by Spain and sold to the United States for $20 million. And Cuba was part of the bargain. The fact is that we became a colony of the United States. So there is that lingering doubt about that now.

We are thankful for the lessons of representative democracy, elections, starting with the better-educated classes as favored appointees or candidates to the two houses (Senate and House); we have the same system as the United States, and as well as in the courts. We are thankful for the gift of English and public school instruction. I was one of those beneficiaries because I grew up during that time, in a public school, and that system was better than the one we have now. But that lingering thought that the United States exploited the Philippines in the earlier years and did not allow it to grow up industrially is still there. And we are very much behind some former colonies like Malaysia. Thailand was never a colony, but they are well ahead of us in terms of GDP per capita.

Did you refer to the experience of transitions in other countries such as Spain, Portugal, or Latin American countries when you were undergoing transition in the Philippines?

No, we were just thinking as Filipinos, and it was a "do or die" situation. We either succeeded against Marcos or we didn't, and if we didn't, we would be put in jail or killed. Of course the idea of a coup or rebellion against Marcos had been forming for maybe three years among the military. The Reform the Armed Forces Movement (RAM) started it. Then, later on, some of us were brought into it because the RAM asked us to support it. I advised them to slow down, that they were not yet ready. But we supported them in terms of the reforms because the Marcos regime was already too abusive in terms of human rights and economic development. We had an oligarchy; they were the only ones who had the businesses, which were distributed only among their cronies. The wives of the officials were very extravagant. Marcos was friendly with the Shah of Iran, Gaddafi, and other lifetime strongmen.

The problem that did him in, the gap between the rich and the poor, was very big. As we started to gain support, we started also thinking of governance, and we agreed in the beginning that if we won, governance must return to the civilian, political leadership. But the young colonels did not fulfill that commitment on their own; they wanted to run the government themselves. But some of us fought that idea.

Maybe we looked at the other insurgencies in Latin America that were similar to ours. The liberation movements run by the priests, for example. Our priests here were also against the government, but they had allied with the Communists. There were very similar movements in Central America with the young students. And in Chile, you had a very horrible situation because of the military itself being the ruler. In our case it was always civilians in charge, with military support.

Economic Management for Development

What were your economic and development priorities?

One of the most pressing problems at the time was energy; there were frequent power outages, which was very detrimental to the economy and to the quality of life. So in December 1992, the Department of Energy was created to plan and manage the supply and use of energy. Short-, medium-, and long-term plans were developed for addressing the energy crisis, and the energy shortage was resolved ahead of schedule. The private sector was an important partner in addressing the energy crisis.[14] Liberalization of the telecommunications and banking industries was also a priority to increase investment and competition.[15]

Corruption is a drain on the economy; I tried to address this by limiting the role of the state in the economy through deregulation, thus opening up our economy to foreign investment and competition.[16] We should allow "the private sector to do what it can do better than government."[17] Greater domestic competition will allow the Philippines to be globally competitive, which will promote economic growth. But in order to create greater domestic competition we must address the monopolies and cartels that dominate certain areas of the economy.[18] Job growth will come from small- and medium-sized enterprises, which provide more jobs than capital-intensive investments.[19]

Our weak infrastructure also held back growth and development and discouraged foreign investment. Investment in infrastructure improvements was (and continues to be) important, including in clean power.[20] We built over 6,000 km of new roads and bridges.[21] These are long-term investments that require long-range planning.

There is a large gap between the rich and poor in the Philippines. We invest too large a proportion of our education budget in university education, which the poor do not benefit from at the same rate as the middle class.[22] But education is the engine that will lift people from poverty and increase the Philippines' competitiveness, so greater resources should be focused on education, as well as primary health care, especially for those at the lowest income levels.[23] This will contribute to a "simultaneous bottom–up / top–down approach" to narrowing the income gap.[24]

Managing Multiple Peace Processes

How did you manage the multiple domestic armed conflicts that were ongoing when you became president?

Peace and reconciliation was a priority of mine from the outset of my presidency.[25] We started negotiations, even before my term as president, with the three armed dissident groups: the RAM who were "military rebels"; the Moro National Liberation Front separatists in the southern Philippines; and the New People's Army, the armed wing of the Communist Party of the Philippines.[26] Through a proclamation in July 1992, I established the nine-member National Unification Commission (NUC), which was mandated, through a consultative process, to draft and propose an amnesty program and peace process.[27] The NUC conducted consultations in 71 provinces with those who were fighting the government, their families, and community leaders on a range of issues, including the causes of the armed conflicts, what kind of policies and programs are needed for a durable peace, and what the sectors and communities themselves were willing to contribute. On the basis of these consultations, the NUC developed its proposals for a comprehensive peace process.[28]

One of the principles of the general peace process was that we were not pursuing "blame or surrender, but rather dignity for all parties." It was not enough that the violence would end, but that the conditions that created the conflicts would be addressed.[29] "Peace and development must always go together; sustainable development in the areas affected" by conflict was a priority.[30] We can only achieve sustainable development as a nation when there is "peace and progress" in all regions.[31] In 1993, I created the Office of the Presidential Adviser on the Peace Process, which "oversaw the implementation of the NUC" plan. In 1994, a general amnesty for armed groups fighting the government was declared. The National Amnesty Commission received over 7,000 amnesty applications, and many insurgents who were in detention were released. Three peace panels were established to manage the peace process with the RAM, MNLF, and the Communists.[32]

The first formal negotiations with the Communists took place in 1986 with the Aquino government but were not successful. Talks restarted in 1992, and the Communist Party was legalized in 1993. In 1998, a cluster of agreements was signed, but progress stalled after 2001.[33]

After nine coup attempts against Aquino's government, negotiations with RAM began in 1992 with a preliminary agreement to "cease hostilities."[34] In May 1995, an agreement was signed with the forces loyal to Marcos known as ALTAS.[35] A General Agreement for Peace was signed in October 1995. A peace agreement with the MNLF was signed in September 1996, following decades of fighting and unrest.[36] International support to negotiations with the MNLF dates to the early 1970s, including the key role played by the Organization of Islamic Conference.[37] The 1996 peace agreement established the Southern Philippines Council for Peace and Development, headed by MNLF leader Nur Misuari, to oversee development projects.[38] The agreement recognized regional autonomy, provided for a general amnesty, and integrated qualified fighters into the national armed forces and police.[39]

There was a notable incident when I was president. We were campaigning in Mindanao to get the congressional vote to ratify our peace agreement with the MNLF. We had to get it ratified, and eventually it was. But during the period we were campaigning, one of the top US officials the chief of the USAID (US Agency for International Development) was with me. The US ambassador to the Philippines was in the next car. The Christians in Mindanao were very mad at me. They didn't like the agreement because it would have diminished their role, according to them; it's not true. But they were against it and so they had big demonstrations, all throughout the road from the airport to General Santos City, maybe 5 km. I stuck my neck out of the car. I did not hide in the car. I looked out in front and they tried to hit me, so I tried to hit them back. And the story goes that they threw tomatoes at me. It's OK. Throw tomatoes, but don't throw hand grenades. That was one of the most difficult parts of my term, the peace agreement in Mindanao, but we did it. "The lesson I learned is that in any peace effort, the leader must focus on the long-term view . . . the strategic vision of peace and development . . . and to refuse to be stampeded into contrary action by tactical pressures from the enemies of the peace process."[40]

The Chinese philosopher Sun Tzu said, "To win without fighting is best," and I agree. I understand what it means to fight, but "violent confrontation should be only the last resort of a democratic president." In democracy, we must seek "win-win" outcomes in any negotiation. Win-win outcomes tend to "enforce themselves," as opposed to being undermined by the party that seems to have itself been shortchanged.[41]

In 1994, the Philippines—together with Brunei, Indonesia, and Malaysia—created the East ASEAN Growth Area (BIMP-EAGA) to accelerate economic development in our designated contiguous regions, which in the Philippines included Mindanao. Cooperation in various sectors such as agriculture, fishing, tourism, shipping, and energy for the purpose of complementarity and growth was part of a plan for the development of Mindanao, thus reinforcing the peace process by uplifting and empowering the region. The BIMP-EAGA is part of the "peace dividend" of Mindanao.[42]

Did the military agree with the peace agreement with the insurgents?

The military in fact fully cooperated. They carried out the policies of the government.

Time Line

1521: Spanish explorer Ferdinand Magellan arrives and is killed during the Battle of Mactan against the datu Lapu-Lapu.

1565-1898: Spanish colonial rule. The country is named Las Islas Filipinas after Felipe II of Spain.

Aug. 1896: The anticolonial uprising against Spain begins.

Dec. 1896: Famed novelist, scholar, doctor, and political activist Jose Rizal is executed by the Spanish.

Dec. 1898: Spain cedes the Philippines to the United States after the Spanish-American War. Filipino independence fighters, led by President Emilio Aguinaldo, continue their armed struggle against US occupation. More than 4,000 US troops and more than 12,000 Philippine Republican Army soldiers are killed, as well as least 200,000 Filipino civilians.

Mar. 1901: Aguinaldo is captured.

Jul. 1901: William Howard Taft, later a US president, becomes the first civil governor as the United States consolidates its control of the Philippines.

Sep. 1935: Following nearly 30 years of legislative elections, presidential elections begin under US rule, facilitating a stable two-party system, albeit plagued by corruption.

Jul. 1946: The Philippines gains independence from United States, which retains advantageous trading rights and military bases in the country.

Nov. 1965: Ferdinand Marcos is elected president in mostly free elections. He appoints family and friends to military and government posts, excludes other factions of party from power, and incurs heavy national debt on patronage projects.

Mar. 1969: The Communist Party of the Philippines (CPP) founds a military wing with covert support from other opposition groups. It becomes a major insurgency along with the separatist Moro National Liberation Front (MNLF).

Nov. 1969: Marcos is reelected amidst unusually extensive fraud, vote buying, and use of military to intimidate opposition.

Aug. 1971: Marcos suspends habeas corpus after a bombing at an opposition rally. Senator Benigno Aquino Jr., from important Philippine family, becomes a prominent critic of Marcos.

Sep. 1972: Marcos declares martial law and imprisons Aquino and others. He pressures families to sell companies to his friends and alters regulations to benefit allies. He appoints technocrats and strengthens investor rights, winning praise and aid from the US government.

Nov. 1972: Via bribery and blackmail, Marcos gets a constitutional convention (convened before martial law began) to replace Congress with a parliamentary system with no term limits. Congress dissolves without holding new elections.

Apr. 1978: In parliamentary elections the opposition loses badly amidst fraud and violence; many boycott, but Aquino runs regional coalition with the CPP. A day before voting, the opposition holds a major "noise barrage" protest.

Oct. 1980: An Aquino-backed group bombs the US tourism convention in Manila, attracting publicity. Marcos agrees to indirect talks with Aquino and pledges to end martial law and hold elections; the opposition boycotts because voting procedures are unfair. Militant groups are apprehended over next few months.

Jan. 1981: Ronald Reagan's new US administration initially harasses US-based exiles, downplays rights abuses, and resists pressure to cut aid to Marcos regime.

Aug. 1981: Marcos appoints ally Fabian Ver as head of military. Ver clashes with Generals Juan Ponce Enrile and Fidel Ramos, who are seen as more professional and independent.

Feb. 1983: The Catholic Bishops' Conference, led by Jaime Cardinal Sin, calls for democracy.

Aug. 1983: Aquino returns from exile. Exiting the plane, he is assassinated by member of government security detail. Demonstrations erupt, supported by the middle class, businesses, and the Church. Aquino's widow Corazon "Cory" Cojuangco Aquino becomes protest leader. International banks cut lending to the government owing to instability, forcing the government to restrict imports and currency trading.

May 1984: Legislative elections are held. The noncommunist opposition takes part and wins many seats in urban areas and leaders' home regions despite fraud and violence.

Oct. 1984: A government investigation into Aquino's death accuses Ver of leading the plot.

Jan. 1985: Strongly advised by the US State Department and Central Intelligence Agency, Reagan finally calls on Marcos to remove economic controls, appoint a successor, and punish Ver.

Mar. 1985: Officers allied with Enrile and covertly backed by US security forces found Reform the Armed Forces Movement (RAM) to oppose Marcos and Ver.

Nov. 1985: On US television, Marcos calls for presidential elections monitored by civil society and foreign press. The opposition endorses Aquino for president.

Feb. 1986: Watchdog National Citizens' Movement for Free Elections (NAMFREL) declares Cory Aquino winner of election, but the electoral commission gives the victory to Marcos; US observers, the Church, and electoral commission staff denounce the official results. The government uncovers a coup plot by RAM; Enrile and Ramos flee to military camps on Epifanio de los Santos Avenue (EDSA) and endorse Cory Aquino. Cory along with Church and media allies mobilize demonstrations referred to as "people power." Protestors surround camps in support, seize key locations, and swear in Cory as president. The United States withdraws support for Marcos, who flees via US transport and is taken to Hawaii. As president, Cory appoints a cabinet that includes Enrile and Ramos. She frees CPP leaders over the objections of US intelligence and some in the cabinet, creates commissions on rights abuses and illicit assets, and dissolves the Marcos-era Parliament and constitution.

Jul. 1986: Marcos allies attempt a coup. RAM, angry about limited influence and negotiations with CPP, covertly supports plot. Marcos allies later attempt three more coups.

Nov. 1986: After Cory Aquino gives Ramos influence over military policy, Ramos halts the coup attempt by RAM, and Enrile leaves the cabinet. RAM later attempts two more coups.

Feb. 1987: Voters ratify the Cory Aquino–backed constitution. It creates a unitary presidential system with regional autonomy and curbs military's role in internal security and politics.

May 1987: Aquino allies win legislative elections. Parties backed by Marcos, Enrile, and CPP do poorly. Fraud and violence persist but at far lower levels.

Sep. 1991: The Philippine Senate votes against continuing US military bases in Philippines.

Oct. 1991: The legislature devolves new powers to local government.

May 1992: Fidel Ramos, Cory Aquino's designated successor, is narrowly elected president, with 24% of the vote in a seven-candidate race.

Sep. 1996: Ramos signs a peace deal with MNLF. Splinter groups, including the Moro-Islamic Liberation Front (MILF), persist.

Sep. 1997: Ramos calls for a parliamentary system of government. Opponents protest a proposal for abolishing term limits; it is ruled unconstitutional and withdrawn.

May 1998: Vice president and film actor Joseph Estrada is elected president by wide margin. Ramos and other elites see Estrada as a dangerous populist and oppose him.

Jan. 2001: Anti-Estrada protests begin after his Senate allies stymie a corruption investigation. Cory Aquino, Sin, and Ramos call for Estrada's resignation, and many security forces join. Vice President Gloria Macapagal-Arroyo takes office. Estrada resigns but calls the ouster illegitimate.

May 2004: Macapagal-Arroyo is elected for a full term. Allegations of vote buying surface, but impeachment attempts in Congress fail throughout her term.

Oct. 2008: MILF peace talks fail when the Supreme Court blocks an autonomy deal, arguing it illegally commits the government to amending constitution.

May 2010: Benigno "Noynoy" Aquino III, son of Benigno Jr. and Cory Aquino, is elected president. Macapagal-Arroyo issues last-minute judiciary appointments, which are later ruled unconstitutional.

Nov. 2011: Macapagal-Arroyo is arrested on corruption and electoral fraud charges; impeachment proceedings against her chief justice begin, resulting in his removal from office.

Oct. 2012: MILF and the government under Noynoy sign a framework peace agreement.

NOTES

1. Ramos (2012, 23).
2. Ibid.
3. Ramos (2011, 50).
4. Ramos (2012, 59).
5. Velasco (2012, 183–85).
6. Ramos (2012, 25).
7. Velasco (2012, 182).
8. Ramos (2008, 114).
9. Ramos (2012, 12).
10. Ibid.
11. Ramos (2008, 116).
12. Ramos (2012, 46).
13. Ramos (2011, 53).
14. Velasco (2010, 103).
15. Velasco (2012, 293).
16. Ramos (2011, 112).

17. Ibid., 115.
18. Ibid., 54.
19. Ibid., 115.
20. Ibid., 17.
21. Velasco (2012, 291).
22. Ramos (2011, 114).
23. Ibid., 65.
24. Ibid., 55.
25. Velasco (2010, 76).
26. Ramos (2012, 41).
27. Velasco (2010, 76–77).
28. Ramos (2008, 145–46).
29. Velasco (2010, 76–77).
30. Ibid., 91.
31. Ramos (2011, 49).
32. Velasco (2010, 76–78).
33. Ramos (2008, 149).
34. Ibid., 147.
35. Ibid.
36. Ramos (2012, 41).
37. Ramos (2008, 142).
38. Velasco (2012, 266).
39. Ibid., 83.
40. Velasco (2010, 84).
41. Ramos (2012, 29).
42. Velasco (2012, 283–84).

REFERENCES

Ramos, Fidel V. *Empowering the People*, vol. 2, *Bulletin of FVR Sermons*. Manila: Ramos Peace and Development Foundation and the *Manila Bulletin*, 2008.
———. *SONA*, vol. 6, *Bulletin of FVR Sermons*. Manila: Manila Bulletin Publication, 2011.
———. *Towards Our Better Future: Seize the Opportunities*. Manila: Ramos Peace and Development Foundation, 2012.
Velasco, Melandrew T. *10 Years of RPDEV: Teamwork for Enduring Peace and Sustainable Development*. Manila: Ramos Peace and Development Foundation, 2010.
Velasco, Melandrew T., Rafael M. Alunan III, and Reynaldo V. Velasco. *Silver Linings: 25 Years of the 1986 EDSA People Power Revolution*. Manila: Ramos Peace and Development Foundation and Media Touchstone Ventures, 2012.

GUIDE TO FURTHER READING

Abinales, Patricio N., and Donna J. Amoroso. "The Withering of Philippine Democracy." *Current History* 105, no. 692 (2006): 290-95.
Anderson, Benedict. "Cacique Democracy and the Philippines: Origins and Dreams." *New Left Review* 1, no. 169 (1988): 3-31.

Bonner, Raymond. *Waltzing with a Dictator: The Marcoses and the Making of American Policy.* New York: Vintage, 1988.

Clarke, Gerald. *The Politics of NGOs in South-East Asia: Participation and Protest in the Philippines.* London: Routledge, 1998.

Franco, Jennifer C. *Elections and Democratization in the Philippines.* New York: Routledge, 2001.

Hedman, Eva-Lotta E. "The Spectre of Populism in Philippine Politics and Society: Artista, Masa, Eraption!" *South East Asia Research* 9, no. 1 (2001): 5–44.

Hernandez, Carolina G., and Maria Cecilia T. Ubarra. *Restoring and Strengthening Civilian Control: Best Practices in Civil-Military Relationships in the Philippines.* Quezon City, Philippines: Institute for Strategic and Development Studies and National Democratic Institute, 1999.

Hutchcroft, Paul D. "Reflections on a Reverse Image: South Korea under Park Jung Hee and the Philippines under Ferdinand Marcos." In *The Park Chung Hee Era: The Transformation of South Korea,* edited by Byung-Kook Kim and Ezra F. Vogel. Cambridge, Mass.: Harvard University Press, 2011.

Miranda, Felipe B., Temario C. Rivera, Malaya C. Ronas, and Ronald D. Holmes. *Chasing the Wind: Assessing Philippine Democracy.* Quezon City: Philippine Commission on Human Rights and United Nations Development Programme, 2011.

Paredes, Ruby R. *Philippine Colonial Democracy.* New Haven, Conn.: Yale University Southeast Asian Studies, 1989.

Putzel, James. "Survival of an Imperfect Democracy in the Philippines." *Democratization* 6, no. 1 (1999): 198–223.

Quimpo, Nathan Gilbert. "Oligarchic Patrimonialism, Bossism, Electoral Clientelism, and Contested Democracy in the Philippines." *Comparative Politics* 37, no. 2 (2005): 229–50.

Riedinger, Jeffrey M. *Agrarian Reform in the Philippines: Democratic Transitions and Redistributive Reform.* Stanford, Calif.: Stanford University Press, 1995.

Rufo, Aries C. *Altar of Secrets: Sex, Politics and Money in the Philippine Catholic Church.* Manila: Journalism for Nation Building Foundation, 2013.

Sheridan, Greg. "'Steady Eddie' Ramos: People Power Mark II." In *Tigers: Leaders of the New Asia-Pacific,* edited by Greg Sheridan. St. Leonard's, N.S.W.: Allen & Unwin, 1997.

Staniland, Martin. "The Philippines: The Fall of Ferdinand C. Marcos, 1985–1986." In *Falling Friends: The United States and Regime Change Abroad,* edited by Martin Staniland. Boulder, Colo.: Westview, 1991.

Teehankee, Julio C. "Electoral Politics in the Philippines." In *Electoral Politics in Southeast and East Asia,* edited by Aurel Croissant, Gabriele Bruns, and Merei John, 149–202. Singapore: Friedrich Ebert Stiftung, 2002.

Thompson, Mark R. *The Anti-Marcos Struggle: Personalistic Rule and Democratic Transition in the Philippines.* New Haven, Conn.: Yale University Press, 1995.

Thompson, W. Scott, and Federico M. Macaranas. *Democracy and Discipline: Fidel V. Ramos and His Philippine Presidency.* Manila: University of Santo Tomas, 2007.

Youngblood, Robert L. *Marcos against the Church: Economic Development and Political Repression in the Philippines.* Ithaca, N.Y.: Cornell University Press, 1990.

Chapter 7

POLAND

....

Poland's Great Experiment: Creating Democracy through Protests, Repression, Negotiation, Elections, and the Politics of Zigzag

JANE L. CURRY

Poland's transition from authoritarian Communism to free market democracy was slow, complicated, and step by step. It began long before 1989 and went on nearly 10 years until a final constitution was passed. It required more than a shift of power from one group to another. It involved untangling the economy from the political system, removing the Communist Party as a central institution in the constitution, establishing political parties and independent and legal civil society organizations, and transitioning from being a satellite of the Soviet Union to being part of Europe. As this process progressed after the Round Table Talks in 1989, the world around Poland transformed: Soviet control of Central and Eastern Europe ended, the countries around Poland fragmented into seven newly independent states, the Berlin Wall came down, the Soviet Union disbanded, and the Warsaw Pact dissolved. With the help of Western aid, Poland transformed itself and joined Western Europe in the European Union (EU) and North Atlantic Treaty Organization (NATO).

There were four national elections and three different presidents* from the collapse in 1989 to the passage of a full new constitution in 1997. During those years, much happened that was not expected: various political coalitions fell apart, and power shifted from one ideological side to the other as the economy and polity changed dramatically. Only in 2007 did a two-party system emerge.

The Historical Base

Poland's past both facilitated and complicated its move to democratization. Communism in Poland was always less rigid and repressive than in other countries. As a result, beginning in 1956, private farms came to dominate the

---

* Wojciech Jaruzelski, 1989–90; Lech Wałęsa, 1990–95; and Aleksander Kwaśniewski, 1995–2005.

agricultural sector; small businesses and trade were allowed; and Poles turned increasingly to the West, both culturally and socially. Protests occurred and, after repression failed, ultimately brought limited reforms, which created a sense that the regime would give in to popular pressure. The single-house Parliament, the Sejm, had candidates not just from the Communist Party but also from a Peasant Party and a Democratic Party for small business, as well as two small "Catholic" groups: a Catholic intellectual group, Znak, and a more pro-Communist organization, Pax, on its list. Voters could cross names off the list, but this did not really affect the results. Opposition groups also developed, although most were not legal. Professional groups remained under state control even as they defended their interests. As a result, there were known spokesmen and experts who could work together in the negotiations between opposition groups and the regime.

The Catholic Church in Poland, with its nationalist tradition, was allowed to function; it had representatives of its lay groups in the Sejm and organized various groups. Although the state often tried to take away some of the Church's privilege, its power grew from the mid-1950s. When Polish Cardinal Karol Wojtyła was elected pope in 1978 and visited Poland in 1979, the Church's power (and Poles' sense that they could act independently of the state) increased even further, which strengthened popular action. When Lech Wałęsa, the trade union leader of Solidarity (Solidarność), publically signed the 1980 Gdansk Agreement that ended the Solidarity strikes, he used a pencil from the pope's first visit in 1979.

Mass demonstrations of workers in 1956, 1970, and 1976 over price increases were put down, but in each case the government conceded to demands to end price rises and increase workers' benefits. Twice, in 1956 and 1970, the first secretary of the Polish Communist Party was replaced in response to the demonstrations.

Intellectual groups grew out of each of the protests. In 1976, Warsaw-based intellectuals formed the Committee to Protect the Workers to aid the workers jailed in those demonstrations and their families. It expanded to run largely illegal discussions, produce thousands of illegal publications, and run the "Flying University," which filled the holes left by government censorship and control.

Within the Communist Party, a reformist wing developed that helped enact economic reforms and open up the political system. By the end of the 1970s, Poland had borrowed more money from the West to import goods and industrial equipment than it could effectively absorb and pay back. Western creditors pushed for price increases, which triggered the occupation of the shipyards in the Baltic cities in 1980 and provoked demands for a free trade union (Solidarity), the right to strike, and greater transparency in the media. After the government conceded to shipyard workers' demands in the Gdansk Agreement, Solidarity demonstrations around the country resulted in extending concessions to other groups across the country, including peasants, students, and the intelligentsia.

Radical demands for political and social freedoms—and for the economy to provide consumer goods, pay adequate salaries, and modernize—increased in the 1980s because the government could not provide basic food and consumer goods. In response to Soviet pressure, and in order to stem the radicalization of Solidarity in the face of the worsening economic situation (as well as the need to avoid making a major payment on its Western loans that it could not afford), the government declared martial law on December 13, 1981. Solidarity leaders and activists (as well as top party and government leaders responsible for the economic disasters of the 1970s) were interned, police and soldiers were stationed in offices and on the streets around Poland, and international and domestic communications were completely cut. The Reagan administration condemned the imposition of martial law and imposed sanctions barring Polish planes from landing in the United States, freezing Poland's loans, and banning trade. Western European countries did not sanction Poland until later but immediately condemned the attacks.

Over the next seven years, the strictures of martial law were reduced: communications were restored, internees were released, political life and the media slowly opened up, and the government experimented with marketizing the economy to increase production. Yet nothing took away the taint of martial law.

The Final Stage

By the end of the 1980s, Poland's economic situation had improved and most basic goods were no longer rationed, as they had been earlier that decade. Although the Western sanctions had ended, factories had been given more autonomy and workers' wages had increased, the majority of Poles thought their personal situation had worsened. The percentage of the population expressing hope in the future had declined dramatically, from 42% during the early 1980s to 16% in February 1988.[1] The state did not have enough funds to meet its basic obligations and was under pressure from the World Bank and the International Monetary Fund, as well as the United States and Western Europe, to restructure its economy.

The result was popular alienation and even more dramatic economic failures. The party's gradual release of more than 1,000 Solidarity activists, the ending of sanctions, greater privatization in the economy, and invitations to moderate opponents to work with the government did not break the political impasse. By 1988, the situation was so severe that the Communist Party and government saw no choice but to initiate "talks about talks" with the political opposition and the Catholic Church in order to get support for more economic reforms. This initiative was important to Solidarity because, although all of its political prisoners had been released by 1986, the movement had not been legalized and could do little more than participate in strikes and demonstrations.

The Negotiations

The Catholic Church leadership served as the intermediary in 1988 by meeting separately with Lech Wałęsa and with General Wojciech Jaruzelski, the former head of the armed forces and first secretary of the Communist Party who had imposed martial law, to start talks about how to design the negotiations. Lower-level leaders from both sides met regularly. The government made clear that it would legalize Solidarity, even allowing it time on television and the right to publish its own newspaper. Aleksander Kwaśniewski, the minister of youth and sports in what would be the last Communist cabinet and one of the designated negotiators for the preliminary talks, floated a "trial balloon" calling for partially free elections in which 35% of the seats in the Sejm would be open to candidates who had not been members of the Communist Party or its subsidiaries, and 65% of the seats would be reserved for Communist Party candidates, including a National List of 60 top party reformers as well as a new freely elected Senate and a president elected by the two houses. In what seemed to be a concession to the Communist Party, which already had its electoral workers in place, it was agreed that the elections would be scheduled soon after the Round Table Talks ended. Solidarity accepted this offer as the basis for a new system, and the government and Communist Party supported it as well.

One representative from Solidarity and one from the government headed each of the three "tables" that made up the Round Table Talks. These tables in turn were composed of a series of task forces or "subtables" that included some 500 experts and activists. A Solidarity specialist and a specialist representing the establishment parties led each task force. They developed economic and social proposals for consideration by legislators after the election, and worked out agreements on a new government structure and a plan for how elections would be conducted, including free elections for Parliament and the presidency that would take place four years after the 1989 elections. Solidarity also won the concession that a new constitution would be passed only after there was a freely elected National Assembly.

The agreements were signed on April 4, 1989, and elections were held on June 4. Candidates endorsed by Solidarity won all the nonparty seats in the first round. On the Communist Party list, only three candidates got a majority in their districts, and only two on the National List received a majority in the first round. Both sides were shocked and unprepared: Solidarity had not run with a platform for "what next," while Communist Party candidates were prepared to share power, not lose it. The defeat was made more dramatic when the old Peasant Party and Democratic Party defected to Solidarity, creating a 65% majority for this new coalition.

Polish Communist Party leaders accepted these dramatic losses, as did reformist Soviet leader Mikhail Gorbachev. Leaders in Solidarity kept their secret agreement that the assembly and Senate would elect Jaruzelski president by having some deputies not show up for the vote, thus reducing the quorum. Solidarity also agreed to a coalition government that would satisfy Soviet expectations by having established Communist officials lead the Ministries of Interior, Defense, International Trade, and International Transport. At that point, they did not know that Communism would soon collapse elsewhere and the Berlin Wall would come down.

Making Change

Tadeusz Mazowiecki, a member of the Catholic opposition, was nominated to be prime minister by Lech Wałęsa (the titular head of Solidarity) and named by President Jaruzelski. He had been a Catholic editor and member of the Sejm as well as one of Solidarity's leaders in negotiating the Gdansk Agreement and the Round Table Talks. Mazowiecki made it clear that he would serve only if he were able to make his own appointments and decisions. His "grand coalition cabinet" included 12 Solidarity candidates: 7 from the two parties that had defected from the Communist Party and 4 from the Communist Party. Only the Ministry of Foreign Affairs, which the Communist Party wanted to head, went to an expert not aligned with any group.

Mazowiecki, from his initial presentation to the Sejm and Senate in September 1989, made it clear that Poland would focus on the present rather than the past by drawing a "thick line" between the two, and on moving ahead with reforming the political system, stabilizing and privatizing the economy, and "joining Europe." This meant not investigating and punishing people for what they had done in the past. This was necessary because Communists were in the government and still controlled the security services and military. Instead, legislation focused on returning state symbols to what they had been before the takeover, creating electoral laws for free elections and beginning work on writing a new constitution.

Cabinet members held vastly different ideas about what should be done, and cabinet meetings lasted for hours, bringing an uneasy consensus. In the Sejm, the dramatic defeat of Communist Party candidates left them shunned, with little hope of influencing policy. The result was that almost all deputies from both groups voted for Mazowiecki as prime minister, for his cabinet choices, and for the laws his government put forth.

The Communist Party, faced with electoral defeat, disbanded nearly four months after the grand coalition was formed. Most members joined the new

Social Democratic Party of Poland, which inherited the Communist Party's property and funds. Kwaśniewski was one of its founding members and its chair. It began to regroup for the 1991 parliamentary elections as the Democratic Left Alliance (SLD) and was a close second to Mazowiecki's party, the Democratic Union. In 1993, this legacy party to the Communist Party, together with the Peasant Party, led the Sejm because Solidarity had fragmented into many small parties that did not gain enough votes to reach the requisite threshold to hold seats. Then, only six years after the Communist Party's electoral debacle of 1989, Kwaśniewski won the presidential election as the SLD candidate against Wałęsa even though his party's resources had been confiscated and despite attacks in the press and by other politicians.

Joining Europe turned out to be easy, particularly after the Berlin Wall fell. The borders were opened, and Poles were allowed to travel freely. Pope John Paul II became engaged and helped convince other states to agree to Poland's entry into European bodies. Poland was invited to join the Council of Europe in 1990. Until the Soviet Union collapsed and Germany was formally reunified, there was no real possibility of Poland's joining NATO or becoming part of the EU. But by 1991, when the Soviet Union imploded, there had been enough Western engagement for Poland to move toward these goals.

Rescuing and transforming the economy was a more difficult challenge. The last Communist government had attempted to gain popular support by giving substantial pay increases and allowing state enterprises to raise their prices. These policies, coupled with the increasing burden of paying back Poland's large debt from the 1970s, resulted in an inflation rate of 55% by October 1989.[2] Western public and private lenders, as well as international institutions, flooded Poland with experts on the economy and governance, all of whom called for rapid and dramatic economic reform. To restructure the economy, the Sejm voted overwhelmingly at the end of December 1989 for the Balcerowicz Plan, proposed by Minister of Finance Leszek Balcerowicz. This "shock therapy" resulted in a 572% increase in prices, while real wages fell 24% compared to the preceding year, even though Poland received a massive influx of foreign aid and investments, including a billion-dollar "stabilization fund" provided by the United States and Western Europe. Aid and trade, such as food "donations" and imports of food and consumer goods, kept Poland's economy going but also weakened its agribusiness and industry because the Western goods that came in were cheaper, better packaged, and more appealing to Poles.

The government had little money to address the new social problems brought about by these changes, hurting Solidarity's electoral base because there was no real social safety net for those most affected by the closing or sale of state industries and farms. For others, what was terrifying was the drop in their purchasing power and insecurity about what would happen as privatization increased and the government reduced its "footprint."[3] The result was a dramatic loss of support for Mazowiecki and his government, and the fragmentation of Solidarity.

Transformation by Elections

This fragmentation caused Jaruzelski to succumb to pressure to resign so that Poland could hold early elections and have a democratically elected president. In his campaign, Lech Wałęsa attacked Mazowiecki and the intellectuals for bringing Poland's economy down and for letting the Communists off lightly. Mazowiecki ran against Wałęsa's erratic posturing. In the end, an unknown Polish businessman from Canada beat Mazowiecki, but he lost in the second round to Wałęsa. This was the beginning of what would be the increasingly bitter fragmentation of Solidarity. It also set the stage for Wałęsa's attacks on other politicians and his defiance of the constitutional provisions limiting presidential powers.

The 1991 parliamentary elections were initially held to ensure that a constitution could be passed by a freely elected legislature. They also reflected Poland's international need to "play catch up" with the East European states, which had democratized later when they were less encumbered by fear of the limits the Soviets might impose. Because their initial elections were free, they were eligible before Poland to elect representatives to the Parliamentary Assembly of the Council of Europe.

The results of this first free parliamentary election in 1991 were disastrous for political stability. Solidarity had fragmented into many parties; the strongest of these were populist and steeped in religious nationalism. After a battle over the election rules, the thresholds were set so low that more than 111 parties qualified to run; 29 passed the 5% threshold to gain seats in the Sejm, and 22 placed in the Senate. No party or coalition had a safe majority. That outcome, coupled with Wałęsa's desire to control all decisions, led to constant battles over appointments and fierce debate over erasing the "thick line." Poland no longer had a cabinet of different views that unified on critical policy issues or a Sejm that respected the government's decisions.

The Sejm collapsed after radicals close to the minister of the interior accused prominent members of the government and Sejm, as well as Lech Wałęsa, of being secret police agents. As the Sejm dissolved, a new temporary "small constitution" was passed that specified the roles of the various institutions and set a higher threshold for seats in the Sejm. In the 1993 snap election that resulted, the right wing was so divided that few parties made the threshold for seats. The SLD gained new electoral support from being outside the battles and for building a reputation as "rational modernizers"; its supporters also included those who remembered the benefits of Communism and those who were attacked for their involvement in Communist rule. The SLD and the Peasant Party dominated the resulting Sejm.

Two years later, Kwaśniewski defeated Wałęsa in the presidential election. During his term, a new constitution was adopted that reflected the lessons learned from the preceding seven years. It circumscribed the powers of the presidency and gave all legislative powers to the two houses of the Sejm, including the power to override a presidential veto. The president was left with only limited powers to disband the Sejm. Poland joined NATO and later the EU, after receiving massive amounts of aid to meet the standards for EU membership and to align the Warsaw Pact Army and its equipment with NATO requirements.

Although many still suffered in the new economy, Poland became a prosperous member of the European community. Yet dealing with the abuses of the Communist past remained unsettled and unsettling. Claims and counterclaims—and exposures of what the secret police had done—became tools of the radical right. Until legislation was passed in 1998 that established an Institute of National Memory, "wild lustration" revelations about who was an agent spying on whom were the stuff of political battles and created profound instability. The past haunts Poland even today, undercutting the Church with revelations of priests as agents and diminishing the respect people have for the Sejm and (during the Wałęsa and Kaczynski presidencies) for the presidency. The focus has been on who did what (and when) rather than on how to solve current problems.

The Polish public has been much less interested than the politicians in punishing people for the past. The trials that began in 2006 against Jaruzelski and those around him for imposing martial law and attacking demonstrators in 1970 drew no real public interest. Candidates for public office and political appointments are required to admit to having been agents (if they were), but many whose admissions were posted at the polling stations have been elected.

Lessons Learned

When Communist Party leaders reached out to Solidarity in 1988 to devise a way to include the opposition in the system, they were pushed by the need to engage Solidarity in what they knew would be painful economic changes. After all, despite making reforms and opening up the system, the declaration of martial law in 1981 had not been forgotten or forgiven.

They took a unique path that moved from engaging Catholic Church leaders as supporters of negotiations to informal talks with intellectual supporters of Solidarity and then a formal roundtable process. For Solidarity's leaders, the Round Table Talks were a chance to reemerge as a legal organization that could take some credit for improvements in people's lives. This process happened because Solidarity had a ready base of negotiators and experts who were known for their opposition work; individuals on both sides knew each other and could work together. In addition, the government and party leadership who committed to change were the very people who had declared martial law and controlled the security services, so there was no question of effective rearguard opposition from the old Communist establishment. From the beginning, the process was public. Once the talks started, experts representing both sides conducted discussions on not only how to open and restructure the system but also social and economic issues, ranging from education reform to workers' rights, that mattered concretely to people.

The election results, which were a surprise to both sides, changed the process, but because Communist leaders had designed the election rules, there was nothing they could do but accept defeat and the defection of their allies. Neither side knew what would happen next. Solidarity leaders brought all the parties into the cabinet, and those who had run as Communist Party members then voted for the dramatic political and economic changes.

Because neither side had a plan for what should be done, it was possible to make irreversible, drastic economic and political changes, but these changes also led to a bitter fragmentation of Solidarity and irresolvable fights about dealing with the past. Poland's political system evolved on the basis of what had worked (or not) in the first decade of the transition. These lessons were reflected in its 1997 constitution.

While Poland's transformation was its own, outside actors played major roles. The demise of Soviet control over Central and Eastern Europe in 1989 and the Soviet Union's dissolution in 1991 opened the doors for previously unimaginable changes. Western engagement with Poland from the mid-1950s let Poles know there were alternatives to Communism and that the outside cared about them. Western economic ties put pressure on Poland's rulers to reform both the political and economic systems.

For the new government, Western advisors as well as loans and aid from Western governments and international institutions were significant in determining the direction of economic reform and holding the economy together after the reforms. Becoming "European" sped up the process of economic and political change. Along with membership in NATO and the EU, this also legitimized the new system for the population, even though many had suffered initially from the reforms.

In the end, this Western engagement and the support it provided, as well as the early and irreversible steps taken to transform the economic and political structures of the old system, led to Poland becoming perhaps the most stable and prosperous of the post-Communist states. It serves as one of the most successful cases of transition from authoritarian rule to democracy. Poland's economy has outperformed most of Europe during the post-2008 recession, and Polish politics have survived the bumpy ride to become democratic and institutionalized on an enduring basis.

Biosketch of Aleksander Kwaśniewski, President of Poland 1995–2005

PHOTO: ADAM CHELSTOWSKI / SCANPIX

Aleksander Kwaśniewski, a career politician, rose through the Polish United Workers' Party (Communist Party) to a minor cabinet position in the last Communist government. He was a major player in the transition from authoritarian Communist rule to democratic governance and a market economy and led reformed Communists to electoral success, serving two terms as president in a semipresidential system.

He began as a leader of a Communist student organization in Gdansk in 1976, and then was editor of the party's two national student periodicals. In the last years of Communist rule, from 1985 to 1990, Kwaśniewski served as a cabinet minister for youth and sports, and then as head of the government's Social-Political Committee from late 1988 to 1989. In 1989, he co-chaired, with Tadeusz Mazowiecki, the Round Table group dealing with trade union affairs.

When the Communist Party disbanded in 1990, Kwaśniewski was a co-founder and chairman of its successor, the Social Democratic Party, and its parliamentary caucus, the SLD. Under his leadership, the SLD did well in Poland's first fully free elections in 1991 and won the 1993 parliamentary elections; Kwaśniewski then led the governing coalition. This electoral victory and his subsequent victory over Lech Wałęsa in the 1995 presidential election resulted from both public dissatisfaction with Poland's "shock therapy" economic program and Kwaśniewski's emphasis on efficient nonideological political leadership, which was focused on economic transformation.

As president, Kwaśniewski was able, by concentrating on effective administration, to bridge the gaps between left and right in his first term, both when the SLD was the ruling coalition and after the right defeated the SLD in 1997. He won parliamentary agreement and popular approval for a new constitution in 1997—with limited presidential powers—to replace the "small constitution" that had followed the transition. He continued the economic transition to capitalism, brought Poland into NATO and the EU, and won reelection as president in 2000. In 2001, Kwaśniewski helped the SLD return to parliamentary power in coalition with the Polish Peasant Party in 2001, only to have the SLD collapse in 2006.

During his presidency and after, Kwaśniewski promoted cooperation among Central and Eastern European countries and encouraged democratization in the larger region. He led the mediation efforts that ended the Orange Revolution in Ukraine in 2004 and headed delegations to observe the subsequent trials of Ukrainian political figures accused of human rights violations. He has also lectured widely.

....

Interview with President Aleksander Kwaśniewski

Poland has been described as one of the most successful cases of transition—from a repressive state apparatus and an inefficient state-controlled economy to a market-based economy and democratic political system. Why was Poland so relatively successful?

I agree that Poland is an example of success. Even during the most recent economic crisis, Poland experienced economic growth and continued political stability, and it has well-regulated relations with all its neighbors.

The issue of neighbors is important because hardly anybody notices that over the years Poland has not moved its borders, while all our neighboring countries have changed. We used to have three neighbors; now we have seven. We managed to establish good relations with all of them. For the last 20 years, Poland has been an exporter of stability in the region.

Why was it possible to achieve a lasting transition to democracy? With regard to the level of political activity of the people, the changes within the Communist Party, and early attempts to reform the previous system, Poland was certainly better prepared for the changes than other countries in this region. Also, Poland had more links with the West than other countries in the region through the Polish diaspora and through contacts between people, such as international scholarships funded for Poles that supported people who later played a vital role in the reforms.

In Poland there was an additional factor that encouraged dialogue and mitigated extreme behavior: the Catholic Church. For practically the entire time after World War II, Poland had permanent political crises, reoccurring about every 10 years; the first one was in 1956, the second in 1970, the next in 1976. Those took their toll on the Communist Party. Then in 1980–81 the Solidarity movement entered the picture.

Generally speaking, Polish Communism changed for the better after each of these crises. In 1956, Stalinism ended and a Polish national path was introduced, which was led by Władysław Gomułka [Communist leader and de facto leader of Poland 1945–48, 1956–70]. One may criticize him for much, but his efforts helped gain Poland some independence from the Soviet Union. Gomułka fell in 1970, and in the 1970s Edward Gierek [leader of the Communist Party 1970–80] brought a partial liberalization of the political system and opened up more to the West. Gierek modernized Poland. Of course, one may criticize him for the loans he took, but on the other hand this was the period when Poland made a modernizing leap. We can joke about it, but this year marks the 40th anniversary of producing the first Polish mini Fiat, which became the typical Polish car. It was also my first car. This was a big step because, thanks to that, Poland became a society of people driving.

The year 1980 marked the end of the Gierek period and the birth of the Solidarity movement—which was without precedent in the Soviet bloc. It was final proof that society expected not "democratization" but democracy, and that the half measures were not enough. The slogan repeated by the party for years—"socialism yes; distortion no"—was no longer accepted.

Social Mobilization

Can you explain the difference between what you refer to as "democratization" and "full democracy"?

Democratization means that we still have only a partial democracy, something that is close to democracy but still is not democracy. In Poland, we had a system that was described as a democracy: "Socialist democracy." There was a very famous joke at this time: "What is the difference between democracy and Socialist democracy? The same as the difference between a chair and an electric chair." One word changes the substance of the idea. And this was Solidarity's main challenge to the system in 1980–81, because the rise of a new generation, a better-educated generation, the people in the big cities, and even the working class, meant that the fighters against the Communist Party were not intellectuals; they were not professors in the academies or dissidents. No, the main fighters against this Communist Party and its program were workers, and that undermined the claims of the Communist Party. The party put the working class at the core of everything it represented. So this period of 1980–81 was very important.

Of course, the revolution of the Solidarity movement was very much connected with the election of Pope John Paul II in 1978. The pope's first visit to Poland in 1979 contributed to this huge movement. Millions of people attended his masses and meetings. Everything was organized not by the government or by official structures but by the people, through the self-organization of society. For the first time in this period of Communism, the people finally realized that they could do something alone, and something great, like an event for one million people.

In 1980, the atmosphere changed very much. The majority of those in Solidarity didn't speak about changing the system because it was still too risky. Brezhnev [general secretary of the Central Committee of the Communist Party of the Soviet Union 1964–82] was still in the Kremlin. But it was a fight for dignity; it was a fight for freedom; it was a fight for democracy as such, not just democratization. Not partial solutions. The people asked for real solutions. And they did so at a time of very deep economic crisis.

Weakening of the Authoritarian System

What was the response of the Polish Communist Party to widespread demands for democratic opening and economic advancement in the context of constraints imposed by the Soviet Union?

Two elements were decisive for the collapse of Communism, in a political and social sense. First were the events of 1968 in Prague, Czechoslovakia, and the subsequent Soviet invasion in response to the reforms proposed by the Czech Communist Party. It was the beginning of the ideological deterioration of the system, because if you have Communist leaders speaking about reforms and you have to use soldiers to stop them, it means that ideologically this system doesn't work. The second element that was decisive for the collapse of Communism was Solidarity, a movement with 10 million people, the majority of whom were Polish workers fighting against the system.

In 1981, the answer of [Wojciech] Jaruzelski, the first secretary of the Communist Party of Poland at this time [1981–89], was martial law. Instituting martial law was one of the most dramatic decisions in Polish history. Today if you ask Polish people what they think about that decision, opinions are very divided: 50% are sure that it was necessary because the situation was extremely dangerous and a Soviet invasion was very likely, and 50% believe that it was not necessary and that Jaruzelski didn't explore all the other possibilities to find a solution. If you ask me, I am sure that fear of a Soviet invasion was very, very strong. It is quite possible that if the situation in Poland had continued in this way, the next month the Soviets, or Warsaw Pact troops, would have decided to intervene. Of course, this would have been a very special kind of "invasion," because at this time 200,000 Soviet soldiers were already on Polish soil. It would not have been necessary to send troops from Vladivostok to Warsaw. It would have been enough to use the soldiers staying in Rembertów, 20 km from the center of the city.

So the 1980s was a time of major problems for Jaruzelski and for Solidarity. For the first time, society was extremely split. After the imposition of martial law, the majority of Poles were disappointed, frustrated, and passive. The position of the Communist Party, of the government, was weak. Despite some reforms, the economy was going badly. Poland had problems with all its Western partners: no money, no credit, no normal relationships. The Soviet Union's situation was deteriorating, so it could not offer any kind of assistance to Poland.

Establishing the Basis for Dialogue and Negotiation

The situation was quite dramatic, and Jaruzelski understood more and more that he needed a real breakthrough. He needed to have some dialogue with the opposition, and of course he first asked the Church to start this dialogue because, for Jaruzelski at the beginning of the 1980s, the Polish Catholic Church was a representation of society. In my opinion, he overestimated the Church's role and position. I had the impression that Jaruzelski, who had good contacts with the Church, was sure that working with the Church would be enough to find a solution. But it wasn't enough because there were many political opposition groups that were not connected with the Church.

Changes happening in the Soviet Union were another important factor, with Gorbachev introducing perestroika in 1986. Until 1986, of course, it was very difficult in all Communist countries to think about a more open dialogue with the opposition. After 1986, Gorbachev gave Jaruzelski a green light. He said, "OK, if you want to make some extra reforms, of course respecting Socialist ideas and values, etc., go ahead." Gorbachev was not so advanced in the beginning. He knew that it was necessary to do something, but he had the problem of explaining the necessity of perestroika and other changes.

By the end of the 1980s, Jaruzelski was absolutely sure that it would only be possible to solve Poland's problems through dialogue. The timetable was very bad for him, because the next elections in Poland were to take place in 1989. Of course it wasn't a normal democratic election because all the candidates were approved by the Communist Party. The real issue was participation. The level of voter turnout would indicate the scale of support for the party. In many cases, the numbers made public had been invented. But the leaders knew very well what the real results of the elections were. In the party, it was obvious that in the upcoming election there was no chance of having a turnout higher than 30% or 40%. A low turnout would be a strong signal that the system was not accepted and that people were looking for change.

The convergence of these factors—the economy, the divided society, the upcoming election—made Jaruzelski determined to start to speak with the opposition. The first very discreet talks started in 1988, and we officially started our Round Table Talks in 1989, from February to April. After that, the system changed.

Explaining the Success of the Polish Transition

Going back to the main question—what was the source of our success—first I think Poland was better prepared for the reforms than other countries. The "permanent" crises in Poland had changed the Communist system, making it in some ways more liberal than others in the Eastern bloc. In Poland we had a very strong opposition and a traditional opposition movement that had been in existence for quite a long time. We had some dissidents in the Communist Party in 1956, and after that we had quite strong opposition organizations, such as the Workers' Defense Committee (Komitet Obrony Robotników) in 1976 with Jacek Kuroń [a prominent leader of the democratic opposition] and others. Gierek was liberal enough to tolerate these groups, and they were active at the end of the 1970s. And of course we had a quite huge, strong opposition with Lech Wałęsa as the leader of Solidarity, and many others were involved. So in the 1980s Poland was really divided, but the non-Communist part of society was quite well organized, especially the Solidarity movement, but even some of the other small groups. These movements established a good organizational infrastructure, recognized alternative political organizations, established opposition leaders, and represented years of discussion about how Poland should be run for the changes that would follow.

The next important element is that there were people who were prepared to lead and implement changes. They were very well educated here in Poland; they had some experience from the West, and all these people were in their late 30s or early 40s, which is the best age to take a political role and to start such reforms. Many were educated abroad, especially in the West. And when they had the opportunity, they were ready to propose reforms. Leszek Balcerowicz [deputy prime minister and minister of finance 1989–91 and 1997–2000, architect of "shock therapy" economic reforms known as the Balcerowicz Plan] is a good example. He spent some time in the United States at St. John's University. Marek Belka [prime minister 2004–5, minister of finance 1997, 2001–2], who is governor of the Central Bank now, also studied in the United States.

In addition, the last Communist government, the government of Mieczysław Rakowski—the famous editor in chief of *Polityka*, a good Polish newspaper, and the last first secretary of the Communist Party [1989–90]—was the prime minister before the transition [1988–89]. His government, of which I was a member, introduced a lot of very important reforms and new laws that very much helped the Polish economy. The most important of these was the so-called Bill of Wilczek. Mieczyslaw Wilczek was minister of industry, and his idea was to create a good climate for entrepreneurs. In my opinion, everything that Wilczek proposed 25 years ago was much better than what our government is proposing now. So we had a better climate for business in terms of taxes, bureaucracy, etc., than other Communist countries. Of course, it is necessary to say that the economic situation of Poland was tragic those days. But despite this, we were courageous enough and determined enough to make these reforms.

Establishing the Basis for Dialogue and Negotiation

In terms of how the key actors approach negotiations such as the Round Table Talks, much depends on their relative strength. In some cases you have a strong government and a weak opposition, or the opposite. You explained that Jaruzelski took the initiative, but you had one main opposition actor, Solidarity. How did the discussion among hard-liners and with reformers unfold?

You can have a strong government with weak opposition or a weak government with strong opposition. The best situation, which happened in Poland, is if you have weaker partners on both sides, not stronger partners. Before the Round Table negotiations, the two main partners were totally weak. The Communist Party was weak and without a plan for what to do or how to manage the ineffective economy. For a majority of the people, and even for many in the Communist Party, it was absolutely obvious that it was necessary to make some very deep political reforms. Solidarity was also quite weak. It wasn't the Solidarity of 1980 and 1981 with 10 million members. It was Solidarity after 10 years: very exhausted and not as popular. I think that the success of the Polish Round Table was possible because we had two not very strong sides, but both had a deep conviction and feeling of responsibility that it was time to do something important for the future, because the situation could not continue. That is quite an important element. In my opinion, if you have one side that is strong and the other quite weak, compromise is impossible to reach. You can see this in the Israel-Palestine conflict today, for example.

The Communist Party in Poland was two million people, with various tendencies inside, but two major groups. There was the group of "reformers," who realized that change was needed and that without really profound changes we would have no chance. Of course among the reformers there were some that were more cautious reformers, others more aggressive reformers, and still others more courageous. The leader of this group was Jaruzelski; if Jaruzelski had not been convinced of the necessity of reforms, nothing would have happened. The other leaders of Communist parties in the region—Erich Honecker [general secretary of the Central Committee of the Socialist Unity Party of Germany 1971–89] and Gustáv Husák [president of Czechoslovakia 1975–89] never accepted reforms—only János Kádár [general secretary of the Hungarian Socialist Workers' Party 1956–88] did. Jaruzelski understood that martial law was necessary in the early 1980s, but after martial law, he saw that his only option was dialogue. He did not have any way to be tougher, stronger, or more repressive. For him, the only way forward was to be a more liberal leader, not a more repressive one. Of course, there were members of the party who were against these reforms, who spoke about the huge risk connected with them. Their main argument was that if we continued with all these reforms, the Communist Party would lose power. We can say now in hindsight that they were right. The reformers were not right regarding the future of the party. When we started the reforms—Gorbachev with perestroika, Jaruzelski here in Poland—it turned out to be the beginning of the end of the party.

Creating the Consensus for Change

Jaruzelski decided to pursue the Round Table Talks and reforms in the latter part of the 1980s. Gorbachev encouraged and supported him, which was important for Jaruzelski. It was a tense situation. During one of the meetings of the Central Committee, when the debate was very dramatic, hard-liners started to attack Jaruzelski about the Round Table dialogue, saying that it was wrong and that it would destroy the party. For the only time in his long political career, Jaruzelski decided to use a kind of blackmail. He said that he saw that many of his comrades were against the dialogue, so he was ready to resign, and they could elect a new first secretary. Some of his closest collaborators said they would also resign. Then of course the Politburo decided to follow the decision of the Central Committee. When they voted, the result was that Jaruzelski should stay, and with that there was acceptance of the pro-reform line of the party. In Communist parties, such dramatic situations, with threatened resignations and revolts, simply do not happen. The offer to resign was a very important signal of Jaruzelski's determination, and that of his team, to make these reforms.

At this time I was 31 or 32; I was the youngest minister in the Polish government because I was nominated as minister for youth and sport when I was only 31. I was young and quite well educated, and I had traveled around the world. In 1976, I spent three months as a student in the United States. So for me it was quite easy to understand what it looked like to compare Communism and the Soviet Union with the West, with the developed countries. And it was absolutely a disappointing observation and an extremely frustrating situation. I also spent time as a student in West Germany. At that time, it was terrible to compare Poland to West Germany. There was nothing to compare; Poland was so underdeveloped.

For my generation it was absolutely obvious that Poland needed to change, that we needed modernization. We wanted to be part of this better-developed world. The problem was how to do it. What should be the approach? I and my colleagues in the university had two or three general positions. The first, which was my position, was that we should do everything possible to support reforms, to change the system as much as possible, but at the same time to accept the situation that we had the Warsaw Pact, the Soviet Union, all these limitations that were the result of World War II, and that these were impossible to change. Some colleagues from the opposition (and the opposition was quite active at this time at the end of the 1970s) said that the system was impossible to reform. They thought it was necessary to fight against this system, even if we would pay a very high price.

The third position of many of my colleagues was that neither of the above strategies would work. We were not ready to change and to reform the system from the inside. We were not ready to pay a high price to be new revolutionaries or to be jailed as dissidents. The only option was to leave. Many of my colleagues did leave Poland at the beginning of the 1980s, and this wave of Polish immigration, especially after martial law, was quite large. Many Poles are still in the United States, Australia, South Africa, and in many European countries.

I was a member of the Communist Party and a minister in the government, and for me everything that was happening in the last years of the 1980s, before the Round Table Talks, was fascinating—a chance to do something that was close to my thinking. I was involved in all these processes from the very beginning, because one of the first decisions Rakowski made in order to change the situation and to make some political reforms was to discuss the new Law of Associations with the Church and the opposition. At the end of the 1980s, this new law allowed various kinds of associations to organize outside the state's control. This was a big step forward.

I was the chairman of the dialogue with the Church. I remember meeting with some bishops and their advisers. One of the advisers of the episcopate was Jan Olszewski [prime minister 1991–92]. They were extremely surprised because we were such a young team. The first reaction of our interlocutors was quite negative because they were sure that Rakowski was joking, that he was not serious in sending such young ministers to discuss this Law of Associations. For my generation it was a wonderful opportunity; for us it was not a big problem that our old party would not be able to be active in the new era.

Process and Mechanism for Negotiation

How did General Jaruzelski and his team understand the situation heading into the Round Table Talks?

Jaruzelski had the minister for interior, Czesław Kiszczak [1981–90], on his team as the leader of the Round Table Talks. It was a very good idea that the minister of interior, the most hated person from the standpoint of the opposition, was the government's leader in the talks, because the opposition saw him as a man who could make decisions. He had the closest contact with Jaruzelski and he, as the main oppressor, was now responsible for democracy and liberalization. So from a political and psychological point of view it was, in my opinion, a very correct decision. Florian Siwicki, minister of defense; then Prime Minister Rakowski; three members of the Politburo (Stanislaw Ciosek, Wladyslaw Baka, and Janusz Reykowski); and I were also on his team.

I was never a member of the Politburo; I was only a member of the government, a minister in Rakowski's government, but I was one of the co-chairmen of the three groups in the Round Table. The general structure of the Round Table had all delegates sitting around a table; these meetings had two chairmen, Kiszczak and Wałęsa. For all documents and decisions we had three committees. I was co-chairman with Mazowiecki, and we discussed trade unions and how to legalize Solidarity. Reykowski, a member of the Politburo, and Professor Bronisław Geremek were co-chairmen of the political committee. The third group discussed the economy; [Wladyslaw] Baka, a member of the Politburo, and Professor Witold Trzeciakowski, an opposition member, were co-chairmen. So Jaruzelski worked with this team, and his role was absolutely crucial.

In my view, there were several elements in Jaruzelski's thinking. The first was that after martial law it was very important to find a new solution, because organizing something similar to what existed again would be a disaster; the situation was totally different. I think the idea of democratization and liberalization was close to Jaruzelski's heart. I am not so sure that Jaruzelski was thinking about full democracy. I think he thought much more about democratization. But I very much respect his determination because I saw it. He is one of very few politicians who started his career with martial law and finished it with dialogue and a peaceful transition of the political system. It is much more common to have a democratically elected prime minister or president who ends up imposing martial law or some other very repressive response. I think that among dictators or quasi-dictators he is really a very special person.

What was the strategy of the Communist Party going into the Round Table Talks?

The idea was very simple: to invite the opposition and propose to share power and responsibility. The idea at the beginning, and of course we were not right, was that the process of transition would take at least four years. And the election, according to the constitution, was to be in 1989. The 1989 election was not fully democratic. The idea was to give 35% of seats in the Parliament to the opposition in a free election, with 65% of seats reserved for the Communist Party and its allies. Then there would be a presidential election, and from the very beginning (though we never officially discussed it) it was absolutely clear to everybody that the presidential candidate during the transition period would be Jaruzelski. I proposed the idea of organizing a Senate, a second chamber of Parliament. The opposition was very much against it because they said that they could accept one not fully democratic election to Parliament, but how many such elections could they accept? And then I proposed an absolutely free election to the Senate, and it was accepted. It surprised the opposition leaders as well as my colleagues, but I explained to them that the party, which had been ruling the country for almost 50 years, should be prepared to participate in one absolutely free election for Senate. Even if 100% of the senators were from the opposition, there would still be a small majority to elect Jaruzelski president. My argument was demagogic. I said, "Look, if this party is not ready even to undertake such a small experiment, it means it is not a political party. Then it will be necessary to admit that our party is not able to win anything. So how can we say that we are ready to run the country but we are not interested in such an exercise with the election?" Of course, I was not so pessimistic. I was sure that in the Senate election at least 30% or 35% of seats would be in the hands of the Communist Party. With Jaruzelski as president, even with a freely elected Senate, we would still have control of the majority of Parliament, and it would have worked for the next stage [freely elected bodies four years later].

Everything changed after the election in June. It was impossible to ignore the results, which were in favor of the opposition. Again, **Jaruzelski was quite responsible, because many in the Communist Party and especially in the coalition parties—in some of the small groups and especially the groups connected with the Church—pressed him to declare that the election was illegal and invalid. He said no, that it was necessary to accept the results and even more to accept that it was a bad result for the Communist Party and therefore necessary to think about new solutions for the future. The election accelerated the process, but it would have happened in time anyway.**

Role of Authoritarian Leaders in Fostering the Transition

It does not always require that someone be a lifelong democrat to play an important role in making democracy possible. Would you agree that General Jaruzelski would be a good example of that?

Absolutely. Among all the leaders of the Soviet bloc, Jaruzelski stands out as clever, well educated, very cultured, and dignified. He had a very pragmatic approach. He realized that without dialogue and change he would have no chance to do something about the economy or incorporate the views of the opposition. Another important element was Gorbachev, no doubt, because Jaruzelski had extremely good, close contact with Gorbachev. The personal relationship between them was very good, and I think that for Gorbachev, perhaps, Jaruzelski and Poland were a very important laboratory to see how some experiments would work.

Jaruzelski is a man of many paradoxes. He was born into a very noble Polish family. His schools before the war were Catholic, including the very Catholic school of Marianów here in Warsaw. He lost his father during the Second World War; he died somewhere inside the Soviet Union because the family was deported to Siberia when the Soviet Union invaded Poland. He spent the war years there. Then he started his career in the Polish Army, which was connected with the Communist government. He became a general, minister of defense, and finally prime minister.

Nobody is ideal; he made a lot of mistakes, and in his life there was also a lot of opportunism. But a very special element that I want to underline is his strong patriotism. This is a man of deep feeling for the Polish state. His sense of responsibility for everything that he did and his patriotism were, in my opinion, extremely important for him and for his decisions, especially his last decisions. When he was elected president in 1989, by one vote in the National Assembly, he resigned a year later. He understood very well that his time was finished, and in the most peaceful way he resigned as president of Poland. This made it possible to organize the general election of 1990, and Wałęsa was elected as his successor. If you ask the people who worked with Jaruzelski during those times, like Mazowiecki, everyone would say that his was an extremely loyal cooperation. He still had a lot of influence in the Army and in some parts of the Ministry of Interior, but he never used it to impose his will. He was extremely loyal to the new prime minister and to his successor, Wałęsa. And really it was the end of his political life because after one year he resigned, but it shows that it is possible to start as a dictator and finish as a very pro-democratic statesman.

Building New Political Parties

Why did you decide that you should move ahead, leave the old party, and create a new one?

I decided to organize a new party because I saw that the Communist Party of Poland was a party of the past. It existed in a repressive system without democratic rules. This party (and even its type of thinking) had become absolutely ineffective and, frankly speaking, unacceptable in the new era now that we had democracy. One of the first statements in our documents for the new party, Social Democracy of Poland (SdRP), was that we wanted to have a political impact that was proportional to our support, that we respected the rules of democracy. If we receive 5% of the vote, that's our role: 5%. If we got 55%, then we would have a majority and we would be responsible for the country.

The first coalition, which I organized with Włodzimierz Cimoszewicz [presidential candidate in 1990 elections and prime minister 1996–97], was SLD (Sojusz Lewicy Demokratycznej), the Democratic Left Alliance. This party became part of the Social Democracy of Poland coalition [which became the singular post-Communist legacy party]. I am proud that during these 23 years this party has never caused any democratic problems. This is one of the most pro-democratic and cleanest parties. All aspects of democracy are completely accepted by the party.

Did you expect that there would have to be a new party when the negotiations began?

No, not exactly. During the negotiations, nobody spoke about new parties because the process was very fragile. We were good negotiators, but we were not prophets. None of us was prophetic enough to know that Soviet Union would collapse, Germany would be united, and the Polish Communist Party would collapse. Frankly speaking, it was probably better that way. If you have too many visions during such negotiations, it is not very helpful, because what will such a change mean?

Thank God we didn't discuss the unification of Germany. We only discussed how to change the political system and the economy in Poland. During a very long and exhausting discussion with the opposition I said to them, "Look, I know that to fight for power is complicated. But why is it so complicated to resign from power?" For me it was absolutely obvious that this dialogue between the opposition and the Communist Party meant that we would at least share power and responsibility. The opposition was coming into politics, and that was important. In the election of June 1989, Solidarity won in a very spectacular way; they won 99 out of 100 seats in the Senate. For me the result was clear: the Polish Communist Party was a party of the past that had no chance to be an effective and respected element in the new democratic Poland.

Economic Reform

The crucial period for our success was after the 1989 election. The new government of Tadeusz Mazowiecki [first noncommunist prime minister 1989–91] was, formally speaking, a coalition government because representatives of all political groups were sitting in the Parliament. This Parliament, elected in 1989, was not fully democratically elected, but it was extremely dedicated to making all these reforms. It was very bipartisan in its approach to all the issues.

The positive atmosphere of the transition, this eruption of hope, and positive expectations were used by the government of Mazowiecki and Balcerowicz to implement economic "shock therapy." Shock therapy means very tough measures in the economy, so people lost money and in many places jobs. We closed a lot of big factories. Unemployment increased very much. But if you want to do shock therapy, it is necessary to find the right time. Without good timing, shock therapy will not succeed. In some countries they decided to implement shock-therapy measures two to three years after the return to democracy. But by then it was too late because the people were not so enthusiastic and less prepared to sacrifice.

There were important social factors as well. In this new environment, Poles showed something that surprised even us: a strong spirit of entrepreneurship. It was unbelievable. Now Poland is probably one of the most pro-entrepreneur-oriented societies in Europe. We have around two million small- and medium-sized companies with seven or eight million people working in them, and these companies are very flexible, which is why during the recent financial crisis we managed the situation so effectively. If you have two or three big companies and you have problems with trade, it can be hard for the government to manage the situation. If you have two million small companies, you may not know what they are doing, but they find some niche. This rise of small-scale entrepreneurs was extremely positive for Poland.

Decentralization

The next important change that contributed to our success was decentralization. One of the main mistakes of many post-Communist countries is that they have a problem with decentralization. We decided to change the system and give more prerogatives to local and regional authorities. We organized the first fully democratic local elections in May 1990, 11 months after the first partially free election of the Polish Parliament. So we can say that, by May 1990, in Poland we had a much more decentralized state with a lot of new power and new money for counties, regions, and provinces.

What was the effect of this decision? First of all, there was much more energy at the local level because the people who wanted to do something could now do it. They had the instruments and they had the funds. Second, people could elect local leaders, people who were well known in the city or the region. They had their own mayors, their own leaders of councils, etc. Decentralization was also very important to get better control over the problems of corruption. Of course, corruption is still a problem everywhere. But if you have a decentralized state structure, it is easier to control corruption. First of all, the bureaucracy is not as developed. If you want to make a decision, it is not necessary to go through many offices and levels. Decision making is closer to the people and the citizens. And if you have strong local communities, they can observe what is going on in these local authorities. It is easy to find out that the mayor of the city one year had a very modest car and the next year had a very good car. This is a simplification, but it illustrates the mechanism.

Consensus for Change

Finally, on any list of reasons for Poland's success, it was important that in the first 20 years it was possible to find very broad political consensus on the main strategic elements of Polish politics, including the democratic changes in 1989–91, the Balcerowicz Plan, and our membership in NATO, which was important for Polish security. We organized a broad consensus for the new constitution that was adopted by referendum in 1997. Then finally we won the referendum for EU membership, with 75% voting in favor. That was probably the last time we had such wide consensus and bipartisanship.

Economic Reform

In all transitions the leading force is political, and leaders decide on economic policies based on their effects on the political evolution of the transition. Although in some countries economic changes were made gradually to avoid backlash, in Poland you applied shock therapy. Why did you make that choice?

Timing is probably the most important element, and it is important to repeat that there is no one answer for all situations everywhere. It would be nice to have two or three prescriptions like you get from the pharmacy to give to Cuba, Myanmar, and others, but that is impossible. But if you want to analyze the Polish case, it is crucial to remember that we had an economic situation that was so bad, so dramatic, that it expanded the space for risky decisions. We were experiencing hyperinflation and had a huge foreign debt. Drastic reforms were the way forward to a better situation. But I think we were lucky because the government decided it was obliged to do something with the economy. They found the right man and the right people, quite a big group of people working with Balcerowicz, and they were intellectually and professionally prepared to do it. **Sometimes it is necessary to perform drastic surgery, but if you do not have good doctors, it can result in tragedy. In Poland, we found good "doctors," specialists who were very determined. During the first months of the new democracy the political situation was full of mutual understanding. There were representatives from the former Communist Party in Parliament. The atmosphere was full of responsibility, full of understanding of the necessity of the situation, of the future.** Since then we have had several fully democratically elected Parliaments, but if you ask many people which Parliament was the best, the answer will be the 1989–91 Parliament, the first and not fully democratically elected Parliament, because there was a special spirit of understanding and commitment.

This combination of major changes in the political system and quite tough decisions regarding the economy was possible in the first two years;

after that it would have been totally impossible. The first fully democratic election for Parliament in 1991 was organized without the 5% threshold so that any party, even a party that won just 1% of the vote, had a chance to be in Parliament. As a result, we had 23 different political parties in Parliament. Can you imagine that these 23 political parties would agree to support a program that was so painful and so complicated that it would cost jobs and create poverty in some regions? It would have been impossible. So therefore timing is important. The people on the streets in North Africa or in other places today are fighting for freedom, for democracy, for dignity, for everything. Of course they are not prepared to accept (or even to discuss) some very complicated economic problems. And of course, when the system changes and they are in power, the first reaction will be more political parties, less dialogue, and more conflict. **It is very difficult to find this small window of opportunity for necessary but painful economic reforms; they are, both practically and theoretically in my view, the main challenge of democratic transitions.**

So how to combine these two elements—a new political system with an eruption of (sometimes very unrealistic) expectations and a very pragmatic economic approach? How to generate support and understanding from the new political leaders, many new political parties, and the people in the streets for these difficult reforms?

What I know from other countries in this region is that when they decided to go step by step without shock therapy (and many leaders were programmatically very much against such policies), they created a lot of problems, because it is still necessary to take many very painful decisions. It is like surgery: you can accept even very risky and tough surgery for a very limited time, but if you have less painful but still very unpleasant surgery every month for five or seven years, that will be intolerable. That is a little bit of what we have in Greece now, for example.

Constitutional Reform

In most transitions, building a new constitution and a new social pact is critical. In Poland, there were some changes to the constitution in 1989, and further changes in 1992 with the Small Constitution. During his presidency, Wałęsa was not able to pass significant constitutional reform, but you did in 1997. What was the process that enabled Poland to reach agreement to pass a new constitution?

Adopting a new constitution was absolutely crucial and very difficult. Frankly speaking, Poland was very close to having a situation like Chile's [which lacked the political consensus to replace the Pinochet-era constitution]. We had the old Communist-era constitution with more and more amendments because it was difficult to organize a two-thirds constitutional majority in the

National Assembly. It is actually easier to organize support in a referendum. In Poland, the reason to fight for a new constitution was very clear because our old constitution was from the 1950s; it had been sent to Moscow and reviewed by Stalin. So for many people in Poland it was absolutely natural and necessary to change what seemed to be a Stalinist constitution. It was politically important to change it, but it also needed to be changed because of its substance.

My predecessor as the chairman of the Constitutional Committee in Parliament was Professor Geremek, an extremely intelligent and respected person. He was unsuccessful because it was difficult to finish this job in the 1991–93 Parliaments; there were too many political parties with different views. For the election in 1993, we decided to accept a 5% threshold for parties to gain seats in Parliament. With this threshold, and because of the disintegration of forces on the right, no parties from the extreme right were elected to Parliament. The SLD together with our coalition partner, the Polish Peasants' Party (PSL, or Polskie Stronnictwo Ludowe), had a majority in the Sejm. And I [as head of the SLD] was made head of the Constitutional Commission. So I immediately invited a very pro-constitutional party from the opposition, the party of Mazowiecki and Geremek, the Freedom Union, to be part of this constitutional majority, and we started to work together.

When Parliament is considering proposed bills just before its term is finished, they can be thrown out in the new session because the new Parliament is not obliged to discuss bills from the previous Parliament. It was the same with the constitution. We had five or six very useful projects, some of them prepared by conservative parties, which were not in the new Parliament. But I decided that we would work with all these projects.

The idea was to discuss and debate all projects and all proposals. Of course it took a lot of time, but we controlled the agenda because we had the majority. Then we started to speak with the Catholic Church, which was an important actor. We organized a good dialogue with the Church and finally prepared a draft constitution. I was elected president in 1995. In 1997, we put the draft constitution to a vote in a national referendum, and it was approved. That had never happened in Poland. I think that if we hadn't done it at that time, between 1993 and 1997, it would have been extremely difficult to prepare a new constitution because the Parliaments elected later did not have constitutional majorities.

System of Government

It appears that Poland is the only country in Eastern Europe that has a semipresidential system. In your own government, when Jerzy Buzek was prime minister [1997–2001], it was a kind of "cohabitation," whereby the president and prime minister are from different political parties or different coalitions. What is your opinion about the semipresidential system? Are you satisfied with this system today?

Yes, quite satisfied. Why the semipresidential system? That is a long story, but to make it brief, we had two possibilities. The first option was to organize a parliamentarian cabinet system, but there were very strong arguments against this, especially that it would be unstable due to the disintegration of the Polish party system. How could we give all this power to the Parliament and political parties if in the first democratically elected Parliament we had 23 parties? We had governmental crises every six months, and we changed prime ministers many times. It would have been totally irresponsible.

So why didn't we decide to organize a presidential system in Poland? First of all, we were afraid, knowing our history and the history of our neighboring countries, of a presidential system which is strongly centralized, and, frankly speaking, we had the very negative example of the presidency of Mr. Wałęsa. Because the quality of his presidency was so bad, we felt that giving a president more prerogatives, more power, would be dangerous.

Given our experience during these years in Poland, from 1993 to 1995, we decided to propose a semipresidential system. This was not totally unknown; it is in place in France and Finland, for example. In my opinion this system is OK; I am sure that it is the best that we can propose for Poland. I would be very cautious about changing it. I worked for four years in a "cohabitation" with Mr. Buzek, and it was quite effective and manageable. Sometimes, indeed, I had the impression that it is easier to work with a government that is not one's own than to work with one's own government.

We have had some real conflicts, including conflict between Lech Kaczyński [president 2005-10] and Donald Tusk [prime minister 2007-14] in the last few years. This was not a constitutional problem. It was a problem of political conflict between two persons. **My experience has been that if you have good, responsible people in the highest positions of the state, even an imperfect constitution will work. But if you have the best constitution but you have bad people in these positions, it will not work. The quality of the constitution is absolutely important, but it is not enough. It is very important to have positive relationships between the people who are responsible for the country.** If they want to fight each other, the best constitution cannot help, because they will use the constitution how they want.

I think this semipresidential system in Poland is absolutely correct. It created checks and balances, more than in some one-sided systems. When we have a strong government with a majority in the Parliament, it is better if the president is not necessarily from the same party. This element of balance is sometimes necessary to block wrong ideas proposed by the government, which is quite powerful in our system. In our semipresidential system, the roles of government and the prime minister are both strong. For example, the prime minister cannot be removed simply with a vote of no confidence. Before a government can be brought down, the prime minister's opponents must have the votes to elect their own candidate, which is not easy to do. The budget is totally the responsibility of the government and Parliamentary majority; the president has nothing to do with it. The president can veto a bill, but that veto can be overridden by a three-fifths majority in Parliament. It is possible to change some elements of the constitution, and perhaps some should be changed, but generally speaking this constitution is very effective. It stabilizes the Polish political situation and the state.

My message for many new members of Parliament is that, if they want to change something in the constitution, they should consider whether it is better to make changes or to fight for continuity and stability. After all, the stability of the constitution is a value in itself. In the Ukraine, for example, they are changing the constitution almost every three or four months. Theirs is a piece of paper, not a constitution. It is important that people respect the constitution, that there is a constitutional culture as there is in the United States. You can only create such a culture if you refrain from changing it every year or every term.

International Influence

You moved Poland toward membership in NATO and the EU. A few years previously, Felipe González [1982–96] led Spain to join the European Economic Community [forerunner of the EU] and to remain in NATO. Did Spain's experiences serve as a model for you?

Felipe González was a very useful adviser to me. I met him for the first time with Rakowski, during the last days of the Polish People's Republic. We visited González, I think in 1988 and then in 1989 when he was president of the government, and it was very instructive to speak with him. Later I met him several times when I was chairman of the Social Democratic Party and then as president of Poland. Spain was a very inspiring example because there were a number of similarities to our case. We both had dictatorships, then a peaceful transition, and now we have democracy, and this democracy is developing in a very peaceful way without revenge. González explained to us how this was possible in Spain. For example, he described the Moncloa Pact [an agreement in 1978 among political parties, trade unions, and business organizations to address inflation, unemployment, and capital flight and therefore to facilitate the transition]. I remember that we also discussed with González why he was not interested in opening the Pandora's box of history, revisiting the conflicts between the Republicans and others.

We also discussed joining the EU. For us that was an important reason for our respect for Spain. At this time, during the 1990s, Spain was really the best European country. González gave me an important piece of advice. We discussed what the EU calls "homework," the reforms all candidate countries have to make in order to join. You hear so many times, "homework, homework, homework" that you feel like a child, and you hate this description. I said to González once, "Felipe, look, we are so tired of all this homework. Everybody speaks about homework." And he told me a very important thing. "This is absolutely true, I understand you. You can be tired, but look, if you do this homework well, then the benefits will come to you sooner and you will have more benefits after your membership. If you do your homework poorly, you will have a lot of problems in gaining access to the funds and subsidies, everything that will come from the EU after membership." And he was absolutely right. That is one of the reasons why Poland is OK today, because we did our homework almost perfectly. During the first 6 years of membership we received approximately €30 billion. Now we are waiting for the next €30 billion, which is a fantastic injection for us, for modernization, for everything. And it was great advice from González. What is happening in Greece is the result of poor homework and then poor results. If you are not prepared, then the system does not have absorptive capacity, and you have no chance of effective membership in the EU.

How did EU membership influence Poland's democratic transition?

EU membership was very important because it came with a lot of consequences —for the economy, the modernization of Poland, open borders, and trade. But from a political point of view, EU membership meant that finally, after so many years, Poland was part of Europe. It took a lot of effort. Our Association Agreement was signed in 1991; we organized a referendum in 2003, in which 75% voted to join the EU; and our membership formally came into force on May 1, 2004.

These memberships helped strengthen our democratic transition. Another important factor was our regional position, because everything around Poland changed. We went from three to seven neighbors on our borders, and there was a very dramatic conflict, very close to us, in the Balkans. Our thinking was: how can we create the best contacts with all of our neighbors, sign new treaties, and generally create an atmosphere of understanding, friendship, and cooperation—a good neighborhood?

I think one of my successes is that I created such good relationships with our neighbors, including of course Germany, Lithuania, Ukraine, and others. We still have our problems with the Russians, but that is a different story. Our next goal was how to manage this new situation in the region, to create contacts and export stability. During the first period after the transition, our region was a fantastic example of dialogue, cooperation, and stability. But it was not so easy and natural; if you took a plane from Warsaw to Belgrade, you would have seen in the beginning of the 1990s the war in the Balkans with ethnic cleansing and thousands of victims. So you can see two regions that are very close to each other, both formerly part of the Soviet bloc, with two totally different situations. Here stability and good relationships, and there war and drama.

How did the Soviet Union first and Russia later—which was historically important and influential in Poland—continue to influence Poland's transition?

Gorbachev was strategically important to us for many reasons. The first was security. In Poland the security problem is extremely sensitive because our history is one of wars. Frankly speaking, being the country between Germany and Russia has not been easy. There were discussions at the beginning of the 1990s about what would be better for us: neutral like Finland or to join NATO. At this time the Soviet Union still existed, and it was very much against Poland joining NATO. The problem was even more complicated because, during the discussion of the superpowers in 1989-90 concerning the unification of Germany, Thatcher, Mitterrand, George H. W. Bush, and others promised that NATO would not enlarge. But the situation changed and the choice between neutrality and NATO was decided by a majority in Poland. It was decided that we should ask for NATO membership because, for us, in this part of the world, to be neutral means to stay in some kind of gray area, without guarantees or allies. For Finland, for many years, it was a different story because it is not located in such a strategic place, and a neutral Finland and a neutral Austria were very useful for both the Soviets and Americans. But what would neutrality mean in the 1990s?

When we decided to join NATO, we began very difficult discussions with Mr. Yeltsin. We argued that it was possible to enlarge NATO due to the collapse of the Soviet Union; all those promises from the superpowers had been made to the Soviet Union. Now that the Soviet Union was no longer, we could speak about enlarging NATO. Of course, Russia was very much against it. But the Americans and Europeans took a very strong position that NATO enlargement was possible and needed. Poland was in the first group of new members, along with Hungary and the Czech Republic.

I had a meeting at the Kremlin in 1997. The Kremlin has large rooms, and Yeltsin has a very strong voice. He said in Russian, "Why do you want to join NATO? You don't need NATO. I can give you all the necessary guarantees. Why do you want to do this?" So I explained why, and it was a very dramatic discussion. Finally, I said, "Boris Nikolayevich, tell me. What are your relationships with Germany?"

"Very good."

"And with Italy?"

"Fantastic."

"And with the UK?"

"Splendid."

"And with Holland, Denmark, others?"

"Great."

"And with Poland, Czech Republic, and Hungary?"

"Bad, because you all want to join NATO. Why do you want to go to NATO?"

And I said, "Look, Mr. Yeltsin, I mentioned all the members of NATO and you have fantastic, splendid, great, excellent, very good relationships with them, and you have problems only with Poland, Hungary, and the Czech Republic. I promise, if we become members of NATO, we will have the same splendid, great, fantastic, excellent relationships." And he started to laugh and he finally accepted that we would pursue membership in NATO.

I respected Yeltsin very much because he was one of very few Russian leaders with a genuine democratic instinct. He was in an extreme situation, and when he had to choose whether to go in a much more democratic direction, he generally chose the democratic direction. Regarding NATO, he helped us very much.

So, in 1999, Poland joined NATO, which was extremely important to us for three reasons. The first was security, because NATO membership is the best guarantee of our security from the strongest countries in the world. The second was Poland's image abroad: NATO membership helped us attract more foreign investment. The third, historical, element of this decision was that for the first time, after a thousand years, Poland and Germany were in the same military and political alliance. If you know the history, the wars, conflicts, occupation, all the difficult problems between Poland and Germany, this was very important.

What was the US role in Poland's democratic transition?

After the collapse of the Soviet Union and the end of the Cold War we had a unilateral world, with the United States in a leading position. I know there is a lot of criticism of American unilateralism and its arrogant policies, with military actions in Iraq and Afghanistan and so on, but from the standpoint of Central and Eastern Europe, this period was very positive. The Americans helped us earlier, supporting Solidarity and our democratic ambitions. And then, after the transition, they supported us through investments in Poland, helped us to become a member of NATO, and strongly encouraged their European partners—the most important partners, like the United Kingdom, Germany, and France—to enlarge the EU. That was not so easy because we were talking about enlargement by 10 countries, 7 of which were from the former Soviet bloc. The situation in the Baltic states was even more complicated. Poland was a post-Communist country, but Lithuania, Latvia, and Estonia were post-Soviet republics, previously not separate countries but part of the Soviet Union. To offer these countries membership in NATO and the EU, with such strong resistance from the Russian side, was absolutely an American success. As president, Bill Clinton was very supportive. He had Secretary of State Madeleine Albright on his team, a person who knows this region very well, and her role was absolutely crucial.

Contemporary Transitions

Imagine if you were to have meetings with three young leaders from Cuba, Jordan, and Myanmar, and they each come to you because by reputation you are a Felipe González–like figure who has lived through a transition and has insights and wisdom. They come to you and they say, "We know that you are not an expert on Cuba or Jordan or Myanmar but you are an expert on transitions, and we would like to know, at the most general level, what advice you would give us about our responsibility as we move forward." What you would tell them, and would you tell each of them the same thing?

The first thing I would say would be to repeat that there is no one path, no single prescription for all these situations. I think it is a mistake for people who are coming from abroad to say, "This is what worked very successfully in Poland, so you should do it and everything will be OK." No. It is very important to understand local factors and the local situation. But I understand that these young people who come to me will know something about their own countries and that they are responsible for understanding what is going on there.

So I would say, "Ok, let us look at your situation. What are the chances? What are the limits? What are the hurdles?" Second, I would then say to them, **"You should have a strategy, because if you want to change your country, it is necessary to have a vision. And the vision cannot be only that you want to be in power or want to run the country. There is an element of that, but this cannot be the main vision. The vision should be freedom, the vision should be democracy, the vision should be social justice, the rule of law, peace, good relationships with neighbors,** and so forth." A vision and a strategy are extremely important. Poland was lucky because we had a strategy, and it was not just the strategy of one party. But for the majority of people it was freedom, it was security, it was Europeanization, modernization of the country, democracy.

The third element is about the method. Dialogue is the best method of politics. It is necessary to have it, even with opponents, even with enemies. Of course, the idea of dialogue is easier to accept for the opposition, and not so easy for those in authoritarian governments, but dialogue is absolutely the basis of almost everything, because without it you have no chance of going forward.

My fourth piece of advice would be to **understand the various positions of those you are dealing with. You need to understand that, even in your group and especially when you start to speak with others, you will find different types of thinking, different experiences, different sensitivities. In** this very pluralistic world we are different, and it is necessary to recognize and respect all these differences and not to be surprised or disappointed by them.

Speaking more concretely, Cuba's case is closer to my understanding, because I know what it means to transition after Communism. In Cuba, I think the situation is similar, to some extent, to what we had in many European countries, because the first challenge is for the opposition to be more united and to develop a strategy. Castro's ideology was so inspiring that it not only inspired millions of Cubans but also many millions of people around the world. Today, after so many years, the ideology is almost empty. The prospects for Cuba depend a great deal on whether they have groups of reformers inside the Communist Party because, in my opinion, everything that will happen in Cuba in the next few years will primarily be the result of what is happening inside the party, and less the result of relations between the party and the opposition. The experience from our part of the world is that it is necessary to work with groups inside the government and the party that are more open and are prepared for some reforms and transition. It would not be a big surprise if Castro's successor were one of the younger generals who could be quite a strong reformer. The Cuban diaspora can also play a role. But I would be very cautious with the diaspora, because in my opinion the transition should first of all be decided by the people living in the country. A diaspora can support some processes, but it cannot replace the local people.

Role of the Military

In most cases of transition the military has played an important role. What can be learned from the Polish experience concerning the military and police in a transition?

Military structures are a strong part of an authoritarian regime. If the regime grows ideologically and economically weaker, then the power of the security forces, especially the secret police, increases. That is why you had an increasing number of generals in all political bodies, like the Politburo. It is also often the case that you have a bad economic situation, and the people are disappointed. You have disorganization in many sectors of society, and the Army or other security structures serve as a contrast: they have order, discipline, people are working hard. There is a psychological element that is very often used to show that the Army is really the pillar of the system, the pillar of the state, which is the pillar of everything. The secret police is the most dangerous because they are very well organized, well paid, and motivated to resist change. In all dictatorships, the secret police have a one-way ticket because they have soiled hands with so much blood; they can only go forward by becoming more aggressive.

But the Army is in a totally different situation. Armies are huge organizations, and in good armies you have a lot of people with some type of positive, pro-state thinking. They are not happy to participate in military actions against the opposition, but they feel some responsibility for the country's future and security. In most countries, a majority of the people in the Army is from very simple families. They are not sons of aristocrats; they are boys from normal houses—workers, peasants, clerks. As a result, the Army is closer to the normal life of the people. The Army in authoritarian systems can play a very negative role if the political leaders so decide. The Polish experience is that in the Army we found a lot of people prepared for reforms and transition.

In terms of good advice for opposition leaders, in Poland we had two approaches. If one day the representative of the opposition becomes the new prime minister or new president of the country, he cannot change the role of the Army overnight. He cannot say that "now this old Army is finished and I will organize a new Army," or that "the police are out of business and I will organize a new force." Transition means that it is necessary to find some balance between the old system and the new system, but it is not easy. It is necessary from the very beginning to say, "Look, the first thing we expect from all the structures is loyalty to the new government, to the newly elected president," and then, step by step, it is possible to make changes and transform these institutions. If you try to make a revolution from the very beginning, I think it will be ineffective. In Poland we have quite a strong group of politicians—Kaczyński and some of his colleagues, for example—that is absolutely sure that the Polish mistake was that, after the Round Table Talks and the election, a revolution did not happen. In all transitions, there is an element of revolution, an element of revenge: a desire to penalize representatives of the ancien régime in order to feel that real change has taken place. I am very much against this type of thinking. In my opinion, evolution, even if it takes more time and is sometimes quite costly, is better than revolution. Especially now with modern communications, evolution can be quite successful. The transition can be really manageable and can finally, at the end of the day, create very positive results.

The Meaning and Popular Appeal of Democracy

What do you think drives the transition toward democracy in countries as diverse as Poland and Chile, Spain and South Africa, Indonesia and Brazil?

I had discussions with Gorbachev when he was still sure that perestroika was a great idea and that the Soviet Union should still exist. He was, in fact, really the last believer in the Soviet Union. And I said, "Mikhail, you should accept finally that if you are speaking with the people, the question is about freedom of democracy, and of dignity. (Perestroika was in fact about all these values.) You can have only two situations. In one, the doors are closed; in the other, the doors are open. If your idea is to open the door for all these values, for all these expectations, for all these needs of the people, you will have to open it wide. You can't just open the door a little bit. After some time, you will have to totally open it or else have your population burst through the doors, because these are very strong values. These values are animating people, especially young people." We then spoke for a long time about all the crises of the Communist Party in Poland. We agreed that Poland needed more democratization. But that was not enough. Poles and others in 1989 said, "please don't speak about democratization—we want to have genuine democracy, not Socialist democracy, not some other kind of democracy, but *real* democracy." **They instinctively knew very well, even if they were not so well educated, what democracy meant: that we can vote, that we accept the democratic rules, that we have free media, access to the media, etc. You can ask even a simple man on the street what democracy means and he will know.**

....

Biosketch of Tadeusz Mazowiecki, Prime Minister of Poland 1989–91

PHOTO: JANEK SKARZYNSKI / SCANPIX

....

Tadeusz Mazowiecki played important roles in Poland's Catholic opposition from the 1950s until Communism ended in 1989, and then as postwar Poland's first noncommunist prime minister. Mazowiecki studied law but made his career as a Catholic activist and editor. After Poland's liberalization in 1956, he was one of the founders of the lay Catholic intellectual organization, Znak, and edited their monthly, *Wiez*, until 1981. In the 1960s, he was a deputy in the Sejm until he demanded an investigation of the killings of shipyard workers who demonstrated in 1970. He also helped found the Committee to Protect Workers, which brought Catholic and non-Catholic opposition intellectuals together to press for human and labor rights. In 1980, Mazowiecki advised Lech Wałęsa during the Gdansk shipyard demonstrations, and remained as an adviser to Solidarity and edited its weekly publication. When General Jaruzelski declared martial law in December 1981, Mazowiecki was interned for many months, and the weekly was shut down.

Eight years later, Mazowiecki became a representative of Solidarity and its chief negotiator in the political reforms section of the Round Table negotiations. After the stunning defeat of the Communists in the partially free elections of 1989, Mazowiecki was named, on Lech Wałęsa's recommendation, Poland's first noncommunist prime minister. He oversaw the transition from Communist rule to multiparty democracy, the economic reforms necessary for a market economy, the country's turn to the West and NATO, and the initial reforms of political institutions. He designed and ran his cabinet to include the perspectives of all groups that won seats in the 1989 election: he drew on Communist ministers of defense, interior, and transport as well as Solidarity activists and specialists. His leadership style involved listening respectfully to divergent views and then making hard choices.

The immediate negative impact of rapid economic liberalization on many Poles undermined Mazowiecki's popularity, and he lost to Wałęsa in the 1990 presidential election. His personal commitment to "drawing a thick line" under the past rather than punishing former members of the regime facilitated the first democratic transition in the Soviet bloc, though it also meant that recriminations about the past would haunt Polish politics for many years. Mazowiecki remained a deputy in the Sejm until 2001. He served as the United Nations' special rapporteur on human rights for Former Yugoslavia, resigning in 1995 to protest the weak international response to atrocities in Bosnia.

Interview with Prime Minister Tadeusz Mazowiecki

Fundamental Principles

What can a young political leader from a country undergoing a transition from authoritarian rule toward democracy learn from your experiences and those of Poland? What should leaders understand about democratic transitions in order to be able to play positive roles in the history of their own countries?

Those who want to learn from our experience have to decide what is important to them, of course. I'd say that **the most important message I have for a young leader in such a situation is that, when introducing change, you cannot just step into the shoes of those you are overthrowing; you cannot just take power and continue as they did. In other words, it's about intending to change the course of history rather than just swapping one government for another**, which is not a solution. We often speak to people from the Arab Spring countries, and we find out that in some countries one form of persecution is just replaced with another. I don't think that can be called a real change, and that is why I would advise against simply stepping into the shoes of those you overthrow. If you want to make a historic change, that change has to be fundamental. The second important lesson is that we made changes in Poland by peaceful means.

Social Mobilization

How was it possible to make such major changes peacefully?

It certainly didn't happen overnight—it was a complex process. In Poland there were various attempts to change the situation, but the most important one was the creation of Solidarity in 1980, not only as an independent trade union but also as a kind of national independence movement. We were the first country from the Soviet bloc to organize large-scale resistance to the Communist government. We couldn't win by force, could we? Despite the introduction of martial law, Solidarity fought the authoritarian regime exclusively by peaceful means. Peace was our only way to victory. Solidarity was formed while Leonid Brezhnev [general secretary of the Central Committee of the Communist Party of the Soviet Union] was still in power in the Soviet Union, and Soviet military intervention in Poland was a real danger. General Jaruzelski imposed martial law from December 1981 to July 1983, and afterward the Communist authorities did not want to see Solidarity reinstated. But for us the fundamental precondition for entering into the Round Table Talks [1988-89] was the legal restoration of Solidarity. Those were our terms—we would not take a seat at the Round Table otherwise. The government found that difficult to accept. They spent a long time trying to get around it and didn't want to accept it, but for us it was a fundamental precondition.

Defeating the Authoritarian System from Within

Solidarity was legally restored by peaceful means as a result of the Round Table negotiations. We were given back the right to participate in political life. We agreed to what were called "contract elections" to the Sejm, the lower house of Parliament. The ruling party and its satellite parties were guaranteed a majority, and we could only gain 35%. However, entirely free elections were to be held for the upper house of Parliament [the Senate], which hadn't existed under Communism but was now to be restored. We assumed that we would remain in opposition, but events quickly accelerated. It was clear that the Communist Party couldn't form a government that would be able to bring Poland out of its dire economic situation. Inflation was very high, and the economic situation was very bad. The Communist Party was unable to form a government, and their two satellite parties broke away from them. As a result, it was possible to create a new parliamentary majority.

When Lech Wałęsa, the leader of Solidarity, offered me the post of prime minister, I said that he should take that office himself, but he decided against it. I told him that I expected support from him, and that Solidarity would be a protective umbrella over the government. I also said that I would be a real prime minister, not a puppet. This part is important, because in the Communist system the actual power was held by the Politburo, and the government had a purely administrative function. I said that if I were to take such a role and become the head of a government making such important changes—the first of its kind in the Eastern bloc—then the center of power would have to be in the government. I wasn't going to be a puppet prime minister, which meant that no new Politburo, not even our own, could be pulling the strings. I said I would be a real prime minister just as the government would be a real government, and that's how it was. Of course, in time Wałęsa and I began to have our differences, but at this initial stage he gave me a lot of support.

For a few months we were the only country in the Eastern bloc implementing such major changes. Other countries followed later. I knew our changes would have an impact on the situation in these other countries, but I didn't expect this to happen so fast, or that the changes in other countries would be so profound. I thought we might be the only country in the Eastern bloc to implement such changes for some time.

We should also bear in mind that at that time in Poland the Communist Party had 2.5 million members and the satellite parties had about half a million members. So **I thought the government would have to consist of all parties represented in Parliament. The Communist Party couldn't be in the opposition. It wasn't an option because they had a decisive influence on the security apparatus and Army. Imagine an opposition that has control of the military—it's never been seen before. That's why I believed that they also had to join the government.** All the powers represented in Parliament had to be a part of the government. **At some point I realized that it would be a government of fundamental change in three main areas: building a democratic state; changing the economic system—here we faced the question of whether to fix the existing ineffective system of a centralized economy or** shift into a free market economy (we firmly chose the latter), and redirecting foreign policy and opening up to the West.

Establishing the Basis for Negotiation and Dialogue

One element that appears in many successful transitions is the opportunity for trust to develop between the different sides and to get to know each other. How did you create those conditions for trust and dialogue before the Round Table Talks?

An essential element was that we knew changes could only be made if we linked the restoration of Solidarity to a change in the country's economic situation. This was the crucial factor. It's very hard to talk about trust. There was no trust. There was one factor that guaranteed there wouldn't be any cheating, and that was the Church. The existence of such an actor in the negotiations between the people in power and the opposition proved to be very important in our case. Up until the end of the Round Table Talks, I wasn't sure whether they might make stipulations for the restoration of Solidarity that we would find unacceptable. When you sit down to talk, your partner gets to know your capabilities and you get to know theirs: what they can do, and what they can't. Gradually, that knowledge of each other's capabilities becomes important.

Justice and Reconciliation

What essential political reforms were priorities at the beginning of your term as prime minister? What was your vision, and what actions did you and your government take?

I should start by saying that I wanted everyone to embrace the changes, and therefore I said that we would draw a thick line under the past, and we would be responsible only for what we did from that point forward. We knew the past lingered heavily over us, but we wanted to be responsible only for our own actions. I must emphasize here that initially everyone was in agreement on this. Later, it became the pretext for criticism of me, claiming that I supposedly didn't want to hold the Communists accountable for their past actions. I did want to hold them accountable, but I believed that it was an issue for historical debate, and also an issue for the courts when it comes to crimes committed. I didn't think it was an issue for the government. **I believed that the role of the government was to offer democracy to all.**

As I've already mentioned, the most important experience that I would share with others is that you shouldn't step into your predecessor's shoes. This is the heart of the matter. In the previous system, as Catholics, people of faith, we were treated as second-class citizens in relation to party members.

Thus we didn't want to now start treating members of the Communist Party as second-class citizens, because we believed that democracy meant democracy for all, that freedom was freedom for all, and that historic progress would only occur if these rules were followed. **This is the crucial and fundamental assumption upon which my government implemented reforms—it opened up democracy to everyone. Literally, what I was saying meant that from that point forward there would be a new beginning. The deeper meaning was that everyone had a future in democracy.** That was an important part of those policies, and it later resulted in many disputes, but above all it ensured an evolutionary transition.

Setting Policy Priorities

Regarding essential changes, I would say that practically everything needed changing, in all areas. Let's take universities as an example. Higher education institutions wanted us to provide them with autonomy and freedom. But we also needed to provide freedom of education, to implement very important changes in the teaching of history, for example, which affected schools. Actually there wasn't a single area in which changes weren't necessary. I wanted to include everyone.

One of the most important reforms by my cabinet was the reform of local government, meaning the introduction of local democracy. The first completely free democratic local elections took place in the spring of 1990. The long tradition of local democracy had been crushed by the Communist system. It didn't exist anymore, so we had to start from the beginning.

Political and Social Rights

The second issue was ensuring freedom of the press and freedom of assembly. As I was forming my government, there were different political organizations in opposition that were not legal, but I spoke of them as if they were. In a way, you could say that I was making them legal in practice. It wasn't until 1997 that we made constitutional changes. Attempts had been made by the Parliament before that. Maybe it was a mistake, but I thought a fundamental change was the most important thing and that changing the constitution would follow as a result. The fundamental changes we made, however, were democratic.

Economic Reform

Another critical area was the economy. We had to deal with rampant inflation but at the same time create laws that would fundamentally change the economic system. This was done by passing a series of laws. These changes were implemented between 1989 and 1990.

International Influence

What was your foreign policy strategy? How did external actors and circumstances influence the Polish transition?

In terms of foreign policy, it was very important to reorient ourselves to the West, even though we had to reckon with our neighbor to the east, which at the time had military bases in Poland with about 200,000 Soviet soldiers. However, it was already a different era—the era of Gorbachev and perestroika. The head of the KGB (Committee for State Security) [the main security agency for the Soviet Union], Mr. Vladimir Kryuchkov, came to Warsaw unexpectedly. I had already been appointed prime minister, but the cabinet hadn't been formed yet. I was told that it would be good if I met him, that his visit was part of some prior exchange that enabled him to come, and so I received him. It was important for me that the essence of our conversation be conveyed to Gorbachev: we would be a friendly country, but decisions would be made here, in Warsaw. That was the main message.

I was keen that my first foreign visit would be to Pope John Paul II in Rome. It was tremendously significant for me. Under the Communist system, leaders used to go to Moscow, but I went to Rome. It was symbolic partly because I didn't go to Moscow, but it was even more important because I went to visit the pope. Furthermore, the first call I made from the prime minister's office was to the pope. It happened when Parliament appointed me prime minister but before the cabinet had been formed. I got through to Monsignor Dziwisz, and to my surprise he said, "please wait a moment," and then the pope came to the phone. I was surprised that he came to the phone. These days popes are on Twitter, but back then I wasn't used to it. Cardinal Wojtyła [Pope John Paul II] was preceded by Cardinal Sapieha, who I knew never came to the phone, so I was surprised that Wojtyła did. He knew that Parliament had appointed me to form a government, and we had a short but very heartfelt conversation.

The Church played a very significant role in this transition. Under martial law we had lectures in church buildings and so on. When it came to the Round Table discussions, representatives from the Church also participated. It was very important to us that they were there, because they somehow added credibility to the negotiations. Their presence was a guarantee for us in a way. So the role of the Church was very important for our transition.

John Paul II supported Solidarity when it was banned. He talked about the notion of solidarity when preaching in different countries and on different continents. His role was therefore very important to me, to us, to Poland. Foreign journalists have often asked me what I consider to be the most important causative factor in our transition: the role of the pope, Reagan, Gorbachev, or Solidarity. I've always said that all of these elements contributed to that historic moment when transformation became possible. As for the role of the pope, take Stalin's famous quip, "How many divisions does the pope have?" The pope didn't have any divisions, but he had great moral strength. The fact that he was Polish gave great moral strength to this nation, kept it alive, maintained its spirit, made people believe it all made sense. And he never faltered in that. During my internment I wrote to the pope illegally in January 1982. There is a reproduction of the card the pope sent me in the internment camp. It says, "I've read your letter several times. I share your thoughts." I had written that no significant change could happen without the restoration of what the nation achieved in 1980. It must be stressed that the pope, unlike some bishops, never withdrew his support for Solidarity. We knew we could rely on him; he was like a rock. So that was very important.

You could say that President Reagan [1981–89] won the technological race and that the Soviet Union couldn't keep up with the pace. Gorbachev was very important. It was a time of high hopes and big change, the time of perestroika. It was no longer Brezhnev's era. Perestroika created a new atmosphere. Another point I can add about those days are my impressions from my first visit to the Soviet Union. I saw how much resistance there was to perestroika. And nothing would have been possible without Solidarity, which was the movement sustaining and fighting for these changes within Poland. That's why I say that all these elements had an impact.

So, let's return to the issue of change. I had said to the Soviet Union that we would be a friendly country, but that decisions would be made here. We were still part of the Warsaw Pact, but our stance was clearly set out in my first speech—the Warsaw Pact cannot be used to play games when it comes to our internal affairs. In a way, the pact still exists. We believed that Europe would be changing, that the events in Poland would subsequently change Europe. However, we also believed that it was a gradual process, and that's why the idea was that relations with our eastern neighbor shouldn't cause problems. With time, Polish foreign policy resulted in the establishment of diplomatic relations not only with Moscow but also with Vilnius [Lithuania], Tallinn [Estonia], Riga [Latvia], and Kiev [Ukraine]. We gradually established relations with Soviet republics that later became independent.

As far as the West was concerned, Europe at that time was moving toward consolidation, whereas we saw a possibility for expansion. EU membership, of course, was not even mentioned at the time. However, there were different concepts and ideas about how to shape Europe. We simply rebuilt our relations with the democratic countries in the West and showed them that our aim was to create a fully democratic system.

Economic Reform

Reflecting on that period, what were the most difficult decisions you had to take? Why were they difficult?

There were very general as well as very specific decisions that were difficult. When it comes to the general decisions, certainly a very important and difficult one was the decision to steer toward a free market economy, radically changing the system. My beliefs pushed me toward humanist Socialist solutions, but then I faced the challenge of restoring capitalism. Nobody had gone back that way before. However, my advisers convinced me that we had to make a fundamental change toward the tested system of a free market economy. As that change was being implemented, I realized that these great creations of socialism, these great industrial workplaces, would go bankrupt because they wouldn't be competitive. And yet they were the foundation that Solidarity was built on. It was therefore a very difficult decision for me morally. I assumed that as the economy developed and once we'd repaired it, we would pay more attention to social issues, but the costs of the transition were unquestionable. This is an example of a general decision, a very difficult one for me morally. There were other, more specific, decisions of course. At some point, protests broke out and an international road was blocked. I had to have it cleared by police forces. Nothing very bad happened there, but for me it was a difficult decision.

Is there one decision or judgment that, if you had to do it over again, you would do differently?

One of our very difficult decisions was closing the state agricultural farms. They wouldn't have been able to survive, as they were subsidized through the state budget and such subsidies were unsustainable. We had to close them down. We hoped the agricultural workers would be willing to take over the land. However, it turned out that they didn't want to take the land, that they didn't feel it was their own; they felt like laborers. They didn't have a farmer mentality. The same thing happened in Czechoslovakia as well. The result was that the transition was really hard for those families, those groups of people, especially in the north and west of Poland where there were many such farms. So, certainly, I wish I had drawn upon the knowledge at the time that came from that experience—I think we were lacking some program for motivating those people, but it was all very difficult. There are still some pangs of remorse there.

What can we learn from the Polish experience regarding economic changes?

When it comes to economic affairs and changes to the system, decisions have to be made quickly in the first phase of governing. The longer you postpone these changes, the harder they are to implement. So they are difficult decisions, but you have to face them resolutely and early on.

Fundamental Principles

Some leaders follow the advice of their advisers in most matters because they are more specialized. Others do not consult much with others when they have a very difficult decision. How did you approach making difficult decisions?

I'd say that in my case there were two integral factors: my beliefs and my openness to listening to different opinions. When it comes to religious faith, I can say that in Catholic social teaching there is a concept of the state of grace. This means that if someone takes on an important responsibility, they get some kind of help. I must say that I felt that help, also in a purely physical sense. Never before had I been able to switch off during the day, relax for a minute, and then get back to work—I would just work until I was tired. When I was prime minister, though, I could switch off for half an hour, relax, and get back to work feeling refreshed. Perhaps that's a mundane example, but it's a very important one to me.

I used to get criticized because the cabinet meetings were very long; they would drag on late into the night. I always organized cabinet meetings on Mondays. They would start in the afternoon and last until late at night. This was because I let ministers voice their opinions. I really wanted these people to be aware of the responsibility that had been entrusted to them. I had a small group of key advisers—an economic adviser, a political adviser, and a foreign affairs adviser. I had close contact with Deputy Prime Minister Balcerowicz and Jacek Kuron, the minister of labor, who was very important because he had this great connection with people. I believed the whole government had to be aware of their responsibility. It was important to me that cabinet meetings weren't just a briefing, but that they generated consensus in the government as well. That was very important. But of course I had the final say as prime minister.

Political Parties

Solidarity played a very important role as an opposition movement, but then had problems governing. You received Wałęsa's support at first, and then there was the separation when you competed for the presidency. What is the difference between functioning well as an opposition movement and functioning well as a government? Why were Solidarity and Wałęsa not able to transform from the role of opposition to being a good coalition leader to stabilize a government?

Solidarity, as I've mentioned already, was not only a trade union but also a great national independence movement. We realized that the differences in opinions within Solidarity were massive. It had both rightwing and leftwing factions. We knew it was a very broad range. I underestimated the need for the early formation of political parties. I didn't create any political parties myself, but they started emerging around me. For some time we thought that the traditional division into political parties wouldn't happen quickly, and that Solidarity would exist as a coherent movement for quite some time. However, these differences started to appear, and political movements started to emerge.

For us, the reforms we implemented were for the good of the whole country. We put the good of the country first. The first thought was about the state, not the party. It was both our strength and our weakness that we didn't create a party system. It was a strength because the interests of the state were put before the interests of the party. As prime minister, I realized how weak the country was and that it had to be strengthened. I realized that the interests of the state were more important than the interests of different parties. I felt strongly compelled to go in that direction. I would never have run in the presidential elections against Wałęsa if he hadn't attacked the government's political program, and even then I was very hesitant, but I was afraid he would destroy it. Thus I decided to run for the presidency to defend the government's program, which was a program for the whole country, not just for one political faction. Furthermore, I considered Wałęsa to be an excellent people's leader, but not necessarily the best person for state office. But, of course, the problem of Wałęsa was real. Nobody denied the great role he played, but finding the right place for him in this new structure became a big problem.

Role of the Authoritarian Leader in Fostering the Transition

What is your evaluation of the changes within the Communist Party, and the role of Jaruzelski?

General Jaruzelski as president was a loyal partner to me. I never agreed with him about his decision to impose martial law in Poland. When we met—I as prime minister and he as president—he often referred to that issue. He said he wanted to talk about it because he was the one who imposed martial law and I was the one who was interned. I told him we had differing opinions on that, since I still believed he could have done more to avoid imposing martial law. However, it was true that he feared Soviet intervention. And as president he was a loyal partner to me. He certainly realized that the power was within the government, not with the president. He came round and understood the sense of these transitions and was quite loyal. The party collapsed, and some of its former members created a new party. The deeper internal transitions took a long time and weren't always implemented in this post-Communist party, but they undoubtedly understood the significance of the transition and played their part.

Reforming the Security Forces

During the authoritarian regime in Poland the security forces played a very important role. Then Poland transitioned to a new, open, democratic political system, but a democracy also needs security forces. How did you approach reforming the security forces?

The initial structure of the government retained the Ministry of the Interior and Ministry of National Defense [and their ministers, who initially remained in their positions until the middle of the 1990s]. But I wanted to have a say in these ministries as well. The initial idea was that a political committee comprised of civilians would be created, but I quickly realized that this was just for show. Thus, in the spring of 1990, I appointed deputy ministers to each of these departments: Krzysztof Kozlowski to the Ministry of the Interior, and Janusz Onyszkiewicz and Bronislaw Komorowski (the current president) to the Ministry of Defense. It was something completely new for them, as they didn't have any experience in that area. The only help I could give them was just general instructions that they should establish themselves, find out what was going on, and gradually make changes.

Let me focus for a moment on the security services. The changes proposed by General Kiszczak [minister of the interior 1981–90] were just for show and we weren't satisfied. The cabinet rejected them. In the middle of 1990, General Kiszczak left and Krzysztof Kozlowski became the minister of the interior, which was already a fundamental change. When Kozlowski came in, we replaced the existing security services with the Office for State Protection (Urząd Ochrony Państwa, or UOP) and vetted the officers. About 16,000 officers left; some retired and some left because they didn't pass the vetting process. The ranks of the UOP were comprised of some Communist-era security service members and some new ones—young, inexperienced people who quickly gained experience. And that's how we initiated change in that ministry.

As far as the Army was concerned, we removed the group of political officers that was typical of the Soviet system. We restored various traditional elements, and by referring to the traditions of the Polish Army, which was very deeply connected to the nation, the morale of the Army gradually changed. We gradually introduced civilian control over the Army; we didn't just swap one military man for another. Introducing civilian control was a hard process because it had never been done before. Between the two world wars, there had been no civilian control over the Army. Then it was military figures who were getting into politics rather than the other way around. And so the process took longer.

In general, we opted to vet the security services and remove people who had disgraced themselves, above all by fighting the opposition and the Church. We opted for new people.

Did you fear, in your government, any military intervention?

No. What I was afraid of, as prime minister at the time, was some kind of provocation. Under the previous system a terrible crime had been committed. The priest Jerzy Popieluszko was kidnapped and brutally murdered by two officers of the security services. I was afraid of this kind of provocation against us, which might be aimed either at me or at their own leaders, who had sat down with us at the Round Table. So **I kept General Kiszczak as head of the Ministry of Interior because I thought he was a kind of guarantee against provocation. Now you might also say, "Well, all right, but the Communist Party had collapsed." Yes, it had collapsed, but its influence in the military was still very strong, and we had to reckon with it. He took responsibility for the Round Table agreements on their behalf. However, I didn't expect him to reform his ministry. I knew this had to be done by my representatives, my people.** And that is indeed what happened.

Constitutional Reform

What was your approach to constitutional reform?

Constitutional reforms were introduced between 1989 and 1990. All provisions of a totalitarian state were removed from the constitution. You have to understand one thing—the constitutions of Soviet bloc countries were very nice, very democratic on paper, but practice was another issue entirely because there were superior forces: the Communist Party and above it "big brother," the Soviet Union. So we removed the undemocratic provisions. By the end of December 1989 we had removed all provisions that were characteristic of satellitism or that represented undemocratic legislation. We reformed the existing constitution, and thus constitutional reform was carried out immediately. We didn't, however, pass a new constitution, although there were plans to do so. Moreover, **I didn't rush the constitution because I was afraid that if a new one was passed by that Parliament—which was not yet entirely democratically elected—there would always be complaints that it wasn't a proper constitution. I thought we should therefore postpone writing and passing a new constitution until after the fully democratic elections to Parliament.**

System of Government

Do you have second thoughts about choosing the semipresidential system as opposed to a parliamentary or presidential system?

Our system gives the government the advantage, but there is a balance between the functions of the president and the government. Although some often criticize it, I think this system works, provided there is a spirit of cooperation. If that spirit is not there, then no legislation can replace it. I would point out that every presidential system that was introduced in post-Communist countries soon slid into oligarchy with little difficulty. We managed to avoid that. Here our democratic foundations are firmly established. I also think we have successfully entered Western democratic structures such as the EU and NATO. That happened later, though, and in my time the idea was to open up toward Western democratic states and create a democratic system. At the same time, Western leaders were afraid that we might stand in the way of transformations in the Soviet Union and Gorbachev's perestroika. That was one of the major concerns. We warmly welcomed Gorbachev's reforms. We didn't want to stand in their way, but it turned out that the transitions were too much for him to manage.

Time Line

Dec. 1970: Shipyard workers protest price increases on basic goods. Police, following the orders of the Polish United Workers' Party (PZPR) government, violently repress demonstrations.

Jun. 1976: Workers demonstrate against new price increases on food. Warsaw intellectuals form the Workers' Defense Committee to aid arrested activists and later expand to underground publishing.

Oct. 1978: Polish Cardinal Karol Wojtyła becomes Pope John Paul II, the first non-Italian pope in 455 years. He advocates against repression in Poland and elsewhere.

Jun. 1979: John Paul II makes his first trip to Poland as pope, organized by the Church and its supporters. He draws huge crowds and television audiences, giving many people confidence in their ability to organize outside government.

Aug. 1980: The government increases prices, prompting a sit-in strike at Lenin Shipyards in Gdansk, led by worker-activist Lech Wałęsa. Workers in nearby enterprises join. Strikers and advisors demand lower prices, better benefits, the right to strike and form a trade union (Solidarity), and freer media. The regime negotiates the Gdansk Agreement, which concede to protesters' demands, with strikers and advisors including future Prime Minister Tadeusz Mazowiecki, Catholic intellectual and magazine editor.

Sep. 1980: Branches of Solidarity spring up across Poland. Membership increases rapidly, reaching over 10 million people during the autumn. Solidarity publications appear, and official media expand their coverage. Conflicts arise over the legalization of student and peasant unions, triggering Solidarity-led strikes and protests. The head of PZPR, Edward Gierek, is ousted.

Oct. 1981: General Wojciech Jaruzelski, prime minister and former commander of the military, is appointed head of the PZPR amidst continued strikes and Soviet pressure to ban Solidarity. Jaruzelski meets with Solidarity and Church leaders, but the strikes continue.

Dec. 1981: Under Soviet pressure, Jaruzelski imposes martial law. Solidarity is banned, its leaders interned, and communications within and outside country are cut. In response, the United States imposes economic sanctions on Poland.

Jun. 1983: The pope visits Poland, calls for calm, and meets with government leaders and Wałęsa.

Jul. 1983: Martial law ends, although many opposition leaders remain detained. The PZPR initiates economic and political reforms, including easing restrictions on the Church.

Mar. 1985: Mikhail Gorbachev becomes leader of the Soviet Union. He liberalizes the Soviet political and economic system and eases Soviet control of Eastern and Central Europe.

Sep. 1986: Jaruzelski declares total amnesty for political prisoners. Solidarity leaders reemerge, although the organization is still not legal. The government introduces new market-oriented economic reforms.

May 1988: The largest wave of strikes and protests since 1981 begins and continues throughout the summer. The protests have few clear goals or leaders.

Aug. 1988: The government initiates talks with Solidarity, with the Church as intermediary. Jaruzelski meets with Wałęsa. Interior Minister Czesław Kiszczak holds talks on how to run negotiations.

Jan. 1989: Jaruzelski, Kiszczak, and other key PZPR ministers force PZPR leaders to support negotiations by threatening to resign otherwise.

Feb. 1989: Round Table Talks begin between representatives of the authorities and Solidarity. The government announces that it has legalized Solidarity in its first statement.

Apr. 1989: Round Table Talks conclude with a sweeping agreement to include Solidarity representatives by allowing candidates who do not belong to Communist-era parties to compete for 35% of Sejm (lower house) seats, with the remaining 65% of seats reserved for members of the PZPR and its subsidiary parties; establishing a freely elected Senate (upper house) open to all candidates; and implementing a nonpartisan presidency elected by members of both houses. Most economic and social issues discussed in the Round Table Talks are left for the upcoming legislature and government to address.

Jun. 1989: Poland holds semifree legislative elections. Solidarity-endorsed candidates win in a landslide, receiving 99 of 100 seats in Senate and all 35%

of Sejm seats reserved for candidates who had not been in Communist-era parties.

Aug. 1989: PZPR subsidiary parties desert PZPR and align with Solidarity. After PZPR fails to form a grand coalition, Solidarity's Tadeusz Mazowiecki, advisor to Wałęsa and Solidarity and Round Table leader, is elected as the first noncommunist prime minister in the Warsaw Pact. In keeping with its initial promise, Solidarity allows Jaruzelski to become president. Under Maziowecki's government, extensive political and economic reforms are enacted.

Nov. 1989: The Berlin Wall falls; Mikhail Gorbachev makes clear that the Soviet Union will not intervene to support allied Communist regimes. By the end of the year, Communist rule in all of Eastern Europe has ended.

Jan. 1990: Led by Finance Minister Leszek Balcerowicz, "shock therapy" (the so-called Balcerowicz Plan) of market-oriented liberalization to stabilize the economy and prepare for privatization begins to significantly decrease the value of Polish currency and individuals' wages. The PZPR dissolves. Many reformist PZPR politicians later join the Democratic Left Alliance (SLD), led by former Round Table subgroup leader Aleksander Kwaśniewski.

May 1990: Solidarity candidates win overwhelmingly in free local elections. Solidarity's leadership begins to splinter, with tensions growing between Mazowiecki and Wałęsa.

Dec. 1990: Direct presidential elections are held after Jaruzelski steps down. Solidarity splits; Wałęsa easily defeats Mazowiecki and others to win the presidency.

Oct. 1991: The first free parliamentary elections are held. Twenty-nine parties win seats; both conservative populists and post-Communists do well.

Dec. 1991: Following parliamentary elections, Jan Olszewski is elected prime minister. Wałęsa and Olszewski clash over military appointments and how to deal with past abuses until Olszewski steps down the next year. Poland and the European Union (EU) sign an Association Agreement, an important step toward membership.

Aug. 1992: Following Olszewski's ouster, the Sejm passes the Small Constitution, which defines the powers of the president and prime minister and increases the threshold for parties to win seats in the Sejm.

Sep. 1993: The SLD and Polish Peasants' Party (PSL), a former subsidiary party, win early parliamentary elections, partially because of the fragmentation of the post-Solidarity right. The leader of the smaller (but less controversial) PSL becomes prime minister.

Nov. 1995: SLD's Kwaśniewski narrowly defeats Wałęsa in presidential elections.

Apr. 1997: A new constitution is passed. It preserves most existing political institutions but eliminates legislative seats that were previously elected on a nationwide basis and limits presidential power.

Jul. 1997: Poland is invited to join NATO. Kwaśniewski strongly supports membership. Poland accepts the offer and joins following two years of talks.

Oct. 2000: Kwaśniewski is reelected, defeating the highly fragmented opposition.

May 2004: Poland joins the EU a year after a referendum on accession. Poland is the only EU economy to grow immediately following the 2008 international financial crisis.

Sep. 2005: The SLD, plagued by several scandals, collapses. Center-right and rightwing post-Solidarity parties gain support.

Oct. 2005: Lech Kaczyński, former mayor of Warsaw, is elected president. Kwaśniewski is unable to run owing to presidential term limits.

Apr. 2010: Kaczyński, other senior officials, and 15 members of Parliament are killed in a plane crash. Successors are installed smoothly, and new presidential elections are scheduled.

NOTES

1. Antoni Dudek, *Historia Polityczna Polski 1989-2012* (Krakow: Wydawnictwo "Znak," 2013), 75.

2. Ibid., 77.

3. Tadeusz Kowalik, *From Solidarity to Sellout* (New York: Monthly Review Press, 2011).

GUIDE TO FURTHER READING

Ash, Timothy Garton. *The Polish Revolution: Solidarity*. New Haven, Conn.: Yale University Press, 1983.

Bernhard, Michael. *The Origins of Democratization in Poland*. New York: Columbia University Press, 1993.

Blejer, Mario I., and Fabrizio Coricelli. *The Making of Economic Reform in Eastern Europe: Conversations with Leading Reformers in Poland, Hungary, and the Czech Republic*. Brookfield, Vt.: Aldershot, 1995.

Castle, Marjorie. *Triggering Communism's Collapse: Perception and Power in Poland's Transition*. Lanham, Md.: Rowman & Littlefield, 2003.

Coughlan, Elizabeth P. "Democratizing Civilian Control: The Polish Case." *Armed Forces and Society* 24, no. 4 (1998): 519-33.

Curry, Jane, and Luba Jafjer, eds. *Poland's Permanent Revolution: People vs. Elites, 1956 to the Present*. Washington, D.C.: American University Press, 1996.

Domber, Gregory F. "International Pressures for a Negotiated Transition, 1981–1989." In *Transitions to Democracy: A Comparative Perspective*, edited by Kathryn Stoner and Michael McFaul. Baltimore, Md.: Johns Hopkins University Press.

Ekiert, Grzegorz, and Jan Kubik. *Rebellious Civil Society: Popular Protest and Democratic Consolidation in Poland, 1989–1993*. Ann Arbor: University of Michigan Press, 1999.

Fitzmaurice, John. "General Wojciech Jaruzelski: Hardline Patriot." In *Leaders of Transition*, edited by Martin Westlake. New York: St. Martin's Press, 2000.

Goodwyn, Lawrence. *Breaking the Barrier: The Rise of Solidarity in Poland*. New York: Oxford University Press, 1991.

Kubik, Jan. "Who Done It: Workers, Intellectuals, or Someone Else? Controversy over Solidarity's Origins and Social Composition." *Theory and Society* 23, no. 3 (1994): 441–66.

Lewis, Paul G. "Political Institutionalisation and Party Development in Post-Communist Poland." *Europe-Asia Studies* 46, no. 3 (1994): 779–99.

Michnik, Adam. *The Church and the Left*. Chicago, Ill.: University of Chicago Press, 1993.

Ost, David. *Solidarity and the Politics of Anti-Politics: Opposition and Reform in Poland since 1968*. Philadelphia: University of Pennsylvania Press, 1990.

Sachs, Jeffrey. *Poland's Jump to the Market Economy*. Cambridge: Massachusetts Institute of Technology Press, 1994.

Szczerbiak, Aleks. "Dealing with the Communist Past or the Politics of the Present? Lustration in Post-Communist Poland." *Europe-Asia Studies* 54, no. 4 (2002): 553–72.

Taras, Raymond. *Consolidating Democracy in Poland*. Boulder, Colo.: Westview, 1995. On events from the 1970s onward.

Wałęsa, Lech. *The Struggle and Triumph: An Autobiography*. New York: Arcade, 1994.

Chapter 8

SOUTH AFRICA

....

Democracy as By-Product: South Africa's Negotiated Transition

STEVEN FRIEDMAN

South Africa's journey from racial oligarchy to universal franchise differs sharply from most (or all) transitions to democracy: the issue was not whether an authoritarian regime would give way to a democratic order, but whether the entire population would achieve the benefits of citizenship that were already enjoyed by a racial minority.

This meant that while both sides insisted that they valued democracy, it was not a prime goal of either. Like whites in other former British colonies, the racial minority enjoyed multiparty democracy: commitment to "white democracy" was an important element in the calculations of the last white president, F. W. de Klerk, and is reflected in the interview published here. But the white leadership's core goal was preserving white interests, not democracy. The black-led resistance sought an end to white rule—democracy was not a necessary condition. Many leaders of the African National Congress (ANC), which led the fight against apartheid, were committed democrats, but the movement included Leninists and African nationalists, who were more concerned with defeating white power than achieving democracy. Negotiations produced a democratic constitution because that seemed the most tolerable outcome for both sides. The transition thus conformed to Dankwart Rustow's thesis that democracy emerges from bargaining between parties that did not see it as their first choice but settle for it as the best available option.[1]

Democracy grew out of an engagement between political organizations that represented defined constituencies: de Klerk presided over a National Party (NP) that was routinely reelected by whites, while the ANC (on whose behalf Mbeki negotiated) was the oldest "liberation movement" in the world, enjoying the trust of most black South Africans for almost a century. Both sides assumed that the ANC would win a free election, which ensured that the transition resembled a labor dispute in which the bargaining power of the parties determined the outcome. John Rawls's "veil of ignorance," in which parties to a constitution have no idea who will emerge victorious and so protect "the losers" in case they need protection themselves, was absent. This made for a difficult transition, but also one in which constituencies' support for compromises could be obtained. It also ensured that civil society, while by no means irrelevant, was not a direct party to the formal negotiations that produced democracy.

The Process

South Africa's transition was the result of a protracted struggle between white colonizers and the indigenous black inhabitants. Conflict began when whites arrived in 1652. In 1910, white elites formed the modern state of South Africa at the expense of black claims. In 1948, the NP won a white election and introduced apartheid, which denied black citizenship rights in the 87% of the country designated white. The ANC, which was formed in opposition to the dispossession of black people at the state's inception, led the resistance to apartheid: it was banned in 1960 and then forced underground and into exile. A decade earlier, the South African Communist Party, later to become an ANC ally, had been banned. From 1960 to 1990, the ANC operated underground, with its leaders in prison or outside the country.

The state had the military might to crush black resistance, but apartheid proved unsustainable. It began to unravel in the late 1960s when a shortage of white workers forced the government to allow firms to employ black workers in more skilled posts. Blacks could no longer be treated as foreigners in the cities, and workers acquired the bargaining power that comes with skilled status. In 1973, strikes triggered reforms that culminated in the extension of bargaining rights to black trade unions in 1980. In 1976, pupils in the Soweto township outside Johannesburg rebelled against instruction in Afrikaans, the language of most whites. This prompted a reform process in which the government tried to abandon peripheral aspects of apartheid in hopes of retaining white political dominance. But each concession became a retreat, which ultimately forced majority rule. Heightened resistance in the 1980s reduced the segregated townships (where black people were forced to live) to battlefields and prompted the government to declare two states of emergency in an attempt to quell the uprising. International pressure against apartheid isolated white society: business began to question the system's workability, and doubts surfaced in the white Afrikaner establishment.

President P. W. Botha, alarmed by increasing resistance, shifted power from the NP to the security establishment to resist the pressure. But his government's concession that black consent was necessary to stability changed the parameters within which the white establishment operated: winning this consent would prove impossible so long as apartheid survived; the attempt to gain black consent forced new retreats. No black politician with a constituency would negotiate until the ANC and its leader, Nelson Mandela, were free to participate. And so the reforms did not shore up the system—they divided the elite and provided new openings for the resistance. In public, the ANC denounced the reforms. Away from the public gaze, contacts between Botha's security establishment and ANC strategists began.

The End of the Beginning

Initial contacts between government security officials and ANC delegations headed by Thabo Mbeki began in the mid-1980s and broadened during the decade. The initial talks became secret discussions facilitated on behalf of the mining company Consolidated Goldfields. From 1985, when a white business delegation traveled to the Zambian capital, Lusaka, to meet the ANC, it became increasingly common for white South African elites to meet with the ANC. Frederick van Zyl Slabbert, a white Afrikaner sociologist who had become leader of the white opposition in Parliament, resigned in 1986 to form an institute committed to facilitating contact between key figures in white society and the ANC, which built legitimacy for negotiation. The ANC adopted a statement in 1987 agreeing to negotiate an end to apartheid, while the NP policy began to recognize that black people should enjoy political rights—if whites retained a veto. Calls grew for the release of Mandela and other political prisoners.

Botha, who had reached the limit of his reform agenda, impeded momentum for a settlement. The logjam was broken when he suffered a stroke in 1989 and was replaced by de Klerk. This shifted decision making from the security establishment back to the NP, de Klerk's power base. Strategy was now the domain of Afrikaner nationalist political thinkers: because this nationalism was born of the fight against British colonialism, it had an egalitarian streak, which assumed that members of a political community should enjoy equal rights, which is why blacks were denied entry to the community. Once the principle of racial interdependence was established, it became acceptable, in theory, for black people to demand citizenship. De Klerk was open to this line of reasoning because he was far more deeply rooted than his predecessor in the political traditions of Afrikaner nationalism. Also, despite a reputation as a hard-liner, de Klerk was a pragmatist who, in the mid-1980s, had begun stressing to private audiences his aversion to nonnegotiables: the issues on which whites were not prepared to negotiate, he argued, would shift if circumstances changed. This meant, of course, that he was open to the argument that the white government's negotiating position would need to shift. These two factors ensured that, within months of taking office, he had begun to play a key role, along with key figures in the Afrikaner nationalist establishment, in initiating the negotiations that ended apartheid.

The Beginning of the End

The process began in February 1990, when de Klerk ended curbs on political activity. "Talks about talks" began weeks after this announcement. The NP was nudged toward negotiation by Western powers, most notably Britain, whose prime minister, Margaret Thatcher, was fighting sanctions against apartheid. The British ambassador to South Africa, Robin Renwick, played a key role in persuading the NP to speed changes to head off further sanctions. The ANC was pushed in the same direction by the former Soviet Union, which had funded its guerrilla war but could do so no longer. It was easier for the ANC to shift its position because it was able to call on a strong tradition of propensity to negotiate that was articulated in a much-quoted speech by Mandela from the dock of his trial for treason.

Diplomats played an important role in ferrying messages between the sides, and international intervention broke the first logjam that had prevented negotiation: the NP government's insistence that it would not talk to the ANC until it renounced violence and the ANC's response that it would not do so until the government committed "irreversibly" to majority rule. By unilaterally lifting the ban on the ANC, de Klerk signaled a willingness to talk without renouncing violence. The ANC responded by unilaterally suspending its "armed struggle." An even more important decision came later—the ANC suspended international sanctions, signaling that it believed that progress to majority rule was irreversible. The fall of the Berlin Wall influenced de Klerk significantly, because fear of Communism had been an important influence on NP thinking.

In 1991, a negotiating forum, the Congress for a Democratic South Africa (CODESA), was convened. It included a wide range of political parties—a concession to the NP's bargaining position. Because the ANC expected to win an election, it wanted an elected assembly to draft the constitution. The NP knew the ANC would win, so it insisted that an elected assembly would decide the outcome of negotiations, because the key issue was whether there would be majority rule. It insisted on an unelected negotiation forum and, in an attempt to dilute the ANC's impact, urged that parties join the talks: this enabled the NP to include parties that participated in apartheid's political institutions—the ANC's only potential allies were other "liberation" movements, which refused to join the talks. The most significant other participant was the Inkatha Freedom Party (IFP), which was embedded in the traditional power structures of the Zulu ethnic group and powerful enough to ensure itself a place at the table in its own right. Civil society organizations were not invited—this was a bargain between political blocs, not an open-ended attempt to develop a new social contract.

Although CODESA remained in session into 1992, the parties were wedded to nonnegotiables that seemed to make compromise impossible: the ANC insisted on majority rule, while the NP demanded a white veto on change. The IFP governed KwaZulu, the ethnic "homeland" reserved for Zulu people, although it had helped make negotiations possible by refusing to negotiate a constitution until the ANC and Mandela were free. The IFP was engaged in violent conflict with the ANC: it wanted a settlement that allowed it to hold on to its regional power base, which meant diluting majority rule. The parties had to remain mindful of their constituencies, and this made compromise elusive. In early 1992, the NP lost a by-election that was considered a key test of white support for negotiations. De Klerk responded by calling a referendum in which whites were asked to give the NP an open mandate to negotiate a settlement. Whites, worried about international isolation and the rising costs of apartheid, agreed. The referendum meant that de Klerk and the NP could claim to speak for white South Africa, but it indirectly destroyed CODESA. The ANC and NP were now engaged in a contest for the support of the United States, United Kingdom, and Western Europe. NP strategists believed the referendum showed the West that the rightwing threat was real and that the NP alone could defuse it, which, they concluded, strengthened the NP's bargaining power. The NP dug in, and by mid-1992 CODESA had deadlocked.

The following months were the most crucial of the negotiation period. After CODESA's collapse, violence that had continued throughout the process escalated as the parties tested their strength on the streets. The battle for international support also continued: a key moment was a statement in July by US Under Secretary of State for African Affairs Herman Cohen to the House of Representatives African Subcommittee that whites should seek protection in nonracial federalism rather than a white veto. By September, the ANC and NP had accepted that they needed to return to the table: they signed a Record of Understanding that involved compromises, which allowed talks to resume in early 1993. But the IFP's leader, Mangosuthu Buthelezi, was not party to the record. For the remainder of the process, Buthelezi made common cause with the white right in an attempt to derail it. Violence continued, and the prospect that the transition might be threatened by rightwing resistance hung over the process for the entire negotiation period.

The Settlement

The negotiations resumed in early 1993. In April, Chris Hani, a pivotal ANC and Communist Party leader, was assassinated by white right-wingers who hoped the killing would spark violence that would derail negotiations. It had the opposite effect: the NP feared that violence might spiral out of control if it did not send a clear signal that the process was irreversible. The parties thus agreed to set an election date—April 27, 1994—which compelled them to reach a settlement before then. Negotiations acquired a sense of purpose, and an agreement was reached in October. But the IFP and the white right refused to join this second round of talks.

Although the resumed negotiations remained a multiparty forum, the ANC and NP were the only parties whose consent was essential. There was no direct civil society influence, although organizations linked to political parties were able to wield influence. The women's lobby, working through ANC women activists, won substantial gains, while trade unions linked to the ANC won a constitutionalized right to strike and frustrated business attempts to win the right to lock out workers. Much was made of the chemistry between the chief negotiators—Cyril Ramaphosa, a former trade unionist for the ANC, and Roelf Meyer, a reformist minister (who later joined the ANC) for the NP. While their personal relationship was a factor, a mutual recognition that stability required a settlement, and the fact that a deadline had been agreed to, concentrated minds.

The divide between the ANC's demand for majority rule and the NP's demand for a minority veto narrowed during the negotiations. The issue of whether the constitution was to be negotiated by an elected assembly or an unelected forum was settled by agreeing on an interim constitution. An elected Parliament would draft the permanent constitution, but it would be governed by agreed-upon principles that limited the scope of possible changes: the ANC could say that an elected assembly drafted the document, and the NP that it had won constraints on majority rule. The negotiators also agreed that parties would be entitled to one cabinet post for each 5% of the vote and a deputy presidency if they won 20%. ANC support for this concession, and for other temporary safeguards for white interests, was won by ensuring that Communist Party head Joe Slovo became the chief advocate of "sunset clauses" offering guarantees for the first five years. The key outstanding issue was whether minorities in the cabinet would enjoy a veto: in the last hours, Meyer (with de Klerk's approval) agreed that they would not, and the interim constitution was adopted the next day. While some in the NP saw this as a betrayal, it was the result of the continuing evolution of its bargaining position: faced with the reality that no settlement was possible without majority rule, NP strategists concluded that their control over the military, police, and bureaucracy—as well as skills and capital—would ensure continued white influence even if majority rule was agreed.

Buthelezi and his white allies remained outside the settlement. But first the white right decided to contest the election. Then Buthelezi and his IFP agreed a week before the poll. Although the immediate reason is unclear, his dream of an independent enclave was doomed because white business and black workers in his home province were too integrally linked with the South African economy to accept partition.

A Note on Leadership

Accounts of the negotiation process usually emphasize the role of leadership in shepherding South Africa away from racial oligarchy to constitutional democracy. De Klerk and Mandela were awarded Nobel Prizes for their role in steering their constituencies to compromise, while Ramaphosa and Meyer's chemistry and mutual commitment to a settlement are often cited as key factors. (Mbeki, who was pivotal in charting the ANC's strategic direction, rarely receives the credit he deserves.)

Leadership clearly did play a role. The costs of apartheid to whites may have been rising, but there is no iron law that decrees that de Klerk and his colleagues had to see that—the white elite in Rhodesia (now Zimbabwe) never saw it. The ANC could only end apartheid by compromising, but Mandela and Mbeki (with Slovo and others) ensured that it entered the negotiations with a much more inclusive notion of a new polity than its counterparts in Zimbabwe. Meyer did much to nudge a reluctant NP to accept majority rule, and Ramaphosa's negotiation skills ensured a bargain that the ANC's base could support.

But the role of leadership can be—and often is—exaggerated. South Africa was not saved from interminable bloodshed simply by a few wise leaders. A complicated mix of economic interdependence, as well as cultural and political influences, meant that support for a common society was far greater than most analyses expected. Key social interests such as business and organized labor, as well as institutions such as the church, also created pressures for compromise. South Africa was, despite surface appearances, ripe for compromise. But it certainly required political skills and vision to turn that potential into reality. Without these skills a transition might have happened, but it would have been more violent and less able to produce the conditions for a workable society.

After the Settlement

The settlement and election were key moments in the transition from white minority rule to a majoritarian democracy, which will remain incomplete for decades. The NP won 20% of the vote in 1994, which gave it one deputy president—de Klerk—and four cabinet ministers. The IFP won 10% and two cabinet members. But the NP left the Government of National Unity in 1995 frustrated by its inability to influence decisions: the three white constituencies whose consent the ANC needed—business, bureaucrats, and the military—negotiated their own deals with the ANC and did not need the NP. But whites still control the lion's share of capital and skills, which continues to constrain ANC options.

The romantic notion that the settlement could produce national unity proved elusive. Despite deep divisions, all parties share a South African identity. But the racial identities that underpinned apartheid have not disappeared. The Truth and Reconciliation Commission, partly modeled on its Chilean precursor, was convened to investigate apartheid-era rights abuses and grant amnesty to perpetrators who fully disclosed what they had done. It helped consolidate a process in which apartheid was delegitimized, but only in the sense that defending it openly has become taboo—expressing racial prejudice in coded language has not. South Africa is still racially divided, and white dominance over the economy and society has not ended.

Like all democratic projects, South Africa's remains unfinished. Racial divisions still inhibit cooperation between the still largely white leadership of business and the professions and the mainly black government. Poverty and inequality, much of it still racially determined, continues to divide the society. And while elections are acknowledged to be free and fair, the fact that race plays a strong role in shaping voter preferences—and that whites still dominate the affluent suburbs while most blacks live in low-income townships—means that there is little party competition. Most residential areas are uncontested fiefdoms of either the governing or opposition party. And, while everyone now votes, millions are denied an effective voice by a society in which around one-third (white and black) live in a noisy democracy, while the remaining two-thirds (entirely black) contend with grassroots power relations that still largely silence them.

This is not to deny democracy's achievements. Freedoms have been preserved and the constitution remains intact, enforced by court rulings that the government unfailingly accepts. Apartheid strategists hoped that creating a black middle class would deflect political demands—it has now emerged as a consequence of the democratization it was meant to forestall. But democratic settlements do not end the journey toward democracy; they open possibilities for it to proceed and to become gradually institutionalized. Although the challenges facing democracy in South Africa are formidable, democratization has proved more enduring than seemed likely when the process began.

Biosketch of F. W. de Klerk, President of South Africa 1989–94

PHOTO: TORBJÖRN SELANDER / SCANPIX

F. W. de Klerk, the son of a prominent Afrikaner political figure, is a lawyer and political leader of the National Party who served in several different cabinet positions in the 1980s. He was steeped in the Afrikaner commitment to racial apartheid and white parliamentary government, which denied national political representation to nearly 90% of South Africa's population. After the previous president, P. W. Botha, suffered a major stroke, de Klerk was generally considered the more conservative of the potential appointees, but he had opposed the half-measures Botha had taken to reform and defend apartheid because he believed they could not work. Reaching the presidency in 1989, de Klerk moved the government away from Botha's reliance on the internal security apparatus and toward those in the National Party who favored stronger reforms in order to protect longer-term Afrikaner interests; they understood that apartheid could no longer be sustained in a transformed economy, an increasingly urbanized society, and a new international environment.

In a February 1990 policy address that took the country and the world by surprise, de Klerk announced the unbanning of the opposition ANC, the release of Mandela and all other political prisoners, and the beginning of negotiations with Mandela and the ANC to develop a new constitution and open the way to the full participation of the black majority. Although this initiative seemed sudden, it was built upon careful preparation, including years of "talks about talks" between government officials and Nelson Mandela that were unknown to many cabinet members, as well as several retreats with his cabinet to build consensus. De Klerk managed to maintain his political base, exert control over the hard-liners and security forces, and make timely concessions to the ANC while projecting a sense of continuing authority, even as the fundamental bases of his power eroded and nonracial democracy emerged. When Mandela and the ANC won national elections and took office in April 1994, de Klerk served for a time as deputy president in a national unity government under Mandela, but then resigned to lead the renamed New National Party in opposition.

Interview with President F. W. de Klerk

Fundamental Principles

Could you briefly summarize some main points about how to make transitions to democracy that capture basic principles you think should be understood and remembered?

Lessons from the South African experience may be relevant in other contexts. The first very basic lesson is **you cannot resolve a conflict without the parties involved talking to each other. Negotiation is the only route to achieve a lasting peace.**

Second, **the main parties to the conflict must realize that it is necessary to change, that a compromise is required. The negotiation must be genuine and have integrity, and should not develop into playing games with each other.** In South Africa, this meant that we needed to get to the point of saying, "We need to change—not because of the pressure, not to satisfy others, but because of our inner conviction that the present situation cannot continue." This is what happened in the National Party before I became president.

Under my predecessor during the 1980s, we went through a period of deep self-analysis, having reached the conclusion that we needed to change. In that process of self-analysis we asked ourselves what is right, and we came to the conclusion that we could not build a future for our own people on the basis of injustice toward the majority of the people in the country. We had to admit to ourselves that the effort to bring justice, to achieve full political rights that were equal in quality for all the people in South Africa through nation-states, had failed. We came to the conclusion that to cling to that principle would never bring justice to all and therefore, from inner conviction, we concluded that we needed to change fundamentally.

But looking at the rest of Africa, we were worried that such change might lead to anarchy rather than a healthy democracy, and therefore we realized we had to achieve a negotiated settlement that would secure proper democracy, ensure security for everybody, secure well-balanced economic policies, and ensure that there would be no further discrimination on the basis of race, color, or any other grounds.

Another lesson we have learned is that **to defuse a situation that seems insolvable, initiatives are required**. I realized that if I took the step-by-step route—if I only made five concessions on five important points but left some unresolved—the ANC (as the other main party to the conflict) would counter that, unless I also made concessions on other issues, they would not come to the negotiation table. So I came to the conclusion, in interaction with my cabinet and the broad leadership of the party, that it was fundamental to put together a package that would force the ANC alliance to accept an invitation to come to the negotiation table.

For example, if I were only to release Mandela and six other prominent people but all the other political prisoners were retained, they would say, "Thank you very much, but until you release all political prisoners, we will not negotiate with you." It was for that reason that we put together a package that tried to address all the ANC's concerns which we could think of and which could be described as reasonable.

In order to succeed with negotiations, you have to put yourself in the other party's shoes. One must think through their case and determine what could be regarded as minimum requirements in order to ensure their cooperative, constructive participation in the negotiation process. We did this, and the speech of February 2, 1990, encapsulated such a package. It helped us to gain, for the moment, the moral high ground. It would have been unreasonable of the ANC, after those announcements, to refuse to negotiate. It would have turned the international community totally against them; they had to accept.

A South African journalist, after reading my speech, which was provided beforehand, exclaimed, "My God, he's done it all." Indeed, the purpose of the package of announcements was to do it all. We took a tremendous risk. We did not impose any preconditions. Then the ANC, after a first round of very broad-based discussions at Groot Schuur in April 1990, took an initiative. It was not negotiated, just as my package was not negotiated with them. They took an initiative to unilaterally suspend the armed struggle. Those two initiatives laid the foundation for the negotiations, which in the end proved to be successful.

Establishing the Basis for Dialogue and Negotiation

Before delivering your crucial speech at the beginning of 1990, there had been previous conversations with the ANC. How did these talks help you design a strategy and move ahead? Also, to negotiate and achieve results, you needed a counterpart and persons that you knew and could trust. How did this happen?

Not all of us in the cabinet under my predecessor knew what was happening behind the scenes. President Botha kept that in a small circle. I did not know about it. I was the leader of the National Party in the Transvaal province, so I was an important player in the party and in the cabinet, but I was not part of his inner circle. When I became leader on February 2, 1989, Kobie Coetsee—a minister in the cabinet and, for some time, a minister in the Office of the State President and later minister of justice—briefed me. He was leading this; he was part of the group of four that was speaking to Mandela. Coetsee—together with Niel Barnard of National Intelligence; General Willemse, the head of the prisons; and Mr. Fanie van der Merwe, the secretary (or, in today's terms, the director general) of the Department of Justice—were talking to Mandela. Mandela was allowed to write to the national executive of the ANC to obtain a mandate to explore the possibility of talks. But substance was not discussed; it was "talks about talks," talks about the possibility of negotiations. Only when I became leader was I fully briefed about all of this.

The official position in public speeches was "We don't negotiate with terrorists." So, in retrospect, all that contributed to prepare the scene for the initiatives that I took. It strengthened my hand. The preparatory work that had been done convinced me that I could be bold.

In the different cases we have looked at, there are actors who do not fully get on board and who try to undermine the transition process. How did you become confident by February 1990 that you could introduce such a bold agenda for change?

We were helped by the fact that, through the very firm action that was taken in 1985-87—the firm security steps, with thousands of people held without trial, clamping down effectively from a military and security point of view—a situation was brought about in which the ANC realized that they could not overthrow the government and that the solution would not be through the barrel of a gun. Although I am not defending what was wrong about our methods, **the best starting point in the resolution of a conflict is that the main parties to the conflict must realize that carrying on with the conflict will end in the devastation of the country, and that there is no real hope of winning the "war."** That, I think, was our situation. We realized that we needed a political solution; the solution did not lie in military or security acts. I think the ANC came to the same conclusion. The firm steps that we took, but also those previous "talks about talks," convinced them of that fact, in my view.

Creating a Consensus for Change

How did I take my team along with me? I don't want to present myself as a hero. My predecessor started with the concept of "bush conferences." A bush conference means taking your fellow leaders, the cabinet, your executive team away from the city, and that is why we call it "to the bush," to a place where sometimes even the cell phones didn't work. Nobody could have an excuse; everybody was in an island situation, forced to really talk to each other in this process of self-analysis. I continued with this practice from the moment I became leader of the National Party, and even before I became president we had conferences like that. In the early months of my presidency, as late as early December 1989, we had a few bush conferences where our approach was, "We've crossed the bridge of acknowledging that we need to change fundamentally. The question is how do we do it? What should our plan of action be? What is our vision?"

Change for the sake of change is not good. You need to develop a vision. And our vision was one united South Africa with all forms of discrimination scrapped from the statute book, with a vote of equal value for all, with a strong constitution. The new South Africa should have a strong Constitutional Court, with checks and balances to prevent the misuse of power or any future domination by any one group over another group. That was the vision that emanated from these heart-to-heart open discussions. In any group of talented executive leaders, whether it is in business or politics, you have diverse views, but through this process we reached an internal consensus.

I spent as much energy on building this internal consensus as I did on anything else during my leadership of the party and during my presidency. My whole cabinet took co-ownership for the package that we announced. They weren't all participating in finalizing the exact wording at each and every step. However, on the broad principle of fundamental change, of putting together a package, of taking an initiative, there was consensus. And then I called them together shortly before I made the speech and said, "This is what I am going to announce. Are we as one?" And they said, "Yes." I also made them promise not even to tell their wives. And I did not tell my wife exactly what I was going to announce. I just said, "South Africa will never be the same again." And the secret was kept.

I followed a top–down process after that. Having secured the support and acceptance of co-ownership for our initiatives from the broad leadership of my party—because the cabinet contained all the leaders of all the provinces and all the leading figures within the party—their task was to sell this to the second tier of leadership. And through the second tier to constantly interact with the grassroots level to convince them that we needed fundamental change to avoid a catastrophe, and that we needed to change for the sake of what is right.

I constantly had to renew this acceptance of co-ownership. As we started negotiating, the typical divisions that you find in any group of executives arose again. Some said, "We can't make this concession." Others said, "We need to make this concession." Others were hesitant to make the concession, and at every week's cabinet meeting we spent an hour or two on the details of the ongoing negotiation process, building a consensus, allowing each member to fully speak his or her mind. Then it was my task as the leader to say what I thought we should do, and see if they accepted. And if they said yes, I could rely on consensus for taking the next step.

Surely there must have been, on some occasion, somebody who found it difficult to get on board. Did you find you had to displace some people so that you had the support of the cabinet?

During my presidency, I did bring about a few changes in the cabinet. I fired one minister because he did too much on his own without clearing it with the cabinet. Other ministers, because of ongoing violence, would have become a problem if they had continued in their security portfolios, and I shifted the minister of police to a civil department and General Malan from defense to a civil department and replaced them with new ministers. I don't think the consensus we achieved was always for everybody a happy consensus, but in the end a cabinet system works that way, and it is a good system. In the end each participant must decide, "Is this an issue of principle?" and then one's conscience will tell you, "I can't go along with this; it is an issue of principle, therefore I will offer my resignation," or "I am prepared to make a compromise."

So you make compromises between parties to a conflict. But also within each party's deliberations, preparing itself for the negotiations, compromises are constantly being made. Many people were not happy with everything we were doing, but they compromised.

Establishing the Basis for Dialogue and Negotiation

You have affirmed that the preparation to transform South Africa was a process and not an abrupt change. When you were thinking about the solutions you were not informed of the conversations with the ANC, so it was a process without all the information. Botha himself was not a man open to move in the direction that you moved. How did this process take place in your mind? In order to be prepared to act when you had the power, what did you know about the talks with Mandela and Mbeki?

Botha was a more dictatorial type of leader. Mbeki's talks, as I understand it, were more focused on talking to people outside the party political circle. He was talking to cultural and religious leaders. He had built a relationship with Willie Esterhuyse, the professor from Stellenbosch who took a delegation to England to meet with Mbeki. My brother was part of that delegation. Having been uninformed, I was critical of my brother for going. **What was helpful**, from my point of view in the early 1980s, **to make us ripe for accepting the necessity of far-reaching fundamental change, were the internal mechanisms that were created.** One was the President's Council, which was a public body that had its meetings in a building adjacent to Parliament. It contained people from all races, and their task was to deliberate about the necessity of, and the possible substance of, constitutional change. And members from the opposition were appointed, so it was a fairly representative body although black participation was, if I remember correctly, very limited.

Creating a Consensus for Change

Another mechanism was the Constitutional Cabinet Committee that was appointed. I served on it. The chairman was Chris Heunis, who was minister of constitutional affairs, and if I remember correctly all the lawyers in the cabinet served on that committee. The Constitutional Cabinet Committee's task was to deliberate on constitutional change and report back to the cabinet. That was not public; that was not a transparent process. The President's Council was a transparent process. And it is from this cabinet committee that emanated the formulation of a vision, which was reported back at cabinet meetings but also at one or two bush conferences to say, "We have identified this needs to be done. These departure points need to be accepted, etc." And this cabinet committee played a very important role in shaping the process of self-analysis and of forward thinking.

I was accused of being a stumbling block in this committee because I played the role of devil's advocate. The late Mr. Heunis, for whose intellect I have the highest respect, had a tendency to try and move on a step-by-step basis. At times he and I clashed because he would say, "We should recommend to the cabinet, the cabinet must decide A." And I would say, "I can live with A, but then we must tell the cabinet that on A will follow B and C and D, and we must spell out what B and C and D will mean. We must think through the logical consequences and we must not hide them." And in that process I became regarded as sort of a troublemaker on this cabinet committee.

So my approach to put together a total package grew within my own heart and mind long before I became president.

Did you have at that time the conviction that the ANC was strong enough to lead the negotiation from the other side? Did you have feedback about how they might react to your project?

At those early stages, no. And of course we needed to stay in power in order to achieve anything, and therefore we had to constantly take into account what the white electorate would accept and what they would reject. Because we had quite an active and growing rightwing opposition that broke away from the National Party in the early 1980s and established what they called the Conservative Party. Their leader was Dr. Andries Treurnicht, and they were making inroads in the electoral process. In 1987, there was an all-white election although there was already a three-chamber Parliament. We stayed in power by presenting a manifesto at that stage to say, "We stand for fundamental change." The Conservative Party, however, showed great growth. So the other reality, which we had to constantly keep in mind, was that we had to take a majority of the white electorate along with us.

Processes and Mechanisms for Negotiation

You also had to put yourself in the shoes of the other, as you say, and know that the opposition also had to satisfy their constituency.

We recognized the importance of the ANC, but **at all times our belief was that we needed inclusive negotiation.** Therefore the very first meeting, which was called at the end of 1990, was fully inclusive. Even small parties unrepresented anywhere were invited. **All political entities and political parties were invited. Inclusivity is extremely important. But we could not allow the very small parties to have a veto. So we developed the concept of "sufficient consensus."**

What did the idea of "sufficient consensus" mean for this process?

Sufficient consensus meant that the major participants in the negotiation process—the government, National Party, ANC, and IFP—reached consensus. The ANC's approach was more generally "forget about the IFP." They were enemies; they were killing each other. Sufficient consensus in their lexicon meant between the government and the ANC. Then, when the IFP withdrew from the negotiation process in September 1992, sufficient consensus became an agreement between the National Party, the government, and the ANC.

Civilian Control over Security Forces

Your autobiography makes it clear that you took measures to achieve control of the security apparatus, but that you were not entirely successful because there were activities of which you were not aware. Do you have any advice for how to deal with recalcitrant security forces?

There were actions that I was not aware of, and times when elements in the security apparatus acted against their instructions from the government and against my policies and principles.

My predecessor—before he became prime minister and later executive president—was minister of defense, and throughout his time as prime minister, and then as state president, he gave the military the inside track. He built up a "securocrat" system under the State Security Council on which he co-opted me because of my political leadership position, not because of my portfolios.

And he relied on them to come with plans affecting other departments. So the State Security Council also became almost a cabinet within a cabinet.

The Defense Force would come with an action plan about socioeconomic change, and this big body, the Secretariat of the State Security Council, would manage the implementation of socioeconomic programs. This caused great resentment in the normal Departments of Health, Housing, Local Affairs, etc., because the securocrats were interfering in their affairs.

When I became president, I reduced the Security Council to the status of just another cabinet committee. I reduced the size of that office to a normal size, a normal secretariat for a normal cabinet committee. And I abolished this inside track that the military especially had (not the police so much) under P. W. Botha. And if the State Security Council had something, they had to come to the cabinet, not to me, not go quietly through the Security Council, and then present the cabinet with a fait accompli. **I insisted that we had to have government by cabinet. I consulted the full cabinet on all important decisions; proposals could come through that committee but had to go to cabinet, where the final decisions were taken.**

Why did you make these efforts to ensure that the military and Security Council were subject to the cabinet and the regular decision-making process?

Throughout my years in cabinet (I became a cabinet minister in 1978, and within less than a year P. W. Botha became prime minister and then president) I was irritated by this. I was highly critical of the preeminence he gave to the military. I was sort of leading the opposition against this tendency. Even as a young minister I was against it. Long before I became president I said to myself if ever I became president I would normalize this situation and I would restore cabinet government again.

So, coming back to the security forces, South Africa never had a history of military coups. Because of our history, the Defense Force and the police were there to fulfill their particular tasks—the Defense Force to secure the borders of South Africa and its security internationally, the police to maintain law and order inside the country—I never felt that the top echelon of those two institutions would lead a coup.

In the years of P. W. Botha, the security forces always adopted the attitude that the politicians' task was to find a political solution and for them to create an atmosphere and a situation that would create space in which political solutions can be brought forward and promoted. So I called two meetings. The first meeting was with the top 400 police officers in the whole country, and the second was with the Defense Force. I said to them, "In the past you have been drawn into things that you should not have been. You will return to your basic tasks. I am taking all your involvement in matters with political implications out of your hands. I am ending all these covert operations unless they are necessary for the state." I appointed an Advisory Committee on Special Secret Projects under Professor Kahn. All the covert programs had to be reported, and this committee would recommend to the cabinet which programs should continue and which should be discontinued. I did the same with the Defense Force. And when there was evidence that elements in those forces continued to act against this policy and this instruction, I appointed the Harms Commission [to investigate the activities of the South African Defense Force Army and South African police counterinsurgency]. But the Defense Force misled the Harms Commission. Then I appointed the Goldstone Commission [officially the Commission of Inquiry Regarding the Prevention of Public Violence and Intimidation]. When Goldstone did discover some facts, I acted very firmly—suspending some senior officers, putting some under investigation, ordering early retirement for others—to break that group that was guilty of what Goldstone found.

But the real risk of destabilization came when a former chief of the Defense Force, General Constand Viljoen, formed a new party, the Freedom Front. Because he had the loyalty of the middle order of military officers, it posed a grave risk. In the end that risk was defused by Mandela, who reached an agreement with Viljoen, promising him that the possibility of a white nation-state could be considered after the first elections. And we wrote into the first transitional constitution of 1993 clauses that said this could be explored. And then Viljoen participated in the elections, and their threats to destabilize the election by creating no-go areas—where the government was not capable of maintaining law and order—fell away. I salute Mandela for achieving that. But I wasn't popular with the defense leaders, and I am still not popular with most of the former chiefs of the Defense Force.

Social Mobilization

Black people also saw the police as a repressive force. How did you address police reform and repair their relationship with the people?

What helped in that regard was a church initiative called the National Peace Accord, which was a separate negotiation. Mandela, Buthelezi, I, and others attended the meeting at which it was established. It was not government controlled; it was civil society controlled. Local community committees were formed in which the police interacted with the community leaders at the grassroots level. In many places it worked to defuse this antipathy and resulted in better cooperation and better understanding, and it played a very good and helpful role. Bishop Tutu played an important role in this process.

It is important under such circumstances to involve the Defense Force and the police. **It is important to depoliticize the security forces and stop them from being used to achieve political goals,** such as subjugating the ANC.

Justice and Reconciliation

How did you approach the issue of amnesty for those who had committed acts of violence?

I was in favor of the Norgaard principles, which handled extremely violent or premeditated crimes separately, which would exclude amnesty for crimes such as assassination, rape, and the like. I reject those methods as being outside the rules of war. But I had to make a compromise within my party, because the ministers of police and defense were very concerned about things that I did not know about, about what their members did in previous years. I reluctantly made the compromise and agreed to a broad amnesty without applying the Norgaard principles. It pained me to release Barend Strydom, who shot so many black people in Strijdom Square in Pretoria just because they were black. It pained me to release a man who threw a bomb into a bar, where people were quietly having a drink, from the ANC side.

But unqualified amnesty provided that there was full disclosure of the crime and that it was clear that the crime was committed with a political motive. Those were the two preconditions. In the end, the amnesty during my presidency, as far as it went, went well. It wasn't completed. Then the amnesty under the Truth and Reconciliation Commission (TRC) followed. It is one of the good things they did. I have criticism of some other things the TRC did, but their role in hearing amnesty applications and adjudicating upon them was a good role, which they performed with integrity and success.

What aspects of the TRC were you critical of?

Well, they were biased. If you analyze what they concentrated on in their investigations, it becomes clear that they never really came to grips with black-on-black violence. They never really came to grips with political crimes committed by the ANC. Most of their efforts were concentrated on misdemeanors on the side of the security forces. This was the one occasion on which Mandela and I could not reach consensus. I was then deputy president. He had to consult me when we first negotiated the institution of a TRC in the Government of National Unity. Originally it was just a Truth Committee, and originally the late Minister Dullah Omar, minister of justice, came with a proposal that a different, easier test would apply to liberation factions, and a more stringent test would apply to members of the security forces. We successfully negotiated that the same test would apply to everybody. We successfully negotiated that it would not just be a Truth Commission but a Truth and Reconciliation Commission.

But then, when the commission was to be appointed, after a consultation process, I was given a list of names, and there was not one member on that list who supported the National Party. There was one who had deserted the National Party. The rest were all ANC sympathizers. I put together a small team and we researched, and I went to Mr. Mandela and said that the list of proposed commission members was too one-sided. I gave him some good names and asked him to consider putting these names in, in place of a short list of names that was on the original list. And he said he would not do it, and that if I insisted he do that then he would insist on certain other things. And then I said to him, "Announce. I don't want to prevent you from announcing the commission, but I will make a public statement that I do not agree with the composition of the commission, that we could not reach consensus on it. And in that sense of the word it will be your commission and not a commission with the full support of all the participants in the Government of National Unity." That is how it went. So from the beginning there was bias.

I often say Chile's example of how it dealt with its equivalent of the TRC was more representative of the parties to the previous conflict. They achieved understanding about what happened on all sides, and theirs was a better method than ours.

Human rights violations and corruption are legacies from dictatorships and authoritarian governments that have to be dealt with; otherwise, people will not regard the subsequent democratic system as legitimate. What are the lessons from your experience?

It would have been better if we had succeeded in reaching clearer agreements about how to deal with political crimes before we had our election in 1994. It is the one issue on which there were constant delays and that caused tension between Mandela and me, where the negotiations were not brought to a sufficient conclusion before we agreed on the transitional constitution of 1993. This constitution left the issue of political crimes open to be dealt with after the first election in 1994. **There should be definitive agreements about how to deal with political crimes and how to deal with the issue of amnesty before implementing a new dispensation.**

Processes and Mechanisms for Negotiation

But in some situations creative ambiguity may be better than premature clarity; would you agree?

Let me qualify what I have said. That is why I used the word "sufficient" agreement. The whole transitional constitution complies with the concept of creative ambiguity. It was not the final agreement, and it contained 34 principles to which the final constitution would have to adhere. It contained an agreement that the new Constitutional Court would have to certify that the final constitution complies with the 34 principles. We did not try to have full clarity on everything.

Constitutional Reform

The constitution is the jewel of the crown of the transition. The question is always how to reform the constitution. The ANC was willing to have a Constituent Assembly, and you preferred a commission. What are the lessons from South Africa on how to write a constitution?

This was an initiative that I took in the first big, inclusive meeting at which all parties were together. The ANC's starting position was that the present system should be suspended; we would form an unelected Government of National Unity, and that government would organize an election for a Constituent Assembly that, in an unfettered way, would write a new constitution. Our starting point was that a new constitution should be negotiated, and only then should there be an election. It was my and my government's initiative to propose a transitional constitution, which would lead to the election of a new Parliament. Everybody would vote for it. And such a new Parliament would also write a final constitution. And this is what took place between 1994 and 1996.

What was for me fundamentally important, and what I am very happy with, is the final package. I insisted there should never be a constitutional vacuum. South Africa's government, with all its faults in the old system, was, constitutionally speaking, a legitimate government recognized by the rest of the world.

And I insisted that any new constitution would have to be accepted by Parliament as it was then constituted, and we achieved this. So **I think when you have a legitimate government, never have a constitutional vacuum where you suspend the present constitution, it should be replaced by a negotiated new constitution.**

And the Constituent Assembly would not comply with those requirements?

A Constituent Assembly can play a role, but once again I think there is a positive lesson to be learned from our experience: that such a Constituent Assembly needs to have boundaries; those boundaries were encapsulated in the 34 immutable principles, and those immutable principles were negotiated on an inclusive basis. Then a Constituent Assembly can add flesh to the skeleton of such a charter. **The purpose of the 34 principles was to be a solemn agreement about the parameters of any new constitution.**

Role of Private Sector

What was the role of business in South Africa's transition? Please tell us about the National Economic Forum.

We could not give a formal role to business during the negotiations, because then it becomes difficult to identify who to include and who to exclude in the formal negotiation process. Why not, then, give a formal role to the church? Why not give a formal role to charitable organizations? Why only to business? So we restricted the structure of the negotiation process to political parties. **But each political party had to develop a way of interacting with outside interest groups, and we worked closely with business.** Business was involved in the negotiation process by providing the Secretariat for CODESA; they paid for it. They helped with all the logistics; they managed it.

I gave a role to business by appointing one of the top industrialists, Derek Keys, as my minister of finance. He had to prepare a budget that we knew an ANC majority Parliament would have to adopt within six weeks after the election. He had to sell that budget and the economic principles contained in it, to the ANC beforehand, and he did so.

The anecdote is that he had discussions with Trevor Manuel [member of the ANC and at that time head of the Department of Economic Planning] and others at a private old Cape residence that belonged to the Rembrandt Group, and just the day after Keys gave a PowerPoint presentation to the cabinet. Just as he and Manuel walked to the car, he said, "You know, I have here in my car this PowerPoint presentation that I showed to the cabinet yesterday. Let's go back. I want to show it to you." And he showed it outside the normal structured negotiations, and this played a key role in moving the ANC from nationalization to privatization, from a centralized economy to recognizing the role of the free markets.

So in an informal (but unstructured) way, my policy was to involve business.

Civil Society

South Africa's civil society was very active; for example, you mentioned Bishop Tutu. Was the church or the religious sector also important?

With the National Peace Accord, yes. The church played a very important role in helping maintain good racial relations and promoting goodwill, but business and organizations such as the judicial professions and so on played a more important role, because their roles relate more to issues that would be contained in a negotiated constitution. I include business in civil society. And in the case of the ANC, trade unions (which can be regarded as civil society) played a very important role in inputs to the ANC and in negotiations from the ANC side.

International Support

When you became president, the Berlin Wall was gone. How did the new international context and international actors influence your vision and actions?

The fall of the Berlin Wall and the breakdown of the Soviet Union as an expansionist world power that sought control over southern Africa really opened a window of opportunity. I don't think I could have included everything that I did in the package of February 2, 1990, if the Berlin Wall had not come down.

It was extremely important because there was a real Communist threat to South Africa. There were thousands of Cuban troops on our borders. We fought a war against them. The Communist Party was giving weapons and military training to the liberation movements. It had infiltrated the liberation movements. Most of them had dual membership of the ANC and the Communist Party. So there was a threat, and when that threat lost the sting in its tail, it opened a window of opportunity that we identified and used to put together the reform package.

Before I became president, I was, in a sense, president-elect when I became leader of my party in terms of our tradition in South Africa. I did a world tour. I briefed Margaret Thatcher, François Mitterrand, and Helmut Kohl. I briefed the Portuguese Prime Minister Cavaco Silva, who became a good friend of mine, and early in the process I also developed a very good relationship with George H. W. Bush. The ANC was insisting that sanctions must continue until they take over power. I said, "No. We've proven our integrity. We are doing everything that can be asked of us in a reasonable way. Sanctions must be lifted now."

And the international community supported me on this issue and lifted sanctions, accepted our bona fides and became supportive of the process, which was very important for us.

Neither we nor the ANC ever considered bringing in international arbiters to the negotiation process. **We agreed very early on that we would negotiate as South Africans with each other. However, the background role that other governments played was important.** From my viewpoint it was more the European governments and America that gave all sorts of support. Some of their ambassadors played important roles behind the scenes when deadlocks were reached at CODESA, and later on at the renewed negotiation forum they helped to build bridges. Some of them claim more credit than they are entitled to in this regard, but I acknowledge the role they played. But it was a role from the sidelines and behind closed doors, not a structured role.

Fundamental Principles

You observe in your autobiography that Mandela was without self-doubt. We have interviewed a number of political leaders, and certainly one quality that comes across is that to play the kind of historic transformational role that high-level political leaders—including yourself—have played, having the capacity to take decisions without then rethinking every decision is a crucial quality. Is that an innate quality that some people just have? Or is it something that is learned through the political process?

I think all the elements you mention form part of it. In my particular case, I think my training as a lawyer played a role, and specifically the university I attended played a role. It was called the Potchefstroom University for Christian Higher Education, and in the legal faculty its focus was when you have to resolve a problem, first ask yourself which principles apply to this case. When a client comes in and says, "Here's my problem," don't run to your library and say, "what has the court in the past decided about this problem?" First, before you go and check, answer yourself as a lawyer, "what are the principles? What does the law say about this?" It taught me logic. I never took far-reaching decisions without proper consultation beforehand, without thinking it through. On far-reaching decisions I never rushed into a decision. I thought it through and then—having consulted properly, having thought it through, having asked, "What is right and what is wrong? What principles apply to this?"—I would come to a conclusion, and then I would not have self-doubt about that conclusion.

Power Sharing

How did you apply the criteria you stated, when you decided to leave the Government of National Unity? What was your thinking at the time and the impact on the future of South Africa?

During the first 18 months of the Government of National Unity it worked well. The ANC realized they did not have governing experience, so they leaned heavily on my experience and the experience of people like Pik Botha and others who were with me in the Government of National Unity in the cabinet. But at some point they felt they had gone through a learning process and no longer required our experience to the same extent.

I had a dual role. I was deputy president and member of the Government of National Unity as well as leader of the main opposition party. They wanted to silence me and said that I could criticize proposals in the cabinet, but because I was deputy president, once a decision is taken, even though I opposed it, I could not publicly attack that decision. This was not in the spirit of how the Government of National Unity should have operated.

Second, in the election of 1994, I promised the voters that in the negotiation of the final constitution we would continue to try and negotiate a system that would take the principle of consensus seeking beyond the first five years. Although we agreed that there would be a Government of National Unity for five years, I promised the voters some sort of consensus-seeking model for the future beyond 1999 in the final constitution.

On two occasions I said to Mr. Mandela, "Unless you make a concession to me in this regard I will have to leave the Government of National Unity." And Roelf Meyer, our main negotiator, assures me that he executed my instructions and on many occasions he told this to Cyril Ramaphosa [head of the ANC negotiation team and chairperson of the Constitutional Assembly]. Our final proposal was a very mild proposal. It said that after the first five-year term of the Government of National Unity we would normalize the situation. There would no longer be a Government of National Unity. If a party gets 50% of the votes, it forms the government, like in any normal democracy. But we proposed that in the final constitution a National Consultative Council should be established to sit next to the cabinet, and that there should be a constitutional duty on any future government to refer issues of national importance to such a Consultative Council, which would represent all major parties in an effort to reach consensus on what the country's policy should be with regard to that issue. Let's say the framework of the budget, for instance.

And we went further and proposed that if consensus is reached within the Consultative Council, then it should become incumbent on the governing party to adopt that as the policy of the government. If no consensus is reached, then the government carries on as in any normal democracy. The Consultative Council would have no veto. So I said that if the ANC would not accept this, I would be forced to consider leaving the Government of National Unity. And they said no. For me it was an issue of conscience. I had promised the voters. On that specific issue I failed to deliver a consensus-seeking model at the executive level of government, and therefore I resigned.

Do you have second thoughts about leaving the Government of National Unity?

I think it is the one issue in which even many of my supporters feel that we should have stayed on. But let me tell you an anecdote. When the ANC said no, I called the executive committee of my party together. This is now something different from my cabinet. I no longer had a full cabinet. And I said, "Look, we must now decide, do we stay in or do we go out?" And there were two schools of thought. One school of thought was led by Pik Botha and Roelf Meyer. They said we should stay. There was another school that thought we should leave.

I offered to leave the Government of National Unity and lead the opposition, the National Party, from the Parliamentary benches. One of the other leaders could become deputy president. The party would remain part of the Government of National Unity, but I would leave. Pik Botha then said no.

International Support

The main responsibility and the main leverage are always with national actors. Taking that into consideration, do you have advice for how international actors can be helpful and not counterproductive in their efforts to support processes of transition toward democracy in different situations?

That's a question I will have to think about a bit more. I think **well-established successful countries should refrain from trying to impose their model on countries that are wracked by conflict. The people of countries trying to resolve conflict should be allowed to work out solutions that are in step with their traditions and with religion where religion plays a part. The successful countries should not regard their constitutional models as an export product and try to impose it on others.** America I think sometimes makes that mistake.

Second, I think **the international community, and specifically countries with a long history of association with countries wracked by conflict, have a role to play.** A good example is Israel and Palestine. I think the Arab countries should do more to bring the Palestinians to a more acceptable position with regard to the right of the State of Israel to exist and with regard to the parameters of all Palestinians returning. I think America and the European countries, but specifically America with its long association, should do more to get the Israelis to take initiatives. They have the power; they are in a position, like I was, to take initiatives, and America should do more to put pressure on the Israeli government to take initiatives to stop this expansion of settlements. They should come to a point where they can offer a country to the Palestinians of which the Palestinians can be proud, and not just a number of cities linked by tarred road. I think there is a duty of governments with links to the Israeli government to use their influence to that effect.

I think this model can be followed in the case of countries like Syria and the like. Neighboring countries that have a very big interest in what is happening in a troubled country on their borders should try to find a constructive role, but not a prescriptive one.

Biosketch of Thabo Mbeki, President of South Africa 1999–2008

PHOTO: RODGER BOSCH / BLOOMBERG VIA GETTY IMAGES

Thabo Mbeki, the son of a prominent South African Communist Party and ANC leader, received political and military training in Moscow and continued his studies at the London School of Economics and the University of Manchester. He then participated in 28 years of political activity in exile in London and several African countries, working as chief assistant to ANC president Oliver Tambo. Mbeki became a leading strategist of the ANC's highly successful campaign to secure international sanctions against apartheid, and he took the lead in facilitating conversations outside South Africa between the ANC and white South African leaders.

Returning to South Africa shortly after Mandela's release from prison, Mbeki played a central role in the subsequent negotiation process that led to the 1993 elections won by Mandela. Mbeki served as first deputy president—and, in effect, chief operating officer—of the new South African government. He drew upon his political position within the ANC, the relationships he had built with South African white elites—first in the confidential discussions prior to the de Klerk reforms and then in the negotiation process—and his own strategic instincts to help manage the transition. Although not without difficulty, Mbeki successfully built national and international confidence from investors that made it possible to reform and strengthen South Africa's economy. Elected president in 1999 and 2004, Mbeki eventually lost some of his national and international stature, in part because of his response to the HIV/AIDS epidemic, and was forced out of office in 2008. He has since become a leading spokesman for sub-Saharan Africa and a trusted mediator of conflicts in the region.

···

Interview with President Thabo Mbeki

What was the strategy beginning in the 1980s to end apartheid? How was an international network of support for the ANC created?

The ANC was banned in 1960. Soon after, some ANC leaders were sent out of the country because **it became clear to the leadership that we needed international support to end apartheid, and therefore needed to develop an international antiapartheid movement.** So, from 1960 onward, the role of the international community in the struggle against apartheid had a higher profile.

We were trying to organize everybody in the world—governments, citizens, religious people, trade unions, political parties, everybody—to stand up against apartheid. Direct support to the ANC in various forms from countries like the Soviet Union and Cuba enabled us to pursue the struggle even by military means. Support for the struggle also came from countries like Sweden, particularly when Olaf Palme was prime minister. They supported other opposition forces in the country.

The second element, apart from direct support to the ANC, was the boycott of apartheid South Africa and the imposing of sanctions. Ordinary citizens refused to buy South African products, governments imposed sanctions, and companies said they would no longer invest in South Africa.

The third element was humanitarian support. International organizations provided humanitarian assistance to refugees. International support became an important part of our struggle. We later said that the South African struggle rested on four pillars. One pillar was popular mobilization within the country. The second pillar was the military struggle with, in our case, the military wing of the ANC, Umkhonto we Sizwe, carrying out military operations. The third element was reconstituting the ANC because the ANC was illegal, and forming branches and organizing specifically as the ANC beyond the mass political struggle. This involved many elements, specifically the ANC underground machinery to continue the struggle by various means. The fourth pillar was international solidarity, expressed in the various ways that I've indicated. It was the activation of all four pillars that resulted in the defeat of the apartheid system.

International Influence

How did changes taking place in the Soviet Union and the United States in the 1980s influence your strategy for obtaining international support?

The 1980s reflected the crisis of the apartheid system. It became clear to everybody, including the apartheid regime, that change was inevitable. For instance, the Chase Manhattan Bank had lent money to the South African government. In 1985, when the time came for the loans to be paid back, normally the loans would have been rolled over and extended, but the bank insisted on being paid back. However, the government was bankrupt; it did not have the money. The government went to the biggest corporation in South Africa at the time, the Anglo American Corporation, to borrow money in order to pay this debt.

That was an important moment. The Chase Manhattan Bank demanded payment because their reading of the political situation in South Africa at the time was that the government could not last; sooner or later it had to go. As business people, they understood that the money they had lent to South Africa was in danger of being lost.

The United States had a policy they called "constructive engagement," which essentially meant isolating the ANC and trying to talk to the South African government to introduce gradual reforms to the apartheid system. But once a major US bank said that the reality of the matter is that the apartheid government would collapse, the US government changed its position. Later, US Secretary of State George Shultz invited the president of the ANC, Oliver Tambo, to visit Washington in 1987 to discuss relations between the US government and the ANC.

During the same period, the position of Namibia changed as a result of the end of the war in Angola. The South African Army had been in Angola essentially fighting with the Cubans. It became clear to the South African government that there was no way to win the war in Angola, and they actually didn't have the money to continue it. The war became unaffordable to the South African economy and became unwinnable on the battlefield, so the United States intervened. The US facilitated the negotiations between the Cubans, the Angolans, and the South Africans to end the war. The possibility for the independence of Namibia was created because once the South African troops and the Cubans pulled out of Angola and Angola returned to peace, this created very big opportunities for the Namibian liberation struggle led by SWAPO (South West Africa People's Organization) to intensify the struggle in Namibia from Angola. Rather than be faced with a situation in which peace would be achieved in Angola but result in an intensified military struggle in Namibia, the international community decided to solve these two questions together. That process continued until Namibia got its independence in 1990. Once Namibia was put on the course toward independence, it was clear that ending apartheid in Namibia would have an effect on apartheid in South Africa. So the events were linked.

International Support

With respect to the Soviet Union, an important supporter, the practice was that every year a delegation of the ANC would visit Moscow and we would have a conversation with the Soviet leadership. We went to the Soviet Union in 1989 in a delegation led by Oliver Tambo, who met with Gorbachev. Gorbachev explained what was going on in the Soviet Union with respect to perestroika and glasnost, why those things were necessary, what they meant, and what they were intended to achieve. In that context he raised the issue of resolving regional conflicts, and said that this is one of the matters they were discussing with the Americans. He said that the case of South Africa was a regional conflict, because although it was a struggle in South Africa, it also impacted Angola, Botswana, Swaziland, and other countries in the region. The only basis for solving this conflict in that region was to end the system of apartheid. Basically, they had agreed with the Americans that the system of apartheid must come to an end, and each country would then do whatever it could to help achieve that outcome. So Gorbachev said that the Soviet Union would continue to support the ANC in the way that it had been supporting us in the past. The Americans (this is after the meeting between George Shultz and Oliver Tambo) would then do whatever they could to bring an end to the system of apartheid, depending on what they thought was possible for them.

The position of the Soviet Union did not change during the Gorbachev years. The difference was that by this time the US had changed its position. The US was now talking directly to the ANC and was looking for its own ways to contribute to end the system of apartheid. During the period between 1985 and 1990, the global antiapartheid movement had become very strong. For instance, the US Congress introduced what was called the Comprehensive Anti-Apartheid Act, which imposed sanctions against South Africa. The bill was approved by the US Congress, but Reagan vetoed it. Then Congress overrode Reagan's veto, so it became law. What was important about that was that the campaign to override Reagan's veto was led by Republican senators—two in particular, Richard Lugar and Nancy Kassebaum—who said the Republican president was wrong and mobilized the Senate to override the veto. Even the US administration could not go against the US Congress on this issue.

The imposition of sanctions had become strong globally, and this contributed to a deepening of the crisis of apartheid. There were big mass struggles, one of the four pillars I was talking about. There were various military actions taking place within the country. Many of the ANC structures within South

Africa had recovered. While still illegal, the ANC could operate in South Africa and direct the struggle. The international dimension, the fourth pillar, had also come to a certain level of maturity.

By this time, with regard to the South African liberation struggle, all the major forces that opposed apartheid accepted the leadership of the ANC. It didn't matter whether you were in the trade unions or in the church or among the Islamic community, the student movement, the youth movement, or were women, traditional leaders, business people, etc.; everybody opposing the apartheid system accepted the leadership of the ANC. Therefore the ANC could exercise leadership using both its structures within the country and its leadership outside the country.

The global antiapartheid movement also accepted the leadership of the ANC. So when the ANC said, for instance, "We need to intensify a campaign for the release of political prisoners," it resulted in the campaign to free Mandela. Other governments, like Sweden and Norway, had come to that position much earlier. The United States and the United Kingdom came later. But they also came to recognize that they had to deal with the ANC.

The ANC led the global campaign, but there were not that many ANC people outside of South Africa. The mobilization of the solidarity movement, the organization of the British or Swedish antiapartheid movement, became the responsibility of the people of that country. They did not need ANC structures in Sweden to do that. There were ANC people in Sweden; maybe six to ten, but no more. But the bulk of the work of organizing the campaign was taken on by the Swedes themselves, because they had taken it as their own responsibility that they could not allow the system of apartheid to continue. They felt a responsibility to do something.

We did not have that many ANC people outside the country except with regard to the pillar of the armed struggle. The armed struggle required that training and weapons acquisition were done outside the country. Therefore the military cadres of the ANC were outside the country, but the bulk of them never engaged in any military action. But this communicated the message that the capacity was there for the ANC to intensify the military struggle.

Establishing the Basis for Dialogue and Negotiation

How did the discussions begin between the ANC and white members of South African society, including members of the National Party?

It was clear to us that the ANC had to increase its support among the South African population. Part of the problem was that the ANC had been banned since 1960 and was therefore not able to speak for itself. The apartheid regime treated the ANC as its enemy. It said the ANC was a terrorist organization, an instrument of the Soviet Union that wanted to impose Communism on the country, and so on. So this was the image of the ANC, particularly among the white population within the country.

In order for us to move forward toward finding a resolution to this conflict, it was important to get the top layer of society to understand the nature of the South African conflict, and that it was not a conflict between a pro-Western, democratic, anticommunist South African government and a terrorist or Communist organization.

One of the important changes was when the upper echelons of South African society—the whites, businesspeople, the intelligentsia, religious leaders, and people in the media—also understood that change was coming and that South Africa could not continue with the system of apartheid. After Chase Manhattan refused to roll over the loan, white South Africans, including businesspeople and the intelligentsia, started coming to see the ANC outside the country. Significant sections of the opinion makers in the country were abandoning the positions of the apartheid regime. Even Afrikaners were defying P. W. Botha and starting coming to visit the ANC. Botha began to see that people from his own National Party constituency were saying that the policy to isolate and destroy the ANC was not going to work, and that they must talk to the ANC. Among the Afrikaners in South Africa, rugby is a very important sport, and there were even representatives of white rugby coming to visit the ANC.

This came as a big shock to people like P. W. Botha. It became inevitable that the National Party itself said, "If we don't catch up with what is happening, we are going to be left behind." So they decided they had to talk to the ANC.

There was an important organization among the Afrikaners called the Broederbond. I met the chairman of the Broederbond, Dr. Pieter de Lange; I had two days of discussions with him in New York in 1987. The Broederbond is the heart of National Party power, and the chairman was explaining to me what was happening within Afrikaner society. He made it very clear in 1987 that they had come to understand that if the process of change had not started in South Africa by 1990, then it was inevitable that South Africa would be caught in a very bloody civil war in which many people were going to die. To avoid that, we should move to end apartheid.

The Gold Fields mining company, which at that time was British, had met Oliver Tambo in London to talk about South Africa. Gold Fields said their view was that there must be change, and that the ANC and the government should talk. Oliver Tambo said that was our view as well. Gold Fields then asked if they could arrange for some of these Afrikaners to begin talking to the ANC, and the ANC agreed. Gold Fields arranged for us to meet with these Afrikaners who were coming from within the National Party stable, without being representatives of the government.

We started a number of meetings with a delegation led by Professor Willie Esterhuyse from the University of Stellenbosch. Esterhuyse at the time was a member of the Broederbond and very close to P. W. Botha. He led a delegation of Afrikaners, and I led the ANC delegation. From 1987 until 1990, we had a number of meetings organized by Gold Fields. During the second or third meeting between us, Esterhuyse told me that our interaction had been approved by P. W. Botha, and he had asked the National Intelligence Service to keep in contact with him. So before Professor Esterhuyse left South Africa to come to our meetings, he would meet with the National Intelligence people, who would then ask him to raise a number of issues that they wanted to understand. He would raise those questions as though they were coming from him. And then when he came back to South Africa, he would report back to National Intelligence and say, "All right, we had a meeting with regard to the questions you said I must pose. These are the responses," and so on.

Until 1989, the National Party was trying to get as good an understanding of the ANC as they could. They understood that for over 20 years they had presented the ANC in a very negative light, and had manufactured an image of the ANC that was not correct. They wanted to know what the ANC stood for, and what it thought about the future of South Africa. They also wanted to know our response to current events, such as developments in Angola and Namibia. They did this in order to prepare themselves for direct official contact between the National Party and the government and the ANC, because they were already talking to Nelson Mandela by this time.

Human relations are important in all those processes. What was your experience in terms of building those human relations with leaders from the National Party and the government of South Africa?

What happened from about 1985 was a process of interaction between the ANC leadership in exile and the senior echelons in white South African society—not only white, but now I am just talking about white society. We had regular interaction with white business, white religious leaders, white academia, white professionals, lawyers, and so on, even white sportspeople. While we were in Lusaka, in exile, we no longer felt like we were outside of South Africa because we were sitting every day with other South Africans. For example, with Professor Esterhuyse, we would discuss various issues and then one of their delegation may say, "Let me tell you about the minister of finance, he is somebody very interesting. Now you see Barend du Plessis is like this and that and that." The result is that by the time one meets him face to face, the atmosphere had been created because of this extensive interaction between us.

This atmosphere had been created to the extent that all of us felt that we actually knew one another, though we had not met. And in some instances, before we came home, we would even speak with some of these white leaders on the phone. So there was no sense of big distance among us. We met for the first time in Cape Town in 1990. They knew our names and we knew their names, and even beyond that we even knew something about each one of them personally. So to interact and communicate was not difficult. We had to negotiate with people from National Intelligence about the list of political prisoners and so on. We finished our discussions and then would have dinner together, and we were chatting away about what kind of man de Klerk is, etc. So by the time we met him it was not difficult to build personal relations with him.

What did you know about the conversations that were taking place inside South Africa?

There was contact between Nelson Mandela and Oliver Tambo. So indeed we had a sense of what Mandela was discussing with the regime. But everybody understood that any decision to formally engage with the government would be taken in Lusaka, because this decision required the whole leadership.

Then, in 1989, Professor Esterhuyse delivered a message from National Intelligence that they were now ready to meet the ANC directly. So we then met with a delegation from the National Intelligence Service in Switzerland.

At that time we were discussing a demand that the ANC had been making for many years: in order for negotiations to take place, they had to first create a climate that was conducive to negotiations. There were questions about the lists of political prisoners because we said that in order for us to have negotiations with the government, the leadership that is in jail must be released so they can be part of the process of negotiations. We discussed the release of political prisoners and the unbanning of political organizations such as the ANC, the Communist Party, all of these organizations. It was necessary to unban them so that people could be active politically. That is what we were negotiating with this group in 1989. Botha was already out of government by then; de Klerk had taken over. These were the two main issues: the release of political prisoners and unbanning organizations in order to begin negotiations.

We had provided leadership to the international community to act against apartheid, and it was also important that we provide leadership to the same international community about the matter of negotiations as a new form of struggle. So we decided in 1989 to draft a policy document on negotiations in South Africa, got the countries in our region in southern Africa and the Organisation of African Unity to agree to it, and ultimately took it to the United Nations (UN) General Assembly in December 1989. So the General Assembly adopted a position about the negotiations in South Africa.

An important part of that decision was that negotiations should be left to South Africans. In particular, we were trying to avoid what had happened in Namibia. In that context, the Security Council adopted Resolution 435, which said Namibia is the responsibility of the UN, and therefore the process for resolving the Namibian conflict would be in the hands of the UN. They appointed Martti Ahtisaari to lead this process for the peaceful transition of Namibia to independence. We wanted to avoid that because our fear was that, given the way the whole global community had become involved in the struggle for the liberation of South Africa, once we were into negotiations then the whole international community would want to be involved, and then we would get a result that we did not necessarily want.

So we said, "No, let the South Africans themselves handle this and the rest of the world will support." The process of negotiations in South Africa from 1990 onward, when the direct negotiations started, broadly kept to what had been agreed. It gave us the possibility to produce a South African outcome, not an outcome dictated from the outside. South Africans sat across the table without this external intervention that we wanted to avoid. Even with regard to the issue of the negotiations, the rest of the world accepted the leadership of the ANC, in the same way they had accepted the leadership of the ANC when the ANC said that they must impose sanctions and boycott South Africa. The world responded positively.

By the end of 1989, the ANC and the regime had agreed that these banned political organizations were going to be unbanned, political prisoners were going to be released, including Mandela, and negotiations would start inside South Africa.

Social Mobilization

It was a major achievement of the ANC to build an organization that put together social movements, students, workers, women, and political groups. What are the lessons from the ANC and South Africa on building a big coalition of political and social forces?

After the ANC was banned in 1960, there followed a very intense and severe campaign of repression, including arrests and killing people in detention. Nelson Mandela was arrested, as were my father and others who ended up in the Rivonia trial as part of this campaign of repression.

One consequence of that was the ANC became very weak inside the country. There were virtually no ANC structures inside South Africa because of that campaign, but the party structure continued to exist outside the country. So there is a period from about 1962 to 1973 in which the ANC was ineffective within South Africa. Its structures had been destroyed; people were in jail, in exile, and so on. This was a very bad period in terms of our struggle, because at this time there was a general demobilization of everybody. There were no student strikes, there were no workers' strikes, there was no activity; the political struggle died.

Then around 1973 the popular struggle inside the country picked up again.

What was the relationship between politics and social movements?

The student movement reorganized itself toward the end of the 1960s and re-appeared in public at the beginning of the 1970s as activists—antiapartheid, progressive, for liberation, and so on. Many of those students had been with us in the ANC Youth League, but during this particular period they had to keep their heads down but were very much part of the remobilization of the students. So while the structures of the ANC were destroyed, there were still individuals in the country who were ANC, who became involved in the process of remobilizing the people, starting with the students and the workers, and then later religious people and so on.

From around 1973, the popular mobilization reappeared again, and it co-incided with the process of rebuilding the structures of the ANC inside the country. By the 1980s, the ANC, still illegal, had succeeded for more than a de-cade in reestablishing itself within the country. So when it came to the ques-tion of negotiations and what to do in terms of the mass democratic movement, the institutional system already existed between the ANC and everybody in the country by this time—trade unions, religious people, sportspeople, aca-demics, intellectuals, media, and government.

We drafted the Harare Declaration in Zimbabwe, a document about the ne-gotiations, and then took it around our region in southern Africa, talked to all of the heads of state and heads of government to say, "Look, we must plan for these negotiations, because they are coming and this is what we are pro-posing," and they agreed. There was a meeting of the Organisation of African Unity (OAU) because we had to put this matter to the OAU so the continent as a whole could support us. In that meeting in Harare, we ensured that there were representatives from South Africa's trade unions, religious people, women's movement, and youth movement. We had a delegation from inside the country that joined us when we met with the OAU in Harare to approve the program and the plan for negotiations. The mass movements inside the country were party to the decision. So when that delegation went back home, they said, to-gether with ANC headquarters, "all of us have joined forces and we have pre-sented a position about negotiations." So it became a position of the movement as a whole, not just the ANC.

Building a Coalition

When negotiations started in 1990, was the political power of the ANC enough to ensure that all sectors felt represented? Some black movements, not only the Inkatha Freedom Party, did not agree with the ANC. What was your strategy to bring all the groups in?

It would not have been correct for the ANC to move alone on the important strategic issue of whether and how to enter into negotiations with the regime. It was important to ensure that the broad democratic movement was party to this decision. That is why we went to Harare with the declaration. In the process of the negotiations we had to ensure that we kept the broad movement involved in the struggle. That was first. The second thing was that there were other black organizations, outside the ANC, that were not part of this broad movement; they were small, but we did not want to ignore them because of the strategic nature of the decision to negotiate in order to produce a new South Africa. In order for that new South Africa to be owned by as broad a section of the South African population as possible, you need as broad a process of involvement as possible. We knew how to deal with ourselves and the broad democratic movement, but there were other organizations such as the Pan-Africanist Congress, the Azanian People's Organisation, and the various Bantustans. During the course of the struggle, we had linked up with some of the leadership in the Bantustans to try and move them away from the apartheid regime toward our side. So we said that we need all of these forces on our side.

We convened a conference of all of them to establish a united front. We needed to make sure that these other organizations, small as they were but representative of certain black constituencies, were brought on board. They came to the conference, and we discussed a united front and its principles, the common objectives, and so on. Then, when we went into the actual negotiations, we insisted that these could not just be negotiations between the ANC and the National Party or the ANC and the government; they had to be inclusive. In the end I think we had 19 political organizations there. We tried to make sure that at all times we carried the majority of the population of the country, even people within political formations that were outside the ANC.

Processes and Mechanisms for Negotiation

When you began negotiations, what were the major issues in the debate leading to the interim constitution, and what procedures did you follow? What are the constitution-building lessons for countries that are entering this process now or in the future?

When we were preparing the Harare Declaration, we first consulted the heads of state and heads of government in the region of southern Africa before we took it to the OAU. One of the consultations we had in the region was with Julius Nyerere [president of Tanzania 1964–85]. Our proposal at that time was that an elected Constituent Assembly should draft the constitution. Julius Nyerere engaged us on that issue. He said that we had not defeated the National Party, and they had not defeated us. However, in our proposal for an elected Constituent Assembly, we were trying to impose a victor's solution on the other side, because it is inevitable that when there was an election in South Africa the ANC would win. So in reality what we were saying was, "Let's have an election to prove that you are democrats." But in fact we would have taken for ourselves the exclusive power to decide the South African constitution. He asked us why we thought the other side would accept that. So he proposed that the ANC and its supporters, and the National Party and its supporters, get together and draft a set of constitutional principles. We must negotiate them because neither side had defeated the other. Afterward, we could then elect a Constituent Assembly, but it must draft the constitution within the parameters of these agreed constitutional principles. In this way the National Party would be reassured that its fundamental positions in the new constitution, drawn up by people elected by our supporters, would be guided by these agreed principles.

Mechanisms for Constitutional Reform

The very first thing we did in the negotiations relating to the constitution was to agree on a set of principles. When the interim constitution was drafted, it had to be consistent with those principles that had been negotiated. Then came the 1994 elections, and we agreed that the democratically elected Parliament in 1994 would serve as the Constitutional Assembly. As an elected body, when it then drafted the final constitution, it was guided by the same principles. The final constitution had to adhere to the principles that had originally been agreed for the drafting of the interim constitution. So in terms of the principles and the core about democracy, multiparty politics, separation of powers, an entrenched bill of rights, independence of the judiciary, all of those things, they could not be changed even though there was an elected Constitutional Assembly.

This is an important point, because what Julius Nyerere was arguing was that South Africa was a very deeply divided society; divided in all sorts of ways in terms of racial divisions, disparities in wealth, etc. But when you draw up a constitution, you are drawing it up for the whole country. **It was important that the constitution be owned by the people of South Africa as a whole, and therefore that the process of drawing up the constitution be inclusive.**

Of course, in elections, one party wins and the other party is defeated. But **you can't draft a constitution on the basis of majorities and minorities. Even the minority must get a sense of ownership of the constitution.** Hence you had to negotiate the principles that would govern the writing of the constitution. These must be drafted and agreed by everybody, including people who represent the minority.

So there is no significant difference between the interim constitution and the final constitution, except that the interim constitution was negotiated by a group of people that was not elected. They were party representatives. The final constitution was negotiated by an elected body. To this day, South Africans don't differ about the constitution. They are all agreed.

Setbacks

There was a critical interruption during those negotiations. What were the main differences? Were disagreements on the issue of majority rule?

There was a problem of violence in the country that disrupted negotiations. The ANC said that we could not continue to negotiate in these conditions when so many people were being killed. When we came back to the negotiations, one of the issues that then arose was that we needed to find a way to negotiate in a manner that would speed up the process without changing its essence.

Mechanisms for Constitutional Reform

Together with writing a new constitution, you decided to create a Constitutional Court, which would supervise the application of the constitutional principles. Why was that a priority?

It was decided that, although there was a democratically elected body that had every right to draft a constitution, the final constitution had to be submitted to the Constitutional Court. The Constitutional Court could then determine whether the provisions in the constitution were consistent with the constitutional principles. If there were any provisions in the constitution that were not consistent with the negotiated principles, the Constitutional Assembly would have to meet again to correct that, because it was important that the negotiated constitutional principles be respected. Even though the ANC had a majority in the elected body, that did not mean the ANC could use its power to impose something on the minority outside of the context of the principles. So the agreement was that the elected body would complete the constitution but would then give it to the Constitutional Court to take a decision as to whether it was consistent with the negotiated principles.

Justice and Reconciliation

How did those negotiated principles apply to the issue of amnesty and human rights, and what are the lessons that could be relevant to others?

In South Africa, the two sides did not defeat each other, so there was no victor to impose a victor's justice on the other. Yet the issue of justice remained; you could not ignore the wrong things that had been done during the course of the struggle. We had to negotiate that.

In our racially divided society, regardless of the basic principles, the fact is that this division became a division between a white minority and a black majority. We said we wanted to build a nonracial South Africa. To do this, you need reconciliation between black and white. The ANC could have said that F. W. de Klerk and others had committed crimes and that we would take them to court. But these are leaders of a whole community who would then feel that they had no place in this new democracy because we were taking their leaders to prison.

In the end, even more pragmatically, there is a situation in which the South African Defense Force is commanded by these white generals appointed by the apartheid regime. The police, the same. Leadership of the civil service, the same. Business is in white hands. So while the ANC represented the majority, many centers of power were elsewhere. So if you want this democratic transition to succeed, you need these people on board. **You can't say two things at the same time. We could not say that we wanted the white minority to join us so that we could establish this democracy together, and at the same time arrest them. We had to find a way to solve this problem.**

The South African solution, which we borrowed from Chile, was the TRC. If people told the whole truth and nothing but the truth, then they could be granted amnesty. Those who did not could still be tried. So the victims were then able to know what happened to their relatives, where they were buried so they could be exhumed and buried properly, and they could receive an apology. To the perpetrators we said, "Because you have told the truth and apologized and you are repentant, commit yourself not to repeat these crimes." Then we granted amnesty.

There were white people charged with crimes who are serving sentences and so on, because some of them applied for amnesty but were refused and were charged. Some of them did not even apply for amnesty because they knew that it was not possible for them to get it through that process. But we had to find a balance between the issue of justice and a peaceful transition to a democratic South Africa. If there was to be a peaceful transition to democracy in South Africa, we had to make sure that we took with us those who might have committed crimes against humanity. If we had said no, that we were going to take them to court, then you had to be ready for the continuation of the war. So we had to take a decision.

National Reconciliation

You mentioned two major initiatives: the final constitution and the TRC. What else contributed to consolidate democracy once the ANC won the national elections in 1994?

During the course of the negotiations, we found that there were certain things that we had expected to be easy to solve but that became difficult in the negotiations. There had been minority regimes in South Africa for a long time during the National Party regime from 1948. They were used to the exclusive exercise of power, and they had abused their power as the white minority to oppress. So we came to the conclusion that the white minority was now afraid. Now that we had a democratic system, it was clear that the ANC was going to win. How did they know we were not going to do the same thing to them, the things they did to us? So they were fearful of democracy.

We put ourselves in their shoes and understood that we would also have the same fears. The only way to address this was to acknowledge that there must be democracy but it does not mean that they would lose power totally; irrespective of the outcome of the elections, they would remain in the government. So we offered a Government of National Unity. We said that even if the ANC received 98% of the votes, we would agree that the National Party must continue to serve in the government, so we would form a Government of National Unity so they could continue to exercise power. They were very surprised by this initiative. That is how the Government of National Unity was formed in 1994.

This is important, because it informed the thinking of the ANC right through. All of these issues about reconciliation and national unity derived from the need to ensure that this very divided and fractured society, which had existed in this form for 350 years, could find a way to remake South Africa and build a new nation. That requires national reconciliation. Thus one finds, for instance, a very controversial clause in the South African constitution. It is called the Property Clause, which is entrenched. It maintains that the state has no right to take away anybody's property without proper reason and compensation. The white minority knew that they had taken the land of the indigenous people, and now they were concerned that the government would take their land and factories. We had to send a message as part of the process of building this new united South Africa, a message that would address what was called "white fears."

The pursuit of the objective of national reconciliation and national unity was a focus of Nelson Mandela during his single term. He would very rarely come to cabinet meetings because he thought that while the rest of us attended to the practical matters of governing the country, he must continue with the message of national reconciliation and national unity. The TRC became an important part of that process, but it was not the only element.

Economic Management for Development

The second important issue related to the divided society was poverty. It was clear that we had to attend to poverty very quickly, and it was very clear that the only way to address this issue in a manner that would make an immediate impact was through the state. Poverty reduction means job creation, employment, etc., that is true. But if we said, "We will develop the economy, create more jobs, and so on and that will address the issue of poverty" and stop there, it would not work. We had to create a safety net. In that way, at least you are able to address the poorest so they get a sense that their lives are improving.

There was a related problem that came with the apartheid system. As the crisis of apartheid worsened, the regime—apart from spending a lot of money on the military and police for repression and to keep itself in power—also thought they could buy people. So suddenly they find money, for instance, to spend in the Bantustans, and they employ more people in the civil service and so on. As a result of this, when we come into government in 1994, the budget deficit was over 10%. We decided that it was not possible for us to continue to sustain such a high budget deficit, particularly when we needed to depend on the state to immediately establish a safety net for the poor. If the budget deficit was allowed to continue increasing, in the end we would have to pay back to the banks the money that we needed in order to produce clean water and schools and clinics. So we needed to cut down the budget deficit and manage it properly. That is one of the difficult things we had to do, because of course the popular opinion was that we should issue bonds, but we felt that route would destroy the economy.

It became a controversial matter. Today people say we took the wrong decision, but it was the correct decision. As a consequence, we were able to cut the budget deficit, and it actually generated more resources for the safety net. The government was still able to introduce a very big public housing program, particularly in the urban areas but also in rural areas. We addressed access to clean water, electrification, and access to health services, and education. We did not have to raise taxes to service a large public debt. That was an important intervention, because poverty and inequality in South Africa are defined in racial terms. So inequality relates to race, and therefore conflict, and is therefore directly relevant to the matter of whether you can achieve any level of national reconciliation. It cannot just be a political matter to say, "Look, we are one nation, let us forget the past," and so on. **We also had to show a change in the lives of the people who had been the disaffected and disadvantaged under apartheid.**

The third issue was rebuilding the South African economy, which was a challenge then and remains a challenge now. Historically, the South African economy has depended too much on minerals. Then there is the land question, because the patterns of land ownership in South Africa to this day retain the features that developed during the colonial period. To address the matter of land redistribution in a manner that does not negatively affect agricultural production is a continuing challenge. But it was part of what we had to address in the beginning.

Setting the Reform Agenda

The next issue has to do with the state machinery. **We did not have a revolution; we had a negotiated transition. So we inherited existing state structures, with the personnel, rules and regulations, traditions, and so on. We wanted to transform these institutions so that they would serve a democratic state. It was not easy, but necessary.** We inherited a functioning state machinery, starting with the cabinet. When we sat in the cabinet, we conducted cabinet meetings according to how they did so during the apartheid years. The cabinet secretary who was keeping records was the same fellow who served under the apartheid years. So we inherited a functioning system that we had to change over time.

The last issue I will mention is the system of international relations. We came from a period when South Africa was a pariah, isolated by the rest of the world. When we took over, we had to build a new system of international relations between South Africa and the rest of the continent and between South Africa and the rest of the world.

The formal negotiations between the ANC and the government started in 1990 and concluded in 1994. This period gave the ANC the opportunity to think about how South Africa should be governed when it became a democratic country and what kind of programs we wanted to have. It was not a matter that arose only because we had to draft an election manifesto in 1994. There was a lot of discussion, and it was not only a discussion within the ANC. The discussion on what happens to South Africa after liberation had to take place among the broader democratic movement. Two particular documents were adopted. One was called *Ready to Govern* and the other was called the *Reconstruction and Development Programme*.

By the time we came into government, we had a good idea of where we wanted to go. If we had come into government without having done that preparatory work, I think we would have had trouble developing a consistent approach to addressing the problems of poverty, reconciliation, state reconstruction, etc. We had the time to prepare. While we were negotiating, we were also doing this other important work.

Reform of the Security Forces

Reform of the security sector is a critical issue during transitions. Was there a risk of a military coup at any point? De Klerk has said that when he took over from Botha he decided to dismantle the power of the State Security Council. How did you manage to build a police force and intelligence system that was closer to the people and helpful for democracy?

We inherited a functioning state administration constructed for the purposes of apartheid, but institutionally it was functioning. The South African military and police, under the apartheid system, were trained and brought up to be loyal to the constitution and to the government of the day. Thus they continued to be loyal when we had a new government and a new constitution. I don't think there was ever a danger of a military coup because of that.

There were officers within the military and the police who were against change, but they did not have the ability to mobilize the entire South African Defense Force or police. Those elements within the military and the police who were against change acted outside of the military and the police to try to destabilize the situation by setting off bombs and killing people. They acted on their own and emerged as an Afrikaner right wing.

De Klerk is correct when he says that he dismantled a particular system, a state security infrastructure with a State Security Council, which really was the top government body because the state was faced with a threat. It was the State Security Council that really managed everything. He closed it down and returned political authority to the cabinet. However, there was the danger that people from these institutions would form rightwing armed counterrevolutionary groups to destabilize the country.

When we agreed we were going to have a democratic South Africa, and that we must change the police and military, our military people met with the apartheid military forces and agreed on a program. Members of our military became part of the new military; our people also joined the police force and the intelligence agency. We handled this transition in a way that was inclusive. We kept the chiefs of the Defense Force and police, and the governor of the Central Bank, from the apartheid years. We changed the head of intelligence immediately. We kept incumbents in a number of important posts for three to four years and then changed them.

Power Sharing

Why did de Klerk leave the position of vice president of the Government of National Unity? Did this surprise you? Did it have any implications for the rest of the period of the transition government?

We did not expect de Klerk to leave the Government of National Unity and were against it. The National Party by this time was calling itself the New National Party and was part of the government. The Reconstruction and Development Programme, which was adopted by the ANC and the broad democratic movement before the elections, became our election manifesto. When we won the election, we then submitted the Reconstruction and Development Programme to the cabinet, to the government as a whole including the National Party, to say, as the majority party, now we must transform this electoral platform into a government program. It was then discussed in the cabinet and a white paper was produced, submitted to Parliament, debated in Parliament, adopted in Parliament, and came back to the executive for implementation.

De Klerk and others were part of that process, as they were part of the government. But there was a small party called the Democratic Party that put on the clothes of the National Party. For instance, in order to raise the standard of black people, we needed to adopt affirmative action to accelerate that process. The Democratic Party, which was a small white party, took the place of the National Party and started talking to the whites in the way that the National Party used to talk to them. It was previously National Party policy to be against affirmative action, though they had used affirmative action to raise the Afrikaner people. They even have an Afrikaans expression for affirmative action; they understand it very well, but they didn't want it anymore. But once they became part of government, it also became their policy.

The Democratic Party then went to the white population, which was the constituency of the National Party, and said that the National Party was betraying them and selling out. They pointed out that the National Party was talking about affirmative action, while the Democratic Party stood for white minority rights. The National Party was in the Government of National Unity and had to speak about the rights of all South African people. Because the Democratic Party, as part of the opposition, could speak in defense of white rights, the National Party feared that the Democratic Party was taking away their constituency and electoral support. That is why the National Party left.

There was a state banquet to celebrate the adoption of the constitution in 1996. A journalist told me that the National Party would meet that night to discuss leaving the government. So I spoke to de Klerk. I asked him if they would meet that night to discuss leaving the government. He said there was a meeting but it was really not to discuss that; it was just to make an assessment about how the government was working. I said to him that the view of the ANC is that they should stay in the government. When we came to the elections in 1999, we would have made progress with regard to many issues, such as housing, clean water, health, and education. So when they campaigned as the National Party, they could say to the people, "look at the progress we have made, because we were part of this government, and Mandela could never have achieved this progress without me, because I am experienced in government." So I asked him to stay, but they did not stay.

Setting Policy Priorities

In your own government, starting in 1999, what were the main issues that you considered, as a president, to be critical to consolidating the progress of the constitution and democracy?

The fundamental issue was to address poverty and inequality, because without that you could not guarantee political stability and acceptance of the new constitutional order. It was critically important that the people got a sense that there was a post-apartheid dividend. That is, not only were you able to vote, but something material was changing in your life.

Of course it was also important to address the issue of the stability of the democratic system. In particular, it was important to make sure that we addressed the issue of political violence. Throughout this period of negotiations there was a lot of violence; a lot of people died. Even after the 1994 elections people continued to be killed; it was a threat to the very system. Rightwing forces—people who broke away from the military, the police, and so on—set up groups and set off bombs. That was a serious matter we really had to attend to. We had to make sure that we ended this process and showed the people that we were now in a democratic system, and that they did not need force in order to bring about the changes they wanted. They could bring about those changes peacefully in a democratic manner.

Political Participation and Advancement of Women

How did the government address the issue of women's participation in a new democratic setting?

There were a number of ways. First, we took a deliberate decision to have a certain number of women in government. Because in many instances you find that if you select based on merit, you are discriminating against women because it is the society which discriminates against them. Therefore you might very well find that there are more males who have these qualifications, because society discriminates in their favor to some extent. But as step number one, we said that one-third of the members of Parliament must be women and that's it; it must happen. After five years or so, you could reach parity.

In the case of the ANC, we have been defending the system of party lists for elections and proportional representation. There has been a lot of debate in South Africa—it continues up to now—about single-member constituencies. Part of our argument is that when you put up one man and one woman, the greatest likelihood is that the man will win. Sure, it's "democratic," but in the end you are going to end up with a system that discriminates against women. But if you have a party list system, and insist that there will be a certain percentage of women in the party lists, women's representation is guaranteed.

Second, it is necessary to understand the nature of the process of discrimination against women. In South Africa there is a lot of poverty, especially rural poverty, among the black population, and the majority of the rural population is women and children because the men are working in the urban areas. So when we commit to eradicate poverty, we must focus first of all in the rural areas and hence concentrate on women. One of the challenges that faces women, which is a manifestation of women's disempowerment in terms of the sociology of rural life, is that it is the women who fetch water from the river, who fetch wood for cooking, who cook, who look after children. If you understand that sociology, what you then understand is that in order to reduce the burden on rural women you must provide clean, piped water. Now they no longer have to go to the river, which is 10 km away. Even if it is still not in the house but there are taps in the village, you take a big burden off the women. Then electrification of the rural areas is important. But let's say you electrify, but they can only afford this electricity for the purposes of lighting, not cooking. What do we do about that? So you must then introduce tariffs, so that for these rural communities there is no payment for electricity until a household has used above a certain amount. What you will then find is that, after you introduce these things, suddenly the women have time to study. They can now go to school and have some time, because they no longer have to go to the river to fetch water or to the forest to look for wood.

Understanding the sociology that relates to women's development and women's empowerment is very important to understanding what interventions to make. It is not enough that a certain number of members of Parliament are women or that there are members of the cabinet who are women. This is important and necessary. But you must go beyond that in order to affect the masses of ordinary women. So I think consistently you would need affirmative action. One of the issues that the ANC Women's League kept discussing was the feeling of disempowerment among women. It comes from the culture, it comes from society, and so they would say that they would encourage the members of the Women's League to stand up and speak, express their views, and not to continue to allow the men to do the talking.

All of this requires a definite intervention. You must ensure that women are represented in Parliament. You must ensure that we change the conditions of life for women. You must find a way to create a space for these women to go to school. In South Africa there was one particular advantage, which was that there has been a women's movement engaged in the struggle in South Africa since 1913, for over 100 years. So there has always been a women's movement in the democratic process.

Fundamental Principles

What are your thoughts about how institutions and governments can help support democracy today? We have a world with a multipolar system, with new technologies and new forms of communication. It is a new world for democracy and for transitions. What are your thoughts about the future of democracy and especially of its future in African countries?

The internal struggle in South Africa for liberation activated millions of people. It was a popular struggle, like the struggle in Egypt and Tunisia and so on, a mobilization of people for change. Consciously they may not be clear about what will happen tomorrow, but they are active for change. It involved millions of people, and that indeed was the engine of change. I am not discounting the role played by political parties, political leaders, and all of that, but I am saying **the ordinary people who were active in that struggle for democracy were the real agents of change**. So democracy comes and the people are very excited. They have elected their own government and they have got their own president, Nelson Mandela. What that did was it also demobilized these millions of people. For example, a very important institution throughout the course of our struggle was the South African Council of Churches. The majority of the population of South Africa is Christian, and the Council of Churches brought together all the various denominations and was very active. People like Bishop Tutu came from this organization. Today it is almost dead. The effect of the change was a demobilization of the people.

Now the government that we have elected must deliver. Then we have a related problem. A lot of the leadership that was part of that mobilization of the people then left to join Parliament and government. They are no longer mobilizing the people; they are sitting in government. Some of them have gone into public service and are now bureaucrats. You take away a lot of this leadership and it weakens the popular institutions, without which you cannot have a properly functioning democratic system. **As the masses are demobilized, and the leadership drifts further and further away from the people, all sorts of things start going wrong. In order to sustain democratic systems, you need political organizations that are properly organized and in touch with the ordinary people, and clear ideas about where to go.** You need strong trade unions and strong civil society organizations engaged with these processes. You need an educated media, not a media that is just after sensational stories, in order to keep the population engaged in the process of change.

Once the people demobilize, the government loses the pressure from the people. Then you get people in government who begin to act in their own interest and not in the interest of the people who elected them. And I think that is very fundamental. That certainly is the South African experience.

....

Time Line

Jan. 1912: The South African Native National Congress, later the African National Congress (ANC), is founded to combat discrimination against blacks.
May 1948: The National Party (NP) wins power on a platform of segregation to favor Dutch-speaking Afrikaner whites. The government confines blacks

to remote areas, segregates schools and public areas, ends nonwhites' limited voting rights, and expands its powers to ban opponents.

Jun. 1955: The ANC, the South African Communist Party (SACP), and allies adopt the Freedom Charter, calling for nonracial democracy and radical economic change.

Apr. 1960: The government bans the ANC as Communist. ANC leaders flee or are arrested, and discuss creating an armed wing—Umkhonto we Sizwe (MK)—founded the following year under youth leader Nelson Mandela.

Aug. 1962: Mandela is arrested, leading to his conviction. His arrest, and those of other ANC leaders the next year, incapacitates the ANC for a decade.

Jan. 1973: A widespread factory workers' strike in Durban demonstrates the power of the growing nonracial trade union movement.

Jun. 1976: There are massive youth protests in the black "township" of Soweto, near Johannesburg. Police respond by killing hundreds. MK escalates attacks from neighboring black-controlled countries.

Oct. 1978: P. W. Botha becomes prime minister. He promotes a "total strategy" of incremental reform combined with violent suppression and shifts power toward the State Security Council.

Mar. 1982: Opponents of Botha's reforms, led by Andries Treurnicht, defect from the NP to found the rightwing Conservative Party (CP).

Aug. 1983: Church, labor, and civil society activists who support nonracial democracy (many of whom are associated with the ANC) launch the United Democratic Front (UDF).

Nov. 1983: White voters approve a new constitution with a presidential system and limited representation for Asian and mixed race ("coloured") voters via a "tricameral" Parliament. The CP and UDF oppose the new constitution.

Sep. 1984: Tricameral elections, combined with a poor economy, spark protests over the next year coordinated by the UDF. They are inspired by the ANC call to make the country "ungovernable."

Nov. 1985: Justice Minister Kobie Coetsee begins secret talks with Mandela. These, and talks with ANC international affairs chief Thabo Mbeki in Lusaka, explore the conditions for legalizing the ANC.

Dec. 1985: Antiapartheid unions found the Congress of South African Trade Unions.

May 1986: South Africa bombs ANC camps in neighboring countries, derailing the Commonwealth Eminent Persons Group (EPG). In response, the EPG calls for new international sanctions.

Jun. 1986: As civil unrest worsens, the government declares a state of emergency and arrests UDF leaders, crippling the UDF. Strikes and insurgency continue, and the UDF is succeeded by the similar Mass Democratic Movement.

Oct. 1986: After the state of emergency and EPG failure, the US Congress enacts new sanctions on South Africa.

Feb. 1989: Botha resigns as party leader after suffering a stroke. The NP parliamentary caucus chooses F. W. de Klerk, minister of education, as the new party leader.

Aug. 1989: As the violence continues, de Klerk and the cabinet force Botha to resign as president. De Klerk assumes the presidency.

Dec. 1989: Following military defeats and US-led diplomacy, South Africa agrees to independence for Namibia, returning it to black rule.

Feb. 1990: In his first address to Parliament, de Klerk calls for negotiations on a new constitution, legalizing the ANC and SACP, and releasing Mandela and other political prisoners.

May 1990: The ANC and the government pledge to end the fighting and release the prisoners. The violence escalates, driven by poor policing and armed conflict between the ANC and Mangosuthu Buthelezi's Zulu nationalist Inkatha Freedom Party (IFP).

Dec. 1991: The Congress on a Democratic South Africa (CODESA) begins to negotiate a new political system. Talks including the NP, ANC, IFP, and others last over a year but reach no consensus.

Mar. 1992: After the NP loses by-elections to the CP, de Klerk calls a whites-only referendum on continuing talks. Observers expect a close vote, but 68% support talks, bolstering de Klerk's mandate.

Jun. 1992: IFP partisans massacre 45 ANC supporters in the township of Boipatong. Mandela accuses the government of supporting the IFP and not policing townships. Deadlocked on constitutional issues, Mandela announces the ANC's withdrawal from CODESA.

Sep. 1992: A Record of Understanding is signed between the ANC and the government, resuming negotiations. The ANC agrees to temporary power sharing and limited amnesty; the NP promises police accountability.

Mar. 1993: The Multi-Party Negotiating Forum (MPNF), the successor to CODESA, begins. The ANC and NP pursue a two-party "sufficient consensus" that excludes the IFP.

Apr. 1993: Someone from the white right assassinates ANC leader Chris Hani. The ANC continues negotiations and calls for calm despite popular outrage. The assassination spurs parties to agree to April 1994 elections, a deadline that accelerates negotiations.

Jun. 1993: White right activists storm the MPNF, but rightwing leader and former general Constand Viljoen persuades them to leave.

Nov. 1993: Parties agree on an interim constitution with bicameralism, proportional representation, and binding "constitutional principles." The Multiparty Transitional Executive Council is formed.

Mar. 1994: The homeland military fend off an attack by a far-right paramilitary in Bophuthatswana. The paramilitary's defeat deters intransigence by homeland leaders and the white right, and prompts Viljoen to contest the election.

Apr. 1994: The IFP stays out of the elections, threatening the settlement, but is pressured to contest one week before the election. Open elections are held. The ANC wins 62%, NP 20%, and IFP 10%. Parties form a coalition with Mandela as president, Mbeki and de Klerk as deputy presidents, and Buthelezi as home minister.

Jul. 1995: The legislature creates the Truth and Reconciliation Commission, chaired by Anglican archbishop Desmond Tutu, to investigate apartheid-era crimes, hold televised hearings, and grant amnesty in exchange for the disclosure of crimes.

Jun. 1996: The NP pulls out of the government to protest their lack of influence. Mbeki becomes the sole deputy president, assuming day-to-day control of the government. The government introduces a market-oriented growth, equity, and redistribution economic policy, which achieves economic growth and stability but fails to resolve unemployment and inequality.

Dec. 1996: A permanent constitution is signed, preserving most interim political institutions and upholding earlier constitutional principles.

Sep. 1997: De Klerk retires as NP leader and returns to private life.

Oct. 1998: The Truth and Reconciliation Commission presents a report criticizing all sides of abuse after granting amnesty in less than 20% of cases.

Jun. 1999: Elections are held under the new constitution. The ANC wins 66%, and the liberal Democratic Party becomes the largest opposition party. Mbeki becomes president, promoting South Africa's regional leadership.

Sep. 1999: The African Union is established as the successor to the Organisation of African Unity, with the extensive involvement of Mbeki and South Africa.

Aug. 2003: Following civil society pressure and court rulings, Mbeki's decision not to supply antiretroviral drugs to state hospitals is reversed.

Jun. 2005: Mbeki fires Deputy President Jacob Zuma, presumed future president, citing corruption allegations. This angers Zuma's ANC supporters.

Dec. 2007: Zuma defeats Mbeki in a contest for ANC party leader and presumed next president.

Sep. 2008: Mbeki resigns as president under pressure from ANC leaders. An interim president takes office until 2009, when Zuma is elected.

NOTE

1. Dankwart A. Rustow, "Transitions to Democracy: Toward a Dynamic Model," *Comparative Politics* 2, no. 3 (1970): 337–63.

GUIDE TO FURTHER READING

Adler, Glenn, and Edward Webster, eds. *Trade Unions and Democratization in South Africa, 1985–1997*. New York: Palgrave MacMillan, 2000.

De Klerk, F. W. *The Last Trek—a New Beginning: The Autobiography*. New York: St. Martin's Press, 1999.

Dlamini, Jacob. *Native Nostalgia*. Auckland Park, South Africa: Jacana Media, 2009. On townships during apartheid and transition.

Friedman, Steven, ed. *The Long Journey: South Africa's Quest for a Negotiated Settlement*. Johannesburg: Ravan Press, 1993.

Friedman, Steven, and Doreen Atkinson, eds. *The Small Miracle: South Africa's Negotiated Settlement*. Johannesburg: Ravan Press, 1994.

Gevisser, Mark. *A Legacy of Liberation: Thabo Mbeki and the Future of the South African Dream*. New York: Palgrave MacMillan, 2010.

Gilliomee, Hermann. "Democratization in South Africa." *Political Science Quarterly* 110, no. 1 (1995): 83–104.

Habib, Adam, Devan Pillay, and Ashwin Desai. "South Africa and the Global Order: The Structural Conditioning of a Transition to Democracy." *Journal of Contemporary African Studies* 16, no. 1 (1998): 95–115.

Jung, Courtney, and Ian Shapiro. "South Africa's Negotiated Transition: Democracy, Opposition, and the New Constitutional Order." *Politics and Society* 23, no. 3 (1995): 269–308.

Lodge, Tom. *Politics in South Africa: From Mandela to Mbeki*. Oxford: James Curry Press, 2003.

Lyman, Princeton. *Partner to History: The US Role in South Africa's Transition to Democracy*. Washington, D.C.: US Institute of Peace, 2002.

Mandela, Nelson. *Long Walk to Freedom: The Autobiography of Nelson Mandela*. New York: Little, Brown, 1995.

Marais, Hein. *South Africa: Limits to Change—the Political Economy of Transition*. Kenwyn, South Africa: University of Cape Town Press, 1998.

Massie, Robert. *Loosing the Bonds: The United States and South Africa in the Apartheid Years*. New York: Nan A. Talese / Doubleday, 1997.

Sparks, Allistair. *Tomorrow Is Another Country: The Inside Story of South Africa's Road to Change*. Chicago, Ill.: University of Chicago Press, 1996. Journalistic overview.

Welsh, David, and Jack Spence. "F. W. de Klerk: Enlightened Conservative." In *Leaders of Transition*, edited by Martin Westlake. New York: St. Martin's Press, 2000.

Wilson, Richard A. *The Politics of Truth and Reconciliation in South Africa: Legitimizing the Post-Apartheid State*. Cambridge: Cambridge University Press, 2001.

Wood, Elisabeth Jean. *Forging Democracy from Below: Insurgent Transitions in South African and El Salvador*. Cambridge: Cambridge University Press, 2000.

Chapter 9

SPAIN

··

Spain: Transition by Transaction

CHARLES POWELL

Spain's checkered political history has given rise to the notion of "Spanish exceptionalism," a concept often associated with an allegedly structural inability to develop stable democratic institutions. But this concept obscures the fact that Spain's political development was not unlike that of many other European states. Admittedly, the 19th and early 20th centuries saw considerable turmoil, including severe dynastic disputes, frequent military uprisings, and extreme social and political polarization. The parliamentary monarchy established in 1874 presided over several decades of stability and prosperity, though its efforts at democratization were finally cut short by a bloodless military coup in 1923. The ensuing Primo de Rivera dictatorship failed to solve major deep-rooted problems and collapsed without resistance. It was replaced by the Second Republic (1931–36), Spain's first attempt at democracy, which was plagued by chronic cabinet instability, party-system fragmentation, and ideological polarization. It also promised far-reaching socioeconomic reforms that it failed to deliver. Nevertheless, the Second Republic did not succumb of its own accord; it was violently overthrown by an only partially successful military coup led by General Francisco Franco, which plunged Spain into a bloody three-year-long civil war (1936–39) that claimed some 400,000 lives.

The Franco Regime

Following the defeat of the Republican armies in April 1939, Franco established a political regime that was authoritarian, extremely confessional, half-heartedly corporatist, deeply conservative, and Spanish nationalist. Franco exercised supreme authority as head of state, commander in chief (Generalissimo) of the armed forces, and head of the artificial single party he had created by decree in 1937. This organization, which later came to be known as the Movement, gradually lost much of its early influence, to the extent that Franco's political system has been described as a no-party state. The Catholic Church, whose leaders saw the civil war as a "crusade" against Marxists and atheists, was initially among Franco's staunchest allies and was rewarded for its support in 1953 with a generous Concordat. In the wake of the Second Vatican Council, however, the Church gradually distanced itself from the regime. Abroad, Franco's major ally was the United States, which offered considerable military and economic assistance in return for access to Spanish bases as of 1953. Because of both its association with the Axis powers in World War II and its authoritarianism, the Franco regime was initially excluded from the European integration process, though the European Community finally granted it a preferential trade agreement in 1970.

Franco's regime constitutes a rare example of limited institutionalization combined with relatively elaborate constitutionalization. Although its institutions never really acquired a life of their own, its constitutional provisions were taken seriously, and some would play a crucial role during the transition. Most importantly, the 1947 Law of Succession declared Spain to be a kingdom, with Franco as regent for life with the power to name his successor. (This provision allowed him to appoint Juan Carlos his successor in 1969.) Similarly, although the 1958 Law of Fundamental Principles declared these to be "permanent and immutable," the Law of Succession stated that all fundamental laws could be reformed so long as they met the approval of two-thirds of the Cortes (Parliament) and were later put to a referendum, a clause that was put to good use during the transition.

In spite of its conservatism, the regime proved compatible with significant social and economic change. Much of this took place after the Stabilization Plan (1959) was adopted in response to the failure of the regime's former autarchic economic policy. Over the next decade and a half, Spain experienced unprecedented economic growth (averaging 7.3% per year during 1960-73), with gross domestic product (GDP) per capita rising from $300 to $3,260. Between 1950 and 1975, the share of the labor force engaged in agriculture declined from 48% to 22%, while that employed in industry and the service sector rose to 38% and 40%, respectively. These changes produced a significant expansion of the middle class, which grew from 14% to 43% of the population. Spaniards also became better educated: adult illiteracy rates, still at 44% in 1930, had dropped to 5% by 1975.

By the 1970s, Spain was a modern, urbanized, relatively prosperous society, with a political culture substantially different from that of the 1930s. This transformation fed a growing demand for democracy: between 1966 and 1976, support for democratic institutions rose from 35% to 78%. Attitudes favorable to democracy were particularly strong among the working class, which largely turned its back on revolutionary ideologies. Modernization did not make the advent of democracy a foregone conclusion, however; economic growth may have delayed it by making the regime more acceptable to an increasingly prosperous population.

These changes also had a significant impact on the role and nature of the state and its relationship with the regime. As economic modernization progressed, the state administration became increasingly professional and meritocratic —as well as predominantly apolitical—which largely explains why it did not later oppose democratization. Similarly, although military officers initially occupied important positions in the state bureaucracy, by the early 1970s they had been displaced from all but the military ministries. As a result of these trends, there was no need for a purge of the bureaucracy during the transition, nor was there a need to extricate the military from the political arena.

These far-reaching changes had complex political consequences, most of which were unintended by the regime. The rapid expansion of university education led to the emergence of a new student movement that was predominantly hostile to Franco. Rapid industrialization favored the emergence of a new, increasingly self-confident labor movement, led by Comisiones Obreras (Workers' Commissions), which were outlawed in 1967. Though theoretically illegal, the number of strikes increased sharply, from 500 in 1969 to 3,156 in 1975; some were accompanied by significant police brutality, resulting in 11 deaths in 1969–74. In Catalonia and the Basque Country, the arrival of hundreds of thousands of immigrants from poorer parts of Spain and unprecedented economic prosperity combined to foster a renewed interest in their autochthonous languages and cultures, often with the active support of the local Catholic clergy. This revival also partly explains the radicalization of the university students who founded ETA (Euskadi Ta Askatasuna, or Basque Homeland and Freedom) in the late 1950s, which soon became a sophisticated urban terrorist organization that claimed 45 victims in 1960–75.

The regime's twilight years also witnessed a significant increase in opposition activity. The largest and best-organized group was the Communist Party of Spain (PCE), which was particularly strong in the labor and student movements as well as in the new neighborhood associations that had emerged in the 1960s. The PCE had been advocating a policy of national reconciliation since 1956, and in 1970 it formally embraced the goal of a multiclass "pact for freedom." When such a pact finally materialized in 1974 as the Junta Democrática, however, it fell far short of the intended goal of uniting the entire democratic opposition. The Spanish Socialist Workers' Party (PSOE), which rapidly overcame its former insignificance after Felipe González's election as party leader in October 1974, deeply resented the PCE's efforts to dominate the Spanish left, just as its sister trade union, the Unión General de Trabajadores (UGT), was suspicious of Communist influence in the Comisiones Obreras. González did not share the PCE's faith in a *ruptura democrática* (democratic break), a process in which large-scale popular mobilizations would somehow result in the peaceful overthrow of the regime and its replacement by a representative provisional government that would call elections to a Constituent Assembly.

Instead, he favored a gradualist approach, resulting in the conquest of *parcelas de libertad* (plots of freedom). González's refusal to join the Junta Democrática and his decision to sponsor an alternative Plataforma de Convergencia Democrática in mid-1975 turned out to be crucial in guaranteeing the PSOE's autonomy during the transition.

The immediate crisis of the Franco regime was due to a number of factors. The economic boom of the 1960s came to an end with the 1973 oil crisis, resulting in "stagflation" and growing social unrest. The assassination of Franco's alter ego, Admiral Luis Carrero Blanco, in December 1973, only six months after his appointment as prime minister, raised fresh doubts about the regime's continuity. In January 1974, Carrero Blanco was succeeded by Carlos Arias Navarro, who presented a modest blueprint for liberalization (*apertura*), but this only deepened the growing rift between hard-liners, who believed the regime's continuity should be guaranteed by an authoritarian monarchy under Juan Carlos, and soft-liners, who assumed the future monarch would need to bring Spain's political system in line with those of its European neighbors. Although it was the product of colonial wars that Franco had largely avoided, many Spaniards regarded the collapse of the Portuguese dictatorship in April 1974 as an indication of what might happen unless significant reforms were implemented immediately. Finally, in September 1975, the execution of five anti-regime militants (as a result of the draconian antiterrorist legislation introduced after Carrero Blanco's assassination) led to an unprecedented international outcry. But it was ultimately Franco's death on November 20, 1975, that triggered the transition process.

The Transition to Democracy

Spain's democratizing process is a paradigmatic case of a "transition through transaction," characterized by the following features: the (paradoxical) use of the former regime's institutions and constitutional procedures to initiate the democratization process; negotiations between soft-liners in the outgoing authoritarian regime and representatives of major opposition groups; the inclusion of representatives of all key political forces in the decision-making process; and private face-to-face deliberations at crucial stages involving a relatively small number of participants. Some have argued that relatively low levels of popular mobilization also characterize transitions through transaction, but the Spanish experience suggests they are compatible with relatively high levels of pressure "from below" if political actors are willing and able to modulate this in response to concessions made "from above." Some also claim that transitions through transaction can only succeed in the absence of political violence, but Spain experienced 460 deaths from political violence in 1975–80; it was partly the fear that this violence might derail the transition process that encouraged political elites to negotiate in the first place.

Spain's relatively brief transition to democracy was launched from above, but it accelerated in response to mounting pressure from below. It was essentially driven by domestic actors, though the European Community—and some of its member states, notably Germany—actively supported democratization (through its parties, trade unions, and political foundations). Its origins largely reflect the political dilemmas facing King Juan Carlos, who needed to acquire a new democratic legitimacy for the monarchy in order to guarantee both his survival as head of state and the continuity of his dynasty. (The fate of his brother-in-law Constantine, who had lost the Greek throne in 1967, offered a salutary warning.) The monarchy that Juan Carlos inherited in 1975 was not the institution embodied by his grandfather Alfonso XIII until 1931, but rather an entirely artificial, authoritarian monarchy designed to perpetuate the regime. Juan Carlos did not inherit Franco's powers, however: the Organic Law of the State (1967) had designed a monarchy in which the combined authority of the prime minister and the president of the Cortes, who shared effective control over the political system, severely curtailed the king's role. Paradoxically, this meant that from the outset the king had a vested interest in a constitutional reform that would free him from the tutelage of unelected officials.

In the first stage of the transition, Prime Minister Carlos Arias Navarro, who increasingly identified with the regime's hard-liners, advanced a blueprint for limited reform that would have led to the election of a semi-democratic Cortes and the legalization of some parties (such as the PSOE) but not others (above all, the PCE). An increasingly active opposition, mass mobilizations (which sometimes resulted in the loss of life), new media outlets, and the European Parliament rejected this plan outright. Nevertheless, it was also during this period that González began to appear regularly in public, and the UGT was able to hold its first public gathering since the civil war in April 1976.

The king's decision to replace Arias Navarro in July 1976 with Adolfo Suárez, a 44-year-old apparatchik of the former regime known for his ambition and audacity, was a crucial turning point. Suárez quickly produced a Law for Political Reform that called for the election of a two-chamber Cortes by universal suffrage: a Congress of Deputies elected according to principles of proportional representation and a majoritarian Senate. In keeping with the procedure envisaged by the Francoist fundamental laws, the bill was first approved by the existing Cortes in November by 425 votes in favor and 59 against. In December, it was ratified by a referendum that registered a 77% turnout (with 94% of votes in favor) in spite of the opposition's decision to abstain on the grounds that it had been excluded from the entire process. Secret talks between Suárez and González, however, enabled the PSOE to hold its party congress immediately after the referendum, paving the way for its legalization in February 1977.

The referendum considerably strengthened Suárez's hand; it was only after it that he engaged in formal talks with the opposition's Committee of Nine, including González. The talks centered on the seven conditions the opposition demanded be met if it was to take part in future elections, which included the legalization of all political parties and trade unions, the political neutrality of public employees, a generous amnesty, the negotiation of an electoral law, and the acknowledgment of regional political identities. As González has acknowledged, these did not constitute formal negotiations; rather, Suárez listened to the opposition's demands and skillfully translated them into legislation. Most importantly, the talks led to the legalization of the Communist Party in April 1977, whose exclusion would have rendered the process illegitimate in the eyes of many Spaniards. This paved the way for the first democratic elections, held in June 1977, which in turn produced the ideal outcome: the high turnout (79%) confirmed their legitimacy, and the strong showing by Suárez's Unión de Centro Democrático (UCD), which obtained 34% of the vote and 165 out of 350 seats, allowed him to remain in office. At the same time, the PSOE emerged as the leading opposition party with 29% of the vote and 118 seats, well ahead of the PCE, which obtained a mere 9% of the vote and 20 seats.

The final stage of the transition consisted of a series of agreements involving all the major political actors. The first of these were the Moncloa Pacts signed in October 1977, which sought to restore growth to an ailing economy and curb inflation by means of far-reaching structural reforms and negotiated wage restraint. In return for the latter, the pacts introduced a new system of direct income tax, which would largely finance the spectacular growth of Spain's health and education systems in the 1980s. Another major initiative requiring a broad political consensus was the Amnesty Law, which benefited all those tried for political crimes committed against the Franco regime prior to the 1977 elections, including ETA terrorists who had been convicted of murder. It also guaranteed that former servants of the regime would not be investigated or prosecuted for human rights violations they might have committed in the past, thereby ruling out the possibility of purging the armed forces, the police, or the judiciary. This law has come under growing criticism in recent years, but at the time it was the major leftwing parties that advocated it most enthusiastically.

By far the most important product of this consensus was the new democratic constitution adopted after 16 months of negotiations between the representatives of all parliamentary parties, which was put to a referendum in December 1978. The debates that dominated the constituent process centered on the same issues that had plagued the Second Republic, but on this occasion they were dealt with far more pragmatically. The Socialists initially put forward an amendment that would have made Spain a republic, but once it was defeated by the other major parties (including the PCE, which had agreed to recognize King Juan Carlos in return for its legalization), they quickly endorsed the new parliamentary monarchy. The constitution disestablished the Catholic Church while at the same time acknowledging the right of all children to receive religious instruction in public schools and the state's obligation to support religious schools. In its treatment of economic issues, the new text balanced the preferences of the right against those of the left. It explicitly acknowledged the market economy and protected private property and inheritance rights against unlawful confiscation, but also contained guarantees of the right to strike and commitments to provide a broad range of social services, including social security, health, education, disability and unemployment benefits, and the promise of a more egalitarian distribution of income. The constitution also included provisions regulating the devolution of powers from the central government to the autonomous communities, paving the way for the development of Spain's future semifederal State of Autonomies. Although these efforts proved sufficient to accommodate Catalan nationalists, they failed to satisfy their Basque counterparts.

Consolidating a New Democracy: The Role of Felipe González

Felipe González contributed more to the consolidation of democracy than to the transition process itself, mainly by preparing his party for office. After narrowly losing to Suárez in the second parliamentary elections, held in March 1979, the PSOE took control of several major cities in local elections in April. In May, González's authority as party leader was unexpectedly challenged following his decision to remove explicit references to Marxism from the PSOE's program, leading him to resign in protest. In September, however, he was reelected secretary general on the understanding that he would be free to run the party in a manner that would broaden its electoral appeal.

Some of González's efforts to undermine the UCD government may have had negative consequences for Spain's political stability overall. In early 1980, for example, the PSOE challenged Suárez by demanding that Andalusia be allowed to attain the same level of autonomy as that recently granted to Catalonia and the Basque Country, effectively triggering the extension of devolution to all regions. González was also relentless in his criticism of Suárez's handling of the recession resulting from the 1979 world oil crisis, and of his failure to curb ETA terrorism. In May 1980, he even tabled a motion of no confidence in Parliament, despite knowing that it would fail.

In the wake of Suárez's resignation and the attempted coup of February 1981, González agreed to support his successor, Leopoldo Calvo Sotelo, in an effort to restore stability. Most significantly, in July 1982, the PSOE endorsed a major law that sought to impose limits on the regional devolution process, though important sections of this law were later declared unconstitutional. In spite of the government's growing weakness, however, González vigorously opposed its decision to apply for NATO membership, a highly controversial decision approved by Parliament in October 1981. Additionally, the Socialists accelerated the disintegration of the ruling party by offering jobs under a future PSOE government to some of its more leftwing leaders.

González truly came into his own upon becoming prime minister after his landslide victory in October 1982. Once in office, his first priority was democratic consolidation, though he also sought to advance his reformist social democratic program. His immediate challenge was to bring the military fully under civilian control; the defense law of 1984 gave him greater powers over the armed forces, and the military code introduced in 1985 limited its jurisdiction to the military sphere. González was also reasonably successful in his dealings with the Catholic Church, even though both his education reforms and the legalization of abortion in 1985 were controversial. Most importantly, his government undertook a major overhaul of Spain's economy, which required slimming down (and subsequently privatizing) much of its highly inefficient heavy industry and liberalizing the banking sector. This process was both demanded and facilitated by the prospect of membership in the European Community, a goal finally realized in January 1986, which was probably his greatest achievement. Reforms paved the way for a period of unprecedented growth (1986–91), which also made possible the rapid expansion of Spain's fledgling welfare state, though the severe 1992–94 recession raised doubts about its viability.

Other aspects of González's legacy were less positive. He unexpectedly reversed his initial support for withdrawal from NATO, convening and winning the March 1986 referendum confirming Spain's membership, a decision that unnecessarily traumatized society. And in spite of having condemned illegal antiterrorist activity under UCD, in 1983–87, his government condoned a "dirty war" against ETA, which failed to curb it and seriously undermined the rule of law. In institutional terms, the PSOE's decadelong absolute majority in Parliament (1982–93) provided much-needed stability but also resulted in the politicization of the judiciary and state-owned media, which had negative long-term consequences for Spanish democracy. The absence of adequate checks and balances largely accounts for the numerous corruption scandals that, combined with the economic downturn of 1992–94, finally resulted in González's defeat in the 1996 elections.

Spain's transition to democracy has come under increasingly critical scrutiny in recent years and is routinely blamed by some for many of Spain's (real or imagined) ills, including its difficulties in dealing with the past, the failure of its allegedly semifederal system, and growing public disaffection with its political system. Much of this criticism is both unfair and misleading, however; it assumes that the transition settlement was cast in stone, and that subsequent generations of Spaniards remained frozen in time.

Biosketch of Felipe González, President of the Government of Spain 1982–96

PHOTO: JOSÉ BALLESTEROS PALENCIA / EFE / SCANPIX

Felipe González studied law at Seville University and then at Louvain in Belgium, becoming a labor lawyer and joining the then-illegal PSOE in 1964. Having developed some visibility in his twenties, both in Spain and in the Socialist International, González challenged the established leadership of the PSOE at the 1970 party congress, thus precipitating a split in the party. The Socialist International eventually recognized González's faction. He was elected party leader in 1974 and was briefly detained by Spanish police in 1975. He set up the PSOE's party structure in Madrid that year with assistance from Germany's Friedrich Ebert Foundation and advice from Olaf Palme and Willy Brandt. González refused to join the Communist-sponsored Junta Democrática, setting up the rival Platform for Democratic Convergence instead, and established a rapport with President Adolfo Suarez after Franco's death, which paved the way for the PSOE's first public congress in Spain since the civil war of the 1930s. González was a member of the Committee of Nine that negotiated the rules for the first free national elections in 1977, and played an important role in the negotiations with Suarez, encouraged by King Juan Carlos, which produced Spain's pacted transition. He led the PSOE to impressive electoral results in 1977 and 1979, and then to a massive victory in 1982, bringing him to the Spanish presidency.

As president of the Spanish government from 1982–96, González consolidated civilian control of the armed forces, negotiated a complex semifederal system for devolution to calm demands for autonomy in Catalonia and the Basque region, and oversaw an ambitious modernizing agenda that included economic liberalization and social reforms; new health, education, and pension systems; Spain's accession to the European Community; and, more controversially, its continued membership in NATO. Having successfully renewed the PSOE's majority in the elections of 1986, 1989, and 1993, González and his party were defeated in 1996, victims of a severe economic downturn and a succession of corruption scandals. Since leaving office, González has been frequently consulted on international governance and transitional issues in many countries.

Interview with President Felipe González

What lessons can be drawn from the Spanish experience for contemporary transitions?

One important lesson is to be familiar with the individual workings of each country, because the processes are not going to mimic one another. What will happen in each country will derive from how the political, social, and economic forces, which differ from case to case, respond to issues that arise in all cases, such as how to control the armed forces.

Role of the King

The Gulf monarchies have asked me what the role of the monarchy was in Spain, and I advised them of something one doesn't study in history books: the king inherited all the powers of the absolute monarchy from the Franco dictatorship. Not only did he have the powers of an absolute monarch, but also the powers of a personal dictatorship. His role was not yet a formal one because it was not consolidated in the constitution. He was like a soldier-king, chief of the armed forces and head of the government. That being the case, at the moment of Franco's death and the proclamation of the monarchy, within a few months the king had the opportunity to designate Adolfo Suárez as prime minister [in 1976, and then Suárez was elected 1977–81]. In the Spanish transition, this step is not much studied: when the king received power and made the decision not to exercise that power absolutely, but rather to delegate it to Adolfo Suárez, as if the constitution were in force. In July 1976, Suárez was designated, for the elections weren't until 1977. At that moment **the king served as a constitutional monarch, without there yet being a constitution. It was a magnificent intuition of the king who, vested with full powers, chose not to exercise them.** Adolfo Suárez also began his term as if he were a constitutional prime minister, in terms of the responsibilities he exercised.

This turned Suárez into the protagonist of the whole process and of the dialogue, of what we could call the Spanish transition. The king gained prestige and space as a moderating force, and his role was very important as a referent for the armed forces.

Shifting Power within the Authoritarian Regime

Like all long-lasting political regimes, when there are 30 to 40 years of a personal dictatorship, as in the case of Spain with 35 years of the exercise of authoritarian power by Franco, even if there were different groups coexisting within, the process of personal dictatorship ran its course, including for biological reasons. So a position is taken by the "reformers" within the system who actually did nothing other than respond to a biological instinct—their life horizon is much beyond that of the representatives of the dictatorship—therefore they had to take a gamble as to what would happen after the disappearance of the dictatorship. Hence the reformers were born, the people who could negotiate with the opposition, and there emerged what could be considered a process of transition to democracy. In Spain this group included Adolfo Suárez, Rodolfo Martín Villa [minister of labor 1975-76, minister of the interior 1976-79, deputy prime minister 1981-82]—people 45 years old in a regime such as that of Franco, a dictator who was 75 years old and sick. They thought, "What is our remaining life expectancy compared to theirs?"

Those are positive forces at play in all countries; it is a common element in all of them. If one scrutinizes any authoritarian regime—for example, Cuba—one finds that there is a generation of political leaders over 50 years of age, some reaching the age of 60, who have been marginalized from power. Those leaders see their own life horizon extending beyond that of the Castro brothers, for example. Therefore they are attempting to take more or less prudent positions to respond to the question of what is going to happen afterward, what their role will be, and how to avoid being liquidated along with the possible liquidation of the regime. That creates a positive dynamic of resistance, which should be analyzed in keeping with the specific workings of each country.

In thinking about the role of the armed forces, I distinguish privilege from status. If one looks at Arab countries such as Morocco or Egypt, there is an oligarchy that, in addition to status, has huge privileges that they associate with the survival of the regime and of power. But there are people who are not fighting because they fear losing their privileges, but because they fear losing something much more modest yet important: their status.

Let's imagine the Guardia Civil [federal police force with military status] in Spain or the armed forces in Egypt. I'm not talking about the chiefs of the armed forces; I'm talking about the armed forces as such, which have their commissaries and preferential access to housing. In Chile you saw it as well: the armed forces had and kept, despite everything, a certain status. It is not a privilege, because from the standpoint of what we consider privileges in Spain the armed forces today have a better way of life—enhanced possibilities for a professional career, an opening to the world—than what they had before. Nonetheless, the fear of losing their status was greater than their fear of other possible losses due to the democratic change. Therefore one must understand the workings of each country and the elements of resistance to change, which at times feed into one another. In Spain there were two key elements of resistance to change on the table, and others under the table. On top of the table one found the situation of the backward looking armed forces, and beneath it a terrorist threat that called into question the unity of Spain. This was a phenomenon that fed back into itself: the more terrorist attacks, the more backward movement in the armed forces.

In the 1982 electoral campaign, when I won, it was still said of me, or my platform, that I was ready to nationalize even the soil in the flowerpots. There was resistance on the part of the large landowners and the industrial sectors, who feared a change that would generate uncertainty. **This is what I think needs to be looked at in each country: what are the forces that can join a dynamic of change that is more or less orderly, how can one build consensus among those forces, and what forms of resistance might be encountered.**

The Need for Intelligence Capability in Democratic Transitions

When we appeared before the Chilean Congress, in 1990, a few hours after Pinochet placed the presidential sash on Aylwin—a ceremony I did not wish to attend, so we arrived a few hours later—all heads of state attending met with the recently inaugurated president of the republic. One by one we each had a cordial interview. By then Aylwin was already a patriarch, and I told him: "President, I don't want to be impertinent, but I would like to put an issue to you that concerns me at the very startup of the government, because I went through it in Spain with great anguish, I experienced it with Adolfo Suárez, and as prime minister." I told him, "President, it's very difficult for me to put myself in Pinochet's place, but you have to make the effort. If I were Pinochet and I had lost the referendum, and I were now under an obligation to place the presidential sash on a democrat, bringing an end to my regime or at least the political part of my regime because I continue to be the chief of the armed forces, I would have taken the measures necessary to know what you are doing minute by minute, and what your minister of interior is doing, and what's going on in the entire state apparatus. If I were Pinochet, I would have absolutely made sure that I had that intelligence capability, and I would find it unusual if Pinochet, if he is who I think he is, hasn't done so."

He told me that I was putting a very serious problem to him, and he asked me if I really thought that this scenario was possible, and I answered that yes,

I did believe that; and he asked for my cooperation because I had experienced this. President Aylwin actually thought, in absolute good faith, that this could not happen; nonetheless, the offer remained. He thanked me, we discussed other issues, and I again offered to help him, for you have to find out whether the ground you're walking on is safe or whether it's mined, and to remove as many mines as possible.

For example, the day before the elections that I won, on October 27, 1982, the last movement in favor of a coup surfaced in Spain. On that day there was a coup attempt that was aborted immediately, when Calvo Sotelo [1981–82] was prime minister. I won the elections on October 28 with an absolute majority, but there was still an effort to stop that process one day earlier; therefore I had plenty of reasons to be on the alert.

One year after Aylwin took office, Senator Jaime Guzmán [Chilean senator and adviser to Pinochet] was assassinated. President Aylwin had planned a trip to Europe to go to Spain and Brussels, but the assassination and the situation that ensued made him doubt whether he should go forward with the trip. He finally decided that he was not going to suspend the trip because it would accord too much importance to what happened, as if the democratic process could be interrupted, and he called me to say he was coming. He reminded me of what we had discussed the day of his inauguration, and he told me that it was a matter he wanted to discuss, bearing in mind what was happening. We met and he told me that he was disconcerted about where those blows might be coming from. He wasn't certain about what was happening, and he asked me if I could provide cooperation. He told me, among other things, that the outgoing people likely had systems for surveillance and wiretapping of the state security apparatus, including the presidency. I told him that one must also have an intelligence structure at the service of the president, and a security apparatus for a democratic president. I sent him three persons who enjoyed my trust who looked into whether the conversations he was having in his office were secure or whether they were being wiretapped. Two weeks later he had a report of what was going poorly, with photographs of all the systems by which he was being watched or listened to. This problem is very common in transition processes.

If what García Márquez [Nobel Prize–winning Colombian author] says is right, no book is instructive for people if it doesn't tell anecdotes, by which human beings understand the categories behind the anecdote. For example, Raúl Alfonsín [president of Argentina 1983–89] was a classic old-school politician for whom inflation or the deficit were problems for technocrats, not for real politicians; therefore, for him, those were matters to be handled by technocrats. That was a time of democratic opening, and since we had experienced some very complicated moments, there was a great willingness to engage in cooperation, to bolster democracy in fundamental areas such as intelligence, to understand acquired practices and pass them on. I never achieved this with Raúl, even though he said that I did. We warned him that the coup attempt of La Tablada was going to happen.

I even informed Carlos Andrés Pérez [president of Venezuela 1974–79 and 1989–93]; in November 1991, I sent him a message saying that we had important information. We knew that a coup was being planned to be carried out in a number of weeks, not years. In response, he sent a person who told us that he knew about it and that we needn't worry. That was five or six weeks before the entry of Hugo Chávez and company to the palace, shooting their way in, and he insisted that we not worry about it. We were getting that information from five persons who were following the ETA [armed Basque nationalist and separatist group] people who had been expelled [from Spain] and were living in Venezuela and who were embedded in the Venezuelan Army's security system. I told Carlos Andrés this, but he didn't pay any attention. Each president has his characteristic way of being. In contrast, Carlos Menem [president of Argentina 1989–99], from day one of his term, wanted to control domestic intelligence activities.

Another anecdote that reflects the differences among democratic transition processes happened to me with Vaclav Havel [last president of Czechoslovakia 1989–92 and first president of the Czech Republic 1993–2003]. While the Czechs and Slovaks still had a legal marriage—the separation had yet to occur—we had a relationship of much trust and affection because he came into politics from the world of culture, theatre. I arrived on a visit when a discussion was under way on an issue that must be analyzed in processes of change. In the legislature presided over by Alexander Dubček [first secretary of the Communist Party of Czechoslovakia 1968–69 and chairman of the Parliament 1989–92], who had been the head of government rolled over by the Soviet tanks in 1968, there was a discussion of the law on vetting officials of the previous Communist governments. While a law such as this is being discussed, a sort of back-and-forth dynamic emerges to see who asks for more, because the more one demands the more democratic you appear to be, so the least democratic were those who were the most demanding. Those who had something to lose were the ones most furiously calling for accountability, to the point of holding Dubček himself accountable as head of government in 1968. He was the man who chaired the legislature, and therefore he had to sign the law on vetting officials.

When I was on an official visit, I met with Vaclav Havel in the Slovak part of the country. He knew I had spoken with Dubček. He told me that he was very interested in my telling him something that he thought the speaker of the legislature had heard about the Spanish transition. I told him the story without hesitating, because I believe it is an anecdote that reveals characteristics of the transition in Spain. I came into office on December 2, 1982, and on January 5, 1983, my wife's father died, so I traveled from Madrid to Seville in a presidential aircraft to attend the funeral. When I reached the airport in Seville, a police commissioner met me and placed himself under my orders as the person responsible for my security while I was there. I shook his hand and greeted him by his name, to which he responded with surprise and he asked me if I knew him; I said yes, that he had arrested me in 1974. One year before Franco's death, this man had arrested me as I was arriving in Seville from Portugal. I crossed the border undercover, I reached Seville, where they were expecting me, and they arrested me for a matter pending from an earlier time. And now the commissar didn't know what to say; that is, he was the chief of security for the man who he had arrested seven years earlier. Vaclav Havel told me: "Now I understand much better how it was in Spain." The person who was protecting me was not from the national police corps in charge of investigating robberies; he was from the political police.

So one must understand what forces are capable of creating a positive dynamic for the transition. Those forces depend on the correlations of power within and outside the regime, the opposition, and to what extent one does or does not draw a line that says "any collaborator, at any stage of the prior regime, is disqualified forever." If that were the case, it would be a practically insurmountable obstacle to reaching a great national accord that makes possible an orderly democratic transition. I'm not saying that it's the same everywhere; I am talking about democratic transitions with a greater or lesser degree of success.

Possible Transition in Cuba

You referred to the difference in expected longevity between those who run Cuba and a younger generation that is thinking about the future. The Castro brothers have never shown an interest in creating a bridge to the future. How do you see the conditions for a transition in Cuba?

There was a special circumstance in Cuba, which was the rise to power of Gorbachev with all his worldwide successes and internal failures. These were so costly to him that only 1% of Russian public opinion approved of him, while 80% of world public opinion held him in esteem because he brought about a historic change. In Cuba as in Russia, only 1% of the people in the regime appreciated him. During the 1991 crisis stemming from the consequences of Gorbachev's policies and the fall of the Berlin Wall, Cuba was left without the backing of the Soviet Union and then of Russia, which was vital for Cuba. Fidel himself began to seek solutions in his own way and encouraged the coming to power of a generation with a different outlook, but maintaining the revolutionary discourse. There were various attempts to bring about an opening in 1991-92, but they went back and forth. When some of our people, such as Carlos Solchaga [minister of industry and energy 1982-85 and minister of economy and finance 1985-93], who were very involved in the economic arena, spoke with Fidel about a certain degree of economic openness, he had a fit of anger because those who had some degree of private initiative earned money, and so he cut off that source of "capitalist corruption," going backward.

In 1995, my last year in government, I held the rotating presidency of the European Union, and I was responsible for attempting to reach a bilateral agreement between the European Union and Cuba, with strong resistance from the United States. It was based on a template for agreements that already existed, such as the bilateral agreement between the European Union and Vietnam. One can observe even Raúl Castro's fascination with the Vietnamese model. For Raúl Castro, China seemed somewhat far away, but he understood the importance of Vietnam's success, that it has taken off economically like an arrow and still has a single party in power, and despite that has cooperation agreements with the European Union, and European bank loans and investments.

I had one last conversation about this possible agreement with Fidel Castro in Bariloche (Argentina), at an Ibero-American summit, in October 1995. December would be the last European Council meeting that I could preside over. In the conversation with Fidel, among other things we discussed the last opportunity they had to sign a bilateral agreement with the European Union, which was possible despite the enormous resistance of the Eastern European countries, which objected to the relationship with Cuba. The two key points of the agreement were economic and political. On the first point, the Cubans were undertaking to open up the economy at the base, the Vietnamese model, which is based on a statist capitalist economy that creates a dynamic of growth with much-improved social well-being for the people. The political point was that the criminal code had to be reformed, which the Vietnamese had accepted very willingly. The offense of "crime against the revolution" was removed from the books—or I should say the idea was to guarantee individual freedom of expression. Pluralism of political parties was not demanded in that agreement, nor was it demanded of Vietnam; it was simply established that people who criticized the regime would not go to prison. It was freedom of expression and, therefore, freedom to criticize. So much progress had been made on the agreement that the French Council of State undertook to draft its report on the reform. In that conversation in Bariloche in October 1995—apart from it being a tough conversation for other reasons—the conditions of the agreement were spelled out.

In December, I reported to the European Council, and in February, Fidel decided to shoot down two small aircraft that were dropping propaganda from Miami over Havana in the form of leaflets. Once he did that, any possibility of an agreement or negotiation vanished. That was how Fidel resolved a commitment he did not want to take to its ultimate consequences. His reasons were that in Cuba, people take up individual liberties even if they don't have them, not like in Vietnam, which is a completely hierarchical society in which the collective prevails over the individual, where demonstrations in favor of liberties only attract radical minorities, as in China. It is a completely different mentality.

Contemporary Transitions

How is the Spanish experience relevant to contemporary transitions?

You can't generalize; each case is unique. I have been present in the evolution of the situation in Tunisia, and it has unfolded in an entirely different way than in Morocco. In Chile as well; the most representative elite was that of the Chilean exile community. Few people had put up resistance to the authoritarian government; the most important were forced to leave the country. Something similar had happened in Tunisia. A part of the Tunisian bourgeoisie was not with the regime, but the regime was not interested in wiping out that part of the bourgeoisie, for it did not consider it a threat to the regime's stability, its business, or its corruption. The government was more focused on wiping out the opposition movements, which they labeled terrorists, and it really did wipe them out. The West never sought to hold the regime accountable for that. After the Algerian experience, the West was very reluctant to do so.

I participated in the agreements for a new cooperation policy with the Mediterranean that was to accompany the peace plan, in 1995, after the first Gulf War. We designed a European policy of bilateral accords with all the countries concerned, from Morocco to Syria. Those agreements had three components. One involved economic cooperation, opening, and liberalization; another related to security; and the third concerned democratic conditionality. Respect for human rights and democratic liberties was the package that was left out, because in the second half of the 1990s what was really of concern to the West was the threat of international terrorism. So, in the case of those heads of state and dictators who guaranteed security, the West looked the other way on the question of freedoms. Therefore the dialogue was very complicated with the elites who wanted freedoms and democracy. I kept the dialogue going, but they were very much in the minority. They were exasperated when they saw democratic conditionality fall by the wayside; indeed, one of the causes of the intervention in Libya was France's failure to support the Tunisian transition.

People rejected France's relationship with Ben Ali and his regime. For France, Tunisia is its own territory, its own culture. When the revolt began, the French ambassador could not appear anywhere, whereas the Spanish ambassador had no problem doing so. So I could speak with the youth that had carried out the revolt, those who "let the genie out of the bottle." In fact, they weren't the ones who led it; it was the Islamists, who had a territorial structure, and to some extent the traditional political parties, who often did not come to agreement. I was very engaged in that process with the absolute certainty that the protagonists whom I knew from before were not going to be the protagonists of the change. I spoke with the Islamists who were making an effort to come off as moderate and democratic—for example, pledging not to alter the rights women have acquired in Tunisia—which were the most advanced in the Arab world. Yet the protagonists of the revolution disappeared, as in Egypt. Those who were in Tahrir Square, constantly calling for, well, it is not exactly known what, because after the revolt the vote gave legitimacy to the new emerging Islamist power, which would win the backing of 40% of the moderates and 20% of the radicals. Even if the radicals can be excluded from power, the moderates would have to make an agreement with the real power in Egypt, which continues to be the armed forces, to ensure stability.

Therefore it's hard to say who the interlocutors are. For example, in the relationship with Morocco, I was exasperated that my natural interlocutors, who had been co-governing for years, were the Moroccan social democrats. They went from being in the opposition, when King Hassan II died, to forming part of the government; they exercised power with the Nationalist Party and with other political forces that had a certain democratic tradition. But my discussion with them always started from the same point: they are elites who are so well educated that they seem to be *trop Sorbonne* (too Sorbonne) for the country, because the reform and modernization came from people educated at the Sorbonne, although the reality of Morocco has little to do with the reality of France. They were very surprised that when I arrived in Morocco I visited neighborhoods and rural towns to see how the people lived, what their lives were like, while they never went to those places, not even during election campaigns. The consequence is that the first time the votes were really counted, in the last election, an Islamist prime minister was elected. With free elections the votes counted, and in the legislature elected the prime minister turns out to be Islamist, because the Islamists are in places where the leaders in suits and ties don't go.

Justice and Reconciliation

What lessons from the Spanish experience in handling the issues of justice, reconciliation, and amnesty might prove useful to others?

On the issue of the amnesty, which is now being reviewed and criticized, those of us who were asking for it knew that it would also benefit the ETA prisoners. What we sought was to get out of jail those who were still awaiting trial, including me, as I was facing a request from the prosecutor for a sentence of 8 years in prison, which they were going to increase to 20 years.

It was Manuel Fraga who, as minister of interior, ordered that the case be reviewed and charges thrown out after a conversation with me. The first time I saw Fraga was at a dinner. At that time there were not yet any political parties; no election had been convened. We met on April 30, 1976; it was a very tense moment in which he really threatened me, and I told him that if he was willing to do so, I would give him an easy way to carry out his threat. I was still on probation, facing an eight-year prison sentence, which he could activate the next day. I told him, "Don't keep threatening me, just recall what I am going to say: within eight years you are going to depend on me more than I will depend on you."

Therefore the view today is that we were offering amnesty for the crimes of the Franco dictatorship, including those that may have been committed by Fraga, but the reality is that we wanted to get those who had been struggling for democracy out of prison, and end the judicial proceedings. Since the 1960s the Communists had been talking about national reconciliation, about making an agreement to that effect. It was their proposal; they were the pioneers. At that time it didn't occur to anyone that we were in a position to demand accountability for the crimes and misdemeanors of the dictatorship; that was unimaginable.

Obviously, when you have an amnesty you don't distinguish whether it is an amnesty or a pardon, and it was clearly a mistake to release the ETA prisoners, thinking that this would lead to the deactivation of that terrorist group and its struggle against the state, just because at that time the state allowed their release and was beginning to draw up a constitution for democracy. Under the administration of Adolfo Suárez, in 1979–80, the largest number of crimes committed by the ETA occurred, 90 to 100 per year. Under my administration a slight decline began that was much more pronounced at the end of my term.

On the issue of the amnesty, the same thing is being experienced in South America every day. Events that occurred 25 years ago are not seen in historical perspective; decisions are not understood in the context in which they occurred.

The great difficulty of political processes that are not transitional, but that come much later, is how to continue revisiting this issue time and again. For example, in Uruguay, there have been two referendums, and the president of the republic himself [José Mujica] was a member of the guerrilla forces, and as such he understands that the responsibility was shared, and he does not want to conduct a vetting of officials because he is responsible for having pointed his weapon and firing outside of the law, and even of having provoked the rise of regressive forces. In Spain there was not the least intention of reviewing and calling for persons to be held accountable for the crimes of the Franco dictatorship.

Decentralization

In addition to the Basque separatist movement, several regions have sought varying degrees of autonomy from the central government. How did the government approach these demands?

The twofold transformation was the democratization and decentralization of the state. Decentralization, which impacted the issue of autonomy, was really demanded by only two and a half communities: Catalonia and the Basque Country, and to a lesser extent Galicia. I am referring to communities with their own languages, though Galicia, even though it is a less rooted sentiment, had the beginnings of autonomy during the Second Republic (1931–39) and considers itself to be what is called a historical community even though there was no social demand for autonomy. In all the other communities there was simply no such demand.

There was a very positive dynamic of political decentralization, but it engendered comparative harms: why should Andalusia enjoy less autonomy than Catalonia, for example. By way of contrast, in Castile-La Mancha there was no claim for autonomy, or in Murcia, and in so many regions of Spain. Therefore the constitution provides for two levels of autonomy: one for the historical communities and another for all others involving decentralization that is more administrative than political, but with an access route to what we could call "category one" autonomies. When people vote between category one (political) and two (administrative), everyone prefers one. Therefore a dynamic of emulation is created, and political decentralization ensues. While it has been very positive for Spain for many years, a time comes when decentralization allows the decentralized powers to assume their role as small monarchs, and the elements of national cohesion weaken. This is the situation we've reached now, beyond the economic crisis, which has accelerated it.

What were the primary challenges that had to be addressed for the success of the democratic transition?

Since the 19th century we have had an agenda that was called the four basic questions. The first was the military question: how does the military power become subordinated to the civilian authorities, with the contempt the generals always felt for the politicians? This point was unavoidable. The second was the social question [class divisions that contributed to the Spanish Civil War], which was the drama of the Republic. The third was the territorial question, the unresolved problem of Catalonia and the Basque Country. Even in the First Republic of the 19th century (1873–74), the idea was that Spain should be a federation. That lasted two years. The last question was the religious one: clericalism and anticlericalism, and the role of the Church.

When the transition came, the social question was the easiest to resolve because society had advanced much more in that area. Therefore in Spain, even in crisis situations, social tensions have not been all that great. The social question was the least complicated in Spain.

Civilian Control of the Armed Forces

The military question was very complicated, yet it was the one that was best resolved in the constitution, with the consolidation that was brought about by the reform that my administration implemented with Narcis Serra, the minister of defense [1982–91]. **For the first time in the contemporary history of the Spanish state, military power was not considered as a power or branch of the state but as an institution, and defense and military policy came to be considered a responsibility of the politicians.** I had a very good experience in relation to the military, better than my experience with the judiciary.

Did you ever fear a military intervention during your administration, as there had been interventions before your administration, in 1981 and 1982?

There was one attempt in 1981, and another in October 1982, and one that occurred just before signing the treaty of accession to the European Union, on Armed Forces Day, which we very quickly thwarted with intelligence. In La Coruña, an attack was planned that would have involved blowing up the reviewing stand with all the authorities of the state, including the royal family, thereby setting in motion an unstoppable dynamic. There were preparations for a similar type of attack provoked by ETA, with the assassination of Carrero Blanco when he was head of the Franco government in December 1973.

So the relationship of the administration of Adolfo Suárez with the military was much more fraught with tension at all times. I'm not saying that there were no such tensions during my administration, but the method used to resolve them was reform, for which we had a large majority and considerable support in the legislature. This made it possible for us to approve all the military reforms: the military code, military jurisdiction, reforms in training, and participation in international missions, all of which gradually produced a complete transformation in the armed forces. Certainly the experience was not free of incidents that we would resolve by entirely different means, as happened in Valladolid.

Adolfo's background was in the state apparatus, and he was secretary general of the Movimiento Nacional, the single party, when the king appointed him prime minister. Every time there was an impertinent pronouncement by a military chief, he had the tendency to get into a debate; there were heated debates in the legislature. The same thing happened to me at first.

I experienced this in Chile when I was there, when talk began of the candidacy of Ricardo Lagos, and they asked Pinochet what he thought about my going to Chile to support the candidacy of Lagos—which really was not posed in those terms, as I was going to a seminar—and Pinochet made that impertinent remark at the Lions Club that "if there is a Socialist candidate, there may be another September 11" [the date in 1973 when Pinochet staged a military coup that overthrew the elected government of President Salvador Allende], a comment very typical of him, arrogant. Obviously the press asked if I had come to support Lagos, and I told them that it was not my intention to answer Pinochet, for in order to speak with Mr. Pinochet he has to lay down his pistol. So long as he's holding one in his hand there's no possibility of dialogue, for he is in an advantageous position. If he wants to compete in elections, he should renounce the use of threats. A scandal ensued.

In my country I did not have a single discussion with the military officers. There were one or two declarations in Valladolid, one of which was in an interview for the magazine *Interviu*, which was not appropriate for military officers. Antonio Asensio, the owner of the magazine, sent me a statement by an officer that was to be published the following Monday. He was frightened; he wanted me to ask the person being interviewed to please withdraw his statement. I told him I would not, because I don't engage in censorship. He should publish it, and I didn't give any further explanation. But I called the minister of defense and the vice president and I told them that on Monday, at the same time as that magazine was to come out, they had to sign a decree transferring this gentleman into the reserves, and to already have designated the new Capitán-General de Valladolid. When people read it in the kiosks, they will see the statement of a man who is already in the reserves, because this is what the government has decided by decree.

That happened to me twice, and what at the time was called the Junta de Jefes del Estado Mayor de la Defensa (Joint Chiefs of Staff) thanked me. These **chiefs of staff, some of them still hardcore *franquistas*, thanked me for not getting into a debate, for not mounting a public spectacle. If that man did not carry out his obligations as a military chief, he should simply be moved to the reserves, stripped of his command authority, and replaced with someone else, and that's it.** What's more, I took the members of the junta with me to the inauguration of Sanguinetti [president 1985-90 and 1995-2000] in Uruguay, and on the plane they asked me what I wanted them to do, for they were going to meet with their counterparts there who were turning over power at the end of the dictatorship. I did not give them any instructions; I simply told them to talk with them and tell them to visit Spain, and see how things are going.

I had only two such coup attempts, although Adolfo had one each week or each month. Once Adolfo called me to his office to tell me he had decided to deploy part of the Army to the border with France in Basque Country and Navarra. I told him it seemed to me a mistake, but he said he wasn't doing it for ETA but due to military pressure. I told him that part of the border could not be that well controlled, even during the Second World War, and that trying to do so now, with terrorists crossing from France to Spain and vice versa, would be a futile effort, a mistake. I told him, "You're going to give legitimacy to ETA, which says that it fights the military, so I don't agree." And he told me that he didn't agree either, but he had no room for maneuver with the military. He would authorize them in order to shut them up—they should know that this wasn't going to be resolved as they said—and he wanted to make them share responsibility. He knew that it was of no use and could even result in the ETA killing a few soldiers. It was a mistake as a strategy, but there was no political room for maneuver, and it had to be done. In other words, he didn't ask me to be in agreement, but rather not to criticize him. I told him, "Do so and you'll have my silence."

So **we would make agreements even on matters on which we didn't agree. This is fundamental for seeing why and how the transition worked.** Therefore we resolved the military problem well, but we have never come up with a satisfactory resolution of the religious question.

Role of the Security Forces

How did the king contribute to the democratic transition and ensure a constitutional monarchy? Why there were coup attempts when the king was the chief of the government?

I'm going to answer by telling you two things that are hard for me to discuss. In the military, there was a generation completely bound to Franco that considered the steps the king had taken [toward democratization] as a betrayal of the legacy received, and therefore they did not question the king but rather the steps he was taking. So they rallied against the government and were upset that the king was facilitating its work. The king also had that moderating power as chief of the armed forces. There was a resistance to change, and it is likely that without the king the coup would have succeeded.

I experienced the transition when all the intelligence services were under the military. Later they were mixed in with civilian intelligence. In countries like Spain, in contrast to the English-speaking world, most democratic civilians did not want to get their hands dirty by getting involved in intelligence problems. The history of Great Britain is full of great intellectuals who have provided services in the area of intelligence for their country, or out of pure patriotism, with strong democratic convictions. When some criticized me saying that the intelligence services were fundamentally military, I would tell them that this was the case because people like them didn't want to dirty their hands working in intelligence to defend the interests of the democratic state. That is a reality, a historical carryover, but there is another more interesting reality.

When Franco died, the intelligence services, which were very complex, fractured into groups driven by two discernible perspectives. According to the first, the function of the intelligence services is to defend the regime

they serve, while the second faction, quite notable, approached me when Franco was still alive because they believed that they served the Spanish state, not the Franco regime, and therefore their task was to facilitate, at the least possible cost to the state, the new democratic stage. That split, marked by very difficult tensions, was vital for pushing forward the democratic proposals and undoing some of the regressive tendencies.

Role of Social Forces

What was the role of the Catholic Church?

In the first phase of the transition the Church wasn't a serious problem, although there was major tension in that the state was considered Catholic. The constitution recognizes the Catholic Church as the majority religion. At the moment of the democratic transition, the Catholic Church had evolved from being the ideological and religious support structure for the Franco regime to having an elite that favored the dynamic of change and democratization. The issue of the Church was resolved reasonably but not definitively. At first it played an important role in facilitating the transition. The cry of the extreme right is sometimes recalled; it was *Tarancón al paredón* ["Tarancón to the firing squad"; Cardinal Tarancón was archbishop of Madrid 1971–83 and played a mediating role during the transition to democracy]. That was their war cry.

The arrival of Pope John Paul II marked the beginning of a regressive process in terms of a part of the doctrine of the Church. There was backsliding, for the Church was very militant in promoting legislation against abortion and divorce, which was being taken up in the time of Adolfo Suárez, with our support, for he alone would not have been able to get it passed. The Church is recalcitrant on these issues by nature. In more recent years, the Zapatero administration, with some of the expansions of freedoms, has seen demonstrations of bishops and priests in the streets, something hitherto unknown, in opposition to bills that enjoy majority support in the legislature.

Why has it been difficult to handle the relationship with the Catholic Church?

The Church has historically felt itself to have more power in Spain than in any other country. The civil war was characterized as a crusade, as a war against the infidels, much more so than in Italy. The Church-state relationship, even during my government, has been much more beneficial from the economic point of view for the Church in Spain than in Italy, Belgium, or any other Catholic country. Now there is a small polemic due to the economic crisis, because the Church does not pay taxes for its properties, whether an apartment, a high school, a business, or any other building that it has leased, even when those operate as businesses.

I was in the government when I received a visit from Agostino Casaroli, a man from the Second Vatican Council, who continued to serve as secretary of state after the election of Pope John Paul II, from 1979 to 1990. He was a very sophisticated man, very intelligent. One day he came to voice some financial concerns, which the Nuncio in Spain, Mario Tagliaferri, had put in a document. I told him, "I know you are concerned about the issue of the financing of the Church. I'm going to resolve that once and for all, so that you see that those who give you your information are deceiving you," as I knew that they were precisely the persons seated beside him. "First, ask them to give you the information on how much state financing of the Church has grown since the Socialists, nonbelievers such as myself, have been in the government." In addition, I asked him with how many states the Vatican has formal diplomatic relations. "With 104," he answered. "So you tell me what model is most favorable to you, and from this moment I will undertake to change Spain's agreements with the Holy See to conform to the model that you choose." He never again raised the problem with me. That was in 1986; I resolved it in a single conversation, once and for all.

Social Mobilization

What was the significance of social mobilization in the transition? What role did women and women's organizations play?

Part of the success of the transition in Spain is due to a very large, broad social majority that was prepared for it. The mobilization was very intense, with an active presence of trade unions, students, neighborhood and community associations. For example, for years there were worker-employer agreements that were beyond the control that the dictatorship exercised over some official trade unions. Indeed, my professional activity as an attorney was defending workers, in a labor law office set up in several parts of the country, outside of the regime's official union structure, working with the Workers' Commissions (Comisiones Obreras) and the General Union of Workers (Unión General de Trabajadores), the two largest unions that were not legal at the time. The representatives of business knew, when they sat down to negotiate, that they were not negotiating with the official vertical trade union but with the workers' real representatives.

The transition was quite peaceful except for some acts of terror by the extreme right. The vast social majorities were completely prepared and ready to engage in a dialogue to facilitate democratic life. They would go into the streets, for the neighborhoods were very organized; the neighbors' associations, including women's associations, led many of those neighborhood movements.

Women were also embedded in the trade unions, apart from the feminist movement that struggled to advance its demands. **There was considerable** participation of women, to the point that during the democratic process Spain was the country that most quickly approached parity in the political representation of women in the legislature, comparable to Nordic countries such as Sweden and Norway. Women were directly favored by the democratic changes, for they went from being considered "disabled" to recovering rights. Under Franco, women could not purchase an apartment or a car, nor could they take out a loan; they had to have the sponsorship of their husband or father. That was resolved in Spain with the democratic transition.

Responding to Economic Crisis

How was the transition affected by the economic situation, and what was the significance of the Moncloa Pact?

The Moncloa meeting paved the way for a great constitutional pact. It was a national pact to address a very serious economic crisis with political factors that posed the danger of regressive [political] forces advancing. The significant thing about that pact was the economic question. The pact was accepted by part of the left and some of the trade unions in order to put an end to runaway inflation that was destroying the Spanish economy so that wage negotiations would be based on anticipated inflation, not on past inflation. It was absolutely crucial that, for the first time, those leading the government who came from the Franco dictatorship sat down with the leaders from outside the system. Immediately after the first elections, held in June 1977, they sat down in October to engage in dialogue to reach agreements to save the country from an economic crisis, because the government wasn't strong enough and did not have the legitimacy required to impose an economic policy without an agreement with the opposition.

There was considerable risk stemming from the deterioration of the economy, but it was further driven by the terrorist attacks; together, these created risks of backsliding. For Adolfo Suárez, prime minister, the priority was mainly political; it was to get past the political pitfalls to consolidating the transition: drafting and implementing the constitution. The economic priority was secondary. He didn't want to have, in addition to political problems, social problems, including major strikes and conflicts, in the midst of an economic situation that was very tough to handle. Therefore, since he couldn't do it alone, he sought certain agreements.

The great achievement of the Moncloa Pact was that it signaled to the country that the opposition, from the Communists to the Socialists and Christian Democrats, was reaching agreement with the reformists of the regime to define the areas in which the country needed consensus to get ahead. This put an extraordinary brake on social conflict when inflation was running at 26% or 27% and rising, with a huge imbalance in public accounts.

One must recall that Franco died immediately after the first oil shock. And the reforms undertaken in the Netherlands or Germany before the oil shock were not adopted in Spain. So there were huge cost overruns for energy, an economic failure that accompanied the political difficulties we have analyzed.

The Moncloa Pact entailed, above all, a clear expression of will vis-à-vis the citizens that the political forces, wherever they were coming from, were defining a space. What is the content of a consensus that strengthens a country? It entails knowing how to define, like a good parent, what to eat, and deciding that one doesn't play with what you eat. You can observe that all the countries in the world that have done so, though this is not part of a formal agreement, are consolidated democracies. In the United States this was done one way; in Great Britain another. There are certain issues that transcend party interests, which become part of the national interest that is not called into question. That's what I call the things you eat, that must be preserved. These have to do with foreign policy, with the tremendous economic disequilibria, or with the need for an agreement such as that on the decentralization of the state. That is why the Moncloa Pact prepared us for a constitutional negotiation.

Economic Management for Development

Do you think that such a pact is necessary and feasible now, given the current economic crisis in Spain?

Not necessarily, but it is more necessary than before because it affects several aspects. There has always been a discussion in Spain on how long the transition lasted. I think it lasted until we had a constitution and democratic alternation in power. When we came into the government, the transition, the rules of the game, were already established. What we did in our stage was not to continue the transition—that's what we had done with Adolfo Suárez. The protagonist was Adolfo Suárez and we [the PSOE, or Partido Socialista Obrero Español] helped as we could: with the Moncloa Pact, the constitution agreed upon, and so on.

We consolidated democracy and modernized the country in addition to opening it up to the world. **If there is one way to describe the stage of government that I presided over, it was one of democratic consolidation, military reform, and deepening of democracy**—opening up to the outside world, joining the European Union, and opening up to Latin America and the Mediterranean, which were our main areas of action, and modernizing the Spanish productive apparatus, which involved industrial restructuring to bring the Spanish productive apparatus up to date. I inherited the administration of Leopoldo Carlos Sotelo [prime minister 1981–82], who told me: "Don't fool yourself. Spain, for structural reasons, will never have less than double-digit inflation." Leopoldo told us that we were never going to have a low rate of inflation, as in Germany or France, because in Spain there is a structural problem and a cultural problem, which do not allow us to drop below double-digit inflation. So he told me that one must work on the structure and the culture. When I was elected, we were at 14% inflation; thanks to the Moncloa Pact, we had brought it down from 26%. When I left the government, inflation was similar to what it was when Aznar [prime minister 1996–2004] ended his term and when Zapatero [prime minister 2004–11] ended his (3.7%), and it seemed very high to me.

Challenging Entrenched Interests

Did the business interests that were close to the Franco regime threaten the transition?

During the election campaign they were very combative; indeed, the interpretation of the 1981 military coup d'état, in which civilians were involved, was that it was an effort to keep the left from reaching the government, which they thought seemed very likely. In 1979, they campaigned, but the toughest moment was when the UCD party of Adolfo Suárez sank and the business community saw our triumph as almost inevitable. One of the things they would say in the 1982 campaign was "they are even going to nationalize the soil in the flowerpots." So it was a ferocious, very negative campaign, with announcements in the press that showed a rotten apple being eaten by a worm. It was of no use, and I never paid much attention to it.

When I came into the government, I did some things that people were not accustomed to. Since the 19th century, the successive governments had not had a minister of economy and finance who was not nominated by the banks; likewise, no minister of industry had been appointed who did not have the electric power companies behind him. We broke with that tradition; I had full autonomy in making these decisions.

It was tougher to establish the autonomy of the government with respect to the trade unions due to a conflict with sister unions directed by Nicolás Redondo [secretary general of UGT 1971–94]. The unions wanted to maintain the tradition of deciding who would be the minister of labor and social affairs. I told them that there were no quotas for anyone. I decided who had to be part of the government team; the constitution required that of me. Of course there were tensions, but the business interests only began to get fed up with the government when the second legislature was ending.

Ricardo Lagos still recalls when they compared him to me on relations with business. In one meeting he said, "If Felipe González was a good model of reference, as you business executives say, 'don't forget that the tax burden increased 1% of gross domestic product each year he was in government.'" This is absolutely so; I was in the government for 14 years, and when I left, the tax burden had increased 14% compared to when I came into office. If we had not done that, how else would we have put in place universal public education or a public health system? In 1988, the business sector already wanted a change of government, so much so that, before the elections, the unions called a general strike that was very successful and agreed upon with the employers, even to recoup the hours lost. The employers facilitated the strike, and the country was brought to a standstill. Even Televisión Española was shut down. In 1989, there were elections, and once again I won a majority in the legislature.

Differences within the Opposition

With respect to the political parties, why did the UCD [the coalition led by Adolfo Suarez that existed 1977–83] sink and a rightist party emerge, the Partido Popular, heir of Fraga's Alianza Popular? How did you handle the relationship with the Communist Party?

I didn't trust the Communists, but I wasn't an anticommunist. I opened up the relationship with them. I was the first one, after 30 years, who made contact with Santiago Carrillo, secretary general of the Communists, in France, which resulted in my receiving hundreds and hundreds of letters from Socialist colleagues in exile, some inside Spain, rejecting that contact.

At the time I did not accept Mitterrand's theory on the unity of the left. It was accepted by Mario Soares [Socialist prime minister of Portugal 1976–78 and 1983–85, and president 1986–96] in Portugal because he was forced to; he wanted the platform in Portugal and all of southern Europe to be the unity of the left, which brought him to the presidency. Mitterrand couldn't believe that the Communists won 9% and we, the PSOE, 30% in the first elections. He thought we were going to get 12% or 14%, and that the Communists were going to win 24% or 25%. However much I explained to Mitterrand that France wasn't Spain, that the reality was that for every vote cast for the Communists we would have three votes, he couldn't believe it until the July 15, 1977, elections, when he saw things in a completely different light and invited me to the Congress of his party four days later.

Mitterrand was very intelligent and at the same time cunning. He made unity with the Communists to do them in; they brought him to power, and then he brought the Communist Party down. He then nationalized what remained to be nationalized of the banking system, the high-tech companies in France, and the big technology companies. Above all he nationalized those that did not help him in the election campaign, with some exceptions.

In July 1982, I received Kissinger in Madrid, a visit that appears in his book of memoirs. In a lengthy conversation he told me, "You're going to do what Mitterrand did; you're going to nationalize the banking system." The United

States feared the Mitterrand model; they were scared because of his victory in France and because Portugal, Greece, southern Europe in general could end up in the hands of the Communists, with the strategy of unity of the left, which was also how they were working in Italy. Kissinger was sent by the US State Department to see what was happening in Spain; they knew little about me, and they wanted to find out which direction the government was going to take, what it was going to do. He finished off with a funny comment, for he told me, "If you do not nationalize the banking system and other things, well you're not a Socialist." I told him that his problem was that he identified Socialist with fool, and they don't always coincide. What I was going to do was give the central bank autonomy, have the banks compete with one another, with regulation and oversight, but I wasn't going to nationalize them; I wasn't going to make credit more costly or bureaucratize it, and I also had a plan to denationalize the industries that the Franco regime nationalized. To me it seemed unbearable that the state was making cars at SEAT, which is a state-owned enterprise, and that private companies were building highways; I preferred the opposite. He left very much impacted by the conversation of what was happening in southern Europe.

There's a very interesting phenomenon, more generational than about specific political instincts. From the first election in 1977, after so many years of dictatorship, the vote from center-left to center-right was similar to that of a European country that had been voting for a long time. The social behavior was the same. In that first election [1977], Adolfo Suárez got 34% of the vote and I got 29%. There was still the Socialist Party of Tierno Galván, which got 4.4%; it was a social and moderate party. Therefore the Social Democrats had 1% more of the vote than Adolfo Suárez of the UCD. The Communists obtained more votes than Fraga with the Alianza Popular, which then became the People's Party (Partido Popular). Nonetheless, the Communist Party continued to be a minority party, along with the Catalan nationalists. It so happens that the first vote gave the forces of the regime 43% or 44% of all the votes, and the forces contrary to the regime 50-something. Thus the election law gave Adolfo Suárez power, but not the votes.

This is key to understanding Spain. The vote always represents a yielding of individual sovereignty. You vote for certain acronyms and a tradition, an ideological sympathy, which is often familiar, but at the same time you vote for a face that does or does not inspire confidence. The great accomplishment of the king was that, even though Suárez had been the secretary general of the movement, the immense majority of the population did not consider him responsible for the Franco regime, the war, or their consequences. It was a generational option. Adolfo Suárez and I, clearly belonging to a postwar generation, got the votes to give us two-thirds of the legislative representation between the two of us. Carrillo, representing the recalcitrant Communist Party, got 9% of the votes, and Fraga 8%. In other words, the faces the people identified with the past didn't get the votes, and the faces identified with Spain's future as a democracy won the majority of votes. It was a generational change: the people did not vote for the past, they voted for the future, and Carrillo and Fraga were the past.

Leadership Qualities

Do you see the political and intellectual qualities of leadership as innate or learned? And if they are learned, how did you learn?

There is no school for that. When one exercises political power, whether or not you have institutional power, one does not propose a theory of leadership to oneself. John Kennedy [US president 1961–63], who was one of the few [presidents] who was educated in political science, had a conversation with his secretary of defense that is worth recalling. When McNamara rejected the position of secretary of defense and told Kennedy to put him in commerce, because he didn't have the slightest notions about defense, Kennedy told him, "You say that you are not prepared to be secretary of defense, nor am I to be president of the United States." **No one is prepared for that; with one or two exceptions, no one who comes from political science has become the leader of a country, they have been brilliant political analysts or they have been the number two person giving direction to a country. Therefore there is no school of leadership.**

A political leader has to have a strong commitment to what he or she proposes and believe in it, and the commitment has to be the least mercenary possible. A leader should be not only a political leader, but also a social leader like Mother Teresa of Calcutta, who gave her whole life in exchange for nothing, without any mercenary aspect. So the credibility of a political, social, or business leader is fundamentally based on a serious commitment to what one proposes, believing in it without self-interested motives.

The second characteristic of a political leader is that he has to take stock of the mood of the others. For example, what was Zapatero's mistake? When the whole country was aware that we were going through a frightful crisis, he appeared time and again saying that it was not all that serious, and that there was no crisis. He did not take it upon himself to consider the mood of the people. Once he has taken charge, the obligation of the political leader is to change the mood. If it's negative, make it positive, which one never does if one is not taking stock of the people's mood. The major political blunders are always the same. Therefore, if a leader considers the mood of the people and is strongly committed to offering a solution, in which everything is at stake in exchange for nothing, he or she will be capable of changing that negative mood to a positive one. Therein lies the magic of politics, because in the end power is no more than the administration of expectations.

The third condition is selecting teams of people and coordinating them with moral authority and persuasion, not threats, because having the power to decide who will hold a cabinet post or cease to hold one is a very strong power. Yet coordinating people with a lot of talent requires not only the political power to appoint, but also a moral authority for them to respect you. That was what Adolfo lost, and then the UDC broke down. He lost moral authority over his team; they did not appreciate him, and they did not respect him as a moral authority. I had on my team, whose members were all more brilliant than myself in their areas, people like Miguel Boyer [minister of economy, treasury, and commerce 1982–85], Alfonso Guerra [deputy prime minister 1982–91], and José María Maravall [minister of education and science 1982–88]; first-rate people. Someone once said to me, "One must choose the best people, including the brilliant ones, to accompany you in governing, but you have to know that geniuses have their temperament, and putting up with them is very difficult; you have to be very patient." It was fantastic advice. If you have someone with a first-rate mind like Boyer, how do you limit the arrogance of an exceptional person if you don't have the moral authority to decide not to take their advice, but rather to proceed with another plan or course of action?

The mistake of some political leaders is that they don't want to have a single collaborator who might cast a shadow over them, who is smarter than they are, because they don't feel they have the moral authority to govern them. And it should be just the opposite. The opposite example is President Reagan, who was a man of encyclopedic ignorance. But there was one area in which he had superior intelligence. He had clear priorities and he chose first-rate people to implement them, beginning with the man who helped cast his image, for I've never seen anyone better. He also chose first-rate people to serve as secretary of state and secretary of defense. He might not have known where Paraguay was in relation to Argentina, but he had a very well-prepared team. He was a very ignorant person, but aware of that, and that is the principle of knowledge that comes from "I know that I know nothing."

In contemporary society, which is being reshaped by globalization and the information revolution, for the first time in human history and in the history of political power, what we've always thought about "information is power" has changed. Today, information is a good like the air—it's available to everyone. Everything that happens, including the most secret, is known. The WikiLeaks scandal is a scandal not because of what it reveals, but because it reveals everything in a package. Yes, if one breaks it down, everything it reveals is known in the corresponding ambit. Information is like water, a good with no owner, and available all at once. The problem is, how do you process that information to obtain a result for you? Intelligence for leadership means coordinating excessively abundant information and giving it operational meaning that serves your purpose.

For example, there was plenty of information indicating the September 11th attack on the United States was going to happen. That is the great discovery of the congressional investigative commission; in the United States they do a good job of obtaining information. They had plenty of data, yet their team was unable to discern which data were relevant to anticipate and prevent the attack. Therefore the problem is that information is not power. Power is coordinating the relevant information for your purpose in running the government. That is the great revolution that has taken place, and it's one of the major reasons why leadership is eroding.

This is part of the crisis of leadership. Leaders have the same *power* that they had 30 years ago, but they have less *authority* vis-à-vis society than they had 30 years ago. The same *potestas* (power through coercion) exists, and there is a crisis of *auctoritas* (authority, prestige). Leadership without *auctoritas*, with *potestas* alone, is a very fragile leadership. There are political leaders who exercise *potestas* with *auctoritas*, and a time comes when they cease to be leaders with power, they are "ex-," yet they maintain *auctoritas* even though they don't have *potestas*. Nonetheless, there are political leaders who have had all the *potestas*, and then when they step down from office they don't have *potestas*, nor do they have *auctoritas*. And the world is full of such former political leaders.

One trains for leadership; that is clear. There may be people better or worse qualified in terms of where they are coming from, that is also true, but one does not learn from books; one trains by leading. You can do a great job explaining to kids, in books, how one can run 100 meters in 10 seconds, but if you don't have them run, none of them will ever do it in that time.

International Influence

You had wide international contact during the transition, including contacts with Willy Brandt [Social Democratic chancellor of Germany 1969-74, vice chancellor 1966-69], Mário Soares, Olaf Palme [Social Democratic prime minister of Sweden 1969-76, 1982-86], and François Mitterrand [Socialist president of France 1981-95], and then with people in NATO and the European Union. What was the impact of external actors in Spain? And what conclusions can you draw for today's transitions?

The Spaniards wanted to be like the rest of Europe, and that went beyond economic considerations. The 1.5 million Spaniards who were forced to leave in the 1960s [because of economic reforms and job loss] had a European experience of trade union freedoms, freedom of expression, freedom of political parties. They brought in their wake 10 million Spaniards who were their family members. Therefore the treaty of accession to the European Union, which had burdensome and serious conditions because it was, after all, a treaty of accession, was approved unanimously by the legislature. People who hadn't believed in Europe fell under the influence of Ortega y Gasset [Spanish philosopher], who said: "Spain is the problem, Europe the solution." And it was very beautiful.

For Spain, Europe was the international influence; but how do you translate that to the current context? Europe has become dramatically less important, as has the United States, albeit to a lesser extent. Let us recall what Lula [president of Brazil 2003–11] said in October 2011—"You built a European democratic and social model that we considered a heritage of humankind; you don't have a right to spoil it"—and we are spoiling it. In other words, Europe is failing and is becoming a small southwestern corner of "Eurasia," which is less and less relevant. This holds for social democracy, and for Christian democracy. It holds for the political forces that have articulated society and well-being and Europe's success after the Second World War.

Europe is failing, and at this time it continues failing because there are inconsistencies in constructing the shared public space; these became dramatically manifest when the world financial crisis broke out. That, in turn, is a reflection that the West—that is, the United States and Europe, what we call the developed West, because Latin America is the developing West, with growth potential—has spent what it's going to have to pay in the next 25 years, while the emerging East and West have saved what they're going to be able to buy in the next 25 years. This is the big change in the world scene.

This change has resulted in Europe becoming less relevant. So Tunisians would like to be, with their own identity, like the Europe they dreamed of when emigrating. They now see it weakened and hardly relevant; the same thing holds for the Egyptians, even the Moroccans, who today are seeking to join the European Union. It is the only country of the Arab world that wants to be part of Europe. For the Turks are not Arabs and are part of the European continent, yet Turkey, due to European mistakes, is less and less interested in integrating with the European Union because Turkey is growing while the European Union is in recession. Therefore integration into Europe, which had been the on the horizon for Turkey, is no longer such an aspiration.

It is particularly unfortunate that Europe as a concept has lost its capacity to seriously influence the processes of transition to democracy that we are witnessing today. The United States has also lost that capacity to a great degree. When the press asked Hillary Clinton [US secretary of state 2009–13], when preparations were under way for a visit by Obama to China, whether he would raise the problem of human rights in China, she answered, "You never want to poke a stick in your banker's eye."

Spain has been a reference not only because of its transition but because of its success over the last 30 years. When I came into government, we had per capita income of $4,500, and when I left government it was $15,000, and amidst the full-blown crisis we are at $30,000 per capita. Even if we drop to $25,000 due to the crisis, an increase from $4,500 to $25,000 is a radical change. The success has been expressed in the physical capital, the evolution of human capital, which has been a point of reference in Latin America and North Africa. Nonetheless, the relevance of Spain as a model is absolutely in crisis.

Like Spain, Europe has lost relevance. It has now gone more than 15 years with less than 1% growth in GDP; Spain has overtaken Italy in per capita GDP. Great Britain is an industrially ruined country. Therefore the heritage of humankind that was the European and democratic socioeconomic model, as Lula put it, is in a profound crisis, and the European leaders don't know how to climb out of it. I was at the helm of European issues with Mitterrand, with Helmut Kohl [chancellor of West Germany 1982–90, chancellor of Germany 1990–98] and Jacques Delors [president of the European Commission 1985–95] in the commission for 10 years, and we knew how decisions were processed: with rigor and efficacy. Those circumstances have disappeared completely.

The voice of the European countries does not exist in Egypt; it does exist in Tunisia. We are in a very complicated situation when it comes to helping democratic processes, as is the United States. The Saudis reached the conclusion, seeing how after 30 years of unconditional services by Mubarak the United States let him fall like an old shoe, that Arabs have to look out for themselves. They are acting accordingly, making agreements with China, among other things. They have an operational security agreement that includes oil and a weapons exchange. This is a very serious change in the world. Revolutions with a democratizing impetus, mostly peaceful except for Libya and Syria, as people are fed up with an authoritarian direction, full of corruption, that leave 80% of the citizens under 35 years of age without hope, lack serious support; they are without direction or lack a point of reference.

For all these reasons, the role of international influence—at least from Europe and the United States—may be less in the future, but even in the past, outside influence may have accounted for 15% of what was happening, while domestic factors accounted for 85%.

Time Line

Apr. 1939: The Spanish Civil War ends in a victory for Francisco Franco's Nationalists.

Jun. 1968: Separatist group Basque Homeland and Freedom (ETA) begins violent attacks against the Franco regime by murdering a policeman.

Jul. 1969: Franco, aged 76, appoints Prince Juan Carlos to succeed him as head of state; he plans to leave other powers to the prime minister.

Dec. 1970: A trial of 16 ETA supporters, including two priests, accused of murdering three policemen, is held in Burgos. Under pressure from the Church and foreign governments, the death sentences are finally commuted.

Dec. 1973: ETA murders Franco's right-hand man, Prime Minister Luis Carrero Blanco, who is replaced by former Minister of the Interior Carlos Arias Navarro.

Feb. 1974: With Franco's health declining and the economy struggling, Arias Navarro attempts a modest (and ultimately unsuccessful) liberalization of the regime.

Apr. 1974: Portugal's rightwing regime is overthrown in leftist military coup, beginning the democratization of Portugal.

Jul. 1974: The Communist Party of Spain (PCE) forms a new antiregime opposition platform, the Junta Democrática.

Sep. 1974: An ETA bomb near police headquarters kills 11. The attack divides ETA, prompting the eventual breakup into ETA-M (military) and the more moderate ETA-PM (political-military).

Oct. 1974: The Spanish Socialist Workers' Party (PSOE) elects young labor lawyer and politician Felipe González as its new leader.

Sept. 1975: Five anti-Franco militants (two from ETA) are sentenced to death and executed, prompting a major international outcry.

Nov. 1975: Franco dies, and Juan Carlos is proclaimed king. Arias Navarro pledges to preserve Franco's legacy while enacting reforms.

Jul. 1976: Juan Carlos, after forcing the resignation of the unpopular Arias Navarro, appoints Adolfo Suárez prime minister. Suárez, a former regime apparatchik, pledges major reforms, political amnesty, and free elections.

Nov. 1976: Franco's Cortes passes the crucial Law for Political Reform, which paves the way for democratic elections.

Dec. 1976: The Law for Political Reform is approved via referendum. The PSOE, though still technically illegal, holds its first Congress in Spain since the Civil War.

Jan. 1977: Fascist guerrillas murder five PCE labor lawyers in their office.

Feb. 1977: The government legalizes the PSOE and other political parties.

Mar. 1977: The government legalizes strikes, enacts a new electoral law, and adopts partial amnesty, aimed at encouraging Basque parties to take part in elections.

Apr. 1977: Suárez legalizes the PCE in exchange for the acceptance of elections and the monarchy. The military peacefully criticizes the decision.

Jun. 1977: The first free general elections since 1936 are held. Suárez and Franco-era reformists in the Union of the Democratic Center (UCD) win plurality; PSOE becomes the main opposition. The PCE and rightwing People's Alliance (AP) each receive less than 10%.

Jul. 1977: A new Ministry of Defense is created under Deputy Prime Minister Manuel Gutiérrez Mellado. Spain applies for membership in the European Community.

Sep. 1977: Suárez agrees to an autonomy plan for Catalonia in exchange for Catalan leaders' recognition of Spanish state and monarchy.

Oct. 1977: To revive the stagnant economy, the government and opposition negotiate Moncloa Pacts to restrict wage increases, cut spending, and raise taxes in exchange for new social benefits. The democratically elected Parliament passes an Amnesty Law.

Nov. 1978: The government uncovers a military conspiracy, Operation Galaxia. To avoid angering the military, the government gives coup leaders minor sentences and does not prosecute accomplices.

Dec. 1978: A new democratic constitution, drafted by Parliament, is approved by referendum.

Mar. 1979: The UCD wins a plurality in elections, and the PSOE consolidates its status as the main opposition party. The PCE and AP do poorly.

Apr. 1979: The first municipal elections are held. The UCD wins nationally, but the PSOE-PCE pact allows Socialists to govern major cities.

May 1979: Felipe González resigns as leader after losing a vote, taken at the party conference, over dropping the party's Marxist identity. He is reelected in September on his own terms.

Oct. 1979: Basque and Catalan voters approve statutes of autonomy for the Basque Country and Catalonia via referenda, with the support of respective mainstream nationalist parties.

Mar. 1980: The first regional elections are held in Basque Country and Catalonia. Mainstream nationalists form governments in both regions.

May 1980: As UCD popularity drops, Suárez reshuffles the cabinet, favoring conservative factions over social democrats. The PSOE presents a motion of no confidence in Parliament, which Suárez narrowly survives.

Jan. 1981: Suárez resigns amidst UCD infighting and defections.

Feb. 1981: Military officers in Valencia and paramilitary civil guards led by Tejero attempt a coup on February 23, known as "23-F," apparently confident of royal support, taking over the Spanish Parliament while in session. King Juan Carlos maneuvers to stop the coup, dissuade officers from joining, and preserve the constitution. Former UDC Minister Leopoldo Calvo Sotelo replaces Suárez as prime minister.

Oct. 1981: Parliament votes to join NATO despite PSOE and PCE opposition, expanding the Spanish military's cooperation with Western armies.

Feb. 1982: The trial begins for the 23-F coup plotters. The coup leaders are eventually given 30-year prison terms, but other defendants receive lighter sentences.

Oct. 1982: The PSOE wins a landslide victory in the elections, and González becomes prime minister. The PCE and UCD collapse; the AP, after moderating, comes second. As prime minister, González promotes economic liberalization and social welfare, leading to sustained economic growth.

Jan. 1986: Spain, along with Portugal, joins the European Community, spurring economic growth and affirming its commitment to democracy.

Mar. 1986: In a referendum, voters endorse remaining in NATO. The PSOE, reversing its earlier position, campaigns for continued membership.

Jun. 1986: The PSOE wins a second absolute majority in general elections.

Dec. 1988: A one-day general strike against the PSOE government's economic policy brings Spain to a standstill.

Oct. 1989: The PSOE wins a third general election but narrowly loses an absolute majority in Parliament.

Jun. 1993: Against all odds, the PSOE wins a fourth general election, but with a significantly reduced majority.

Mar. 1996: The PSOE loses the election to José María Aznar's Popular Party, successor to the AP. Felipe González stands down as party leader a year later.

GUIDE TO FURTHER READING

Aguilar, Paloma. *Memory and Amnesia: The Role of the Civil War in the Transition to Democracy*. New York: Berghahn Books, 2002.

Bermeo, Nancy. "Sacrifice, Sequence, and Strength in Successful Dual Transitions: Lessons from Spain." *Journal of Politics* 56, no. 3 (1994): 601–27.

Encarnación, Omar G. "Social Concertation in Democratic and Market Transitions: Comparative Lessons from Spain." *Comparative Political Studies* 30, no. 4 (1997): 387–419.

Fishman, Robert. *Working-Class Organization and the Return to Democracy in Spain*. Ithaca, N.Y.: Cornell University Press, 1990.

Gunther, Richard, José Ramón Montero, and Joan Botella. *Democracy in Modern Spain*. New Haven, Conn.: Yale University Press, 2004.

Gunther, Richard, José Ramón Montero, and José Ignacio Wert. "The Media and Politics in Spain: From Dictatorship to Democracy." In *Democracy and the Media: A Comparative Perspective*, edited by Richard Gunther and Anthony Mughan. Cambridge: Cambridge University Press, 2000.

Harrison, Joseph. "Economic Crisis and Democratic Consolidation in Spain, 1973–1982." Working Papers in Economic History. Madrid: Universidad Carlos III de Madrid, 2006.

Linz, Juan J. "Innovative Leadership In the Transition to Democracy and a New Democracy: The Case of Spain." In *Innovative Leaders in International Politics*, edited by Gabriel Scheffer. Albany: State University of New York Press, 1993.

Linz, Juan J., and Alfred Stepan. "The Paradigmatic Case of Reforma Pactada-Ruptura Pactada: Spain." In *Problems of Democratic Transition and Consolidation: Southern Europe, South America, and Post-Communist Europe*, edited by Juan Linz and Alfred Stepan. Baltimore: Johns Hopkins University Press, 1996.

McDonough, Peter, Samuel H. Barnes, and Antonio López Pina. *The Cultural Dynamics of Democratization in Spain*. Ithaca, N.Y.: Cornell University Press, 1998.

Muro, Diego, and Gregorio Alonso, eds. *The Politics and Memory of Democratic Transition: The Spanish Model*. New York: Routledge, 2010.

Pérez-Díaz, Victor. *The Return of Civil Society: The Emergence of Democratic Spain*. Cambridge, Mass.: Harvard University Press, 1993.

Powell, Charles. *Juan Carlos of Spain: Self-Made Monarch*. New York: Palgrave, 1996.

——. "International Aspects of Democratization: The Case of Spain." In *The Interna-

tional Dimensions of Democratization: Europe and the Americas, edited by Laurence Whitehead. Oxford: Oxford University Press, 2001.

Preston, Paul. *The Triumph of Democracy in Spain*. London: Methuen, 1986.

Serra, Narcis. *The Military Transition: Democratic Reform of the Armed Forces*. Cambridge: Cambridge University Press, 2010. By a former defense minister.

Tezanos, José Félix, Ramon Cotarelo, and Andrés de Blas, eds. *La Transición Democrática Española* [The Spanish democratic transition]. Madrid: Sistema, 1989.

Chapter 10

Women Activists in Democratic Transitions

GEORGINA WAYLEN

This chapter considers the role that women's movements and key female actors played in fostering transitions from authoritarian rule toward more democratic governance. It examines how they supported and enhanced political participation by different groups of women and promoted policies that strengthened women's rights and gender equality. **The transitions examined in the *Democratic Transitions* project are widely thought to have been "successful," but they vary considerably in terms of their gender outcomes, a dimension that mainstream analyses of transitions have largely ignored. The overall success of particular transitions might be assessed differently if their gender dimensions are taken into account.**[1] The leaders interviewed for International IDEA's *Democratic Transitions* project are all men, primarily because the top authorities in transitions during the past 30 years have almost invariably been men. In the immediate aftermath of transitions, few women became executive leaders, and the few who did (such as Cory Aquino in the Philippines [now deceased] and Megawati Soekarnoputri in Indonesia) were not elected on the basis of their political platforms or party affiliations alone (related to gender or not) but also because they had close family connections to former political leaders.

Yet, **like all political processes, transitions are gendered—men and women play different roles within them, and the processes have different impacts on men and women.**[2] Women played significant roles in many transitions and attempted to ensure that their outcomes were favorable to women, but with varying degrees of success. These differences are a result of a variety of factors: the importance of women's organizing; the ability of female activists to build broad coalitions involving allies in the bureaucracy, political parties, legislatures, and civil society; and activists' ability to frame their issues effectively. **Many women who actively sought to ensure positive gender outcomes during transitions were active in social movements, the bureaucracy, and academia—not just in political parties or the inner circles of men who became democratic presidents when elections were held** (as these arenas often remained relatively closed to women). In addition to drawing on the wider literature on the subject, this study incorporates interviews with some of these key female activists to determine what strategies they used and how they assessed their efficacy.

Today there is renewed interest in transitions as a result of the Arab Spring and events in Myanmar. At first glance, many of these new cases seem to be repeating earlier patterns of women's activism and subsequent exclusion. For example, women participated in many of the demonstrations that brought down the authoritarian regimes in Egypt and Tunisia, but (as was true in most earlier transitions) few women were elected in the "founding elections" or appointed to cabinets or constitutional commissions. In the Egyptian case, the period between the first parliamentary and presidential elections in 2012 and the removal of the Muslim Brotherhood president from power by the military in July 2013 saw high levels of polarization between more secular and religious sectors, increased levels of sexual violence, and the approval of a constitution that did not promote gender equality, suggesting that policies that critically affect women—such as a minimum age for marriage—might be under threat and that efforts to impose sharia law might pose more challenges to women than earlier activists had faced.

This chapter examines the experiences of female activists during transitions covered in this project to determine why some but not others were able to achieve outcomes (including constitutional, policy, and program changes) favorable to women's equality. To explain complex outcomes, wide-ranging analyses are necessary that do more than examine women's movements and their interactions with institutions, which was initially the focus of much of the gender and transitions literature. We need to assess the opportunities and constraints that arise from the nature of the prior authoritarian regime (and from the timing and dynamics of the transition itself) and to look at the effects of changes on different groups of women that vary by class, race, ethnicity, and sexuality.

This volume analyses a range of "third-wave" transitions that took place from the 1970s to the 1990s; some were rapid and others prolonged, some pacted and others not, some occurred in countries that had prior democratic traditions, while others had little or no democratic experience to draw upon. Some took place in a context that emphasized human rights and the participation of marginalized groups, including women. The cases involved varying degrees of social mobilization by women, and different levels of visibility of female activists opposing authoritarian rule. In a few cases, a posttransition elected government sympathetic to gender reforms played a crucial role. In some, transitions brought immediate gains; in others, gains did not occur for some time. It was also not uncommon for early gains to be reversed. At various points, many feminists became disillusioned with the outcomes of the transition process because they did not result in the desired gains for women. This led some to conclude that transitions to democracy had failed women in general (and some groups of women in particular), and therefore that the promise of democracy was not fulfilled.

The Chilean case provides a good example of both gains and constraints.

Organized groups of women played an important role in the broad movement that opposed Pinochet in the 1980s. Human rights and popular organizations also involved large numbers of women, although not all were feminists or on the left.[3] Female activists organized prior to the 1989 elections to ensure that their demands were included in the manifesto of the winning center-left coalition. Hopes were high when the new government took office and a women's ministry (Servicio Nacional de la Mujer, or SERNAM) was established. But in contrast to several other cases, there was no constitutional convention, and for the first decade after the transition, many reforms proved more difficult to achieve than expected. Although divorce was legal elsewhere in the region, for example, it was not legalized in Chile until 2004.[4] Chile's experience contrasts with that of South Africa, where in the immediate posttransition period female activists seemed to have achieved many of their aims—including a gender policy machinery and policy reforms related to women's reproductive rights.[5] In South Africa, substantial numbers of women were elected to Parliament, and the new constitution included gender equality clauses. But female actors face different opportunities and challenges, as well as different institutional and structural constraints in each transition; these make possible some reforms but not others. This chapter explores the strategies activists used to deal with these challenges and the contexts in which they were operating, and highlights the importance of broader international efforts to promote democracy and gender equity.

The challenges of the 1980s and 1990s differ from those today in several important ways. Changes in the geopolitical context after the end of the Cold War and the collapse of state socialism changed the ideological divide between left and right. Globalization has affected levels of inequality, and neoliberal reforms have reduced the role of the state, with differential consequences for women. The "war on terror" has altered the security environment, resulting in increased militarization and securitization. In earlier transitions, many activists drew on their links to leftwing and social democratic ideologies, parties, and political practices. And some key female actors returned from exile with new feminist ideas and approaches. For example, the Spanish Socialist Carlota Bustelo was introduced to the work of Simone de Beauvoir while living in France in the 1960s, and Chilean feminist activist and Socialist Deputy Adriana Muñoz describes her "political transformation" in exile in Austria. Muñoz had come "from a Marxist-Leninist strand of the Socialist Party," but after participating in feminist and environmentalist groups in Europe, she "began to understand how to do politics differently and abandoned Marxism-Leninism." When she returned to Chile, she began organizing with "other women who had also returned from exile with this new vision of politics and of the position, status, and role of women in political processes."

The United Nations (UN) Women's Conference in Beijing held in 1995 marks the high point of the international women's movement.[6] By the early 1990s, global women's movements had succeeded in framing women's rights as human rights and violence against women as a human rights violation, making it easier for many female activists in transitions to emphasize that their gender demands enhanced democracy and human rights. In some authoritarian regimes, feminists were part of the democratic opposition that campaigned for an end to state violence. **Linking women's rights and human rights put gender issues on the political agenda of many posttransition democracies.**[7] In contrast, the transitions in Eastern and Central Europe rejected many state Socialist policies that enshrined "equality" and eliminated quotas for women in Parliaments and severely curtailed access to abortion. Women also lost employment and state-funded child care.[8] Today, female activists face new constraints as the acceptability of a discourse on universal human rights has been eroded, while opposition to gender-progressive measures (such as improved reproductive rights) has increased, particularly from the political right and a range of religious groupings. Issues such as women's dress, movement, and bodily autonomy have become more highly contested in many parts of the contemporary world, particularly where fundamentalist religious beliefs have a significant influence.

Causal patterns can explain much of the variation in the gender outcomes of these earlier transitions. Examining the different actors involved in each case, the political opportunity structure in different transitions, and the strategies that activists employed helps explain the range of gender outcomes in the constitutional, electoral, bureaucratic, and policy arenas. These patterns will help us assess the implications of women's experiences in past transitions on women's rights and participation in current and future transitions.

Women's Organizing in Transitions

In most cases in this volume, women were an active and visible part of the public opposition to authoritarian regimes, and participated alongside men in the mass demonstrations (such as "people power" in the Philippines) that contributed to the breakdown of nondemocratic rule.[9] But the number of women organizing *as women* was smaller, and varied during different stages of each transition. The types of women's organizations involved also varied greatly, from religious and community groups organizing around neighborhood issues and economic survival to human rights organizations and more overtly feminist ones. **In Latin America, the suppression of the political sphere facilitated the growth of women's organizing, as social movements and civil society became the sites of resistance and opposition.**[10] Women's activism in human rights organizations demanding the return of their disappeared family members, and feminist activism such as the International Women's Day demonstrations calling for "democracy in the country and in the home," were important early examples of public opposition to dictatorship in Chile.[11] And in some cases, such as the Madres of the Plaza de Mayo in Argentina, women's activism had an important political impact but did not necessarily bring feminist perspectives to the fore.

In Brazil, Chile, the Philippines, and South Africa, however, **women's organizations brought feminist issues onto the agenda prior to the transition itself.**[12] According to Sheila Meintjes, a South African who was active in the United Women's Organization in Cape Town in the late 1980s,

> At the time of the transition, women were very well organized in antiapartheid organizations, both as women and also in civic organizations in the United Democratic Front (UDF). It was very significant that, within the UDF, women had been making demands about gender equality and personal transformation. It wasn't just about gender equality; it was about the fact that women needed to be treated appropriately—in public and in private.

Jacqueline Pitanguy, a Brazilian feminist activist since the 1970s, maintains that "the women's movement that emerged in Brazil was one of the first social movements to really work to bring to discussions of social justice and democracy issues such as the inequality of women under legislation, particularly the issue of violence against women and the issue of the reproductive rights—and under the ambit of inequality."

In some transitions it was therefore possible to strategically frame gender issues in ways that resonated with powerful discourses of human rights and equality. But in Eastern and Central Europe the opposite was true, as many female activists rejected feminism as another "ism" and reacted against the top-down imposition of "women's equality" associated with the post–World War II state Socialist regimes.[13]

Where women's organizing had been less long-standing and widespread, the periods of liberalization that took place immediately prior to and during the transitions often saw a huge growth in the number of women's organizations —including feminist ones—even if the number of preexisting organizations had been small, such as in Ghana. In Spain, Carlota Bustelo describes how, two weeks after Franco's death:

> The first National Conference for the Liberation of Women took place clandestinely in Madrid. It was attended by about 500 women from across the country. By the end, two different manifestos—an equality feminist one (equality with men) and a difference feminist one—were approved, although they were in agreement about specific demands. These were presented to the political parties, which were then being set up or renovated, making them aware that feminism also existed in Spain, and that as a result women were making demands that should be taken into account.[14]

In Indonesia, the first Women's Congress took place in 1998 during the transition process. It included women from 25 provinces and resulted in the formation of the Women's Coalition for Justice and Democracy.[15] Its founder, Nursyahbani Katjasungkana, describes how

> Demonstrations started almost every day and then students started coming, then it became bigger and bigger, and then in May '98 we managed to push Soeharto to step down. And then the idea of having a mass organization came to mind. Again I discussed this with other activists and we formed the committee, consisting of (I think) 12 female activists in Jakarta to prepare for the first mass Women's Organization Congress, which would focus on increasing the participation and representation of women in politics. Then, in December, making our women's movement history, we conducted a congress attended by almost 600 women from all over Indonesia.

In Ghana, the large-scale murder of women in the late 1990s helped catalyze women's organizing,[16] leading to the formation of broad-based alliances such as the Network for Women's Rights in Ghana (NETRIGHT) in the run-up to the 2000 election in which opposition candidate John Kufuor finally defeated Jerry Rawlings's designated successor.[17] Dzodzi Tsikata, a founder of NETRIGHT, suggests that in effect there were two transitions in Ghana: the first in 1992, in which women played little part, and the second in 2000, in which women were more active:

> Constitutional rule led to a slow opening up of the base, and many small organizations began to start up. People were questioning more policies and getting more confident because there was constitutional rule, and people were testing spaces and opening up a bit more, and I think women benefitted from that. So, along with other spaces, women's organizations started to attack, to push for the further promotion of women's rights and increased attention to particular issues they were interested in. There were discussions about violence against women as a huge issue. All the organizations became a bit more conscious of their weaknesses: they were small, they were not mass-membership organizations, and they were not able to influence the state much, and therefore they began to take a decision to begin to establish coalitions among themselves to increase their influence.

These cases suggest that, even when women's organizations did not contribute significantly to creating civil society pressures for transitions, the transition process itself often contributed to the emergence of women's organizations, including broad alliances and umbrella organizations.

In many cases, however, the posttransition period decreased the activity of many mass social movements, including women's movements. "Politics as usual" (favoring parties over social movements) took over in many cases where women's organizing had been quite strong. In Brazil, Chile, and South Africa, women's organizations lost much of their leadership as female activists moved into the state (including the newly created women's ministries) and national legislatures.[18] Teresa Valdés, a Chilean feminist, comments:

Many women went from the women's movement to central government, ministries, and local government. Thus the installation of a democratic government had a negative impact on the women's movement, as many organizations were left without leaders. In addition, international organizations moved resources that were previously given to civil society to the state.

Pregs Govender argues that, in South Africa, "it was something that happened to all organizations with the elections: people came into government for the first time in 1994, and some political movements, political organizations, and community movements came into government and the Parliament. There was a depletion of the leadership of these organizations. And I don't think there had been any proper plan to deal with this—you couldn't plan for this."

The professionalization—or the "NGO-ization"—of many remaining women's organizations (and their dependence on state or international funding) also changed their character, divorcing them further from the grassroots; some were co-opted by the state to provide services, and all had to compete for declining sources of international support.[19] Valdés argues that "the relationship established by the government with civil society, especially with women's organizations, was on the condition that we were experts, technical professionals on this subject, and that we removed the political contents of what we were proposing." All these factors reduced the activist capacity of women's organizations.

But women's mobilization alone is no guarantee that women's political participation will increase or that gender-progressive measures will be adopted. Strategic organizing by key actors—and a favorable institutional context—are both crucial to achieving positive outcomes and challenging retrenchment. In some cases, women's organizations formed coalitions prior to the founding election. More commonly, they came together in broad alliances to campaign for new policies on particular issues, such as domestic violence. Gender activists also formed strategic alliances with women (and sympathetic men) operating in different arenas, including legislatures, governments, parties, and women's organizations and umbrella groups. With some exceptions, these women tended to come from the political and economic elite, which gave them access to male leaders but could also lead to divisions between female leaders and their mass base. The broad-based organizing that brought women onto the streets during the transitions could not easily be replicated after the transition to provide mass support to press for new legislation on gender issues or to counter the various forms of backlash that emerged. The women's movements involved in (or emerging from) the transitions were very heterogeneous, including women with different class, racial, sexual, and religious identities. In Indonesia, feminist activists included both secular and religious women, and in South Africa race and class were salient issues.[20] Thenjiwe Mtintso remembers that, for female activists, "there was an issue of race even among us . . . the white women and the black women, but even among the black women there was a class differentiation."

In part because of such differences in backgrounds, beliefs, and experiences, there was often conflict among different female actors and sectors of the women's movement over goals, tactics, and strategy. Not all women who had participated in transition mobilizations supported feminist goals (the meaning of which was subject to controversy), particularly those related to reproductive rights. In some cases, feminism was considered a Western concept that was relevant only to "elite" women. Sheila Meintjes notes that "among antiapartheid women's organizations, there was also the sense that feminism was a Western import that didn't have a lot to do with African women, who didn't share the same problems with their men that Western women seemed to be driving at." In other cases there were conflicts between those who sought "autonomy" from the political system, seeing it as inevitably patriarchal and male dominated, and those who wanted fuller participation, often seeing themselves as both feminists and party activists.

In Brazil and Chile (and to some degree in Spain), differences among political parties also divided female activists along party lines. Teresa Valdés recounts:

> There was a very difficult moment in Mujeres por la Vida (the group I participated in) because the Communist Party and others on the left rejected the 1988 plebiscite [requiring a vote for or against Pinochet]—or more accurately they did not agree with accepting the institutional route from dictatorship that had been proposed in the 1980 constitution [adopted under military rule]. So inside our group we had to take action that was very sad and politically difficult: we could either opt for the unity of the group or for political advocacy within the coalition that had formed, which would exclude the Radical Party and the Party of the Revolutionary Left.

A number of other factors also affected the extent and form of women's activism in the cases analyzed. The institutional legacy of nondemocratic regimes (and the gender regime that each embodied) varied considerably. The dictatorships in Chile and Spain (and to a lesser extent Brazil), for example, had very conservative views of gender relations, while some other nondemocratic regimes (state Socialist regimes in particular) had introduced legal reforms that benefitted women.[21] These different nondemocratic regimes also facilitated different levels of women's organizing. State Socialist regimes offered few opportunities for women's autonomous organizing.[22] For example, in Poland, the only women's organizations that were allowed to exist, like the Women's League, were sanctioned by the state and part of the Communist Party apparatus. Yet while some authoritarian regimes inadvertently provided space for autonomous organizing, others successfully co-opted major women's organizations, thus reducing the capacity for autonomous organizations to develop.[23] Nursyahbani Katjasungkana argues that in Indonesia "Kowani, the most progressive women's organization since before independence, was co-opted by Soeharto. And Soeharto sponsored a new women's movement called Dharma Wanita, which promoted Ibuism—the state ideology that "women have to be first wife, second mother, third educator of the children, fourth social worker, and fifth citizen."

This also happened in Ghana, where the state-sponsored 31 December Women's Movement played a dominant role for a number of years, even after the transition was well underway.[24] Tsikata argues that in Ghana

> those organizations that were more directly in support of the regime fared better than those that were slightly removed or a bit more independent. By 1984–85, the only surviving women's organization was the 31 December Women's Movement, and it came to be led by the first lady. It had superior access, state support, and all sorts of other privileges, and so it came to dominate the scene. Donors also gave it resources, and very soon it was the only organization to be reported in the media. So, in a sense, it took up all the space, and many women's organizations found it difficult to bring their issues to bear or to publicize their activities. For a long time, it seemed to be the only organization on the scene; its superior access to power was definitely key in its dominance of the women's movements.

The space available to voice gender concerns within the opposition to nondemocratic rule also varied considerably. Some opposition parties and movements—for example, on the left and those organizing around human rights abuses—were more open to women's issues, which they saw as part of their broader agenda of equality, rights, and justice. Female activists in some political parties, such as the Spanish and Chilean Socialists and some other leftwing parties like the Brazilian Social Democratic Party and the Workers' Party in Brazil and the African National Congress (ANC) in South Africa, organized extensively, often in separate women's bodies as well as within the parties themselves.[25] Carlota Bustelo describes her return to Spain:

> I made contact with the Spanish Socialist Workers' Party (PSOE), where a group of us created "Women and Socialism," through which we wanted to influence party policy toward women. As we discussed and acted, we became more feminist and more belligerent. The party's secretary of education, Luis Gomez Llorente from the left wing of the PSOE, gave us a part of his budget and encouraged us to contribute our efforts to shaping the groups that were emerging. We were able to do this in part by giving talks or lectures clandestinely in different districts of Madrid and other cities, and we also had some money to produce leaflets and "cassettes" to spread our feminist ideas and enable others who also shared them to increase their dissemination.

Thenjiwe Mtintso (at that time an ANC/Umkhonto weSizwe activist in exile) claims that during the 1980s an active women's section within the ANC was "a very critical step in the struggle for gender and inclusion because it mobilized women who had been in the liberation movement itself, and raised the consciousness of the liberation movement as a whole on the place, role, and status of women and the need to ensure that women's liberation and gender equality are not a by-product." Adriana Muñoz recounts that in Chile:

> Some feminists installed themselves in the political parties while others remained outside. Those of us who were in the political parties thought we had to be inside where the negotiations happened, because if it was left to men to define the program of a Chilean transition to democracy, we were sure that the women's agenda would not be there. So we struggled to be represented at all levels of party power—I in the Socialist Party and the Party for Democracy. Together with other women, we became involved in all the programmatic commissions and advocated our women's agenda and women's rights.

Some culturally traditional and religious groups, such as the Roman Catholic Church, were opposed to authoritarian rule but were less open to gender claims (and more likely to mobilize against them), as occurred in Chile and Brazil.

The pace of the transition processes was also a factor. With the exception of Indonesia and perhaps the Philippines, where the prior regime fell relatively swiftly, the majority of transitions reviewed in this volume were relatively slow, negotiated, and pacted, or "guided," as in Brazil, Chile, Ghana, South Africa, and Spain. Pacted transitions involved negotiations among a relatively narrow elite, but some were more open to incorporating the demands of social movements. In Chile, Ghana, Poland, and Spain, the prior regimes and their allies maintained considerable control over the transition and negotiations were closed (or even secret), and therefore few women participated. Brazil and South Africa had relatively more open and participatory negotiation processes, and women organized as women had greater possibilities for access. These differences help explain why it was sometimes possible for women's movements to get women's issues on the agenda and bring about some degree of gender-friendly policy change and institutional reform, while in other contexts gender reforms were shut out or set back.

Outcomes

The Constitutional Arena

Institutional design was an important focus of many of the negotiations that took place in negotiated and pacted transitions. In some cases, newly elected Parliaments sat as constitutional assemblies, and new constitutions were designed to carry out the broader goals of the transition. In other cases, prior or modified versions of existing constitutions were retained or there were no significant constitutional reforms, as in Chile, where the electoral system functioned under the constitution imposed by the military in 1980. The extent to which women organized as women intervened in these processes varied widely. In Brazil and South Africa, organized women actively participated in the formal processes and the Parliaments that formed Constituent Assemblies, and helped develop gender-sensitive constitutions. In Spain and the Philippines, organized women and feminists lobbied from outside, but few women were involved directly in the design processes. There was virtually no involvement by organized women in the limited Chilean constitutional renegotiations that took place after the plebiscite (despite the existence of an active women's movement), nor were women active in writing the new Ghanaian constitution. And although the constitutions in Poland, Indonesia, the Philippines, and Spain contain some form of gender-equality clause, women's organizations had little overall impact.

In both Brazil and South Africa, the constitution was drafted as part of a gradual pacted transition. In South Africa, drafting the interim constitution was central to the multiparty negotiations dominated by the ANC and the apartheid government from 1992 to 1994. **After few women were involved in the initial negotiations in the Convention for a Democratic South Africa, women (particularly ANC women) fought to ensure that they were part of all negotiating teams in the subsequent multiparty talks.** The Women's National Coalition (WNC), a broad independent alliance of women's organizations, was created.[26] WNC coordinator Pregs Govender (1992-94) argues:

> The WNC began with the ANC Women's League initiating a meeting with women from other political parties and organizations across society, from a range of diverse backgrounds, to look at the question of women being left out of the negotiation process and the fear that although women had been so active against apartheid, the issues that directly affected women and impacted on women's lives ... would actually fall off the table completely and that issues such as non-sexism, gender equality, ... substantive gender equality, socioeconomic rights, bodily integrity, and reproductive rights would not appear in the constitution. ... The combination of people who were negotiators, people who were lawyers, people who were good at research, and people who were good at mobilizing and building women's movements came together in a very effective manner.

The WNC played a key role in negotiations involving traditional leaders on the relationship between customary law and the equality clause.[27] Sheila Meintjes, part of the WNC research supervisory group, claims that this "was a very, very important moment in the coalition and we played a very important role in making sure that customary law did not trump the constitution with what the chiefs wanted. They wanted customary law to hold, but it made all [African] women minors under the law." The interim constitution was then considered by the newly elected Parliament acting as a Constituent Assembly. Female members of Parliament, particularly from the ANC, pushed successfully to get specific clauses—for example, on domestic violence—inserted alongside the more general commitments to gender equality.

In Brazil after the election of a civilian president in 1985, the newly elected Parliament acted as a Constituent Assembly between 1986 and 1988. Female members of political parties caucused together and were lobbied by (and worked with) women from civil society. **The new federal women's body, the National Council for Women's Rights (Conselho Nacional de Direitos da Mulher, or CNDM), included representatives from both the state and civil society and acted as a women's lobby; it coordinated women's organizations and feminist activists to pressure Congress as the Constituent Assembly.**[28] Jacqueline Pitanguy, chair of the CNDM, described how "we created a department specifically to work for the constitution. We started to . . . go to state level, mapping the groups of women in each state so that we could organize together to launch a campaign in each state. The ownership of the campaign, although it was a CNDM campaign, was also at the state level." Among their efforts was a Women's Letter, a set of demands drawn from women's organizations that was presented to the National Assembly (and to individual states). They also ensured that assembly members were strategically lobbied at the constituency, regional, and federal levels. Pitanguy describes how "there was face-to-face work within the Congress":

> Every day we were in the National Congress and we talked to the leaders of the political parties . . . And I remember walking through those corridors. It was constant. We also had telegrams from the states. We were always connected to local women's groups. This campaign was not only a federal-level campaign; it was a national campaign. So we would visit representative so-and-so and we would see how reluctant he was on this issue, so we would immediately contact the women's groups in that particular state.

Female legislators (the so-called lipstick lobby) from a range of parties also acted together within the assembly and worked with the CNDM. As a result, Pitanguy notes that 80% of their demands were included in the 1988 constitution, and that attempts to enshrine the "right to life" were defeated. But the resulting constitution was an unwieldy document that required enabling legislation in order to be effective.

In Spain's pacted, negotiated transition, an elected Parliament acting as a Constituent Assembly designed the new constitution in 1977–78. Few women were involved in the relatively closed and elite-driven process led by Adolfo Suarez, leader of the Union of the Democratic Center (UDC) and prime minister.[29] An all-male panel selected from the members of the Constituent Cortes (the Spanish Parliament when acting as a Constitutional Assembly) drafted the constitution; three of its seven members were from the governing center-right UCD, and one was from the PSOE. The constitution was then discussed by a 35-member parliamentary constitutional committee that contained only one woman and approved by both houses, which contained only 27 women. Feminist organizations did lobby the proceedings from the outside, and some female deputies were active inside. Bustelo notes that she "collaborated with one of the *ponencia* (panels) in drafting articles 9 and 14, which refer to equality." Clauses on equality and divorce were thus included, although efforts were less successful regarding reproductive rights and rules of primogeniture.[30]

In the Philippines, the newly elected Corazon Aquino appointed a 50-member Constitutional Commission (composed of less than 15% women but with a female chair) to draft a new constitution. A broad alliance of women's organizations, including the feminist group Gabriela, came together to lobby, but with mixed results. Although an equality clause was included, it was not as far-reaching as the one proposed by the women's organizations. A pro-life clause was also passed, supported by a strong Church lobby and pro-life women's organizations, but as a concession to women's organizations it referred to the right to life of the mother as well as the unborn child from conception.[31]

In Indonesia, constitutional reform took place gradually. Some women representing NGOs and women's organizations were appointed members of the People's Consultative Assembly (PCA) that initiated changes between 1999 and 2002, and feminists made efforts to ensure that affirmative action was included in the constitutional reforms, but few unequivocal gains were made. Nursyahbani Katjasungkana, who was a member of the PCA as a representative of lawyers' organizations, recounts that, learning from South Africa's experience, they did "manage to put a special chapter in the constitution on human rights, including the nondiscrimination principle and affirmative action principle."

Toward the other end of the spectrum, women were not involved in the initial Chilean constitution produced by the military in 1980; hence it was not a gender-sensitive document. Women also played no part in the minimal (closed) constitutional renegotiations that took place after the plebiscite between the key political parties and the military government prior to the presidential and parliamentary elections of 1989. This marginalization of women occurred despite the active role of a large number of women's organizations, including relatively long-standing umbrella organizations like Mujeres por la Vida and the Women's Concertación, which was created in response to the low numbers of women selected to compete in those elections to ensure that gender equality remained on the Concertación agenda.[32]

In Ghana, the new constitution was drafted in 1991 in a Consultative Assembly created by the Rawlings regime relatively early in the top–down transition process. Therefore few women's organizations actively attempted to influence the process, and gender issues did not feature in the resulting document. Dzodzi Tsikata recalls, "we didn't get many of our issues in the constitution. We were not very active in the constitutional process. There was a lack of female activists, and I don't recall that there were discussions about the constitution."

In Poland, in the somewhat different context of a transition from state socialism, organized women also did not have a significant impact on designing the 1997 constitution, although some women's NGOs—such as the Women's Rights Center—did make submissions.[33] **The final document included clauses guaranteeing the equality of men and women, but these were hard to enforce because they were not backed up by specific legislation or civil codes; in some areas, such as labor law, legislation directly contradicted the constitution.** In common with some other Eastern European cases, after much controversy and debate, the new constitution included a right-to-life clause. The Catholic Church succeeded in including language on the protection of the unborn fetus, which the constitutional tribunal subsequently upheld.[34]

The Electoral Arena

The posttransition levels of women's numerical representation in legislatures varied considerably. Women initially had low levels of representation in Brazil, Chile, Ghana, Indonesia, Poland, and Spain (around 10% or less); South Africa was a notable exception with 27.7%. As was typical of many third-wave transitions, the number of women elected to national legislatures has increased over time, particularly where effective quotas were introduced. In South Africa, for example, the ANC introduced a 33% quota for the 1994 election. In other cases, electoral quotas, often a significant institutional reform in their own right, were introduced. In Brazil, however, a poorly designed and implemented quota had little impact on women's representation—indeed, it was higher in the Senate (which did not have a gender quota) than in the assembly (which did).[35] Levels of women's representation are also related to both the nature of the electoral system and the degree of political parties' institutionalization.[36] Leftwing parties often nominate and elect more women than rightwing parties, as their relatively more egalitarian ideologies make them more likely to adopt positive measures that increase the selection and representation of excluded groups and to ensure a more sympathetic environment for feminist activism.

But we should not just look at women's numerical representation. It is also important to consider the extent to which female legislators "act for" women (substantive representation) in different transitions. This can take several forms. Female legislators may introduce bills to strengthen women's rights and gender equality or try to prevent the implementation of retrogressive measures. They can also engage in cross-party organizing within the legislature or form alliances with women's organizations in civil society. Substantive representation varied among our cases. In Ghana, for example, few women were elected, few had feminist convictions, and few had ties to organized women outside the legislature, so there was little activity on gender issues.

Dzodzi Tsikata claims there was a lack of links because "it's been a one-way street . . . There are activists who have tried to reach out to the women in Parliament, but not the other way around."

In Brazil, Chile, Indonesia, and Spain, few women were elected, but some key feminist actors pushed for progressive gender legislation; their success depended in large part on whether a sympathetic government was in power.[37] Nursyahbani Katjasungkana claimed that when she was in the Indonesian Parliament from 2004 to 2009, a small progressive group of women from her party and several others (some of whom had activist backgrounds) managed to enact at least 14 laws. In Brazil and South Africa, women's organizing within legislatures proved significant at certain points, such as when the lipstick lobby helped shape the Brazilian constitution. In the first multiracial South African Parliament, female members of Parliament (MPs), many with a background in civil society and feminist organizing (and who often knew each other from previous activism such as in the WNC) formed a cross-party women's caucus that was initially active on a range of gender issues including violence.[38] Thenjiwe Mtintso, an ANC MP in this first Parliament, confirms the WNC's lasting impact:

> We had a women's caucus across political parties to find each other. And we then had what we called the Committee on the Improvement of the Status and Quality of Life of Women, which was not your usual committee, but we insisted on having that. These things that happened in Parliament were facilitated by what we did before: negotiation, the Women's Coalition, and the Women's Charter.

Feminist MPs tended to have more extensive connections to women's organizations outside legislatures and were more likely to be members of leftist parties. The strength of party discipline and how the party system works can also have an impact: cross-party organizing can be easier where party systems are fractured and party discipline is weak. It was relatively easier to establish a cross-party women's bloc in Brazil, for example, but this was more difficult to sustain in South Africa, particularly after the first few years, when party discipline and loyalty grew stronger. There are also few examples of effective women's caucuses within parties except in South Africa's ANC. The formal parliamentary committee, the Joint Monitoring Committee on the Quality of Life and Status of Women, also benefitted from effective leadership from key feminist actors like Pregs Govender in the first nonracial Parliament; as a result, Govender believes that 80% of the gender legislation on their agenda had been passed by 1999.

Cross-party organizing was also easier on certain issues such as domestic violence; the opposite was true for reproductive rights, on which women (and men) were divided. For example, women on the right and left were able to form alliances to support measures for child maintenance in Chile despite their deep differences on reproductive rights. In Indonesia, female MPs were able to organize together on many issues, but not around an antipornography bill that split secular and moderate Islamic female politicians from more conservative ones.[39] Nursyahbani Katjasungkana's own party was divided over the bill, which she personally disagreed with; for her, "the hardest time I had in Parliament was discussing that bill."

The Bureaucratic Arena

The extent and types of gender change in the bureaucratic arena also varied greatly among posttransition cases. In some, women's policy agencies (WPAs or, in UN parlance, "women's machineries") had already been established by the prior regime in response to UN influence during the 1970s. This was true in Ghana and the Philippines, where Imelda Marcos headed the agency [the National Commission on the Role of Filipino Women]. **Over time, WPAs were created, redesigned, or replaced in all countries, facilitated by an increasingly favorable international climate, particularly after the 1995 UN conference in Beijing. But WPAs were set up for different reasons, with different structures, powers, and resources—and therefore different capacities to represent women's interests in the policy-making process.** In Eastern Europe, for example, some governments set up WPAs in part to help gain accession to the EU. In order to assess their utility and effectiveness, we must look at how (and why) they were set up, the resources allocated, their accountability, and the participation of groups outside the state as well as the wider political context in which they were operating.

In Brazil, Chile, and South Africa, WPAs were set up as a direct result of the activities of organized women during and prior to the transition process, while in Spain one was created in 1983 (headed by Carlota Bustelo) after the election of a Socialist government. Sympathetic newly elected governments set up these machineries as a result of campaigning by female activists in political parties, legislatures, and women's organizations. In Chile, the Women's Concertación called for a women's ministry prior to the founding elections.[40] Teresa Valdés, feminist activist and researcher, recalls that one of the committees preparing the women's program within the Women's Concertación "developed the proposal to have an institutional framework for women, understood as a ministry or service. We learned from all the experiences of the Instituto de la Mujer in Spain, the Women's Council in Brazil, and other friends who came from exile; this was pivotal." In South Africa, detailed consideration was given to the experience of other countries, leading to the design of a package of focal points in state agencies and Parliament.

In Ghana, President Kufuor established a new women's ministry (Ministry of Women and Children's Affairs, or MOWAC) against the wishes of women's organizations.[41] Tsikata notes that after the antigovernment women's mobilizations prior to the 2000 elections:

400 DEMOCRATIC TRANSITIONS

The new government came and said they would reward women with this ministry, and our response set the tone for tensions because women's groups, based
on their experiences of other ministries around the continent, said that what
we needed was not a ministry and that ministries tended to be weak with no
budget. We made all these arguments, and I think the person who was to be
appointed as minister did not appreciate our efforts to pull down the ministry
even before it had started. So it set the wrong tone, and for a long time things
were very bad.

The MOWAC, headed by an antifeminist minister, battled with women's organizations throughout her tenure from 2001 to 2005. But even bodies that were
supported by female activists faced problems. **With few resources and little
power, WPAs often faced high expectations and sometimes troubled relationships with groups outside the state, while their control of resources
also contributed to the NGO-ization of women's organizations, which relied more on government and international funding than on grassroots
mobilization.** The political context in which WPAs were operating was also
important. In less institutionalized political systems, changes of government
and broader ideological trends could both negatively affect them. New or less
sympathetic governments could eliminate, withdraw funds from, or down-
grade WPAs. Budget cuts, neglect, and marginalization weakened the South
African gender machinery (in the view of Thenjiwe Mtintso, the first head of
the Commission for Gender Equality). This also occurred in Brazil at the end
of the 1980s, resulting in the mass resignation of Pitanguy and her colleagues,
and several times in Poland with the frequent changes in government, particularly after the rightwing Solidarity Electoral Alliance defeated the Democratic Left Alliance in 1997.[42] A WPA is therefore more likely to be effective if
it is part of a government that is relatively sympathetic to a gender-equality
agenda, as was the case in Chile, Spain, and South Africa; yet even then it can
face significant problems.

Gender Policy Reform

**Gender rights are not a single homogenous category. Policy reform is eas-
ier to achieve in some less contested areas of gender rights than others.[43]
Gender-based violence, divorce, electoral quotas, and property rights were
in general easier to address than reproductive rights.** Some gender rights
produce strong opposition, particularly from those identified with the right or
from religious organizations that, for example, see such reforms as a threat to
the sanctity of the family. Abortion reform proved divisive in many posttransition polities, and impossible to achieve despite mobilization and lobbying.
Of the countries analyzed in this volume, it occurred only in South Africa in
the transition's immediate aftermath, and in Spain a decade later (after the

victory of a Socialist government). There were also examples of retrenchment. In Eastern Europe, as noted, women lost many rights they had enjoyed, at least on paper, under socialism. In Poland, access to abortion—which had been relatively widespread—was severely restricted in 1993.[44] And, despite some liberalization in 1996, abortion levels remained low. In Indonesia, a decentralization program increased restrictions on women in some localities where local (often more Islamic) measures were introduced.[45] Nursyahbani Katjasungkana, founder of the women's legal organization APIK (Asosiasi Perempuan Indonesia untuk Keadilan, or Indonesian Women's Association for Justice), claims that "according to the National Commission on Violence against Women, there are around 250 rigid bylaws that discriminate against people and 78 that discriminate against women; for example, about clothing, the veil, or that women cannot go outside the home without a male relative, or get papers for their land or identification if they do not wear a veil." Even changes to property rights and measures to counter domestic violence have met with serious opposition in some cases.

Where reforms have occurred, the initiatives of key female actors in creating alliances in the bureaucracy, legislature, and civil society as well as a favorable political context—particularly a sympathetic government in power—are critical factors.[46] Domestic violence legislation illustrates this point. It is an issue that resonates with feminists and has wide female support across class and ideological lines. From the beginning of the UN Decade for Women, 1976–85, there has been growing international consensus about the need to confront this issue and the mechanisms that are needed to do so. But there are differences in the speed and extent to which posttransition governments adopted anti–domestic violence legislation and implemented policies to prevent and ameliorate it. In virtually all cases, coalitions of activists formed, but some were more effective than others. In Ghana, a coalition of activists against domestic violence was formed from a range of organizations in 2002. The campaign faltered despite the support of the attorney general, however, as one of its main opponents was the controversial head of MOWAC, the minister for women's affairs. The legislation did not pass until 2007 after a younger (more progressive) minister replaced her.[47] Tsikata observes that relations with MOWAC had become

> even worse around the struggle around the domestic violence law, because it was strange for a minister to be the one to draw attention to the things in the law that were not good for men. It took the coalition seven years to get the domestic violence law passed. All the groups were very insistent and pushed and pushed, but the government was not fazed by the strength of the coalition and its demands, and took its time to pass the law.

In Chile, a sometimes-troubled alliance of feminists inside and outside Parliament and the women's ministry SERNAM achieved the passage of domestic violence legislation in 1994.[48] But women's organizations and feminist legislators believed that the final bill had been toned down by SERNAM, which was operating in a conservative political context and influenced by the Christian Democrats in the governing Concertación, who were themselves subject to pressure from the Catholic Church. Adriana Muñoz, the Socialist deputy who proposed the original bill, argues:

> Our biggest problem was our situation as a center-left alliance. We passed a law on "intrafamily violence." The law that I presented instead prohibited violence against women (i.e., violence inflicted on women because of their gender). We could not get anywhere with this because Christian Democrat women felt it was necessary to emphasize the problem as a domestic problem. We had to give in. This was a concession; we could not get any further because we simply did not have the votes in Parliament. The right was a barrier—a permanent opposition—and feminist women and those on the left were very concerned to have Christian Democrat votes to at least get as far as we could.

In Indonesia, according to Nursyahbani Katjasungkana,

> Fortunately, the Domestic Violence Act was drafted by APIK. I and others (of course we asked other groups and also researchers) used a "triangle of empowerment"—women who were researchers, activists, and femocrats had to work together for change. And we managed to form a coalition to promote the Domestic Violence Act. But from the beginning, the challenge came from religious groups because they said this law would ruin our family harmony and the concept of the family. It took seven years from the drafting in 1997 until it was enacted in 2004.

South Africa and Brazil passed measures against domestic violence more easily in their posttransition periods. In both cases, activists had put domestic violence on the agenda prior to and during the transition. In South Africa, it was taken up by the WNC, female activists in the ANC, and the ANC Women's League. A document on the subject had been submitted to the constitutional negotiations by the ANC and, as part of its preparations for the Beijing women's conference, the ANC government committed itself to action, partnering with a national network. The parliamentary committee on women argued that a measure had to be passed in the first Parliament, and the ANC women's caucus expedited its passage.[49] In Brazil, an anti-domestic violence clause was inserted into the constitution and a number of federal- and state-level initiatives, such as women's police stations in Sao Paulo, had been established as a result of feminist activism both within and outside political parties and the state; Brazilian feminists also played a key role in raising the issue at the international level.[50] But the weakening of the National Council for Women's Rights by the end of the 1980s had a detrimental effect on the efficacy of many of these measures. **Like other laws and constitutional measures, those in-**

volving women's rights depend on effective implementation, which has varied considerably in the cases reviewed here.

Conclusions: Lessons Learned?

All the cases illustrate the central importance of women's organizing. Valdés argues that, in Chile, "if there had not been this show of strength on the streets and in different situations, it would not have been possible to get what we got from the transition . . . the articulation of the social and political worlds created the power and possibility that women's proposals for democracy were part of the program of the Patricio Aylwin's government." Pitanguy also stressed the central importance of mass women's movements organizing within Brazilian civil society. But many of those interviewed also stressed the danger of losing touch with the mass base of women's movements, and losing momentum and commitment as female leaders move into government roles. **Maintaining women's mobilization, one of the most difficult challenges, proved important for achieving positive gender outcomes over the longer term.**

Broad coalition building that connects a range of different actors— including academics, movement activists, and political women (labeled the "triple alliance" in South Africa)—was also vital for bringing together diverse knowledge (even when, as in South Africa and Indonesia, this process was fraught). But Nursyahbani Katjasungkana emphasized that, despite their differences, secular and Islamic feminists worked together. Pregs Govender stressed the strength of the WNC and emphasized the importance of the coalition's "ability to complement each other's skills, experience, and expertise—and to value all the different contributions and work together across all divides." Many of those interviewed (e.g., from South Africa) stressed that having worked together prior to the transition made cooperation easier, even among women from different backgrounds and views.

It was also important for broad alliances to develop a common agenda that appealed to (and mobilized) a range of women. Ideally, broad-based coalitions and umbrella organizations included both feminists and nonfeminists, and women of different political and religious persuasions—these were the basis of effective campaigns around specific issues in Chile, Indonesia, and South Africa. Meintjes noted that within the WNC "we recognized that gender equality was what united us. There were differences that we could all live with, and that we would have to live with because this was politics. But if we didn't get gender equality into the constitution, we were sunk." Muñoz pointed out that there were different political visions even within the Women's Concertación in Chile:

Certainly, we Socialist feminists wanted more radical measures such as abortion and divorce. However, as it was a center-left alliance, and Christian Democrat women had a different view, we created a common platform. Because the important thing at that time was to build a coalition of parties for democracy and a Women's Concertación for Democracy, with the intention of getting a lot of power and promoting democracy for women in each of our parties. So from that point of view **we were pragmatic; we said, "what matters is unity, having a united platform. And we will leave out everything that divides us,"** so we left out many issues such as divorce, sexual and reproductive rights, abortion. We put aside all issues that were controversial between the center of the Concertación and the left and more feminist groups in order to put forward a united program that would give us sufficient power that each of the political parties would promote our objectives in the negotiations on the transition program.

The Chilean case in particular shows that framing issues such as violence and rights of children in terms of strengthening the family helped to build support for reform across political divides, even if this meant that many feminists believed that issues such as socioeconomic change, redistribution, and the more profound transformation of gender relations (including the empowerment of both women *and* men) had not been addressed.

Women's organizations were also more effective if their platforms, proposals, and demands were developed before any intervention into political processes. Pitanguy stressed that **women's organizations**

> have to build alliances within themselves, and they have to come to the constitution ready with a set of proposals and demands that is nonnegotiable and a set of proposals that can be negotiated . . . the first thing for any women's movement in countries that are going through democratic transitions is to have a consensual base among themselves. They cannot waste time, energy, and strength by resolving internal conflicts. They have to come into the political arena as a cohesive group.

Pitanguy stressed that female actors "have to be part of the constitutional process." Active participation in the opposition and in posttransition transition processes was an absolutely fundamental condition for successfully asserting gender claims; where it was weak, as in Ghana and Poland, fewer positive gender outcomes resulted. Despite fears of co-optation, some actors felt that women had to intervene from the earliest stages of the transition. Mtintso argued that, from the beginning, the issue of transforming gender power relations in society has to be part of theorizing and practical and organizational considerations, because if these "don't happen at the preparatory stages, it's very difficult to integrate them at the stage of transformation . . . of change. You have got to prepare, and we did in the ANC. Not satisfactorily, but we did it, and that did a lot to influence the outcome: the constitution, the legislation, and the institutions." Pitanguy also believes that "**it's very important not to** let the moment pass. You need political timing, and you have to be organized for that timing, but you have to start organizing before it arrives."

Successful intervention overall requires several conditions to be met. First, appropriate strategies and tactics must be devised. For example, participants felt that efforts to shape the Brazilian and South African constitutions were relatively successful because of targeted lobbying and monitoring, and building alliances with other key actors. As Pitanguy says, "We arrived with a mission, but we knew how to negotiate. We knew how to make alliances. We were, in a sense, politicians. **We were doing politics. We were working with the instruments of politics,** you know, not with the instruments of authoritarianism, of radicalism; we were opposed to that. **We knew how to negotiate and how to build alliances within the government.**"

Alliance-building and intervention strategies are also needed to prevent retrenchment and the introduction of measures that threaten women's rights, such as "right-to-life" clauses. In countries like Indonesia—but also in Eastern and Central Europe and Latin America, where the Catholic Church was active in the opposition—religious conservatives had a high level of support, and it was difficult to avoid retrenchment. Seeking allies in other arenas—such as influential political parties, legislatures, bureaucracies, or key ministers—was therefore important. It was crucial for gender actors to be involved in political parties, campaigning and changing them from within at every level. Policy change is easier to achieve if the governments and parties in power are relatively sympathetic to gender-progressive measures. Some transitions were more open than others, which made it more likely that women's organizing would have positive effects. Political parties have therefore played a key role in this process. Their openness to female activists and gender issues varied greatly between countries. Some parties provided a more positive environment than others, enabling women to more effectively organize for change both within and outside the parties—and in some cases achieve significant results.

Finally, the importance of a favorable international context is clear. Many female activists reported learning from experiences elsewhere, for example, how to design effective WPAs. They emphasized that **interactions with activists from other countries in regional and international forums had been energizing, allowing them to share strategies and develop feasible goals that were suited to their local political and cultural situations.** Pitanguy stressed the importance of transnational alliances that "reinforce one another . . . even if national groups work on national constitutions." Women's organizations in Ghana had close ties with other African groups and looked to Botswana, Nigeria, and South Africa for appropriate models. Tsikata stressed the importance of the Botswanan example, which provided inspiration for a women's manifesto that was presented to political parties. And according to Nursyahbani Katjasungkana, Indonesian activists were influenced by the Women's Decade conferences, UN Committee on the Elimination of Discrimination Against Women (CEDAW), and the Beijing Platform for Action, as well as by Indian feminism and ideas, while Chilean feminists drew on the Brazilian and Spanish experiences. Most stressed the importance of all international support that facilitated knowledge sharing and did not simply comprise financial support. Both the Chilean Women's Concertación and the WNC in South Africa received significant international funding and technical support. Interviewees in Ghana, Indonesia, and South Africa reported that posttransition reductions in international funding for NGOs had hit many women's organizations hard, often occurring either because these countries ceased to be priorities for international donors as attention shifted to other regions or because they were judged to be too affluent for continued support. The international context was perhaps relatively more favorable to women's issues between 1975 and 1995, when these earlier transitions were taking place. Since then, factors such as the continuing conservative stance of the Catholic Church on social issues and the increased salience of religious and ethnic identity politics suggest that the international context may provide less support for those who would fight for gender equality today.

Key actors who intervene in transitions from the earliest stages can facilitate positive gender outcomes. Women's organizations need clear agendas that are developed by a range of actors and backed by broad coalitions within civil society. They must endeavor to work together with strategic allies—for example, in potentially sympathetic political parties, governments, and bureaucracies—and, if possible, to frame issues in ways that fit the dominant ideas of the transition. Transitions from nondemocratic rule can offer important openings for social movements that are trying to reshape the rules of the game. Despite setbacks and frustrations, there are lessons to be learned on strategies that are likely to be effective. Today's transitions present new and different challenges, but they can also offer some important opportunities for strategic intervention and action.

Options for Action

Activists and Advocates

- *Organize as early as possible in transition processes.* The earlier that women begin to organize, the greater their chances of positively influencing the transition process. Ideally, women will begin to organize before the "official" process begins, so they are prepared to input or engage during the "prenegotiation" phase (the "talks about talks"). This allows time to develop an organizational infrastructure, form alliances, build trust and confidence, and identify a shared agenda and strategy.
- *Form a range of alliances.* Movements that form alliances with a broad range of actors can leverage larger networks, which mobilize more people to ac-

tion, apply pressure to critical institutions and individuals, and draw on an array of talents and resources. Expansive alliances include various women's groups and activists (drawn as widely as possible within civil society, including groups that can offer strategic support such as social justice and environmental groups); feminist politicians, academics, and lawyers; sympathetic allies in political parties; and executives such as government ministers and bureaucrats.

- *Intervene in the full range of political processes.* Participate in all stages of the transition process—constitution writing, institutional design, and implementation—as members of constitutional review committees, technical and drafting committees, Constituent Assembly and Parliament members, lobbyists, and advocates. Activism within political parties that are likely to be sympathetic to gender concerns can promote the selection of women as candidates and appointees. Many critical negotiations take place, however, outside of formal structures and procedures. Women's access to informal decision-making spaces will in part depend on the range of alliances they have built.

- *Develop a platform that can unite different groups of women.* There is a range of possible positions on political, social, and economic issues, and it will not be possible to agree on every aim. But in order to maintain a broad alliance—and to intervene strategically during transition processes—it is helpful to identify a common platform of positions and goals to unite diverse actors and focus advocacy efforts.

- *Maintain momentum during the implementation and consolidation phases.* As female civil society leaders and academics are recruited into government roles, proper succession planning and intergenerational transmission within organizations is critical to ensure that movements are not "beheaded" and that momentum is sustained in the posttransition phase. As organizations become more professionalized, links with grassroots movements should be maintained to ensure their continued relevance to the needs of women at all levels.

Leaders and Political Parties

- *Ensure that transition processes are as open as possible to female actors.* In particular, leaders and political parties should ensure that women are included in parties, negotiations, and governments, and participate on equal terms with men at all levels. Where this looks unlikely to happen, they should consider implementing mandatory quotas with effective sanctions—for example, for negotiations teams—to ensure the presence of women in active/speaking roles.

- *Make sure that posttransition constitutions, policies, and institutional designs reflect equality concerns.* These should be well drafted and formally enshrined in ways likely to be long-lasting, unambiguous, and enforceable.

International Actors

- *Support activists who are working to ensure that gender concerns are included in transitions.* This support should include financial assistance, facilitation of knowledge exchange and sharing among activists (both regionally and internationally), and capacity-building initiatives.
- *Decouple support for gender activists from wider country support.* Support for gender activists should not depend on a country's eligibility for international support (e.g., gross domestic product levels, etc.). Such support can mitigate the vulnerability of gender activists to changing donor preferences and help consolidate gains and prevent backsliding.
- *Exert pressure on other actors.* International actors can pressure political actors to ensure that gender concerns and female actors are included in transition processes and outcomes.

....

Biosketches of Interviewees

Carlota Bustelo is a Spanish politician and women's rights activist. She has been a leading figure in the leftist feminist movement in Spain since the 1970s and was involved in the creation of the Spanish Women's Liberation Front. In 1974, she joined the PSOE. From 1977 to 1979, Bustelo was a member of the Cortes Constituyentes, the Constituent Assembly that drafted Spain's new constitution, contributing to the debate on the sexual and reproductive rights of women. In Congress she was a strong advocate of gender quotas and parity in political parties and played a pivotal role in creating the Divorce Act of 1981. From 1983 to 1988, Bustelo served as the first director-general of the Instituto de la Mujer, an autonomous governmental body to promote equal opportunities between women and men. Bustelo was a member of the UN Committee on the Elimination of Discrimination against Women .

Pregaluxmi (Pregs) Govender has been deputy chair of the South African Human Rights Commission since 2009 and leads its work on socioeconomic rights, CEDAW, and the Access to Information Act. A political activist against apartheid since 1974, Govender joined the trade union movement in the 1980s and headed South Africa's first Workers' College. During the country's transition, Govender managed the Women's National Coalition, which united South African women to ensure that the constitution addressed women's demands. She also worked in the Reconstruction and Development Program (RDP) Office, integrating women's concerns into the RDP. An African National Congress Party member, Govender was elected to Parliament in 1994. She chaired the Parliamentary Committee on Women and initiated the country's Women's Budget. During President Mbeki's term, she chaired HIV and AIDS public hearings and was the only MP to register opposition to the arms deal in the 2001 budget vote before resigning.

Nursyahbani Katjasungkana is an Indonesian human rights lawyer, former parliamentarian, and gender activist. She has worked for 30 years with NGOs focusing on human and women's rights and environmental issues. She was the first secretary general of the Indonesian Women's Coalition for Justice and Democracy, the first women's mass organization in Indonesia since 1965. Katjasungkana is the cofounder of the Indonesian Women's Association for Justice, which provides direct legal aid to female victims of violence and discrimination. She is cofounder of the Kartini Network for Women's/Gender Studies in Asia and was a member of the Advisory Board of the National Commission on Human Rights. She cofounded the Women's NGO Network to Monitor the Indonesian Government's Implementation of CEDAW. From 1998 to 2005, she was a commissioner on the Commission of Violence against Women. She was elected as member of the People's Consultative Assembly (1999-2009), where she drafted the Domestic Violence Act.

Sheila Meintjes is a South African academic and women's rights activist. Meintjes has been active in feminist and women's politics since the 1970s. In the 1980s, she was a member of the United Women's Organization, a mass-based community organization affiliated with the United Democratic Front, one of the most important antiapartheid organizations. From 1989, she was a lecturer at the University of the Witwatersrand in Johannesburg. She was research coordinator for the Women's National Coalition, which played a significant role in the negotiations that were part of the transition to democracy in South Africa. Meintjes was appointed a commissioner on the Commission on Gender Equality (2001-4). She led the commission's governance program and was responsible for the Commission in Gauteng Province. A professor at Wits University, her research interests include democracy in multicultural societies, feminist theory, gender politics, and violence and conflict transformation.

Thenjiwe Mtintso is a South African political party leader, former diplomat, and a women's rights defender. Born in Soweto, Mtintso became an activist in the South African Student Organization and Black Consciousness Movement while a student. Because of her political activities, she was expelled from university, detained, and tortured by the security services in the 1970s. Mtintso went into exile in 1978, joining the ANC and the Umkhonto weSizwe, where she became a commander. Mtintso returned to South Africa in 1992 and was appointed to the Transitional Executive Committee. She participated in the Convention for a Democratic South Africa negotiations, and during the first democratic elections in 1994 she was elected an MP. In 1997, she served as the first chairperson of the Commission for Gender Equality. In 1998, she was elected deputy secretary general of the ANC. She is a member of the ANC's National Executive Committee and has served as South Africa's ambassador to Cuba and Italy.

Adriana Muñoz is a Chilean politician, sociologist, and women's rights defender. Muñoz joined the Socialist Party of Chile in 1967. Following the 1973 coup, she went into exile in Austria, returning to Chile in 1982. In 1986, she joined the Political Commission of the Socialist Party of Chile; in 1987, she participated in founding the Party for Democracy (PPD). From 1988 to 1990, she was president of the Federation of Socialist Women, and between 1991 and 1992 served as vice president of the PPD. From 1990 to 1994, and again since 1997, Muñoz has served as a deputy on behalf of the PPD in the Chilean Chamber of Deputies. She was the first female president of the Chamber of Deputies of Chile (2002–3). As an advocate for women within the Chamber of Deputies, she has proposed legislation on issues such as divorce, abortion, and domestic violence. In November 2013, she was elected to the Senate, the upper house of the National Congress, to represent the region of Coquimbo. Muñoz has also worked as a researcher and participated in numerous projects on gender-related issues.

Jacqueline Pitanguy is a Brazilian academic, policymaker, and gender activist. One of Brazil's best-known feminists, Pitanguy was an opponent of the military junta in Brazil, fought for the democratization of the country, and struggled at the same time for women's rights. Following the return to democratic governance in 1985, Pitanguy worked to ensure the inclusion of issues of concern to women in the new constitution. She was president of the National Council for Women's Rights, a cabinet position, from 1986 to 1989, where she designed and implemented policies to improve the conditions of women. Pitanguy is a co-executive director of CEPIA (Citizenship, Studies, Information and Action), an NGO she founded in 1990 that focuses on issues of health, sexual and reproductive rights, violence and access to justice, poverty, and employment from a gender perspective.

Dzodzi Tsikata is a Ghanaian academic and gender advocate. Tsikata has been active in the Ghanaian women's movement since the 1980s. She is one of the founding members of the Network for Women's Rights in Ghana, has been a past convenor of the network, and is currently a member of the steering committee. Tsikata is an associate professor at the Institute of Statistical, Social and Economic Research and former director of the Centre for Gender Studies and Advocacy at the University of Ghana. Her research interests include gender and livelihoods, gender and development policies and practices, rural and urban livelihood systems, and the politics of land tenure.

Teresa Valdés is a Chilean sociologist, human rights defender, and women's rights advocate. Valdés was imprisoned by the Pinochet regime for her political activities. Following her release, she became a leader in the women's movement and in 1983 cofounded Mujeres por la Vida (Women for Life), which organized demonstrations against the dictatorship. She was a researcher and professor at the Latin American Faculty for Social Sciences in Chile for 25 years, where she was the founder and coordinator of the Gender Studies Area. Valdés was a senior researcher and member of the Board of Directors at the Center for the Study and Development of Women in Chile. She is currently the coordinator at the Observatorio de Género y Equidad (Gender Equality Observatory), an independent research and advocacy foundation.

NOTES

1. Paxton (2000).
2. Waylen (2007).
3. Baldez (2002).
4. Haas (2010).
5. Waylen (2010).
6. Molyneux and Razavi (2005).
7. Waylen (1994).
8. Jaquette and Wolchik (1998).
9. Roces (2010).
10. Jaquette (1994).
11. Waylen (1994).
12. Alvarez (1990); Aquino (1994); Baldez (2002); Hassim (2006); Quindoza Santiago (1995).
13. Einhorn (1993); Gal and Kligman (2000).
14. See also Duran and Gallego (1986).
15. Blackburn (1999).
16. Fallon (2003).
17. Mama (2005).
18. Alvarez (1990); Franceschet (2005); Hassim (2006).
19. Alvarez (1999).
20. Blackburn (2010).
21. Htun (2003); Threlfall (2004).
22. Einhorn (1993).
23. See Blackburn (2010).
24. Mama (2005).
25. Valiente (2003); Waylen (2007).
26. Albertyn (1994).
27. Ibid.
28. Alvarez (1990); Htun (2003).
29. Threlfall (2004).

30. Bonime-Blanc (1987, 95).
31. Abao and Yang (2001).
32. Baldez (2002).
33. Waylen (2007).
34. Ibid.
35. Marx, Borner, and Caminiotti (2009).
36. Waylen (2007).
37. Blackburn (2010); Haas (2010); Valiente (2003).
38. Geisler (2000).
39. Brenner (2011); Wieringa (2006).
40. Franceschet (2005).
41. Mama (2005).
42. Matynia (2003).
43. Htun and Weldon (2010).
44. Zielinska (2000).
45. Brenner (2011); Wieringa (2006).
46. Tripp (2013).
47. Tsikata (2009).
48. Haas (2010).
49. Hassim (2006).
50. Alvarez (1990).

INTERVIEW REFERENCES

Author's correspondence with Carlota Bustelo, April 2013
Author's interview with Pregaluxmi Govender, January 2013
Author's interview with Nursyahbani Katjasungkana, January 2013
Author's interview with Sheila Meintjes, January 2013
Author's interview with Thenjiwe Mtintso, January 2013
Author's interview with Adriana Muñoz, December 2012
Author's interview with Jacqueline Pitanguy, December 2012
Author's interview with Dzodzi Tsikata, December 2012
Author's interview with Teresa Valdés, December 2012

REFERENCES AND FURTHER READING

Abao, Carmel, and Elizabeth Yang. *Women in Politics, Limits and Possibilities: The Philippines Case.* Manila: Friedrich Ebert Stiftung, 2001.

Albertyn, Cathi. "Women and the Transition to Democracy in South Africa." In *Gender and the New South African Legal Order,* edited by Felicity Kaganas and Christina Murray, 39–63. Cape Town: Juta, 1994.

Alvarez, Sonia. *Engendering Democracy in Brazil.* Princeton, N.J.: Princeton University Press, 1990.

———. "Advocating Feminism: The Latin American Feminist NGO Boom." *International Feminist Journal of Politics* 1, no. 2 (1999): 181–209.

Aquino, Belinda. "Philippine Feminism in Historical Perspective." In *Women and Politics Worldwide*, edited by Barbara Nelson and Najma Chowdhury, 591–604. New Haven, Conn.: Yale University Press, 1994.

Baldez, Lisa. *Why Women Protest: Women's Movements in Chile*. Cambridge: Cambridge University Press, 2002.

Blackburn, Susan. "Gender Violence and the Indonesian Political Transition." *Asian Studies Review* 23, no. 4 (1999): 433–48.

———. "Feminism and the Women's Movement in the World's Largest Islamic Nation." In *Women's Movements in Asia*, edited by Mina Roces and Louise Edwards, 21–33. London: Routledge, 2010.

Bonime-Blanc, Andrea. *Spain's Transition to Democracy: The Politics of Constitution Making*. Boulder, Colo.: Westview Press, 1987.

Brenner, Susanne. "Private Moralities in the Public Sphere: Democratization, Islam and Gender in Indonesia." *American Anthropologist* 113, no. 3 (2011): 478–90.

Duran, Maria Angeles, and Maria Teresa Gallego. "The Women's Movement and the New Spanish Democracy." In *The New Women's Movement*, edited by Drude Dahlerup, 200–216. London: Sage, 1986.

Einhorn, Barbara. *Cinderella Goes to Market: Citizenship, Gender and Women's Movements in East Central Europe*. London: Verso, 1993.

Fallon, Kathleen M. "Transforming Women's Citizenship Rights within an Emerging Democratic State: The Case of Ghana." *Gender and Society* 17, no. 4 (2003): 525–43.

Franceschet, Susan. *Women and Politics in Chile*. Boulder, Colo.: Lynn Rienner, 2005.

Gal, Susan, and Gail Kligman, eds. *Reproducing Gender: Politics, Publics, and Everyday Life after Socialism*. Princeton, N.J.: Princeton University Press, 2000.

Geisler, Gisela. "'Parliament Is Another Terrain of Struggle': Women, Men and Politics in South Africa." *Journal of Modern African Studies* 38, no. 4 (2000): 616–19.

Haas, Liesl. *Feminist Policymaking in Chile*. University Park: Pennsylvania State University Press, 2010.

Hassim, Shireen, *Women's Organizations and Democracy in South Africa: Contesting Authority*. Madison: University of Wisconsin Press, 2006.

Htun, Mala. *Sex and the State: Abortion, Divorce, and the Family under Latin American Dictatorships and Democracy*. Cambridge: Cambridge University Press, 2003.

Htun, Mala, and Laurel Weldon. "When Do Governments Promote Women's Rights: A Framework for the Comparative Analysis of Sex Equality Policy." *Perspectives on Politics* 8, no. 1 (2010): 210–17.

Jaquette, Jane, ed. *The Women's Movement in Latin America: Participation and Democracy*. Boulder, Colo.: Westview Press, 1994.

Jaquette, Jane, and Sharon Wolchik, eds. *Women and Democracy: Latin America and Central and Eastern Europe*. Baltimore: Johns Hopkins University Press, 1998.

Mama, Amina. "In Conversation: The Ghanaian Women's Manifesto Movement." *Feminist Africa* 4 (2005).

Marx, Jutta, Jutta Borner, and Maria Caminiotti. "Gender Quotas, Candidate Selection and Electoral Campaigns." In *Feminist Agendas and Democracy in Latin America*, edited by Jane Jaquette, 45–64. Durham, N.C.: Duke University Press, 2009.

Matynia, Elizabieta. "Provincializing Global Feminism the Polish Case." *Social Research* 70, no. 2 (2003): 454–71.

Molyneux, Maxine, and Shahra Razavi. "Beijing plus Ten: An Ambivalent Record on Gender Justice." *Development and Change* 36, no. 6 (2005): 983–1010.

Paxton, Pamela. "Women's Suffrage in the Measurement of Democracy: Problems of Operationalization." *Studies in Comparative International Development* 35 (2000).

Quindoza Santiago, Lilia. "Rebirthing Babaye: The Women's Movement in the Philippines." In *The Challenge of Local Feminisms*, edited by Amrita Basu, 110–30. Boulder, Colo.: Westview Press, 1995.

Roces, Mina. "Century of Women's Activism in the Philippines." In *Women's Movements in Asia: Feminisms and Transnational Activism*, edited by Mina Roces and Louise Edwards. London: Routledge, 2010.

Threlfall, Monica. "Gendering the Transition to Democracy: Reassessing the Impact of Women's Activism." In *Gendering Spanish Democracy*, edited by Monica Threlfall, Christine Cousins, and Celia Valiente. London: Routledge, 2004.

Tripp, Aili Mari. "Political Systems and Gender." In *Oxford Handbook of Gender and Politics*, edited by Georgina Waylen, Karen Celis, Johanna Kantola, and Laurel Weldon, 514–29. Oxford: Oxford University Press, 2013.

Tsikata, D. "Women's Organizing in Ghana since the 1990s: From Individual Organizations to Three Coalitions." *Development* 52, no. 2 (2009): 185–92.

Valiente, Celia. "The Feminist Movement and the Reconfigured State in Spain." In *Women's Movements Facing the Reconfigured State*, edited by Lee Ann Banaszak, Karen Beckwith, and Dieter Rucht, 30–47. Cambridge: Cambridge University Press.

Waylen, Georgina. "Women and Democratization: Conceptualizing Gender Relations in Transition Politics." *World Politics* 46, no. 3 (1994): 327–54.

———. *Engendering Transitions: Women's Mobilization, Institutions and Gender Outcomes.* Oxford: Oxford University Press, 2007, esp. 163.

———. "Gendering Policy and Politics in Transitions to Democracy: Chile and South Africa Compared." *Policy and Politics* 38, no. 3 (2010): 337–52.

Wieringa, Saskia. "Islamization in Indonesia: Women Activists' Discourses." *Signs* 32, no. 1 (2006): 1–8.

Zielinska, E. "Between Ideology, Politics and Commonsense: The Discourse of Reproductive Rights in Poland." In *Reproducing Gender: Politics, Publics, and Everyday Life after Socialism*, edited by Susan Gal and Gail Kligman. Princeton, N.J.: Princeton University Press, 2000.

Chapter 11

From Authoritarian Rule toward Democratic Governance

Learning from Political Leaders to Shape the Future

....

ABRAHAM F. LOWENTHAL AND SERGIO BITAR

Opposition movements, often calling for democracy, have been challenging authoritarian governments in such different countries as Egypt, Tunisia, Yemen, and Myanmar. Some of these governments have given way, and others are likely to follow, as undemocratic regimes are facing (or will face) growing demands for participation and representation in east and west Asia, North and sub-Saharan Africa, and Latin America and the Caribbean.

Building democracies to replace authoritarian regimes has not been easy or quick, nor will it be, in current and future cases, easy or quick. Yet, for several decades, currents of change, sometimes subject to undertows, have generally moved toward more open, participatory, and accountable politics. Higher levels of urbanization, income, education, and literacy have often reinforced heightened expectations of personal autonomy and political expression. These tendencies, in turn, have been accelerated by new information and communications technologies that make opposition movements easier to mobilize.

People everywhere want their voices to be heard and heeded. This aspiration for political expression puts the question of transitions from authoritarian rule toward democracy squarely back on the international agenda, and makes it timely to study how prior democratic transitions were achieved. This is especially important because successful prior transitions were not at all inevitable, and in many cases were surprising.

This chapter draws on our interviews with 13 political leaders (12 former presidents and 1 former prime minister) from 9 countries who helped end autocracies and craft democracies in their place during the last quarter of the 20th century.* These nine countries all achieved democratic governance—unevenly and in some cases incompletely—but without reversal.

---

* We conducted face-to-face interviews between January 2012 and June 2013 with Fernando Henrique Cardoso of Brazil, Patricio Aylwin and Ricardo Lagos of Chile, John Kufuor and Jerry Rawlings of Ghana, B. J. Habibie of Indonesia, Ernesto Zedillo of Mexico, Fidel V. Ramos of the Philippines, Aleksander Kwaśniewski and Tadeusz Mazowiecki of Poland, F. W. de Klerk and Thabo Mbeki of South Africa, and Felipe González of Spain.

Although attempted transitions to democracy have failed in several other countries, we focus on these nine successful cases in order to capture insights from leaders, most of them now long retired from partisan political struggles, who played leading roles in guiding their countries to democracy. We seek to distill principles that can be helpful for those who want to achieve future transitions.*

We begin by presenting some of the contours of these nine transitions, highlighting their main similarities and differences. We highlight several difficult issues that recurred repeatedly, albeit in various forms. We then show how political leaders, both incumbents from authoritarian regimes who were ready to support a transition toward democracy and challengers from opposition movements who aimed to achieve such transitions, perceived and addressed these recurrent issues. We examine the strategies the leaders developed, the obstacles they confronted, and what lessons can be learned from their experiences. We consider how the circumstances of current and future transitions will differ from those of the late 20th century, and what these differences may imply for the future. We conclude by identifying the distinct qualities of political leadership that are illustrated in these interviews and are very much needed in our time. Leaders cannot by themselves bring about democracy, but their contributions are essential.

The Broad Contours of Nine Successful Transitions

- Most of these transitions from authoritarian rule toward democracy were extended processes rather than single events. Dramatic moments of visible change—the inauguration of Nelson Mandela in South Africa, the "People Power" outpouring in the Philippines, the decisive victory of the "NO" campaign in Chile's 1988 plebiscite, or the surprising defeat of the Polish Communists in the partially free elections of 1989—captured broad attention. But these and most of the other nine transitions occurred gradually over considerable time. Iconic events can play a vital role in catalyzing or symbolizing political transformation, but the road toward democracy often begins years before (and extends years after) these moments. Those who want to undertake or support democratic transitions should keep this in mind. These transitions typically had their origins long before the memorable moment when the authoritarian regime finally ended. The first steps toward transition often took place quietly, even invisibly: in the political opposition, within the authoritarian regime itself, in civil society, or in multiple places.

---

* We do not offer this essay as a contribution to political science theory, for which other methods and additional cases would be necessary. We aim to learn about making democratic transitions from key leaders who contributed importantly to successful transitions, and to make accessible their political wisdom.

For opposition movements, these pretransition phases—sometimes involving political parties, study groups, think tanks, labor unions, women's and student movements, and other domestic nongovernmental organizations (NGOs)—helped establish or deepen personal connections and fostered trust among disparate opposition sectors. In some cases, they also improved communications and developed mutual understanding between figures within the authoritarian regime and leaders in the opposition.

- Once they begin, transitions proceed at different speeds, with advances and retreats, and often with zigzags. Unexpected events can have major effects. Brazil's president-elect Tancredo Neves, who had been chosen by the opposition movement as its candidate in the indirect elections of 1985, became fatally ill on the eve of taking office as the first civilian president after two decades of military rule. As a result of a political deal that had been struck to enhance the opposition's electoral prospects, Neves's death unexpectedly brought to the presidency vice president elect Jose Sarney, a conservative civilian figure from the military regime; this slowed—but in some ways facilitated—the transition process. The failed assassination plot by left extremists against Augusto Pinochet in Chile in 1986 forced the democratic opposition to break definitively with those willing to use violence. The assassinations of Luis Carrero Blanco in Spain, Chris Hani in South Africa, and Benigno Aquino (leader of the political opposition to the Marcos regime in the Philippines, who was slain on the airport tarmac as he returned from exile to Manila in 1983) helped trigger important political choices. The fall of the Berlin Wall in 1989—as well as the subsequent changes within and ultimate dissolution of the Soviet Union—radically transformed the context for change in Poland and South Africa, and the Asian financial crisis of 1997–98 undermined Soeharto in Indonesia. Political leaders did not anticipate any of these surprises, many of which presented unforeseen obstacles. These events required nimble responses but did not derail the possibilities for achieving democracy.

- On rare occasions, authoritarian regimes collapsed abruptly in the face of economic crisis, as in Indonesia in 1998, or popular outrage triggered by inflammatory events, such as the assassination of Aquino followed by the grossly fraudulent "snap" elections staged by Marcos in 1986.* Even in these exceptional cases, however, an extended process of social mobilization against the regime, followed by tacit or explicit negotiation, often helped produce agreements on the principles and procedures necessary to make

---

* In other cases that we did not review, authoritarian regimes sometimes collapsed after military defeat, as was the case in Argentina, Greece, and Portugal. The perception in the Philippines that the New People's Army (MPA) insurgency was gaining strength contributed to the weakening of the Marcos regime and to the Reform the Armed Forces Movement (RAM), which helped topple Marcos.

democratic governance possible. Democracies did not directly emerge from crowds in the street, however impressive they might have been.

- Most of these transitions took many years to reach maturity and institutionalization. In some countries—including Brazil, Chile, the Philippines, Poland, South Africa, and Spain—many years of pressure from opposition movements were needed to end authoritarian rule. There were multiple stages and occasional setbacks. In Brazil, Ghana, Poland, and South Africa, autocratic regimes (or sectors within them) reached out to moderate opposition elements, in part to enhance international legitimacy or respond to external pressures, and built relationships with opposition forces that were willing to negotiate an opening of those regimes. In Poland, Spain, and South Africa, for instance, long-gestating processes of dialogue and negotiations among elites emerged from extended conflicts, with periodic demonstrations of force by one or both sides. These negotiations established parameters and enabled the gradual elaboration of core principles and rules of engagement that allowed democratic movements to gain broad support and eventually take hold.

- The transitions had some common features, but they differed in their inception, sequence, and trajectory. The circumstances in which they arose included personal dictatorships with military backing in Indonesia, the Philippines, and Spain; institutional military rule in Brazil and Chile; quasi-military rule by a charismatic autocrat in Ghana; one-party-dominant systems of different types in Mexico and Poland, in the latter case bolstered and constrained by external support from the Soviet Union; and exclusionary rule by a white oligarchy that had long repressed the black majority in South Africa.*

These regimes differed in a number of other ways that influenced how they ended and conditioned the prospects for democracy. They varied in the degree to which they controlled their national territory and commanded the allegiance of their citizens, including those of different ethnic backgrounds, religious beliefs, and regional loyalties. Such differences significantly influenced the transitions in Spain, South Africa, Ghana, Indonesia, and the Philippines, where particular regions and ethnic groups demanded greater autonomy and resources.

Several authoritarian governments had been reasonably successful at achieving economic development, promoting social welfare, and protecting national and citizen security, at least for dominant segments of the population; others had not. Transitions from relatively successful regimes and from

---

* In other cases, transitions have taken place after civil wars or in the wake of foreign occupation, or from monarchies or patrimonial regimes. Each of these transitions presented special issues, but many of the recurrent challenges considered here were also relevant.

badly faltering ones took different courses, shaped by the relative power of the governments vis-à-vis the opposition forces. The transitions in Brazil, Chile, and Spain, for example, were affected by the perceived success of the incumbent authoritarian governments in providing citizen security and economic growth.

The degree of professional discipline and coherence of—as well as the level of public support for—the armed forces, police, intelligence, and other security services also shaped these transitions. They were conditioned by the relative strength of civilian institutions, including political parties, legislatures, and judiciaries. The persistence and recovery of preexisting political parties, institutions, and traditions facilitated the transitions in Chile and Brazil. Prior constitutional or legal norms and networks were also important in Indonesia, the Philippines, Ghana, Mexico, and Spain. In some countries, aversion to recent experiences of violence, repression, and corruption, or else nostalgia for valued aspects of the past, affected the transitions.

They were also influenced, to a greater or lesser degree, by the relative strengths and distinct qualities of civil society organizations (CSOs) such as trade unions, religious communities, student federations, and women's groups. It mattered, too, how these groups had related to the authoritarian regime, security forces, and business sectors. The African National Congress (ANC) in South Africa; the Coalition for the No and then the Concertación in Chile; the Spanish Socialist Workers' Party (PSOE) and the Communist Party of Spain (PCE); Solidarity in Poland; and other parties, political movements, and CSOs in other countries helped mobilize pressure on authoritarian governments. The broader the organized support for the opposition movement and its leadership, the more likely it was to secure important concessions in the explicit or tacit negotiations with the authoritarian government that often took place.

- Some of these transitions were initiated at least in part by mutual approximation by sectors within the upper ranks of the authoritarian regime and elements of the opposition, as was the case in Brazil, Spain, Mexico, Poland, and Ghana. In some cases, regimes responded mainly to pressures from bottom-up social mobilization, as in Chile, Indonesia, the Philippines, Poland, and South Africa. Many transitions emerged from tacit or explicit negotiation between elements of the incumbent government and the opposition, as occurred in different ways in Brazil, Chile, Indonesia, Mexico, Poland, South Africa, and Spain. A few transitions (but not many) involved formal accords among elites, such as Spain's Moncloa Pacts on economic policies, which later led to political agreements.
- All these transitions were the result of domestic forces and processes, but they were also affected, in different ways, by the broad international context and specific external actors. Regional tendencies, prevailing interna-

tional ideologies, and linkages to long-established democracies were relevant, as were the nature and degree of each country's integration into the global economy.* So, in some cases, were specific pressures by major powers, neighboring countries, international institutions, and other external actors, including NGOs, business, labor and media organizations, and diaspora communities. In many countries, the personal experience abroad of political leaders, often in exile, and the ideas and networks that resulted, were also relevant, as illustrated in the interviews of Cardoso, Habibie, Lagos, and Mbeki.

In some (but by no means all) cases, political leaders, political parties, and other participants learned from the experiences of earlier transitions and the international exchange of ideas. Mbeki emphasizes how the advice of Tanzania's Julius Nyerere on building a new constitution influenced the ANC's thinking in South Africa and how Chile's experience with its Truth and Reconciliation Commission helped inform South Africa's work on transitional justice. Lagos notes how important the advice of Spain's González on how to deal with the armed forces, police, and intelligence services was for Chileans. Poland's Mazowiecki and Kwaśniewski both mention how the Soviet invasions of Czechoslovakia and Hungary affected the approaches of both General Jaruzelski and the opposition in Poland.

The Cold War competition between the United States and the Soviet Union, and its end, profoundly affected all these transitions. Although international actors alone were not decisive in any of the transitions, in virtually all these cases, international reinforcement of (and interactions with) local actors and the withdrawal of external support from the authoritarian regime were important.

But none of these structural, historical, and contextual factors by themselves determined when and how autocracies ended, or whether and how democracy could ultimately be fashioned. Critical decisions had to be made by political leaders in governments, parties, and movements, often among unattractive options. Both skill and luck played a role.

In these nine countries, all the transitions from authoritarian rule led to constitutional democracies—institutionalized through regular, mainly free, and reasonably fair elections, combined with meaningful restraints on executive power and practical guarantees of essential political rights, especially of free speech and assembly, and individual freedoms.† Some of these countries

---

* For comparative views of the external role in democratic transitions, see K. Stoner and M. McFaul, *Transitions to Democracy: A Comparative Perspective* (Baltimore: Johns Hopkins University Press, 2013).

† Other transitions during these years have produced different outcomes, including hybrid semiauthoritarian regimes that combine competitive elections with serious ongoing violations of democratic procedures, as well as highly uneven and incomplete democratic

still have important issues related to (or limits on) the nature or degree of effective democratic governance, but basic democratic institutions remain in place in all nine cases. The fact that all these countries managed to achieve constitutional democracies that have not been reversed in a generation (or longer) makes it particularly useful to learn from the political leaders who helped guide these historic transformations.

Given the diverse circumstances and trajectories of transitions from authoritarian rule toward democracy, there can be no "one size fits all" model or simple manual of "best practices" for such transitions. But we can learn a great deal from the leaders who shaped these transitions, especially by identifying and exploring how they perceived and handled key issues that arose in virtually all cases.

Recurrent Challenges of Transitions

Four broad clusters of challenges stand out: preparing for the transition, ending an authoritarian regime, making and managing the transfer of power, and stabilizing and institutionalizing the emerging democracy. These challenges did not emerge in linear fashion or in necessary chronological order, but they appeared in all these cases and are likely to be present in future transitions.

Preparing for the Transition

Domestic forces seeking to end an authoritarian regime typically had to achieve enough broad support, coherence, legitimacy, and other resources to challenge the regime's capacity to govern, as well as to become plausible contenders for national power. In some cases they also had to become viable interlocutors for those within the authoritarian regime who realized that the regime needed a partner to facilitate a possible exit strategy. Sometimes they also had to become credible to international actors who wanted to support a transition. Achieving these goals often required bridging deep disagreements about aims, strategies, tactics, and leadership among those opposed to the authoritarian regime. Convincing diverse opposition groups to work out their major differences in order to confront an authoritarian regime typically was not easy. Building a broad coalition capable of ousting an authoritarian regime, and with a strong commitment to democratic values, often required working assiduously to overcome divisions within the opposition, while at the same time understanding and taking advantage of divisions, evident or latent, within the regime. Knowing both how to unite the opposition and how to split the incumbent regime was at the heart of many transitions, as discussed by

---

governments that have been subject to reversion. See S. Levitsky and L. A. Way, *Competitive Authoritarianism: Hybrid Regimes after the Cold War* (New York: Cambridge University Press, 2010).

Cardoso, for example, who emphasized his core strategy: not to oust the military but to induce them to reach out in search of an exit.

Ending the Authoritarian Regime

Authoritarian governments did not relinquish power until at least one important sector within the regime perceived that doing so was the only way to avoid major unwanted consequences: severe loss of public support, civil violence, a split of the armed forces, serious economic damage, international ostracism, or threats to the nation's territorial integrity. The humiliation of military defeat, economic collapse, or electoral debacle sometimes hastened a regime's exit. But these traumas usually led to democratic transitions only when segments of the authoritarian government tolerated or supported opposition demands for democracy.

Opposition forces had to craft approaches that could induce such elements within the authoritarian government to be open to a transition. This often required assuring them that wholesale revenge against the former rulers and their main supporters would not be undertaken; that economic and other interests of established power centers would be respected, although blatant corruption and gross privileges would not be accepted; and that the individual rights of the former ruling elites would be protected under law as the new authorities took power. It was not easy to reconcile such assurances with the understandable aspirations of long-excluded opposition forces that had taken great risks to combat the authoritarian regime. But this *was* possible, and it often seemed to transition leaders, both from incumbent governments and opposition movements, to be necessary.

Making and Managing the Transfer of Power

Implementing successful transitions required dealing with multiple, often interconnected, tensions and dilemmas. Those who took power had to foster civic order and end violence while at the same time striving to assure that all security and intelligence forces, including some that were at the heart of previous repression, would henceforth act within the law and be subject to control by the new civilian authorities.

They also had to inspire domestic trust and gain international legitimacy. In many cases, this involved developing electoral procedures to ensure that the will of the majority of voters would be recorded and respected, but also reassuring key political minorities (often including some associated with the outgoing regime) that they would be represented and that their core interests would be protected, according to the rule of law.

A third need was to assure that those who took office would be well prepared, technically and politically, for their new governing responsibilities: by acquiring the necessary training and skills, attracting officials who already had those skills, or keeping on some personnel from the previous regime, as

González, Mazowiecki, and Mbeki emphasize. On a range of issues—from macroeconomic policies to the delivery of social services and the quest for transitional justice—governing required perspectives, competencies, and expertise that was quite different from those of opposition. In many cases, this meant learning on the job.

Oppositions-turned-governments had to balance the need for bureaucratic, technocratic, security, and judicial expertise against the aim to curb the influence of the former regime. They had to refocus the bureaucracy and the security and police forces from controlling subjects to serving citizens. They needed to persuade citizens, in turn, to accept and begin to trust a state that many had understandably rejected as illegitimate and hostile.

Transition leaders had to balance the conflicting imperatives of responding to those whose human rights had been violated by the previous regime and holding accountable those who had committed gross violations on the one hand, while preserving the loyalty of security forces (some of whose members had been involved in these violations) on the other. At the same time, they had to assure citizens that these forces could effectively deal with crime, violence, and, in some cases, separatist and insurgent movements. They had to find ways to foster peaceful mutual acceptance by former bitter enemies, which is no easy matter.

The new authorities typically inherited long-standing patterns of corruption and impunity. They needed to establish or protect the autonomy and authority of independent judiciaries and independent media that could hold national executives and others accountable while avoiding the creation of veto centers that could block all the new government's initiatives.

They also needed to achieve economic growth and expanded employment, and control inflation, while improving the provision of housing, health, and education and expanding public expenditures to meet the long-deferred needs of the poor. Doing so required the new authorities to engage national and foreign investors without fueling fears that they were selling out to the privileged. Often the new governments had to gain public support for macroeconomic policies that were intended to produce long-term benefits but imposed painful sacrifices and uncertainties in the short term. Leaders of all these transitions adopted market-oriented approaches and prudent monetary and fiscal policies. They accepted—even those who were not originally so inclined—that these were necessary in an ever more globalized economy, in tandem with strong social policies that could produce more equitable economic development.

Stabilizing and Institutionalizing the Emerging Democracy

As democratic transitions took hold, political leaders frequently faced other thorny issues. After some years, the public often blamed democratic leaders—and sometimes democracy itself—for the failure to meet economic or political expectations. Movements that had united in opposing the authoritarian regime often fragmented, creating challenges for governments, or else decayed over time into conformism and complacence.

By the same token, civil society organizations—including human rights groups and women's movements—that had contributed importantly to anti-authoritarian opposition sometimes atrophied or else moved to extreme and disruptive positions after many of their most talented and pragmatic leaders entered government or party politics. In these circumstances, it was not easy to maintain active and independent nongovernmental organizations . Building mutually beneficial relationships between a new government and new opposition forces (that sometimes included the former authorities), as well as with independent social forces and civil society organizations, was not simple. It required especially sensitive and sustained attention.

Learning from Political Leaders

In the particularly uncertain circumstances of systemic transitions, political leaders often have to take decisions with strictly limited information or assurance about their consequences.* Many of these leaders emphasized the apprehensions that pushed them to fashion compromises that some at the time (as well as some in succeeding generations) criticized as too timid. Their testimony explains how and why they made the hard choices they did on such questions as civil-military relations, transitional justice, and reserved domains.† Fear of reversion or violence also shaped their approaches to crafting constitutional provisions, electoral systems, and economic policies. Risks, uncertainties, and tough decisions were inevitable, but they did not necessarily prevent leaders from taking actions that could break through stalemate.

Moving Forward Incrementally

All these leaders believed that it was important to take advantage of even partial opportunities to move forward rather than reject incremental progress in the hope of later being able to make a possible (but not assured) greater change. They emphasized their determination to ameliorate undesirable situations rather than to imagine a way to start from scratch or simply

---

* In their groundbreaking study of transitions from authoritarian rule, Guillermo O'Donnell and Philippe Schmitter emphasized the special uncertainties of such transitions and how and why they differ from "normal politics." See G. O'Donnell and P. Schmitter, *Transitions from Authoritarian Rule: Tentative Conclusions about Uncertain Democracies* (Baltimore: Johns Hopkins University Press, 1986; republished with a new preface by Cynthia Arnson and Abraham F. Lowenthal, Johns Hopkins University Press, 2013).

† Reserved domains are special concessions to previous power groups to preserve certain privileges, such as guaranteeing budget levels to military institutions, putting parts of the economy under the control of specific groups, and assuring political representation to designated individuals, institutions, or interest groups.

wish away the tough constraints that slowed progress toward their ultimate goals.

Aylwin, for instance, discusses the debate within the opposition on whether (and on what terms) to participate in the 1988 plebiscite in Chile, mandated by the constitution Pinochet imposed in 1980, and his ultimately prevailing arguments for challenging the regime within its own rules rather than continuing to insist on its illegitimacy. Lagos recalls the advice that Felipe González gave him and his colleagues about "getting out of the well"—that is, achieving greater strength and leverage—before formulating additional demands. Cardoso explains his inclination, opposed by many others in the Brazilian opposition, to accept that direct presidential elections would not be permitted by the military regime and instead to work within the regime's rules to contest the elections of 1985.

De Klerk and Mbeki discuss the crucial decision to agree on the principles for a provisional constitution before the first national democratic election, to be debated, improved, and approved by the Congress that would be elected later in South Africa. Mazowiecki and Kwaśniewski both emphasize the agreement to proceed with partially free "contract" elections in Poland in 1989 on terms intended to guarantee that the Communists would have a majority of seats and that General Jaruzelski would be confirmed as president, in order to assure gradualism. Kufuor explains why he rejected his party's boycott of the 2000 Ghanaian elections. Zedillo underlines the importance of incremental reforms in electoral procedures proposed by the National Action Party (PAN) and accepted by the ruling Institutional Revolutionary Party (PRI) over the course of several previous years before his presidency, when the PRI seemed unlikely ever to cede national power.

These leaders consistently gave priority to gaining ground wherever possible, even when some vital priorities could only be partly achieved and when some important constituents and supporters were making demands that the leaders considered unviable. **Rejecting maximalist positions sometimes called for more political courage than adhering to those goals or hewing to attractive but perhaps impractical principles.**

In order to combat repression and push for openings, opposition leaders had to mobilize protests; challenge the established order and rules; denounce the imprisonment, torture, and expulsion of dissidents; and combat the regime's national and international legitimacy. They always had to be prepared, however, to make compromises that would improve their position. Incumbents in authoritarian regimes who were open to a democratic transition, in turn, had to find ways to maintain authority and the support of their core constituencies while providing space for opposition partisans. They had to be willing to take risks to do so, as de Klerk did, for instance, by calling and winning an all-white referendum to support his approach to negotiations with the ANC. Aylwin, Lagos, Cardoso, de Klerk, Mbeki, González, and Mazowiecki all stress, from different perspectives, that leaders on both sides had to combine exerting continuous pressure with a real willingness to work out compromises. Transition making is not a task for the dogmatic.

The Need for a Hopeful and Inclusive Vision

Although accepting unsatisfying compromises was sometimes necessary, these leaders also understood the need to consistently project a broad and hopeful vision of what the transition would signify. They emphasized the way forward rather than concentrating on past grievances. A compelling vision of the longer-term future for the whole society, combined with modest promises for more immediate gains, helped sustain complex transitions through stressful periods that involved dangers, costs, and disappointments. Such visions were needed to combat the fear that could demobilize social organizations and paralyze people. Overcoming pervasive fear was an enormous challenge for many of these leaders, as de Klerk, González, Lagos, and Mazowiecki emphasized. The anecdote told by Lagos, about a Socialist woman who had reluctantly decided to vote for a conservative candidate in order to avoid a return to polarization, is particularly poignant.

Building Convergence and Coalitions

Encouraging convergence, forging consensus, and building coalitions among opposition forces were all vital both for achieving these transitions and for beginning to construct democratic governance. It was important to connect the opposition's political actors to social movements—including workers, students, women, human rights groups, and religious institutions—in the process of defining and achieving the opposition's overarching aims. Connections at the elite level were obviously important, both within opposition forces and between opposition forces and some of those who were opposed to regime change. But so was the sense among the wider public that democratic movements were truly inclusive and not merely vehicles for particular individuals or groups. It was vital to build on the participation of social movements in mobilizing opposition to the authoritarian regime and then in framing a new constitution, protecting human rights, and building political parties and civil society. In many cases, the participation of women and women's organizations was critical to achieving these objectives, as mentioned by Cardoso, Habibie, Lagos, Mbeki, Ramos, and Rawlings, and discussed in detail in Georgina Waylen's essay (chap. 10, this volume).

Accomplishing convergence required focusing sharply on what united people rather than on what divided them, as Aylwin, González, and others emphasize. But it also required making difficult decisions to exclude some groups that refused to renounce violence, or that insisted on uncompromising demands for regional, ethnic, or sectarian autonomy. Incorporating these would likely have hurt the chances for a successful transition in Chile, Indonesia, the Philippines,

South Africa, and Spain. Political leaders had to nurture reciprocal acceptance among the often mutually hostile opponents of an authoritarian regime, and find ways to reconcile differing positions or establish a basis for mutual tolerance with those from the incumbent government and their supporters, and at the same time isolate those who remained intransigent on both sides.

Opposition leaders often had to build bridges to moderate elements within the old regime and to other power centers in society, especially key business interests. In many cases it was also necessary to try to reconcile the views of members of the opposition living in (or just returned from) exile with those who were organizing within the country, or sometimes to choose between them, as Cardoso, González, Lagos, and Mbeki all observed.

Personal style and deference were important for building consensus. Habibie went himself to the National Assembly to seek its support immediately after the fall of Soeharto, and he authorized General Wiranto to retain the extraordinary emergency powers that Soeharto had granted, thus assuring Wiranto's loyalty. Ramos adopted a highly consultative and deliberative approach to policy formulation. Cardoso went with his wife to the promotion ceremonies of Brazil's military officers in order to strengthen the personal relationships he would need to draw on later to remove service heads from the cabinet and establish a civilian minister of defense, as he intended. Aylwin individually and actively recruited members of Chile's Truth and Reconciliation Commission who had credibility in different sectors, going to their private residences at times. Mazowiecki presided over long consensus-building sessions of his cabinet and worked consistently to make his government broadly inclusive. Zedillo accepted proposals from the opposition PAN and Party of the Democratic Revolution (PRD) parties to change Mexico's electoral laws and procedures. All these initiatives took self-confidence, vision, patience, persistence, and precious time. They also reflected conscious and thoughtful efforts to signal to contending forces that all would have a stake in the new regime.

Creating and Protecting Spaces for Dialogue

Creating and protecting spaces for direct dialogue among opposition groups and between government and opposition leaders were often critical. Such explorations sometimes required secrecy that temporarily exacerbated distrust among opposition groups. It was vital to build bridges between political movements and other sectors—including business groups, professional associations, religious groups, and civil society organizations—some of which had cooperated earlier with the authoritarian regime but now seemed ready for neutrality or perhaps even to defect. These leaders thought that it was much more important to invest in future-oriented relationships than to sort out disputes about the past.

Such future-oriented dialogues often sharpened the opposition's vision and programs, built incipient consensus, and developed shared commitments, including those to democracy and human rights; they also helped clarify the issues that would be the hardest to negotiate. These dialogues provided ideas and analysis and even helped craft the norms and rules of the game for eventual democratic governance. This was illustrated by the secret "talks about talks" held outside South Africa between government officials and ANC leaders, as well as the "bush retreats" de Klerk held with National Party leaders to build consensus for the negotiations with the ANC. Other examples included the roles of the Group of 24, the Center for Christian Humanism, Corporación de Estudios para Latinoamérica (CIEPLAN) and Vector in Chile; the Brazilian Center for Analysis and Planning (CEBRAP) and other centers of reflection in Brazil; the Round Table Talks and the pre–Round Table private discussions at Magdalenka between Solidarity and the Communist government in Poland; the talks between Adolfo Suárez and the Committee of Nine before the 1977 elections in Spain; and the roles of Islamic organizations in Indonesia and of the Lawyers' Association and other civil society groups in Ghana. It was important not to shortchange or truncate the prolonged discussions often required to construct coalitions and forge consensus.

Constitution Making

Drafting a new constitution or amending an existing one was typically an essential—but difficult and sometimes dangerous—task. That process inevitably opened important debates on fundamental issues: from social and economic rights to the design and details of the electoral system; from the role of the military to the reform of the justice system; and the issue, in some cases, of regional autonomy. Electoral systems and procedures were often matters of strong contention, as was the legalization of previously banned political groups that authoritarian governments had considered subversive.

Several alternative approaches were employed for designing a new constitution: electing a Constitutional Assembly, establishing a special commission, or delegating that function to the Parliament, sometimes before submitting the resulting document to the public for approval by referendum. Each process makes sense in certain circumstances. Whatever the process chosen, leaders emphasized the importance of engaging a wide range of participants in drafting a constitution and trying hard to accommodate the core demands of key contending groups.

This was important even when it meant reluctantly accepting (at least for some time) such cumbersome procedures as Chile's undemocratic provisions: appointed senators and especially the designation of former President Pinochet as commander of the armed forces for eight years after his presidency and as senator for life. In some cases, transition leaders determined that building broad support for the new constitutional document required incorporating certain aspirations that might eventually need to be revised. This was true, for example, of the lofty but fiscally unsustainable socioeconomic guarantees of

Brazil's 1988 constitution, as well as its provision to entitle the various armed services to participate in the cabinet, which was revised during the Cardoso presidency.

Sometimes it was necessary to proceed through multiple stages. In Spain, the Suárez government secured approval of provisions to hold democratic elections from a Parliament that was still dominated by supporters of the former dictator Francisco Franco, and deferred the drafting of a new constitution until after those elections. In Poland, proposed constitutional reforms that were not approved by the sitting Parliament were revived by President Kwaśniewski and presented to (and approved by) the next Parliament, which was democratically elected. South Africa's experience was perhaps the most complex. The de Klerk government and the ANC negotiated a provisional constitution based on 34 agreed-upon principles. They deferred the drafting of a permanent text until after the first democratically elected Parliament constituted itself as a Constitutional Assembly, and then subjected the permanent text to approval by the Constitutional Court in order to ensure compliance with the 34 principles.

All these leaders understood that whether the constitutional text would be truly permanent mattered less than whether its framers could achieve broad "buy-in" regarding its main terms and legitimacy, establish consensus on a framework for moving forward, and agree on a way—that was neither too easy nor practically impossible—to amend the document at a later stage, when conditions warranted. Although the exact wording of a constitution obviously matters, it also matters how, when, and by whom it is adopted.*

Providing assurances to elements and supporters of the former regime that their economic and institutional interests—as well as their individual rights—would be protected was often vital in the constitution-making process, despite the foreseeable protests such assurances provoked among those who were previously excluded (and often repressed). An important principle was that assurances should be transparent and consistent with democratic and constitutional procedures in order to allow the possibility of further review under these procedures at later stages. Tough issues such as transitional justice and civil-military relations did not necessarily have to be resolved in a single step but could be tackled in stages over time. In announcing the establishment in 1990 of the Truth and Reconciliation Commission in Chile, for example, Aylwin promised to seek justice only "insofar as is possible," but he hoped that what was possible might expand over time, as it eventually did.

---

* Philippe Schmitter emphasized this point in "Contrasting Approaches to Political Engineering: Constitutionalization and Democratization" (unpublished manuscript, February 2001).

It was more important to reach agreement on the procedures by which political power could be obtained and challenged than to specify in advance the precise details of political representation. Compromises were often required in order to achieve broad participation in the political process, even if these reduced the authority of elected officials and created the need for further adjustments in the future.

Debate continues to this day about whether such compromises went too far. In Chile, for example, the 2005 constitutional revision did not change the binomial electoral system adopted under Pinochet after the 1988 plebiscite but before the Concertación took power. It made it possible for a minority party that obtained one-third of the vote in district elections to Congress to gain representation equal to that of the majority party that got 60%, making it difficult for any president to win a comfortable legislative majority. This controversial provision remained until 2015—25 years after the end of dictatorship—when Congress approved a new electoral law. There is no doubt, however, that such compromises helped draw highly polarized movements into peaceful electoral competition, and thus helped create stable democracies that were open to further evolution at later stages.

The Political Economy of Transitions

The Asian financial crisis of 1997–98 precipitated the fall of Soeharto and thus the Indonesian transition toward democracy. In Brazil, Poland, and South Africa, long-term economic stagnation, short-term decline, and fiscal deficits and high inflation helped convince some important economic groups that had prospered under authoritarianism that a political change was now necessary, or at least acceptable, as Cardoso discusses. Unemployment, recessions, and in some cases inflation also mobilized many people to oppose authoritarian governments. The most direct precipitants of transitions were usually more political than material, but adverse economic conditions certainly weakened some authoritarian governments.

Regardless of how a transition began, once a new government was in place, economic issues became a priority. In Poland (and in other former Communist economies), welfare subsidies for most people were reduced or eliminated in order to achieve fiscal balance. The need to alleviate poverty as well as address concerns about inflation and unemployment conflicted in many countries with the need to impose economic reforms and fiscal discipline in order to promote future growth, as emphasized by Habibie, Mbeki, and others. But fiscal austerity risked strong political backlash, as Mazowiecki and Zedillo point out. González, Habibie, and Mazowiecki highlight the need for quick action to alleviate poverty and undertake economic reforms while there is strong popular support for political change. Aylwin and Lagos emphasize that the Concertación commitments to reducing poverty and achieving economic "growth with equity" won support from both business and labor while affording the government the political authority needed to restrain wage demands—from the powerful miners' union, for example.* In many cases, special social measures were needed to mitigate the hardships endured by the most vulnerable.

The Importance of Political Parties

Political parties, old and new, played a major role in most of these transitions. They established regional and territorial networks, developed ties with social movements and civil society organizations, helped craft and implement strategies to combat the authoritarian regime, and mobilized international support. Parties helped to choose candidates for, organize, and conduct electoral campaigns; prepare platforms and programs for electoral competition and governance; train cadres for public service; mediate conflict among political allies; and assure that governments did not lose touch with their popular base.

Authoritarian regimes generally banned parties or tried to weaken or destroy them. Exceptionally, as in Brazil and Indonesia, they created "official" parties to support themselves. They sometimes allowed circumscribed official "opposition" party activity in order to legitimate the ruling party's hegemony, as in these two countries and in Poland and Mexico. Authoritarian regimes usually restricted the access of such opposition parties to campaign funding and the media, and often repressed or intimidated opposition leaders. They generally discredited and hampered politics, parties, and politicians.

Most of the leaders who worked to end authoritarian regimes and foster democratic governance began by building or reviving political parties. They sought to legalize parties and assure their fair access to media exposure and campaign finance, and helped them reduce atrophy, division, or marginalization. In several cases, leaders mobilized international solidarity and support for all these purposes. They devoted substantial effort to developing electoral rules and procedures to help parties avoid fragmentation, and to enable them to broaden and institutionalize their appeal. Aylwin, Lagos, Cardoso, de Klerk, Mbeki, González, Habibie, Kufuor, Rawlings, and Ramos all invested heavily in party-building efforts. (Mazowiecki, who did not make this goal a priority during his short tenure as prime minister, observed in retrospect that this was a mistake.) Zedillo, from the long-ruling PRI, played an important role in Mexico's transition by supporting reforms that created more favorable conditions for opposition parties, helping them become strong enough to compete with the PRI. He also introduced primary elections as the means of choosing

---

* For an illuminating discussion of the political economy of market-opening transitions, see T. Besley and R. Zagba, eds., *Development Challenges in the 1990s: Leading Policymakers Speak from Experience* (Washington, D.C., and New York: World Bank and Oxford University Press, 2005).

the PRI presidential candidate, thus "cutting off his finger (*dedo*)" to end the *dedocracia* by which Mexican presidents had personally chosen their successors for more than six decades.

Indonesia, Ghana, Poland, and the Philippines all illustrate problems that democracies face when strong parties are not developed. Political parties have lost credibility and strength, even in many established democracies, and attacks on *partidocracia* are common in many countries. **But parties can play and have played important positive roles when they are not merely the vehicles of individual political figures and their cronies. Institutionalizing parties takes time and continuing attention, but early and sustained investment can pay rich dividends.**

Achieving Democratic Civilian Control of the Military, Police, and Intelligence Services

In almost every case, a key challenge was to bring the armed forces and other security institutions under civilian authority while recognizing their legitimate roles, their appropriate claim on some level of resources, and their need to be protected from reprisals by former opposition forces.* These issues were handled differently from case to case, but it was generally necessary to remove or retire top officers responsible for torture and brutal repression; to place top military commanders under the direct authority of civilian ministers of defense; and to insist firmly that active duty military officers refrain entirely from political commentary and partisan involvement. Aylwin, Lagos, Cardoso, de Klerk, Mbeki, González, Habibie, Kufuor, Kwaśniewski, Mazowiecki, and Ramos provide fascinating testimony on how these important goals were accomplished in diverse circumstances. The anecdotes these leaders recount about their own relations with military leaders speak volumes about the qualities required to manage this difficult issue. It took judgment and courage to determine when a ranking officer needed to be removed and when to look the other way, and more generally how best to harness military discipline to strengthen democratic governance.

It was necessary to recognize and enhance the professionalism and self-esteem of the armed forces, help them focus on external defense rather than internal security, and provide them the equipment and facilities they required. It was also important that senior civilian officials charged with overseeing defense policy be knowledgeable about security matters and respectful of their military peers. This was challenging in countries where democratic movements had clashed violently with the armed forces, and mutual distrust, even disdain, persisted.

* A recent and comprehensive study of civil-military relations and their importance for building and consolidating democracy is Z. Barany, *The Soldier and the Changing State: Building Democratic Armies in Africa, Asia, Europe and the Americas* (Princeton, N.J.: Princeton University Press, 2012).

González, Habibie, Mbeki, and Ramos all emphasize the need to separate both police and domestic intelligence functions from the armed forces. It was crucial to reorganize, redefine, and limit the role of the police by inculcating new attitudes toward the general population and substituting protection for repression while maintaining their capacity to dismantle violent groups. The domestic intelligence services also had to be brought under civilian control. This was by no means simple. Civilians had to be encouraged to enter and staff the intelligence services, previously not considered a suitable professional career, as González emphasizes.

Being aware of, and consistently clear about, communicating all these points was vital for constructing democratic governance. **Subjecting all security and intelligence forces to firm civilian control was often one of the most protracted challenges new democracies faced. It sometimes took repeated confrontations over several years between democratic governments and elements of the armed forces or the intelligence and police agencies—some highly visible, others not—to firmly establish civilian control.** Aylwin did not at first take advice from González to establish his own intelligence capability, for example, but over time he learned the wisdom of this counsel.

Achieving Transitional Justice

There was strong political and social pressure in all cases to hold accountable members of the former authoritarian regime for human rights violations and blatant corruption. It was critical, however, to balance the need for truth and justice with the requirement to provide assurances and safety to those leaving power. In some cases, this involved transparent legal processes, carried out over time, to extract the truth (to the extent possible) about violations of rights; to provide recognition and even reparation to victims; and, when feasible, to bring major violators to justice. It was also important to guarantee those leaving power that there would be no wholesale prosecution of former officials.

There was no simple formula for handling these complex questions. These interviews underline how important it was to address them openly, emphasizing both recognition of victims and measures to achieve mutual tolerance, if not reconciliation. In Brazil and Spain, amnesties allowed members of the democratic opposition who had been operating clandestinely to enter open political competition. In Chile, Ghana, and South Africa, Truth and Reconciliation Commissions and recognizing violations were vital steps. The tension between drawing a "thick line" between the past and the present (as Mazowiecki and Kufuor emphasized) and recognizing and remembering the abuses that had occurred so that they would not be repeated (as stressed by Aylwin, Lagos, de Klerk, and Mbeki) cannot easily be resolved; most of these leaders struggled to respect and reconcile both objectives. In Indonesia, where human rights violations were swept under the rug, the unresolved issues remain problematic.

Mobilizing External Support

External actors—governments, international and multilateral institutions, corporations, trade unions, religious organizations, international associations of political parties, and other nongovernmental entities—helped support most of these transitions. In some cases, they provided the necessary venue and conditions for dialogue among different opposition sectors, as well as between them and representatives of authoritarian regimes and other social forces. These contributions were illustrated in South Africa, where a major mining corporation provided funding and safe venues outside the country for secret meetings between government officials and ANC leaders, as Mbeki discusses, but they were also significant in Spain and Chile.

External actors helped reinforce civil society organizations by sharing expertise and providing encouragement and support, often long before a challenge to authoritarian rule was actually mounted or the time for turnover arrived. External actors facilitated the exchange of experiences from different countries on political party organization, electoral systems and conduct, coalition building, constitution making, and advancing the rights of women. They provided training on community organization, communications and information, public opinion polling, exit polling, quick counts, election monitoring, and other practical aspects of democracy building. In some countries, international electoral monitoring missions helped bolster the credibility of elections and their results. External organizations also provided educational and networking opportunities on substantive issues that helped opposition cadres prepare for the eventual responsibilities of government. These activities were important in Poland, for instance, where a generation of economists was trained abroad in how to liberalize an ineffective statist economy and promote markets. The policy decision to build a market economy was made in Poland, but international cooperation helped make possible its implementation.

International actors facilitated access to prior experience in the recurrent issues that put transitions at risk: civil-military relations, transitional justice, the conduct of credible elections, police reform, and the oversight of domestic intelligence agencies, right down to the details of disarming hostile surveillance and intelligence activity, which González vividly described. They also promoted peer group communication and training opportunities with counterparts in the armed forces, business and labor groups, professional associations, and other sectors, which sometimes helped reinforce democratic attitudes and behavior among these groups. And they provided reassurance, broad counsel, and, on occasion, detailed practical advice.*

---

* Foreign governments also provided asylum to threatened opposition leaders and later to exiting members of authoritarian regimes (as occurred with Marcos in the Philippines); furnished advanced voting machines and personal identification techniques to facilitate clean elections (as in Ghana); and pressed local authorities to assure that the opposition

Concerted external pressure to curb repression and respect human rights, including those of free expression and assembly, were often important. Economic sanctions were critical in South Africa and Poland. Various trade, investment, aid, and cooperation programs were significant in Poland, Indonesia, Ghana, and the Philippines. In addition to pressure, international recognition of Rawlings for accepting multiparty elections, reasonably fair electoral procedures, and term limits reinforced his contributions to Ghana's democratic transition.

Finally, international organizations, governments, foundations, and NGOs sometimes played significant roles in responding to critical social and economic needs during transition periods. In Ghana, Poland, South Africa, Spain, and they provided resources to mitigate the social impact of necessary economic reforms, invested in infrastructure development and capacity building, and offered other financial and technical assistance. The European Union (EU) and the US government were crucial in helping Poland (and other Central and Eastern European countries) move toward democracy in the 1990s. Such international economic assistance can be critical when it is provided in response to local needs, in cooperation with local actors, and leaves policy choices to local political debates and decisions.

Aspiring transition makers and external actors need to understand both the potential contributions and the limits of external involvement. Democracy can take root in a society only after it becomes the most accepted way to contend for political power. International actors can often do a good deal—patiently, quietly, and at the request of local actors—to reinforce movement in that direction, but they cannot take the place of domestic actors. Having a broader understanding of the many difficult challenges and obstacles that must be faced, and of the considerable time it may take for democratic governance to take hold, should help international actors avoid impatient, ineffective, and counterproductive interventions and instead enable them to contribute more consistently over the longer term. They are most likely to be effective when they listen, raise questions that arise from comparative experience, and encourage local actors to consider issues from various perspectives rather than promote prepackaged answers.

Changing Contexts for Transitions

The contexts of current and future challenges to authoritarian rule differ importantly from those in which the transitions of the late 20th century and early 21st century took place. The world continues to change, ever more rapidly.

---

would have reasonable access to the media (as in Chile's 1988 plebiscite). International organizations offered technical assistance for economic management (as the German Central Bank and the International Monetary Fund did in Indonesia) and reinforced local pressures for free and fair multiparty elections (as in Ghana and Mexico).

Transformed Geopolitics and International Norms

Today's challenges to authoritarian rule are mostly free of the Cold War's pressures to contain social mobilization, limit changes to property regimes, and determine political alignments in light of international geopolitical balances. Since the Cold War's end, the major powers have become less inclined to see political change in authoritarian allies as threatening, thus opening up more space for democratizing movements, but also perhaps diminishing international support for such forces in specific situations.

The strengthening of international legal norms and institutions to protect individual human rights and prosecute crimes against humanity, as well as the creation of the International Criminal Court, have somewhat reduced the possibility that outright repression can take place without repudiation or sanctions; brutal repression continues in several notorious cases, but at least there are international standards that somewhat discourage such practices. The breakup of the Soviet Union and the decline of US international influence in recent years have produced a more multipolar international system. International constraints on democratic openings have diminished, but so has the international capacity to respond to internal violence and gross repression, or to help broker solutions. Some rights, including those of women, have been much more widely accepted.

The collapse of the Soviet economic system and China's rise in the international economy reinforced global turns toward economic liberalization, market-oriented reforms, private foreign investment, and the globalization of world production, finance, and trade. Most governments today seek to expand international trade and respect international financial and investment norms and regulations, leaving little room in the global economy for closed economies, especially for small and midsized countries. Some countries have strengthened the state's role in avoiding economic concentration, improving income distribution, promoting regional development, and protecting the environment.

Democratic governance has become more widely accepted internationally as the most legitimate basis for political order. But there are different concepts regarding what democracy entails and requires. "Competitive authoritarian" regimes have been established in several countries that are not incomplete or decaying democracies, but rather deliberate efforts to present alternatives to liberal democracy by combining reasonably free plebiscitary elections with authoritarian governance.* The pressures of globalization, the consequent openness to international influence, and the strengthening of international legal regimes and institutions may make it harder over time for authoritarian

---

* For a full discussion, see Levitsky and Way, *Competitive Authoritarianism*.

governments to maintain systematically antidemocratic practices and suppress human rights, including the rights of women, but this is certainly not yet the case.

Legacies of Prior Democratic Experiences

Many authoritarian regimes in the 1970s and 1980s, and a few in the 1990s, came to an end in countries that had some prior experience with constitutional democratic governance; in several cases some democratic institutions were still formally in place. Political actors in these countries had networks, experience in negotiating and fashioning compromises, and confidence that they could compete effectively under democratic rules. Future transitions from authoritarian rule will often take place in countries with little or no such prior experience, and in some cases with leaders who have long suppressed dissent. Some national traditions of responsive government—at local levels, for example—can be invoked against such regimes. The universal and powerful appeal of participation in self-government, which is perhaps rising with income levels and capacity for political expression, can also be energizing. But developing the culture and institutions of democratic politics takes time, effort, and skill.*

Socioeconomic, Class, and Demographic Differences

The transitions of the 1970s and 1980s, and some in the 1990s, mainly took place in countries with a growing and educated middle class that was often favorably disposed toward expanded political expression and had training in law, public administration, and economics, which helped build effective democratic governance. Transition attempts in countries with low income and development levels, fragile trade unions and social organizations, small middle classes, weak states incapable of providing social services and citizen security, and few people trained in public administration may be more difficult, especially in the face of popular pressure for quick "bread and butter" economic gains. Other attempts—especially in the Gulf States, Middle East, and North Africa—will occur in resource-rich countries with high incomes and expanding middle classes. Many of these countries, however, also have bloated states and high levels of clientelism and corruption. For geopolitical reasons related

---

* As the late European social scientist Ralf Dahrendorf observed in his *Reflections on the Revolution in Europe: In a Letter Intended to Have Been Sent to a Gentleman in Warsaw*, "The formal process of constitutional reform takes at least six months; a general sense that things are looking up as a result of economic reform is unlikely to spread before six years have passed; the third condition of the road to freedom is to provide the social foundations which transform the constitution and the economy from fair-weather into all-weather institutions capable of withstanding the storms generated within and without, and sixty years are barely enough to lay these foundations" (New York: Times Books, 1990), 99–100.

to their strategic location or their natural resources, they experience little sustained external pressure to open their political systems. Such regimes are more able to buy off or stifle opposition movements.

Many contemporary authoritarian regimes in Asia and Africa are in societies that have strong ethnic or religious and regional divisions and inequalities, which contribute to polarization. Some have increasing numbers of frustrated and educated young people who are unable to find gainful employment and can thus be readily mobilized for protest. Engaging young people in political organizations, parties, and other institutions—not merely in street demonstrations—is a major challenge to governance in many countries, including long-established democracies. Today's leaders must relate well to new generations and encourage them to organize democratically and to stay involved.

All these and other difficulties—including the presence of powerful organized crime syndicates and transnational extremist political movements—put intense pressure on weak political institutions. It will therefore be challenging to formulate approaches and build institutions that can facilitate dialogue and convergence, establish checks and balances and the means of accountability, build independent judiciaries and the rule of law, establish civilian control of all security forces, and lay the other foundations for democracy. Democratic governance will be harder to achieve in countries with weak states and institutions, but it can be constructed, as illustrated by Ghana's experience.

International Efforts to Promote Democracy

Many European transitions, including Poland's, Spain's, and others in Central and Eastern Europe, were strongly aided by the prospect of incorporation into the EU and by proffered economic assistance from the EU and the United States that was conditioned on political reforms. Several Latin American openings toward democracy, including Chile's, were facilitated first by the US administration's new emphasis on human rights in the late 1970s (under Jimmy Carter) and then by the return of US policy to actively promoting democracy and human rights in the mid-1980s during the second Reagan administration. Democratic openings were also reinforced by the consensus for human rights and political freedoms developed in the Organization of American States and by the strengthening of international legal norms and institutions, including the Inter-American Commission on Human Rights and the International Criminal Court. Mexico's democratization was bolstered by the general integration of labor markets, production processes, and popular culture between Mexico and the United States, and by the mobilization of US and Mexican businesses and NGOs to support democratic opening and the rule of law, reinforced by the passage of the North American Free Trade Agreement.

Regional institutions, today and in the future, may be equally, more, or in some cases (such as the Gulf Cooperation Council) less supportive of democratic governance. The slow but growing engagement of regional intergovernmental organizations is promoting and protecting the integrity of elections. The African Union Charter on Democracy, Elections and Governance has come into full effect. The Association of Southeast Asian Nations (ASEAN) Political and Security Blueprint includes common language on democracy standards, and the ASEAN Secretariat provided observers for the 2012 Myanmar by-elections. Such regional partnerships provide important resources on which transition leaders can draw.

Regional and Cultural Differences

A number of potential transitions are being (or may be) attempted in countries with Muslim majorities at a time when there are salient divisions between fundamentalist and moderate interpretations of Islam, and when the civil state, the role of the armed forces, and popular sovereignty are all highly contested concepts. Indonesia, the world's largest Muslim-majority nation, has built increasingly effective democratic governance over the past generation, and pro-democracy sectors are influential in many other Muslim-majority countries. In some countries, however, powerful conservative sectors contend that law should be derived solely or primarily from sharia, and that the state should enforce religious orthodoxy and traditional gender roles. Both religious conservatives and secular liberals see compromise on the role of religious law and the status of women as morally unacceptable. Thus they may both support authoritarian solutions, but of different types and for opposite reasons.

Armed forces in the Middle East have mainly been committed to civil rather than religious states, and today they are challenged by both secular democrats and religious fundamentalists. International peer discussions with military leaders should focus on the principles and practices that are most conducive both to ongoing political stability and to the coherence and integrity of military institutions.

Religious institutions have often acted as bulwarks of authoritarian regimes, but in the late 20th century they sometimes fostered democratization, particularly in Roman Catholic countries such as Brazil, Chile, the Philippines, Poland, and Spain. The roles of Cardinals Raúl Silva Henriquez and Juan Francisco Fresno in Chile, Paulo Evaristo Arns in Brazil, Vicente Enrique Tarancón in Spain, Jaime Sin in the Philippines, and Pope John Paul II in his native Poland were all important. In South Africa, Bishop Desmond Tutu, the Anglican Protestant Church, and clergy from other churches, including some Dutch Calvinist ministers, also supported the transition toward inclusive democracy. Muslim organizations, movements, parties, and individuals in Indonesia also helped build the country's nonsectarian democracy; the role of Abdurrahman Wahid (Gus Dur) deserves special mention.

Muslim religious authorities will doubtless play major roles in other countries, but these are likely to vary from case to case, and in Arab and non-Arab cultures, just as the political roles of various Christian denominations and political leaders have varied between (and sometimes within) countries. Finding ways to engage Muslim religious authorities more actively in support of democratic governance is an important challenge. Such engagement may also benefit from international exchanges of relevant experiences, including consultations about how best to cope with transnational organizations with extremist visions that promote violence in support of sectarian causes.

The Information and Communications Revolutions

The revolutions in information and communications technology (ICT) have eroded the capacity of governments to control information, reduced the costs of sharing alternative views and news, facilitated popular organizing, and made it easier to draw upon external sympathy and support. Anyone anywhere with a mobile phone camera can spark protests by recording egregious behavior. These processes will accelerate as smartphones and broadband become available to most of the population, especially youth. Social networks using these technologies cannot replace political organizations in governing, but they can shake up political systems, requiring political parties and institutions to adapt or be severely weakened.

Innovations in ICT are not always good for democratization, however. They may help create short-lived bursts of popular involvement that give democratic organizers undue confidence in their ability to move ahead without persistent and organized negotiation and compromise. They may also enable extremists to expand their support, and may help give the perception that fringe groups are major actors. Technologically sophisticated governments, sometimes aided by multinational companies, can use the same technologies to repress citizens. Governments can now intercept electronic communications, identify protesters filmed on security cameras, and threaten or imprison opposition members.

Those who want to undertake or support democratic transitions must learn how to harness new technologies and combine them with the more time-consuming but vital processes of deliberation, negotiation, coalition building, compromise, and consensus building. They must also learn how to protect democratic forces from the manipulation of ICT, both by authoritarian regimes and by antidemocratic extremist elements.

Qualities of Political Leadership

There is no prescribed "central casting" model for a transition leader. The leaders we interviewed, who were opposition activists and incumbents from authoritarian governments, included experienced politicians, lawyers, and economists; a senior military figure; a junior military officer; a journal editor; an academic sociologist; and an aeronautics engineer. They had different religious beliefs and practices, ranging from devout to nonbelieving, and included Catholics, Protestants, and a Muslim. Their physical presence and personal styles differed remarkably.

Some were not, in fact, democrats by temperament, conviction, experience, or reputation. Jerry Rawlings ruled for a decade as a military dictator and agreed to hold open, multiparty elections, under domestic and external pressure, only when secret polls showed that he would win easily. His interview reveals the complex attitudes Rawlings had and still has toward representative liberal democracy. F. W. de Klerk was committed for many years to apartheid and its exclusion of South Africa's large black majority until he became convinced, late in the day, that this system was no longer sustainable for economic, political, and moral reasons. B. J. Habibie was an intimate associate of Soeharto, Indonesia's long-term dictator. Habibie's respect for democratic institutions, apparently acquired during his 20 years as an aeronautical engineer in Germany, was not evident until he was thrust into power when Soeharto fell. Starting without any political base or significant support, and with strident opposition in the streets, Habibie worked quickly to achieve legitimacy through a number of dramatic democratizing steps.

Aleksander Kwaśniewski, a junior minister in the Communist government in Poland who played an important role as a representative of that regime in the Round Table Talks, later launched a social democratic party, was elected president after the transition, and eventually helped strengthen Poland's new democratic institutions and practices. Successive Polish political leaders brought very different qualities to the changing challenges of transition. Lech Wałęsa was a dissident trade union leader who articulated bold demands and mobilized broad popular support, but later lost much legitimacy when he pushed to acquire more personal power. Mazowiecki concentrated on tough political and economic policy choices, inclusionary and conciliatory approaches, and managing Poland's important link with the Vatican and its delicate relations with the Soviet Union. Kwaśniewski focused largely on effective administration and institution building.

Ernesto Zedillo had democratic inclinations from an early age but held important posts in Mexico's ruling PRI at a time when it had controlled virtually all political positions for many decades. Previous electoral procedures had been designed to assure that this domination would continue. Zedillo's willingness as president to accept changes in the procedures and conditions for elections opened the way for alternation of power in Mexico and progress toward effective democratic governance—what Zedillo called "normal democracy."

All these leaders—even those with autocratic backgrounds—concluded, for diverse reasons, that government based on popular sovereignty and constitutional restraints was a better path for their country and themselves than available alternatives. Some had strong democratic principles. Some developed or strengthened their commitment to democracy in response to social pressures in unfolding circumstances. Others adopted democracy-opening approaches only when it became politically advantageous. None of these particular leaders was a saint. They were all pragmatic politicians who looked for ways to gain or maintain influence and solve problems, bet on democratic processes to do so, and helped bend their countries toward democracy.

Whatever their backgrounds or motives, these leaders shared some common qualities that helped them succeed.

- All of them had—some from the beginning, others developing over time— a strategic sense of direction toward more inclusionary and accountable governance, and a fundamental preference for peaceful and incremental (rather than violent or convulsive) transformation.
- They captured the mood and spirit of citizens and reinforced the efforts of political parties and social organizations to move toward democracy.
- They diversified and expanded their own bases of support and worked to weaken intransigent elements, both within the regime and within the opposition. They were able to assess the interests and influence of multiple power centers and interest groups, and often found paths toward political compromise and accommodation.
- Many showed resolution and courage, sometimes even risking their lives in conditions of polarization and violence that took the lives of colleagues. Often these leaders mustered great patience, persistence, and stamina in the face of opposition, obstacles, and setbacks, and were able to persuade others not to lose heart.
- They had the self-confidence needed to make difficult, decisive, and timely decisions with calm conviction. Some were by nature highly analytical and reflective, but even they managed consistently to look forward rather than second-guess their prior decisions.
- Most relied heavily on competent associates who shared political values and specific expertise in order to deal with difficult issues. Although they could (and did) make key choices personally, most of them concentrated mainly on building consensus, forging coalitions, constructing political bridges, and communicating consistently with key constituencies and the broad public.
- They were generally able to persuade others to accept their decisions. Although some were eloquent or charismatic, they mainly did so by understanding and responding to the core interests of diverse actors, including adversaries, rather than primarily by fiat or the force of their personalities.
- Although they were deeply grounded in their respective national societies and relied primarily on domestic relationships, each of these leaders knew how to mobilize external support without becoming foreign instruments.
- Above all, these leaders adjusted rapidly to events and used unexpected turns to seize the initiative. They piloted in turbulent waters: bending into

the current, steering left or right, to and fro, as the rapids required, while ultimately moving forward. They did not determine the direction and pace of the currents, but they managed to help guide their countries to calmer waters and toward eventual democratic governance.

It is hard to imagine that these transitions would have been so successful without these leaders and their decisions. They and other individual leaders in these countries—including Nelson Mandela, Roelf Meyer, Cyril Ramaphosa, Oliver Tambo, and Desmond Tutu in South Africa; Corazon Aquino in the Philippines; Lech Wałęsa, Wojciech Jaruzelski, Czeslaw Kiszcak, and Adam Michnik in Poland; Ulysses Guimarães, Tancredo Neves, Luiz Inacio (Lula) da Silva, and Generals Golbery do Couto e Silva, João Figueiredo, and Ernesto Geisel in Brazil; Clodomiro Almeyda, Manuel Bustos, Gabriel Valdés, and Andrés Zaldivar in Chile; Cuauhtemoc Cárdenas, Manuel Clouthier, Porfirio Muñoz Ledo, Ernesto Ruffo, and Vicente Fox in Mexico; King Juan Carlos, Santiago Carrillo, Manuel Fraga, and Adolfo Suárez in Spain—helped open their countries' paths toward democracy.* The top political executives did not work on their own, and they could not have achieved success without social, political, and civic forces, but they worked creatively and constructively with many others, within tight constraints, to build new realities.

The prospects for building democracies in other countries, now and in the future, depend in considerable measure on the emergence and performance of such leaders. As Samuel Huntington observed, "A democratic regime is installed not by trends but by people. Democracies are created not by causes but by causers."[1] These interviews provide ample evidence.

Looking Forward

In his interview, Felipe González makes two points worth emphasizing. He notes that leadership is not learned in university courses, but rather in actual practice, by applying broad principles to concrete circumstances. And, citing the late novelist Gabriel García Márquez, González suggests that people often learn such broad principles from anecdotes, from narratives of remembered experiences. That is the fundamental premise of this volume.

New actors, technologies, institutions, norms, challenges, and opportunities have emerged and will no doubt continue to do so. But though actors and technologies change rapidly, the imperatives of political expression and action are much more permanent. Mobilizing for political freedom, building spaces for dialogue, constructing convergence and consensus, forging agreement on procedures and rules of engagement, and reassuring opposing forces

* The role of King Juan Carlos of Spain, for instance, is concisely highlighted by Charles Powell in "Abdication Is the King's Final Gift to a Grateful Spain," *Financial Times*, June 4, 2014.

that their fundamental interests will be protected will remain vital priorities. Establishing mechanisms to deal with issues of transitional justice and memory; to assure civilian control of military, police, and intelligence forces; and to protect both civic order and individual human rights will continue to be central challenges. That is true both for those seeking to end authoritarian governments and for those trying to counter a reversal of democratic gains by governments that are fairly elected but then weaken or ignore the checks and balances of democracy.

Social movements and civil society organizations, enhanced by electronic networking, will pressure governments and other institutions. But though these actors and their techniques can be helpful, they cannot replace political parties, social organizations, and political leaders in the difficult tasks of building electoral and governing coalitions, winning public support, preparing viable public policies, calling for sacrifices in the common good, inspiring people to believe that democracy is possible, and governing effectively. The importance of vision, patience, persistence, and openness to compromise will therefore continue.

Future leaders will have to consider carefully which aspects of prior experiences elsewhere are relevant in the specific circumstances of their own countries. Knowing that many of the issues they confront have been experienced before, and understanding the different ways these have been handled, should be immensely helpful. We hope they will be inspired by the qualities and achievements of the political leaders this volume highlights.

NOTE

1. Samuel P. Huntington, *The Third Wave: Democratization in the Late Twentieth Century* (Norman: University of Oklahoma Press, 1991), 107.

ACKNOWLEDGMENTS

International IDEA and the directors of this project, Sergio Bitar and Abraham Lowenthal, express their deep appreciation to the 13 political leaders who granted interviews. We also express our gratitude to their personal staff assistants and other institutional colleagues who facilitated these meetings and the resulting texts.

We gratefully acknowledge the contributions of the nine experts who prepared context-setting introductions to each set of interviews, reviewed and improved the time lines and guides to further reading, helped the project directors prepare for the interviews, reviewed the transcripts, and in most cases commented on the introduction and concluding chapter.

Professor Georgina Waylen's essay (chap. 10) on women in democratic transitions is a vital contribution to this project. We are grateful to the nine eminent women who granted interviews to Professor Waylen for sharing their experiences and insights on women's role in democratic transitions. We also extend our appreciation to the authors of the country background papers that informed the development of this chapter: Maria Esther del Campo Garcia, Jean Franco, Marta Pajarin Garcia, Takyiwaa Manuh, and Ani Soetjipto.

We are grateful to Laurence Whitehead and Alfred Stepan, senior advisors to the project, who helped the project directors prepare for the interviews by framing issues and commenting on their evolving ideas. We appreciate important contributions by our principal research assistant, Benjamin Mainwaring, who helped to review the literature and research specific issues, prepared a first draft of the time lines and guides to further reading, and provided editorial suggestions. We are grateful as well for the research assistance provided by James Loxton, Carolina Larriera, Victor Saavedra, and Consuelo Amat. We acknowledge the assistance of Andrzej Rossa, who provided simultaneous interpretation for the Polish interviews; Charles Roberts, who translated several interviews from Spanish; Kelley Friel, who copyedited the manuscript, and the photographers who are credited with each photograph.

We are especially appreciative of the assistance provided by Mariana Aylwin in facilitating the interview with her father, and by Sergio Fausto in helping edit and condense the extraordinary five-and-a-half-hour interview we had with President Cardoso. We also appreciate the background interviews we had with Alejandro Foxley in Chile; Adam Michnik in Poland; P. V. Obeng in Ghana; Leon Wessels in South Africa; Carolina Hernandez in the Philippines; José Luis Maraval in Spain; and Lázaro Cardenas, Jeffrey Davidow, Carla Hills, Santiago Levy, Luis Maira, Kevin Middlebrook, Carlos Portales, and Carlos Manuel Sada, who helped us prepare for our unprecedented interview with President Ernesto Zedillo.

International IDEA expresses its great appreciation to Sergio Bitar and Abraham Lowenthal for their skillful leadership of so many aspects of this challenging project, and to members of its staff and International Advisory Board for their many helpful suggestions. International IDEA and the project directors are grateful to Dr. Jane Jaquette for numerous contributions to the project, including extensive suggestions for the chapter on women in democratic transitions.

Senator Bitar and Dr. Lowenthal thank International IDEA and its former secretary general, Vidar Helgesen, for initiating and supporting this effort, and for recruiting us to carry it out. We also appreciate the support provided by International IDEA's current Secretary General Yves Leterme, and especially his decisions to make the book available in multiple languages and to help assure its visibility and impact. We are grateful to many members of International IDEA's outstanding staff for their cooperation but must make special mention of Melanie Allen, program officer, whose extraordinary substantive and administrative contributions set an inspiring and demanding standard. Melanie handled countless detailed logistic, diplomatic, and editorial issues with unfailing cheer and timeliness; contributed numerous substantive and editorial suggestions, including much of the editing of the interviews for publication; and undertook the incorporation of materials from the writings of President Ramos to supplement his interview. We are also immensely grateful to Koert Debeuf for his imaginative, energetic, and effective efforts to help ensure that this book becomes known in relevant political, institutional, media, and academic circles.

We greatly appreciate the outstanding logistical support provided by Katarina Jörgensen and Jenefrieda Isberg. Nyla Grace Prieto provided expertise on the Philippines case, Theophilus Dowetin offered insights into the Ghanaian transition, Andrew Ellis provided guidance and expertise on the Philippines and Indonesian transitions, and Rumbidzai Kandawasvika-Nhundu contributed to the initial conceptualization of chapter 10, on women in transitions. Hamdi Hassan and Domenico Tuccinardi contributed briefing papers on religious-secular divisions and the prospects for democratic governance in West Asia and North Africa and on the impact of modern information and communications technology on democracy, respectively. Nadia Handal Zander provided valuable practical guidance throughout the project, and James Lenahan likewise contributed to making this publication a reality. Our special appreciation goes to Kristen Sample and Helen Kavanagh-Berglund, who provided comments on all chapters and provided vital support throughout the project. We are grateful also to Brechtje Kemp, who helped to bring this volume to publication.

We gratefully acknowledge the following persons, listed in alphabetical order, who provided comments on various parts of the manuscript in progress: Manuel Alcantara, Genaro Arriagada, Ayman Ayoub, Mariano Bertucci, Archie Brown, Rt. Hon. Joe Clark, Jane Curry, Jorge Dominguez, Bahtiar Effendy, Louise Frechette, Stephen Friedman, Frances Hagopian, Evelyne Huber, Stephen Levitsky, Soledad Loaeza, Michael Lowenthal, Scott Mainwaring, Cynthia McClintock, Kevin Middlebrook, Gerardo Munck, Philip Oxhorn, Philippe Schmitter, Richard Snyder, Leena Rikkila Tamang, Matthew Taylor, Massimo Tommasoli, Peter Winn, Daniel Zovatto, and participants in seminars at Brown, Harvard, and McGill Universities and Occidental College. Sergio Bitar also thanks the National Democratic Institute as well as its director, Kenneth Wollack, and staff in Cairo for arranging his visits to Egypt and his conversations with leaders of political parties there.

Finally, Sergio and Abe want to thank each other and their wonderful and patient wives. This has been an immensely rewarding experience.

Sergio Bitar is a Chilean engineer, economist, political leader, and public intellectual. He served as Minister of Energy and Mines in the cabinet of Salvador Allende. After the 1973 coup, he was a political prisoner for 14 months and then deported to exile in Venezuela. He is one of the architects of the "Coalition for the 'No'" that defeated President Augusto Pinochet in the 1988 plebiscite. Bitar later served as a Senator, as head of the Party for Democracy, and as a minister in the governments of Presidents Lagos and Bachelet. He is president of Chile's Foundation for Democracy and director of the Global Trends and Latin America's Future project at the Inter-American Dialogue. MPP, Harvard University

Abraham F. Lowenthal, professor emeritus of international relations at the University of Southern California, founded the Woodrow Wilson Center's Latin America Program, the Inter-American Dialogue, and the Pacific Council on International Policy. He has published on Latin American politics, inter-American relations democratic governance, and US foreign policy. PhD, Harvard University

CONTRIBUTORS

Genaro Arriagada is a political scientist and politician. He served as minister of the presidency in the cabinet of Eduardo Frei Ruiz Tagle and as ambassador to the United States. He was chief executive of the "NO" campaign in the 1988 plebiscite vote that defeated Pinochet. He has been general secretary and vice president of the Christian Democratic Party, and has published widely on Chilean and Latin American politics.

Jane L. Curry is a professor of political science at Santa Clara University. A scholar of the Polish transition, she is also a specialist on Central and Eastern European journalism studies and transformation. She has recorded more than 200 interviews with Georgian, Polish, Serbian, and Ukrainian participants in their countries' transitions from Communist rule. PhD, Columbia University

Bahtiar Effendy is the dean of the Faculty of Social and Political Sciences, State Islamic University, Jakarta. As a professor of politics, he has published widely on Indonesian democracy, relations between religion and the state, and politics in the Islamic world. PhD, Ohio State University

Steven Friedman is director of the Centre for the Study of Democracy at Rhodes University and the University of Johannesburg. A former trade unionist, journalist, and an academic, he has published widely on the South African transition to democracy, especially the role of the citizen in strengthening democracy. PhD, Rhodes University

Frances Hagopian is the Jorge Paulo Lemann Visiting Associate Professor for Brazil Studies in the Department of Government at Harvard University. She has published extensively on comparative politics in Latin America, with emphasis on democratization, political representation, political economy, and religion and politics. PhD, Massachusetts Institute of Technology

Soledad Loaeza is a professor at the Center of International Studies at El Colegio de México. Her areas of expertise include political systems and elections as well as presidential power and democratization in Mexico. She is a member of International IDEA's Board of Advisers. PhD, Institut d'études politiques de Paris

Kwame A. Ninsin is professor emeritus of political science at the University of Ghana and is a scholar in residence at the Institute for Democratic Governance in Accra. His areas of expertise include the political economy of Ghana, Ghana's democratic transition, and globalization in Africa. PhD, Boston University

Mutiara Pertiwi is a junior researcher at the Institute for International Studies, State Islamic University, Jakarta. Her publications focus on Indonesian democracy, Asian nontraditional security issues, international relations in Southeast Asia, global governance, and humanitarianism. MA (Hons), Australian National University

Charles Powell is director of the Elcano Royal Institute in Madrid. He is a specialist on Spain's transition to democracy, the role of the king in the transition, Spanish politics, and the political and security relationship between Spain and the United States. PhD, Oxford University

Mark R. Thompson is director of the Southeast Asia Research Centre and professor of politics at the Department of Asian and International Studies at the City University of Hong Kong. His expertise is on authoritarian rule and comparative democratization, particularly in Southeast Asia and Eastern Europe. PhD, Yale University

Georgina Waylen is a professor of politics at the University of Manchester. She is a specialist on comparative politics with a focus on gender and politics, international political economy, transitions to democracy, and governance and institutions. She is co-director of the Feminism and Institutionalism International Network.

SELECTED BIBLIOGRAPHY

....

This bibliography covers comparative and theoretical literature (in English) on transitions from authoritarian rule and the construction of democratic governance. A bibliography on women and transitions is provided in chapter 10.

Alagappa, Muthiah, ed. *Civil Society and Political Change in Asia: Expanding and Contracting Democratic Space.* Stanford, Calif.: Stanford University Press, 2004.

Barahona de Brito, Alexandra, Carmen González-Enriquez, and Paloma Aguilar, eds. *The Politics of Memory: Transitional Justice in Democratizing Societies.* Cambridge: Cambridge University Press, 2001.

Barany, Zoltan. *The Soldier and the Changing State: Building Democratic Armies in Africa, Asia, Europe, and the Americas.* Princeton, N.J.: Princeton University Press, 2012.

Bellin, Eva. "Reconsidering the Robustness of Authoritarianism in the Middle East: Lessons from the Arab Spring." *Comparative Politics* 44, no. 2 (2012): 127–49.

Bermeo, Nancy. "Myths of Moderation: Confrontation and Conflict during Democratic Transitions." *Comparative Politics* 29, no. 3 (1997): 305–22.

Besley, Timothy, and Roberto Zagha, eds. *Development Challenges in the 1990s: Leading Policymakers Speak from Experience.* Washington, D.C.: World Bank; New York: Oxford University Press, 2005.

Bratton, Michael, and Eric C. C. Chang. "State-Building and Democratization in Sub-Saharan Africa: Forwards, Backwards, or Together." *Comparative Political Studies* 39, no. 9 (2006): 1059–83.

Bratton, Michael, and Nicolas van de Walle. *Democratic Experiments in Africa: Regime Transitions in Comparative Perspective.* Cambridge: Cambridge University Press, 1997.

Brinks, Daniel, and Michael Coppedge. "Diffusion Is No Illusion: Neighborhood Emulation in the Third Wave of Democratization." *Comparative Political Studies* 39, no. 4 (2006): 463–89.

Brownlee, Jason. *Authoritarianism in an Age of Democratization.* New York: Cambridge University Press, 2007.

Bunce, Valerie, Michael McFaul, and Kathryn Stoner-Weiss, eds. *Democracy and Authoritarianism in the Postcommunist World.* New York: Cambridge University Press, 2010.

Bunce, Valerie, and Sharon Wolchik. *Defeating Authoritarian Leaders in Post-Communist Countries.* New York: Cambridge University Press, 2011.

Burnell, Peter, and Richard Youngs, eds. *New Challenges to Democratization.* Abingdon: Routledge, 2010.

Carothers, Thomas. *Aiding Democracy Abroad: The Learning Curve.* Washington, D.C.: Carnegie Endowment for International Peace, 1999.

———. "The End of the Transition Paradigm." *Journal of Democracy* 13, no. 1 (2002): 5–21.

Chalmers, Douglas, and Scott Mainwaring. *Problems Confronting Contemporary Democracies.* Notre Dame, Ind.: University of Notre Dame Press, 2012.

Coleman, Isobel, and Terra Lawson-Remer, eds. *Pathways to Freedom: Political and Economic Lessons from Democratic Transitions.* New York: Council on Foreign Relations, 2013.

Collier, Ruth Berins. *Paths toward Democracy: The Working Class and Elites in Western Europe and South America.* Cambridge: Cambridge University Press, 1999.

Collombier, Virginie. *The Political Economy of Transitions: Comparative Experiences.* Oslo: United Nations Development Programme, Oslo Governance Centre, 2013.

Crawford, Gordon. *Foreign Aid and Political Reform: A Comparative Analysis of Democracy Assistance and Political Conditionality.* Houndsmill: Palgrave, 2001.

Diamond, Larry. *The Spirit of Democracy: The Struggle to Build Free Societies throughout the World.* New York: Times Books, 2008.

Diamond, Larry, and Leonardo Morlino, eds. *Assessing the Quality of Democracy.* Baltimore: Johns Hopkins University Press and the National Endowment for Democracy, 2005.

Dobson, William J. *The Dictator's Learning Curve: Inside the Global Battle for Democracy.* New York: Anchor Books, 2012.

Ethier, Diane. "Is Democracy Promotion Effective? Comparing Conditionality and Incentives." *Democratization* 10, no 1 (2003): 99–120.

Fish, Steven M. "Stronger Legislatures, Stronger Democracies." *Journal of Democracy* 17, no. 1 (2006): 5–20.

Gandhi, Jennifer, and Ellen Lust-Okar. "Elections under Authoritarianism." *Annual Review of Political Science,* 12 (2009): 403–22.

Geddes, Barbara. "What Do We Know about Democratization after Twenty Years?" *Annual Review of Political Science* 2, no. 1 (1999): 115–44.

Gunther, Richard, and Anthony Mughan, eds. *Democracy and the Media: A Comparative Perspective.* Cambridge: Cambridge University Press, 2000.

Haggard, Stephan, and Robert R. Kaufman. *The Political Economy of Democratic Transitions.* Princeton, N.J.: Princeton University Press, 1995.

Hamid, Shadi. *Temptations of Power: Islamists and Illiberal Democracy in a New Middle East.* New York: Oxford University Press, 2014.

Hayner, Priscilla B. *Unspeakable Truths: Transitional Justice and the Challenge of Truth Commissions.* New York: Routledge, 2001.

Hobson, Christopher, and Milja Kurki, eds. *The Conceptual Politics of Democracy Promotion.* Abingdon: Routledge, 2012.

Howard, Philip N., and Muzammil M. Hussain. *Democracy's Fourth Wave? Digital Media and the Arab Spring.* New York: Oxford University Press, 2013.

Huntington, Samuel P. *The Third Wave: Democratization in the Late Twentieth Century.* Norman: University of Oklahoma Press, 1991.

Karl, Terry Lynn. "Dilemmas of Democratization in Latin America." *Comparative Politics* 23, no. 1 (1990): 1–21.

Kuran, Timur. "Now Out of Never: The Element of Surprise in the East European Revolution of 1989." *World Politics* 44, no. 1 (1991): 7–48.

Levitsky, Steven, and Maria Victoria Murillo. "Building Institutions on Weak Foundations." *Journal of Democracy* 24, no. 2 (2013): 93–107.

Levitsky, Steven, and Lucan A. Way. *Competitive Authoritarianism: Hybrid Regimes after the Cold War.* New York: Cambridge University Press, 2010.

Lijphart, Arend. *Patterns of Democracy: Government Forms and Performance in Thirty-Six Countries.* New Haven, Conn.: Yale University Press, 1999.

Lindberg, Staffan I. *Democracy and Elections in Africa.* Baltimore: Johns Hopkins University Press, 2006.

Linz, Juan J., and H. E. Chehabi, eds. *Sultanistic Regimes.* Baltimore: Johns Hopkins University Press, 1998.

Linz, Juan J., and Alfred Stepan. *Problems of Democratic Transition and Consolidation: Southern Europe, South America, and Post-Communist Europe.* Baltimore: Johns Hopkins University Press, 1996.

Mainwaring, Scott, and Anibal Perez-Liñán. *The Rise and Fall of Democracies and Dictatorships: Latin America since 1900.* Cambridge: Cambridge University Press, 2013.

McAdam, Doug, Sidney Tarrow, and Charles Tilly. *Dynamics of Contention.* Cambridge: Cambridge University Press, 2001.

McFaul, Michael, and Kathryn Stoner-Weiss. *After the Collapse of Communism: Comparative Lessons of Transition.* Cambridge: Cambridge University Press, 2004.

Miller, Laurel E., Jeffrey Martini, F. Stephen Larrabee, Angel Rabasa, Stephanie Pezard, Julie E. Taylor, and Tewodaj Mengistu. *Democratization in the Arab World: Prospects and Lessons from Around the Globe.* Santa Monica, Calif.: RAND, 2012.

Morlino, Leonardo. *Changes for Democracy: Actors, Structures, Processes.* Oxford: Oxford University Press, 2011.

Munck, Gerardo L., and Carol Skalnik Leff. "Modes of Transition and Democratization: South America and Eastern Europe in Comparative Perspective." *Comparative Politics* 29, no. 3 (1997): 343–62.

O'Donnell, Guillermo, and Philippe C. Schmitter. *Transitions from Authoritarian Rule: Tentative Conclusions about Uncertain Democracies.* Baltimore: Johns Hopkins University Press, 1986; republished with a new preface by Cynthia Arnson and Abraham F. Lowenthal, Johns Hopkins University Press, 2013.

O'Donnell, Guillermo, Philippe C. Schmitter, and Laurence Whitehead. *Transitions from Authoritarian Rule,* 4 vols. Baltimore: Johns Hopkins University Press, 1986.

Ottaway, Marina. *Democracy Challenged: The Rise of Semi-Authoritarianism.* Washington, D.C.: Carnegie Endowment for International Peace, 2003.

Pevehouse, Jon C. *Democracy from Above: Regional Organizations and Democratization.* New York: Cambridge University Press, 2005.

Philpott, Daniel. "Explaining the Political Ambivalence of Religion." *American Political Science Review* 101, no. 3 (2007): 505–25.

Pridham, G., and P. G. Lewis, eds. *Stabilizing Fragile Democracies: Comparing New Party Systems in Southern and Eastern Europe.* London: Routledge, 1996.

Przeworski, Adam. *Democracy and the Market: Political and Economic Reforms in Eastern Europe and Latin America.* Cambridge: Cambridge University Press, 1991.

Przeworski, Adam, and Fernando Limongi. "Modernization: Theories and Facts." *World Politics* 49, no. 2 (1997): 155–83.

Reynolds, Andrew, ed. *The Architecture of Democracy: Constitutional Design, Conflict Management, and Democracy.* Oxford: Oxford University Press, 2002.

Risse, Thomas, Stephen C. Ropp, and Kathryn Sikkink, eds. *The Power of Human Rights: International Norms and Domestic Change.* Cambridge: Cambridge University Press, 1999.

Rustow, Dankwart A. "Transitions to Democracy: Toward a Dynamic Model." *Comparative Politics* 2, no. 3 (1970): 337–63.

Sadiki, Larbi. *Rethinking Arab Democratization: Elections without Democracy.* Oxford: Oxford University Press, 2009.

Sartori, Giovani. *Comparative Constitutional Engineering: An Inquiry into Structures, Incentives, and Outcomes.* New York: New York University Press, 1994.

Schedler, Andreas, ed. *Electoral Authoritarianism: The Dynamics of Unfree Competition.* Boulder, Colo.: Lynne Rienner, 2006.

Sen, Amartya K. "Democracy as a Universal Value." *Journal of Democracy* 10, no. 3 (1999): 3–17.

Stepan, Alfred, and Juan J. Linz. "Democratization Theory and the 'Arab Spring.'" *Journal of Democracy* 24, no. 2 (2013): 15–29.

Stoner, Kathryn, and Michael McFaul, eds. *Transitions to Democracy: A Comparative Perspective.* Baltimore: Johns Hopkins University Press, 2013.

Svolik, Milan W. *The Politics of Authoritarian Rule.* New York: Cambridge University Press, 2012.

Teorell, Jan. *Determinants of Democratization: Explaining Regime Change in the World, 1972–2006.* Cambridge: Cambridge University Press, 2010.

Welzel, Christian, and Ronald Inglehart. "The Role of Ordinary People in Democratization." *Journal of Democracy* 19, no. 1 (2008): 126–40.

Whitehead, Laurence. *Democratization: Theory and Experience.* Oxford: Oxford University Press, 2002.

Whitehead, Laurence, ed. *The International Dimensions of Democratization: Europe and the Americas.* Oxford: Oxford University Press, 1996.

INDEX